D1600211

2018
The Supreme Court Review

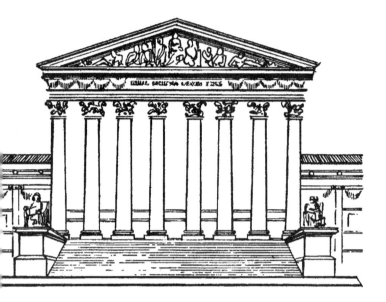

2018
The

"Judges as persons, or courts as institutions, are entitled to no greater immunity from criticism than other persons or institutions . . . [J]udges must be kept mindful of their limitations and of their ultimate public responsibility by a vigorous stream of criticism expressed with candor however blunt."
—*Felix Frankfurter*

". . . while it is proper that people should find fault when their judges fail, it is only reasonable that they should recognize the difficulties. . . . Let them be severely brought to book, when they go wrong, but by those who will take the trouble to understand them."
—*Learned Hand*

THE LAW SCHOOL

THE UNIVERSITY OF CHICAGO

Supreme Court Review

EDITED BY

GEOFFREY R. STONE

DAVID A. STRAUSS

AND JUSTIN DRIVER

 THE UNIVERSITY OF CHICAGO PRESS

CHICAGO AND LONDON

INTERNATIONAL STANDARD BOOK NUMBER: 978-0-226-64622-0

LIBRARY OF CONGRESS CATALOG CARD NUMBER: 60-14353

THE UNIVERSITY OF CHICAGO PRESS, CHICAGO 60637

THE UNIVERSITY OF CHICAGO PRESS, LTD., LONDON

© 2019 BY THE UNIVERSITY OF CHICAGO, ALL RIGHTS RESERVED, PUBLISHED 2019

PRINTED IN THE UNITED STATES OF AMERICA

The paper used in this publication meets the minimum requirements of American National Standard for Information Sciences–Permanence of Paper for Printed Library Materials, ANSI Z39.48-1984. ⊗

TO

*Devoted public servant and distinguished jurist
whose lucid and thoughtful opinions
will endure for generations*

CONTENTS

MARK TUSHNET

TRUMP v HAWAII: "THIS PRESIDENT" AND THE NATIONAL SECURITY CONSTITUTION

When Justice Sonia Sotomayor analogized the majority opinion in *Trump v Hawaii* to *Korematsu v United States*, Chief Justice John Roberts got his back up: "*Korematsu* has nothing to do with this case."[1] Why? *Korematsu* involved "[t]he forcible relocation of U.S. citizens to concentration camps, solely and explicitly on the basis of race. . . ."[2] That's an accurate *description* of the case, but what makes it different in principle from the travel ban upheld in *Trump v Hawaii*?

According to the Chief Justice, the Japanese exclusion orders upheld in *Korematsu*, unlike the travel ban, were "objectively unlawful"—an odd phrase.[3] The Chief Justice continued, "it is wholly inapt

---

Mark Tushnet is William Nelson Cromwell Professor of Law, Harvard Law School.

[1] *Trump v Hawaii*, 138 S Ct 2392, 2423 (2018).

[2] Id.

[3] Id. What does "objectively" add to "unlawful" or "lawful"? Are some statutes or executive actions merely "subjectively unlawful" or "subjectively lawful"? The language of objectivity and (implicitly) subjectivity, then, is something like a language of praise and disparagement. In such a language, calling an action objectively unlawful is not to provide reasons, even implicitly, supporting the characterization. It is more like pounding the table for emphasis. Nor, I think, can "objectively unlawful" be read to mean only that the Japanese exclusion orders were expressly based upon race, because the Chief Justice's next sentence refers to the travel ban as "factually neutral." The Chief Justice added that the executive order in *Korematsu* was "outside the scope of Presidential authority," which again is his *description* of what the case should have held, but not an explanation for the order's illegality.

to liken that morally repugnant order to a facially neutral policy denying certain foreign nationals the privilege of admission." The action
"is well within executive authority"—again, nothing more than a
restatement of the Court's holding—and "could have been taken by
any other President . . ."[4] (emphasis added). Putting aside the conclu-
sory language, we can see several themes in the Chief Justice's defense of the Court's decision.

The first is what I will call, echoing the Chief Justice's language, a
distinction between "this President" and "the Presidency."[5] The
second is that facial neutrality operates as an absolute screen to shield
badly motivated actions from anything but the most minimal scrutiny. That is dramatically at odds with the way facial neutrality has
operated in other cases, where facially neutral statutes can be invalidated if they result from discriminatory animus. The third theme,
then, attempts to explain and limit this apparent departure from settled
principles by suggesting several implicit differences between the travel
ban and the orders in *Korematsu*. (*a*) The *Korematsu* orders operated
within U.S. borders, whereas the travel ban operated outside those
borders. (*b*) The *Korematsu* orders affected U.S. citizens, whereas the
travel ban affected (only) "certain foreign nationals." (*c*) And, with respect to those foreign nationals, the ban dealt only with "the privilege
of admission."[6]

After briefly sketching the facts underlying *Trump v Hawaii* and the
Supreme Court opinions in the case, I turn to these three themes in
order.

I. The Travel Bans

Campaigning for the Presidency, Donald Trump repeatedly
told the public that he would implement a ban on the entry of Muslims
into the United States.[7] Days after his inauguration, he issued what was
described in the litigation as EO-1. EO-1 barred citizens of seven

---

[4] Id.

[5] See 138 S Ct at 2418 ("In [reviewing the executive order], we must consider not only the
statements of a particular President, but also the authority of the Presidency itself.").

[6] The Chief Justice needed to build this third principle into his conclusion because
distinguishing between the "privilege of admission" and entitlement to a visa was essential to
his argument that the travel ban, affecting only the former, was consistent with a statute,
8 USC § 1152(a)(1)(A), prohibiting discrimination on the basis of nationality in connection with
issuing immigrant visas.

[7] See, for example, 138 S Ct at 2417.

Muslim-majority nations from entry into the United States for ninety days, pending a promised review of the United States's ability to rely upon information provided by those nations in its efforts to identify and prevent the entry of potential terrorists.[8] The lower courts enjoined the order.[9]

The Trump administration revoked EO-1 and replaced it with EO-2. Aside from removing one nation (Iraq) from the list of nations in EO-1, EO-2 was mostly indistinguishable from EO-1.[10] Again, lower courts enjoined the order's implementation. The government sought review in the Supreme Court, arguing among other things that plaintiffs in the lower court litigation lacked standing to challenge the order. The Court granted certiorari and stayed the injunction except with respect to people with "credible claim[s] of a bona fide relationship" with someone in the United States.[11] After the ninety-day period specified in EO-2 (as in EO-1) expired, the Court dismissed the case as moot.

Trump v Hawaii involved the travel ban's final form, EO-3. That order placed restrictions on entry of nationals of eight countries. The general rationale stated in the order and its supporting material was that the identified nations were unable to assist the United States adequately in screening potential terrorists from entering the United States. The order provided that there would be no entry for nationals of North Korea and Syria, and no entry for Iranians other than those seeking student visas; restrictions like those for Iranians, for nationals of Chad, Libya, and Yemen, because, although the assistance they provided was inadequate they were "valuable counterterrorism partner[s]";[12] no entry from Somalia for those seeking immigrant visas and "additional scrutiny" for those seeking other visas; and restrictions on entry of some government officials from Venezuela.[13]

EO-3 was developed by the Department of Homeland Security after consultations with the State Department and intelligence agen-

---

[8] Id at 2403. In some applications, EO-1 was as close to a pristine violation of basic rule-of-law norms as one can imagine: It applied to people who had no practical opportunity to shape their conduct with reference to the order—people already on planes flying to the United States with previously issued visas in hand. Prior to the ban they faced some risk that they would be turned away when they presented their visas; after it that risk escalated dramatically.

[9] Id.

[10] Id at 2403–4.

[11] *Trump v IRAP*, 137 S Ct 2080 (2017).

[12] Chad was later removed from the list.

[13] See 138 S Ct at 2404–6.

cies. The consultations focused on how effective nations around the world were in providing information to U.S. officials charged with authorizing entry—specifically, information that would be helpful in identifying applicants who posed terrorist threats to the United States. An initial survey found sixteen nations with "deficient" procedures and thirty-one "at risk" of having such deficiencies. The State Department then worked with foreign governments to remedy identified problems. The result was to reduce the number of problematic nations to the eight ultimately included in EO-3.[14]

EO-3 included two nations—North Korea and Venezuela—that were not included in EO-1 and whose populations are largely non-Muslim. It excluded Iraq because of the close relations between Iraq and the United States in fighting ISIS.[15] That EO-3 resulted from an extensive process of interagency consultation—in contrast to EO-1—played a role in the Court's analysis of its constitutionality.[16] The Court apparently believed that interagency consultation had some bearing on whether EO-3 was unconstitutionally infected with anti-Muslim bias.

A skeptic might describe the inclusion of North Korea and Venezuela as an attempt to put lipstick on the pig—to create the impression that an order directed at Muslims was in fact something else. One could also take a skeptical view of the interagency consultation, as a process intended to generate a foreordained conclusion—a ban that could be presented to the public as fulfilling Trump's campaign promise. The conclusion, that is, was "wired" from the beginning. The "lipstick on the pig" skepticism might properly lead one to ignore the inclusion of North Korea and Venezuela in EO-3, given the substantive constitutional question.

How to deal with the "wired from the beginning" skepticism is a more difficult question. It is related, as we will see, to the Court's implicit distinction between "this President" and "the Presidency." The reason for the difficulty is that many executive and agency actions are similarly foreordained. Consider the most routine but significant agency actions subject to notice and comment rule-making. Comments

---

[14] See id at 2404–5.

[15] See id at 2405.

[16] See id at 2408–9. For a discussion of a norm counseling interagency consultation prior to issuing significant executive orders, see Daphna Renan, *Presidential Norms and Article II*, 131 Harv L Rev 2187, 2221–30 (2018).

elicited in the process sometimes lead to significant changes from the rules put out for comment and sometimes lead to cosmetic changes. Almost always, though, the more significant the proposed rule is to an administration's policy agenda, the more likely it is that the final rule as adopted will be the one the agency proposed at the outset.[17] The "wired from the beginning" skepticism might be legally relevant in some domain where the law requires actual deliberation. It isn't clear that there is any such domain within constitutional law: Sometimes bad motivation or animus is relevant to constitutionality, and perhaps evidence of actual deliberation might shed light on motivation; but absence of deliberation as such doesn't seem constitutionally relevant.

Chief Justice Roberts wrote the Court's opinion upholding EO-3. "Assuming without deciding that [the challengers'] statutory claims [we]re reviewable," he rejected two statutory arguments that were, he said, the challengers' "primary contention[s]."[18] The Immigration and Nationality Act gives the President authority to "suspend the entry of all aliens or any class of aliens" if he "finds that the entry . . . would be detrimental to the interests of the United States."[19] Relying on this provision's "plain language," the Court rejected the challengers' argument that the provision "confers only a residual power to temporarily halt the entry of a discrete group of aliens engaged in harmful conduct."[20] Another provision bans discrimination "in the issuance of an immigrant visa" because of race or place of residence.[21] According to the Chief Justice, this provision dealt only with discrimination in connection with issuing visas, and did not apply at all to decisions regarding actual entry into the United States, the only subject in EO-3. The "basic distinction between admissibility determinations and visa issuance . . . runs throughout" the statute.[22]

---

[17] For some indirect evidence of this, see Susan Webb Yackee, *Sweet-Talking the Fourth Branch: The Influence of Interest Group Comments on Federal Agency Rulemaking*, 16 J Pub Admin Res & Theory 103 (2005) (focusing on changes between original proposals and final rules, but showing indirectly that many proposals are unaffected by comments).

[18] 138 S Ct at 2407, 2415.

[19] 8 USC § 1182 (f).

[20] 138 S Ct at 2408.

[21] 8 USC § 1152(a)(1)(A).

[22] 138 S Ct at 2414. Justice Thomas in a concurring opinion observed that he found "the plaintiffs' proffered evidence of anti-Muslim discrimination . . . unpersuasive," 138 S Ct at 2425 (Thomas, J, concurring), then devoted the bulk of his opinion to criticism of the scope of the remedy—a so-called universal or nationwide injunction—entered in the district court and affirmed by the court of appeals.

Justice Breyer dissented, joined by Justice Kagan. For him, the way in which the administration implemented the order's "elaborate system of exemptions and waivers" would "help" the Court determine whether the order had been "significantly affected by religious animus" or, alternatively, rested on national security concerns.[23] Anyone who got a waiver or exemption obviously could not be the target of anti-Muslim animus. But, if the system was administered so as to provide almost no waivers on a case-by-case basis, "denying visas to Muslims who meet [EO-3's] own security terms would support the view that the Government excludes them for reasons based upon their religion."[24] In Justice Breyer's view the evidence available to the Court "provide[d] cause for concern."[25] The State Department had not issued any guidance about how to administer the waiver system, and statistics suggested that waivers were granted so infrequently that many persons who showed that they did not pose security threats may have been unable to obtain visas.

Justice Breyer argued that the Court should remand the case for further proceedings on these questions about the waiver system. But, he said, "[i]f this Court must decide the question without [such] further litigation," "the evidence of antireligious bias" was "a sufficient basis to set [EO-3] aside" on the basis of the information available to the Court.[26]

Justice Sotomayor also dissented, joined by Justice Ginsburg. She argued that under existing Establishment Clause doctrine EO-3 was unconstitutional because "a reasonable observer would conclude that [it] was motivated by anti-Muslim animus," and that there were no good reasons for refraining from applying that doctrine.[27] The Chief Justice had asserted that it was "problematic" to apply existing Establishment Clause doctrine "in the national security and foreign affairs context" because that doctrine had been developed in "cases involving holiday displays and graduation ceremonies."[28] Justice Sotomayor replied that "just because the Court has not confronted the precise situation at hand does not render these cases (or the principles

---

[23] Id at 2429 (Breyer, J, dissenting).

[24] Id at 2430 (Breyer, J, dissenting).

[25] Id at 2431 (Breyer, J, dissenting).

[26] 138 S Ct at 2433 (Breyer, J, dissenting).

[27] Id at 2433 (Sotomayor, J, dissenting).

[28] Id at 2420 n 5.

they announced) inapplicable." For her, what was "problematic" was the Court's "apparent willingness to . . . forgo any meaningful constitutional review at the mere mention of a national security concern."[29]

II. Devising Doctrine for This President and the Presidency

Chief Justice Roberts devoted three paragraphs occupying a little more than a page to supplying examples of candidate and then President Trump's statements about desiring and implementing a "Muslim ban." The statements were, he said, at "the heart" of the constitutional challenge to EO-3.[30] The issue for the Court, the Chief Justice wrote, was "not whether to denounce the statements," but how to design a doctrine dealing with a presidential action that might have been adopted at least in part because of policy choices influenced by the views expressed in the statements.[31] And, in devising that doctrine, the Chief Justice cautioned that it would apply not only to "a particular President," but would affect "the authority of the Presidency itself."[32]

The Chief Justice's formulation seems unexceptionable. All Presidents claim that their most controversial executive policies are within the scope of the power the Constitution gives them. Faced with a questionable exercise of presidential power, judges must come up with a doctrine that deals acceptably both with that particular action and with other similar actions that, in the judges' view, are closely related (in some way) but are not questionable. One solution is to find the particular action within the scope of presidential authority. That was the solution chosen in *Trump v Hawaii*.

Another solution might be available, though.[33] The judge could identify a line separating the questionable action from the others.

---

[29] Id at 2441 n 6 (Sotomayor, J, dissenting).

[30] 138 S Ct at 2417. Justice Sotomayor's dissent observed that the Chief Justice's account "does not tell even half of the story," and spent about six pages offering her version. Id at 2435–38 (Sotomayor, J, dissenting).

[31] The Chief Justice's words were, "the significance of those statements in reviewing" the policy, which he then described. 138 S Ct at 2418.

[32] Id.

[33] Shalini Bhargava Ray, *Plenary Power and Animus in Immigration Law*, 80 Ohio St L J — (forthcoming 2019), proposes another alternative. She would apply a mixed-motive analysis that asks whether the law in question would not have been promulgated but for the bad motivation. In its strongest form the argument draws on mixed-motive cases arising from situations

Consider a particular President who adheres to an extremely expansive theory of the unitary Presidency. According to this President, that theory implies that any statutory restrictions on the President's power to dismiss officials who have among other duties the enforcement of national law are unconstitutional. Specifically, the President's theory is that a President can dismiss a member of an independent agency because the member has made decisions inconsistent with the President's policy views. So, according to the President, statutes purporting to limit the dismissal power to malfeasance or neglect of duty are unconstitutional.[34]

There is an obvious basis for distinguishing this President from "the Presidency itself." Given that this President's unitary-executive theory is mistaken, the judge can be more skeptical if this President claims that he is dismissing an official for malfeasance and not because of a policy disagreement. The judge can then limit the authority of this President without casting doubt upon the authority of the Presidency itself. Put another way, the distinction *determines* the scope of presidential authority.

This discussion exposes some of the difficulties associated with distinguishing between "a particular President" and "the Presidency." By counterposing "a particular President" to "the Presidency itself," the Chief Justice implicitly assumes, sensibly enough, that the Presidency as an office is occupied at any one moment by particular Presidents. But, if we have a basis for distinguishing a particular President from other occupants of the office, that distinction can be used to shape the doctrine. We have one rule restricting the power of particular Presidents like this one—in the prior example, Presidents who act upon mistaken theories of the unitary executive—and an-

---

that arise often enough to produce a "comparison set" with which the law in question can be compared: We examine cases where the motivation was absent to see whether decision makers made the same decision as the one in question, or what the result was when they followed standard procedures that screened bad motivations out of the process. The difficulty is that the travel ban and, perhaps, problems similar to the one it presented do not arise often enough to create a comparison set. And without one it is extremely difficult to figure out how we could tell whether the same decision would not have been made but for the bad motivation. (One signal of the difficulty is an alternative formulation Ray offers: Would the President have made the same choice anyway? Are we to ask whether President Trump would have made the same choice, or whether some other President, less bigoted than Trump, would have? Answering either question seems to me impossible.)

[34] The President might try to shoehorn his or her views into the relevant statute through an interpretation of the statute according to which policy disagreement is either malfeasance or neglect of duty. Depending on the statute's precise language, this interpretation might just be completely parasitic upon the underlying unitary-executive theory.

other rule that leaves less constrained Presidents who do not share the distinguishing feature of this (and similar) Presidents.

The key here might lie in the fact that the Chief Justice only *implicitly* assumes that this particular President is different from other Presidents. The criterion we might use to distinguish him from others leaps from the page: President Trump's statements show that he is virulently bigoted against Muslims—or, to use a shorthand, that he is a virulent racist.[35] On the face of things it shouldn't be difficult to design a doctrine with two branches, one examining skeptically racially tinged decisions by a virulently racist President and the other taking a less skeptical view of similarly tinged decisions by a somewhat less racist President.[36]

Perhaps, though, there would be something unseemly in shaping doctrine around an assessment of the degree to which a President is racist.[37] Again, pinning down that concern is difficult because the concern can't be disconnected from the fact that the underlying action is itself unseemly. So, perhaps the thought is that there's something especially unseemly about a judicially developed doctrine that names racism for what it is: Particular Presidents might be racists but for some unstated reason the Court as an institution somehow shouldn't call them out for their racism. We might well wonder about what that proposition tells us about the Chief Justice's view of the Court as an institution.[38]

---

[35] Cf. *Shaare Tefila Congregation v Cobb*, 481 US 615 (1987) (holding that the cause of action created by the Civil Rights Act of 1866 for discrimination on the basis of race covered discrimination on the basis of the fact that the plaintiff was Jewish because in 1866 Jews were considered to be a distinctive race).

[36] There is a sense in which the distinction suggested in the text tracks the well-established distinction between claims of disparate race-based treatment, which are subject to more-than-rational-basis scrutiny, and claims of disparate (racially disproportionate) impact of facially neutral rules, which are not unless the court concludes that the facially neutral rule was adopted precisely because of its disparate impact. On the latter qualification, see note 37 below.

[37] I feel compelled to insert a cautionary note here. What follows is an attempt to describe what constitutional doctrine might look like were we to accept two propositions: that there's a lot of racism that affects contemporary policy-making, and that not every policy tinged by racism is unconstitutional. On the latter proposition, see *Washington v Davis*, 426 US 229, 248 (1976) ("A rule that a statute designed to serve neutral ends is nevertheless invalid, absent compelling justification, if in practice it benefits or burdens one race more than another would be far reaching and would raise serious questions about, and perhaps invalidate, a whole range of tax, welfare, public service, regulatory, and licensing statutes that may be more burdensome to the poor and to the average black than to the more affluent white."). One could plausibly reject the proposition that we can't afford to provide too much justice.

[38] In distinguishing the "Muslim ban" from the relocation order in *Korematsu*, the Chief Justice pointed out that the former was facially neutral while the latter was based "solely and

There may be another reason for the Chief Justice's analysis—more defensible perhaps, but even more troubling. In one passage in the opinion, the Chief Justice described how, in his words, "[o]ur Presidents have frequently used th[eir] power to espouse the principles of religious freedom and tolerance on which this Nation was founded."[39] Then he wrote, "Yet it cannot be denied that . . . [Presidents] have performed unevenly in living up to those inspiring words."[40] This suggests that this "particular President" might not be all that different from prior (and perhaps future) ones: They are all a little bit racist.[41] The doctrinal implication of that observation might be to be skeptical about *all* racially tinged presidential policies—at the very least, to evaluate such policies by using a standard requiring the government to justify the policies with more than the justifications sufficient under a "mere rationality" standard.

Justice Sotomayor endorsed such a doctrine in her dissent. There might be some reason to worry about it, though. The view that everyone's a little bit racist treats racism as a graduated continuum, with virulent racists at one end and (perhaps) inadvertent or unconscious or unthinking racists at the other. At the highest level of abstraction, though, U.S. constitutional law tends to abjure graduated scales in favor of more categorical approaches.[42] A categorical approach to racist motivation would almost certainly be quite unseemly. In some cases a judge would have to say, "Yes, this action is a little bit racist, but not enough to require me to ask for strong justifications." We would, I think, rather clearly not want to hear judges saying that. A doctrine that disregards even virulent racism as motivating a policy does avoid this embarrassment.

An alternative path would lie in treating distinctions among Presidents based upon constitutional or other legal theories they hold, on the one hand, and on the other distinctions based upon something like the personal traits that trigger their choices among policies. We might not want a doctrine that barred excessively narcissistic Presidents from

---

explicitly on the basis of race." 138 S Ct at 2423. That distinction allows us to call the relocation order racist without calling Franklin Roosevelt racist.

[39] Id at 2418.

[40] Id.

[41] See "Everybody's a Little Racist," from the musical *Avenue Q*, available at https://perma.cc/9YGB-87KZ.

[42] See Vicki C. Jackson, *Constitutional Law in an Age of Proportionality*, 124 Yale L J 2680 (2015).

acting upon expansive unitary-executive theories while allowing more mature ones to do so, on the theory that personal racism is just like excessive narcissism.

There are two obvious lines of response. First, U.S. history singles out racism as a matter of special constitutional concern in a way that it doesn't single out narcissism. Second, maybe we *should* allow mature Presidents to act upon expansive unitary-executive theories while barring narcissistic ones from doing so. The argument would be that the very fact of maturity means that such a President is unlikely to invoke the expansive theory in ways that threaten the foundations of our constitutional order, whereas narcissistic Presidents might do so.

This is not to suggest that every personal trait will provide a defensible distinction between a particular President and the Presidency itself. Consider, for example, a President who breaks prior norms with seeming abandon. We probably should not use that to distinguish between "this President" and the Presidency. Sometimes norms *should* be broken, when they have become dysfunctional. Sometimes norm-breaking is part of a larger program of instituting a new constitutional order. And, more mundanely, every President breaks norms sometimes, and distinguishing among Presidents based on the degree to which they do so will inevitably be controversial.[43]

The examples of narcissism and norm-breaking suggest that we would have to ask about the implications of using each specific trait as the basis for a distinction. Some—virulent racism, excessive narcissism—might be worked into defensible constitutional doctrine while others, such as norm-breaking and a neurotic fear of seeming "weak" (perhaps) might not. I think it clear that this line of thought should be unsettling. Not, in my view, because it can't be built into constitutional doctrine,[44] but because it calls upon judges to think about a

---

[43] For example, note the account of norm violations by President Obama offered in David E. Bernstein, *Lawless: The Obama Administration's Unprecedented Assault on the Constitution and the Rule of Law* (Encounter Books, 2015).

[44] I suppose it's necessary here to include a note explaining that this line of thought can be incorporated into originalist theory in some of its contemporary versions. A sketch: The Fourteenth Amendment as originally understood requires that courts subject legislation and executive actions resting upon racist premises to careful examination. (As to executive actions, see *Yick Wo v Hopkins*, 118 US 356 (1886).) Racism is a personal trait. Other personal traits are constitutionally relevant if they are sufficiently similar to racism. The measure of similarity is whether acting on the trait is inconsistent either (*a*) with the concept of equality originally understood to be inscribed in the Constitution by the Fourteenth Amendment and, with respect to the national government, by the Fifth Amendment, or (*b*) with the concept of

range of personal traits in ways that are far outside their professional competence.

Might courts treat racism differently? That is, might it be possible to develop a judicially administrable rule that allows careful examination of policies resulting from virulent racism while barring such examination of policies resulting from excessive narcissism or neurotic fear? The claim that racism is historically distinctive suggests that we can. The proposition that everyone's a little bit racist suggests that we ought not.

The distinction the Chief Justice drew between this "particular President" and the "authority of the Presidency itself" shows us what a genteelly racist constitutional law looks like. The analogy to *Korematsu* is well founded.

III. The Role of Facial Neutrality

Chief Justice Roberts rejected the analogy to *Korematsu* because the policy there was explicitly based upon race while that in *Trump v Hawaii* was facially neutral. Coupled with other distinctions, EO-3's facial neutrality "inform[ed the Court's] standard of review," which was the loosest version available of mere rationality: The policy was constitutional if "it can reasonably be understood to result from a justification independent of unconstitutional grounds."[45] Using this standard is defensible given the problematic "this President/the Presidency" framing.

It is true that, independent of the other distinctions—that the order operated outside U.S. borders, for example—the use of mere rationality in *Trump v Hawaii* was nonstandard. The usual formulation is that facial neutrality is not an absolute bar to more searching scrutiny. Rather, a policy with a racially (or in this setting religiously) disparate impact is generally subject to mere-rationality review, but not if the policy was adopted for the very purpose of having that impact. And, of course, those challenging EO-3 claimed that it was indeed adopted for that purpose.

What's the theoretical foundation for a weak "mere-rationality" standard? Some libertarian-leaning constitutional scholars and litiga-

---

equality developed by subsequent constitutionally permissible constructions of the terms "equal protection of the laws" or "due process of law."

[45] 138 S Ct at 2418, 2420.

tors have mounted a challenge to the weak mere-rationality standard.[46] They support "judicial engagement." Judicial engagement starts with the observation that the weak mere-rationality standard at least purports to require a plausible connection between legislation and some public purpose. The next step in engagement involves an at least modest judicial inquiry into the factual predicates linking the legislation to the asserted public purpose.

The theory of judicial engagement fails to grapple with the underlying rationale for the weak mere-rationality standard. That rationale is rooted in an account of pluralist politics. Consider *Railroad Retirement Board v Fritz*, where the Court upheld a revision in a pension plan that gave greater benefits to those with a "current connection" to the railroad industry than to those who lacked such a connection.[47] Applying the mere-rationality test, the Court found that the distinction Congress drew was a rough-and-ready means of identifying "career railroaders" who, it believed, had a stronger equitable claim to the benefits than others. It's clear, though, what was really going on. Congress had to divide a pot of money among several groups. Those with "current connections" simply had more political clout than the others.

And there's nothing wrong with that. Pluralist politics consists of assembling legislative majorities from groups with varying interests and political power. Legislatures make compromises whose defense is that, taken as a group, the compromises—across a range of statutes— allow the legislature to adopt statutes that provide net benefits to society. The key point is that the compromises are justified *systemically*, not one by one. We might not be able to provide a rational justification for the "current connection" rule, but we surely can provide such a justification for a political system in which "mere" political compromises occur. To put the point starkly: Imagine that Congress was considering a major program to improve airport security, but found itself just shy of the necessary votes. The railroaders with current connection tell the bill's sponsors: "We really don't care about airports, but if you give us more from the pot of money, we'll vote for the airport security bill." An interpretation of the Consti-

---

[46] For an introduction, see "What Is Judicial Engagement?," available at https://ij.org /center-for-judicial-engagement/programs/what-is-judicial-engagement/.

[47] 449 US 166 (1980), cited in *Trump v Hawaii*, 138 S Ct at 2420.

tution that cast doubt on that deal would in my view be defective.[48] And, specifically, invalidating one specific compromise on weak minimal-rationality grounds would disrupt the overall system of pluralist politics.

There is a parallel to the pluralist-politics defense of a weak mere-rationality standard in connection with *Trump v Hawaii*. It is that successful presidential candidates need no justification whatever for carrying through on their campaign promises. Those promises may entail adopting foolish or completely ineffective policies, but so what (from a constitutional point of view)? All that should matter is that the promises were made and honored. Campaign promises are the meat and potatoes of appeals to voters, and on any decent account of democracy voters are entitled to get what they vote for even if, again, what they want is foolish or ineffective.

Voters can't get everything they want, though. If a candidate promises to "lock her up," he can't fulfill that pledge because to do so would clearly violate the Constitution without satisfying constitutionally required procedures and standards of proof. But consider a campaign promise to send direct monetary payments to churches to pay for the construction of parking structures to accommodate those attending services. Assume that governing Supreme Court precedent supports the proposition that the program is unconstitutional, but a plausible argument could be made that the Court's understanding of the Constitution is mistaken.

The theory known as departmentalist constitutional interpretation, or the related theory of popular constitutionalism, might suggest that the courts should be deferential to a presidential decision that implemented a campaign promise of this kind. Those theories hold that Presidents and, I think by necessary implication, candidates for the Presidency can offer and act upon rationally defensible constitutional interpretations that differ from otherwise authoritative judicial interpretations. Ordinarily, even on a departmentalist account, the President chooses a policy based upon his or her reasonable constitutional interpretation, the action is challenged in court, and ultimately the Supreme Court decides whether to uphold the challenge or the policy, based upon its independent assessment of the

---

[48] For a contrary view, see Cass Sunstein, *Naked Preferences and the Constitution*, 84 Colum L Rev 1689 (1984).

relevant constitutional arguments. That assessment might give the President's arguments the weight they rationally deserved, but it would not give deference to the President. That is, the Court would not give any weight to the mere fact that the arguments were offered within a defensible departmentalist account of constitutional interpretation.

Arguably the courts should treat campaign pledges differently when they are supported (or supportable) by a departmentalist account. The reason is parallel to that offered in support of weak minimal rationality within pluralist politics. With campaign pledges, independent judicial assessment of campaign pledges' constitutionality might undermine or transform the role of such pledges in democratic politics in unpredictable ways. Voters probably know that some campaign pledges are cheap talk, others not. If the courts did what they ordinarily do, and made their own assessment of the constitutionality of policies that implement campaign pledges, that would further muddy the waters by making it impossible for voters to figure out which promises were cheap talk, which not. So, it might make sense for the courts to give some deference to a departmentalist interpretation supporting a campaign promise. Weak minimal rationality might be the correct standard.

In the typical case of judicial review and departmentalism, courts would engage in an independent evaluation of the evidence supporting the proposition that a facially neutral statute or executive order was badly motivated. It might be, though, that the campaign-promise context matters. That EO-3 fulfilled a campaign pledge played no overt role in the Court's analysis, but that fact might provide stronger support for the use of a weak minimal-rationality test than the arguments the Chief Justice offered.

IV. The Ambiguities of Rational Basis Review in Trump v Hawaii

The Court's formulation of the weak rational-basis standard was, "can reasonably be understood to result from a justification independent of unconstitutional grounds." The verb form appropriate to such a formulation is "could": The policy could have been adopted by a President who lacked unconstitutional animus. Yet, at some points the verb form "is" or its equivalent occurs. So, for example, the Chief Justice wrote, "there is persuasive evidence that the entry suspension *has* a legitimate ground in national security considerations."[49]

"Is" differs from "could" when we consider the scope of executive power in general. Holding that a purely domestic policy resulting from religious bigotry is constitutional if there actually were minimally rational reasons supporting it would transform the law of unconstitutional motivation quite dramatically. Existing law puts several questions about facially neutral statutes. Given facial neutrality, were they nonetheless motivated by racial or religious bigotry? If so, are there sufficiently strong reasons of public policy justifying the statute?[50]

As if acknowledging this difficulty, the Chief Justice seemed to limit the domain of weak minimal-rationality review of badly motivated executive orders and, perhaps, only certain kinds of executive orders. EO-3 involved "national security and foreign affairs," it applied to "foreign nationals" and not U.S. citizens, it dealt with "the privilege of admission,"[51] and—implicit in the Chief Justice's description of *Korematsu*—it operated outside U.S. borders.

Trump v Hawaii can be understood in part as a stage in the development of a rights-affecting National Security Constitution.[52] Its most immediate predecessor is *Holder v Humanitarian Law Project.*[53] That case upheld as consistent with the Free Speech Clause a statute restricting the ability of U.S. citizens to provide information about international law to certain terrorist groups, where the activity was coordinated with those groups. Chief Justice Roberts's opinion for the Court characterized the statute as content-based, thereby triggering a high degree of scrutiny. Yet, in exercising that scrutiny, the Court repeatedly deferred to judgments made by—and sometimes simply imputed to—the executive branch. *Hawaii v Trump* confirms what was apparent when *Holder* was decided: Deference is characteristic of minimal-rationality review, not strict scrutiny.

---

[49] 138 S Ct at 2421 (emphasis added). I think the following qualifies as well, though I concede that others might read it differently: EO-3 *"reflects* the results of a worldwide review process. . . ." Id (emphasis added).

[50] See, for example, *Church of Lukumi Babalu Aye, Inc. v Hialeah*, 508 US 520 (1993).

[51] On this limitation, see note 6 above.

[52] See Harold Koh, *The National Security Constitution: Sharing Power After the Iran-Contra Affair* (Yale, 1990) (primarily addressing separation-of-powers issues).

[53] 561 US 1 (2010).

And, as in *Hawaii v Trump*, in *Holder* the Chief Justice built quali-fications into the Court's holding, qualifications whose justification appears to be solely to ensure that the rights-affecting national security Constitution doesn't threaten constitutional rights in purely domestic contexts. Most notably, the Court asserted that its analysis wouldn't apply in connection with exactly the same information were it to be provided to domestic terrorist groups. One rationale for upholding the statute was that assistance was "fungible," in the sense that the terrorist groups wouldn't have to come up with their own resources to acquire the information and so could use those resources to support their vi-olent actions. The Court said that the statute might be unconstitu-tional were it to apply to support not coordinated with the groups but rather provided entirely independently of them. Yet, the fungibility argument is as strong with respect to independent information pro-vision as it is with respect to coordinated provision.

Perhaps the development of a rights-affecting national security Constitution is a good thing. I think, though, that it should be defended directly on that ground rather than attempting to say that such a Constitution is just the good old Constitution we have had for more than two hundred years.

The rights-affecting national security Constitution has been con-structed to this point to exclude U.S. citizens from its express cover-age.[54] Scholars have devoted substantial attention to whether the U.S. national border is either morally or constitutionally significant, for example in asking whether U.S. officials are bound by the Constitution when they act outside those borders. The rights-affecting national security Constitution might be understood to instruct U.S. officials that their primary concern lies with securing the welfare of people within the nation's borders. It might reflect the view that U.S. officials should give those people's interests more weight because they are within the United States, beyond whatever value attaches to them as human beings. Giving some added weight to the interests of one's family and even one's neighbors seems to many either morally ac-ceptable or morally desirable. I'm agnostic about whether the moral case for this practice extends to "mere" co-citizens: As a resident of

---

[54] But see *Hamdi v Rumsfeld*, 542 US 507 (200) (holding, in a case involving a U.S. citizen, that the Due Process Clause permitted adjudicative bodies dealing with alleged terrorists to rely upon hearsay and similar evidence that would not ordinarily be admissible in similar domestic proceedings). Hamdi's U.S. citizenship was in some sense accidental: He was a birthright cit-izen who had not had significant contacts with the United States for most of his life.

Washington, DC, why should I care more about the human consequences of wildfires in northern California than about bone-chilling
cold in Toronto?

Shift to the institutional level, though, and the case for instructing
officials to pay more attention to co-citizens than others might well
be defensible even in a world with an extremely strong human-rights
culture. Put in the most brutally textualist terms, the U.S. Constitution is a Constitution of *the United States*. The President has a duty
to take care that *this* Constitution be faithfully executed, and the constitutionally required oaths for other offices might be taken as having
the same content.

V. Conclusion

After his summary of Trump's anti-Muslim statements, the
Chief Justice tried to give us a civics lesson. He described the President's "extraordinary power to speak to fellow citizens," specifically
mentioning their use "of that power to espouse the principles of religious freedom and tolerance on which this Nation was founded."[55]
Justice Anthony Kennedy also spoke as a civic educator. Sometimes, he
wrote, "the statements and actions of Government officials are not
subject to judicial scrutiny or intervention." But, he continued, "That
does not mean those officials are free to disregard the Constitution. . . ."
There was "an urgent necessity that officials adhere" to constitutional
guarantees of freedom of religion "in all their actions, even in the
sphere of foreign affairs." These are the words with which Justice
Kennedy ended his Supreme Court career: "An anxious world must
know that our Government remains committed always to the liberties
the Constitution seeks to preserve and protect, so that freedom extends
outward, and lasts."[56]

Things that are sayable at one time sometimes become unsayable
later. Dissenting in *Everson v Board of Education*, Justice Robert Jackson quoted Lord Byron's epic poem *Don Juan* to disparage the majority's long essay—a civics lesson of sorts—on the importance of
keeping church and state separate coupled with its bottom-line holding that New Jersey could supply bus transportation to children attending church-related schools: "The case which irresistibly comes to

---

[55] 138 S Ct at 2417–18.

[56] Id at 2424 (Kennedy, J, concurring).

mind as the most fitting precedent is that of Julia who, according to Byron's reports, 'whispering "I will ne'er consent,"—consented.'"[57] In the #MeToo era no Justice could get away with that quotation.

Still, Justice Jackson's words accurately describe the civics lessons offered by the Chief Justice and Justice Kennedy.[58] The majority expressly repudiated *Korematsu*. The Court's decision in *Trump v Hawaii* is, though, no less racist than *Korematsu*.[59] Perhaps the attempted civics lessons make *Trump v Hawaii* worse than *Korematsu*: They show that the Chief Justice and Justice Kennedy knew—at some level of understanding—that they were doing the wrong thing, and nonetheless did it.

---

[57] 330 US 1, 19 (1947) (Jackson, J, dissenting).

[58] One might defend reprinting them by referring to the distinction between "use" and "mention," but there are enough examples of real-world situations in which speakers have been severely criticized for mentioning unsayable words to suggest that the use/mention distinction no longer has much force in the settings with which we are concerned.

[59] Justice Murphy's dissent in *Korematsu* asserted that the executive order there fell "into the ugly abyss of racism." *Korematsu v United States*, 323 US 214, 233 (1944) (Murphy, J, dissenting). Justice Murphy used the word in three opinions issued on the same day: *Korematsu*; *Ex parte Endo*, 323 US 283, 307 (1944) (Murphy, J, concurring); and *Steele v Louisville & Nashville R. Co.*, 323 US 192, 209 (1944) (Murphy, J, concurring). These are the first uses of the word in the U.S. Reports.

KATE ANDRIAS

JANUS'S TWO FACES

In ancient Roman religion and myth, Janus is the god of beginnings, transitions, and endings. He is often depicted as having two faces, one looking to the future and one to the past. The Supreme Court's *Janus v AFSCME* case of last Term is fittingly named.[1] Stunning in its disregard of principles of stare decisis, *Janus* overruled the forty-year-old precedent *Abood v Detroit Board of Education*.[2] The *Janus* decision marks the end of the post–New Deal compromise with respect to public sector unions and the First Amendment. Looking to the future, *Janus* lays the groundwork for further attack on labor rights—as well as for a broader erosion of civil society and democracy at the expense of corporate power. In that way, *Janus* represents an unequivocal transition to what Justice Kagan termed a "weaponized" view of the First Amendment among the Court's majority—indeed, far more so than her dissent elaborates.

But *Janus* may also have another, more hopeful, forward-looking face. Ultimately, *Janus*'s undoing of the compromise that governed union fees for nearly fifty years provides the opportunity for a sys-

---

Kate Andrias is Professor of Law, University of Michigan Law School.

AUTHOR'S NOTE: For helpful comments, I am grateful to Justin Driver, Sam Bagenstos, Nick Bagley, Don Herzog, and Laura Weinrib. Thanks also to Arianna Demas and Kenneth Sexauer for excellent research assistance and to the Michigan Law Library for help with Justice Frankfurter's archives.

[1] 138 S Ct 2448 (2018).

[2] 421 US 209 (1977).

tematic rethinking of the relationship between labor and the Constitution and, more generally, of the meaning of the First Amendment.

In *Janus*, the dissenters on the Court gestured at this broader project, but their future-facing efforts were partial and unsatisfying. Instead, they looked backward to *Abood*, a precedent the result of which was tolerable, but the reasoning of which was deeply flawed. *Abood* adopted a categorical approach to compelled subsidization of speech. It also fundamentally misconstrued the role of unions and their relationship to politics, the public's interest in labor relations, and the nature of the "public square." In so doing, *Abood* helped lay the groundwork for *Janus*'s demolition of union rights and for its protection of a right to exit from democratic institutions. Though stare decisis counseled in favor of maintaining *Abood*, its demise now opens up space to begin to flesh out what, in this setting, Justice Kagan's promise of a "First Amendment meant for better things" might look like.[3] This essay takes a first step toward that end.

I

There is little dispute that the Supreme Court dealt a devastating blow to unions last Term when it issued *Janus*.[4] At its core, *Janus* overruled *Abood v Detroit Board of Education*,[5] a four-decades-old precedent that allowed public employers to require employees to pay "fair-share" or "agency" fees covering the costs that unions incur in negotiating and administering labor contracts on the employees' behalf. *Janus* invalidated thousands of public sector labor-management contracts in more than twenty states, affecting millions of government employees.[6] The decision will likely have substantial adverse effects on union membership and funding in the short term,[7] while forcing

---

[3] *Janus*, 138 S Ct at 2502 (Kagan, J, dissenting).

[4] See, e.g., Sarah Jaffe, *With Janus the Court Deals Unions a Crushing Blow: Now What?*, NY Times (June 27, 2018), https://www.nytimes.com/2018/06/27/opinion/supreme-court-janus -unions.html; Chris Maisano, *Labor's Choice After Janus*, Jacobin (June 27, 2018), https:// jacobinmag.com/2018/06/labors-choice-after-janus; George Will, *In Janus the Supreme Court Corrects Its First Amendment Jurisprudence*, National Review (July 1, 2018), https://www .nationalreview.com/2018/07/supreme-court-janus-decision-win-for-first-amendment -freedoms/.

[5] 421 US 209 (1977).

[6] *Janus*, 138 S Ct at 2487–88 (Kagan, J, dissenting).

[7] Id at 2487. See Henry S. Farber, *Union Membership in the United States: The Divergence Between the Public and Private Sectors*, in Jane Hannaway and Andrew J. Rotherham, eds,

unions and government to explore new ways of structuring public sector worker representation going forward.[8] At the very least, to remain viable, unions will need to reallocate resources from organizing new workers and advocating for worker-friendly policies to soliciting fees and collecting dues.

Long before *Janus*, labor unions—and American workers—were already struggling. Globalization, the fissuring of the employment relationship, intense employer hostility to worker organizing, a weak labor law regime, and internal union deficiencies all had contributed to declining rates of unionization in the private sector.[9] Meanwhile, decades of austerity politics, the privatization of public services, and systematic conservative attack had put public sector unions on the defensive.[10] For many years, commentators had diagnosed American labor law as ossified and impotent to meet the needs of workers in the face of rising employer resistance and a transformed economy.[11] But with *Janus* and the passage of new "right-to-work" laws prohibiting agency fees in the private sector, even in states once considered union bastions, the American system of labor relations is no longer merely sclerotic and ineffectual. It is now unraveling at its seams.

To understand how momentous *Janus* was for unions and for labor law, one must understand the system of collective labor law that has governed since the New Deal. Both the National Labor Relations Act (the NLRA), which applies to private sector workers, and the

---

Collective Bargaining in Education: Negotiating Change in Today's Schools 27 (Harvard, 2006) (finding that union coverage is significantly higher where unions are allowed to negotiate union security provisions as compared to where agency shop arrangements are prohibited).

[8] See Part V.

[9] See Kate Andrias, *The New Labor Law*, 126 Yale L J 2, 13–45 (2016); David Weil, *The Fissured Workplace: Why Work Became So Bad for So Many and What Can Be Done to Improve It* (Harvard, 2014); Katherine V. W. Stone, *From Widgets to Digits: Employment Regulation for the Changing Workplace* (Cambridge 2004).

[10] On the history of the right-to-work campaign, see Sophia Z. Lee, *The Workplace Constitution from the New Deal to the New Right* 56–78, 115–32, 223–55 (Cambridge, 2014); Joseph A. McCartin and Jean-Christian Vinel, *Compulsory Unionism: Sylvester Petro and the Career of an Anti-Union Idea, 1957–1987*, in Nelson Lichtenstein and Elizabeth Tandy Shermer, eds, *The American Right and U.S. Labor in America: Politics, Ideology, and Imagination* 226 (Pennsylvania, 2012). On the history of austerity politics and the sustained attack on the welfare state, see Paul Pierson and Theda Skocpol, *The Transformation of American Politics: Activist Government and the Rise of Conservatism* (Princeton, 2007); Paul Pierson, *Dismantling the Welfare State?: Reagan, Thatcher, and the Politics of Retrenchment* (Cambridge, 1994).

[11] See, e.g., Cynthia L. Estlund, *The Ossification of American Labor Law*, 102 Colum L Rev 1527 (2002) (arguing that the National Labor Relations Act has ossified); Paul Weiler, *Promises to Keep: Securing Workers' Rights to Self-Organization Under the NLRA*, 96 Harv L Rev 1769 (1983) (detailing the failure of the NLRA to protect workers' right to organize).

vast majority of state-enacted public sector labor laws embrace the principles of majoritarian democracy. When a majority of workers in a given bargaining unit votes to unionize, the union becomes the exclusive bargaining agent charged with representing all workers in the unit, even those who objected to unionization.[12] The union has a duty to represent all of the workers fairly, and the negotiated contract benefits workers collectively.[13] In turn, each worker must pay a fee that covers the union's costs germane to its role as the exclusive bargaining agent. Without such a fee, a classic collective-action problem would arise.[14]

Beginning in the 1950s, however, the Supreme Court ruled that nonmembers could not be forced to pay for any of the union's political or ideological expenses.[15] Such contributions in the public sector, the Court opined in *Abood*, violate workers' First Amendment rights,[16] and, in the private sector, reach beyond what is permitted by statute.[17] In *Abood*, the Court explained the rule as follows: mandatory fees to cover collective bargaining are acceptable on the ground that the state has an interest in negotiating with a single bargaining representative to achieve "labor peace."[18] But, political activity, the Court concluded, is subsidiary to unions' core mission and risks conflicting with individuals' freedom of belief.[19]

This compromise—compulsory dues for the cost of representation and bargaining only—is known as the "agency-shop," or a "fair-

---

[12] 29 USC § 159; *Emporium Capwell Co. v Western Addition Community Organization*, 420 US 50 (1975); *J. I. Case Co. v NLRB*, 321 US 332 (1944).

[13] *Vaca v Sipes*, 386 US 171, 186 (1967); *Steele v Louisville & N.R. Co.*, 323 US 192, 202–3 (1944).

[14] See Mancur Olson, *The Logic of Collective Action: Public Goods and the Theory of Groups* 2 (Harvard, 1971).

[15] *Railway Employees Department v Hanson*, 351 US 225 (1956); *International Association of Machinists v Street*, 367 US 740 (1961).

[16] *Abood*, 431 US 209. See also *Chicago Teachers Union, Local No. 1 v Hudson*, 475 US 292 (1986) (establishing procedures that unions must follow to ensure employees have the ability to opt out of nonchargeable expenses).

[17] *Communication Workers of America v Beck*, 487 US 735 (1988) (interpreting the NLRA); *International Association of Machinists v Street*, 367 US 740 (1961) (interpreting the Railway Labor Act).

[18] *Abood*, 431 US at 224; see *Ellis v Brotherhood of Railway, Airline & Steamship Clerks, Freight Handlers, Express & Station Employees*, 466 US 435, 455–56 (1984) (stating that "[i]t has long been settled that . . . interference with First Amendment rights is justified by the governmental interest in industrial peace" and that compulsory fees are permissible when enabling an exclusive bargaining agreement).

[19] *Abood*, 431 US at 213, 235.

share" system. It existed in relatively stable form for over fifty years.[20] States that wished to prohibit fair-share systems and ban compulsory union fees altogether could do so for both their public and private sector workers. Yet under such "right-to-work" systems, unions must still represent the nonpaying workers, giving rise to a collective-action problem of "nightmarish proportions."[21] Until recently, however, less than half of states—nearly all in regions with little union density—had adopted right-to-work laws.[22]

With the Great Recession of 2008, however, union opponents opened up a new line of attack.[23] Conservatives systematically began pushing the argument that, in the face of stagnating wages, unionized workers, and unionized government workers in particular, constituted an "elite" whose pay and pensions were not sustainable.[24] The proposition that public sector union contracts had become too expensive, and that unsustainable and underfunded union-won pension plans were undermining the finances of cities and states, gained traction.[25] Against this background, the National Right to Work Committee (NRTWC), which had long fought unions, and mandatory

---

[20] Some scholars have argued that the dues settlement was a component of a "roughly even-handed" compromise that reduced constitutional protection for both pro- and anti-union speech. Laura Weinrib, *The Right to Work and the Right to Strike*, 2017 U Chi Legal F 513, 536 (2018); Cynthia Estlund, *Are Unions a Constitutional Anomaly?*, 114 Mich L Rev 169, 184–85, 193 (2015) (describing compromise as a quid pro quo).

[21] *Janus*, 138 S Ct at 2490 (Kagan, J, dissenting); *Abood*, 431 US at 220–22. For further discussion of the collective action problem, see Catherine L. Fisk and Martin H. Malin, *After Janus*, 107 Cal L Rev *6–16 (forthcoming 2019), https://lwp.law.harvard.edu/files/lwp/files/2019-fisk-c-malin-m-after_janus-clr-107.pdf.

[22] *Right to Work States Timeline* (National Right to Work Committee), https://nrtwc.org/facts/state-right-to-work-timeline/.

[23] Joseph A. McCartin, *Public Sector Unionism Under Assault: How to Combat the Scapegoating of Organized Labor*, 22 New Labor F 54, 55–56 (2013); Richard B. Freeman and Eunice Han, *The War Against Public Sector Collective Bargaining in the U.S.*, 54 J Industrial Relations 386 (2012).

[24] For some examples of the recent scholarly attack on public sector unions, see Daniel DiSalvo, *Government Against Itself: Public Union Power and Its Consequences* (Oxford, 2015); Steven Greenhut, *Plunder!: How Public Employee Unions Are Raiding Treasuries, Controlling Our Lives, and Bankrupting the Nation* (Forum, 2009); Steven Malanga of the Manhattan Institute added *Shakedown: The Continuing Conspiracy Against the American Taxpayer* (Ivan R. Dee, 2010); Mallory Factor, *Shadowbosses: Government Unions Control America and Rob Taxpayers Blind* (Center Street, 2012). For a history of the conservative legal movement more generally, see, e.g., Jefferson Decker, *The Other Rights Revolution: Conservative Lawyers and the Remaking of American Government* (Oxford, 2016); Steven M. Teles, *The Rise of the Conservative Legal Movement: The Battle for Control of the Law* (Princeton, 2008); Joseph Fishkin and David E. Pozen, *Asymmetric Constitutional Hardball*, 118 Colum L Rev 915, 951–59 (2018).

[25] McCartin, 22 New Labor F at 56 (cited in note 23).

fees in particular,[26] began a renewed attack on agency fees in state legislatures and in the courts.[27]

In 2012, the conservative majority on the Supreme Court took up the cause, reaching out to grant certiorari in cases presenting the constitutionality of public sector union fees, despite the absence of any circuit splits. Invoking the First Amendment, the Court began to chip away at the agency-fee system. In *Knox v SEIU*,[28] Justice Alito, writing for the majority, constructed new rules that made it harder for unions to collect fees, while warning that *Abood*'s holding is "something of an anomaly."[29] In 2014, in *Harris v Quinn*,[30] he—and the Court—went further. In *Harris*, home-care workers in Illinois contested paying fees to the union elected by a majority of fellow home-care workers. In extended dicta, Justice Alito, writing for the majority, questioned *Abood*'s analysis and suggested that the First Amendment should prohibit fair-share fees in public sector employment generally.[31] But the *Harris* Court stopped short of overruling *Abood*, concluding instead that while the home-care workers could not be required to pay an agency fee, *Abood* did not squarely control their situation because they were only quasi–public sector employees.[32] In 2016, in *Friedrichs v California Teachers Association*,[33] the Court seemed poised to finish what *Knox* and *Harris* began: to hold that the First Amendment prohibits fair-share agreements of any sort in the public sector. With Justice Scalia's death, however, the Court split 4–4, thus affirming the decision below without opinion, and letting stand existing doctrine.[34]

During this same period, the NRTWC and conservative Republicans pushed for anti-union laws in previously union-friendly states,

---

[26] See generally Lee, *The Workplace Constitution* (cited in note 10); McCartin and Vinel, *Compulsory Unionism* (cited in note 10).

[27] McCartin, 22 New Labor F at 57–58 (cited in note 23); Moshe Z. Marvit, *For 60 Years, This Powerful Conservative Group Has Worked to Crush Labor*, The Nation (July 5, 2018), https://www.thenation.com/article/group-turned-right-work-crusade-crush-labor/.

[28] *Knox v Service Employees International Union*, 567 US 298 (2012).

[29] Id at 311.

[30] 134 S Ct 2618 (2014).

[31] Id at 2630–34.

[32] Id at 2634–38.

[33] 136 S Ct 1083 (Mem) (2016) (per curiam).

[34] Id.

bringing the total number of states that prohibit agency fees in the private sector to twenty-seven.[35] Michigan, the birthplace of the once mighty United Auto Workers, enacted an expansive right-to-work law in 2012.[36] That same year, Indiana expanded its prohibition on agency fees to cover all private sector employment.[37] Wisconsin enacted a series of even more far-reaching laws, prohibiting agency fees in the private sector, while stripping most governmental workers of their collective bargaining rights.[38] The right-to-work campaigns were part of a broader, long-running project to undermine unions and to weaken the Democratic Party, with which unions had long been associated.[39]

Janus represents the capstone of the anti-union campaign. With the newly appointed Justice Gorsuch supplying the fifth vote, Justice Alito declared for the conservative majority: "Fundamental free speech rights are at stake."[40] "States and public-sector unions may no longer extract agency fees from nonconsenting employees," he explained.[41] Indeed, Alito went further, holding that the First Amend-

---

[35] *Right to Work States Timeline* (cited in note 22). But see Noam Scheiber, *Missouri Voters Reject Anti-Union Law in a Victory for Labor*, NY Times (Aug 7, 2018), https://www.nytimes.com/2018/08/07/business/economy/missouri-labor-right-to-work.html. The NLRA has been interpreted to allow states to enact "right to work" laws prohibiting agreements under which unions obtain a "union security clause" obliging all employees to pay any fees as a requirement of employment. For reasons eloquently explained by Judge Diane Wood, this statutory interpretation is questionable. See *Sweeney v Pence*, 767 F3d 654, 671 (7th Cir 2014) (Wood dissenting); see also Brief of Law Professors Andrias, Estlund, Fisk, Lee, and Weinrib as Amici Curiae in Support of Appellants, *International Union of Operating Engineers Local 139 v Schimel*, 863 F3d 674 (7th Cir 2017).

[36] Monica Davey, *Limits on Unions Pass in Michigan, Once a Mainstay*, NY Times (Dec 1, 2018), https://www.nytimes.com/2012/12/12/us/protesters-rally-over-michigan-union-limits-plan.html. See Mich Comp Laws § 423.14.

[37] Monica Davey, *Indiana Governor Signs a Law Creating a "Right to Work" State*, NY Times (Feb 1 2012), https://www.nytimes.com/2012/02/02/us/indiana-becomes-right-to-work-state.html. See Ind Code § 22-6-6.

[38] Monica Davey, *Unions Suffer Latest Defeat in Midwest with Signing of Wisconsin Measure*, NY Times (March 9, 2015), https://www.nytimes.com/2015/03/10/us/gov-scott-walker-of-wisconsin-signs-right-to-work-bill.html; Monica Davey, *Wisconsin Senate Limits Bargaining by Public Workers*, NY Times (March 9, 2011), http://archive.nytimes.com/www.nytimes.com/2011/03/10/us/10wisconsin.html. See Wis Stat § 111.04; 2011 Wis Laws 10.

[39] See Lee, *The Workplace Constitution* (cited in note 10); Elizabeth Tandy Shermer, *Sunbelt Capitalism: Phoenix and the Transformation of American Politics* (Pennsylvania, 2015). Compare with James Feigenbaum, Alexander Hertel-Fernandez, and Vanessa Williamson, *From the Bargaining Table to the Ballot Box: Political Effects of Right to Work Laws* (National Bureau of Economic Research, Working Paper No 24259, 2018), http://www.nber.org/papers/w24259.pdf (describing political effects of right-to-work laws).

[40] 138 S Ct at 2460.

[41] Id at 2486.

ment protects not only a right to opt out of union fees but requires that workers affirmatively consent before any fees can be taken from their paychecks.[42]

II

The majority opinion was stunning in its subversion of traditional principles of stare decisis. As Justice Kagan emphasized in dissent, *Abood* was not just any precedent. It was one on which there was extensive and widespread reliance in state law and contract. By overruling *Abood*, the Court "wreak[ed] havoc on entrenched legislative and contractual arrangements."[43] And it did so notwithstanding that the other factors for stare decisis were met.[44] The lower courts had not struggled to apply *Abood*.[45] The *Abood* rule was deeply embedded in federal constitutional law.[46] *Abood* cohered with the Court's approach to reviewing regulation of public employees' speech in the nonunion context, such as in *Pickering v Board of Education*.[47] And *Abood*'s requirement that workers affirmatively opt out of union dues was in line with broader First Amendment doctrine in which the Court has required that dissenters object to compulsory speech; dissent is not presumed.[48] Indeed, the only basis for the claim that *Abood*

[42] Id. Compare with Aaron Tang, *Janus and the Law of Opt-Out Rights*, Harv L Rev Blog (July 2, 2018), https://blog.harvardlawreview.org/janus-and-the-law-of-opt-out-rights/ (emphasizing novelty of the opt-out rule).

[43] 138 S Ct at 2499 (Kagan, J, dissenting). Compare with *Payne v Tennessee*, 501 US 808, 827 (1991) ("Considerations in favor of *stare decisis* are at their acme in cases involving property and contract rights. . . .").

[44] See *Planned Parenthood of Southeastern Pennsylvania v Casey*, 505 US 833, 867–68 (1992) (discussing factors in stare decisis analysis).

[45] 138 S Ct at 2498 (Kagan, J, dissenting).

[46] See, e.g., *Locke v Karass*, 555 US 207, 213–14 (2009); *Lehnert v Ferris Faculty Association*, 500 US 507, 519 (1991); *Teachers v Hudson*, 475 US 292, 301–02 (1986); *Ellis v Brotherhood of Railway, Airline & Steamship Clerks, Freight Handlers, Express & Station Employees*, 466 US 435, 455–57 (1984). The Court had also relied on the rule when deciding cases involving compelled speech subsidies outside the labor sphere, in circumstances involving, for example, bar dues and student association fees. See, e.g., *Keller v State Bar of California*, 496 US 1, 9–17 (1990) (state bar fees); *Board of Regents of University of Wisconsin System v Southworth*, 529 US 217, 230–32 (2000) (public university student activity fees); *Glickman v Wileman Brothers & Elliott, Inc.*, 521 US 457, 471–73 (1997) (commercial advertising assessments).

[47] 391 US 563 (1968) (holding that the First Amendment protects speech on matters of public concern but that public employers have a right to manage their workforces by restricting employment-related speech); *Garcetti v Ceballos*, 547 US 410 (2006) (discussing doctrine); *Janus*, 138 S Ct at 2492–97 (Kagan, J, dissenting).

[48] See *West Virginia Board of Education v Barnette*, 319 US 624 (1943) (striking down state regulation requiring expulsion of schoolchildren who refused to recite the Pledge of Alle-

had become "an outlier among [the Court's] First Amendment cases" was the doctrine Justice Alito had himself penned, in recent years, with the clear aim of weakening *Abood*—and unions.[49] The Court, Kagan charged, was doing far more than overruling a long-standing precedent. It was threatening the rule of law by undermining "the actual and perceived integrity of the judicial process."[50]

But debates about stare decisis ultimately turn on how right or wrong the underlying decision is on the merits. If *Lawrence v Texas*[51] is correct—if *Bowers v Hardwick*[52] was wrong from the day it was decided—stare decisis worries abate.[53] So is *Janus* correct on the merits? And if not, why not?

Kagan's answer to this question was again vehement. Recalling debates from the New Deal, she invoked the relationship between courts and majoritarian institutions: "There is no sugarcoating today's opinion. The majority . . . prevents the American people, acting through their state and local officials, from making important choices about workplace governance."[54] The most "alarming" feature of the majority's opinion, she explained, was that it was using the Constitution to designate winners and losers in what should be understood as a policy debate.[55] The Court was "turning the First Amendment into a sword,

---

giance); *Wooley v Maynard*, 430 US 705 (1977) (holding that a Jehovah's witness could not be criminally prosecuted for obscuring the state motto of New Hampshire, "Live Free or Die," on the prefabricated license plate of his automobile).

[49] *Janus*, 138 S Ct at 2498 (Kagan, J, dissenting).

[50] Id at 2478, quoting *Payne*, 501 US at 827. See Richard H. Fallon Jr., *Foreword: Implementing the Constitution*, 111 Harv L Rev 54, 109, 112 (1997) (describing justifications for the principle of stare decisis as promoting fairness, efficiency, predictability, and stability, and noting that "[t]o invite indiscriminate re-fighting of constitutional battles, and to raise attendant doubts about the stability of doctrine generally, would do more to retard than to advance the project of constitutionalism . . ."); Henry Paul Monaghan, *Stare Decisis and Constitutional Adjudication*, 88 Colum L Rev 723, 742–46, 757 (1988) (noting that in constitutional matters the Court has been relatively unconstrained by its own precedents but arguing that "precedent binds absent a showing of substantial countervailing considerations"). See also Randy J. Kozel, *Precedent and Speech*, 115 Mich L Rev 439 (2017) (critiquing Court's recent willingness to ignore precedent in First Amendment cases).

[51] 539 US 558 (2003).

[52] 478 US 186 (1986).

[53] *Lawrence*, 539 US at 578 ("*Bowers* was not correct when it was decided, and it is not correct today. It ought not to remain binding precedent."). But compare with Frederick Schauer, *Precedent*, 39 Stan L Rev 571, 575 (1987) ("[I]f we are truly arguing from precedent, then the fact that something was decided before gives it present value despite our current belief that the previous decision was erroneous.").

[54] *Janus*, 138 S Ct at 2501 (Kagan, J, dissenting).

[55] Id.

and using it against workaday economic and regulatory policy."[56] It was "weaponizing the First Amendment, in a way that unleashes judges, now and in the future, to intervene in economic and regulatory policy."[57] As Kagan asserted, this was "not the first time the Court ha[d] wielded the First Amendment in such an aggressive way."[58]

Kagan was echoing a charge made by multiple observers that the Roberts Court has used the First Amendment much as the *Lochner* Court did the Due Process Clause—to thwart democratically chosen outcomes and, more specifically, to protect the privileges of the economically powerful while resisting legislative and executive efforts to advance the interests of the less powerful.[59] Kagan cited two recent cases, *National Institute of Family and Life Advocates v Becerra*[60] and *Sorrell v IMS Health Inc.*[61] She could have added numerous others, including *FEC v Wisconsin Right to Life*,[62] *Citizens United v FEC*,[63]

---

[56] Id.

[57] Id.

[58] *Janus*, 138 S Ct at 2501 (Kagan, J, dissenting).

[59] See, e.g., Jeremy K. Kessler and David E. Pozen, *The Search for an Egalitarian First Amendment*, 118 Colum L Rev 1953, 1959–60 (2018); Genevieve Lakier, *Imagining an Antisubordinating First Amendment*, 118 Colum L Rev 2117, 2158–59 (2018); Catherine L. Fisk, *A Progressive Labor Vision of the First Amendment: Past as Prologue*, 118 Colum L Rev 2057, 2062–63 (2018); Jedediah Purdy, *Beyond the Bosses' Constitution: The First Amendment and Class Entrenchment*, 118 Colum L Rev 2161 (2018); Weinrib, 2017 U Chi Legal F at 533–35 (cited in note 20); Amanda Shanor, *The New Lochner*, 2016 Wis L Rev 133 (2016); Charlotte Garden, *The Deregulatory First Amendment at Work*, 51 Harv CR-CL L Rev 323, 323–24 (2016); Elizabeth Sepper, *Free Exercise Lochnerism*, 115 Colum L Rev 1453, 1455–57 (2015); Jedediah Purdy, *The Roberts Court v. America*, Democracy (Winter 2012), http://democracyjournal.org/magazine/23/the-roberts-court-v-america; Joseph Fishkin and William E. Forbath, *Constitutional Political Economy When the Court Is to the Right of the Country*, Balkinization (June 28, 2018), http://balkin.blogspot.com/2018/06/constitutional-political-economy-when.html. See also Jeremy K. Kessler, *The Early Years of First Amendment Lochnerism*, 116 Colum L Rev 1915, 1917–18 nn 5–8 (2016) (collecting sources published from 2011 to 2016 that suggest the First Amendment has been "hijacked" by antistatist, economically libertarian interests).

[60] 138 S Ct 2361 (2018) (invalidating a law requiring medical and counseling facilities to provide relevant factual information to patients).

[61] 564 US 552 (2011) (striking down a law that restricted pharmacies from selling data).

[62] 551 US 449 (2007) (holding that the federal campaign finance law's prohibition on use of corporate funds to finance electioneering communications during pre-federal-election periods violated corporation's free speech rights when applied to its issue-advocacy advertisements).

[63] 558 US 310 (2010) (striking down on First Amendment grounds federal restrictions on corporate "electioneering communications").

Arizona Free Enterprise Club's Freedom Club PAC v Bennett,[64] *Mc-Cutcheon v FEC,*[65] and *Harris v Quinn.*[66]

As scholars have detailed, the Roberts Court's First Amendment cases, taken together, expand the scope of activity that the First Amendment protects, transforming what was previously understood as ordinary business activity into protected speech.[67] The decisions are also increasingly absolutist: once the speech interest is identified, the governmental interest is nearly always insufficient to justify the regulation. The cases thus enable individuals and corporations to opt out of democratically made decisions, while disabling the government from engaging in regulation, frequently, regulation that achieves redistribution.[68] An empirical study recently concluded, "[n]early half of First Amendment legal challenges now benefit business corporations and trade groups, rather than other kinds of organizations or individuals."[69]

III

At the very end of the opinion, Kagan briefly moved beyond critique to gesture toward an affirmative vision for the First Amendment. "The First Amendment," she asserted, "was meant for better things. It was meant not to undermine but to protect democratic governance—including over the role of public-sector unions."[70] But

---

[64] 564 US 721 (2011) (striking down on First Amendment grounds provision of Arizona's Citizens Clean Elections Act which provided matching funds to publicly financed candidates when privately funded opponent's spending exceeds the publicly financed candidate's initial state allotment).

[65] 572 US 185 (2014) (striking down on First Amendment grounds Federal Elections Campaign Act's (FECA) aggregate limit on candidate contributions and other contributions to party committees).

[66] 134 S Ct 2618 (2014) (striking down on First Amendment grounds agency fee requirement for home-care workers).

[67] See sources cited in notes 61–66; see also *Burwell v Hobby Lobby Stores, Inc.*, 134 S Ct 2751 (2014) (holding that the Religious Freedom and Restoration Act permits commercial enterprises to opt out of laws they judge incompatible with their sincerely held religious beliefs).

[68] See Garden, 51 Harv CR-CL L Rev at 332 (cited in note 59); Kessler and Pozen, 118 Colum L Rev at 1960 (cited in note 59); Purdy, 118 Colum L Rev at 2162–63 (cited in note 59). For further discussion of the implications of this doctrine, see Part IV.

[69] John C. Coates IV, *Corporate Speech & the First Amendment: History, Data, & Implications,* 30 Const Comm 223, 224 (2015).

[70] *Janus*, 138 S Ct at 2502 (Kagan, J, dissenting).

what does it mean to say that the First Amendment is meant for better things? Despite Kagan's searing assessment of the majority's approach, her opinion offered scant explanation of what a First Amendment doctrine protecting democratic governance would look like.

Instead, in offering an alternative to the weaponized First Amendment, Kagan looked backward to *Abood*. Her dissent rested on a defense of *Abood*'s essential compromise—its acceptance of compulsory union fees to cover expenses germane to collective bargaining but not to politics. Yet while *Abood*'s outcome was tolerable for unions, the opinion's reasoning was deeply flawed on at least three levels. First, *Abood* overstated the speech harm to dissenting workers. Second, it fundamentally misdefined the role of unions and their relationship to politics, as well as the public's interest in labor questions. Third, it adopted a crabbed understanding of the government's interest in facilitating unions, one that rested on a narrow and one-sided view of the speech rights at stake. Ultimately, *Abood* offered, at best, a feeble defense of public sector unions and their relationship to democratic governance. At worst, the *Abood* compromise helped to sow the seeds for the weaponized, *Lochner*-ized First Amendment.[71]

A

The *Janus* majority and dissent share a basic premise: dues payments are a form of compelled speech protected by the First Amendment. That premise, which lies at the core of the "weaponized First Amendment," long predates the Roberts Court.

Prior to World War II, the lawyers who championed the freedom of speech and expression were concerned, above all, with protecting labor's rights—the right to organize, to picket, to strike.[72] But as early

---

[71] Consider Kessler, 116 Colum L Rev at 1922 (cited in note 59) (arguing that First Amendment *Lochner*-ism long predates the Roberts Court and that economically libertarian tendencies "may be intrinsic to judicial enforcement of civil liberties").

[72] Laura Weinrib, *The Taming of Free Speech: America's Civil Liberties Compromise* (Harvard, 2016). For additional work exploring how progressive lawyers, administrators, and activists invoked a range of constitutional rights, largely but not exclusively outside of the courts, in the hopes of building a more socioeconomically equal, pluralistic, and democratic society, see Jeremy K. Kessler, *The Administrative Origins of Modern Civil Liberties Law*, 114 Colum L Rev 1083 (2014); Risa L. Goluboff, *The Lost Promise of Civil Rights* (Harvard, 2007); Ken I. Kersch, *Constructing Civil Liberties: Discontinuities in the Development of American Constitutional Law* (Cambridge, 2004); Reuel E. Schiller, *Free Speech and Expertise: Administrative Censorship and the Birth of the Modern First Amendment*, 86 Va L Rev 1 (2000); James Pope, *Labor's Constitution of Freedom*, 106 Yale L J 941 (1997).

as the mid-1930s, conservative lawyers and businessmen began to reframe their *Lochner*-era substantive due process arguments in the language of the First Amendment, challenging New Deal regulation and collective labor rights as threats to free expression and individual rights.[73] By the postwar period, liberal lawyers and politicians shared some of conservatives' concerns about growing labor power and the "totalitarian" reach of the administrative state.[74] Ultimately, they coalesced around a compromise that allowed deferential review of ordinary economic legislation but promised active judicial review to protect individual civil liberties.[75] The line between economic policy and individual liberties was, however, contested from the outset. By the mid-1940s, the Supreme Court had already begun to invoke the First Amendment to protect employers' right to oppose unionization—with support from both business groups and the American Civil Liberties Union.[76]

Ironically, the Court's move to constitutionalizing a right to opt out of union dues can be traced to a 1956 case involving a private sector workforce, where the First Amendment typically does not apply.[77] In *Railway Employees Department v Hanson*,[78] the NRTW Foundation argued that the Railway Labor Act violated the First Amendment because it allowed railroad employers to compel employees to join and support unions.[79] The Court found state action, but without deciding

---

[73] Weinrib, *Taming of Free Speech* at 226–310 (cited in note 72); Kessler, 116 Colum L Rev at 1925–36 (cited in note 59); Kate E. Andrias, *A Robust Public Debate: Realizing Free Speech in Workplace Representation Elections*, 112 Yale L J 2415, 2423–26 (2003); Lee, *The Workplace Constitution* (cited in note 10). See also Gillian E. Metzger, Foreword, *1930s Redux: The Administrative State Under Siege*, 131 Harv L Rev 1, 52–62 (2017).

[74] Kessler, 114 Colum L Rev at 757–73 (cited in note 72). See also Weinrib, 2017 U Chi Legal F at 526–29 (cited in note 20) (describing how the Court backed away from its protection of labor's concerted activity).

[75] See Laura M. Weinrib, *The Liberal Compromise: Civil Liberties, Labor, and the Limits of State Power, 1917–1940* (May 1, 2011) (unpublished PhD diss., Princeton University), http://chicagounbound.uchicago.edu/cgi/viewcontent.cgi?article=1005&context=other_publications. The oft-cited judicial encapsulation of this view is *United States v Carolene Products Co.*, 304 US 144, 152 n 4 (1938).

[76] *NLRB v Virginia Electric & Power Co.*, 314 US 469 (1941). See Weinrib, 17 U Chi Legal F at 529 (cited in note 20); Weinrib, *Taming of Free Speech* at ch 8 (cited in note 72); see also Andrias, 112 Yale L J at 2423–26 (cited in note 73).

[77] See Lee, *The Workplace Constitution* at 75–78, 89–93, 103, 124, 166–67, 179–82, 216–17, 245–53 (cited in note 10) (providing a history of the relationship between the state-action doctrine and debates about exclusive representation).

[78] 351 US 225 (1956).

[79] See Lee, *The Workplace Constitution* at 122–29 (cited in note 10).

the First Amendment question it rejected the NRTW's argument on the ground that nothing in the record indicated that the union was actually spending money for political purposes.[80]

A few years later, however, in *International Association of Machinists v Street*, the Court concluded that railroad collective-bargaining agreements requiring payment of union dues or fees do raise First Amendment concerns to the extent that the union spends the money on political causes.[81] The Court then avoided the constitutional issue by reading—or straining to read—the Railway Labor Act (RLA) not to authorize union security provisions that require employees to pay fees to support political causes.[82] In 1977, the Court extended the compelled-speech holding to public sector workers with *Abood*—the case *Janus* overruled. The Court ruled that Michigan could not constitutionally allow expenditure of agency fees on political activities over the objection of Detroit's nonunion teachers.[83] The Court also applied the same logic to state bars in *Keller v State Bar of California*, holding that attorneys' bar dues could not be used for political advocacy that was not "germane" to "the State's interest in regulating the legal profession and improving the quality of legal services."[84] Later, the Court brought its reasoning back to the private sector in *Communications Workers v Beck*, as a matter of statutory construction of the National Labor Relations Act.[85]

Throughout this circuitous line of cases, however, the Court never offered a satisfying explanation for why requiring workers to subsidize a union (or requiring citizens to subsidize another representative organization) constitutes a violation of the First Amendment.[86] Com-

---

[80] The Court found state action on a theory like the one it adopted in *Shelley v Kraemer*, 334 US 1, 20 (1948) (government enforcement of restrictive covenants is state action). According to the Court, the RLA's preemption of a state law invalidating a contract made the contract terms state action. But the Court never extended this theory beyond the RLA. See Lee, *The Workplace Constitution* (cited in note 10).

[81] 367 US 740, 749 (1961).

[82] Id at 750–70.

[83] 431 US at 225–56.

[84] 496 US 1, 13 (1990).

[85] 487 US 735 (1988).

[86] Several scholars have argued that there is no persuasive answer. William Baude and Eugene Volokh, Comment, *Compelled Subsidies and the First Amendment*, 132 Harv L Rev 171 (2018); see also Catherine Fisk and Erwin Chermerinsky, *Exaggerating the Effects of Janus: A Reply to Professors Baude and Volokh*, 132 Harv L Rev F 42 (2018) (agreeing that *Janus* was wrongly decided because paying money for services is not compelled speech that violates the

pulsory payment of fees does not constitute "true 'compelled speech'"
in which an individual is obliged personally to express a message with
which he disagrees.[87] Compulsory payment of fees also does not restrict the payor's own speech. As Justice Frankfurter wrote in his *Street*
dissent, union objectors are not subject to "suppression of their true
beliefs."[88] "The individual member may express his views in any public
or private forum as freely as he could before the union collected his
dues."[89]

From this vantage point, union dues are analogous to the wide range
of circumstances where the government compels speech without
triggering any First Amendment inquiry.[90] For example, legislators
require witnesses to testify at hearings; judges insist that jurors pro-
nounce verdicts; agency heads force regulated entities to report all
sorts of information.[91] Like union dues, these compulsions occur
without attribution of particular views to the speaker and without a
restriction of the speaker's own speech.[92]

First Amendment); Catherine L. Fisk and Margaux Poueymirou, *Harris v. Quinn and the
Contradictions of Compelled Speech*, 48 Loyola LA L Rev 439 (2015) (arguing that the Court
wrongly finds compelled speech in union dues while ignoring the associational rights of
unions). Brishen Rogers disagrees with the *Abood* approach, but he notes that it is broadly
consistent with a mid-century "civil libertarian" approach that emphasized individual rights
and expression in the political sphere but not the economic sphere. See Brishen Rogers, *Three
Concepts of Workplace Freedom of Association*, 37 Berkeley J Empl & Labor L 177 (2016).

[87] Justice Scalia drew the distinction between true compelled speech and compelled subsidization of speech in *Johanns v Livestock Marketing Association*, 544 US 550, 557 (2005). For
examples of cases the Court sees as involving "true compelled speech," see *West Virginia
Board of Education v Barnette*, 319 US 624 (1943); *Wooley v Maynard*, 430 US 705 (1977).

[88] *Street*, 367 US at 805 (Frankfurter, J, dissenting).

[89] Id at 806.

[90] Robert Post, *Compelled Subsidization of Speech: Johanns v Livestock Marketing Association*, 2005
Supreme Court Review 195, 216 (2005). See also Nikolas Bowie, *The Government Could Not
Work Doctrine*, 105 Va L Rev *1 (forthcoming 2019), https://poseidon01.ssrn.com/delivery.php
?ID = 86610507112210308910209112009201707503105407104501708709511010310 11
05001067068114109106101006099105006110085012114086100114098007082094092014
08311510208402201506508609004407612601011707311212002502302607912000511109
81181070920920760910730710260170830 97&EXT = pdf (arguing that applying strict scrutiny
to objectionable compulsion undermines government's ability to function).

[91] Id at *35; Post, 2005 Supreme Court Review at 216 (cited in note 90).

[92] The Court has inconsistently relied on the distinction between compulsions that require
endorsement of speech or imputation of views and compulsions that do not. Compare *Rumsfeld
v Forum for Academic and Institutional Rights*, 547 US 47 (2006) (emphasizing distinction between compelled subsidization of speech and compelled endorsement of speech and upholding
a federal statute that required institutions of higher education to provide military recruiters
equal access to that provided to other employers); *Board of Regents of the University of Wisconsin
System v Southworth*, 529 US 217 (2000) (upholding university requirement that students pay
fees to support organizations as long as university distributed fees in viewpoint neutral manner);

More to the point, if union dues constitute compelled speech, it is hard to see why fees and taxes imposed by the government do not as well.[93] As Justice Frankfurter emphasized in his *Street* dissent, the government requires us to pay for speech by the government all the time.[94] Pacifists must pay taxes knowing some portion will be used to subsidize pro-military expression. Climate change deniers must fund significant environmental measures expressing the contrary. Atheists must fund the speech of numerous government chaplains. None of these individuals has a First Amendment claim.[95] So too, the Court has held that the government may compel us to fund the speech of private actors, including political candidates through the public financing of political campaigns.[96] This is true even though the Court has concluded that restrictions on campaign expenditures violate the First Amendment.[97] In Justice Frankfurter's words, "[o]n the largest

---

Glickman v Wileman Brothers & Elliot, Inc., 521 US 457 (1997) (upholding a federal marketing program for California summer fruits that required private parties to subsidize advertising campaign on ground that program did not require endorsement); *PruneYard Shopping Center v Robins*, 447 US 74, 87 (1980) (holding that state constitutional provisions authorizing individuals to petition on the property of a privately owned shopping center did not raise First Amendment concerns even though it required the property owners to subsidize speech; the views of the persons petitioning would "not likely be identified with those of the owner"), with *Agency for International Development v Alliance for Open Society International*, 570 US 205, 208, 213, 218 (2013) (striking down a statute that prohibited federal funds from going to organizations that did not have "a policy explicitly opposing prostitution and sex trafficking" because the government was "compelling a grant recipient to adopt a particular belief as a condition of funding").

[93] Baude and Volokh, 132 Harv L Rev at 9–13 (cited in note 86); Bowie, 105 Va L Rev at *24–25 (cited in note 90).

[94] *International Association of Machinists v Street*, 367 US 740, 808 (1961) (Frankfurter, J, dissenting).

[95] See *United States v Lee*, 455 US 252, 260 (1982) ("The tax system could not function if denominations were allowed to challenge the tax system because tax payments were spent in a manner that violates their religious belief."); *Lyng v Northwest Indian Cemetery Protective Association*, 485 US 439, 451–52 (1988) (emphasizing that the First Amendment does not allow citizens to veto public programs of which they do not approve); *Johanns*, 544 US at 562 ("[Citizens] have no First Amendment right not to fund government speech. And that is no less true when the funding is achieved through targeted assessments devoted exclusively to the program to which the assessed citizens object."). For further discussion, see Bowie, 105 Va L Rev at *23–25 (cited in note 90); compare with Part IV (discussing developments post *Janus*).

[96] *Buckley v Valeo*, 424 US 1, 91–92 (1976) (per curiam) (rejecting a challenge to the federal campaign finance law that compelled taxpayers to subsidize presidential candidates who asked for public funding and upholding the financing scheme as no different from "any other appropriation from the general revenue").

[97] See Bowie, 105 Va L Rev at *23 (cited in note 90) (analyzing Court's public financing holding in *Buckley v Valeo*); Baude and Volokh, 132 Harv L Rev at 189–90 (cited in note 86) (questioning the analogy between compelling to give money and restricting money).

scale, the Federal Government expends revenue collected from individual taxpayers to propagandize ideas which many taxpayers oppose."[98]

The Court has recognized the tension between the *Abood* line of cases prohibiting compelled subsidization and the obligation to pay taxes and other government fees, but has provided little reasoned justification for the distinction.[99] It has simply asserted that "[c]itizens may challenge compelled support of private speech, but have no First Amendment right not to fund government speech."[100] Notably, the Court has not clarified whether compelled subsidization of government speech does not implicate speech interests or rather whether the government's interest in raising revenue and maintaining its operations outweighs any speech harm.[101]

Justice Powell—who would have restricted agency fees even more than the majority in *Abood*—claimed that subsidization of government speech was different than subsidization of private organizations because government was "representative of the people."[102] But under this logic, compulsion to contribute to a union should be permissible as well: a fundamental tenet of labor law is that the union is a majoritarian body that must represent all workers in the bargaining unit fairly; and the Labor Management Reporting and Disclosure Act of 1959 is designed to ensure that all workers are entitled to rights of democratic participation.[103]

By deeming compelled union fees protected speech, *Abood* helped to lay the foundation for the weaponized First Amendment.[104] For

---

[98] *Street*, 367 US at 808 (Frankfurter, J, dissenting).

[99] Compare *United States v United Foods, Inc.*, 533 US 405 (2001) (holding that mandatory check-off for generic mushroom advertising violated the First Amendment) with *Johanns*, 544 US at 566–67 (because the generic beef advertising at issue was the government's own speech it was exempt from First Amendment scrutiny). See Post, 2005 Supreme Court Review at 197 (cited in note 90).

[100] *Johanns*, 544 US at 562; see also id at 559, quoting *Southworth*, 529 US at 529 ("[I]t seems inevitable that funds raised by the government will be spent for speech and other expression to advocate and defend its own policies.").

[101] Id.

[102] *Abood v Detroit Board of Education*, 431 US 209, 259 n 13 (1977) (Powell, J, concurring).

[103] See 29 USC §§ 411–15; *Sheet Metal Workers' International Association v Lynn*, 488 US 347 (1989); Fisk and Malin, 107 Cal Law Rev at *4 (cited in note 21).

[104] The Court's increasing solicitude for commercial speech also played an important role in the weaponizing of the First Amendment. See *Central Hudson Gas & Electric Corp. v Public Service Commission of New York*, 447 US 557, 566 (1980); *Buckley v Valeo*, 424 US 1, 19 (1976); *First National Bank of Boston v Bellotti*, 435 US 765, 784 (1978); *Virginia State Board of*

if union dues cause a First Amendment harm worthy of strict scrutiny—even though they involve payment to a representative, democratic body and do not require actual speech by the payor, restrict the payor's speech, or risk attribution of a view to the payor—all sorts of other compulsions could too, certainly much governmental regulation and perhaps even some taxes.[105]

B

The problem with *Abood*'s reasoning, however, stems not only from the initial determination that the First Amendment is implicated but also from what followed next. One could grant that union dues constitute an infringement on dissenters' freedom of speech (or association) rights but recognize that the infringement is marginal, while engaging in a reasoned inquiry about the social value of union dues. Here, too, however, *Abood* and the *Janus* dissent fell short.

American constitutional rights over the twentieth century have frequently been framed as absolutes.[106] In the First Amendment area, once a regulation falls into the category of restricting or compelling protected speech, and in particular political speech, the regulation is likely to fail. The work is done by the categorization.[107] At that point, little attention is paid to how burdensome a regime is in practice, or how good a reason the government has for its regulation in light of the particular situation. *Janus* is part and parcel of this approach: once the Court concluded that political speech was burdened, the union objector was destined to win. The government's interests could not outweigh this categorically grievous harm.

Abood and the *Janus* dissent, at first blush, appear to take a different approach, weighing the government's interest in labor peace, and therefore in exclusive representation, against the objecting worker's interest in not being compelled to subsidize speech with which she disagrees. Having so balanced, *Abood* concluded that the government's interest could prevail with respect to matters germane to collective

---

Pharmacy v Virginia Citizens Consumer Council, Inc., 425 US 748, 762 (1976); Garden, 51 Harv CR-CL L Rev at 325 (cited in note 56); Robert Post, *Compelled Commercial Speech*, 117 W Va L Rev 867 (2015).

[105] See Part IV.

[106] Jamal Greene, Foreword, *Rights as Trumps?*, 132 Harv L Rev 28 (2018).

[107] Id at 40. See also Kathleen M. Sullivan, Foreword, *The Justices of Rules and Standards*, 106 Harv L Rev 22, 58 (1992).

bargaining. But, in fact, *Abood* was nearly as categorical as *Janus*, for the *Abood* Court agreed that dues for political speech were absolutely protected. This is the position Justice Kagan defended.

The compromise that divided political activity from matters germane to collective bargaining was understood to be a victory for unions when first announced, and from a financial perspective, it worked fairly well for labor organizations for forty plus years.[108] But as Alito argued in *Janus*, it is untenable to see politics as not germane to unions' work.[109] Indeed, in defining all political activity as not germane to unions' core function, *Abood* fundamentally misdefined unions. It implied that the primary job of unions is that of private business agents whose goal is to resolve narrow disputes for a defined set of members, rather than as organizations participating in a broader deliberation, and sometimes struggle, about the legitimacy of social practices relating to workers' lives, including both the scope of employer authority and the distribution of resources in society.[110]

Throughout its history, the American labor movement's relationship to politics—and to the state—has been complicated and multi-faceted.[111] Yet it has never been so limited as the *Abood* line of cases suggests. As far back as the Gilded Age, broad and radical reform politics characterized the views of the mainstream labor movement.[112] The Knights of Labor in the 1880s, who organized unskilled and skilled workers together, sought to transform an economic system of

---

[108] See Lee, *The Workplace Constitution* at 131 (cited in note 10) ("[l]abor advocates agreed that they had emerged from *Street* relatively unscathed" and describing *Street* as a "major loss" for the right-to-work movement).

[109] The division of the political from the economic characterized other areas of labor law in the post–New Deal era, presenting similar problems. See Karl E. Klare, *The Public/Private Distinction in Labor Law*, 130 U Pa L Rev 1358 (1981); Rogers, 37 Berkeley J Empl & Labor L at 28–29 (cited in note 86). The *Janus* majority also objected to the *Abood* compromise on the ground that the line between matters of public concern and matters germane to collective bargaining is hard to draw. But, as Kagan correctly notes, many lines are hard to draw and courts nonetheless draw them. Moreover, there is little evidence that courts have had significant difficulties separating chargeable and nonchargeable expenses. See *Ellis v Brotherhood of Railway, Airline & Steamship Clerks, Freight Handlers, Express & Station Employees*, 466 US 435 (1984).

[110] See Don Herzog, *Household Politics: Conflict in Early Modern England* 99–100 (2013) (describing politics as the realm of conflict over legitimate authority and, more broadly, over the legitimacy of social practices).

[111] See, e.g., Christopher L. Tomlins, *The State and the Unions: Labor Relations, Law, and the Organized Labor Movement in America, 1880–1960* (Cambridge, 1985); William E. Forbath, *The Shaping of the American Labor Movement*, 102 Harv L Rev 1109, 1185–95 (1989).

[112] Forbath, 102 Harv L Rev at 1121–23 (cited in note 111).

"wage slavery" into one committed to "republican liberty."[113] By the early twentieth century, in response to widespread court injunctions against labor activity, the rising American Federation of Labor (AFL) had adopted a less political, more "voluntarist" approach, the primary goal of which was to remove the coercive power of the state from industrial relations.[114] Yet the AFL, too, used political strategies to achieve its goals, eventually winning the Norris LaGuardia Act and the Clayton Act, which limited the ability of federal courts to enjoin labor action.[115]

The rise of the Congress of Industrial Unions (CIO) in the 1930s and '40s saw the return of a competing approach, as the more radical industrial unions saw politics and economics as inexorably connected, and advanced a vision of social democracy as well as industrial unionism.[116] Their efforts were in line with Progressives and New Dealers who envisioned a broad role for worker organizations and other civic associations in government—and a robust role for the state in enabling such involvement.[117]

Despite the competing visions of unionism, during this period both the AFL and the CIO used legislative and administrative strategies, as well as shop-floor militancy, to advance their goals.[118] In the aftermath of the postwar Taft-Hartley reforms, which constrained labor's ability to engage in militant class-wide collective action and otherwise limited its strength, subsequent decades saw a return toward a

---

[113] Alex Gourevitch, *From Slavery to the Cooperative Commonwealth: Labor and Republican Liberty in the Nineteenth Century* (Cambridge, 2015); William E. Forbath, *Caste, Class, and Equal Citizenship*, 98 Mich L Rev 1, 58 (1999).

[114] Forbath, 102 Harv L Rev at 1118 (cited in note 111).

[115] Id at 1226–33; Nelson Lichtenstein, *State of the Union: A Century of American Labor* 63–65 (Princeton, 2d ed 2013).

[116] Lichtenstein, *State of the Union* at 32, 43–53, 100–05, 185–86 (cited in note 115); Forbath, 98 Mich L Rev at 62–76 (cited in note 113); Kate Andrias, *An American Approach to Social Democracy: The Forgotten History of the Fair Labor Standards Act*, 128 Yale L J *616, 652–53 (forthcoming 2019) (on file with author). The industrial unions also organized across traditional boundaries of job categories, race, and gender in an effort to build a more egalitarian political economy.

[117] Id at *642–51.

[118] Andrias, 128 Yale L J (cited in note 116); Mark Barenberg, *The Political Economy of the Wagner Act: Power, Symbol, and Workplace Cooperation*, 106 Harv L Rev 1379 (1993); Lichtenstein, *State of the Union* at 43–64 (cited in note 115); Forbath, 98 Mich L Rev (cited in note 113). See also *Street*, 367 US at 800 (Frankfurter, J, dissenting) ("The AFL, surely the conservative labor group, sponsored as early as 1893 an extensive program of political demands calling for compulsory education, an eight-hour day, employer tort liability, and other social reforms.").

less political unionism, one focused more on internal representation rather than broad-reaching social change.[119] Yet even in these decades, unions engaged in extensive political activity to advance the interests of working people, from efforts to enact national legislation like the Occupational Safety and Health Act and the Affordable Care Act, to fights to shape trade policy, to local campaigns for public housing and state employment law.[120]

The history of public sector labor unions is similarly political, perhaps more so. Public sector workers in municipal and state government were largely nonunion in the 1950s, but by the early 1960s, their wages had fallen behind their private sector counterparts, public sector labor was in short supply, and large groups of public sector workers had begun collectively demanding improved conditions at work.[121] From the outset, public sector labor leaders understood that political mobilization of their membership and communities was of central import to their ability to win union recognition and to bargain effectively.[122] In response to this mobilization, in 1958, Robert Wagner, the mayor of New York, and then in 1962, President Kennedy, issued executive orders legalizing public employee collective bargaining—and public sector unionism grew rapidly across the country over the next several decades.[123] Teacher unions, in particular, found themselves at the heart of political fights about racial identity, distribution of resources, and school control.[124]

In short, politics have always been inextricably connected to the work of the labor movement in the private and public sectors. When the AFL-CIO filed its brief in *Street*, the railway labor case that was

---

[119] Lichtenstein, *State of the Union* at 114–40 (cited in note 115).

[120] Jake Rosenfeld, *What Unions No Longer Do* 159–81 (Harvard, 2014); Benjamin I. Sachs, *The Unbundled Union: Politics Without Collective Bargaining*, 123 Yale L J 148, 152, 168–71 (2013); Lichtenstein, *State of the Union* at 185–86 (cited in note 115).

[121] Joseph E. Slater, *Public Workers, Government Employee Unions, the Law, and the State, 1900–1962* 193–94 (Cornell, 2016); Lichtenstein, *State of the Union* at 181–82 (cited in note 115).

[122] Lichtenstein, *State of the Union* at 182–83 (cited in note 115).

[123] Id; Slater, *Public Workers* at 193–94 (cited in note 121). See also Slater, *Public Workers* at 158–92 (detailing enactment of Wisconsin public sector labor law).

[124] Marjorie Murphy, *Blackboard Unions: The AFT and the NEA, 1900–1980* (Cornell, 1990); see also Leon Fink and Brian Greenberg, *Upheaval in the Quiet Zone: 1199SEIU and the Politics of Health Care Unionism* (Illinois, 2d ed 2009) (describing politics and organizing successes of insurgent health care union); *Janus*, 138 S Ct at 2475–76.

the precursor to *Abood*, it offered the following encapsulation of the relationship between unions and politics:

> A look at the history of union political action supplies abundant proof that labor's interest in politics is as old as its interest in the closed shop or the union shop. It provides full documentary support for legal commentators who have concluded that "political activity is a legitimate if not indispensable means of advancing the cause of organized labor"; that "political activities may be germane to collective bargaining insofar as favorable legislation, or the defeat of unfavorable legislation, strengthen the union's bargaining position"; and that unions have an "inherent interest" in lending financial support to certain political causes. In a word, even a brief survey of historical and economic data establishes that union political activity is wholly germane to a union's work in the realm of collective bargaining, and thus a reasonable means to attaining the union's proper object of advancing the economic interest of the worker.[125]

The brief continued with an elaboration of union politics beginning in colonial times, and then marched through to the present, drawing on historical sources as well as empirical studies, to show labor's involvement in politics for every time period in American history.

Justice Frankfurter, in his *Street* dissent, underlined the point. After detailing the labor movement's achievements, ranging from the eight-hour day to minimum wages, he wrote, "what is loosely called political activity of American trade unions . . . [is] activity indissolubly relating to the immediate economic and social concerns that are the raison d'être of unions."[126] In an internal memo found in his papers, which did not make it into the final opinion, Frankfurter noted the consistency between the American labor movement and that of the United Kingdom, emphasizing the necessarily intertwined political and economic role that unions play in any capitalist democracy.[127] In

---

[125] Brief for the American Federation of Labor and Congress of Industrial Organizations as Amicus Curiae, *Street*, 367 US at *14 (US filed March 21, 1960) (available on Westlaw at 1960 WL 98532) (citations omitted). Notably, the AFL offered this argument to counter a due process claim; it saw no First Amendment problem for the reasons elaborated in Part III.A of this essay, and therefore disposed of that issue quickly.

[126] *Street*, 367 US at 800 (Frankfurter, J, dissenting).

[127] Felix Frankfurter, microformed on Felix Frankfurter Papers, Harvard Law School Library ("Felix Frankfurter Papers") at Part II: Supreme Court of the United States Case Files of Opinions and Memoranda: October Terms 1953–61, Reel 67, p 305 ("Reference to the English legislative history in dealing with the so-called political uses to which trade-union funds may be put of course duly takes into account that England does not have our constitutional problems. But trade unionism—its origins, its history, its development, its presuppositions and purposes—does not have geographic bounds, and the response to law to it is not determined by parochial considerations.").

the opinion, Frankfurter similarly drew attention to the fundamental nature of worker organizations in capitalist, common-law democracies; he pointed to the political activity of British trade unions "as early as 1867," the Canadian Trades Congress in 1894, and recent political activity by Australian unions:

> That Britain, Canada and Australia have no explicit First Amendment is beside the point. For one thing, the freedoms safeguarded in terms in the First Amendment are deeply rooted and respected in the British tradition, and are part of legal presuppositions in Canada and Australia. And in relation to our immediate concern, the British Commonwealth experience establishes the pertinence of political means for realizing basic trade-union interests.[128]

As Justice Frankfurter concluded, political efforts to improve the lot of workers generally are, or should be, "as organic, as inured a part of the philosophy and practice of . . . unions as their immediate bread-and-butter concerns."[129]

The *Abood* line of cases thus fundamentally misconstrued the role of unions and their relationship to politics, and more broadly the relationship of politics to the economy. The cases also misdefined the public's interest in labor relations and the nature of the "public square." That is, to sustain the fair-share compromise without reducing fees to a paltry amount, the cases adopted a crabbed definition of "public concern." The doctrine excluded from its definition of public concern what Justice Kagan in *Harris* termed the "prosaic stuff of collective bargaining."[130] But workers' wages are neither prosaic nor of only private concern. They are at the heart of how our society distributes economic resources. Again, Justice Frankfurter made this point in dissent in *Street* years ago.[131]

Ironically, it is now the NRTWC and the *Janus* majority who argue that *Abood* misdefines the nature of economic disputes between employers and employees. The wages and benefits of public sector workers, Alito pointed out, are clearly important to taxpayers and

---

[128] *Street*, 367 US at 812–13.

[129] Id at 801 (Frankfurter, J, dissenting). See also id at 812 ("For us to hold that these defendant unions may not expend their moneys for political and legislative purposes would be completely to ignore the long history of union conduct and its pervasive acceptance in our political life. American labor's initial role in shaping legislation dates back 130 years.").

[130] *Harris*, 134 S Ct at 2655 (Kagan, J, dissenting).

[131] *Street*, 367 US at 815 (Frankfurter, J, dissenting).

citizens.[132] Kagan did not contest that employment-related speech has public import, but she countered: "The question is not, as the majority seems to think, whether the public is, or should be, interested in a government employee's speech. Instead, the question is whether that speech is about and directed to the workplace—as contrasted with the broader public square."[133]

Yet speech about and directed to the workplace is also often simultaneously about and directed to the "public square."[134] After all, the wages and benefits of both public and private sector workers are critical matters for public debate. Recent teacher strikes taking aim at chronic underfunding of education provide a vivid illustration of the connection between matters germane to collective bargaining and matters central to the public square.[135] So does the Fight for $15, the remarkably successful union-led campaign to raise the minimum wage in cities and states across the nation.[136] Indeed, in interpreting the NLRA, the Court has recognized that private sector workers' concerted activity regarding employment issues deserves protection whether it occurs through the employee-employer relationship or in the public square.[137]

In short, *Abood* and the *Janus* dissent operate according to a fiction that politics can be separated from economics, while embracing the view that unions' primary function is or should be to resolve discrete workplace disputes.[138] The problem is not merely that this logic is unpersuasive as a descriptive matter. The mistake also fatally infected the rule *Abood* adopted about the permissibility of union fees. The *Janus* majority exploited the weakness of the public/private dichotomy for the position that *no* union fees in the public sector are constitutional. The dissenters might have argued the inverse: union fees

---

[132] 138 S Ct at 2474–76.

[133] *Janus*, 138 S Ct at 2495 (Kagan, J, dissenting).

[134] Kagan differentiated speech directed to the workplace from speech directed only to the public square on the ground that public-square speech does not implicate management interests in labor peace and workplace control. For a critique of this point, see Part III.C.

[135] See Kate Andrias, Feller Memorial Labor Law Lecture, *Peril and Possibility: On Strikes, Rights, and Legal Change in the Era of Trump*, Berkeley J Empl & Labor L (forthcoming 2019) (on file with author).

[136] Andrias, 126 Yale L J (cited in note 9).

[137] *Eastex, Inc. v NLRB*, 437 US 556 (1978).

[138] Compare with *Street*, 367 US at 814 (Frankfurter, J, dissenting) ("The notion that economic and political concerns are separable is pre-Victorian.").

are constitutional, including those spent on political activity about labor-related issues, for such activities are germane to unions' core function.[139]

C

While embracing an overly narrow conception of both unions and the public's concern, *Abood* also adopted too restrictive a view of the government's interest in facilitating unions. With the union framed as an apolitical, workplace problem solver, the Court defined the government's interest in unions as achieving "peaceful labor relations" and "labor stability" with its own employees.[140] In her *Janus* dissent, Kagan elaborated this theory. She detailed how mandatory agency fees promote managerial prerogative: first, she explained, exclusive representation arrangements benefit "government entities because they can facilitate stable labor relations" by eliminating "the potential for inter-union conflict and streamlin[ing] the process of negotiating terms of employment."[141] Second, "the government may be unable to avail itself of those benefits unless the single union has a secure source of funding . . . if the union doesn't have enough [money], it can't be an effective employee representative and bargaining partner. And third, agency fees are often needed to ensure such stable funding. That is because without those fees, employees have every incentive to free ride on the union dues paid by others."[142]

But the government's interest in facilitating well-funded exclusive bargaining representatives in order to promote industrial peace is dangerously thin ground on which to justify the compulsion of political speech. As Alito pointed out, industrial peace and management prerogative can just as well be achieved, and largely have been, through other methods.[143] Moreover, labor peace and managerial efficiency were not the sole or even the primary motivations for the enactment of

---

[139] This distinction would track the line drawn in *Eastex, Inc.*, 437 US, in interpreting section 7 of the NLRA. One might imagine other sensible distinctions, for example, carving out partisan candidate endorsements and contributions from chargeable expenses. The point is that the distinctions would flow from a more realist accounting of the role of unions in society, and would reflect a different judgment about the relative costs of the contested action to union objectors.

[140] *Janus*, 138 S Ct at 2489 (Kagan, J, dissenting).

[141] Id.

[142] Id (citations omitted).

[143] 138 S Ct at 2464–65; *Harris*, 134 S Ct at 2640.

modern labor laws—nor for labor's insistence on the "union shop" and mandatory fees. As scholars have documented, democratic and egalitarian aspirations better explain the labor statutes enacted in the New Deal and in later decades. Supporters of the NLRA and the subsequent labor and employment statutes governing both private and public sector workers sought both to increase workers' economic power and to give workers greater voice on the shop floor and in the broader democracy.[144] The labor statutes were a means toward equal citizenship and social equality.[145] And the closed-shop tradition was part and parcel of this effort.[146]

Theorists of social equality have long recognized the workplace as a key location for egalitarian struggle and for the shaping of democracy.[147] Michael Walzer warns that inequality at work can "corrupt the distributive spheres with which it overlaps, carrying poverty into the sphere of money, degradation into the sphere of honor, weakness and resignation into the sphere of power."[148] Elizabeth Anderson details how employers exercise extraordinary authority over their employees' lives at work and even beyond work, leaving them with little privacy and freedom.[149] John Dewey argued that the workplace is a central location in our society for the development and exercise of citizenship and democracy.[150] Unions have, since their inception,

---

[144] See Andrias, 128 Yale L J (cited in note 116); Forbath, 98 Mich L Rev (cited in note 113); Pope, 106 Yale L J (cited in note 72); Barenberg, 106 Harv L Rev (cited in note 118). The effort to equalize power provoked massive resistance by employers and was ultimately curtailed by Court interpretation and statutory amendment. See, e.g., Karl E. Klare, *Judicial Deradicalization of the Wagner Act and the Origins of Modern Legal Consciousness, 1937–1941*, 62 Minn L Rev 265 (1978); Nelson Lichtenstein, *Taft-Hartley: A Slave-Labor Law?*, 47 Cath U L Rev 763 (1998).

[145] Samuel R. Bagenstos, *Employment Law and Social Equality*, 112 Mich L Rev 225 (2013); Forbath, 98 Mich L Rev (cited in note 113).

[146] Lichtenstein, *State of the Union* at 68 (cited in note 115). Exclusive representation is not the only way to create strong unions. See Rogers, 37 Berkeley J Empl & Labor L at 46–51 (cited in note 86) (explaining how European labor systems take wages out of competition and achieve greater economic equality and workplace democracy through methods other than compulsory dues).

[147] Bagenstos, 112 Mich L Rev at 243 (cited in note 145).

[148] Michael Walzer, *Spheres of Justice: A Defense of Pluralism and Equality* 183 (Basic Books, 1983).

[149] Elizabeth Anderson, *Private Government: How Employers Rule Our Lives (and Why We Don't Talk About It)* (Princeton, 2017); Elizabeth S. Anderson, *What Is the Point of Equality?*, 109 Ethics 287, 289 (1999).

[150] See John Dewey, *The Public and Its Problems* 118–21, 125 (1954); John Dewey, *Liberalism and Social Action*, in Jo Ann Boydston, ed, 11 *The Later Works, 1925–1953* 25 (1987). For a

sought to rectify the imbalances of power at work and to engage workers in the practice of democracy, both in their workplaces and in government.[151]

Today, in an era of staggering inequality, unions still function to increase the power of workers in the economy and the democracy, albeit with less success than in the post–New Deal period.[152] Indeed, Justice Kennedy observed at oral argument that what was fundamentally at stake in *Janus* was worker power in politics. He pressed the union's lawyer to acknowledge that "if you do not prevail in this case, the unions will have less political influence." The attorney conceded the point.[153] Though Kennedy offered this argument as a reason why union fees were unconstitutional, Kagan might have offered the opposite perspective, invoking the significant interest the government has in facilitating workers' collective voice in the democracy as a justification for exclusive representation and union fees.[154]

Yet democratic and egalitarian aspirations—or countervailing speech interests—nowhere appear in *Abood* or Justice Kagan's *Janus* dissent.[155] Rather, Kagan's focus is quite the opposite: she emphasizes

---

modern argument about the relationship of work to citizenship, see Cynthia Estlund, *Working Together: How Workplace Bonds Strengthen a Diverse Democracy* (Oxford, 2003).

[151] See Andrias, 128 Yale L J (cited in note 116); Gourevitch, *From Slavery to the Cooperative Commonwealth* (cited in note 113); Rosenfeld, *What Unions No Longer Do* (cited in note 120); Forbath, 98 Mich L Rev (cited in note 113).

[152] See Rosenfeld, *What Unions No Longer Do* at 10–30 (cited in note 120). Compare with Richard B. Freeman and James L. Medoff, *What Do Unions Do?* (Basic Books, 1984) (describing, as of the mid-1980s, the role of trade unions in the United States). On the relationship between unions and equality, see, e.g., Bruce Western and Jake Rosenfeld, *Unions, Norms, and the Rise in U.S. Wage Inequality*, 76 Am Soc Rev 513, 513 (2011); see also Henry S. Farber et al, *Unions and Inequality Over the Twentieth Century: New Evidence from Survey Data*, National Bureau of Economic Research Working Paper No. 24587 (May 2018), http://tuvalu.santafe.edu/~snaidu/papers/union_sub3.pdf (finding that "unions have . . . a significant, equalizing effect on the income distribution"); Jacob S. Hacker and Paul Pierson, *Winner-Take-All Politics: How Washington Made the Rich Richer—and Turned Its Back on the Middle Class* 142 (Simon & Schuster 2010); Kay Lehman Schlozman, Sidney Verba, and Henry E. Brady, *The Unheavenly Chorus: Unequal Political Voice and the Broken Promise of American Democracy* 325–26 (Princeton, 2012).

[153] Transcript of Oral Argument at 54, *Janus*, 138 S Ct 2448. For a different take on this exchange, see Purdy, 118 Colum L Rev at 2182 (cited in note 59).

[154] This approach would not have persuaded the majority but would have put the dissent on stronger footing both descriptively and normatively. Notably, Kagan has offered similar arguments in her campaign finance dissents. See *Arizona Free Enter Club's Freedom Club PAC v Bennett*, 564 US 721, 756 (2011) ("The program does not discriminate against any candidate or point of view, and it does not restrict any person's ability to speak. In fact, by providing resources to many candidates, the program creates more speech and thereby broadens public debate.").

[155] Contrast with id.

the need to give the government a "free[] hand" in dealing with its employees,[156] underlining the cases' "attitude . . . of respect—even solicitude—for the government's prerogatives as an employer. So long as the government is acting as an employer—rather than exploiting the employment relationship for other ends—it has a wide berth, comparable to that of a private employer."[157] Indeed, to support her position in *Janus*, Kagan defended the focus on management prerogative as the relevant governmental interest in the area of public employee speech more generally.[158] But, as scholars have shown, the public employee speech doctrine systematically underprotects employee speech interests and the broader interest in social equality, for it nearly always permits the government, as manager, to discipline employees for speech made in the context of their employment.[159] Like the *Abood* doctrine, the public employee speech doctrine places employment not within the domain of governance in which the usual principles of free speech apply, but within the domain of management subject to norms of managerial control and efficiency.[160] In the end, for those committed to a more egalitarian democracy, the doctrine is hard to reconcile with Kagan's allusion to a First Amendment meant "for better things."

IV

The *Abood* doctrine is long-standing and the *Janus* dissenters had reason to emphasize stare decisis rather than to challenge long-standing precedent. And unions did not seek *Abood*'s reversal. But the liberal compromise struck in the 1950s over Frankfurter's dissent, extended by *Abood* and defended by the *Janus* dissenters, helped lay the groundwork for the weaponized First Amendment. The *Abood*

---

[156] *Janus*, 138 S Ct at 2492 (Kagan, J, dissenting), quoting *NASA v Nelson*, 562 US 134, 148 (2011).

[157] Id at 2493.

[158] Id at 2492–97 (discussing *Pickering v Board of Education*, 391 US 563 (1968) and *Garcetti v Ceballos*, 547 US 410 (2006)).

[159] George Rutherglen, *Public Employee Speech in Remedial Perspective*, 24 J L & Pol 129, 144 (2008); Bagenstos, 112 Mich L Rev at 265 (cited in note 145). Because of the state-action requirement, the doctrine gives virtually no protection to private employees' speech. See Bagenstos, 112 Mich L Rev at 254–62 (cited in note 145); Anderson, *Private Government* (cited in note 149).

[160] On this categorization more broadly, see Robert C. Post, *Constitutional Domains: Democracy, Community, Management* 199–266 (Harvard, 1995).

doctrine first found a categorical speech harm where, at most, a minimal infringement existed. It then went on to adopt an untenable account of the relationship between politics and economics and, more specifically, a cramped definition of both the union role and the nature of the "public square." Consistent with this approach, *Abood* privileged the government's managerial interests over its egalitarian and democratic functions and took a narrow, one-sided view of the speech interests at stake. Ultimately, *Abood*'s approach vindicated the "right to exit"—the right of dissenters to opt out of the collective, even when guaranteed the right to fair representation and the right to exercise voice through democratic processes.[161]

The roots of union exit rights are in part liberal and egalitarian. In the 1940s–1960s, African-American workers and civil rights litigators rightfully opposed exclusionary unions, and their interests sometimes overlapped with the goals of the NRTWC.[162] But vindicating the right to participate on an equal basis need not have resulted in constitutionalizing a right to exit. By defending this path, by attempting to prop up *Abood* rather than to rethink it, the Court's more liberal members accepted the core of a doctrine that now threatens to eviscerate civil society and fortify corporate power.

Looking to the future, how much further the conservative majority on the Supreme Court will go in weaponizing the First Amendment is unclear. *Janus* raises the possibility that exclusive representation could itself be deemed unconstitutional, further unraveling the U.S. labor law regime. After all, if compelled union fees in the public sector constitute an incurable First Amendment harm, why doesn't compelling a dissenter to be bound by the agreement of a union with which it disagrees? Indeed, in *Janus*, Alito characterized the state's requirement that a union serve as an exclusive bargaining agent for its employees as "a significant impingement on associational freedoms that would not be tolerated in other contexts."[163] Thus far lower courts have declined to read *Janus* so broadly[164]—and the position of the conservative majority on this question is unclear. The *Janus*

---

[161] See Robin West, *A Tale of Two Rights*, 94 BU L Rev 893, 894 (2014).

[162] See Lee, *The Workplace Constitution* (cited in note 10).

[163] *Janus*, 138 S Ct at 2478.

[164] *Bierman v Dayton*, 900 F3d 570 (8th Cir 2018); *Reisman v Associated Faculties of University of Maine*, 2018 WL 6312996 (D Me); *Uradnik v Inter Faculty Organization*, 2018 WL 4654751 (D Minn).

Court did not expressly draw into question *Minnesota State Board for Community Colleges v Knight*, which upheld exclusive representation against First Amendment challenge.[165] Rather, *Janus* spent several pages making clear that the argument that "designation of a union as exclusive representative of all employees in a unit and the exaction of agency fees are [not] inextricably linked."[166]

Also unclear is whether *Janus* will undermine the government's own ability to fund speech with which taxpayers disagree: for example, will the line separating the public financing scheme for elections in *Buckley* from the agency-fee scheme of *Janus* hold? In a case pending before the Washington Supreme Court, the Pacific Legal Foundation (PLF) points to *Janus* to support its challenge to an electoral public financing scheme. The PLF asserts that Seattle's Democracy Voucher Program "compels property owners to bankroll speech they do not wish to support," and that it "disfavors minority viewpoints" by distributing money "at the whim of majoritarian interests."[167] In the immediate term, it seems unlikely that those Justices concerned about the Court's institutional legitimacy will extend *Janus* so far—but the ground is laid.[168]

Another open question is whether *Janus*'s newly manufactured opt-in rule will give rise to a far-reaching presumption of exit from the body politic. Under the doctrine to date, opt-out is the rule: a student who wishes not to recite the Pledge of Allegiance is protected from expulsion, but the school need not affirmatively seek permission from every student or parent before recitation of the pledge.[169] A Jehovah's Witness who obscures the state's motto on a license plate is shielded from criminal prosecution, but the state need not affirmatively seek consent from every driver before distributing the standard plate.[170] In *Janus*, Alito turned the doctrine on its head, holding that workers need not object to union dues; rather, their dissent will be

---

[165] 465 US 271 (1984).

[166] *Janus*, 138 S Ct at 2465–69.

[167] *Elster v City of Seattle*, No 96660-5 (Wash Sup Dec 19, 2018), accepting certification, No 77880-3-I (Wash App).

[168] Linda Greenhouse, *A Supreme Court Divided. On the Right*, NY Times (Dec 20, 2018), https://www.nytimes.com/2018/12/20/opinion/abortion-planned-parenthood-supreme-court.html.

[169] *West Virginia Board of Education v Barnette*, 319 US 624 (1943).

[170] *Wooley v Maynard*, 430 US 705 (1977).

presumed and fees will only be collected if workers affirmatively consent.[171] If such logic were extended, a host of majoritarian decisions and governmental regulations would not apply until regulated entities opt in. But this result seems unlikely. The government simply could not function if it were routinely required to obtain consent from each individual and corporation affected by a regulation. Here, it seems the *Janus* majority was willing to distort the traditional approach to compelled speech in order to weaken unions in particular.

In other ways, the reach of *Janus* as a "weapon" is more evident. As Kagan notes in her dissent, and Alito does not refute, the Court had repeatedly relied upon the *Abood* line of cases to approve mandatory fees imposed on state bar members.[172] In 1961, in *Lathrop v Donohue*,[173] the Court treated the constitutionality of bar dues as having been settled in 1956 by *Hanson*. Then, in *Keller v State Bar of California*,[174] the Court relied on *Abood* in setting the constitutional limits on mandatory bar fees. *Keller* is now in doubt, with the Court having granted, vacated, and remanded related cases.[175] The consequences reach beyond the profession of law. The same principle would bar the government from compelling contributions to, and thereby facilitating the operation of, a host of other civic organizations. Frankfurter foresaw this result way back in *Street*. In an internal memo, he warned his brethren that he would "eat his hat" if the Court's opinion did not lead to a similar ruling for union fees in the private sector (which it did), for integrated state bars (which seems likely), and for other collective bodies.[176]

More generally, *Janus* is unlikely to be the last case in which the Court strikes down regulation on the ground that it requires individuals or corporations to subsidize messages with which they disagree. Conservative judges on the D.C. Circuit have used a similar theory against numerous governmental regulations. For example,

---

[171] *Janus*, 138 S Ct at 2486; see Tang, *Janus and the Law of Opt-Out Rights* (cited in note 42). Even more shocking, perhaps, is that this about-face in the doctrine is stated only briefly in the majority opinion with little explanation, and altogether neglected by Kagan. Thanks to Justin Driver for this point.

[172] *Janus*, 138 S Ct at 2498 & n 3.

[173] 367 US 820, 828 (1961).

[174] 496 US 1 (1990).

[175] *Fleck v Wetch*, 868 F3d 652 (8th Cir 2017), cert granted, vac'd, rem'd, 2018 WL 6272044 (Dec 3, 2018).

[176] Felix Frankfurter, Felix Frankfurter Papers at Part II, Reel 67, p 573.

drawing on First Amendment principles, a panel of the D.C. Circuit concluded that requiring an employer to inform workers of their legal right to organize a union via an official posting violated the NLRA's statutory "free speech" provisions.[177] Another panel concluded that a Securities and Exchange Commission regulation violated the First Amendment insofar as it required publicly traded companies to disclose whether their products contained minerals traceable to African war conflicts.[178] Yet another struck down a regulation mandating that cigarette packages display textual warnings and graphic images regarding the health risks of smoking.[179] To date, the D.C. Circuit sitting en banc has rejected this fully weaponized version of the First Amendment.[180] But in the aftermath of *Janus*, employers are pressing the argument again, arguing, for example, that their own free speech rights are violated when employees are granted rights by the National Labor Relations Act to wear union buttons at work; such buttons, the argument runs, carry a message with which the employer disagrees.[181] *Janus* suggests that at least several Justices on the Supreme Court may sympathize with this claim.

V

What then is *Janus*'s more hopeful, future-looking face for those committed to labor rights? *Janus*'s undoing of the compromise

---

[177] *National Association of Manufacturers v NLRB*, 717 F3d 947 (DC Cir 2013) (concluding that section 8(c) of the NLRA, which protects employers' rights to express "any views, argument, or opinion" prohibited the agency from requiring employers to post a notice informing employees of their rights under their law), overruled by *American Meat Institute v U.S. Department of Agriculture*, 760 F3d 18 (DC Cir 2014).

[178] *National Association of Manufacturers v SEC*, 748 F3d 359, 373 (DC Cir 2014), adhered to on reh'g, 800 F3d 518 (DC Cir 2015), and overruled by *American Meat Institute v U.S. Department of Agriculture*, 760 F3d 18 (DC Cir 2014).

[179] *R. J. Reynolds Tobacco Co. v FDA*, 696 F3d 1205, 1214 (DC Cir 2012), overruled by *American Meat Institute v U.S. Department of Agriculture*, 760 F3d 18 (DC Cir 2014).

[180] *American Meat Institute v U.S. Department of Agriculture*, 760 F3d 18, 23–34 (DC Cir 2014) (rejecting prior panel rulings); *In-N-Out Burger, Inc. v NLRB*, 894 F3d 707 (5th Cir 2018) (affirming NLRB decision that restaurant employees have rights under section 7 of the NLRA to wear buttons displaying union message). See also *National Association of Manufacturers v Perez*, 103 F Supp 3d 7, 17 (DDC 2015) (requiring an employer to post government speech about labor rights is simply not compelled speech in violation of the First Amendment).

[181] See *In-N-Out Burger, Inc. v NLRB*, 894 F3d 707 (5th Cir 2018), petition for cert filed, No 18-340 (Sept 14, 2018) (petitioning for certiorari from Fifth Circuit decision that company violated federal labor law by barring an employee from wearing a "Fight for $15" button on his work uniform and citing *Janus* to support First Amendment argument).

that governed union fees for nearly fifty years is a blow to unions, but it opens up space for innovation and reform. The *Janus* majority suggested that, in order to solve the free-rider problem created by the decision, labor organizations could abandon majoritarian, exclusive representation.[182] They could accept a system in which they no longer represent all workers in a given bargaining unit, offering their services only to supporters. Some scholars have urged the same, with different motivation; they argue that ending exclusive representation would result in more militant and effective unions.[183] A second possible path forward, urged by other scholars and supported by some state legislators, would be for public employers to transmit money directly to unions to support their exclusive representation function.[184] This approach would presumably solve the funding problem created by *Janus*. But neither alternative to worker-funded exclusive representation has gained much traction with the labor movement.[185] The first approach, if pursued without other changes that protect labor rights, risks weakening unions to the point where they might no longer be able to pursue their basic redistributive mission, while the second sacrifices the fundamental nature of unions as membership organizations governed by and for workers.[186]

Unions have instead responded to *Janus* by engaging in renewed internal organizing, with workers explaining to one another why col-

---

[182] 138 S Ct at 2467–69 (observing that unions are not compelled to seek the designation of exclusive representation and suggesting that unions could refuse to represent nonmembers in grievance processing).

[183] James Gray Pope, Ed Bruno, and Peter Kellman, *The Right to Strike*, Boston Review (May 22, 2017), http://bostonreview.net/forum/james-gray-pope-ed-bruno-peter-kellman -right-strike (urging labor to embrace the right to strike and to abandon exclusive representation); Sophia Lee, Forum Response, *The Right to Strike*, Boston Review (May 22, 2017), http://bostonreview.net/forum/right-strike/sophia-lee-lee-responds-pope (arguing that ending exclusive representation should also lead to ending union security agreements).

[184] Aaron Tang, *Public Sector Unions, the First Amendment, and the Costs of Collective Bargaining*, 91 NYU L Rev 144, 183–90 (2016); Aaron Tang, *Life After Janus*, 119 Colum L Rev (forthcoming 2019), https://poseidon01.ssrn.com/delivery.php?ID=8020900990840990270 9811309901106507703400604900409006000708001112511002907200609109303605410 20 6306002304109006902310700110206605605805905400311010003112108803008807906 10020531020960241071110080280980900860021191240750861161130260740971111100 89017081008&EXT=pdf. Compare with Benjamin Sachs, *Agency Fees and the First Amendment*, 131 Harv L Rev 1046 (2018) (arguing that fair-share or agency fees deducted from paychecks should not be conceived as employees' money, but rather should be understood as state money paid to the union for services the state requests, such as collective bargaining and contract enforcement).

[185] Fisk and Malin, 107 Cal L Rev (cited in note 21).

[186] Id.

lective organization should be supported.[187] Some have been successful at maintaining and even growing their membership.[188] A few
unions have also begun to develop campaigns not dependent on exclusive representation, campaigns designed to raise standards for workers throughout an industry, including nonunion workers, while shaping political debate on economic justice issues.[189] Meanwhile, labor
leaders and scholars are engaging in a fundamental rethinking of labor
law, urging reforms that aim to increase worker power in the workplace, the economy, and the democracy.[190] In short, *Janus* has accelerated a process of introspection and reconsideration, leaving labor's
future far from decided but with significant potential for renewal.

The undoing of the *Abood* compromise provides the opportunity
for a similar rethinking of First Amendment doctrine: what would a
more egalitarian and democratic First Amendment look like in the
area of union dues, labor, and beyond? This essay's examination of
the errors of the *Abood* line of cases can help point the way forward.

Justice Harlan wrote to Justice Frankfurter at the end of the *Street*
deliberations: "Dear Felix, So much water is over the dam since
writing first started in this case that your last circulation leads me to
say Amen again to your dissent. It is *so* right!"[191] Harlan had a point.

---

[187] Id; see also Alana Semuels, *Is This the End of Public-Sector Unions in America?*, The Atlantic (June 27, 2018), https://www.theatlantic.com/politics/archive/2018/06/janus-afscme
-public-sector-unions/563879/.

[188] Sarah Chaney, *U.S. Union Membership Rate Declined in 2018*, Wall Street Journal (Jan 18,
2019) (describing growth in public sector union rate among some unions and a decline for others), https://www.wsj.com/articles/u-s-union-membership-rate-declined-in-2018-11547837708.

[189] Andrias, *Peril and Possibility*, Berkeley J Empl & Labor L (cited in note 135). Compare
with Marion Crane and Ken Matheny, *Labor Unions, Solidarity, and Money*, 22 Employee
Rights & Employment Pol J 101, 105 (2018) (arguing that "[i]t is time to divorce the need for
funding from the meaning of solidarity and to relinquish the vision of unions as service
organizations that has . . . contributed to an outsized reliance on law—particularly the ex-
clusivity doctrine and the principle of majority rule—as the source of worker power").

[190] Andrias, 126 Yale L J (cited in note 9); David Madland, *The Future of Worker Voice and
Power*, Center for American Progress (Oct 2016), https://cdn.americanprogress.org/wp-con
tent/uploads/2016/10/06051753/WorkerVoice2.pdf; David Rolf, *Toward a 21st Century Labor
Movement*, American Prospect (April 18, 2016), http://prospect.org/article/toward-21st
-century-labor-movement; Brishen Rogers, *Libertarian Corporatism Is Not an Oxymoron*, 94 Tex
L Rev 1623, 1624 (2016); David Madland and Alex Rowell, *How State and Local Governments
Can Strengthen Worker Power and Raise Wages*, Center for American Progress (May 2017),
https://cdn.americanprogress.org/content/uploads/sites/2/2017/05/01144237/C4-StateLocal
WorkerVoice-report.pdf; Dylan Matthews, *The Emerging Plan to Save the American Labor
Movement*, Vox (Sept 3, 2018), https://www.vox.com/policy-and-politics/2018/4/9/17205064
/union-labor-movement-collective-wage-boards-bargaining; *Clean Slate* (Harvard Labor and
Worklife Program), https://lwp.law.harvard.edu/programs/clean-slate.

[191] Memo signed JMH (6/15/61), Felix Frankfurter Papers at Part II, Reel 66, p 813.

Frankfurter's warning about the antidemocratic effects of expanding the Court's First Amendment jurisprudence was prescient. He anticipated the creep of the compelled-speech doctrine, which became even more damaging to democratic governance with the subsequent growth of protection for commercial speech.[192]

Frankfurter's deference to the majoritarian branches and reluctance to expand the category of absolutely protected speech beyond its obvious core provide a starting point for imagining a better First Amendment. Quoting Justice Cardozo, Frankfurter wrote,

> [C]ountless claims of right can be discovered to have their source or their operative limits in the provisions of a federal statute or in the Constitution itself with its circumambient restrictions upon legislative power. To set bounds to the pursuit, the courts have formulated the distinction between controversies that are basic and those that are collateral, between disputes that are necessary and those that are merely possible. We shall be lost in a maze if we put that compass by.[193]

Adopting a minimalist and deferential approach would give government more room to pursue social democratic aims, including requirements for agency fees, without running afoul of the First Amendment.[194] For those who believe in a more egalitarian political economy, an approach requiring deference to the democratic branches finds support in the empirical reality that courts have long been foes of labor and redistributive legislation more generally.[195]

But minimalism, without more, could have significant downsides, leaving valuable expression and association activity unprotected.[196] What of the rights to organize, bargain, boycott, and strike? An approach that primarily aims to minimize the First Amendment would leave in place, and could even worsen, doctrine that allows significant repression of workers' expressive activity by hostile legislatures—

---

[192] See sources cited in note 104.

[193] *Street*, 367 US at 819 (Frankfurter, J, dissenting), quoting *Gully v First National Bank*, 299 US 109, 118 (1936).

[194] Jedediah Purdy terms such an approach a "jurisprudence of permission." Purdy, 118 Colum L Rev at 2180 (cited in note 59). See Kessler and Pozen, 118 Colum L Rev at 1989 (cited in note 59) (collecting literature debating minimalism and maximalism in First Amendment law).

[195] See Kate Andrias, *Building Labor's Constitution*, 94 Tex L Rev 1591 (2016); Forbath, 102 Harv L Rev (cited in note 111).

[196] Kessler and Pozen, 118 Colum L Rev at 1989 (cited in note 59).

prohibitions on boycotts, pickets, strikes, and even the right of public sector workers to bargain collectively.[197]

And there is an additional problem with a categorically minimalist approach that merely aims to shrink the reach of the First Amendment. Such an approach fails to grapple with the widely held intuition that the First Amendment *is* implicated when government restrains or compels expressive activity that is not "core" speech. More generally, it fails to confront the cultural importance of the First Amendment and the Constitution—the First Amendment's place in our "small-c constitution"—the web of practices, institutions, norms, and traditions that structure American society.[198] In our constitutional culture, the First Amendment has extraordinary power and resonance.[199] Seeking merely to pull back the reach of the First Amendment without engaging in a debate about what it means to protect freedom of speech and expression in our constitutional democracy concedes the terrain of the Constitution.[200]

Understanding *Abood*'s errors allows us to imagine a substantively different labor speech doctrine as well as one more procedurally deferential to democratic decision makers. In the case of agency fees, imagine, for example, a doctrine that recognizes the minimal speech harm to objecting workers, while embracing a more expansive view of unions' social function and government's interest in regulation. The doctrine would recognize that labor organizations serve a role that is not limited to advancing managerial efficiency, nor to the commercial sphere. Rather, unions enable workers' effective participation in the political process, they facilitate worker voice, and they serve as a critical countervailing force to organized business interests in the public square. They also help achieve social equality. This version

---

[197] See Andrias, *Peril and Possibility*, Berkeley J Empl & Labor L (cited in note 135) (describing limits on public employee bargaining rights); Julius G. Getman, *The Supreme Court on Unions: Why Labor Law Is Failing American Workers* 90–100 (2016) (describing law on secondary boycotts by unions).

[198] See Richard A. Primus, *Unbundling Constitutionality*, 80 U Chi L Rev 1079, 1082 (2013) (describing "small-c" constitutionalism and discussing the diversity of small-c constitutional theories); Michael W. McCann, *Rights at Work: Pay Equity Reform and the Politics of Legal Mobilization* (Chicago, 1994).

[199] See Akhil Reed Amar, *The First Amendment's Firstness*, 47 UC Davis L Rev 1015, 1025–29 (2014); Philip Bobbitt, *Constitutional Fate: Theory of the Constitution* 93–119 (Oxford, 1982); Kessler and Pozen, 118 Colum L Rev at 1990 (cited in note 59).

[200] Joseph Fishkin and William E. Forbath, *The Anti-Oligarchy Constitution*, 94 BU L Rev 669, 672 (2014); Andrias, 94 Tex L Rev (cited in note 195).

of the First Amendment would allow democratic processes to pursue these interests at least when incursions on other speech rights are minimal. Indeed, it would recognize these interests as essential to an overall system of free speech, expression, and association.[201]

A doctrine revised along these lines would have implications for a host of issues beyond the scope of this essay, including other aspects of public employee speech and association, and even private employee speech doctrine. It might also draw into question such general First Amendment principles as, for example, the requirement of state action, the definition of rights in negative terms, and the law's claim to neutrality. Indeed, a doctrine valuing the speech interests of workers as a group or the government's interest in social equality would not be neutral. But it would be no less neutral than the system adopted in *Abood* or in *Janus*, which put such considerations off limits, weighing only the government's managerial prerogative and interest in labor peace, or only the speech interests of dissenting workers.

That there is a debate to be had about the social value of unions, about permissible governmental interests, and about what it means to protect the freedom of speech does not mean that the place for such debate is primarily in the courts. Litigation is ill-equipped to drive a more egalitarian First Amendment—or a more egalitarian labor law.[202] Instead, debate and struggle over the content of labor law and the nature of "the freedom of speech" must occur first and foremost in the public square and in the political branches.[203] But such political

---

[201] See Kessler and Pozen, 118 Colum L Rev at 1994–2001 (cited in note 59) (cataloging literature advocating that courts consider speech "on both sides" and ultimately urging an approach that would "attend[] to the perspective of listeners as well as speakers, and tak[e] into account the informational and expressive interests of as many listeners and speakers as practicable"); Lakier, 118 Colum L Rev at 2127 (cited in note 59) (urging a functional, antisubordination approach to the First Amendment, including consideration of the expressive interests of third parties when those interests are directly implicated by the First Amendment case at hand). For earlier variations of the speech-on-both-sides and systemic free speech arguments, see Owen M. Fiss, *Why the State?*, 100 Harv L Rev 781, 783 (1987); Owen M. Fiss, *Free Speech and Social Structure*, 71 Iowa L Rev 1405 (1986). For a critique, see Robert C. Post, *Meiklejohn's Mistake: Individual Autonomy and the Reform of Public Discourse*, 64 U Col L Rev 1109 (1993).

[202] See Andrias, 94 Tex L Rev (cited in note 195); Leslie Kendrick, *Another First Amendment*, 118 Colum L Rev 2095 (2018); Louis Michael Seidman, *Can Free Speech Be Progressive?*, 118 Colum L Rev 2219 (2018).

[203] For past examples of such movements, see Fishkin and Forbath, *Constitutional Political Economy* (cited in note 59); Weinrib, *Taming of Free Speech* (cited in note 72); Goluboff, *The Lost Promise of Civil Rights* (cited in note 72); Pope, 106 Yale L J (cited in note 72). See also Andrias, 94 Tex L Rev (cited in note 195) (discussing contemporary labor movement efforts and their relationship to constitutional change).

debate and political conflict will inevitably be in dialogue with the Court's own work.

Given our constitutional system, courts cannot avoid hard questions about social facts or socially constructed values. They inevitably consider, either overtly or covertly, whether government is responding to a genuine problem, whether it is employing responsive instruments that are relatively nonburdensome to rights-holders or that are in service of other rights.[204] As Justice Frankfurter wrote in *Street*:

> It disrespects the wise, hardheaded men who were the authors of our Constitution and our Bill of Rights to conclude that their scheme of government requires what the facts of life reject. . . . To say that labor unions as such have nothing of value to contribute to that process (the electoral process) and no vital or legitimate interest in it is to ignore the obvious facts of political and economic life and of their increasing interrelationship in modern society.[205]

Ultimately, *Janus*'s destruction of the *Abood* compromise offers an opportunity for the now-dissenters on the Court to rethink what, in the context of the facts of our increasingly unequal political and economic life, a "better" First Amendment regime might entail.

---

[204] See Greene, 132 Harv L Rev at 63 (cited in note 106) (urging more explicit and extensive proportionality analysis in constitutional adjudication).

[205] *Street*, 367 US at 815.

CASS R. SUNSTEIN

CHEVRON WITHOUT CHEVRON

I. On Simplifying Life

Chevron v NRDC[1] has a strong claim to being the most important case in all of administrative law.[2] It is now under serious
pressure, fueled by some serious questions about the legitimacy of
the regulatory state in general.[3]

Cass R. Sunstein is Robert Walmsley University Professor, Harvard University.

Author's note: I am grateful to John Manning, David A. Strauss, and Adrian Vermeule
for valuable discussions and general inspiration, and to Cody Westphal for excellent research
assistance.

[1] 467 US 837 (1984).

[2] For a fascinating account of how this came to be so, see Thomas Merrill, *The Story of
Chevron: The Making of an Accidental Landmark*, 66 Admin L Rev 253 (2014), and in particular
this summary, id at 282–83:

> *Chevron* became a landmark decision due to the cumulative effect of a series of for-
> tuitous events, among them Justice White's assignment of the case to Justice Stevens,
> Justice Stevens' creative restatement of certain principles of judicial review of questions
> of law, the lack of scrutiny given the Stevens opinion by other justices, Judge Patricia
> Wald's quick embrace of the two-step formula in the DC Circuit, Justice Scalia's el-
> evation to the Supreme Court from the DC Circuit two years later, and the Justice
> Department's unrelenting campaign to make *Chevron* the universal standard for ju-
> dicial review of agency interpretations of law. Individually, each of these events is
> readily explicable; cumulatively, they would have to be described as an accident. ...
> The wonder of it all is that the Court that rendered this decision had utterly no in-
> tention of producing such an opinion. Indeed, the Court did not even realize it had
> produced such an opinion until others pointed this out.

[3] For a representative statement, see Christopher DeMuth, *Can the Administrative State Be
Tamed?*, 8 J Legal Analysis 121 (2016). For an extreme version of this view, see Philip

For example, Justice Neil Gorsuch objects that *Chevron* "[t]ransfer[s] the job of saying what the law is from the judiciary to the executive."[4] Invoking the massive power of contemporary regulatory agencies, Chief Justice John Roberts seeks ways to confine *Chevron's* reach.[5] As he puts it, "The Framers could hardly have envisioned today's 'vast and varied federal bureaucracy' and the authority administrative agencies now hold over our economic, social, and political activities."[6] Justice Clarence Thomas argues that *Chevron* is inconsistent with the Constitution.[7] In his view, the decision "wrests from Courts the ultimate interpretative authority to 'say what the law is,'" and instead "hands it over to the Executive."[8]

It seems clear that *Chevron* is entering a period of serious reconsideration. In the fullness of time, it might be seriously qualified or even abandoned.[9] My main topic here is simple: Without the framework established and applied in *Chevron*, how would *Chevron* itself have been decided? In a way, that question seems narrow and backward-looking. But it is larger than it seems. *Chevron*—the case—is representative of the kinds of problems that courts are now addressing and will be addressing for the foreseeable future. An understanding of how *Chevron* might be decided without *Chevron* offers some broader lessons about statutory interpretation in the regulatory state. As we will see, that understanding also suggests the perils of overruling *Chevron* and fortifies the view that administrative law ought to retain it.

I will explore five possibilities: (1) textualism, (2) purposivism, (3) use of canons of construction, (4) *Skidmore* deference, and (5) validation

---

Hamburger, *Is Administrative Law Unlawful?* (Chicago, 2015). For an important statement in the aftermath of the New Deal, see Roscoe Pound, *Administrative Law and the Courts*, 24 BU L Rev 223 (1944).

[4] *Gutierrez-Brizuela v Lynch*, 834 F3d 1142, 1152 (10th Cir 2016).

[5] *City of Arlington v Federal Communications Commissions*, 569 US 290, 327 (2013) (Roberts, CJ, dissenting) ("Our duty to police the boundary between the Legislature and the Executive.... is heightened ... by the dramatic shift in power over the last 50 years from Congress to the Executive—a shift effected through the administrative agencies.... We reconcile our competing responsibilities in this area by ensuring judicial deference to agency interpretations under *Chevron*—but only after we have determined on our own that Congress has given interpretive authority to the agency.").

[6] Id at 313.

[7] *Michigan v EPA*, 135 S Ct 2699, 2712–13 (2015) (Thomas, J, concurring).

[8] Id at 2712 (2015) (Thomas, J, concurring), quoting *Marbury v Madison*, 5 US (1 Cranch) 137, 177 (1803).

[9] A different but complementary perspective can be found in Lawrence Solum and Cass R. Sunstein, *Chevron as Construction* (unpublished manuscript, 2019).

of the agency's decision on the ground that nothing in the Clean Air Act forbids it. Of these, the first two are often useful, but revealingly, they turn out to be essentially useless in *Chevron* itself—a conclusion that helps explain why the Court adopted the *Chevron* framework (without dissent, as if it were a matter of routine). The last three are often useful, and are far from useless in *Chevron*, but the question remains whether their use would represent an improvement over the approach required by *Chevron*.

As these conclusions suggest, textualism and purposivism sometimes fail to give concrete answers to difficult statutory questions.[10] Canons of construction can be decisive but also contentious. More broadly, the discussion offers a significant cautionary note: In many cases, abandoning the *Chevron* framework would impose significant costs for little gain. Abandoning that framework would introduce high levels of confusion in the lower courts and the Supreme Court itself, as judges worked to produce a post-*Chevron* framework and struggled to resolve the many cases that would turn out to be difficult to resolve well, or even at all, without *Chevron*. After a period of struggle, the resulting framework might not turn out to be altogether different from that in *Chevron* itself—which suggests that abandoning long-standing law would not be worth the candle.[11]

II. The Meaning of "Source": "When I am so confused, I go with the agency"[12]

Chevron's two-step framework should be familiar,[13] but the actual dispute in the case casts the origins of that framework in a dis-

---

[10] I am aware, of course, that textualists and purposivists often disagree, and am bracketing that disagreement for present purposes. See John Manning, *What Divides Textualists from Purposivists?*, 106 Colum L Rev 70 (2006).

[11] I am focusing here on how to decide *Chevron* without *Chevron*, and while I draw some general lessons from that discussion, my primary focus is not on the question whether the decision should be overruled. For more detailed discussion of that question, see Cass R. Sunstein, *Chevron as Law*, Georgetown L J (forthcoming 2019).

[12] So said Justice John Paul Stevens, author of *Chevron*, in conference. See Merrill, 66 Admin L Rev at 272 (cited in note 2).

[13] The literature is voluminous. For a highly selective sampling of good work, see, for example, Nicholas Bednar and Kristin E. Hickman, *Chevron's Inevitability*, 85 Geo Wash L Rev 1392 (2017); Lisa Heinzerling, *The Power Canons*, 58 Wm & Mary L Rev 1933 (2017); Michael Herz, *Chevron Is Dead; Long Live Chevron*, 115 Colum L Rev 1867 (2015); Lisa Schultz Bressman, *Chevron's Mistake*, 58 Duke L J 549 (2009); Jack M. Beermann, *End the Failed Chevron Experiment Now: How Chevron Has Failed and Why It Can and Should Be Overruled*, 42 Conn L Rev 779 (2010); Jacob Gersen and Adrian Vermeule, *Chevron as a*

tinctive light. The Clean Air Act[14] contains a stringent "nonattainment program," applicable to areas that have failed to comply with national ambient air quality standards, which are designed to protect public health and welfare.[15] Under the nonattainment program, a permit is required whenever a company builds a new "source" or modifies an existing one, unless the incremental pollution falls within the statutory limits.[16] Before the Reagan administration, the Environmental Protection Agency (EPA) had understood the term "source" to apply to every pollution-emitting apparatus or unit within a plant.[17] If, for example, a single boiler with a smokestack emitted pollution, it would qualify as a "source." Whenever a company constructed a new boiler, it would have to obtain a permit under the stated conditions, and so too if a company modified an existing boiler.

Under President Ronald Reagan, the EPA redefined the term "source" so that it could include an entire plant.[18] This was not a modest or one-off initiative. On the contrary, it was part of a "Government-wide reexamination of regulatory burdens and complexities."[19] A plantwide definition of "source" reduces compliance burdens and complexity and gives companies much greater flexibility.[20] It does so by creating a kind of "bubble" over the plant, allowing companies to build new pollution-emitting devices or to modify old ones, so long as they do not exceed the total statutory limit on emissions (i.e., the limit that triggers permit requirements). Under the plantwide definition, a company might build

---

Voting Rule, 116 Yale L J 676 (2007); Peter L. Strauss, *"Deference" Is Too Confusing*, 112 Colum L Rev 1143 (2012); Matthew Stephenson and Adrian Vermeule, *Chevron Has Only One Step*, 95 Va L Rev 597 (2009); Thomas Merrill, *Judicial Deference to Executive Precedent*, 101 Yale L J 969 (1992); Douglas Kmiec, *Judicial Deference to Executive Agencies*, 2 Admin L J 269, 277–28 (1988); Clark Byse, *Judicial Review of Administrative Interpretation of Statutes: An Analysis of Chevron's Step Two*, 2 Admin L J 255 (1988); Thomas Merrill, *Textualism and the Future of the Chevron Doctrine*, 72 Wash U L Q 351 (1994); Richard Pierce, *Chevron and Its Aftermath: Judicial Review of Agency Interpretations of Statutory Provisions*, 41 Vand L Rev 301 (1988); Note, *"How Clear Is Clear" in Chevron's Step One?*, 118 Harv L Rev 1687 (2005).

[14] Clean Air Act Amendments, Pub L 95-95, 91 Stat 685 (1977).

[15] 42 USC §§ 7501–08.

[16] 42 USC § 7502(b)(5).

[17] See *Chevron, USA, Inc. v Natural Resources Defense Council, Inc.*, 467 US 837 (1984).

[18] Id at 840.

[19] 46 Fed Reg 16281 (1981).

[20] For helpful discussion, see Ellen M. Saideman, *An Overview of the Bubble Concept*, 8 Colum J Envir L 137, 142–48 (1982) (discussing the EPA's definition of "stationary source"); Robert Hahn, *Where Did All the Markets Go? An Analysis of EPA's Emissions Trading Program*, 6 Yale J Reg 109 (1989).

a new pollution-emitting device within its plant, but also take one off-line, and in that way avoid the permit requirements of the act.

As the EPA explained, the previous approach, disallowing a plant-wide definition, "can act as a disincentive to new investment and modernization by discouraging modifications to existing facilities" and "can actually retard progress in air pollution control by discouraging replacement of older, dirtier processes or pieces of equipment with new, cleaner ones."[21] In the EPA's view, the plantwide approach would save a great deal of money and would not be harmful on environmental grounds; indeed, it could be better, because it could remove that disincentive to new investment and modernization.[22]

Environmental groups vigorously disagreed.[23] They believed that the plantwide definition was harmful from the environmental point of view—and also that it was inconsistent with the relevant provision of the Clean Air Act. The United States Court of Appeals for the District of Columbia Circuit essentially accepted their argument.[24] The court acknowledged that the Clean Air Act "does not explicitly define what Congress envisioned as a 'stationary source' to which the permit process and construction moratorium should apply." It added, "Nor is the issue squarely addressed in the legislative history." But it pointed out that another provision of the act, governing new source performance standards (NSPS), defined "source" to mean "any building, structure, facility, or installation."[25]

The court did not rely on the text of that provision. Instead it noted that its previous decisions had distinguished sharply between the Prevention of Significant Deterioration (PSD) program, which was designed for areas that had achieved compliance with national ambient air quality standards, and other programs, where compliance had not been attained.[26] In areas governed by the relatively more lenient PSD program, bubble programs were acceptable and indeed mandatory—but not so in nonattainment areas.[27] In the key passage,

---

[21] 46 Fed Reg 16281 (1981).

[22] See Hahn, 6 Yale J Reg at 109 (cited in note 20).

[23] Merrill, 66 Admin L Rev at 259–59 (cited in note 2).

[24] *National Resource Defense Council, Inc. v Gorsuch*, 685 F2d 718 (DC Cir 1982), rev'd by *Chevron, USA, Inc. v National Resource Defense Council, Inc.*, 467 US 837 (1984).

[25] *National Resource Defense Council, Inc. v Gorsuch*, 685 F2d 718, 723 (DC Cir 1982).

[26] Id at 725–26.

[27] Id at 726.

the court said that "the nonattainment program's raison d'être is to ameliorate the air's quality in nonattainment areas sufficiently to achieve expeditious compliance with the [national ambient air quality standards]."[28] In view of the central purpose of that program—its "raison d'être"—the plantwide definition was invalid.

The Supreme Court had no enthusiasm for that approach, and it offered its two-step framework against the background set by the lower court's reasoning.[29] Like the lower court, the Supreme Court emphasized that the nonattainment program did not include a definition of "stationary source," though that term was defined for other programs.[30] The Court found the absence of a definition highly relevant. As the Court put it, the nonattainment amendments "contain no specific reference to the 'bubble concept.' Nor do they contain a specific definition of the term 'stationary source,' though they did not disturb the definition of 'stationary source' contained in § 111(a)(3), applicable by the terms of the Act to the NSPS program."[31] The only relevant provision said that the terms "major stationary source" and "major emitting facility" refer to "any stationary facility or source of air pollutants which directly emits, or has the potential to emit, one hundred tons per year or more of any air pollutant (including any major emitting facility or source of fugitive emissions of any such pollutant, as determined by rule by the Administrator)."[32] This phrase does not define "source."

The Court thought that this provision "sheds virtually no light on the meaning of the term 'stationary source.'"[33] To be sure, it equates a source with a facility, which is relevant and argued in favor of the EPA's approach: "The ordinary meaning of the term 'facility' is some collection of integrated elements which has been designed and constructed to achieve some purpose. Moreover, it is certainly no affront

---

[28] Id at 726–27.

[29] As I have noted, the framework was not intended to mark new ground, see note 2. As Merrill explains, "*Chevron* was little noticed when it was decided, and came to be regarded as a landmark case only some years later. This may be the most interesting aspect of the *Chevron* story—how a decision that was considered routine by those who made it came to be regarded as one of potentially transformative significance." Merrill, 66 Admin L Rev at 253, 257 (cited in note 2).

[30] *Chevron, USA, Inc. v National Resource Defense Council, Inc.*, 467 US at 851.

[31] Id.

[32] Id, citing 42 USC § 7602(j).

[33] *Chevron*, 467 US at 860.

to common English usage to take a reference to a major facility or a major source to connote an entire plant, as opposed to its constituent parts."[34] But the Court did not rely on this point. It said that the main definition "simply does not compel any given interpretation of the term 'source.'"[35]

That left the Court with the definition in the NSPS program, which "sheds as much light on the meaning of the word 'source' as anything in the statute."[36] Here the Court was equivocal, and its revealingly indeterminate and somewhat frustrated analysis is worth quoting at length:

> As respondents point out, use of the words "building, structure, facility, or installation," as the definition of source, could be read to impose the permit conditions on an individual building that is a part of a plant. ... On the other hand, the meaning of a word must be ascertained in the context of achieving particular objectives, and the words associated with it may indicate that the true meaning of the series is to convey a common idea. The language may reasonably be interpreted to impose the requirement on any discrete, but integrated, operation which pollutes. This gives meaning to all of the terms—a single building, not part of a larger operation, would be covered if it emits more than 100 tons of pollution, as would any facility, structure, or installation. Indeed, the language itself implies a "bubble concept" of sorts: each enumerated item would seem to be treated as if it were encased in a bubble. ... While respondents insist that each of these terms must be given a discrete meaning, they also argue that [the provision governing NSPS] defines "source" as that term is used in [the provision governing nonattainment areas]. The latter section, however, equates a source with a facility, whereas the former defines "source" as a facility, among other items. We are not persuaded that parsing of general terms in the text of the statute will reveal an actual intent of Congress.

Finding the statute and its legislative history ambiguous, the Court relied on its famous framework. "First, always, is the question whether Congress has directly spoken to the precise question at issue. If the intent of Congress is clear, that is the end of the matter; for the court, as well as the agency, must give effect to the unambiguously expressed intent of Congress."[37] In the face of ambiguity, courts must ask a second question. Again in the Court's words, "if the statute is silent or

---

[34] Id.

[35] Id.

[36] Id.

[37] Id at 842–43.

ambiguous with respect to the specific issue, the question for the court is whether the agency's answer is based on a permissible construction of the statute."[38]

The Court concluded that "the EPA's definition of the term 'source' is a permissible construction of the statute which seeks to accommodate progress in reducing air pollution with economic growth."[39] With that conclusion in view, there is real charm in Justice Stevens's remark in conference: "When I am so confused, I go with the agency."[40] An understanding of the full context suggests that this remark is a capsule summary of what happened in *Chevron*.

III. Without Chevron

It should be clear that in *Chevron*, the two-step framework helped to make everything easier.[41] Indeed, the Justices were originally sharply divided about how to resolve the case, and Justice Stevens's opinion, offering that framework, produced unanimity.[42] But suppose that the Court had not adopted that framework. Suppose that it insisted on a competing idea, to the effect that resolution of statutory ambiguities is for courts, not agencies.[43] How might *Chevron* have been or now be resolved?

It should be clear that this question bears directly on the current challenges to the *Chevron* framework. Countless cases are similar to *Chevron*, or relevantly identical, and the question how to decide *Chevron* without *Chevron* is pertinent to all of them.[44] Let us stipulate that without *Chevron*, courts would be required to decide on the meaning of the term "source" without deferring to the agency's interpretation, or at least without deferring in the way that the Court did in *Chevron* itself. What then?

---

[38] Id at 843.

[39] Id at 866.

[40] Merrill, 66 Admin L Rev at 272 (cited in note 2).

[41] Ironically, the author of the opinion, Justice Stevens, did not intend to do anything new. As Merrill reports, when he was asked about the opinion, "Justice Stevens would respond that he regarded it as simply a restatement of existing law, nothing more or less." Merrill, 66 Admin L Rev at 258 (cited in note 2).

[42] Id.

[43] I am bracketing throughout the question of legal authority, pressed by those who think that *Chevron* is not a faithful interpretation of section 706 of the Administrative Procedure Act (APA). For detailed discussion, see Sunstein, *Chevron as Law* (cited in note 11).

[44] For candidates from the Supreme Court, see *Babbitt v Sweet Home Chapter*, 515 US 687 (1995); *City of Arlington v FCC*, 133 S Ct 1863 (2013); *Entergy Corp. v Riverkeeper*, 556 US 208 (2009).

A. TEXTUALISM

Many judges are strongly committed to textualism,[45] and almost all judges agree that the statutory text is the right place to start. Abandonment of *Chevron* would put new pressure on judges to discern the (unique) meaning of the text. In many cases, that would not be so challenging. Indeed, courts often discern the unique meaning under Step One of the *Chevron* framework.[46] The question is how that approach would have worked in *Chevron* itself. Here is a way of sharpening that question. Suppose that no agency was in the picture at all. An issue of statutory interpretation might (and often does) arise, for example, in a private enforcement action. If so, courts would not be able to resort to deference doctrines, and textualism might be the preferred approach.

It might seem tempting to suggest that, in ordinary English, the word "source" has a clear meaning. According to one dictionary, a source is "a point of origin or procurement."[47] According to another, it is "any thing or place from which something comes, arises, or is obtained; origin."[48] We might suggest a simple conclusion: *If air pollution comes from something, that something is a source.*[49] On that view, *Chevron* might seem easily resolved on textualist grounds. A single smokestack, from a single building, is unquestionably a source. Any apparatus is a source. A plant that includes several buildings *contains* sources; it is not a source. We can imagine hard cases, as where two smokestacks are in a single building, but *Chevron* itself is not one; a plantwide definition runs afoul of the ordinary meaning of the statutory term.

In these circumstances, we could easily imagine a court invalidating that definition—and thus not only abandoning the *Chevron* framework but also overruling the decision on its facts. But on reflection, that would be surprising, and not the most admirable form of

---

[45] For sophisticated versions, see Antonin Scalia, *A Matter of Interpretation* (1998); Brett Kavanaugh, Book Review, *Fixing Statutory Interpretation*, 129 Harv L Rev 2118 (2016).

[46] See, for example, *MCI Telecommunications Corp. v American Telephone & Telegraph Co.*, 512 US 218 (1994).

[47] Merriam-Webster, definition of "Source" (2018), archived at https://perma.cc/P9GM-KAS4.

[48] Dictionary.com, definition of "Source" (2018), archived at https://perma.cc/LZB6-FLHJ.

[49] The DC Circuit endorsed this view many years ago. See *ASARCO Inc. v EPA*, 578 F2d 319, 325 (DC Cir 1978).

textualism. In context, the word "source" just does not have a plain meaning. We can accept the dictionary definitions given above and nonetheless insist that a plant can be "a point of origin" or a "place from which something comes." The text does not forbid the plant-wide definition (or require it). If a court were to try to resolve the question in *Chevron* on purely textual grounds in a private enforcement action, without an agency in the picture, it would have a real struggle. It would probably be at sea.

It is useful to distinguish here between textualism in its most honorable and appealing form and its less honorable and less appealing sibling, which H. L. A. Hart called "conceptualism."[50] Sometimes words do have clear meanings and courts rightly insist on them; that is an appealing form of textualism, and it is obviously relevant to and possibly decisive in Step One of the *Chevron* framework. (I am bracketing obvious complexities, such as those that arise when the text produces an absurd outcome, or seems in conflict with the evident purpose.) But sometimes words have several meanings, and it is wrong to insist on one of them. Conceptualism can be found whenever a judge takes a word with two or more meanings and simply proclaims, without further argument or evidence, that one is right.

In the constitutional context, consider, for example, the view that the Equal Protection Clause necessarily forbids affirmative action programs, because its text calls for "equal" protection. That is a form of conceptualism, because the word "equal" can be understood in several ways. Taken by itself, it could ban affirmative action programs, mandate affirmative action programs, or have nothing to say about affirmative action programs.[51]

So too for the word "source." At least in *Chevron* itself, textualism is a dead end.

---

[50] See H. L. A. Hart, *The Concept of Law* (Oxford, 1965): "Different legal systems, or the same system at different times, may either ignore or acknowledge more or less explicitly such a need for the further exercise of choice in the application of general rules to particular cases. The vice known to legal theory as formalism or conceptualism consists in an attitude to verbally formulated rules which both seeks to disguise and to minimize the need for such choice, once the general rule has been laid down." I am using the idea of conceptualism in a somewhat narrower sense than Hart did.

[51] I do not mean, with these claims, to say anything controversial about constitutional law, or to state a view about affirmative action programs or the view that what is authoritative is the "original public meaning." If we insist that the original public meaning is authoritative in *Chevron*, we are still at a dead end.

B. PURPOSIVISM

Some judges say that if the text is ambiguous, its meaning should be determined by ascertaining its purpose.[52] In some contexts, purposivism is helpful in sorting out ambiguities. If a statute forbids vehicles in the park,[53] it ought not to ban the construction of a war memorial consisting of a tank used in the Iraq War. The purpose of the prohibition is to prevent noise, traffic, and pollution. A war memorial does not do anything of those things. But purpose is not always helpful. In some cases, courts are essentially constructing a purpose rather than finding it, and different judges can construct different purposes.[54]

Consider, for example, the question whether exchanging a firearm for drugs constitutes a "use" of a firearm "during and in relation to" a drug offense.[55] It is tempting to think that if the word "use" is ambiguous, the statutory purpose clarifies things. Congress was concerned about using a firearm *as a weapon* in relation to a drug offense, which means that when it is an object of barter, it is not being "used" in the statutory sense.[56] In my view, that argument is convincing. But reasonable people could disagree. Perhaps Congress was concerned about the combination of firearms and drug offenses; perhaps its purpose was to deter that dangerous combination.[57] If so, its purpose was triggered by "use" of a firearm as an object of barter.

---

[52] For an elaboration of a purposive approach, see Stephen Breyer, *Active Liberty: Interpreting Our Democratic Constitution* (Vintage, 2005).

[53] See Hart, *The Concept of Law* at 129 (cited in note 50).

[54] On the virtues and vices of purposivism, see Manning, 106 Colum L Rev at 70 (cited in note 10). One reading of purposive interpretation comes from the Legal Process school, which takes legislators to be "reasonable persons pursuing reasonable purposes reasonably." Henry M. Hart and Albert M. Sacks, *The Legal Process* 1378 (William Eskridge and Philip Frickey, eds, 1994) (1958). On that approach, purpose is a construction, not a matter of finding something, and reasonableness is the lodestar. I am bracketing that view here. To make a long story short, it would probably entail the conclusion that the plantwide definition is *mandatory*, for reasons discussed below. It should be clear that if judges are to decide what reasonable people do, and to interpret ambiguities accordingly, they would be assuming a large policymaking role. It would be possible to think that if the Legal Process school is right, *Chevron* stands on firm ground, because agencies are in a better position than courts to decide as would reasonable persons pursuing reasonable purposes reasonably.

[55] See *Smith v United States*, 508 US 223 (1993).

[56] Compare with id at 242 (Scalia, J, dissenting).

[57] This was the majority's suggestion. See *Smith*, 508 US at 240.

Is purpose helpful in *Chevron*? As we have seen, the courts of appeals thought so.[58] After all, the nonattainment program is designed to ensure attainment, and for that reason it imposes especially stringent restrictions in the areas that it covers. One might think that if the purpose of the program is properly understood, we should read the text consistently with it, which would mean that as between a less stringent and a more stringent approach, the more stringent must prevail.[59] If a purposivist court were trying to resolve *Chevron* without an agency in the picture, it might be tempted to say exactly that.

There is an initial problem with this idea as applied to the problem in *Chevron*. The EPA concluded that a plantwide definition would promote economic goals without harming, and possibly while helping, the environment.[60] If that is so, or if a court cannot know whether that is so, the supposed purpose of the nonattainment program is neither here nor there. The purpose—understood as "produce attainment!"—might not be compromised by the plantwide definition and might even be promoted by it. If the latter, then the plantwide definition is mandatory, given the purpose. We might conclude that in *Chevron*, purpose is unhelpful unless and until we get clear on the economic and environmental consequences of the plantwide definition. To say the least, that is not easy for judges to do.

But the larger problem with purposive interpretation, as a solution to the *Chevron* question, lies elsewhere. Congress expresses its purposes through texts, which typically balance an array of purposes. There is no justification for using one supposed purpose, taken at a high level of abstraction, as a basis for pushing the text in a direction that Congress did not necessarily embrace.[61] The question is whether the text means X or Y. The purpose can be cashed out, so to speak, with either X or Y. It is tendentious to treat a single abstract purpose, compatible with either X or Y, to justify the selection of Y.[62]

---

[58] See *National Resource Defense Council, Inc. v Gorsuch*, 685 F2d 718 (DC Cir 1982), rev'd by *Chevron, USA, Inc. v National Resource Defense Council, Inc.*, 467 US 837 (1984) (cited in note 24).

[59] See *ASARCO Inc. v EPA*, 578 F2d 319, 325 (DC Cir 1978).

[60] For theory, see Merrill, 66 Admin L Rev at 259 (cited in note 2); for evidence, see Hahn, 6 Yale J Reg at 129 (cited in note 20).

[61] For a valuable treatment, see Manning, 106 Colum L Rev 70 (cited in note 10).

[62] Judge Frank Easterbrook puts it well:

> The selection of Y is a measure of what Goal X was worth to the legislature, of how best to achieve X, and of where to stop in pursuit of X. Like any other rule, Y is bound

Textualism's less appealing sibling is conceptualism. Purposivism also has a less appealing sibling, which can be found whenever courts create a purpose, and make it authoritative, entirely on their own.[63] Call it *faux purposivism*. What Gertrude Stein said about Oakland is sometimes true for the purpose: "There's no there there."[64]

C. CANONS

In some regulatory cases, canons of interpretation can be exceedingly useful and even decisive.[65] Suppose that in *Chevron*, one or another interpretation would create a serious constitutional problem. If so, a court might invoke the avoidance canon in order to steer clear of the domain of constitutional doubt.[66] Or suppose that in *Chevron*, one or another approach would apply a rule retroactively[67] or extraterritorially.[68] If so, the case would be simple to resolve.

The problem is that it is not easy to identify a canon of construction to settle the question how to interpret the word "source." In an earlier era, some courts might have said that "remedial statutes should be

---

to be imprecise, to be over- and under-inclusive. This is not a good reason for a court, observing the inevitable imprecision, to add to or subtract from Rule Y on the argument that, by doing so, it can get more of Goal X. The judicial selection of means to pursue X displaces and directly overrides the legislative selection of ways to obtain X.

Frank Easterbrook, *Statutes' Domains*, 50 U Chi L Rev 533, 546 (1983). See also *US v Rodriguez*, 480 US 522, 525–26 (1987).

[63] I am bracketing Dworkin's approach to interpretation. See Ronald Dworkin, *Law's Empire* (Belknap, 1985). Dworkin sees interpretation as an effort to make the best constructive sense out of the relevant legal materials (including statutory text). To simplify a complex story, Dworkin's approach requires judges to respect the constraints of "fit" and, within those constraints, to decide what best "justifies" the existing materials by making the best constructive sense of it. See id. In constitutional law, the meaning of the Equal Protection Clause, as applied to (say) bans on same-sex marriage, would turn on what ruling would make the clause the best that it can be. We could say the same thing about "source." If we adopt Dworkin's conception of interpretation, we might end up embracing *Chevron* on the ground that agencies, with their superior expertise and accountability, are in the best position to undertake the task of interpretation as Dworkin understands it. Law's Empire would turn out to be Agencies' Empire, at least to some degree.

[64] See Gertrude Stein, *Everybody's Autobiography* 298 (1937). Here is the fuller version: ". . . what was the use of my having come from Oakland it was not natural to have come from there yes write about it if I like or anything if I like but not there, there is no there there."

[65] See *Kent v Dulles*, 357 US 116 (1958).

[66] See id.

[67] See *Bowen v Georgetown University Hospital*, 488 US 204 (1988).

[68] See *Equal Employment Opportunity Commission v Arabian American Oil Co.*, 499 US 244, 248 (1991).

construed liberally, to promote their remedial purpose"[69]—which might have spelled doom for the plantwide definition. But contemporary courts rarely invoke the "remedial statutes" canon, and for good reason: The canon places an unjustified thumb on the scales, disconnected from Congress' actual instructions.

It might be tempting to develop or invoke another kind of canon, specifically suited to the modern administrative state. The Court itself has embraced what seems like a relevant canon, in the form of a cost-benefit default principle: *It is unlawful for an agency to refuse to consider costs unless Congress has clearly authorized them to do so.*[70] The principle means that in the face of statutory ambiguity, it will be assumed that Congress instructed agencies to consider costs rather than to ignore them. A version of that principle could well be invoked in *Chevron*, even without *Chevron*.

The key case, *Michigan v EPA*, involved a provision of the Clean Air Act that requires the EPA to list hazardous pollutants, for later regulation, if it is "appropriate and necessary" to do so.[71] The EPA contended that it had the authority to base its listing decision only on considerations of public health (and hence to decline to consider costs).[72] In its view, the words "appropriate and necessary" were ambiguous, and a cost-blind interpretation was legitimate.

By a five-to-four vote, the Court disagreed.[73] It held that the "EPA strayed far beyond" the bounds of reasonableness in interpreting the statutory language "to mean that it could ignore cost when deciding whether to regulate power plants."[74] In a passage of potential relevance to the plantwide definition in *Chevron*, the Court added, "One would not say that it is even rational, never mind 'appropriate,' to impose billions of dollars in economic costs in return for a few dollars in health or environmental benefits. ... Consideration of cost reflects the understanding that reasonable regulation ordinarily requires paying attention to the advantages and the disadvantages of agency decisions."[75]

---

[69] See Rudolph H. Heimanson, *Remedial Legislation*, 46 Marq L Rev 216 (1962).

[70] See *Michigan v EPA*, 135 S Ct 2699, 2710–11 (2015).

[71] Id at 2704–05.

[72] Id.

[73] Id.

[74] Id at 2707.

[75] Id.

While rejecting the majority's particular conclusion on relatively technical grounds, Justice Kagan's dissenting opinion, joined by three other members of the Court, was more explicit on the general point, contending, "Cost is almost always a relevant—and usually, a highly important—factor in regulation. *Unless Congress provides otherwise, an agency acts unreasonably in establishing 'a standard-setting process that ignore[s] economic considerations.'*"[76] Justice Kagan added that "an agency must take costs into account in some manner before imposing significant regulatory burdens."[77]

These ideas could easily be adapted for the *Chevron* situation. Indeed, the adaptation would be a modest tweak. *Michigan* holds that it is unreasonable, in the sense of arbitrary, to adopt an interpretation that would prevent consideration of costs. It would be similarly unreasonable to adopt an interpretation that would impose high costs for little or no benefit (as the *Michigan* Court also said). Hence we can identify another canon of construction, to the effect that *agencies cannot impose high costs for little or no benefit unless Congress has clearly authorized them to do so.* Suppose, as is plausible, that the plantwide definition would save significant sums of money, and that it would be equal or better from the environmental point of view.[78] If so, a failure to adopt that definition would violate the relevant canon. It would essentially impose hundreds of millions or perhaps billions of dollars in costs in return for little or nothing. If so, *Chevron* without *Chevron* would be an easy case: the plantwide definition was obligatory. A relevant, if novel, canon of construction required it.

This approach has considerable appeal. In my view, it is essentially correct. But consider two points. First, it depends on a stipulation about the consequences of the competing definitions of "source." The stipulation might be wrong. Suppose that the consequences are disputed.[79] Perhaps there is a reasonable argument that the plantwide definition would produce serious environmental harm. If so, the relevant canon does not solve the problem. Second, *Chevron* itself

---

[76] Id at 2716–17 (Kagan, J, dissenting) (emphasis added). The dissent rejected the majority's conclusion in large part because the EPA had considered costs at a later stage in its processes, when it was deciding on the appropriate level of stringency. Id at 2719–21.

[77] Id.

[78] See Hahn, 6 Yale J Reg at 128–29 (cited in note 20).

[79] See Merrill, 66 Admin L Rev at 258–60 (cited in note 2).

would produce the same result. After all, *Michigan* itself was an application of *Chevron* Step Two! My conclusion is that while on plausible assumptions the no-high-costs-with-little-or-no-benefits canon (an unruly name, to be sure) produces a sensible resolution of the *Chevron* problem without *Chevron*, it would do exactly the same thing with *Chevron*.

D. SKIDMORE TO THE RESCUE

As the relevant doctrine is now organized, there are three possibilities with respect to judicial deference to agency interpretations of law. (1) Agency interpretations of law may receive *Chevron* deference. (2) Agency interpretations of law may receive no deference at all.[80] (3) Agency interpretations may receive "*Skidmore* deference."

The last of these is named, of course, after the Court's famous 1944 decision in *Skidmore v Swift & Co.*,[81] which presented the question of how to interpret the statutory term "working time." The disputed contexts were those in which employees had to be available to take telephone calls and possibly to report for duty, but were not otherwise "working."[82] The administrator of the Fair Labor Standards Act had views on that question and offered a possible resolution. The Court was keenly interested in those views, on the ground that

> [T]he rulings, interpretations, and opinions of the Administrator under this Act, while not controlling upon the courts by reason of their authority, do constitute a body of experience and informed judgment to which courts and litigants may properly resort for guidance. The weight of such a judgment in a particular case will depend upon the thoroughness evident in its consideration, the validity of its reasoning, its consistency with earlier and later pronouncements, and all those factors which give it power to persuade, if lacking power to control.

It is worth underlining the Court's emphasis on "experience and informed judgment," in the context of an attempted interpretation of an ambiguous term ("working time"). As of now, *Skidmore* is alive and well, and the Court shows no signs of abandoning it. On the contrary,

---

[80] This would be the case if, for example, an agency were interpreting the APA or the Freedom of Information Act.

[81] 323 US 134 (1944).

[82] Id at 139.

the Court has embraced it.[83] The only question—and it can be quite difficult—is when *Skidmore* applies and when *Chevron* applies. We know that if an agency is engaged in rulemaking or adjudication, it receives *Chevron* deference.[84] We know that if an agency is issuing an interpretive rule, the answer is: *It depends.*[85]

Let us put the doctrinal complexities to one side. If the Court abandoned *Chevron*, or scaled it back, perhaps it would retain *Skidmore*. Indeed, it would be likely to do so. The *Skidmore* decision calls for a softer form of deference, if it is deference at all, but it nonetheless gives an agency a significant power: the "power to persuade." Suppose that the issue in *Chevron* were to be examined under *Skidmore* and in terms of the three specified *Skidmore* factors.[86] True, the EPA's interpretation was inconsistent with earlier pronouncements, but it deserves high marks for thoroughness.[87] Was it "valid in its reasoning"? That factor seems to add little; it suggests that courts should simply ask whether the agency got it right, which means that deference would be beside the point. But perhaps we could read *Skidmore* to mean, quite broadly, that a careful and thorough agency explanation deserves careful and respectful judicial attention, with a demerit for inconsistency with earlier pronouncements.

If the *Chevron* Court were to apply *Skidmore* rather than *Chevron*, its ultimate conclusion seems reasonably clear: The EPA's decision must be upheld. Indeed, that conclusion follows, more or less, from the actual holding in *Skidmore*, which was to follow the administrator's reasonable definition of "working time."[88] If *Chevron* were abandoned, courts might well resort to *Skidmore*, which would often produce exactly the same result.

At this point, it is natural to ask: Is *Skidmore* really different from *Chevron*? If it is, is it all that different? The conventional wisdom is that *Skidmore* calls for a markedly lower level of deference. While *Chevron* makes reasonable interpretations "binding," *Skidmore* merely

---

[83] See *United States v Mead*, 533 US 218, 234–35 (2001).

[84] See id at 229.

[85] See *Barnhart v Walton*, 535 US 212, 222 (2002).

[86] The Court referred mysteriously to other factors—"all those factors"—but for simplicity I refer only to the three that are specified.

[87] 46 Fed Reg 50766 codified at 40 CFR §§ 51.18(j)(1)(i), (ii) (1983).

[88] *Skidmore v Swift & Co.*, 323 US 134, 136 (1944).

entitles them to respectful consideration.[89] An outsider might be forgiven for thinking that this is not much of a difference. Both cases suggest that courts should follow the agency's interpretation, if it is reasonable and so long as the statute is ambiguous. But considerable evidence suggests that consistent with conventional understandings, *Chevron* calls for a higher degree of deference than *Skidmore* does.[90]

Fair enough. But in *Chevron* itself, the difference between the two would not seem to matter a great deal. Many cases are relevantly like *Chevron*, and in all of them, *Skidmore* could solve the problem.

E. NO VIOLATION OF LAW

There is a final possibility. The claim in *Chevron* was that the EPA had violated the Clean Air Act. For a violation to occur, of course, it would be necessary for a court to find that the agency acted inconsistently with a relevant provision of law. Did it? Perhaps not—even without *Chevron*. It would be reasonable to say that the agency's definition of "source" did not violate anything at all, because the statute offered no definition that would forbid the use of a plantwide definition.

In a famous article, Judge Frank Easterbrook argued that sometimes a statute does not supply an answer, and so it should not be construed but must instead "be put down and disregarded."[91] I confess that I find his central argument elusive, because any decision to "put down" a statute must depend on some kind of construction, to the effect that the statute is inapplicable. But this passage is helpful:[92]

> My suggestion is that unless the statute plainly hands courts the power to create and revise a form of common law, the domain of the statute should be restricted to cases anticipated by its framers and expressly resolved in the legislative process. Unless the party relying on the statute could establish either express resolution or creation of the common law power of revision, the court would hold the matter in question outside the statute's domain. The statute would become irrelevant, the parties (and court) remitted to whatever other sources of law might be applicable.

---

[89] See *United States v Mead*, 533 US 218 (2001).

[90] See Kent Barnett and Christopher J. Walker, *Chevron in the Circuit Courts*, 116 Mich L Rev 1 (2017).

[91] See Frank Easterbrook, *Statutes' Domains*, 50 U Chi L Rev 533, 534 (1983).

[92] Id at 544.

Now we're talking! Easterbrook's claim here is that if a statute does not give courts the authority to create common law, the reach of statutes is restricted to their "express resolution." Without necessarily adopting that suggestion,[93] courts could say more modestly that nothing in the Clean Air Act forbids the plantwide definition of source (or for that matter its predecessor). The EPA was therefore on firm ground.

It might be tempting to respond that agencies do not have authority unless Congress has allocated it to them. If Congress has been silent, agencies lack the relevant authority, and so must lose. The claim is generally right, but it is not responsive to the particular argument I am making here. By hypothesis, Congress has granted the relevant authority to the agency. We are not speaking of cases in which agencies may lack that authority. The only question is the meaning of some term that is part of the congressional grant ("source"). If the agency's action is not inconsistent with congressional instructions, then the agency has not violated the law.

If this is the right approach, then abandoning *Chevron* need not result in overruling its holding. The revised analysis would not speak of deference to agency interpretations of law. It would point to an absence of any legal violation by the EPA.

One advantage of this approach is that it would be generalizable. Many cases now analyzed under *Chevron* could be treated in just that way.[94] Courts could simply say that agencies had not violated anything in the relevant statute, or exceeded their statutory authority. One question, of course, is whether this approach would be an improvement over *Chevron*.[95] In practice, it would be quite similar, in the sense that agencies would continue to win. But in principle, it would be quite different. Instead of saying that agencies are allowed to interpret ambiguous provisions, it would mean more simply that

---

[93] Judge Easterbrook's approach seems uncomfortably close to the old and long-rejected idea that statutes in derogation of the common law must be narrowly construed. See Jefferson Fordham and Russell Leach, *Interpretation of Statutes in Derogation of the Common Law*, 3 Vand L Rev 438 (1950). In my view, that idea is enjoying a modern revival, though a defense of that proposition would require an extended discussion. See Sunstein, *Chevron as Law* (cited in note 11), for a discussion of the "major questions" exception to *Chevron*, which can be seen as an example.

[94] See, for example, *Babbitt v Sweet Home Chapter*, 515 US 687 (1995); *Entergy Corp. v Riverkeeper*, 556 US 208 (2009).

[95] Importantly, it would avoid the controversy over whether *Chevron* is a violation of Article III or of the APA. For discussion, see Sunstein, *Chevron as Law* (cited in note 11).

agencies have not been shown to violate any provision of law. I acknowledge that some people might find that distinction elusive.

IV. Parallel Worlds

It takes some work to imagine what the world of administrative law would have looked like without *Chevron*, or if *Chevron* had been abandoned in, say, 1987.[96] The best way to do that is to focus on particular cases, and on that count, *Chevron* itself is the most obvious candidate. We have seen that both textualism and purposivism lead nowhere, or at least nowhere good, meaning nowhere concrete—a conclusion that holds for many cases decided with reference to *Chevron*.[97] Something similar can often be said about the use of canons of construction, now available under Step One of *Chevron*. But I have urged that in *Chevron* itself, a current court might well invoke a canon in favor of some kind of cost-benefit balancing in order to mandate the plantwide definition.[98] As we have seen, that same approach would likely be followed, now, under Step Two of *Chevron*.

If *Chevron* did not exist, or if it were abandoned or scaled back, *Skidmore* deference might turn out to be far more important than it is today. In principle, it is weaker than *Chevron* deference, and that appears to be true in practice as well.[99] If *Skidmore* deference were applied in *Chevron*, the agency would undoubtedly win, simply because other sources of statutory meaning did not cut against its interpretation. We have also seen that without *Chevron*, a court might

---

[96] In that year, the Court, or at least Justice Stevens, seemed to have mounted a failed effort to do exactly that. See *Immigration and Naturalization Service v Cardoza-Fonseca*, 480 US 421 (1987): "The question whether Congress intended the two standards to be identical is a pure question of statutory construction for the courts to decide.... The narrow legal question whether the two standards are the same is, of course, quite different from the question of interpretation that arises in each case in which the agency is required to apply either or both standards to a particular set of facts." Id. For discussion, see Merrill, 66 Admin L Rev at 276 (cited in note 2).

[97] See *Babbitt v Sweet Home Chapter*, 515 US 687 (1995); *Entergy Corp. v Riverkeeper*, 556 US 208 (2009). The Court has found the text clear, of course, in important cases rejecting agency decisions under *Chevron*. See, for example, *MCI Telecommunications Corp. v American Telephone & Telegraph Co.*, 512 US 218 (1994); *Massachusetts v EPA*, 549 US 497 (2007). While I cannot prove the point in this space, there is a good argument that in at least some such cases, conceptualism, rather than textualism, was at work.

[98] As noted in text, this depends on stipulations about the likely effects of the plantwide definition.

[99] See Barnett and Walker, 116 Mich L Rev 1 (cited in note 90).

well uphold the agency's interpretation on the ground that it did not violate any provision of law.

One of the lessons of this lengthy exercise is that without *Chevron*, *Chevron* would almost certainly have come out the same way, though through more complicated routes. Another lesson is that the most important resources available for deciding *Chevron* without *Chevron*— text, purpose, canons of construction—remain fully available for deciding *Chevron* with *Chevron*. In these circumstances, the argument for abandoning *Chevron* is weaker than it might otherwise seem.[100] Doing so would introduce new levels of uncertainty, even a degree of chaos, about a recurring issue in administrative law. It would alter the background against which Congress has enacted numerous statutes since 1984. It would result in far more politicized judging.[101] It would require answers to a host of open questions.

In short, there would be a lot of dust to clear. The irony is that after a lengthy and difficult cleanup operation, and after adoption of novel formulations, the framework that would ultimately replace *Chevron* would be likely to operate, in practice, a fair bit like that in *Chevron* itself.

---

[100] Other issues, involving the APA and constitutional constraints, are explored in detail in Sunstein, *Chevron as Law* (cited in note 11).

[101] See Kent Barnett et al, *Administrative Law's Political Dynamics*, 71 Vand L Rev 1463 (2018). I discuss the argument for overruling *Chevron* in more general terms in Sunstein, *Chevron as Law* (cited in note 11).

TRACEY MACLIN

BYRD v UNITED STATES: UNAUTHORIZED DRIVERS OF RENTAL CARS HAVE FOURTH AMENDMENT RIGHTS? NOT AS EVIDENT AS IT SEEMS

No discerning student of the Supreme Court would contend that Justice Anthony Kennedy broadly interpreted the Fourth Amendment during his thirty years on the Court. For example, in *Maryland v King*,[1] a 2013 case that Justice Samuel Alito described as "perhaps the most important criminal case that this Court has heard in decades,"[2] Justice Kennedy's majority opinion rejected a Fourth Amendment challenge to a Maryland law requiring forensic testing of DNA samples taken from persons arrested for violent crimes. *King* was criticized by individuals and organizations across the political spectrum,[3] and it

Tracey Maclin is Professor of Law, Boston University School of Law.

AUTHOR'S NOTE: Thanks to Al Alschuler and Gary Lawson for reading and commenting on a draft of this article. And thanks to Sanjana Dubey and Julia Harper for their research and editing assistance.

[1] 569 US 435 (2013).

[2] Transcript of Oral Argument, *Maryland v King*, No 12-207, at 35 (Feb 27, 2013), archived at http://perma.cc/ZD4J-58YU.

[3] Conservative Republican Senators Rand Paul and Ted Cruz, the *New York Times* editorial pages, the *American Prospect*, and the American Civil Liberties Union all denounced *King*. See Rand Paul, *Big Brother Says "Open Your Mouth!"* (American Conservative, June 10, 2012), archived at http://perma.cc/4YRJ-F4BW; Ted Cruz, *Statement on SCOTUS Decision in Maryland v. King* (June 3, 2012), archived at http://perma.cc/C75J-WKLD; Editorial, *DNA*

has been characterized as "a watershed moment in the evolution of Fourth Amendment doctrine and an important signal for the future of biotechnologies and policing."[4]

A decade before *King* was announced, Justice Kennedy wrote for a majority of the Court in another controversial case dealing with police bus sweeps for drugs and guns. *Drayton v United States*[5] addressed whether passengers on an interstate bus were seized when police approached, asked for identification, and requested permission to search their bodies and luggage for weapons or illegal narcotics, and whether police must inform persons of their right to refuse to cooperate to validate a consent search.[6] Drayton and Brown were companions seated on a bus when officers questioned them and asked to search their luggage and persons at a rest stop. After narcotics were discovered on Brown, an officer said to Drayton, "Mind if I check you?"[7] Without a verbal response, Drayton lifted his hands above his legs, which allowed the officer to pat down his legs and detect narcotics concealed underneath his pants. Kennedy concluded that no seizure had occurred, and that police need not inform passengers of their rights when requesting consent to search because it is the responsibility of citizens to know and assert their rights if they wish not to cooperate.[8]

Lastly, consider Justice Kennedy's position on the exclusionary rule, which requires the suppression of evidence obtained by police in violation of the Fourth Amendment. In contrast to other "moderate"

---

and Suspicionless Searches, NY Times A24 (June 4, 2013); Scott Lemieux, *Scalia Gets It Right* (American Prospect, June 3, 2013), archived at http://perma.cc/55L8-SG8K; American Civil Liberties Union, *Comment on Supreme Court DNA Swab Ruling (Maryland v. King)* (June 3, 2013), archived at http://perma.cc/4XF6-M9LN. More recently, Barry Friedman stated that the "decision in *King* is built on a lie." Barry Friedman, *Unwarranted: Policing Without Permission* 274 (Farrar, Straus and Giroux, 2017) (noting that *King* justified its result because of the State's interest in "identifying" arrestees, but identification had nothing to do with why the State takes DNA samples; "the DNA of arrestees is being checked to solve cold cases").

[4] Erin Murphy, *License, Registration, Cheek Swab: DNA Testing and the Divided Court*, 127 Harv L Rev 161, 161 (2013). See also Tracey Maclin, *Maryland v King: Terry v Ohio Redux*, 2013 Supreme Court Review 359, 402–3 (noting that the logic of *King* "invites law enforcement officials to extend DNA searches to persons arrested for any offense and even to persons merely detained by the police").

[5] 536 US 194 (2002).

[6] Id at 203.

[7] Id at 199.

[8] Id at 207. See Tracey Maclin, *The Good and the Bad News About Consent Searches in the Supreme Court*, 39 McGeorge L Rev 27, 63–65 (2008); Janice Nader, *No Need to Shout: Bus Sweeps and the Psychology of Coercion*, 2002 Supreme Court Review 153, 179.

conservative Justices who have recently sat on the Court, Justice Kennedy has *never* voted to apply the exclusionary rule in a case in which the scope of the rule was contested in a search and seizure case.[9] Tellingly, he provided the fifth vote and concurred in the three key sections of Justice Antonin Scalia's opinion in *Hudson v Michigan*,[10] which held that suppression is never a remedy for knock-and-announce violations.[11] Academic commentators generally agree that *Hudson* is a direct attack on the exclusionary rule from several perspectives and lays the foundation for abolishing the rule as a categorical matter.[12] Justice Kennedy wrote a concurring opinion in *Hudson* in which he stated that "the continued operation of the exclusionary rule, as settled and defined by our precedents, is not in doubt."[13] Justice Kennedy's cryptic comment raised several ques-

---

[9] See Tracey Maclin, *The Supreme Court and the Fourth Amendment's Exclusionary Rule* 346 (Oxford, 2013). Justice Kennedy's votes in exclusionary-rule cases put him in the company of Chief Justice Roberts and Justices Scalia, Thomas, and Alito who have also never voted to apply the exclusionary rule. By comparison, Justices O'Connor and Souter, neither of whom championed the exclusionary rule, voted to enforce the rule at least once during their tenure on the Court. O'Connor voted for the defendant in *Illinois v Krull*, 480 US 340 (1987), and in *Murray v United States*, 487 US 533 (1988) (O'Connor joined Justice Marshall's dissent), while Souter voted for the defendant in *Pennsylvania Bd of Probation & Parole v Scott*, 524 US 357 (1998).

[10] 547 US 586 (2006).

[11] Id at 589.

[12] Wayne R. LaFave, 1 *Search and Seizure: A Treatise on the Fourth Amendment* § 1.6(h) at 281 (West, 5th ed 2012) (arguing that *Hudson*'s cost-benefits analysis was "dead wrong," but also that it has the capacity to metastasize into a much broader limitation upon the suppression doctrine"); Albert W. Alschuler, *The Exclusionary Rule and Causation: Hudson v. Michigan and Its Ancestors*, 93 Iowa L Rev 1741, 1764 (2008) (describing *Hudson*'s attenuation theory as a "formula for abolishing the [exclusionary] rule"); Thomas K. Clancy, *The Irrelevancy of the Fourth Amendment in the Roberts Court*, 85 Chi Kent L Rev 191, 202 (2010) (stating that at its "most fundamental level," the result in *Hudson* "called into question the future of the exclusionary rule," and that abolition of the rule "is Scalia's clear aim; he has planted the seeds in *Hudson* and needs one more vote to reap the harvest"); James J. Tomkovicz, *Hudson v. Michigan and the Future of Fourth Amendment Exclusion*, 93 Iowa L Rev 1819, 1841–47 (2008) (stating that when read broadly, *Hudson* "foreshadows and anticipates outright abolition" of the exclusionary rule). See also Donald Dripps, *The Fourth Amendment, the Exclusionary Rule, and the Roberts Court: Normative and Empirical Dimensions of the Over-Deterrence Hypothesis*, 85 Chi Kent L Rev 209, 210 (2010); David A. Moran, *The End of Waiting for the Exclusionary Rule, Among Other Things: The Roberts Court Takes on the Fourth Amendment*, 2006 Cato S Ct Rev 283; Sharon L. Davies and Anna B. Scanlon, *Katz in the Age of Hudson v. Michigan: Some Thoughts on "Suppression as a Last Resort,"* 41 UC Davis L Rev 1035 (2008). Recently, in *Collins v Virginia*, 138 S Ct 1663 (2018), Justice Thomas questioned the Court's power to impose the exclusionary rule on the states. Id at 1675–80 (Thomas, J, concurring) (explaining first that the exclusionary rule "is not rooted in the Constitution or a federal statute" or federal common law, then stating skepticism that the Court has the authority to impose the rule on the states).

[13] *Hudson*, 547 US at 603 (Kennedy, J, concurring in part and concurring in the judgment).

tions, including why someone who claims to support the "continuing vitality of the exclusionary rule . . . would cast the crucial fifth vote for an opinion that openly declared war on the exclusionary rule."[14]

In light of his previous votes in search and seizure cases, surprisingly Justice Kennedy, in what would be his final Fourth Amendment opinion for a majority of the Court, authored an opinion in favor of a criminal defendant. In *Byrd v United States*,[15] a unanimous Court rejected the government's argument that unauthorized drivers always lack an expectation of privacy in a rental car and thus can never challenge a police search of the car.[16] Byrd was driving a rental car in violation of the rental agreement but with the permission of the renter; the police searched the trunk of the car, allegedly without consent or probable cause, and found heroin and body armor. The Court in *Byrd* held that the search was unlawful because "as a general rule, someone in otherwise lawful possession and control of a rental car has a reasonable expectation of privacy in it even if the rental agreement does not list him or her as an authorized driver."[17]

When *Byrd* arrived at the Court, few would have predicted a victory for Terrence Byrd, let alone a unanimous vote for the defense. Even apart from the Court's general antagonism to Fourth Amendment claims, too many obstacles stood in the way of a victory for Byrd.[18] First, the federal appellate courts had split three ways on whether an unauthorized driver of a rental car could raise a constitutional challenge to a police search.[19] A majority of the court of appeals—the Third, Fourth, Fifth, and Tenth Circuits—had adopted a bright-line rule that unauthorized drivers lacked standing to contest

---

[14] Moran, 2006 Cato S Ct Rev at 308 (cited in note 12).

[15] 138 S Ct 1518 (2018).

[16] Id at 1522.

[17] Id at 1524. In the final section of the opinion, the holding was framed without the caveat: "the mere fact that a driver in lawful possession or control of a rental car is not listed on the rental agreement will not defeat his or her otherwise reasonable expectation of privacy." Id at 1531.

[18] Byrd had the burden of proving that he had a legitimate expectation of privacy in the car. See *Rawlings v Kentucky*, 448 US 98, 104 (1980).

[19] See Darren M. Goldman, Note, *Resolving a Three-Way Circuit Split: Why Unauthorized Rental Drivers Should Be Denied Fourth Amendment Standing*, 89 BU L Rev 1687 (2009); Lisa J. Zigterman, Note, *Live and Let Drive: The Struggle for Unauthorized Drivers of Rental Cars in Attaining Standing to Challenge Fourth Amendment Searches*, 2009 U Ill L Rev 1655; Petition for a Writ of Certiorari, *Byrd v United States*, Docket No 16-1371, *11–18 (US filed May 11, 2017) (available on Westlaw at 2017 WL 2130318) ("Byrd Cert Brief").

a search.[20] By contrast, in the Eighth and Ninth Circuits, "an unauthorized driver *always* had standing to challenge a search, so long as the unauthorized driver had the permission of an authorized driver."[21] In these circuits, the rental contract between the authorized driver and the rental company was irrelevant to the standing issue; what mattered most was whether the driver had permission from the authorized driver.[22] Although the approach of the Eighth and Ninth Circuits could also be characterized as a bright-line rule—that is, the unauthorized driver always has standing when he has the permission of the authorized driver—that directive lacked clarity for both police and judges attempting to apply it.[23] Finally, the Sixth Circuit announced a third rule. While recognizing an initial presumption against standing, the Sixth Circuit embraced a totality of the circumstances test to decide whether an unauthorized driver had standing.[24]

Another apparent impediment for Byrd was the result and reasoning of *Rakas v Illinois*.[25] Frank Rakas and Lonnie King were passengers in a vehicle that was the suspected getaway car in a robbery. After police lawfully stopped the car, a search revealed a box of rifle shells in the locked glove compartment and a sawed-off rifle underneath the front passenger seat. Neither passenger claimed ownership of the vehicle or the rifle or the shells.[26] When these items were in-

---

[20] *United States v Kennedy*, 638 F3d 159, 165 (3d Cir 2011); *United States v Wellons*, 32 F3d 117, 119 (4th Cir 1994); *United States v Seely*, 331 F3d 471, 472 (5th Cir 2003) (per curiam); *United States v Roper*, 918 F2d 885, 887–88 (10th Cir 1990).

[21] Goldman, 89 BU L Rev at 1708 (footnote omitted) (cited in note 19).

[22] Id at 1711.

[23] For example, "the test does not define what 'permission' is, or how it is proven." Id at 1719. Would police "be required to contact the authorized driver or could the officer just take the unauthorized driver's word?" Id. In other words, the test of the Eighth and Ninth Circuits "fails to accomplish its intended goal—ease of use." Id.

[24] *United States v Smith*, 263 F3d 571 (6th Cir 2001). Five factors were considered by the court: (1) whether the unauthorized driver had a valid driver's license; (2) whether the unauthorized driver was able to proffer the rental agreement and had sufficient knowledge about the vehicle and the circumstances surrounding the rental; (3) the nexus between the authorized driver and unauthorized driver; (4) whether the unauthorized driver had permission to drive the vehicle from the authorized driver; and (5) whether the unauthorized driver had a business relationship with the rental company. Id at 586. See also *United States v Winters*, 782 F3d 289, 300–01 (6th Cir 2015) (reaffirming the test from *Smith* and stating that the fact that the defendants were not listed on the rental car agreement was "entitled to some weight" in the totality of the circumstances analysis).

[25] 439 US 128 (1978).

[26] Why the defendants never asserted a property interest in the rifle or the shells remains a mystery. Shortly after *Rakas* was decided, Professor Kamisar offered the following speculation:

troduced at trial, the Illinois courts ruled that the defendants lacked standing to contest the search. The Supreme Court agreed, holding that passengers' lawful presence in a vehicle was not enough, by itself, to confer standing. *Rakas* explained that because neither Rakas nor King had a property or possessory interest in the vehicle or the items, they failed to prove they held a Fourth Amendment privacy interest in the glove compartment or in the area under the front seat. "Like the trunk of an automobile, these are areas in which a passenger *qua* passenger simply would not normally have a legitimate expectation of privacy."[27] In *Byrd*, the government argued that *Rakas* precluded Byrd from claiming a legitimate expectation of privacy in a rental car that he neither owned nor leased.[28] While Byrd's presence in the vehicle was legitimate since he had obtained the keys from the authorized driver, *Rakas* instructed that legitimate presence "is a necessary, but not a sufficient, foundation for asserting Fourth Amendment rights."[29]

Another seeming hurdle for Byrd was that his case would rise or fall on whether he had standing.[30] In the typical search and seizure case,

---

Recall that at the suppression hearing the defense lawyer maintained that his client did not "have to admit" that the items seized were theirs. The way he put that suggests that perhaps the defense lawyer was unaware that testimony given to establish standing to object to illegally seized evidence may not be used against the defendant at his trial on the question of guilt or innocence. [See *Simmons v United States*, 390 US 377 (1968).]

On the other hand, perhaps the defense lawyer was thinking of putting his client on the stand at the trial and was painfully aware that in a few jurisdictions, including Illinois, a defendant's testimony at his pretrial hearing to suppress illegally seized evidence has been admissible for impeachment purposes if and when the defendant testifies at his trial. In these jurisdictions, *Simmons* has been modified in light of *Harris v. New York*, 401 U.S. 222 (1971), which allows statements obtained in violation of *Miranda* to be introduced at trial for impeachment purposes.

See Jesse H. Choper, Yale Kamisar, and Laurence H. Tribe, *The Supreme Court: Trends and Developments* 163–64 (National Practice Institute, 1979) (remarks of Professor Kamisar).

[27] *Rakas*, 429 US at 149.

[28] See *Byrd*, 138 S Ct at 1522.

[29] Brief for the United States, *Byrd v United States*, Docket No 16-1371, *14 (US filed Dec 13, 2017) ("Government Brief").

[30] *Rakas* merged the issue of standing with the substantive merits of a defendant's Fourth Amendment claims. In future cases, *Rakas* explained that "the better analysis forthrightly focuses on the extent of a particular defendant's rights under the Fourth Amendment, rather than on any theoretically separate, but invariably intertwined concept of standing." *Rakas*, 439 US at 139. Interestingly, a year later the Court used the term "standing" notwithstanding what was said in *Rakas*. See *Arkansas v Sanders*, 442 US 753, 761 n 8 (1979). Despite *Rakas*'s instruction, courts still analyze defendants' Fourth Amendment claims under the standing rubric, as did the lower courts in Byrd's case. *United States v Byrd*, 679 Fed Appx 146, 150 (3d Cir 2015). *United States v Byrd*, 2015 WL 5038455, *2 (MD Pa 2015). As Orin Kerr observes,

standing is not an issue. Police illegally enter A's home and seize criminal evidence. Or, police illegally frisk B and discover a weapon in his pocket. A clearly has a basis to contest the intrusion because police entered *his* home, as does B because police searched *his* person. "The basic rule of standing is that a litigant may assert only a violation of his own fourth amendment rights."[31] But in cases where a defendant's nexus to a challenged search or seizure is attenuated or illegitimate, the concept of standing becomes important and sometimes controversial. The Court has left no doubt that the car thief or the "burglar plying his trade in a summer cabin during the off season"[32] lacks standing to contest what would otherwise be an illegal police search because their presence in the stolen vehicle or the cabin is illegal or "wrongful."[33]

Furthermore, lengthy history exists on the interplay of standing and the exclusionary rule. Opponents of the exclusionary rule are generally averse to grant standing to criminal defendants to contest a search or seizure. The best evidence of this phenomenon emerged after the onset of the exclusionary rule. In 1914, *Weeks v United States*[34] ruled that evidence obtained in violation of the Fourth Amendment was inadmissible in federal court.[35] "Almost immediately thereafter lower federal courts began to develop a limitation on the applicability of the exclusionary rule that has become known as the 'standing' requirement."[36] Seven years later, one scholar noted that the standing

---

"judges, practitioners, and academics still talk about standing . . . because the issue of whose rights are being violated is a conceptually distinct question from whether anyone at all has Fourth Amendment rights." Orin Kerr, *Four Thoughts on Byrd v. United States* (Volokh Conspiracy, Jan 2, 2018), archived at http://perma.cc/G78Y-63QN. Forty years after *Rakas* explained that notions of standing were unnecessary and unhelpful for deciding search and seizure cases, the Court now agrees that "[t]he concept of standing in Fourth Amendment cases can be a useful shorthand for capturing the idea that a person must have a cognizable Fourth Amendment interest in the place searched before seeking relief for an unconstitutional search." *Byrd*, 138 S Ct at 1530.

[31] Albert W. Alschuler, *Interpersonal Privacy and the Fourth Amendment*, 4 NIU L Rev 1, 4 (1983).

[32] *Rakas*, 439 US at 143 n 12.

[33] *Jones v United States*, 362 US 257, 267 (1960) (explaining that anyone "legitimately on premises where a search occurred may challenge its legality" when evidence obtained from the search is offered against him, but distinguishing those "who, by virtue of their wrongful presence, cannot invoke the privacy of the premises searched").

[34] 232 US 383 (1914).

[35] Id at 398.

[36] Richard B. Kuhns, *The Concept of Personal Aggrievement in Fourth Amendment Standing Cases*, 65 Iowa L Rev 493, 493 (1980) (citation omitted). While the "precise origins of

doctrine permitted the government to profit from unconstitutional searches.[37] In cases where a defendant's basis for contesting a search is debatable, conferring standing to a particular defendant "is solely for the purpose of determining whether evidence unlawfully obtained should be excluded at trial."[38] For jurists opposed to suppressing illegally obtained evidence, standing is a gateway to invoking exclusion and thus should be discouraged whenever possible.

The interplay between standing and the exclusionary rule was clearly on the minds of some Justices in *Rakas*.[39] Then-Justice Rehnquist's opinion for the majority pointedly noted that "[c]onferring standing to raise vicarious Fourth Amendment claims would necessarily mean a more widespread invocation of the exclusionary rule during criminal trials."[40] Rehnquist also stated that "misgivings as to the benefit of enlarging the class of persons who may invoke that rule are properly considered when deciding whether to expand standing to assert Fourth Amendment violations."[41] Since *Rakas*, the Court has been even less willing to enforce exclusion as a remedy. Thus, Byrd would have to persuade a Court openly hostile to the exclusionary rule that he should be afforded standing.

---

the fourth amendment standing requirement are unclear," Professor Kuhns believes that the "[f]irst and perhaps most important[ ]" factor in the development of the concept of standing was that it "provided courts that were disenchanted with the exclusionary rule with a means of limiting the scope of the rule." Id at 504 n 78, citing Richard A. Edwards, *Standing to Suppress Unreasonably Seized Evidence*, 47 Nw U L Rev 471, 472 (1952).

[37] Osmond K. Fraenkel, *Concerning Searches and Seizures*, 34 Harv L Rev 361, 375 (1921).

[38] Welsh S. White and Robert S. Greenspan, *Standing to Object to Search and Seizure*, 118 U Pa L Rev 333, 356 (1970). See also William A. Knox, *Some Thoughts on the Scope of the Fourth Amendment and Standing to Challenge Searches and Seizures*, 40 Mo L Rev 1 (1975) ("In the past, the Court has often used language which refers to standing to challenge or the scope of the amendment when it is really deciding whether a specific remedy—the exclusionary rule— should be available.") (footnote omitted); Kuhns, 65 Iowa L Rev at 505 (cited in note 36) ("[I]n contrast to a substantive holding that a particular search or seizure is unconstitutional . . . standing cases involve an attempt to preclude a defendant from invoking the exclusionary rule.").

[39] The first sentence of Justice Harry Blackmun's pre-argument memo to himself read: "This case focuses on the exclusionary rule and raises an issue as to its expansion." Harry A. Blackmun, Pre-Argument Memorandum on *Rakas v Illinois, Harry A. Blackmun Papers*, Box 290, Folder 3, Manuscript Division, US Library of Congress (on file with Library of Congress). Likewise, in his pre-argument memo Justice Lewis Powell noted that if the defendants' standing argument prevailed "the result would be a major extension of the scope of the exclusionary rule." Lewis F. Powell, Jr., Papers, Washington and Lee School of Law, Box 60. Finally, during the Justices' conference discussion, Chief Justice Burger remarked that the "only issue is standing." Powell Papers, Box 60.

[40] *Rakas*, 439 US at 137.

[41] Id at 138 (footnote omitted).

Finally, Byrd needed to propose a constitutional test, preferably a workable bright-line rule that would not be too restrictive of police interests, that would resolve his and future cases. As discussed above, *Rakas* foreclosed legitimate presence in the car as a proxy for Fourth Amendment protection. Moreover, for Justices inclined to a textual interpretation of the Constitution, Byrd needed to address the fact that the Fourth Amendment protects people in "their" effects.[42] Byrd could not assert the constitutional rights of the authorized driver because Fourth Amendment rights are personal and cannot be vicariously asserted.[43] Thus, Byrd's test had to show why an unauthorized driver could nonetheless claim a vehicle that he neither owned nor leased was "his" under the Fourth Amendment.

In an attempt to prove his point, counsel for Byrd stated during oral argument that his client "ha[d] the right to exclude others" from the rental car which "bolsters also [Byrd's] reasonable expectation of privacy"[44] in the car. Counsel then accepted Justice Stephen Breyer's characterization of the rule Byrd was proposing: "A person who has possession of and is [the] driver of a car, whoever he is, has a reasonable expectation in privacy of the parts of the car, unless in driving or possessing it or—he's committing a crime."[45] This test emphasizes Byrd's possession and control of the vehicle. A few moments later, however, counsel seemed to offer a different test that emphasized the privacy of items stored in a closed vehicle. When Justice Elena Kagan asked why society should consider Byrd's conduct reasonable, counsel responded: "Because society recognizes that when you put your personal items in a locked space . . . you have an expectation of privacy regarding it."[46] Counsel never reconciled the differences in these formulations.

---

[42] US Const, Amend IV.

[43] *Alderman v United States*, 394 US 165, 171 (1969) ("The established principle is that suppression of the product of a Fourth Amendment violation can be successfully urged only by those whose rights were violated by the search itself, not by those who are aggrieved solely by the introduction of damaging evidence."); id at 174 ("Fourth Amendment rights are personal rights which, like some other constitutional rights, may not be vicariously asserted.") (citations omitted).

[44] Transcript of Oral Argument, *Byrd v United States*, Docket No 16-1317 at 27 (Jan 9, 2018), archived at http://perma.cc/MK9V-TFXN.

[45] Id. At the end of the oral argument, counsel for Byrd restated his proposed bright-line rule. "This Court should adopt a clear bright-line rule that unless you're a criminal trespasser, unless you're a car thief, that you have at least the ability to invoke the Fourth Amendment." Id at 69.

[46] Id at 31.

While the Court generally requires probable cause for automobile searches, *Rakas* demonstrated that with the right set of facts, police do not always need probable cause to search a car. Put differently, vehicle occupants may not be similarly situated under the Fourth Amendment—even when they occupy the same vehicle. Some are protected; some are not. Byrd would need to surmount one or more of the obstacles described above to prove that he was the right type of vehicle occupant entitled to invoke the Fourth Amendment.

I take a closer look at *Byrd* to examine what it means for Fourth Amendment doctrine. Part I summarizes Justice Kennedy's majority opinion and the brief concurrences submitted by Justices Thomas and Alito. Part II scrutinizes *Byrd*'s holding: I demonstrate that the Court's holding is not as simple as it seems, and I consider whether the crucial elements of Justice Kennedy's analysis affect the logic of prior precedents and the Court's view of standing under the Fourth Amendment. Part III contemplates *Byrd*'s impact on the development of search and seizure law in the future.

I. THE COURT'S REASONING IN BYRD

In 1980, the Kentucky Supreme Court remarked that the law on standing was "totally incomprehensible."[47] Though that statement was hyperbole, the Court's Fourth Amendment rulings have not always provided guidance and clarity regarding standing. For example, prior to 1960, "[lower] courts were inclined to hold that neither the bailee-operator of a vehicle nor a passenger therein had standing with respect to a search of a vehicle."[48] Judges who denied standing in such circumstances were not defying Supreme Court precedent. In the Court's first important automobile case, *Carroll v United States*,[49] the Justices reserved the question whether an occupant of a vehicle "who did not own the automobile" could challenge a police search.[50] According to one account, the Court had addressed "fourth amendment standing issues in only a dozen cases" between

---

[47] *Rawlings v Commonwealth*, 581 SW2d 348, 349 (Ky 1979), aff'd 448 US 98 (1980).

[48] LaFave, 6 *Search and Seizure*, § 11.3(e) at 243 (footnote and citations omitted) (cited in note 12).

[49] 267 US 132 (1925).

[50] Id at 162.

1948 and the announcement of *Rakas*.[51] And since *Rakas*, the Court had not heard a case involving standing to challenge a car search until it decided to review *Byrd*.[52]

A. JUSTICE KENNEDY'S OPINION FOR A UNANIMOUS COURT

On September 17, 2014, Terrence Byrd's girlfriend, Latasha Reed, rented a car for him, most likely because Byrd was ineligible to rent a car due to his criminal record.[53] After renting the car from a Budget Rental Company facility in Wayne, New Jersey, Reed gave Byrd the keys. Byrd was not listed as an authorized driver on the rental agreement. Byrd took control of the car and later headed to Pittsburgh, after a stop at his home to gather some personal items which he put in the trunk of the rental car. While driving on Interstate 81 near Harrisburg, Byrd passed a state trooper who was parked in the median.

State Trooper David Long testified that he was suspicious of Byrd "because he was driving with his hands at the '10 and 2' position on the steering wheel, sitting far back from the steering wheel, and driving a rental car."[54] The trooper knew the vehicle was a rental car because one of its windows contained a barcode. Based on these observations, Long decided to follow Byrd. A short time later, he stopped Byrd for remaining in the left lane too long after passing another vehicle.[55] According to Long, Byrd was "'visibly nervous' and 'was shaking and

---

[51] Kuhns, 65 Iowa L Rev at 514 (footnote omitted) (cited in note 36).

[52] A year after *Rakas*, a passenger in a taxi cab challenged a search of his suitcase which police found in the trunk of the cab. See *Arkansas v Sanders*, 442 US 753 (1979). Because the passenger "concede[d] that the suitcase was his property, . . . there [was] no question of his standing to challenge the search." Id at 761 n 8. Before *Rakas*, many of the Court's automobile search rulings "assumed that a mere passenger in an automobile is entitled to protection against unreasonable searches occurring in his presence. In decisions upholding the validity of automobiles searches, [the Court has] gone directly to the merits even though some of the petitioners did not own or possess the vehicles in question." *Rakas*, 439 US at 158–59 (White dissenting) (citations omitted).

[53] Early in the oral argument, counsel for Byrd appeared to concede the point. Oral Argument in *Byrd* at 4 (cited in note 44) ("Justice Ginsburg: Could he have been—could he have been the renter, given his criminal record? Mr. Loeb: Perhaps not, Your Honor.").

[54] *Byrd*, 138 S Ct at 1524.

[55] This was obviously a pretextual stop. Although not mentioned in Justice Kennedy's opinion, Byrd was African American. See e-mail from Joshua E. Rosenkranz, Counsel of Record for Terrence Byrd, to Tracey Maclin, Professor of Law, Boston University School of Law (June 12, 2018) (on file with author). Trooper Long wanted to find a reason to question Byrd and search the vehicle he was driving.

had a hard time obtaining his driver's license.'"[56] After giving Long an interim license and the rental agreement, Byrd told Long that a friend had given permission to drive the car.

Another trooper, Travis Martin, soon arrived at the scene. Realizing that Byrd was not authorized to drive the vehicle, Martin remarked that Byrd "has no expectation of privacy" in the car.[57] After Byrd refused consent to search the car, the troopers told Byrd they did not need his consent because he was not listed on the rental agreement.[58] A search of the trunk revealed body armor and forty-nine bricks of heroin in a laundry bag. The lower federal courts denied Byrd's suppression motion. Specifically, the district court, relying on circuit precedent, ruled that an unauthorized driver of a rental car lacked "standing" to challenge the search of the car.[59]

In the courts below, Byrd argued that his Fourth Amendment rights were violated because he had a reasonable expectation of privacy in the rental car.[60] Addressing that claim, Justice Kennedy began his analysis by noting that "property concepts"[61] would guide the Court in evaluating Byrd's argument. "One who owns and possesses a car, like one who owns and possesses a house, almost always has a reasonable expectation of privacy in it."[62] At the same time, the Court's precedents establish that a "common-law property interest in the place searched" is not essential to claim "a reasonable expectation of privacy in it."[63] Acknowledging that the Court had not offered "a single metric or exhaustive list of considerations" to decide when a person has a reasonable expectation of privacy,[64] Justice Kennedy

---

[56] *Byrd*, 138 S Ct at 1524.

[57] Id at 1525. A computer search of Byrd's name revealed, inter alia, that Byrd "had prior convictions for weapons and drug charges as well as an outstanding warrant in New Jersey for a probation violation." Id. The troopers learned that the State of New Jersey did not want Byrd arrested for extradition. Id.

[58] Id. During the back-and-forth with the troopers, Byrd admitted that he had a "blunt" in the car, which the troopers understood to mean a marijuana cigarette. Id.

[59] *Byrd*, 2015 WL 5038455 *2.

[60] At the Court, Byrd proffered an alternative claim that he "had a common-law property interest in the rental car as a second bailee that would have provided him with a cognizable Fourth Amendment interest in the vehicle." *Byrd*, 138 S Ct at 1526–27. The Court refused to consider this claim because it had not been raised or considered below. Id.

[61] Id at 1527.

[62] Id.

[63] Id.

[64] *Byrd*, 138 S Ct at 1527.

reaffirmed *Rakas*'s instruction that privacy interests "must have a source outside of the Fourth Amendment, either by reference to concepts of real or personal property law or to understandings that are recognized and permitted by society."[65] Positive law and societal understandings, according to Kennedy, "are often linked" and that linkage was evident in this case because "[o]ne of the main rights attaching to property is the right to exclude others," and society recognizes that "one who owns or lawfully possesses or controls property will in all likelihood have a legitimate expectation of privacy by virtue of the right to exclude."[66]

Offering a vastly different perspective and at the same time swinging for a doctrinal home run, the Solicitor General proposed a bright-line rule that would limit Fourth Amendment privacy to those persons listed on the rental contract. The government argued that only authorized drivers of rental cars have expectations of privacy in those vehicles and "drivers who are not listed on rental agreements always lack an expectation of privacy in the automobile based on the rental company's lack of authorization alone."[67] The government's argument was apparently based, in part, on the view that *Rakas* precluded passengers from challenging the search of a car's interior. The Court, however, rejected this stance because it "rests on too restrictive a view of the Fourth Amendment's protections."[68] Though the government believed that *Rakas* supported its position, Justice Kennedy explained the government had misread *Rakas* because it "did not hold that passengers cannot have an expectation of privacy in automobiles."[69] In fact, as Justice Kennedy reminded the government, *Rakas* specifically rejected the dissent's claim that it was "hold[ing]" that "a passenger lawfully in an automobile 'may not invoke the exclusionary rule and

---

[65] Id at 1527, citing *Rakas*, 439 US at 144 n 12.

[66] *Byrd* at 1527, quoting *Rakas*, 439 US at 144 n 12, citing William Blackstone, 2 *Commentaries on the Laws of England*, ch 1 (1765).

[67] *Byrd*, 138 S Ct at 1527. The government's proposed bright-line rule was at odds with the laws of several states. "For example, under state law in Illinois, Iowa, Missouri, Nevada, New York, Oregon, and Wisconsin, spouses automatically are authorized drivers regardless of whether they are listed on the rental car contract." Brief of the American Civil Liberties Union and the National Association of Criminal Defense Lawyers as Amici Curiae in Support of Petitioner, *Byrd v United States*, Docket No 16-1371, *13 (US filed Nov 20, 2017) ("ACLU Brief"). Thus, the government's proffered test was not as workable as it seemed on paper.

[68] *Byrd*, 138 S Ct at 1527–28.

[69] Id at 1528.

challenge a search of that vehicle unless he happens to own or have a possessory interest in it.'"[70] Narrower in scope, *Rakas* merely held that legitimate presence alone was insufficient to assert a Fourth Amendment interest, which was enough to resolve the case.

Furthermore, Justice Kennedy explained that *Rakas* did not control Byrd's case "because this case does not involve a passenger at all but instead the driver and sole occupant of a rental car."[71] Embracing Justice Powell's view in his *Rakas* concurrence, Justice Kennedy agreed that a "distinction . . . may be made in some circumstances between the Fourth Amendment rights of passengers and the rights of an individual who has exclusive control of an automobile or of its locked compartments."[72] This distinction among occupants of automobiles paralleled some of the logic of *Jones v United States*,[73] where Jones was arrested after police found narcotics in the apartment in which he was temporarily residing. The apartment "belonged to a friend" who had given Jones permission to use the apartment along with a key to it.[74] Jones had some clothes in the apartment, had slept there "maybe a night," but the apartment was not his home.[75] Though the apartment was not Jones's home, the Court ruled that Jones had standing to challenge the search.[76]

For Justice Kennedy, Byrd's Fourth Amendment claim was similar to Jones's because both "had complete dominion and control over the [place searched] and could exclude others from it."[77] This understanding of what the Fourth Amendment protects was "also consistent"[78] with the *Rakas* majority's explanation that "one who owns or lawfully possesses or controls property will in all likelihood have a legitimate expectation of privacy by virtue of [the] right to exclude."[79] Relying on these passages from *Jones* and *Rakas*, Justice Kennedy then stated: "The Court sees no reason why the expectation of privacy that

[70] *Rakas*, 439 US at 149 n 17 (citations omitted).

[71] *Byrd*, 138 S Ct at 1528.

[72] Id.

[73] 362 US 257 (1960).

[74] Id at 259.

[75] Id.

[76] Id at 265.

[77] *Byrd*, 138 S Ct at 1528, citing *Rakas*, 439 US at 149.

[78] *Byrd*, 138 S Ct at 1528.

[79] Id, citing *Rakas*, 439 US at 144 n 12.

comes from lawful possession and control and the attendant right to exclude would differ depending on whether the car in question is rented or privately owned by someone other than the person in current possession of it."[80] Put simply, both Byrd and Jones "had the expectation of privacy that comes with the right to exclude."[81] Perhaps offering a slight dig at the government, Kennedy noted that the government conceded that "an unauthorized driver in sole possession of a rental car would be permitted to exclude third parties from it, such as a carjacker."[82]

Of course, Byrd's situation differed from Jones's in at least one significant way: Jones had the permission of his friend to use the apartment, whereas Byrd was expressly barred from driving the vehicle under the rental agreement and his girlfriend had no authority under the agreement to override that restriction. Thus, the government insisted that because Byrd's driving constituted a breach of the rental agreement, he had no standing to complain about the search.[83] In any event, the Court was not persuaded. First, the Court found the government was "misreading" the rental agreement when it argued that the rental company would consider the agreement "void" once an unauthorized driver operated the car.[84]

Second, Justice Kennedy noted that car rental agreements contain many restrictions, including, for example, prohibitions on driving a rental car on unpaved roads or driving while using a handheld cellphone.[85] Even the government acknowledged that such restrictions have no connection with a driver's reasonable expectation of privacy in the rental car.[86] To be sure, the Court observed that violating the authorized-driver provision is a serious breach of the rental agreement, "but the Government fail[ed] to explain what bearing this breach of contract, standing alone, has on expectations of privacy in

---

[80] Id.

[81] Id.

[82] *Byrd*, 138 S Ct at 1529, citing Oral Argument in *Byrd* at 48–49 (cited in note 44).

[83] *Byrd*, 138 S Ct at 1529.

[84] Id. For good measure, Justice Kennedy quoted the rental agreement, which stated: "Permitting an unauthorized driver to operate the vehicle is a violation of the rental agreement. This may result in any and all coverage otherwise provided by the rental agreement being void and my being fully responsible for all loss or damage, including liability to third parties." Id at 1529.

[85] Id.

[86] Id.

the car."[87] Put differently, Kennedy saw no principled distinction "between the authorized-driver provision and the other provisions the Government agrees do not eliminate an expectation of privacy."[88] Such provisions concern "risk allocation between private parties—violators might pay additional fees, lose insurance coverage, or assume liability for damage resulting from the breach."[89] However, these concerns about risk allocation are irrelevant to the issue of whether a person has a reasonable expectation of privacy in a rental car if he "has lawful possession of and control over the car."[90] In other words, the rental agreement's failure to recognize Byrd as an authorized driver did not eliminate the protection the Fourth Amendment provided by his "lawful possession and control and the attendant right to exclude"[91] others from the vehicle.[92]

After explaining why the provisions of the rental agreement did not undermine constitutional protections, Justice Kennedy explained that the Court must focus on "the concept of lawful possession."[93] At this point, Kennedy considered "an important qualification"[94] of Byrd's proposed rule, which he had earlier described as urging that "the sole occupant of a rental car always has an expectation of privacy in it based on mere possession and control."[95] Recalling that prior cases had established that "wrongful" presence at the scene of a search would preclude a person from invoking Fourth Amendment protection, Kennedy observed that "[n]o matter the degree of possession and control, the car thief would not have a reasonable expectation of privacy in a stolen car."[96] He then mentioned an argument that the

---

[87] *Byrd*, 138 S Ct at 1529.

[88] Id.

[89] Id.

[90] Id.

[91] *Byrd*, 138 S Ct at 1528.

[92] See also Orin Kerr, *Byrd v. United States: The Supreme Court Takes a Broad View of Fourth Amendment Standing* (Volokh Conspiracy, May 15, 2018), archived at http://perma.cc/VEK9 -RS6W (explaining that *Byrd* adopted the norm that "the terms in rental car contracts are really about the risk allocation under the contract, not the rental car company's efforts to block the delegation of possession to someone else. Given that, the fact of not having the person's name on the rental car contract doesn't eliminate the otherwise-existing Fourth Amendment right.").

[93] *Byrd*, 138 S Ct at 1529.

[94] Id.

[95] Id at 1528.

[96] Id at 1529.

government did not make below, namely, that Byrd's possession of the car was "wrongful" because he intentionally used his girlfriend to mislead the rental car company.[97] In the government's eyes, Byrd's actions made him the equivalent of a car thief.[98] Observing that it was unclear whether the conduct of which the government accused Byrd amounted to a crime, the Court remanded this claim to the lower court, while intimating that the government should eventually prevail: "[I]t may be," the Court said, "that there is no reason that the law should distinguish between one who obtains a vehicle through subterfuge of the type the Government alleges occurred here and one who steals the car outright."[99] In other words, if the government's view of the facts were true, then Byrd might be "no better situated than a car thief,"[100] and thus lack an expectation of privacy in the rental car.

B. JUSTICES THOMAS'S AND ALITO'S CONCURRING OPINIONS

While joining Justice Kennedy's opinion, Justices Thomas and Alito penned brief concurring opinions. Justice Thomas chided the parties for failing to "adequately address several threshold questions" related to Byrd's claim that he held a property interest in the rental car.[101] According to Justice Thomas, Byrd's argument that the vehicle "was *his* effect"[102] required consideration of at least three issues. First,

---

[97] *Byrd*, 138 S Ct at 1530.

[98] Briefly put, the government argued that Byrd knew he would never be able to rent a car due to his criminal record. Therefore, "he used Reed, who had no intention of using the car for her own purposes, to procure the car for him to transport heroin to Pittsburgh." Id.

[99] Id. Interestingly, the Court instructed the lower courts on remand to address the government's "theft-equivalent" claim despite the government's failure to raise this claim in the proceedings below. By contrast, the Court was silent on whether the lower courts should consider Byrd's alternative claim that he possessed a property interest in the car as a second bailee, which was also not raised below. Id at 1524 (concluding that a "remand is necessary to address in the first instance the Government's argument that . . . Byrd had no greater expectation privacy than a car thief").

Also, the government had argued in its brief in opposition to certiorari that even if Byrd had standing to challenge the search, the troopers had probable cause that the vehicle contained evidence of criminality. The Court of Appeals did not address that issue in light of its ruling that Byrd lacked standing. The Court noted that on remand, the appellate court was free to decide the probable-cause issue if the argument had been preserved by the government. Id at 1530.

[100] Id at 1531.

[101] *Byrd*, 138 S Ct at 1531 (Thomas, J, concurring).

[102] Id.

"under the original meaning of the Fourth Amendment," what type of property interest was necessary to prove that an item was someone's personal "effect"?[103] Second, "what body of law determines whether that property interest is present—modern state law, the common law of 1791, or something else?"[104] Finally, is operating a rental car as an unauthorized driver "illegal or otherwise wrongful under the relevant law," and, if so, does that unlawful conduct impact the Fourth Amendment analysis?[105] In Justice Thomas's view, the answers to these questions are "vitally important to assessing whether Byrd can claim that the rental car is his effect."[106]

Justice Alito had a more nuanced view of the Court's holding. He asserted that the Court had *not* held that the typical unauthorized driver of a rental car can always assert the illegality of a search. Rather, the Court held that "an unauthorized driver of a rental car is not always barred from contesting a search of the vehicle."[107] Justice Alito explained that an unauthorized driver's right to raise a Fourth Amendment claim turned on the answers to several questions, including "the terms of the particular rental agreement," "the circumstances surrounding the rental," "the reason why the driver took the wheel," "any property right that the driver might have," and "the legality of his conduct under the law of the State where the conduct occurred."[108] Put differently, in future cases a defendant would have to do more than simply allege that he was an unauthorized driver who had not committed a fraud on the rental company in order to merit standing. Based "[o]n this understanding," Justice Alito joined Justice Kennedy's majority opinion.[109] But Justice Alito was joining an opinion that did not exist. Factors that Justice Alito considered relevant to whether an unauthorized driver had standing to challenge a search, for example, "the terms of the particular rental agreement,"[110] and "the reason why the driver took the wheel,"[111] were irrelevant to

---

[103] Id.

[104] Id.

[105] *Byrd*, 138 S Ct at 1531 (Thomas, J, concurring).

[106] Id.

[107] Id at 1531 (Alito, J, concurring).

[108] Id at 1532.

[109] *Byrd*, 138 S Ct at 1532.

[110] Id.

[111] Id at 1531 (Alito, J, concurring).

or played no role in Justice Kennedy's analysis. Justice Alito made a point of saying that on remand, the Court of Appeals could reexamine whether Byrd had standing to challenge the search or resolve the appeal on other grounds.[112]

II. Fourth Amendment Protection for Unauthorized Drivers of Rental Cars? Not as Easy as It Seems

The result in *Byrd*—especially from a unanimous Court—was a surprise. And at this point, the Court's motivation is not clear. In the GPS-tracking case, *United States v Jones*,[113] which held that the government conducted a search when it surreptitiously placed a global positioning system (GPS) device on a vehicle,[114] court watchers honed in on the Deputy Solicitor General's concession during oral argument that the government's position would allow FBI agents to place GPS tracking devices on the cars of the Justices without cause.[115] The result in *Riley v California*,[116] which ruled that police could not routinely search an arrestee's cell phone incident to arrest, was driven by the technological advances that allow cell phones to store vast amounts of personal information.[117] There was no similar revelation or magic moment in *Byrd* that appeared to make a difference.[118] I believe that most, if not all, of the Justices would not

---

[112] Id.

[113] 565 US 400 (2012).

[114] Id at 404.

[115] See, for example, Linda Greenhouse, *Reasonable Expectations* (NY Times, Nov 16, 2011), online at http://opinionator.blogs.nytimes.com/2011/11/16/reasonable-expectations (Perma archive unavailable) ("[I]t's not implausible to suppose that the outcome of the GPS case will depend in large part on the justices' view of reasonable government behavior toward a citizenry that includes themselves. In fact, it's implausible to suppose otherwise."). See also Garrett Epps, *Justice Roberts: Could the Government Track My Car?* (Atlantic, Nov 8, 2011), archived at http://perma.cc/9VFP-GNYC; Tamara Rice Lave, *Protecting Elites*, 14 NC J L & Tech 461, 461–63 (2013) (arguing that the Justices in *Jones* could only sympathize with Jones once they realized that the government could target them as well).

[116] 134 S Ct 2473 (2014).

[117] Id at 2493 ("But the fact that a search in the pre-digital era could have turned up a photograph or two in a wallet does not justify a search of thousands of photos in a digital gallery. The fact that someone could have tucked a paper bank statement in a pocket does not justify a search of every bank statement from the last five years.").

[118] One commentator on *Byrd* thinks that the Justices were concerned about the Fourth Amendment rights of innocent drivers:

> [T]he Justices were worried about the interests of the innocent, when confronting the Government's argument for their proposed rule in the case. The Justices were

allow an unauthorized driver to operate a car he or she had rented, nor would they drive a rental car without being listed on the rental agreement. Maybe the best explanation for the result in *Byrd* is that the government overreached in offering a rule that would confine Fourth Amendment privacy only to persons listed on the rental agreement. This was asking too much even for a Court ordinarily unreceptive to Fourth Amendment claims,[119] so the Justices voted for Byrd by default.

A. THE UNCERTAIN BASIS OF THE COURT'S HOLDING

While the result in *Byrd* was a surprise, the basis and scope of its holding is uncertain. The Court held: "[A]s a general rule, someone in otherwise lawful possession and control of a rental car has a reasonable expectation of privacy in it even if the rental agreement does not list him or her as an authorized driver."[120] In a key passage, Justice Kennedy stated that "lawful possession and control and the attendant right to exclude"[121] affords standing to challenge a search. Despite this

---

worried that if the Government got its way, and got them to rule that unauthorized drivers had no privacy rights in the trunks of cars, that rental cars would then always be subjected to being stopped, until it is determined that the driver is authorized, or that unauthorized drivers, who are not committing any crime (only a contract violation) will be subject to having the police rummaging around their belongings on the side of the road, and there will be no need to offer any justification. Police would be authorized to rummage around on a whim.

Don Murray, *Byrd v. United States—Fourth Amendment Applies to Unauthorized, Non-Thief Rental Car Drivers* (Shalley and Murray, May 16, 2018), archived at http://perma.cc/R9U6 -UC7V. Before any motorist can be stopped, police must have probable cause or reasonable suspicion that the driver has committed a traffic offense or other crime. Thus, in one sense, any motorist lawfully seized is not entirely "innocent." Even assuming, however, that motorists who commit traffic offenses are "innocent," if the Justices were truly worried about the Fourth Amendment rights of "innocent" drivers, they would have reversed *Whren v United States*, 517 US 806 (1996), which ruled that pretextual traffic stops do not violate the Fourth Amendment. Pretextual traffic stops do more harm to the Fourth Amendment rights of "innocent" motorists than police stops of rental vehicles operated by unauthorized drivers. See Tracey Maclin and Maria Savarese, *Martin Luther King Jr. and Pretextual Stops (and Arrests): Reflections on How Far We Have Not Come Fifty Years Later*, 49 Memphis L Rev 43 (2018).

[119] Compare Greenhouse, *Reasonable Expectations* (acknowledging that a few Fourth Amendment rulings for defendants, like the GPS case, are exceptions; however, "Fourth Amendment cases involving behavior with which the justices don't instinctively identify, and in which the court rules reflexively for the government, are too numerous" to be considered anything but the norm for the Court) (cited in note 115).

[120] *Byrd*, 138 S Ct at 1524.

[121] Id at 1528.

seemingly straightforward language, *Byrd*'s holding leaves several questions unanswered.

For starters, why was Byrd's operation of the vehicle "lawful"? "Lawful" is not the first adjective that comes to mind if asked to describe Byrd's possession of the rental car. Putting aside his calculated efforts to mislead the rental company and also assuming that his actions did not constitute a criminal offense in most states, it is not obvious why Byrd had "lawful" possession and control of the car. While Byrd may have had his girlfriend's permission to drive the car, certainly, the owner of the car, Budget Rental Company, prohibited Byrd from driving the car by the rental agreement terms.[122]

The uncertain meaning of "lawful" in this context was illustrated during the oral argument. Justice Sonia Sotomayor asked the government's lawyer whether the son of a father who owns the car, but is not an authorized driver on the insurance contract or the car registration, has a legitimate expectation of privacy in the car after the father gives the son permission to drive the car.[123] The lawyer replied that the son possesses a privacy interest because he "has a connection to the owner of the car."[124] But what is the difference between this hypothetical and the facts in *Byrd*? Byrd also had a "connection" to the renter of the car. Imagine that the father in Justice Sotomayor's hypothetical allows his daughter to drive the car, but explicitly tells the daughter and her boyfriend that the boyfriend is forbidden to drive the vehicle. If the daughter allows the boyfriend to drive the car, is he a "lawful" driver? After all, the boyfriend has a "connection" to an authorized driver. But having a "connection" to an authorized driver does not provide much guidance to police who are deciding whether they can conduct a search, or to judges who have to decide

---

[122] Compare Goldman, 89 BU L Rev at 1720 (cited in note 19):

> [T]he unauthorized driver is a willing participant in the misconduct. The unauthorized driver is driving a rental car while well aware that she does not have the owner rental company's permission; she thus knows that she is in wrongful possession of the car. As [*United States v Wellons*, 32 F3d 117 (4th Cir 1994)] noted, the unauthorized driver is in the exact same position as if she had stolen the car from the rental company's premises. Neither person is in *lawful* possession of the car.

(footnotes omitted).

[123] Oral Argument in *Byrd* at 65 (cited in note 44).

[124] Id.

whether a person has standing to challenge the search. Unfortunately, Justice Kennedy's opinion does not explain why Byrd's possession of the vehicle was "lawful."

Perhaps what made Byrd's possession and control "lawful" was the fact he had permission to drive the car from the authorized user, his girlfriend. Orin Kerr thinks that *Byrd* announced a limited holding. "Delegated rights from the legitimate renter ordinarily control, and at least the kinds of rental car contract terms that currently exist don't change that."[125] That fact—permission from the authorized driver—was emphasized in Byrd's brief and had been the overriding factor in the Eighth and Ninth Circuit rulings that granted standing to unauthorized drivers. Likewise, Professor Sherry Colb writes, "the important thing is that Byrd had permission to drive the car from the woman who rented it, and that gave him standing."[126] Colb argues that *Byrd* "recognizes that privacy arises not only from property ownership but from relationships between people who share spaces with one another."[127]

The problem with these explanations, however, is that in the analysis section of his opinion, Justice Kennedy never mentions that Byrd had his girlfriend's permission to drive the car. If permission from the legitimate renter was essential to proving a reasonable expectation of privacy in these circumstances, one would expect the Court to highlight that fact. Perhaps Justice Kennedy did not rely upon this factor because it is too similar to the concept of "legitimately on [the] premises" that was deemed insufficient in *Rakas*.[128]

---

[125] Kerr, *The Supreme Court Takes a Broad View* (cited in note 92).

[126] Sherry F. Colb, *Rental Cars, Privacy, and Suppression of Evidence* (Verdict, June 20, 2018), archived at http://perma.cc/5ZXB-SZW6.

[127] Id.

[128] *Rakas*, 439 US at 143–48. Al Alschuler makes a compelling argument why an owner's permission should be sufficient to show a reasonable expectation of privacy:

> In *Rakas*, the driver of the automobile, who apparently also was its owner, almost certainly had given her passengers permission to use the glove compartment and the area under the seat. In all but the rarest circumstances, a person who stores property in an automobile's locked glove compartment with the automobile owner's permission has a reasonable expectation that the property will remain private in that compartment. Cultural expectations of privacy are changing and uncertain, but not so uncertain as to make a denial of that proposition anything but silly. Nevertheless, it is the owner's permission and not anyone's presence or absence that gives rise to the legitimate expectation of privacy.

Alschuler, 4 NIU L Rev at 12 (cited in note 31).

And, there is no mention anywhere in *Byrd* about privacy arising from relationships between people who share spaces with each other.[129] Moreover, if permission from the legitimate renter or owner is enough to confer standing, then the unlicensed driver would also have standing to challenge a search.[130] There is no suggestion, however, that Justice Kennedy meant his holding to go that far.

B. DO PROPERTY RIGHTS OR SOCIETAL NORMS MATTER MOST?

1. *"The right to exclude."* Rather than emphasize the fact that Byrd had permission from the authorized driver, Justice Kennedy stressed that Byrd had the right to exclude third parties, like a carjacker, from the vehicle. Kennedy suggests that this right is a property interest. Focusing on property interests may be the key to deciphering *Byrd*, because five weeks later, Justice Kennedy asserted that property interests are "fundamental" and "dispositive" in deciding whether a person has a legitimate expectation of privacy against a challenged police intrusion.[131] Assuming a right to exclude others is a property

---

Alschuler further notes that the *Rakas* Court "did not discuss the possible significance of the defendants' failure to establish the owner's permission" as a basis for invoking the Fourth Amendment. Id at 14. Any uncertainty about whether an owner's permission could confer standing was eliminated by *Rawlings v Kentucky*, 448 US 98, 104–5 (1980), where the Court made clear that a defendant does not prove that he had a legitimate expectation of privacy merely because he had the owner's permission to store his effects in her purse.

[129] During the oral argument, Justice Ginsburg asked counsel for Byrd: "Does the familial relationship really matter?" Counsel replied: "No, Your Honor. It simply bolsters the expectation." Oral Argument in *Byrd* at 32 (cited in note 44).

[130] See *People v McCoy*, 646 NE2d 1361, 1365 (Ill App 1995) (Cook, J, specially concurring):

> The fact the relative is not licensed to drive might be relevant on the issue [of] whether the lessee actually loaned out the vehicle, but it is not relevant on the relative's possessory interest. It is possible for an unlicensed driver to possess a motor vehicle, just as it is possible for an unlicensed driver to own a motor vehicle. Even where a vehicle is operated illegally the operator may have a possessory interest in the vehicle.

Compare *People v LeFlore*, 996 NE2d 678, 689 (Ill App 2013) (dicta noting the court's disagreement with the dissent's conclusion that a "defendant's status as an unlicensed driver does not necessarily defeat his expectation of privacy in [his girlfriend's] vehicle"), with id at 706 (Birkett concurring in part and dissenting in part) (stating that "[a]s a revoked driver, defendant clearly had no legitimate expectation of privacy in [his girlfriend's] vehicle or its movements").

[131] *Carpenter v United States*, 138 S Ct 2206, 2228 (2018) (Kennedy, J, dissenting) (noting the "commonsense principle that the absence of property law analogues can be dispositive of privacy expectations").

interest,[132] perhaps the best way to read *Byrd* is that the existence or possession of that right is crucial to establishing an expectation of privacy.

Is the right to exclude imperative to establish Fourth Amendment standing? The answer has been a moving target for over half a century. The Justices have sent conflicting signals on the question. Many years ago, Justice Robert Jackson commented on why a "right to exclude" should not be determinative of one's standing to challenge a police search in *McDonald v United States*.[133] There, police suspected McDonald of running an illegal numbers operation in a room he rented in a rooming house. Without a warrant, an officer opened a window of the landlady's apartment and climbed through. The officer identified himself to the landlady and then admitted his colleagues.[134] After searching rooms on the first floor, the police went to the second floor of the rooming house where McDonald's room was located. An officer stood on a chair and peered through the transom. Inside he saw McDonald and Washington with gambling paraphernalia. The officer ordered McDonald to open the door. McDonald and Washington were arrested and the evidence seized. The government contended that McDonald had no standing to complain about the intrusion into the landlady's premises and the arrest of the defendants was based on evidence seen in plain view from a location where the police were lawfully present.[135]

Although the Court ruled that the warrantless entry, search, and seizure violated the Fourth Amendment, the Court did not directly address the government's argument that McDonald lacked standing to challenge the entry into the landlady's home.[136] Justice Jackson,

---

[132] I agree with Orin Kerr that the Court did not articulate why a "right to exclude" is a property interest. "The Court doesn't grapple with what doctrines or approaches to property law should govern [in this setting]. . . . [I]t's not entirely clear why [an unauthorized driver's right to exclude a carjacker is a property interest] or what kind of property law test the Court has in mind to understand the right to exclude." Kerr, *The Supreme Court Takes a Broad View* (cited in note 92).

[133] 335 US 451 (1948).

[134] According to Justice Jackson, the officer was in plain clothes, "showed his badge to the frightened woman and then brushed her aside and then unlocked doors and admitted two other officers." Id at 457–58 (Jackson, J, concurring).

[135] Id at 453–54.

[136] The Court simply stated: "We do not stop to examine that syllogism for flaws. Assuming its correctness, we reject the result." Id at 454. On a different aspect of *McDonald*, Professor Kuhns states that *McDonald* was "the first case to present a fourth amendment standing issue." Kuhns, 65 Iowa L Rev at 526 (cited in note 36). While not employing the

however, believed that McDonald had standing to challenge the police intrusion into the rooming house. "But it seems to me that each tenant of a building, while he has no right to exclude from the common hallways those who enter lawfully, does have a personal and constitutionally protected interest in the integrity and security of the entire building against unlawful breaking and entry."[137]

Since Justice Jackson proffered this view, the Court has gone back-and-forth on the importance of a right to exclude for standing purposes. Twenty years after Jackson's observation, in *Mancusi v DeForte*,[138] the Court held that a vice president of a local Teamsters Union had standing to challenge a search of an office he shared with other union officials.[139] The Court brushed aside the claim that DeForte lacked standing because he had no right to exclude others from the office. "It is, of course, irrelevant, that the Union or some of its officials might have validly consented to a search of the area where the records were kept, regardless of DeForte's wishes."[140] The Court explained that "capacity to claim the protection of the Fourth Amendment depends not upon a property right in the invaded place but upon whether the area was one in which there was a reasonable expectation of freedom from governmental intrusion."[141]

Similarly, in *Minnesota v Olson*,[142] police entered the home of Robert Olson's girlfriend during the afternoon without a warrant to arrest him for murder.[143] Olson had spent the previous night at the residence and some of his clothes were there. After the Minnesota Supreme Court concluded that Olson had a sufficient interest in the girlfriend's home to contest the police entry, the Court affirmed, holding that a person's "status as an overnight guest is alone enough

---

term "standing," *McDonald* "upheld the right of one defendant [Washington] to exclude illegally obtained evidence solely on the ground that his codefendant [McDonald] was entitled to exclude the evidence." Id (footnote omitted). Eventually, this aspect of *McDonald* was overruled by *Alderman v United States*, 394 US 165, 171 (1969) (rejecting the argument that "if evidence is inadmissible against one defendant or conspirator, because tainted by electronic surveillance illegal as to him, it is also inadmissible against his codefendant or co-conspirator"); id at 172 (stating that "[c]oconspirators and codefendants have been accorded no special standing").

[137] *McDonald*, 335 US at 458 (Jackson, J, concurring).

[138] 392 US 364 (1968).

[139] Id at 369.

[140] Id at 369–70.

[141] Id at 368.

[142] 495 US 91 (1990).

[143] Id at 93.

to show that he had an expectation of privacy in the home that society is prepared to recognize as reasonable."[144] In doing so, the Court rejected the State's argument that Olson's claim of a protected interest in the premises turned on whether he "had complete dominion and control over the apartment and could exclude others from it."[145] The Court noted that the fact that the host "has ultimate control of the house is not inconsistent with the guest having a legitimate expectation of privacy."[146] Reserving constitutional protection only to those with the authority to exclude others was inconsistent with societal norms. "If the untrammeled power to admit and exclude were essential to Fourth Amendment protection, an adult daughter temporarily living in the home of her parents would have no legitimate expectation of privacy because her right to admit or exclude would be subject to her parents' veto."[147]

On the other hand, statements from the Court in other cases appear to condition Fourth Amendment protection on a right to exclude third parties. In a baffling footnote that both emphasized and discounted the importance of property interests to Fourth Amendment protection, Justice Rehnquist stated in *Rakas*, "One of the main rights attaching to property is the right to exclude others, . . . and one who owns or lawfully possesses or controls property will in all likelihood have a legitimate expectation of privacy by virtue of this right to exclude."[148] And in another part of *Rakas*, Rehnquist distinguished car passengers from someone who is allowed to stay in a friend's apartment while the friend is away temporarily or a person using a telephone booth. The person staying at a friend's apartment "ha[s] complete dominion and control over the apartment and could exclude others from it" and the person using the phone booth is able "to exclude all others."[149] Tellingly, Rehnquist over-

---

[144] Id at 96–97.

[145] Id at 98.

[146] *Olson*, 495 US at 99.

[147] Id at 99–100. See also *Bumper v North Carolina*, 391 US 543, 548 n 11 (1968) (stating that there was "no question of [Bumper's] standing to challenge the lawfulness of the search" of his grandmother's home "because the house searched was his home").

[148] *Rakas*, 439 US at 143 n 12 (citations omitted).

[149] Id at 149, citing *Jones v United States*, 362 US 257 (1960), and *Katz v United States*, 389 US 347 (1967). *Katz* held that government eavesdropping on the conversations of someone who uses a public telephone constitutes a search and seizure under the Fourth Amendment. "[A] person in a telephone booth may rely upon the protection of the Fourth

looked whether a passenger in a car could exclude third parties from the vehicle.[150]

One year after *Rakas*, in *Rawlings v Kentucky*,[151] the Court was more adamant about the necessity of having a right to exclude in order to claim Fourth Amendment protection.[152] In that case, police lawfully entered a home to arrest the homeowner. Although the homeowner was absent, police discovered several persons and "smelled marihuana smoke and saw marihuana seeds" in the home.[153] Three persons, including David Rawlings and Vanessa Cox, were detained to await the arrival of a search warrant. When other officers returned with the warrant, an officer ordered Cox to empty the contents of her purse. The purse contained a large quantity of illegal drugs, which Rawlings claimed were his. The Kentucky Supreme Court ruled that Rawlings had no standing to contest the search of the purse.[154] As he did in *Rakas*, Justice Rehnquist authored the Court's opinion. In rejecting Rawlings's argument that he had a privacy interest in the purse because Cox had given him permission to store his drugs in the purse,[155] Rehnquist outlined several factors that undercut Rawlings's claim.[156] One factor was that Rawl-

---

Amendment. One who occupies it, shuts the door behind him, and pays the toll that permits him to place a call is surely entitled to assume that the words he utters into the mouthpiece will not be broadcast to the world." Id at 352.

[150] In fact, Justice Rehnquist's opinion in *Rakas* never bothers explaining "why the passengers did not have a legitimate expectation of privacy in their friend's car, other than on [his] say so. After all, they seemed to do as much, if not more, to maintain privacy in their friend's car as Mr. Katz did in the public phone booth." Nadia B. Soree, *The Demise of Fourth Amendment Standing: From Standing Room to Center Orchestra*, 8 Nev L Rev 570, 601 (2008).

[151] 448 US 98 (1980).

[152] Id at 105.

[153] Id at 100.

[154] *Rawlings v Commonwealth*, 581 SW2d 348, 349 (Ky 1979).

[155] A majority of the Justices expressed skepticism that Cox consented to the transfer of the drugs. *Rawlings*, 448 US at 105.

[156] The Court deemed important the following: (1) When Rawlings placed the drugs in Cox's purse, "he had known her for only a few days." (2) Rawlings "had never sought or received [prior] access to her purse." (3) Rawlings did not "have any right to exclude other persons from access to Cox's purse." (4) The "precipitous nature of the transaction" did not support the inference that Rawlings took "normal precautions to maintain his privacy." (5) Rawlings's admission that "he had no subjective expectation that Cox's purse would remain free from governmental intrusion." Id. Professor Wayne LaFave has cogently explained why none these factors "can withstand close scrutiny" and are irrelevant to the issue decided in *Rawlings*. LaFave, 6 *Search and Seizure*, § 11.3(c) at 218–22 (cited in note 12).

ings lacked "any right to exclude other persons from access to Cox's purse."[157]

Obviously, the Court has not resolved whether a right to exclude others is essential to establish an expectation of privacy. The Court has read *Jones* and *Katz* to mean "that a right to exclude is one way to gain an expectation of privacy."[158] Other cases, such as *DeForte* and *Olson*, establish that an absence of a right to exclude has no bearing on the issue. Finally, *Rakas* and *Rawlings* intimate that "without a right to exclude there can be no legitimate expectation of privacy."[159] Justice Kennedy, the author of *Byrd*, has noted elsewhere that where societal expectations of privacy exist, "the absence of any property right to exclude others" is irrelevant.[160] Unfortunately, *Byrd* makes no effort to clarify the issue or reconcile the tension among these cases.

If the "right to exclude others" is the basis for *Byrd*'s holding, then *Byrd* means that even when an owner who is not present provides consent to search, that consent is ineffective to override an unauthorized driver's refusal to allow a police search. During oral argument, several Justices asked questions that involved purported consent by the owner of the vehicle which appeared to supersede Byrd's privacy in the vehicle. For example, Chief Justice Roberts asked about a rental contract that contained a provision that required the driver to consent to a search if stopped by the police.[161] Justice Alito wanted to know whether Byrd could contest a police search "if the rental agreement said that if any unauthorized person uses the car,

---

[157] *Rawlings*, 448 US at 105, citing *Rakas*, 439 US at 149. Of course, unlike Byrd and the defendants in *Rakas*, Rawlings claimed ownership of the drugs, and thus had a property interest in the items seized. That fact made no difference to the *Rawlings* Court because "*Rakas* emphatically rejected the notion that 'arcane' concepts of property law ought to control the ability to claim the protection of the Fourth Amendment." *Rawlings*, 448 US at 105, quoting *Rakas*, 439 US at 149–50 n 17. The Court's duplicity is obvious:

> *Rakas* had emphasized the defendants' failure to allege ownership of the property seized, and it had said that an owner of property would "in all likelihood" have standing to challenge its search or seizure "by virtue of [his] right to exclude." Accordingly, the defendant in *Rawlings* said to the Supreme Court, "I am the owner." And the Court responded, "Mr. Rawlings, don't be arcane."

Alschuler, 4 NIU L Rev at 15 (cited in note 31).

[158] LaFave, 6 *Search and Seizure*, § 11.3(a) at 181 n 79 (cited in note 12).

[159] Id.

[160] *Minnesota v Carter*, 525 US 83, 101 (1998) (Kennedy, J, concurring).

[161] Oral Argument in *Byrd* at 4–5 (cited in note 44).

[the company] consent[s] to a search by the police?"[162] Finally, Justice Kennedy wanted an answer to the question of whether, if police phoned the car rental company and received permission to search the car, that search violated Byrd's Fourth Amendment right.[163] If a right to exclude is the driving force behind the result in *Byrd*, then the unauthorized driver defendant should prevail in each hypothetical because he has "lawful possession and control [of the vehicle] and the attendant right to exclude,"[164] and thus would have an expectation of privacy to challenge any search. And even if the rental company has a superior property interest over an unauthorized driver vis-à-vis the vehicle, as in Justice Kennedy's hypothetical, the company's property interest does not eliminate the unauthorized driver's reasonable expectation of privacy that comes with lawful possession and control. Curiously, counsel for Byrd told the Justices that "the owner can— can grant [police] consent—to search the—the car."[165] That answer, however, is inconsistent with the Court's precedents.[166]

2. *A change in Fourth Amendment doctrine?* Assuming that the right to exclude is essential to the result in *Byrd*, does this logic signify a change in Fourth Amendment doctrine? Consider the defendants in *Rakas* who were passengers in a vehicle. They too likely possessed a right to exclude third parties. Imagine that the driver of the vehicle in *Rakas* stopped at a convenience store to purchase a cup of coffee, leaving the defendants, Rakas and King, inside the car to await her

---

[162] Id at 9.

[163] Id at 10.

[164] *Byrd*, 138 S Ct at 1528.

[165] Oral Argument in *Byrd* at 10 (cited in note 44).

[166] Counsel's answer is inconsistent with *Chapman v United States*, 365 US 617 (1960), which held that a landlord did not have the authority to consent to a search of his tenant's home, and *Stoner v California*, 376 US 483 (1964), which held that a hotel clerk cannot consent to a search of the room of a hotel guest. Admittedly, *Byrd* seems distinguishable from *Chapman* and *Stoner* because Byrd was not authorized by the rental company to drive the rental car, whereas Chapman and Stoner were authorized respectively by the landlord and hotel to be on the premises. But that distinction brings us back to the relevance of Byrd's status as an unauthorized driver, which Justice Kennedy's opinion finds not to be particularly significant. See notes 83–92 and accompanying text. Finally, if the police called the rental company and got consent, as in Justice Kennedy's hypothetical, the conflict between the company's consent and Byrd's refusal to consent should be resolved in favor of Byrd. *Georgia v Randolph*, 547 US 103 (2006), ruled that where a wife gives police consent to search her home, but the husband is present and objects, the objection of the physically present husband prevails, rendering the warrantless search unreasonable as to the husband.

return.[167] With the driver inside the store, certainly *Rakas* and *King*, like *Byrd*, "would be permitted to exclude third parties from [the vehicle], such as a carjacker."[168] Yet, *Rakas* ruled that passengers lacked privacy interests in the glove compartment and area underneath the front seat, just as passengers lack privacy in the vehicle's trunk. To be sure, as Justice Kennedy reminded us, *Byrd* did "not involve a passenger at all but instead the driver and sole occupant of a rental car."[169] But that difference has no bearing on the right to exclude. If *Byrd* had been a passenger while his girlfriend drove the rental car to Pittsburgh, he would have still possessed a right to exclude third parties from the vehicle during a rest stop while his girlfriend was inside a restaurant buying a cup of coffee.

Similarly, consider whether a right to exclude would affect the result in *Minnesota v Carter*.[170] There, two men, Wayne Thomas Carter and Melvin Johns, came to Kimberly Thompson's home. Relying on a tip from a confidential informant, an officer went to a window of Thompson's ground-floor apartment and was able to observe through a gap in the closed blind Carter and John packaging cocaine. This observation led to a search warrant and the subsequent arrest of the defendants and the seizure of incriminating evidence. Police later determined that Carter and Johns lived in Chicago and came to the apartment "for the sole purpose of packaging the cocaine."[171] The men had never been to the residence before and were there for less than three hours. The Minnesota Supreme Court ruled that the defendants had standing to challenge the officer's observation because they had a legitimate expectation of privacy as guests in Thompson's home.[172] The Court reversed. Writing for five Justices, Chief Justice Rehnquist explained that the defendants' claim straddled between that of an overnight guest who the Fourth Amendment protects and one "merely 'legitimately on the premises'" who has no

---

[167] The driver of the vehicle was apparently King's former wife. See Choper, Kamisar, and Tribe, *The Supreme Court* at 165 (remarks of Professor Kamisar) (cited in note 26).

[168] *Byrd*, 138 S Ct at 1528–29, citing Oral Argument in *Byrd* at 48–49 (cited in note 44).

[169] *Byrd*, 138 S Ct at 1528.

[170] 525 US 83 (1998).

[171] Id at 86.

[172] Id at 87, citing *State v Carter*, 569 NW2d 169, 174 (Minn 1997), quoting *Rakas*, 439 US at 143.

constitutional protection.[173] Ultimately, the Court found that the defendants had no legitimate expectation of privacy in the apartment due to "the purely commercial nature of the transaction," the "relatively short period of time on the premises," and their "lack of any previous connection" with Thompson.[174]

If a right to exclude others matters for standing purposes, Carter and Johns had a valid claim for Fourth Amendment protection. Although *Carter* never mentions the issue, one could reasonably conclude that Carter and Johns, as invitees, could have excluded a vacuum-cleaner salesman or a trespasser seeking entry into the apartment. As Justice Kennedy put it in *Byrd*, they "would be permitted to exclude third parties from [the apartment], such as a [burglar],"[175] while Thompson was out.

The above discussion is not meant to suggest that *Byrd* signals the overruling of *Rakas* or *Carter* or undercuts their holdings. Rather, the discussion is offered to illustrate that *Byrd*'s reliance on a right to exclude to establish a reasonable expectation of privacy proves too much yet too little. Of course, some might say that there were no stops for coffee in *Rakas* or vacuum-cleaner salesmen in *Carter*. But there was no carjacker in *Byrd* either.

C. DO SOCIETAL NORMS CONTROL?

In other parts of the opinion, Justice Kennedy focuses not on property interests but on social norms. For example, he concludes that the rental agreement was not voided by Byrd's operating the car, and he emphasizes that various restrictions in the agreement have no connection with the privacy interests of drivers.[176] Of course, social norms often influence Fourth Amendment cases.[177] Indeed, the "Court has correctly reasoned that the 'security' protected by the Fourth Amendment is not self-defining and takes its meaning from reasonable

---

[173] *Carter*, 525 US at 91.

[174] Id.

[175] *Byrd*, 138 S Ct at 1528–29, citing Oral Argument in *Byrd* at 48–49 (cited in note 44).

[176] *Byrd*, 138 S Ct at 1529.

[177] See, for example, *Katz*, 389 US at 352 (noting that persons who use pay phones are entitled to assume that their conversations are not being recorded by the government; a contrary result would ignore the "vital role that the public telephone has come to play in private communications"); *Olson*, 495 US at 98–99 (explaining that staying overnight in another's home is a "longstanding social custom that serves functions recognized as valuable by society").

expectations of privacy that the community's shared way of life sustains."[178] Justice Kennedy's opinion, however, is scant on the social norms that support the view that Byrd had a reasonable expectation of privacy in the rental car.

Are there social expectations or normative principles that support the result in *Byrd*? The law is well established that in routine cases police are not permitted to search a car without probable cause.[179] But *Byrd* does not rest on that legal norm. If it had, the Court would have issued a short opinion explaining that unauthorized drivers of rental cars possess the same Fourth Amendment rights as other drivers. Another possible answer is that everyone knows that unauthorized drivers frequently drive rental cars. Yet, Justice Kennedy does not mention or embrace this possible societal understanding as the basis for *Byrd*. Nor does Justice Kennedy ground his holding on the norm that Byrd's lawful presence in the vehicle secured him constitutional privacy. When pressed on the normative claim he was making, counsel for Byrd stated that:

> society recognizes that when you put your personal items in a locked space, . . . you have an expectation of privacy regarding it. . . . If someone is wrongfully present and creating a criminal act by being present, that's different. But the government concedes [Byrd] was not wrongfully present in the car, he had his personal items locked in the trunk, and as an objective matter, someone has a . . . reasonable expectation of privacy in those circumstances.[180]

This answer sounds like a mixture of privacy and "legitimately on [the] premises" norms, which was once enough to support Fourth Amendment standing, but was disavowed in *Rakas* as being sufficient, standing alone, to assert a Fourth Amendment interest.[181] *Byrd* reaffirms this aspect of *Rakas*.[182]

---

[178] Lloyd L. Weinreb, *Your Place or Mine? Privacy of Presence Under the Fourth Amendment*, 1999 Supreme Court Review 253, 274.

[179] See *Carroll v United States*, 267 US 132 (1925); *California v Acevedo*, 500 US 565 (1991); Justice Sotomayor was thinking about this norm when she asked during oral argument: "And absent probable cause, there's no right to search. So why are we here?" Oral Argument in *Byrd* at 21–22 (cited in note 44).

[180] Oral Argument in *Byrd* at 31–32 (cited in note 44).

[181] *Rakas*, 439 US at 143–48.

[182] "[I]t is also clear that legitimate presence on the premises of the place searched, standing alone, is not enough to accord a reasonable expectation of privacy, because 'it creates too broad a gauge for measurement of Fourth Amendment rights.'" *Byrd*, 138 S Ct at 1527, citing *Rakas*, 439 US at 142.

Moreover, Justice Kennedy's opinion does not substantively apply the traditional *Katz* test, which measures privacy rights by asking whether the claimant has a subjective expectation of privacy that society deems reasonable. Even assuming Byrd thought he had a privacy interest in the car, why would society consider that expectation reasonable? Does society endorse an unauthorized driver operating a rental car? Or is this behavior reasonable because unauthorized drivers frequently drive cars they should not? Neither proposition is supported by a deep-seated societal understanding or any other obvious form of societal consensus. As noted above, the only societal norms or property interests remotely supportive of Byrd that were offered by the Court were that he had his girlfriend's permission to drive the car, and he had a right to exclude third parties. Unfortunately, Justice Kennedy does not provide a clear explanation for the *Byrd* holding.[183] Ultimately, lower courts will have to improvise when deciding future cases raising issues related to *Byrd*.

III. THE CONSEQUENCES OF BYRD

While the basis of *Byrd*'s holding is undefined and "leaves a little bit unclear what test lower courts should [be] applying" in future cases,[184] one immediate result of *Byrd* is clear: in future cases, the typical unauthorized driver has standing to challenge a search of the rental vehicle he is operating.[185] Without saying so directly, Justice Alito refused to join this interpretation of *Byrd*. Rather, he took the position that "an unauthorized driver of a rental car is not always barred from contesting a search of the vehicle."[186] Whether an unauthorized driver could challenge a search, according to Alito, required consideration of multiple factors, including the provisions of the rental agreement, the circumstances surrounding the rental, why

---

[183] See Kerr, *The Supreme Court Takes a Broad View* (cited in note 92) (stating that *Byrd*'s holding is "a bit difficult to pin down. . . . At times it sounds like not just property-like concepts but actual property law—property's right to exclude—that controls. . . . And at other times, the Court seems to not be applying property law at all. . . . So which is it, property? Social norms? . . . [T]he test itself isn't clearly resolved in *Byrd*.").

[184] Id.

[185] Lower courts have ruled that unauthorized drivers of rental vehicles have standing to contest the legality of a *seizure* of the vehicles they are driving. *United States v Starks*, 769 F3d 83 (1st Cir 2014); *United States v Worthon*, 520 F2d 1173 (10th Cir 2008). See also Bradley Michelsen, Comment, *Think Twice Before Borrowing a Friend's Rental Car: A Look at Fourth Amendment Standing Analysis in United States v. Worthon*, 34 Okla City U L Rev 263 (2009).

[186] *Byrd*, 138 S Ct at 1531 (Alito, J, concurring).

he was driving the vehicle, any property interest the driver possessed, and the lawfulness of the driver's conduct in the jurisdiction where it occurred.[187] "What this [instruction] permits in a variety situations is entirely unclear."[188] For example, how should police officers and judges apply two of the considerations suggested by Alito—the circumstances surrounding the rental and why the driver is behind the wheel? Answers to these questions will initially come from the unauthorized driver and are obviously subject to manipulation or falsehoods. For someone who favors workability and bright-line rules regarding police searches of vehicles,[189] Justice Alito's position promotes neither.

Byrd's holding mandates that in the run-of-the-mine case, an unauthorized driver of a rental car will be afforded the same constitutional protection as an authorized driver. Practically speaking, this is important because of the potential impact to society. One amicus brief informed the Court that there are "2.3 million rental cars currently in service" nationwide.[190] Further, "as of 2014, there were estimated to be about 19,115 car-sharing" vehicles in the country "shared by about 996,000 members."[191] *Byrd* means that the Fourth Amendment applies even when unauthorized drivers of rental vehicles and unregistered drivers of car-sharing programs take the wheel.

Moreover, the logic of *Byrd* is unlikely to be confined to cases involving rental cars.[192] One topic that *Byrd* may affect is whether a defendant has standing to challenge the installation and use of a GPS tracking device to locate a vehicle. In *United States v Jones*,[193] the Court unanimously agreed that this police conduct constituted a

---

[187] Id.

[188] *Arizona v Gant*, 556 US 332, 361 (2009) (Alito, J, dissenting).

[189] See id at 360 (Alito, J, dissenting) (criticizing the majority's ruling because it eliminates a rule that was "relatively easy for police officers and judges to apply" and for adopting a test that requires "case-by-case, fact-specific decisionmaking").

[190] ACLU Brief at *20 (cited in note 67).

[191] Id at *21.

[192] Orin Kerr thinks *Byrd*'s analysis will impact the privacy protection afforded e-mail. According to Kerr, lower courts have ruled that "terms of service can eliminate Fourth Amendment rights that otherwise exist in a person's e-mail." Kerr believes that this view is wrong because "terms of service can at most control who has third party consent rights rather than who has a reasonable expectation of privacy in e-mail. *Byrd*'s explanation of why the terms of a rental contract don't control expectations of privacy in a car seems custom-made to bolster the argument that terms of service don't control expectations of privacy in e-mail." Kerr, *The Supreme Court Takes a Broad View* (cited in note 92).

[193] 565 US 400 (2012).

search under the Fourth Amendment, though the Justices were divided as to why. Five Justices adopted a property-based trespass analysis and emphasized that the government "physically occupied property for the purpose of obtaining information."[194] A different set of five Justices applied *Katz* to conclude that the defendant's "reasonable expectations of privacy were violated by the long-term monitoring of the movements of the vehicle he drove."[195] Since *Jones* was announced, lower courts have grappled with who may contest GPS installation and monitoring. As Professor Wayne LaFave has helpfully explained, three categories of defendants have been afforded standing by the lower courts:

> (1) only those persons with a sufficient property interest in the vehicle at the time of the initial "trespass" by which the GPS device was attached; (2) only those persons using or with an interest in the vehicle at the time the tracking information was obtained; or (3) only those persons qualifying in *both* respects.[196]

Regarding the first category, lower courts have suggested that unless a defendant has a property interest in a vehicle when police attach a GPS device, that defendant lacks standing to contest the installation.[197] After *Byrd*, however, a defendant challenging installation of a GPS device would not need a formal property interest in the vehicle or even proof that he is the regular driver of the vehicle. Under *Byrd*, it is enough that the defendant has "lawful possession and control"[198] at the time the GPS device is installed to merit standing.

---

[194] Id at 404.

[195] Id at 415 (Sotomayor, J, concurring) (joining Justice Alito's opinion that long-term GPS monitoring constitutes a search); id at 430 (Alito, J, concurring in the judgment) (explaining that "the use of longer term GPS monitoring in investigations of most offenses impinges on expectations of privacy").

[196] LaFave, 6 *Search and Seizure* § 11.3(e) Pocket Part at 30 (2017–18) (cited in note 12).

[197] See *United States v Sparks*, 711 F3d 58, 62 n 1 (1st Cir 2013) (dicta noting that Sparks did not own the vehicle, "but was its usual driver"; "on the other hand, [Michaud] seems to have had no equivalent interest in the" vehicle); *United States v Hernandez*, 647 F3d 216, 219 (5th Cir 2011) (concluding, before the decision in *Jones*, that defendant lacked standing to challenge installation of GPS because the truck was registered to his brother, defendant was not a regular driver and no proof that defendant had possessory interest in the house where truck was located when the GPS was attached). But see *People v LeFlore*, 996 NE2d 678, 688 (Ill App 2013) (concluding that if the defendant borrowed the vehicle with his girlfriend's consent, he has standing to contest "the State's use of the GPS device and any evidence obtained from that use, despite not being in possession of the vehicle when the GPS device was installed").

[198] *Byrd*, 138 S Ct at 1524.

When determining whether a defendant may challenge the monitoring (as opposed to the installation) of a GPS device attached to a vehicle, some lower courts have required that the defendant prove that he was either operating the vehicle or had a possessory interest in the vehicle at the time the tracking data are obtained. For example, in *United States v Gibson*,[199] the Eleventh Circuit concluded that a defendant lacked standing to challenge the use of a GPS tracking device to locate a vehicle on a particular day because he was neither the driver nor a passenger in the vehicle and held no possessory interest in the vehicle. Responding to the dissent's argument that the defendant had a reasonable expectation of privacy in the vehicle because he had the status of a co-owner of the vehicle, the court emphasized that the defendant failed to prove "that he had exclusive custody and control of the [vehicle]."[200] Requiring "exclusive custody and control" of a vehicle to claim a legitimate privacy interest seems inconsistent with *Byrd*. Certainly, Terrence Byrd did not have "exclusive custody and control" of the rental car that he was not authorized to drive. Byrd merely obtained the keys from a legitimate renter and drove away. Under typical conditions, that is enough to establish standing, notwithstanding the fact that Byrd could not bar the legitimate renter or the rental company from regaining control of the vehicle.

Moreover, a strong argument can now made that "a passenger *qua* passenger"[201] has a reasonable expectation of privacy that the vehicle he is traveling in is not subjected to GPS monitoring solely at the discretion of the police. Decided five weeks after *Byrd*, *United States v Carpenter*[202] leaves no doubt that an individual has a "reasonable expectation of privacy in the whole of his physical movements."[203] Specifically, *Carpenter* held that "an individual maintains a legitimate expectation of privacy in the record of his physical movements as captured through [cell-site location information] CSLI."[204] And

---

[199] 708 F3d 1256 (11th Cir 2013).

[200] Id at 1278 (explaining that defendant lacked a privacy interest in the vehicle "because he was not the legal owner of the [vehicle], he has not established that he had exclusive custody and control of the [vehicle], and he was neither a driver of, nor a passenger in, the [vehicle] when it was searched").

[201] *Rakas*, 439 US at 148–49.

[202] 138 S Ct 2206 (2018).

[203] Id at 2217.

[204] Id.

though the Justices in *Carpenter* debated whether CSLI data are more or less precise than GPS tracking information, Chief Justice Roberts's opinion for the majority left no doubt that the constitutional issue was not going to turn on which type of technology was more accurate.[205] Instead, what mattered was that the government's access to CSLI related to Carpenter "invaded Carpenter's reasonable expectation of privacy in the whole of his physical movements."[206]

Under *Carpenter*'s logic, even a mere passenger should have standing to contest the use of a GPS device to monitor a vehicle in which he is traveling.[207] To the extent that *Rakas*'s holding is inconsistent with this position, then its holding—that legitimately being inside a vehicle is not sufficient to establish standing to contest a search of the vehicle—does not survive either *Jones* or *Carpenter*, which have clearly refashioned and extended Fourth Amendment protection. As explained by the Chief Justice, five Justices in *Jones* concluded that GPS monitoring of a vehicle violates the Fourth Amendment rights of persons who have a reasonable expectation of privacy "in the whole of their physical movements."[208] *Carpenter* reaffirmed that conclusion and extended constitutional protection to the gathering of CSLI by the government. Nothing in the reasoning of either *Jones* or *Carpenter* supports denying the protection of those rulings to passengers.[209] After *Carpenter* and *Jones*, "everyone inside the car—everyone whose location becomes known" due to GPS monitoring or CSLI data collection, should have standing.[210] Put differently,

---

[205] Id at 2210 (stating that "the rule the Court adopts 'must take account of more sophisticated systems that are already in use or in development.' . . . [T]he accuracy of CSLI is rapidly approaching GPS-level precision.").

[206] *Carpenter*, 138 S Ct at 2219.

[207] See, for example, *Commonwealth v Rousseau*, 990 NE2d 543, 553 (Mass 2013) (concluding, before the *Carpenter* decision, under the state constitution that "the government's contemporaneous electronic monitoring of one's coming and goings in public places invades one's reasonable expectation of privacy" even in the absence of a property interest in the vehicle).

[208] *Carpenter*, 138 S Ct at 2217, citing *Jones*, 565 US at 430 (Alito, J, concurring in the judgment); id at 415 (Sotomayor, J, concurring).

[209] Justice Scalia's opinion in *Jones* did not address Jones's standing to challenge the installation of the GPS device on his wife's vehicle. The government acknowledged that Jones was "the exclusive driver" of the vehicle. Scalia did comment that while Jones was not the owner of the vehicle, he "had at least the property rights of a bailee." *Jones*, 565 US at 404 n 2.

[210] See Orin Kerr, *Does Fourth Amendment Standing Work Differently for Jones Trespass Searches, Traditional Katz Searches, and Long-Term Katz Searches?* (Volokh Conspiracy, Feb 14, 2012), archived at http://perma.cc/9DTK-GU49 ("If the theory is about privacy rights in one's public physical location, not what is inside the car, I'm not sure that the standing

the "seismic shifts in digital technology"[211] and the government's ability to obtain vast amounts of personal information by using modern technology have rendered *Rakas*'s view of a passenger's privacy interest obsolete in the twenty-first century.

IV. Conclusion

In the final section of his opinion, Justice Kennedy intimates that we should have predicted the result in *Byrd*. "Though new, the fact pattern here continues a well-traveled path in this Court's Fourth Amendment jurisprudence."[212] In Justice Kennedy's view, the Court's precedents support *Byrd*'s holding "that the mere fact that a driver in lawful possession or control of a rental car is not listed on the rental agreement will not defeat his or her otherwise reasonable expectation of privacy."[213] The Court's precedents on standing are indeed "well-traveled." But that path is not clearly marked. The Court's rulings offer myriad directions and they lack guidance for judges and lawyers. While Justice Kennedy wants us to think that the reasoning and holding in *Byrd* is obvious, his opinion relies on property interests and societal norms that are hardly evident.

Some current Justices and scholars insist that property law has had and should continue to have an overriding influence in deciding Fourth Amendment cases.[214] *Byrd* regrettably follows that approach when Justice Kennedy states that "property concepts" will guide the

---

analysis still focuses on rights to the inside of the car (as it traditionally does). Under the logic of [Justices Alito and Sotomayor in *Jones*] rationale, shouldn't everyone inside the car—everyone whose location becomes known, have standing? Why should rights in the inside of the car matter under the long-term search inquiry?").

[211] *Carpenter*, 138 S Ct at 2219.

[212] *Byrd*, 138 S Ct at 1531.

[213] Id.

[214] See, for example, *Carpenter*, 138 S Ct at 2239 (Thomas, J, dissenting) ("The concept of security in property recognized by Locke and the English legal tradition appeared throughout the materials that inspired the Fourth Amendment."); William Baude and James Y. Stern, *The Positive Law Model of the Fourth Amendment*, 129 Harv L Rev 1821, 1837–39 (2016) (noting that the key episodes in the historical development of the Fourth Amendment focused on property law). In the context of a case addressing "conversational privacy," the Justice responsible for the *Katz* test, Justice John Harlan, urged his colleagues to "reject traditional property concepts entirely, and reinterpret standing law in the light of the substantive principles developed in *Katz*." *Alderman v United States*, 394 US 165, 191 (1969) (Harlan, J, concurring in part and dissenting in part). For Harlan, that meant "[s]tanding should be granted to every person who participates in a conversation he legitimately expects will remain private—for it is such persons that *Katz* protects." Id (footnote omitted).

Court's decision making.[215] But property rights should not control the meaning and scope of the Fourth Amendment. Orin Kerr has convincingly shown that—over the course of the Court's Fourth Amendment jurisprudence—concepts of property law have not been decisive for the Court.[216] And as a policy matter, property rights should not control who has standing to invoke the Fourth Amendment. Rather, the "capacity to claim the protection of the Amendment depends not upon a property right in the invaded place but upon whether the area was one in which there was a reasonable expectation of freedom from governmental intrusion."[217] As the Court's precedents demonstrate, when the Justices rely upon property concepts like a right to exclude third parties to decide who has standing, inconsistent results and confusion are inevitable because officers in the field cannot easily determine remote property interests. Accurate measurement of property rights often requires extensive fact-finding post hoc.

There was another "well-traveled path" available to the Court in *Byrd*. Police cannot search a motorist's vehicle unless probable cause exists that the vehicle contains evidence of criminality. If Byrd's operation of the vehicle was not a crime, why should he not have the same Fourth Amendment rights as other lawful drivers? The Court could have ruled *simpliciter* that unauthorized drivers (who are not car thieves) occupy the same seat as other drivers: police cannot search their vehicles without probable cause. Period. No need to ponder "property concepts"[218] like a right to exclude third parties. If there is no probable cause, there can be no search. That approach would have avoided future confusion for police, judges, and the public. And it would have promoted a traditional view of the Fourth Amendment: police should not have "unbridled discretion" to invade the privacy of motorists.[219]

---

[215] *Byrd*, 138 S Ct at 1527.

[216] Orin S. Kerr, *The Curious History of Fourth Amendment Searches*, 2012 Supreme Court Review 67, 69 ("To the extent the early cases reveal any consistent methodology, they suggest a mix of property, privacy, and policy concerns not entirely dissimilar to those that have influenced the *Katz* test."); id at 87 (noting that despite claims made by the Justices in the 1960s, "the Court had never held that 'property interests control' Fourth Amendment law. Property traditionally had played a role in Fourth Amendment law, just as it continues to play a role today. But it was never the exclusive test.").

[217] *Mancusi v DeForte*, 392 US 364, 368 (1968).

[218] *Byrd*, 138 S Ct at 1527.

[219] *Delaware v Prouse*, 440 US 663, 648 (1979).

FREDERICK SCHAUER

STARE DECISIS—RHETORIC AND REALITY IN THE SUPREME COURT

I. Prologue—A Conversation Cut Short

For a while it appeared likely that the hearings on the Supreme Court nomination of then-Judge Brett Kavanaugh would be remembered principally for focusing on the role of precedential constraint in Supreme Court decision making. Given that at least three and probably four Justices believed that *Roe v Wade*[1] had been wrongly decided,[2] and that none of those Justices had, unlike, Justice Kennedy,[3] expressed a willingness to adhere to any of the important

---

Frederick Schauer is David and Mary Harrison Distinguished Professor of Law at the University of Virginia.

Author's note: I wish to express special thanks to Justin Driver for comments and editing that were as helpful as they were perceptive.

[1] 410 US 113 (1973).

[2] For Justice Thomas, see *Gonzales v Carhart*, 550 US 124, 168 (2007) (Thomas, J, concurring); *Stenberg v Carhart*, 530 US 914, 980, 982 (2000) (Thomas, J, dissenting); *Planned Parenthood of Southeastern Pennsylvania v Casey*, 505 US 833, 944 (1992) (Rehnquist, CJ, concurring in the judgment and dissenting in part, joined by, inter alia, Thomas, J). For Justice Alito and Chief Justice Roberts, their views can be inferred, although far less clearly than for Justice Thomas, from *Whole Woman's Health v Hellerstedt*, 136 S Ct 2292, 2330 (2016) (Alito, J, dissenting, joined by Roberts, CJ, and Thomas, J). And for the typical speculation about Justice Gorsuch, see Amy Howe, *Gorsuch on Abortion, Religion and Reproductive Rights*, http://www.scotusblog.com/2017/03/gorsuch-abortion-religion-reproductive -rights (March 17, 2017).

[3] *Planned Parenthood v Casey*, 505 US at 843 (opinion of O'Connor, J; Kennedy, J; and Souter, J).

aspects of *Roe*, it seemed for a time that the nomination and the hearings would be situated in history as the locus of a senatorial and public conversation about the degree to which, if it all, a Supreme Court Justice should be willing to abide by earlier decisions that he or she believes mistaken.[4] When, in response to questions posed to the nominee prior to the hearings by Senator Susan Collins, Judge Kavanaugh said that he considered *Roe* to be "settled law," the stage was set for a public discussion and then Senate Judiciary Committee hearings about just what he meant by that phrase, about what it is in general for an earlier decision to establish settled law, and about the extent to which settled law should be overturned or modified in light of changes in social conditions, in national politics, in medical or other technology, or in the ideological makeup of the Court itself.[5]

Although this discussion of the place of precedent in Supreme Court decision making was launched both in the Senate and in public debate, that discussion came to an abrupt end. As we now know, the charges of sexual misconduct against now-Justice Kavanaugh, and his response to those charges, eventually overwhelmed all other considerations in the hearings of the Senate Judiciary Committee, in the debates in the full Senate, and in public discussion.[6] Whatever value there might have been in a continued sustained public and senatorial conversation about the idea of precedent and its role in constraining Supreme Court decisions was, not surprisingly, overwhelmed by the tsunami of other and highly volatile considerations.

The continuing political salience of abortion in general, and *Roe v Wade* in particular,[7] as exemplified by Senator Collins's initial concerns about Judge Kavanaugh, coincides with a seemingly divided

---

[4] See *Factbox: Kavanaugh's View on Precedent Central to U.S. Abortion Debate*, https://www.reuters.com/article/us-usa-court-abortion-factbox/factbox-kavanaugh's-viewAlthough-on-precedent-central-to-u-s-abortion-debate-idUSKCN1LL14M (Sept 5, 2018); Mark Sherman, *Stare Decisis? Roe? A Supreme Court Confirmation Glossary*, Associated Press, https://www.yahoo.com/news/stare-decisis-roe-supreme-court-143648078.html (Sept 3, 2018).

[5] See Robert Barnes and Michael Kranish, *Kavanaugh Advised Against Calling Roe v. Wade "a Settled Law" While a White House Lawyer*, Wash Post, Sept 6, 2018, at 1; Jordain Carney, *Kavanaugh: Roe v. Wade Has Been "Reaffirmed Many Times,"* The Hill, Sept 5, 2018, https://thehill.com/homenews/senate/405135-kavanaugh-roe-v-wade-has-been-reaffirmed-many-times.

[6] See Seung Min Kim et al, *Kavanaugh Hearing: Supreme Court Nominee Insists on His Innocence, Calls Process "National Disgrace,"* Wash Post, Sept 27, 2018, at 1.

[7] The issue of abortion surfaces persistently in the context of contemporary judicial confirmation proceedings, and is plainly of great concern to a portion of the electorate in political campaigns. Yet it is persistently a less publicly (as opposed to politically) salient issue

and acrimonious Supreme Court[8] in which the likelihood of compromise among the Justices seems ever more elusive. It is perhaps not surprising, therefore, that the question of precedential constraint on the Court still looms large, as it did for two cases in the 2017 Term in which the majority and dissenting Justices debated not only the merits of the substantive controversies that divided them, but also the extent to which Justices should subjugate their own considered views to the views of those who occupied the same seats in years past.[9] That is the question of precedent, or, more precisely, of stare decisis, and the public, political, and judicial visibility of that question suggests that the time is ripe for a careful consideration of the extent to which, if at all, the Supreme Court is constrained by its earlier decisions, and the extent to which, if at all, the Court should in fact be so constrained.

II. PRECEDENT 101

The idea of precedent is fundamentally about authority, and authority is, in the context of law, about the source of a directive and not about its content.[10] The Constitution is authoritative just because

---

than is often believed. See Frederick Schauer, *Foreword: The Court's Agenda—and the Nation's*, 120 Harv L Rev 4, 12–24 (2006).

[8] The Court does appear to be more divided than it has been at many times in even the recent past, but the extent of the increase in that division may not be as great as the conventional wisdom supposes. One indicator might be the percentage of 5–4 decisions, in which that percentage for the 2017 Term was 24%, with eighteen of the Court's seventy-one decisions being decided by 5–4 majorities. By comparison, the average annual percentage of 5–4 decisions from the 1981 Term through the 2016 Term, based on the *Harvard Law Review*'s annual statistical recap, was 19.9%, with the percentage of 5–4 decisions being higher in the 1986, 2000, 2006, 2008, and 2014 Terms than it was in the 2017 Term, and the remainder being lower. Obviously there are substantial selection effects cautioning against taking these statistics as indicating very much about the degree of underlying divisions, but a plausible conclusion is that the degree of division on the Court is increasing in recent years, but perhaps less dramatically so than some observers might have concluded. And although there is also now a perception of increasing acrimony in reported opinions, again the perception of a recent increase might be overstated. For somewhat earlier acrimonious opinions, see, for example, *Romer v Evans*, 517 US 620, 636 (1996) (Scalia, J, dissenting); *DeShaney v Winnebago County Department of Social Services*, 489 US 189, 212 (1989) (Blackmun, J, dissenting); *United States v Kras*, 409 US 434, 464 (1973) (Marshall, J, dissenting); *West Virginia State Board of Education v Barnette*, 319 US 624, 646 (1943) (Frankfurter, J, dissenting).

[9] *Janus v AFSCME, Council 31*, 138 S Ct 2448 (2018); *South Dakota v Wayfair, Inc.*, 138 S Ct 2080 (2018).

[10] On authority as content-independent, the *locus classicus* is H. L. A. Hart, *Commands and Authoritative Reasons*, in *Essays on Bentham: Jurisprudence and Political Theory* 243 (Clarendon/Oxford, 1982). See also Joseph Raz, *The Morality of Freedom* 23–69 (Clarendon/Oxford, 1986); Joseph Raz, *The Authority of Law: Essays on Law and Morality* (Clarendon/Oxford,

those whom it directs are expected to follow it even if they disagree with what it says,[11] and so too with statutes, official regulations, and the entire panoply of legal rules and principles.[12] Seen from the perspective of addressees—subjects—who accept the authority of the law, the law's directives provide reasons for action and reasons for decision solely because of where they come from. It is the provenance[13] and not the wisdom of a directive that provides a reason to follow it, and thus there is, for those who accept the authority of the law, a (not necessarily conclusive[14]) reason to follow legal directives that have little or no wisdom supporting them.

Just as directives from the Constitution or a statute may be authoritative in just this content-independent way, so too might a directive from a court have a similar kind of content-independent authority.[15] This observation is banal when we are thinking of the authority of courts over citizens, but courts can have authority over other courts as well. When what is at issue is the authority of a higher

---

1979); Frederick Schauer, *Authority and Authorities*, 95 Va L Rev 1931 (2008); Scott J. Shapiro, *Authority*, in Jules Coleman and Scott Shapiro, eds, *The Oxford Handbook of Jurisprudence and Philosophy of Law* 382 (Oxford, 2002). A valuable recent analysis is Laura Valentini, *The Content-Independence of Political Obligation: What It Is and How to Test It*, 24 Legal Theory 135 (2018).

[11] Think of the parent who, in a moment of exasperation, says to the child, "because I said so!"

[12] The standard view in Anglo-American jurisprudence is that authority is something that is accepted by the subjects of that authority, and thus exists only insofar as such acceptance is manifested. H. L. A. Hart, *The Concept of Law*, Leslie Green, Penelope A. Bulloch, and Joseph Raz, eds (Oxford, 2012) (1961); Raz, *Morality of Freedom* (cited in note 10); Raz, *Authority of Law* (cited in note 10). But it is important to bear in mind, as Hart acknowledged, that acceptance of authority need not be entirely voluntary, and can be the result of threats of sanctions or other forms of coercion. See Frederick Schauer, *The Force of Law* (Harvard, 2015).

[13] Ronald Dworkin, who disliked the idea, referred to this as the "pedigree" of a legal rule. Ronald Dworkin, *Taking Rights Seriously* 17 (Duckworth, 1977).

[14] On the now-familiar distinction between what we have a reason to do and what we should do, all things considered, see Gilbert Harman, *Change in View* 132 (MIT, 1986); Barry Loewer and Marvin Belzer, *Prima Facie Obligation: Its Deconstruction and Reconstruction*, in Ernest Lepore and Robert Van Gulick, eds, *John Searle and His Critics* 359 (Blackwell, 1991); John Searle, *Prima Facie Obligations*, in Joseph Raz, ed, *Practical Reasoning* 238 (Oxford, 1978). In the philosophical literature, overridable—not conclusive—reasons, obligations, rights, and duties were traditionally referred to as "prima facie," but the modern tendency is to use the term "pro tanto." See Maria Alvarez, *Reasons for Action: Justification, Motivation, and Explanation*, in *Stanford Encyclopedia of Philosophy*, https://plato.stanford.edu/entries/reasons-just-vs -expl/ (April 24, 2016).

[15] Larry Alexander, *Constrained by Precedent*, 63 S Cal L Rev 1 (1989); Frederick Schauer, *Precedent*, in Andrei Marmor, ed, *The Routledge Companion to Philosophy of Law* 123 (Routledge, 2012); Frederick Schauer, *Precedent*, 39 Stan L Rev 571 (1987).

court over a lower one, the idea of a precedent is rarely controversial. In a hierarchical organization, those lower in the hierarchy are expected to obey those above them, and lower courts are expected to follow the rulings and interpretations of higher courts in the same way that privates are expected to follow the standing orders and particular commands of sergeants and captains. The idea of *vertical* precedent, as it is sometimes called,[16] is a widely accepted feature of a judicial system in which lower courts are called "lower" for a reason, and one of those reasons is that these lower courts are expected, to put it loosely and roughly, to treat higher court decisions on matters of legal interpretation and application as if they were law themselves. From the standpoint of a vertical-precedent-accepting court other than the Supreme Court, the Constitution truly is what the Supreme Court says it is.[17]

When we switch from vertical to horizontal authority, however, things are neither so easy nor so well accepted. Horizontal precedent—stare decisis—is the obligation of a court to follow the previous decisions of the same court, hence the idea that this obligation is horizontal and not vertical. The core idea is that stare decisis grants authority to the past simply because of its pastness. Unlike vertical precedent, moreover, stare decisis is a relatively recent invention in the history of the common law,[18] and is a practice far from universally accepted in nonjudicial decision-making domains. Issues of path dependence and genuine learning from the past aside,[19] we do not ex-

---

[16] See Alexander, 63 S Cal L Rev (cited in note 15); Charles L. Barzun, *Impeaching Precedent*, 80 U Chi L Rev 1625, 1661 (2013); Steven J. Calabresi and Gary Lawson, *Equity and Hierarchy: Reflections on the Harris Execution*, 102 Yale L J 255, 276 n 106 (1992); Lewis A. Kornhauser, *Adjudication by a Resource-Constrained Team: Hierarchy and Precedent in a Judicial System*, 68 S Cal L Rev 1605, 1605 (1995); Randy J. Kozel, *The Scope of Precedent*, 113 Mich L Rev 179, 204 (2014); Jeffrey C. Robbins, *Structure and Precedent*, 108 Mich L Rev 1453 (2010).

[17] "We are under a Constitution, but the Constitution is what the judges say it is, . . ." Charles Evans Hughes, speech at Elmira, New York, May 3, 1907, as quoted in John Bartlett, *Familiar Quotations* 700 (Emily Morison Beck, ed, 15th ed, 1980). See also Eric J. Segall, *The Constitution Means What the Supreme Court Says It Means*, 129 Harv L Rev F 176 (2016).

[18] See Thomas R. Lee, *Stare Decisis in Historical Perspective: From the Founding Era to the Rehnquist Court*, 52 Vand L Rev 315 (1999); Edward M. Wise, *The Doctrine of Stare Decisis*, 21 Wayne L Rev 1043 (1975). But for the view that the origins of stare decisis go back farther than Wise and others claim, see Thomas Healy, *Stare Decisis and the Constitution: Four Questions and Answers*, 83 Notre Dame L Rev 1173, 1177 (2008).

[19] Past decisions can influence current ones in multiple ways, and not all of those ways count as authoritative. Sometimes we simply learn from the past, and treat the lessons of the past as constraining only insofar as those lessons are ones we accept and respect on the basis

pect presidents or members of Congress to make the same decisions as their predecessors. Even when we disagree with the decision of an incumbent who makes a decision different from what the previous occupant of his or her office would have decided, we couch our criticism in the language of content-based rightness and wrongness, and not in the language of legitimacy. A member of Congress who votes "no" on an issue that the previous incumbent of her seat had voted "yes" may be criticized for casting a substantively wrong vote, but in the normal course of things it would be surprising to see her criticized for not accepting a content-independent obligation to vote the same way as her predecessor merely because that was the way in which her predecessor had voted.[20]

When we turn to the courts, however, the idea of stare decisis counsels a different attitude. Here the expectation embodied in the idea of stare decisis is that judges of a court will, presumptively even if not conclusively,[21] follow the previous decisions of that court—by hypothesis and by definition no higher in the judicial hierarchy— even if and when they think the previous decisions are mistaken.[22] And when put this way, it is understandable that not everyone would accept that courts should be bound to their past mistakes in ways that members of the legislative and executive branches of government are not.[23] Perhaps most prominently, Justice Scalia often criticized the idea of stare decisis for the Supreme Court, although acknowledging

---

of their content and not of their provenance. And sometimes past choices, in life as well as in law, make what would otherwise have been available options unavailable. This is the phenomenon of path-dependence, and it has frequent importance in law. See Oona Hathaway, *Path Dependence in the Law: The Course and Pattern of Change in Common Law Legal Systems*, 86 Iowa L Rev 601 (2001). But both path-dependence and learning from the past must be distinguished from treating the past as authoritative in a content-independent way—as treating the past as important or authoritative and constraining just because of its pastness. And when we understand the distinction, we get closer to understanding the idea of precedent in law, and perhaps understand as well why its virtues are far from self-evident.

[20] This is not to say that only courts can be bound by ideas of stare decisis. See Trevor Morrison, *Stare Decisis in the Office of Legal Counsel*, 110 Colum L Rev 1448 (2010). And every younger child who complains that "it's not fair" when he or she does not get something that was previously given to older siblings is relying on stare decisis as well.

[21] See Steven J. Burton, *The Conflict Between Stare Decisis and Overruling in Constitutional Adjudication*, 35 Cardozo L Rev 1687 (2014).

[22] See *Fong Foo v Shaughnessy*, 234 F2d 715, 719 (2d Cir 1955); Richard A. Wasserstrom, *The Judicial Decision: Toward a Theory of Legal Justification* 52 (Stanford, 1960).

[23] See *Guardians Ass'n v Civil Service Comm'n*, 463 US 582, 618 (1983) (Marshall, J, dissenting) (objecting to allowing stare decisis to stand in the way of sound substantive principle).

that a commitment to stare decisis may have purely pragmatic,[24] even if not principled, virtues.[25] Implicit in Justice Scalia's skepticism is the view that a Justice's oath and obligation is to the Constitution itself and not to the previous Justices of the Supreme Court, and thus, implicitly, that the norm[26] of stare decisis has a nonconstitutional and thus inferior status.[27] And although Justice Thomas has rarely opined publicly on the subject, Justice Scalia claimed that Justice Thomas's views about stare decisis are even more skeptical—or even more dismissive—than were his own.[28] As were, it is worth noting, Justice Douglas's, whose criticism of stare decisis for the Supreme Court foreshadowed Justice Scalia's: "It is the Constitution which [we

---

[24] Justice Scalia long harbored serious doubts about whether the so-called Dormant (or Negative) Commerce Clause power was at all legitimate (see *Itel Containers Int'l Corp. v Huddleston*, 507 US 60, 79 (1993) (Scalia, J, concurring in part and concurring in the judgment)). Nevertheless, he was willing solely on stare decisis grounds to agree to the use of that power where there had been explicit discrimination against interstate commerce (explicit protectionism, more or less) or where the challenged impediments to interstate commerce were the same as those that the Court had previously invalidated. *United Haulers Ass'n v Oneida-Herkimer Solid Waste Management Authority*, 550 US 330, 348 (2007) (Scalia, J, concurring in part).

[25] See Antonin Scalia, *A Matter of Interpretation: Federal Courts and the Law* 139–40 (Princeton, 1997) ("[T]he whole function of the doctrine is to make us say that what is false under proper analysis must nevertheless be held to be true, all in the interest of stability."). See also Antonin Scalia, *Originalism: The Lesser Evil*, 57 U Cin L Rev 849, 869 (1989); David A. Strauss, *Tradition, Precedent, and Justice Scalia*, 12 Cardozo L Rev 1699 (1991).

[26] Throughout this article, I will use "norm" to refer to a standard that has both an empirical existence and some degree of "oughtness." Unless there is some basis for criticism of departure from a standard, it is little more than a habit. And unless that standard is widely accepted, it is little more than an abstract prescription. But when there is both widespread acceptance (and practice) of a form of behavior and widespread belief that departure from this behavior is grounds for criticism, we have a norm, or at least what I will take to be a norm for purposes of this article. See generally Cristina Bicchieri and Ryan Muldoon, *Social Norms*, Stan Encyc Phil, www.plato.stanford.edu/entries/social-norms (Sept 4, 2018); Richard McAdams, *The Origin, Development, and Regulation of Norms*, 96 Mich L Rev 338 (1997); Elinor Ostrom, *Collective Action and the Evolution of Social Norms*, 4 J Econ Perspectives 137 (2000).

[27] See Randy Barnett, *Trumping Precedent with Original Meaning: Not as Radical as It Sounds*, 22 Const Comm 257 (2006); Gary Lawson, *The Constitutional Case Against Precedent*, 17 Harv J L & Pub Pol 23 (1994); Michael Stokes Paulsen, *The Intrinsically Corrupting Influence of Precedent*, 22 Const Comm 289 (2005). For an opposing view, arguing for the compatibility of originalism and stare decisis, and containing a careful documentation and analysis of Justice Scalia's views on stare decisis, see Amy Coney Barrett, *Originalism and Stare Decisis*, 92 Notre Dame L Rev 1922 (2017).

[28] See Lincoln Caplan, *Clarence Thomas's Brand of Judicial Logic*, New York Times, October 22, 2011, at SR10.

swear] to support and defend, not the gloss which [our] predecessors may have put on it."[29]

Justice Scalia's skepticism, the relative newness of stare decisis in the common-law world, and the rarity of stare decisis in the full panoply of decision-making environments should come as little surprise. For stare decisis to be of genuine importance, it must tell decision makers to make decisions they think mistaken on first-order substantive grounds. Stare decisis is little more than excess baggage for a decision maker who believes a previous decision to be correct and wishes to follow it for that reason. And thus, as Justice Kagan has recently put it, "[r]especting *stare decisis* means sticking to some wrong decisions."[30] This is not to say that there are not second-order institutional (and possibly subconstitutional) reasons for a decision-making environment to adopt and enforce a stare decisis norm, and thus to encourage or compel decision makers to make what they believe to be mistaken decisions in order to serve larger institutional goals. The arguments from settlement and reliance are familiar,[31] and in addition there may be the less familiar virtues of cross-temporal integrity and consistency, virtues that may at times produce strong community-building or community-reinforcing practices.[32] But all of these virtues compete,

---

[29] William O. Douglas, *Stare Decisis*, 49 Colum L Rev 735, 736 (1949).

[30] *Kimble v Marvel Entertainment, LLC*, 135 S Ct 2401, 2409 (2015).

[31] See *Alleyne v United States*, 133 S Ct 2151, 2164 (2013) (Sotomayor, J, concurring); *Planned Parenthood of Southeastern Pennsylvania v Casey*, 505 US 833 (1992); *Payne v Tennessee*, 501 US 808, 828 (1991); Alexander, 63 S Cal L Rev at 13–14 (cited in note 15); Aaron-Andrew P. Bruhl, *Following Lower-Court Precedent*, 81 U Chi L Rev 851, 879–81 (2014); Randy J. Kozel, *Precedent and Reliance*, 62 Emory L J 1459 (2013); Michael Stokes Paulsen, *Abrogating Stare Decisis by Statute: May Congress Remove the Precedential Effect of Roe and Casey?*, 109 Yale L J 1535 1553–56 (2000); Schauer, *Precedent* (cited in note 15), and Schauer, 39 Stan L Rev (cited in note 15).

[32] The integrity (see Ronald Dworkin, *Law's Empire* (Harvard, 1986)) or internal cohesiveness function of stare decisis is stressed in Randy J. Kozel, *Settled versus Right: A Theory of Precedent* (Cambridge 2017), and is skeptically discussed in Christopher J. Peters, *Foolish Consistency: On Equality, Integrity, and Justice in Stare Decisis*, 105 Yale L J 2031 (1996). It is important to note, however, that a regime of stare decisis achieves this cohesiveness or community-creating function not by treating like cases alike, as is often alleged, for that constraint is a largely empty one. See Larry Alexander and Emily Sherwin, *The Rule of Rules: Morality, Rules, and the Dilemmas of Law* 135–56 (Duke, 2001); H. L. A. Hart, *The Concept of Law* 159 (Penelope A. Bulloch and Joseph Raz, eds, 3d ed, Oxford, 2012) (Clarendon/Oxford, 1961); Kenneth I. Winston, *On Treating Like Cases Alike*, 62 Cal L Rev 1 (1974). Rather, stare decisis (and vertical precedent as well) achieves this coherence or community-reinforcing function by treating unlikes as being alike—as treating as alike decisions that are in some respects different. Cohesiveness or community is achieved by grouping together particulars that are in some ways different and thus by suppressing potentially relevant differentiating factors. See Frederick Schauer, *On Treating Unlike Cases Alike*, 33 Const Comm 437 (2018). More broadly, see John E. Coons, *Consistency*, 75 Cal L Rev 59 (1987).

from the perspective of the putatively constrained decision maker, with the virtues of getting things right, and of rendering a substantively correct judgment. It should come as little surprise, therefore, that the virtues of stare decisis are hardly self-evident to the decision maker who is urged to make what she perceives to be an incorrect decision. And thus it should also come as little surprise that stare decisis is a virtue, as the following section will explain, that is far more often preached than practiced.

III. The Evidence

The concluding phrase of the previous section was but an introduction to an examination of what the empirical evidence tells us about the existence of actual stare decisis constraint, especially in the Supreme Court. So if we pose the question as just framed, we then need to inquire how often Supreme Court Justices actually do suppress their own best legal (and, at times, constitutional) judgment in deference to past judgments by the Court that they now believe (and may then have believed) are legally mistaken. That, after all, is what a norm of stare decisis would require, but the question is about the extent to which that norm is in fact followed, or, to put it differently, about the extent to which such a norm actually exists.

The conventional empirical answer to that question as provided by those who study Supreme Court decision making systematically is well captured by the title of a book by two of the leading political scientists who have examined Supreme Court decision making. *Stare Indecisis* is what political scientists Saul Brenner and Harold Spaeth entitle their 1995 book,[33] and the title conveys their conclusion that a stare decisis norm seldom causes the Court as a whole or individual Justices to prefer the stare-decisis-indicated outcome to what would otherwise be their preferred legal or constitutional outcome. And because the Brenner and Spaeth research builds on Spaeth's earlier conclusions that the votes of individual Justices are more determined by the Justices' prelegal ideologies and policy preferences than by the legal factors of text, precedent, history, and the traditional methods of

---

[33] Saul Brenner and Harold J. Spaeth, *Stare Indecisis: The Alteration of Precedent on the U.S. Supreme Court, 1946–1992* (Cambridge, 1995). See also Saul Brenner and Mark Stier, *Retesting Segal and Spaeth's Stare Decisis Model*, 40 Am J Pol Sci 1036 (1996); Jeffrey A. Segal and Harold J. Spaeth, *The Influence of Stare Decisis on the Votes of United States Supreme Court Justices*, 40 Am J Pol Sci 971 (1996).

legal reasoning,[34] it is fair to conclude that their research points to these prelegal ideologies playing a larger role than stare decisis in determining and predicting Supreme Court outcomes.

Not surprisingly, the Brenner and Spaeth findings have spawned a substantial research agenda for both themselves and others. But with few exceptions,[35] the basic conclusions of the attitudinal model, both with respect to Supreme Court decision making in general and with respect to the role of stare decisis in particular, have withstood scrutiny. Indeed, the most extensive subsequent study, Thomas Hansford and James Spriggs's *The Politics of Precedent on the U.S. Supreme Court*, published in 2006, although focusing primarily on the way in which the strength of policy preferences influences the Court's tendency to broaden or narrow an existing precedent,[36] and although acknowledging a role for the so-called legal variables, nevertheless starts with the premise that the "[r]esearch consistently indicates that the justices' policy preferences are the primary determinant of their votes on the merits of cases."[37] Similarly, an important study by Jack Knight and Lee Epstein concludes that a genuine stare decisis norm influences how cases are argued, how opinions are written, and how Supreme Court decisions are received by lower courts, but does not disturb the conclusion that the stare decisis norm has little effect on the Justices' actual votes.[38]

These findings from the quantitative research are largely consistent with the conclusions that can be drawn from a more qualitative and anecdotal examination of the Supreme Court's recent and not so recent decisional history. What that history strongly suggests is that

---

[34] See Jeffrey A. Segal and Harold J. Spaeth, *The Supreme Court and the Attitudinal Model Revisited* (Cambridge, 2002). See also, and earlier, David W. Rohde and Harold J. Spaeth, *Supreme Court Decision Making* (Freeman, 1976); Jeffrey A. Segal and Harold J. Spaeth, *The Supreme Court and the Attitudinal Model* (Cambridge, 1993). It is important to note that Spaeth and others do not claim that legal factors play no role, but only that the role they play is less than is often believed, and less than the role played by prelegal or extralegal social, moral, or political attitudes.

[35] See Youngsik Lim, *An Empirical Analysis of Supreme Court Justices' Decision Making*, 29 J Legal Stud 721 (2000) (finding that stare decisis is of limited importance in Justices' decision making when the Justice was a member of the Court that decided the precedent case, but more important when the Justice was not on the Court at the time of the earlier decision).

[36] See also Richard Re, *Narrowing Precedent in the Supreme Court*, 114 Colum L Rev 1861 (2014).

[37] Thomas G. Hansford and James F. Spriggs II, *The Politics of Precedent on the U.S. Supreme Court* 17 (Princeton, 2006).

[38] Jack Knight and Lee Epstein, *The Norm of Stare Decisis*, 40 Am J Pol Sci 1018 (1996).

in cases in which either the Court as a whole or individual Justices are inclined, precedent aside, to make a particular decision, the presence of an opposed precedent is rarely a barrier to reaching the precedent-independent outcome. Forty years ago, Henry Monaghan lamented the unwillingness of the Supreme Court to take its own previous decisions seriously,[39] and with characteristic bluntness he observed that the Court's observations about the lesser weight of stare decisis in constitutional cases[40] "usually means that stare decisis has no weight when the constitutional law on a particular subject seems, to a majority of the Court, to be in need of correction."[41]

Little evidence suggests that Monaghan's observations are less relevant or accurate today. As long as there are available in the decisional toolbox of the Justices multiple ways of rationalizing the avoidance of a seemingly applicable previous decision, the existence of that decision seldom stands as a significant barrier to what seems now to the Court or to individual Justices as the better decision to make, precedent aside, for the case before them. Sometimes this avoidance will be justified by efforts to distinguish the obstructive precedent, but just as often that precedent will be pushed aside or explicitly overturned because it is believed that conditions have changed,[42] or because it is thought that the precedent has proved itself unworkable,[43] or because it has been effectively overruled by intervening decisions,[44] or because its theoretical or doctrinal foundations have been eroded,[45] or because the precedent is simply a rule of procedure,[46] or because the precedent is not recent,[47] or because the precedent is constitutional

[39] Henry P. Monaghan, *Taking Supreme Court Decisions Seriously*, 39 Md L Rev 1 (1979).

[40] "[I]n cases involving the Federal Constitution, where correction through legislative action is practically impossible, this court has often overruled its own decisions. The court bows to the lessons of experience and the force of better reasoning, recognizing that the process of trial and error, so fruitful in the physical sciences, is appropriate also in the judicial function." *Burnett v Coronado Oil & Gas Co.*, 285 US 393, 306–08 (1932) (Brandeis, J, concurring).

[41] Monaghan, 39 Md L Rev at 3 (cited in note 39).

[42] *Planned Parenthood of Southeastern Pennsylvania v Casey*, 505 US 833, 860 (1992) (opinion of O'Connor, J; Kennedy, J; and Souter, J).

[43] *Swift & Co. v Wickham*, 382 US 111, 116 (1965).

[44] *Patterson v McLean Credit Union*, 491 US 164, 173–74 (1989).

[45] *Hurst v Florida*, 136 S Ct 616, 623 (2016); *Leegin Creative Leather Products, Inc. v PSKS, Inc.*, 551 US 877, 887–89 (2007).

[46] *Hohn v United States*, 524 US 236, 252 (1998).

[47] *Montejo v Louisiana*, 556 US 778, 792 (2009).

and not statutory,[48] or simply because the Court or Justice who rejects the precedent believes it to have been wrongly decided or badly reasoned.[49] Indeed, the foregoing list—lengthy though it may be—is likely incomplete, for there appears to be little limit on the range of justifications that the Court has used and can continue to use in order to justify ignoring, overriding, rejecting, overruling, distinguishing, or otherwise refusing to follow a previous decision that it finds mistaken. And thus it is difficult to take issue with then-Justice Rehnquist's assertion in his dissenting opinion in *Garcia v San Antonio Metropolitan Transit Authority*[50] that the willingness of the Court to reject a previous decision is simply a function of whether there is a majority of the Court willing to take that course.[51]

The tissue-thin character of the stare decisis constraint in the Supreme Court is further exemplified by the general unwillingness of dissenting Justices to abandon their dissents in subsequent cases.[52] If stare decisis operated as a serious constraint, we would expect Justices who were not on the prevailing side in some previous case to accept that the case that they thought wrongly decided was nevertheless an authoritative precedent despite their views about its correctness. And thus if there were in place a strong norm of stare decisis, we would expect those Justices to abandon their dissenting posture in deference to what had become the law over their objections. But we know that such a course is highly unusual, and the ubiquitous practice of persistent dissent[53] provides further support for the conclusion that stare decisis is a norm far more often touted than followed.

---

[48] *Burnet v Coronado Oil & Gas Co.*, 285 US 393, 406–07 (1932) (Brandeis, J, concurring) (stating that stare decisis is less stringent "in cases involving the Federal Constitution, where correction through legislative action is practically impossible").

[49] *Pearson v Callahan*, 555 US 223, 233–36 (2009). Thus, Justice Thomas, concurring in the judgment in *Randall v Sorrell*, 548 US 230, 267 (2006), forthrightly observed that "the Court has never felt constrained to follow governing decisions it believes are 'unworkable or badly reasoned.'" (quoting *Vieth v Jubelirer*, 541 US 267, 306 (2004) (plurality opinion), quoting *Payne v Tennessee*, 501 US 808, 827 (1991)).

[50] 469 US 528 (1985).

[51] 469 US at 580 (Rehnquist, J, dissenting).

[52] See Maurice Kelman, *The Forked Path of Dissent*, 1985 Supreme Court Review 227. See also Earl M. Maltz, *Some Thoughts on the Death of Stare Decisis in Constitutional Law*, 1980 Wis L Rev 467; Henry P. Monaghan, *Stare Decisis and Constitutional Adjudication*, 88 Colum L Rev 723 (1988). For Justice Brennan's explicit defense of the practice, see William J. Brennan Jr., *In Defense of Dissents*, 37 Hastings L J 427 (1986). And on persistent dissent in death penalty cases, see Laura K. May, *Justice Brennan and the Jurisprudence of Dissent*, 61 Temple L Rev 307 (1988); Michael Mello, *Adhering to Our Views: Justices Brennan and Marshall and the Relentless Dissent to Death as a Punishment*, 22 Fla St U L Rev 592 (1995).

[53] See Richard Re, *Promising the Constitution*, 110 Nw U L Rev 299, 349–51 (2016).

There are, of course, exceptions to the foregoing generalizations. Among the most prominent of these exceptions is Justice Stewart's approach to, first, *Griswold v Connecticut*[54] and then *Roe v Wade*.[55] As is well known, Justice Stewart memorably dissented in *Griswold*, observing that a law being "uncommonly silly" offered insufficient basis for invalidating it in light of the fact that, to him, there was no "general right of privacy."[56] But eight years later, in *Roe*, Justice Stewart was willing to join the majority because of what he took to be the controlling force of a precedent with which he disagreed,[57] even though there was no indication that even by 1973 Justice Stewart had disavowed or regretted the position that he took eight years earlier in *Griswold*.

The empirical virtue of Justice Stewart's *Griswold-Roe* path derives from the fact that Justice Stewart was plainly on record as having disagreed with an outcome that he was then plainly willing to accept on stare decisis grounds. To the same effect is Justice White's decision in *Edwards v Arizona*,[58] where he wrote for the majority in both applying and extending *Miranda v Arizona*,[59] a decision from which he had dissented.[60] Similarly, Justice Kennedy, in *Ring v Arizona*,[61] joined the majority opinion even as he made clear his continuing disagreement[62] with *Apprendi v New Jersey*,[63] the decision on which the majority opinion in *Ring*, and thus Justice Kennedy's concurrence, was based.

Although there are other examples of the same phenomenon,[64] they remain extraordinarily rare. Far more common are instances in which Justices who refer explicitly to stare decisis as a justification are Justices who did or would have agreed with the earlier decision, thus making, for them, the reference to stare decisis as causally inert for

---

[54] 381 US 479 (1965).

[55] 410 US 113 (1973).

[56] 381 US at 530 (Stewart, J, dissenting).

[57] 410 US at 170 (Stewart, J, concurring).

[58] 451 US 477 (1981).

[59] 384 US 436 (1966).

[60] Id at 504 (White, J, dissenting).

[61] 536 US 584 (2002).

[62] Id at 613 (Kennedy, J, concurring).

[63] 530 US 466 (2000).

[64] On Justice Harlan, see Henry J. Bourguignon, *The Second Mr. Justice Harlan: His Principles of Judicial Decision Making*, 1979 Supreme Court Review 251, 279.

their conclusions and little more than makeweight in their opinions. In *CBOCS West, Inc. v Humphries*,[65] for example, Justice Breyer relied heavily on stare decisis in upholding a civil rights action based on a claim of retaliation,[66] but it seems highly improbable that Justice Breyer disagreed on the merits with the decision[67] whose stare decisis effect he argued demanded the result in *CBOCS West*. Similarly, Justice Powell appealed explicitly to stare decisis in his opinion for the Court in the Eleventh Amendment immunity case of *Welch v Texas Department of Highways and Pubic Transportation*,[68] but the role of stare decisis is undercut by his observation that the earlier decisions on whose stare decisis effect he purported to rely were ones in which the underlying substantive conclusion was one that had, he believed, "ample support."[69] And, most notably, although perhaps least clearly, the now-prominent[70] stare decisis analysis of Justices O'Connor, Kennedy, and Souter in *Planned Parenthood of Southeastern Pennsylvania v Casey*[71] was offered in support of the stare decisis effect of *Roe v Wade*, but we do not know how any of those three Justices would have voted in *Roe* itself in 1973, nor do we know whether in 1992 any of them thought that *Roe* was rightly decided, nor how any of them would have decided *Roe* has it been first presented for decision in 1992. All we do know is that the joint opinion, despite its reliance on stare decisis, reads like an opinion defending the relevant parts of *Roe* on the basis of its merits and not its provenance, and thus that, at the very least, it is far from clear just how much causal influence stare decisis in fact exerted in the case.[72]

---

[65] 553 US 442 (2008).

[66] Id at 451–52.

[67] *Sullivan v Little Hunting Park, Inc.*, 396 US 229 (1969).

[68] 483 US 468, 478–79 (1987).

[69] Id at 482.

[70] See, e.g., Deborah Hellman, *The Importance of Appearing Principled*, 37 Ariz L Rev 1107 (1995).

[71] Cited in note 2.

[72] Some commentators would include *Dickerson v United States*, 530 US 428 (2000), in the group of cases in which at least some Justices voted to affirm on stare decisis grounds a decision with which they had in past explicitly disagreed. See Richard H. Fallon Jr., *Stare Decisis and the Constitution: An Essay on Constitutional Methodology*, 76 NYU L Rev 570 (2001). But a more persuasive reading of *Dickerson*, in my view, is as a reaffirmation of the Court's authority against efforts by Congress to reverse Supreme Court decisions, and stare decisis as such appears to be doing little work in the case. Indeed, this reading is reinforced by *Nevada Department of Human Resources v Hibbs*, 538 US 721 (2003), in which Chief Justice Rehnquist,

It would be misleading to conclude from the foregoing that stare decisis does absolutely no work in Supreme Court decision making. First, there are the examples, noted above,[73] rare but not nonexistent, in which Justices with reasonably clear first-order substantive preferences have set them aside in the service of second-order stare decisis preferences. Second, we simply do not know the extent to which a causally effectual stare decisis norm influences votes to grant or deny certiorari. Third, and related to the second consideration, we do not know and cannot know the extent to which the selection effect distorts some of the large n empirical conclusions about the seeming noneffect of a stare decisis norm.[74] And, fourth, we cannot know the extent to which stare decisis considerations, even when not vote- or outcome-determinative, nevertheless shape opinion writing in ways that may have longer-term incremental effects—incremental effects that may, over time, ultimately shift at least some votes or some outcomes away from where they otherwise would have been.[75]

All that said, however, it is difficult to escape the conclusion, supported both by the systematic empirical research and the more qualitative examination of numerous examples, that the stare decisis norm, even if one exists, is far weaker than most of the commentators and most of the Justices appear to have asserted. And this conclusion is reinforced by two decisions from the 2017 Term, decisions in which stare decisis rhetoric played a prominent role but in which, again, that rhetoric may have had less effect than the Justices who used it encouraged their audiences to believe.

IV. Two Cases

These skeptical conclusions about the existence of a genuinely consequential stare decisis norm find support in two recent Supreme Court decisions in which stare decisis rhetoric figured prominently. One of these, *Janus v AFSCME*,[76] held, by a 5–4 majority decision,

---

again writing for the Court as he did in *Dickerson*, stressed the importance of the Court's constitutional authority against claims that that authority should be shared by Congress.

[73] See above, text accompanying notes 54–64.

[74] See Frederick Schauer, *Stare Decisis and the Selection Effect*, in Christopher J Peters, ed, *Precedent in the United States Supreme Court* 121 (Springer, 2012).

[75] See Richard H. Fallon Jr., *Constitutional Precedent Viewed Through the Lens of Hartian Jurisprudence*, 86 NC L Rev 1107, 1155–58 (2008).

[76] 138 S Ct 2448 (2018).

that requiring public employees to pay union agency fees to support collective-bargaining activities violated the First Amendment rights of dissenting employees to refuse to support speech-related activities with which they disagreed. In doing so, the Court reversed its earlier decisions in *Abood v Detroit Board of Education*[77] and, less directly, *Keller v State Bar of California*,[78] both of which had been understood to stand for the proposition that compelling union members to support political activities with which they disagreed violated the First Amendment, but that requiring those members to pay agency fees to support collective-bargaining efforts lay outside the First Amendment's prohibitions.

I will leave to others the substantive analysis and evaluation of *Janus*.[79] In the context of this article, what is especially germane is not the debate about the merits of the First Amendment claims, but the way in which the majority and the dissent treated the question of stare decisis. Writing for the majority, Justice Alito predictably acknowledged the "importance of following precedent,"[80] but immediately added that this importance would not prevail when there were "very strong reasons"[81] for not following a precedent. He then proceeded to list five such reasons, concluding that all of them applied here. Perhaps principal among these reasons, for Justice Alito and the majority, was that *Abood*, the case that *Janus* explicitly overruled, was "poorly reasoned."[82] But the majority had much more to say about stare decisis, including the conclusion that stare decisis was also not dispositive when the earlier decision involved free-speech rights, when the potential stare decisis import of an earlier decision was undermined by other decisions and subsequent empirical developments, when practical problems in application made clear that the early decision was not workable, and when there had been little reliance by primary actors on those decisions.[83] And having announced these as

---

[77] 431 US 209 (1977).

[78] 496 US 1 (1990).

[79] See Kate Andrias, *Janus's Two Faces*, 2018 Supreme Court Review (in this volume). See also William Baude and Eugene Volokh, *Compelled Subsidies and the First Amendment*, 132 Harv L Rev 171 (2018).

[80] 138 S Ct at 2460.

[81] Id.

[82] Id.

[83] For the majority, any reliance concerns were alleviated by the Court's prior signal of its potential overruling of *Abood*, those signals appearing in *Knox v SEIU, Local 1000, 567 US*

grounds for overruling a precedent, Justice Alito then framed the balance of his opinion around demonstrating that each of these factors applied to *Abood*,[84] thus leading to the necessity, for him, of it being overruled.

Justice Kagan's dissent, joined by Justices Breyer, Ginsburg, and Sotomayor, angrily accused the majority of reaching a decision that "subverts all known principles of *stare decisis*."[85] "The majority has overruled *Abood* for no exceptional or special reason, but because it never liked the decision," Justice Kagan wrote. "It has overruled *Abood* because it wanted to."[86] And to support such strong language, Justice Kagan proceeded to frame *her* opinion in exactly the same way as had the majority, tracking the majority's application to the issue in *Abood* and *Janus* of each of the majority's grounds for overturning a precedent, and finding that none of them applied to this case and to this issue.[87]

In addition to presenting a sharp debate so focused on stare decisis, and offering a lengthy catalog of the many ways in which the constraints of stare decisis could be overcome, *Janus* is notable for the majority's conclusion that *all* of these ways applied to the case before the Court. In doing so, the majority not only avoided confronting the admittedly challenging but arguably more honest process of weighing the reasons for following a precedent against the reasons for rejecting it, but also, and potentially more importantly, appeared to reaffirm that any of the reasons for rejecting a precedent might be available in future cases. After *Janus*, it would appear to take an especially unimaginative Court, or an especially unimaginative Justice, to find that not one of these reasons justifying overruling applied to some case that the Court or a Justice thought required overruling. Although none of the justifications in *Janus* for disregarding or overruling a precedent was entirely new in that case, the very act of listing and purporting to use all of them lays the groundwork in future cases

---

298, 302, 320–23 (2012), and then in *Harris v Quinn*, 134 S Ct 2618, 2632–34 (2014). For commentary on this idea of signaling reversal in advance to give affected parties "one last chance" to adapt, see Richard Re, *Second Thoughts on "One Last Chance,"* 66 UCLA L Rev (forthcoming 2019).

[84] 138 S Ct at 2478–86.

[85] Id at 2497 (Kagan, J, dissenting).

[86] Id at 2501 (Kagan, J, dissenting).

[87] Id at 2497–2500 (Kagan, J, dissenting).

for a further weakening of whatever strength a norm of stare decisis may hold.

Of potentially even greater importance to the issue of stare decisis was the Court's decision in *South Dakota v Wayfair, Inc.*,[88] which overturned the Court's previous decisions in *National Bellas Hess v Department of Revenue*[89] and *Quill Corp. v North Dakota*,[90] and accordingly held that states could impose and collect taxes on sales to state residents by out-of-state sellers who had no physical presence in the taxing state.[91] But lurking behind the merits of the decision was the Court's familiar assertion that stare decisis was strongest for statutory cases because of the ability of Congress to step in and correct a decision it deemed mistaken, and, conversely, that the constraints of stare decisis were weaker in constitutional cases because of the inability of Congress to correct an erroneous constitutional decision.[92] Although a Dormant Commerce Clause decision such as *South Dakota v Wayfair* is subject to revision or rejection by congressional action and thus resembles a decision interpreting a statute, it is also a decision that is based on the Constitution and not on a statute. For Justice Kennedy, this aspect of the earlier cases entitled those cases to less stare decisis respect, and thus made the path to their overruling especially easy to traverse.

In some respects, Justice Kennedy's opinion for the Court in *Wayfair* is of a piece with Justice Alito's in *Janus*. Like Justice Alito, Justice Kennedy relied heavily on the perceived wrongness of the decisions that were overruled, criticizing *National Bellas Hess* and *Quill* as having been based on an "incorrect interpretation of the Commerce Clause."[93] And Justice Kennedy also made much of the way in which

---

[88] 138 S Ct 2080 (2018).

[89] 386 US 753 (1967).

[90] 504 US 298 (1992).

[91] For commentary on the merits of the decision, see *Leading Cases—Constitutional Law—Article I—Stare Decisis for Constitutional Default Rules—Dormant Commerce Clause—South Dakota v. Wayfair, Inc.*, 132 Harv L Rev 277 (2018).

[92] See *Kimble v Marvel Entertainment, LLC*, 135 S Ct 2401, 2409 (2015); *Michigan v Bay Mills Indian Community*, 134 S Ct 2024, 2034 (2014); *Agostini v Felton*, 521 US 203, 235 (1997); *Patterson v McLean Credit Union*, 491 US 164, 172–73 (1989); *Gidden v Zanok*, 370 US 530, 543 (1962); *Burnet v Coronado Oil & Gas Co.*, 285 US 393, 405–10 (1932) (Brandeis, J, dissenting); William N. Eskridge Jr., *Overruling Statutory Precedents*, 76 Georgetown L J 1361 (1988); Lawrence C. Marshall, *"Let Congress Do It": The Case for an Absolute Rule of Statutory Stare Decisis*, 88 Mich L Rev 177 (1989).

[93] 138 S Ct at 2092. Perhaps this is an excessively fine parsing of the language chosen by different Justices, but Justice Alito's "poorly reasoned" characterization of the decision that

the earlier decisions had failed the test of workability,[94] had not induced legitimate[95] detrimental reliance,[96] and, most importantly, had been undercut by intervening cases and by intervening technical developments, especially the rise of Internet commerce.[97]

As in *Janus*, Justice Kennedy's opinion in *Wayfair* lists and uses so many different grounds for rejecting a precedent that it is difficult to imagine an "incorrect" previous opinion that would be able to withstand all of these grounds. And because the way in which Justice Kennedy places a ruling that can be overturned by Congress on the constitutional side of the constitutional/statutory divide, there is some risk that *Wayfair* further weakens stare decisis considerations of whatever force they may ever have had. Taken together, *Wayfair* and *Janus* thus hardly inspire confidence that the Court views stare decisis as a serious and sometimes insurmountable hurdle, however often the Justices mention stare decisis and however often claims for its virtue appear in the Court's opinions.[98]

Janus overruled seems a bit stronger than the "incorrect interpretation" language that Justice Kennedy used in *Wayfair*. Insofar as this fine distinction actually embodies a real distinction, it suggests that *Wayfair* makes it even easier to overturn a precedent than did *Janus*. And see also Caleb Nelson, *Stare Decisis and Demonstrably Erroneous Precedents*, 87 Va L Rev 1, 3 (2001). Nelson's "demonstrably erroneous" standard seems closest to the notion that the Court should be "convinced" of its prior error before overruling, *Smith v Allwright*, 321 US 649, 665 (1944), but it is hardly obvious that Justices bent on overruling either perceive or are willing to follow previous decisions they think are wrong but not demonstrably so, or that they suspect are wrong but are not convinced are wrong.

[94] 138 S Ct at 2097.

[95] Implicit in Justice Kennedy's discussion of legitimate reliance was the view that reliance by tax evaders and those who built their business models around them was not a form of reliance that the Court should respect. 138 S Ct at 2098. On balancing reliance interests against the virtues of reaching a correct decision, see Randy J. Kozel, *Stare Decisis as Judicial Doctrine*, 67 Wash & Lee L Rev 411, 414–15 (2010). And for the place of stare decisis within larger issues of legal transition, issues that necessarily implicate reliance, see Jill E. Fisch, *The Implications of Transition Theory for Stare Decisis*, 13 J Contemp Legal Issues 93 (2007).

[96] 138 S Ct at 2098.

[97] Id at 2096.

[98] Some commentators find it curious and revealing that none of the opinions in either *Janus* or *Wayfair* discussed or even mentioned the discussion of stare decisis in *Planned Parenthood v Casey* (cited in note 3). See Adam Liptak, *Playing with Precedent: How Justices Can Set a Trap for Roe v. Wade*, New York Times, Sept 17, 2018, at A12. But the stare decisis discussion in *Planned Parenthood* arose on the context of a sharply divided series of opinions on a highly controversial issue, and the Court's treatment of stare decisis there was itself challenged by the four Justices in dissent, in part because of its selectivity about which aspects of *Roe* to follow and which to ignore. And thus, apart from the question of which side got the better of the stare decisis analysis in *Planned Parenthood*, it is plain that the stare decisis discussion there is far more controversial and far less iconic than the discussions of stare decisis in, to take the two most prominent examples, Justice Brandeis's opinion in *Coronado Oil* (cited in note 40) and the Court's opinion in *Payne v Tennessee* (cited in note 49). Ac-

V. "Weaponizing" Stare Decisis

In her discussion of the merits of the First Amendment arguments in *Janus*, Justice Kagan described the challengers to the agency fees at issue as having "weaponized" the First Amendment.[99] In doing so, she appeared to be arguing, following the lead of then-Justice Rehnquist's dissent in *Virginia State Board of Pharmacy v Virginia Citizens Consumer Council, Inc.*,[100] that the First Amendment was being opportunistically and strategically deployed to serve argumentative purposes other than those that lie at or near the First Amendment's core goals, functions, and justifications.

In light of what we know about the actual constraining capacity of precedent, we might well conclude that the norm of stare decisis itself has been weaponized. Justices and commentators who disagree with the merits of some proposed change in Supreme Court doctrine will in similar fashion weaponize the idea of stare decisis as a way of adding rhetorical emphasis to their disagreement, and they will typically be met with an equally weaponized justification for avoiding or overruling a previous decision drawn from the capacious arsenal of available stare-decisis-avoiding justifications. And at the end of the day, there is a standoff, with stare decisis rarely, and these days hardly ever, awarding victory to one side or another. At least within the array of currently-sitting Justices, there do not appear to be any who have demonstrated the ability to combine their accusations of ignoring stare decisis with a willingness to adhere to stare decisis when its effect is to reinforce or perpetuate decisions they believe mistaken, or to support their sometimes vehemently professed adherence to stare decisis with a willingness to relinquish their own proclivity to persistent dissent.

Once we see that the essence of a stare decisis claim is a content-independent appeal to respecting mistaken decisions despite their being mistaken, we can understand that a stare decisis norm, if one

---

cordingly, the failure to discuss *Planned Parenthood* in either *Janus* or *Wayfair* seems best explainable by the conclusion that all of the Justices, including Justice Kennedy, co-author of the *Planned Parenthood* joint opinion, believe that *Planned Parenthood* is at best a fragile precedent on the subject of precedent.

[99] 138 S Ct at 2501.

[100] 425 US 748, 772 (1976) (Rehnquist, J, dissenting). The point has been influentially elaborated in Thomas Jackson and John C. Jeffries Jr., *Commercial Speech: Economic Due Process and the First Amendment*, 65 Va L Rev 1 (1979). See also Frederick Schauer, *First Amendment Opportunism*, in Lee C. Bollinger and Geoffrey R. Stone, eds, *Eternally Vigilant: Free Speech in the Modern Era* 175 (Oxford, 2002).

were to exist, could do its work only if those who wield the weapon of stare decisis would be willing to accept the bitter with the sweet. A stare decisis norm that is available to support the results that one believes sound on first-order substantive grounds but that is easily rationalized away when it would perpetuate results that he or she believes unsound on first-order substantive grounds is in reality no stare decisis norm at all. Perhaps regrettably, this conclusion is consistent with what the empirical political science research on stare decisis tells us, it is consistent with what more qualitative and anecdotal observations of the Court's decisions tell us, and it now appears consistent with what even the most recent appeals to stare decisis by the Justices reveal.

VI. Conclusion: The Rhetoric and the Reality

For generations, judges and scholars have argued for the virtues of horizontal precedential constraint—stare decisis.[101] And for a long time, even if not for quite as long, empirical political scientists have concluded that such constraint is not to be found in the reported decisions of the Supreme Court of the United States.

These two bodies of thought are not logically inconsistent. Like world peace and nonfat bacon, there are things we would like to have exist but which do not yet exist, and genuine precedential constraint in the Supreme Court may well be one of them. Although my claims in this article are located in the vicinity of the traditional legal realist skeptical take on precedent and its ability to constrain,[102] my con-

---

[101] In addition to the references scattered throughout this article, see also, inter alia, *Precedent in Law* (Lawrence Goldstein, ed, Clarendon/Oxford, 1987); Deborah Hellman, *An Epistemic Defense of Precedent*, in Christopher J. Peters, ed, *Precedent in the United States Supreme Court* (Springer, 2014); Henry P. Monaghan, *Stare Decisis and Constitutional Adjudication*, 88 Colum L Rev 723 (1988); Gerald J. Postema, *On the Moral Presence of Our Past*, 36 McGill L Rev 1153 (1991); Stephen R. Perry, *Judicial Obligation, Precedent and the Common Law*, 7 Oxford J Legal Stud 215 (1987). Consistent with the theme of this article, I do not want to claim that the nature of the normative pleas for, or the defenses of, stare decisis has been consistent over time. Although I have not undertaken a serious empirical analysis, it nevertheless seems obvious that academic arguments for the virtues of stare decisis, and criticisms of Justices for ignoring stare decisis, have been far more frequent in the era of the Rehnquist and Roberts Courts than they were in the era of the Warren and even Burger Courts. But if stare decisis is to be taken out of mothballs to be used only during periods of (from the perspective of the user) generally disagreeable judicial outcomes, it is unlikely that a stare decisis norm will ever become seriously entrenched, and thus equally unlikely that appeals to stare decisis will ever be taken particularly seriously.

[102] See, for example, Felix Cohen, *Ethical Systems and Legal Ideals: An Essay on the Foundations of Legal Criticism* 33–40 (Falcon, 1933); Karl N. Llewellyn, *The Theory of Rules* 124–25

clusions are more modest. The claim here is not that stare decisis constraint is impossible, which some of the realists sometimes tended to believe. Nor is it that stare decisis constraint is not desirable, which some of the realists—Jerome Frank particularly[103]—on occasion also contended. Rather, it is simply that for the Supreme Court of the United States, with its small and self-selected docket heavily populated by issues of high moral and political valence, there does not appear to be in place a stare decisis norm—a norm pursuant to which most of the Justices most of the time would feel compelled by internal belief or external pressure actually to adhere to past decisions even when those Justices believed those decisions to be mistaken. In a different world such a norm might exist and have substantial force, but that is not our world. And it does not appear to have been our world for some considerable period of time. Moreover, although such a genuinely efficacious stare decisis constraint might be desirable, it might not. Especially for the Supreme Court, given the ideological nature of most of the cases to which the Court gives plenary consideration, and given the increasingly public political role that the Court seems to play, the arguments for getting things right (from the perspective of the decider) rather than deferring to those who got things wrong in the past seem far from frivolous. Still, it would be mistaken to infer from the nonexistence of a robust stare decisis norm for the Supreme Court that such a norm is either impossible or undesirable.

But perhaps this conclusion is too quick. Perhaps what the contemporary and not-so-contemporary disconnect between the increasing number of normative arguments in favor of stare decisis and the decreasing, if that is possible, instances of actual stare decisis constraint tells us is not only that there may be only a weak stare decisis norm in practice, but also that entrenching and enforcing a stare decisis norm may not, at least in the Supreme Court, be such a good idea after all. If a stare decisis norm is about stability for stability's sake, then perhaps we should consider whether stability is what we want and what we can expect from a body that decides only roughly seventy cases a year. And if a stare decisis norm is necessarily about

---

(Frederick Schauer, ed, Chicago, 2011); Herman Oliphant, *A Return to Stare Decisis*, 14 ABA J 71, 159 (1928). A valuable overview and analysis is Charles Collier, *Precedent and Legal Authority: A Critical History*, 1988 Wis L Rev 771.

[103] Jerome Frank, *Law and the Modern Mind* (Brentano's, 1930). When Frank became a federal judge, however, his opinions often looked quite traditional.

entrenching previous decisions just because of their temporal priority and not because of their substantive merit, then, again, perhaps it is worth considering and revisiting whether (and when) granting a content-based authority to the past is or is not a good idea.

This is hardly the place to resolve this question. But perhaps it is the place, finally, to face up to the weakness, verging on impotence, of the widely referenced but rarely followed stare decisis norm. Such facing up, a task for commentators as much as for the Court, might, as just suggested, produce an increasing willingness to reject the importance of stare decisis. Or it might produce a renewed internalization of the stare decisis norm such that Justices—and to a lesser extent commentators, who play a different role[104]—across the ideological spectrum might be willing to accept on stare decisis grounds past decisions they plainly think wrong. I suspect, however, that neither of these paths will be followed, and that for some time to come, as it has been for some time in the past, stare decisis will serve almost entirely as a rhetorical weapon against opponents of what the wielder of the weapon believes to be the right result, questions of stare decisis aside. Stare decisis will continue not to constrain, and accusations of failure to adhere to stare decisis will continue to be part of the rhetorical arsenal of those who agree with a past decision and lament its overturning. So it has been in the past, and so it is likely to continue in the future.

---

[104] But I do not wish to let the commentators off too easily. Commentators who criticize Supreme Court decisions they do not like for ignoring stare decisis ought to be willing either to go on record with decisions they think mistaken but which they believe ought to be accepted on stare decisis grounds, or in the alternative recognize that their appeals to stare decisis will ring hollow if they do not themselves accept the necessarily content-independent idea of a genuine stare decisis constraint.

PAMELA S. KARLAN

JUST DESSERTS?: PUBLIC
ACCOMMODATIONS, RELIGIOUS
ACCOMMODATIONS, RACIAL EQUALITY,
AND GAY RIGHTS

In the summer of 1964, several African American individuals were
denied service at Piggie Park's barbecue joints. They sued under the
public accommodations provisions of the newly enacted Civil Rights
Act of 1964, which forbid discrimination on the basis of race. Piggie
Park's owner, Maurice Bessinger, raised a constitutional defense: "the
Act violate[d] his freedom of religion under the First Amendment

Pamela S. Karlan is Kenneth and Harle Montgomery Professor of Public Interest Law and
Co-Director, Supreme Court Litigation Clinic, Stanford Law School.

Author's note: I presented some of the material in this article at the University of Illinois
College of Law, the University of Minnesota Law School, the University of California Irvine
School of Law, the University of Chicago Law School, the University of Southern California
Gould School of Law, and Stanford Law School. Each time, I received exceptionally helpful
suggestions, comments, and criticisms. I also thank Viola Canales, Beth Heifetz, Marty Led-
erman, and Geof Stone for their contributions.

In the interest of full disclosure, I note that I participated in the following cases discussed in
this essay: *Obergefell v Hodges*, 135 S Ct 2584 (2015) (counsel for the United States as amicus
curiae); *United States v Windsor*, 133 S Ct 2675 (2013) (counsel for respondent); *Shelby County v
Holder*, 133 S Ct 2612 (2013) (counsel for Representatives F. James Sensenbrenner Jr., John
Conyers Jr., Steve Chabot, Jerrold Nadler, Melvin L. Watt, and Robert C. Scott as amici
curiae); *Lawrence v Texas*, 539 US 558 (2003) (counsel for law professors as amici curiae); *Romer
v Evans*, 517 US 620 (1996) (counsel for several civil rights organizations as amici curiae); and
North Carolina State Conference of NAACP v McCrory, 831 F3d 204 (4th Cir 2016) (counsel for
the United States).

'since his religious beliefs compel him to oppose any integration of the races whatever.'"[1] In *Newman v Piggie Park Enterprises, Inc.*, the district court made short work of that argument:

> Undoubtedly defendant Bessinger has a constitutional right to espouse the religious beliefs of his own choosing, however, he does not have the absolute right to exercise and practice such beliefs in utter disregard of the clear constitutional rights of other citizens. This court refuses to lend credence or support to his position that he has a constitutional right to refuse to serve members of the Negro race in his business establishments upon the ground that to do so would violate his sacred religious beliefs.[2]

The Supreme Court was even more dismissive. In the course of a short opinion regarding the plaintiffs' entitlement to attorney's fees, the Court declared Piggie Park's defense "patently frivolous."[3]

A half-century later, the Supreme Court revisited the question of when a public accommodations statute must give way to a claim of free exercise. This time around, the case involved a gay couple who wanted a cake for a party celebrating their upcoming marriage.[4] The shop's owner, Jack Phillips, refused to provide one. When the couple filed a complaint under Colorado's public accommodation statute, which protects individuals against discrimination "because of disability, race, creed, color, sex, sexual orientation, marital status, national origin, or ancestry,"[5] Phillips raised a First Amendment defense premised on his belief that "God's intention for marriage is that it should be the union of one man and one woman."[6] Requiring him to use his "gifts, time and talents" to create the cake "would violate my core beliefs, the instructions of the Bible and [be] displeasing to God."[7] Citing *Newman v Piggie Park*, the Colorado Court of Appeals rejected Phillips's free exercise claim.[8] It also rejected his claim that requiring him to make and sell wedding cakes to gay and straight

---

[1] *Newman v Piggie Park Enterprises, Inc.*, 256 F Supp 941, 944 (DSC 1966), aff'd in part and rev'd in part, 377 F2d 433 (4th Cir 1967), aff'd, 390 US 400 (1968) (per curiam).

[2] Id at 945.

[3] *Newman v Piggie Park Enterprises, Inc.*, 390 US 400, 403 n 5 (1968) (per curiam).

[4] Because same-sex marriage was not then legally available in Colorado, they planned to marry in Massachusetts and then return home for a celebration with friends. *Masterpiece Cakeshop, Ltd. v Colo. Civil Rights Comm'n*, 138 S Ct 1719, 1724 (2018).

[5] Colo Rev Stat § 24-34-601(2)(a) (2017).

[6] Joint Appendix at 157, *Masterpiece Cakeshop*, 138 S Ct 1719 (2018) (No 16-111).

[7] Id.

[8] *Craig v Masterpiece Cakeshop, Inc.*, 370 P3d 272, 292 (Colo Ct App 2015).

couples on equal terms involved compelled speech in violation of the First Amendment's speech clause.[9]

When the Supreme Court granted review in *Masterpiece Cakeshop v Colorado Civil Rights Commission*, after a long period of irresolution,[10] it seemed as if the Court was poised to revive a version of the question Herbert Wechsler infamously posed with respect to *Brown v Board of Education*: "Given a situation where the state must practically choose between" the claims of individuals who want equal access to goods and services and actors who object to being forced to associate with the claimants, "is there a basis in neutral principles" for holding that claims for access "should prevail?"[11]

But in the end, the case fizzled out, even the Court admitting that its decision—which rested entirely on the proposition that Colorado's administrative proceedings had been tainted by antireligious bias—left articulation of any general rule to "further elaboration."[12] Despite a suggestion at oral argument from Phillips's counsel that the First Amendment objections of bakers have greater merit than those of chefs,[13] the Court's perplexity about the "difficult questions as to the proper reconciliation of at least two principles"[14] was surely not the product of an inability to distinguish between entrées and dessert. Rather, like the Court's struggle that same Term over the justiciability of political gerrymandering claims,[15] the Court's decision in *Masterpiece Cakeshop* reflected its reluctance, or inability, to draw a clear,

---

[9] See id at 285–88.

[10] *Masterpiece Cakeshop* was "relisted" sixteen times before the Court granted certiorari. See *Masterpiece Cakeshop, Ltd. v Colo. Civil Rights Comm'n*, No 16-111, https://tinyurl.com/PKJD01 (reflecting the Supreme Court's docket for the case). See also text accompanying notes 110–11 (discussing relisting).

[11] Herbert Wechsler, *Toward Neutral Principles of Constitutional Law*, 73 Harv L Rev 1, 34 (1959).

[12] *Masterpiece Cakeshop, Ltd. v Colo. Civil Rights Comm'n*, 138 S Ct at 1732. For criticism of the Court's this-day-and-this-train-only approach, see, e.g., Richard Epstein, *Symposium: The Worst Form of Judicial Minimalism—Masterpiece Cakeshop Deserved a Full Vindication for Its Claims of Religious Liberty and Free Speech*, SCOTUSblog (June 4, 2018, 8:29 p.m.), available at https://tinyurl.com/PKJD06.

[13] Tr of Oral Arg 14, *Masterpiece Cakeshop, Ltd. v Colo. Civil Rights Comm'n*, 138 S Ct 1719 (2018) (No 16-111).

[14] *Masterpiece Cakeshop*, 138 S Ct at 1723.

[15] See *Gill v Whitford*, 138 S Ct 1916 (2018) (not reaching the merits of a partisan gerrymandering claim due to the plaintiffs' lack of standing); *Benisek v Lamone*, 138 S Ct 1942 (2018) (per curiam) (not reaching the merits of a partisan gerrymandering claim due to the procedural posture of the case as a request for preliminary injunction).

manageable line—here, between situations where public accommodation statutes must accommodate conscientious objection and those
where they need not. In fact, as Justice Kagan suggested at oral argument, the problem was not deciding whether and how to draw *a* line,
but rather whether and how to draw *three* lines, along separate "axes."[16]
First, does baking a cake fall on the "speech" side of the speech/con-
duct line that determines whether an activity is entitled to First
Amendment protection? Second, is there a relevant distinction between statutes that prohibit discrimination on the basis of sexual orientation and those that forbid other forms of status-based discrimination? And, finally, is there something about *weddings* that justifies a
broader accommodation for conscientious objections there than for
other situations?[17]

The connection between the second and third axes takes us back to
a second Warren Court decision, *Loving v Virginia*.[18] There, the
Court condemned Virginia's ban on interracial marriage as violating
both equal protection, because it was "designed to maintain White
Supremacy,"[19] and due process, because it denied the Lovings "[t]he
freedom to marry [that] has long been recognized as one of the vital
personal rights essential to the orderly pursuit of happiness by free
men."[20]

That "stereoscopic" view of the Fourteenth Amendment, in which
values of equality and liberty reinforce one another, served as a
cornerstone of the Court's gay rights decisions up through *Obergefell
v Hodges*.[21] But as much as Justice Kennedy's opinion for the Court
there drew on *Loving*, it is important to note two stark differences
between *Loving* and *Obergefell* that were to play an important role in
Masterpiece Cakeshop.

First, as it had in *Newman v Piggie Park*, the Court in *Loving* gave no
weight to religious bases for discrimination. To the contrary: the

---

[16] Tr of Oral Arg 34, *Masterpiece Cakeshop, Ltd. v Colo. Civil Rights Comm'n*, 138 S Ct 1719
(2018) (No 16-111).

[17] See id at 34–35.

[18] *Loving v Virginia*, 388 US 1 (1967).

[19] Id at 11.

[20] Id at 12.

[21] 135 S Ct 2584 (2015). For discussions of the stereoscopic view, particularly as it relates to
the Court's gay rights–related decisions, see Pamela S. Karlan, *Equal Protection, Due Process,
and the Stereoscopic Fourteenth Amendment*, 33 McGeorge L Rev 473 (2002); Pamela S. Karlan,
Foreword: Loving Lawrence, 102 Mich L Rev 1447 (2004).

Court's quotation, without comment, of the trial judge's invocation of "Almighty God" in the Lovings' case was almost certainly intended to condemn those views.[22] By contrast, Justice Kennedy's opinion for the Court in *Obergefell* went out of its way to state that "[m]any who deem same-sex marriage to be wrong reach that conclusion based on decent and honorable religious or philosophical premises, and neither they nor their beliefs are disparaged here."[23]

Second, *Loving* was a unanimous decision. It came after a decade in which the Court had "largely completed the project of dismantling formal Jim Crow."[24] And that unanimity extended to the degree of official respect due to private beliefs regarding racial equality.[25] By contrast, *Obergefell*, like each of the Court's landmark gay rights decisions, involved a sharply divided Court.[26] And the lead dissent by Chief Justice Roberts charged that the Court's opinion contained a series of "assaults on the character of fairminded people" that "portray[ed] everyone who does not share the majority's 'better informed understanding' as bigoted."[27]

---

[22] *Loving*, 388 US at 3 (quoting the trial court stating that "Almighty God created the races white, black, yellow, malay and red, and he placed them on separate continents. And but for the interference with his arrangement there would be no cause for such marriages. The fact that he separated the races shows that he did not intend for the races to mix."). For discussion of the religious bases for segregation, and a comparison to religious claims regarding the rights of LGBT persons, see William N. Eskridge Jr., *Noah's Curse: How Religion Often Conflates Status, Belief, and Conduct to Resist Antidiscrimination Norms*, 45 Ga L Rev 65 (2011).

[23] *Obergefell v Hodges*, 135 S Ct 2584, 2602 (2015).

[24] See Pamela S. Karlan, *The Gay and the Angry: The Supreme Court and the Battle Surrounding Same Sex Marriage*, 2010 Supreme Court Review 158, 163.

[25] See, e.g., *Palmore v Sidoti*, 466 US 429, 433 (1984) ("The Constitution cannot control such prejudices but neither can it tolerate them. Private biases may be outside the reach of the law, but the law cannot, directly or indirectly, give them effect."); *Norwood v Harrison*, 413 US 455, 469–70 (1973) ("[A]lthough the Constitution does not proscribe private bias, it places no value on discrimination. . . . Invidious private discrimination may be characterized as a form of exercising freedom of association protected by the First Amendment, but it has never been accorded affirmative constitutional protections.").

[26] See *Romer v Evans*, 517 US 620 (1996) (6–3); *Lawrence v Texas*, 539 US 558 (2003) (6–3); *United States v Windsor*, 570 US 744 (2013) (5–4).

[27] *Obergefell*, 135 S Ct at 2626 (Roberts, CJ, dissenting); see also id at 2638 (Thomas, J, dissenting) (claiming that "the majority's decision threatens the religious liberty our Nation has long sought to protect"); id at 2642–43 (Alito, J, dissenting) (charging that the Court's decision will be "used to vilify Americans who are unwilling to assent to the new orthodoxy" and that "those who cling to old beliefs" will "risk being labeled as bigots and treated as such by governments, employers, and schools"). Professor Stone described the potential conflict between marriage equality and traditional religious belief as "a central theme of those who denounced the decision" in *Obergefell*. Geoffrey R. Stone, *Sex and the Constitution: Sex, Religion, and Law from America's Origins to the Twenty-First Century* 526 (2017).

Masterpiece Cakeshop was Justice Kennedy's final opinion involving the rights of gay people—and the antepenultimate opinion of his three decades on the Court. Given his pivotal role over the past generation, his departure raises the question where we find ourselves in the "life cycle" of gay rights claims.[28]

I started to think seriously about that question while waiting to watch the oral argument in *Obergefell*. Demand for the seats in the Bar section was going to be high, so I arrived at the Court early in the afternoon the day before. There were already dozens of people in line.[29] Most of them were not, however, lawyers eager to see the arguments. They were paid line standers, hired by firms like linestanding.com and billed out to clients at upwards of $50 per hour, to hold lawyers' places. And these line standers were largely middle-aged people of color, who had mostly been recruited from nearby shelters.[30]

As the evening wore on, it got dark, and then cold; it drizzled. Late in the night, some of the line standers asked me and the few other lawyers in the line whether we would hold their places while they went back to their shelter to freshen up. So for several hours in the darkest, coldest part of the night, we sat there keeping an eye on their empty chairs. I later heard that although the paid line standers had been promised $10 an hour, some of them were told midway through their stints that they would receive only half their payment immediately; they would need to return a fortnight later to receive the rest.[31]

---

[28] See Reva B. Siegel, *Foreword: Equality Divided*, 127 Harv L Rev 1, 76 (2013).

[29] Practically speaking, there are three sorts of seating for members of the public who want to watch oral arguments at the Court. Members of the Supreme Court Bar can sit in "chairs just beyond the bronze railing" (the "Bar section"). There are also seats, behind the railing, for the general public. Some of those seats are available for an entire argument session, but most are allocated to the "three-minute line," whose occupants are shuffled in and out of the courtroom during a session. See US Supreme Court, *Visitors' Guide to Oral Argument*, "Courtroom Seating," available at https://www.supremecourt.gov/visiting/visitorsguideto oralargument.aspx ("*Visitors' Guide to Oral Argument*").

[30] For accounts of paid line standing for Supreme Court oral arguments and the prices charged, see generally Robyn Hagan Cain, *Need a Seat at Supreme Court Oral Arguments?: Hire a Line Stander*, FindLaw, Sept 2, 2011, available at http://tinyurl.com/zxtoq48; Adam Liptak, *Supreme Court Spectator Line Acts as a Tollbooth*, NY Times, April 15, 2013, available at http://tinyurl.com/h37vcqd; Sarah Kliff, *Supreme Court and the Business of Waiting in Line*, Wash Post, March 25, 2012, available at http://tinyurl.com/hbzm4hk. For photographs I took to reflect the composition of the Bar line for *Obergefell*, see https://tinyurl.com /JustDess1 and https://tinyurl.com/JustDess2.

[31] In light of the difficulties homeless individuals often face in navigating complex processes to vindicate their rights, see, e.g., *Veasey v Perry*, 71 F Supp 3d 627, 675 (SD Tex 2014) (discussing the barriers they face in obtaining government documents), aff'd in relevant part, 830 F3d 216 (5th Cir 2016) (en banc), and their general lack of connection to financial in-

While I was on line, both Monday afternoon and Tuesday morning, I spoke to a number of officials from the Court who had come to take in the scene. They seemed genuinely surprised and taken aback.[32] There were also several press reports, nearly all of them critical.[33] The next fall, the Court forbade line standers in the Bar line.[34]

During the twenty hours I stood and sat outside the Court, I was struck by a tremendous irony: By 7 a.m. on the day of argument, when the Court police began to monitor the Bar line, the column consisted of (primarily white) lawyers eagerly awaiting an expected milestone in the struggle for gay equality. But in the night, the line had consisted of homeless people of color, for whom the promises of equality made over a century before had not yet been realized. In short, that cold spring evening and morning represented, as Charles Dickens long ago wrote, both "the season of Light" and "the season of Darkness"; it was simultaneously both a "spring of hope" and a "winter of despair."[35]

What accounts for the fact that, to paraphrase Dickens again, one set of claims for justice seemed to be "going direct to Heaven" while the other seemed to be "going direct the other way"?[36] And looking back from the vantage point of *Masterpiece Cakeshop*, are we likely to see the convergence of claims for racial and sexual orientation equality over the next Terms?

I. Gay Rights and Racial Justice in the First Roberts Court

The Term before Justice Kennedy joined the Supreme Court, the Court took starkly different positions regarding the inclusion of gay people and people of color within fundamental American insti-

---

stitutions, see Mehrsa Baradaran, *How the Poor Got Cut Out of Banking*, 62 Emory L J 483 (2013), it seems quite plausible that many of the line standers never received the full pay promised for their service.

[32] See Robert Barnes, *Supreme Court Tells Lawyers: Stand in Line Yourselves; You Can't Pay Others to Hold a Spot*, Wash Post, Oct 6, 2015, available at http://tinyurl.com/h2kw4oa.

[33] See, e.g., Dahlia Lithwick and Mark Joseph Stern, *Not All Must Rise*, Slate, April 27, 2015, available at http://tinyurl.com/lsojz3t.

[34] E-mail from Kathy Arberg to Adam Liptak et al, Oct 5, 2015 (on file with the author) (the Supreme Court's Public Information Officer sent an e-mail to the Supreme Court press corps noting some "new procedures). See also *Visitors' Guide to Oral Argument* (cited in note 29) ("Only Bar members who actually intend to attend argument are allowed in line for the Bar section; 'line standers' are not permitted.").

[35] Charles Dickens, *A Tale of Two Cities* (1859).

[36] Id.

tutions. Over the previous generation, the Supreme Court had issued a series of decisions providing constitutional protection to individuals' decisions about intimate relationships.[37] Those decisions had not, however, extended to marriage equality for gay people: in 1972, the Court had dismissed an appeal from a Minnesota decision denying a marriage license to a gay couple "for want of a substantial federal question."[38] But in *Bowers v Hardwick*,[39] Justice Byron White's opinion for the Court went quite a bit further in excluding gay people from the constitutional protections that other individuals enjoyed. He declared that "majority sentiments about the morality of homosexuality" were sufficient to justify, at least with respect to gay people, a Georgia statute that imposed a mandatory prison term for private, consensual sexual activity between adults.[40]

The Court, however, was still committed to the project of fully integrating racial minorities into the key institutions of civil society. The same day it issued its opinion in *Bowers v Hardwick*, the Court also handed down *Thornburg v Gingles*.[41] The Court's embrace there of amended section 2 of the Voting Rights Act, which forbids election practices based on "discriminatory effect alone,"[42] reflected a willingness to enforce antidiscrimination statutes even when those statutes went decisively beyond providing a remedy solely for unconstitutional conduct.[43] Earlier in the Term, the Court had upheld race-conscious affirmative action remedies in employment discrimination cases that

---

[37] See *Griswold v Connecticut*, 381 US 479 (1965); *Loving v Virginia*, 388 US 1 (1967); *Eisenstadt v Baird*, 405 US 438 (1972); *Roe v Wade*, 410 US 113 (1973); *Carey v Population Services Int'l*, 431 US 678 (1977).

[38] *Baker v Nelson*, 409 US 810, 810 (1972).

[39] 478 US 186 (1986).

[40] Id at 196. See id at 188 n 1 for the terms of the statute. The Court declined to consider whether Georgia's statute, which forbade the specified acts without regard to the sex of the participants, could constitutionally be applied to acts involving opposite-sex couples. Id at 188 n 2.

[41] 478 US 30 (1986).

[42] Id at 35.

[43] Section 2 of the Voting Rights Act, 52 USC § 10301, was adopted to respond to the Court's holding in *City of Mobile v Bolden*, 446 US 55 (1980), that plaintiffs challenging an electoral practice—there, the use of at-large elections—must show both a racially discriminatory purpose and a disparate impact. Enforcement of the "results" test of section 2 dramatically reshaped electoral bodies throughout the nation. See National Commission on the Voting Rights Act, *Protecting Minority Voters: The Voting Rights Act at Work*, 1982–2005 (2006), available at https://tinyurl.com/PKJD09. See also Ellen Katz et al, *Documenting Discrimination in Voting: Judicial Findings Under Section 2 of the Voting Rights Act Since 1982*

benefited individuals who had not themselves been the victims of discrimination.[44] And in *Batson v Kentucky*,[45] the Court had overturned a Warren Court–era precedent to hold that prosecutors could not take race into account in exercising peremptory challenges to remove minority citizens from juries.

A quarter-century later, things were quite different. During the same week that the Supreme Court struck down the Defense of Marriage Act,[46] the Court also struck down a key provision of the Voting Rights Act and tightened the scrutiny for race-conscious admissions policies in higher education.[47]

A number of scholars, most notably Reva Siegel in her *Harvard Law Review Foreword*[48] and Russell Robinson in *Unequal Protection*,[49] have located the differences in how claims for gay and racial inclusion have fared in long-term doctrinal movements within antidiscrimination law, such as the rise of the discriminatory-purpose requirement or the emergence and evolution of the tiers of scrutiny. But there are more particular explanations as well that focus on the different positions gay people and people of color occupy in contemporary society and on the legal claims they were advancing before the first Roberts Court. Understanding those explanations both sets the stage for the Court's decision in *Masterpiece Cakeshop* and provides some hints as to how doctrine may develop going forward.

Final Report of the Voting Rights Initiative, University of Michigan Law School, 39 U Mich J L Reform 643 (2006).

For a discussion of the Court's now-abandoned willingness to give Congress wide scope in enforcing the equality values of the Fourteenth Amendment, see Pamela S. Karlan, *Foreword: Democracy and Disdain*, 126 Harv L Rev 1, 22–25 (2012).

[44] See *Sheet Metal Workers v EEOC*, 478 US 421 (1986); *Local No 93, Int'l Ass'n of Firefighters, AFL-CIO C.L.C. v City of Cleveland*, 478 US 501, 515 (1986). In *Wygant v Jackson Bd. of Educ.*, 476 US 267 (1986), however, the Court rejected a school board's policy of extending preferential protection against layoffs to minority teachers.

[45] 476 US 79 (1986).

[46] See *United States v Windsor*, 133 S Ct 2675 (2013).

[47] See *Shelby County v Holder*, 133 S Ct 2612 (2013) (holding unconstitutional the coverage formula subjecting jurisdictions to the requirement that they preclear election changes to ensure that the changes would have neither a discriminatory purpose nor a discriminatory effect); *Fisher v University of Texas at Austin*, 133 S Ct 2411, 2420 (2013) (holding that universities should receive "no deference" with respect to the means they use to pursue their compelling interest in selecting a racially diverse class).

[48] Siegel, 127 Harv L Rev (cited in note 28).

[49] Russell K. Robinson, *Unequal Protection*, 68 Stan L Rev 151, 171 (2016) (challenging the "conventional wisdom by asserting that sexual orientation is presently in a more favorable position than race and sex").

A. INSULAR VERSUS NONINSULAR MINORITIES

Thirty years ago, Bruce Ackerman published a foundational article, "Beyond Carolene Products."[50] There, he challenged the idea that "discrete and insular minorities"—to use footnote 4's famous formulation[51]—were especially disadvantaged in the political process and therefore particularly deserving of judicial solicitude. He suggested that, all other things being equal, being discrete and insular might make it easier for a minority to organize and press its demands. By contrast, being invisible and diffuse might make it harder for a group's members to find one another and to organize. Thus, Professor Ackerman suggested that "[t]he victims of sexual [orientation] discrimination or poverty, rather than racial or religious minorities, will increasingly constitute the groups with the greatest claim upon *Carolene*'s concern with the fairness of pluralist process."[52]

But while Professor Ackerman has turned out to be spot on about the ways in which poor people are excluded from effective participation in governance, his prediction was less accurate with respect to the relative position of gays and racial minorities. And, ironically, the relative success of the gay rights movement relative to racial justice movements may be precisely because gay individuals are *less* insular in a particularly relevant sense than are people of color.

Thirty years on, gay people are no longer invisible; they have come out. Even at the Supreme Court. In 1985, during the conference discussing *Bowers v Hardwick*,[53] Justice Lewis F. Powell, who cast the deciding vote, could tell his colleagues (quite mistakenly) that he had never met a gay person.[54] In 2003, the counsel who successfully argued on behalf of the petitioners in *Lawrence v Texas* was . . . Paul Smith, an experienced Supreme Court advocate, a former clerk to Justice Powell, and an openly gay man. I was in the courtroom that

---

[50] Bruce A. Ackerman, *Beyond Carolene Products*, 98 Harv L Rev 713 (1985).

[51] *United States v Carolene Prods. Co.*, 304 US 144, 152 n 4 (1938). The operational language of footnote 4 described three potential situations in which courts might be more skeptical of the constitutionality of challenged legislation: first, "when legislation appears on its face to be within a specific prohibition of the Constitution"; second, when the legislation "restricts those political processes which can ordinarily be expected to bring about repeal of undesirable" laws; and third, "whether prejudice against discrete and insular minorities may be a special condition, . . . which may call for a correspondingly more searching judicial inquiry."

[52] Ackerman, 98 Harv L Rev at 718 (cited in note 50).

[53] 478 US 186 (1986).

[54] John C. Jeffries Jr., *Justice Lewis F. Powell, Jr.* 521–22 (1994).

day, and after the argument (which had gone very well), I was standing with Walter Dellinger, a leading Supreme Court advocate and constitutional law professor, when we were approached by the *New York Times*'s Supreme Court correspondent, Linda Greenhouse. Walter asked Linda what she had thought was the most interesting part of the argument. Without missing a beat, Linda replied "the Bar section." What she meant was that those seats—some of the ones that needed $6,000 worth of line-standing time for later gay rights arguments—were filled, in significant numbers, by former clerks and other frequent participants in the Court's business who were openly gay. When the Justices came out from behind the velvet curtain to take their seats, it was clear that at least some of them recognized this fact.

To paraphrase former Secretary of Defense Donald Rumsfeld, in the seventeen years between *Hardwick* and *Lawrence*, gay people had moved from being unknown unknowns to being known unknowns to being known knowns. The Justices had always known people who were gay, but now they knew it. These were people who had worked for them, people they respected, people who had become in some cases virtually a part of their families. Two decades of gay people coming out meant that the Justices, like the rest of the American people, now understood that LGBT people were their children, their friends, their colleagues, their employees.[55]

The relationship between the Justices' experiences and their decisions extends across a range of constitutional law domains. Consider, for example, the Court's Fourth Amendment jurisprudence. In *United States v Jones*,[56] the Court confronted the question whether the government needs a warrant to attach a GPS device to an individual's car. At oral argument, the Chief Justice asked the deputy solicitor general whether, under the government's theory, the police could "put a GPS device on all of our cars" or "monitor[ ] our movements for a month."[57] When the deputy solicitor general replied that "the justices of this Court when driving on public roadways have no greater expectation" of privacy than suspected drug dealers like Antoine

---

[55] See Adam Liptak, *Exhibit A for a Major Shift: Justices' Gay Clerks*, NY Times, June 8, 2013, available at https://tinyurl.com/PKJD68.

[56] 565 US 400 (2012).

[57] Tr of Oral Arg 9, *United States v Jones*, 565 US 400 (2012) (No 10-1259).

Jones,[58] the case was essentially over: it was no surprise the Court ruled unanimously in favor of the warrant requirement.[59]

It may be precisely because gay people are in one very important way *not* insular that they have been so successful in the struggle for marriage equality. The vast majority of gay children are born to straight parents.[60] As a result, many straight people have intimate family ties to gay people. Those ties can be powerful levers for changing attitudes.[61] On the eve of the arguments in *Perry* and *Windsor*, for example, Republican Senator Rob Portman, a longtime opponent of same-sex marriage, announced "a change of heart" on the question of marriage equality that he attributed to learning that his son was gay and "want[ing] him to have the same opportunities that his brother and sister would have."[62] And one of the most memorable and effective advertisements in the campaign against California's Proposition 8 showed the straight parents of a lesbian daughter discussing how they wanted her to be treated fairly.[63] In this sense, the gay community stands in a relationship to the straight community that parallels in important features the experience of the disability rights community. That has been another movement for civil rights and civic inclusion that has had marked successes, at least as a political matter, over the past several decades.[64]

---

[58] Id at 9–10.

[59] And in *Riley v California*, 134 S Ct 2473 (2014), and *Carpenter v United States*, 138 S Ct 2206 (2018), the Court gave greater Fourth Amendment protection to cellphone-derived information than to nondigital analogs because "cell phones and the services they provide are 'such a pervasive and insistent part of daily life' that carrying one is indispensable to participation in modern society," *Carpenter*, 138 S Ct at 2220 (quoting *Riley*, 134 S Ct at 2484)—surely a reflection of their own experience.

[60] And the vast majority of gay parents have children who are straight.

[61] See Siegel, 127 Harv L Rev at 85 n 429 (cited in note 28) (noting a study that found that among adults whose views about gay people had become more favorable over the last five years, "79% attributed the change in some part to knowing a gay or lesbian person"). See also Stone, *Sex and the Constitution* at 449 (cited in note 27) (describing how revelations in the wake of the AIDS epidemic created a "great awakening" among straight people of their connection to gay people); id at 499 ("sometimes familiarity breeds, not contempt, but acceptance").

[62] Kevin Cirilli, *Portman for Gay Marriage After Son Comes Out*, Politico (March 15, 2013), available at https://tinyurl.com/PKJDA01.

[63] See David Fleischer, *The Prop 8 Report: What Defeat in California Can Teach Us About Winning Future Ballot Measures on Same-Sex Marriage* (finding 3), available at http://tinyurl.com/yc3s3atq; see Melissa Murray, *Marriage Rights and Parental Rights: Parents, the State, and Proposition 8*, 5 Stan J Civ Rts & Civ Liberties 357, 394 (2009) (discussing the "Thorons" advertisement).

[64] As a matter of constitutional law, the Supreme Court has not required heightened scrutiny of laws that discriminate on the basis of disability. See *City of Cleburne v Cleburne*

By contrast, it is hard to imagine the modal politician waking up to discover that his children are African American or poor or undocumented. The continued residential and socioeconomic isolation of minority communities means that their claims are less likely to resonate with decision makers and are less likely directly to affect non-group members. The intimate connections that gay people have with the majority community thus not only change the sorts of legal claims and legal theories they seek to advance, but also increase their chances of success.

Gay rights in the Supreme Court thus offers an illustration of Derrick Bell's famous "interest-convergence" hypothesis.[65] Professor Bell argued that "[t]he interest of blacks in achieving racial equality [would be] accommodated only when it converges with the interests of whites" in "policymaking positions."[66] At the oral argument in *United States v Windsor*, the Chief Justice told Windsor's counsel that "[a]s far as I can tell, political figures are falling over themselves to endorse your side of the case."[67] He implicitly suggested that gay political success was a point *against* judicial intervention or heightened scrutiny. But what the interest-convergence hypothesis tells us is that only once a group can make some common cause with already powerful elements of society can it expect judicial intervention under the Equal Protection Clause.[68] For gay people, this occurred once they ceased to be discrete and insular.

B. DISCRETE FORMAL EXCLUSION VERSUS SYSTEMIC BARRIERS

The director John Waters famously remarked that he had "always thought the privilege of being gay is that we don't have to get married or go in the Army."[69] And yet, the two most striking legal victories of

---

Living Ctr., 473 US 432, 446 (1985). But the form of rationality review courts have applied in the wake of *Cleburne* has more "bite" than traditional, extremely deferential rationality review. And statutory protections for people with disabilities are in important ways more robust than protections against race and sex discrimination. See Pamela S. Karlan and George Rutherglen, *Disabilities, Discrimination, and Reasonable Accommodation*, 46 Duke L J 1, 2 (1996).

[65] Derrick A. Bell Jr., *Brown v Board of Education and the Interest-Convergence Dilemma*, 93 Harv L Rev 518 (1980).

[66] Id at 523, 524.

[67] Tr of Oral Arg 108, *United States v Windsor*, 570 US 744 (2013) (No 12-307).

[68] See William N. Eskridge Jr., *Destabilizing Due Process and Evolutive Equal Protection*, 47 UCLA L Rev 1183, 1186 (2000); Cass R. Sunstein, *Sexual Orientation and the Constitution: A Note on the Relationship Between Due Process and Equal Protection*, 55 U Chi L Rev 1161 (1988).

[69] Rebecca Mead, *The Groom Reaper*, New Yorker, March 26, 2007.

the gay rights movement at the national level have been the arrival of marriage equality and the repeal of Don't Ask, Don't Tell.[70]

These victories share a number of characteristics. They sought to strike down formal, facially discriminatory legal barriers. They sought access to fundamentally conservative public institutions. And while it might seem that there would be greater resistance precisely for that reason, in another sense claims to inclusion in bedrock institutions can actually be less threatening to the existing order.[71] As Justice Kennedy framed it in the conclusion to *Obergefell v Hodges*: "It would misunderstand these men and women to say they disrespect the idea of marriage. Their plea is that they do respect it, respect it so deeply that they seek to find its fulfillment for themselves."[72]

The gay rights cases that preceded *Masterpiece Cakeshop* shared a particular structure: they each involved litigation between gay people and the government over laws that overtly discriminated against gay people. *Romer v Evans* involved a challenge by gay people to a Colorado constitutional amendment that prohibited any government actor within the state from taking action to protect gay people as a class.[73] *Lawrence v Texas* involved a challenge to a state criminal statute that criminalized only gay sex. *United States v Windsor* challenged a federal statute that expressly restricted "marriage," for purposes of federal law, to straight couples.[74] And *Obergefell v Hodges* challenged a state statute that restricted marriage to opposite-sex couples and declared marriage between persons of the same sex to be "against the strong public policy of [the] state."[75]

---

[70] See Don't Ask, Don't Tell Repeal Act of 2010, Pub L No 111-321, 124 Stat 3515. For an account of the process leading up to the act, see Stone, *Sex and the Constitution* at 455–59 (cited in note 27).

[71] Indeed, the division in the gay community over whether to seek marriage responded to this potentially homogenizing tendency. The potential of marriage to domesticate and align gay sexuality with straight sexuality led some gay rights activists to downplay or resist the importance of marriage. See, e.g., Paula Ettlebrick, *Wedlock Alert: A Comment on Lesbian and Gay Family Recognition*, 5 J L & Pol'y 107 (1996); Nancy Polikoff, *We Will Get What We Ask For: Why Legalizing Gay and Lesbian Marriages Will Not "Dismantle the Legal Structure of Gender in Every Marriage*,*"* 79 Va L Rev 1535 (1996). For the argument on the other side, see, e.g., Tom Stoddard, *Bleeding Heart: Reflections on Using the Law to Make Social Change*, 72 NYU L Rev 967 (1997). For reflection on the debate in light of the Court's marriage equality decisions, see, e.g., Suzanne B. Goldberg, *Obergefell at the Intersection of Civil Rights and Social Movements*, 6 Cal L Rev Circuit 157 (2015).

[72] 135 S Ct 2584, 2608 (2015).

[73] *Romer v Evans*, 517 US 620, 624 (1996).

[74] 1 USC § 7.

[75] Ohio Rev Code Ann § 3101.01(C)(1).

With respect to marriage equality, the remedy was issuance of marriage licenses. This discrete interaction with the government offered a clear focal point for judicial action. To be sure, a series of later more potentially complex consequences flows from that interaction—that was the point, in some sense, of the more than 1,100 federal laws impacted by DOMA[76]—but they flow almost mechanically from the existence of the marriage; they generally don't require further judicial intervention. And while there were some early hiccups of resistance,[77] de jure equal access to marriage seems to have arrived relatively smoothly.[78] As a matter of constitutional law, it is unclear whether there remain other *public* institutions to which individuals can be denied access because of their sexual orientation: at the oral argument in *Hollingsworth v Perry*—the challenge to California's marriage restriction—Justice Sotomayor asked the attorney defending the restriction whether, "outside of the marriage context," he could "think of any other rational basis, reason for a State using sexual orientation as a factor in denying homosexuals benefits or imposing burdens on them? . . . Denying them a job, not granting them benefits of some sort, any other decision?" His reply was categorical "Your Honor, I cannot."[79]

Formal de jure legal exclusion, by contrast, is no longer the primary barrier that people of color face to full civic inclusion. Broadly speak-

---

[76] See *Windsor*, 133 S Ct at 2683 (describing how DOMA affected everything from who can be buried in national cemeteries to how political candidates can use campaign funds).

[77] See, e.g., Carl Tobias, *Implementing Marriage Equality in America*, 65 Duke L J Online 25 (2015) (discussing the issue generally); Howard M. Wasserman, *Crazy in Alabama: Judicial Process and the Last Stand Against Marriage Equality in the Land of George Wallace*, 110 Nw U L Rev Online 201 (2015) (discussing the judicial resistance in Alabama).

[78] That is not to deny the existence of rear-guard resistance. For example, the Arkansas Department of Health refused to put the name of a married woman's spouse on the birth certificate as a second parent in cases where the pregnancy was the product of sperm donation if the second spouse was a woman, but not if the second spouse was a man. See *Pavan v Smith*, 137 S Ct 2705, 2077 (2017) (per curiam). And Mississippi enacted a statute providing, among other things, that state employees could not be required to license or celebrate marriages that are inconsistent with their belief that "[m]arriage is or should be recognized as the union of one man and one woman." Miss Code Ann § 11-62-5(8)(a).

[79] Tr of Oral Arg 14, *Hollingsworth v Perry*, 570 US 639 (2013) (No 12-144). This article does not address the question whether public institutions can deny access to particular public institutions or benefits to individuals on the basis of gender identity or gender expression. My view is that denying access to an institution or a benefit generally available to women to an individual because she is a transgender woman violates existing prohibitions on sex discrimination; so, too, would denying access to an institution or a benefit generally available to men to an individual because he is a transgender man. See, e.g., *Whitaker v Kenosha Unified Sch. Dist. No 1 Bd. of Educ.*, 858 F3d 1034, 1049 (7th Cir 2017), cert dismissed, 138 S Ct 1260 (2018); *Glenn v Brumby*, 663 F3d 1312, 1316 (11th Cir 2011); *Schwenk v Hartford*, 204 F3d 1187, 1201–2 (9th Cir 2000).

ing, there are three sorts of exclusionary practices. Formal exclusion involves practices that, as a matter of express law, deny individuals particular benefits or impose on individuals particular burdens.[80] As far as I know, the last two examples of this sort of practice that the Supreme Court confronted were the Virginia prohibition on interracial marriage struck down in 1967 in *Loving v Virginia*[81] and the California state prison policy of using race in temporary cell assignments struck down by the Court in 2005.[82]

The other two forms of exclusion arise from either disparate treatment under ostensibly neutral laws or from disparate impact. Proving purposeful disparate treatment can be difficult, and may require retail, rather than wholesale, litigation.[83] Moreover, because disparate treatment often arises from the way law is *administered*, there are numerous opportunities for government officials to engage in disparate treatment; it is therefore harder for courts to police this form

---

[80] Professor Robinson makes the point that the restrictive marriage statutes did not, on their face, discriminate on the basis of sexual orientation. Robinson, 68 Stan L Rev at 178–80 (cited in note 49). True enough, although they did expressly discriminate against same-sex couples. And he is surely right that to the extent the Court thought that DOMA and the restrictive marriage laws were illegitimate because they discriminated against gay people, the idea that the laws involve discrimination on the basis of sexual orientation is hard to square with the notion in *Geduldig v Aiello*, 417 US 484 (1974), that discrimination against pregnant persons cannot be understood as discrimination on the basis of sex. But my point here is not about the identity of the group that is being denied access. Rather, it is that access to an identifiable, discrete benefit is being denied as a matter of formal legal rules. To be sure, judicial sympathy for the excluded individuals may stem from a sense that the excluded individuals form a cognizable class—an issue to which I return below.

[81] 388 US 1 (1967).

[82] *Johnson v California*, 543 US 499 (2005). Thus, as I have pointed out elsewhere, "[i]t wasn't until 1964, after the Court had largely finished the job of striking down explicit racial classifications, that the Court 'both articulated and applied a more rigorous review standard to racial classifications.'" As a result, almost all the racial classifications the Supreme Court sees arise in the context of race-conscious affirmative action. Pamela S. Karlan, *John Hart Ely and the Problem of Gerrymandering: The Lion in Winter*, 114 Yale L J 132, 1344 (2005).

There do remain some laws that expressly exclude individuals from certain benefits on the basis of race—most notably laws that provide preferences to individuals descended from pre-European inhabitants of what became the United States. In 2000, the Supreme Court struck down, on the grounds that it violated the Fifteenth Amendment's prohibition on denying the right to vote "on account of race," a Hawaiian law that limited who could vote in elections for the Office of Hawaiian Affairs to citizens descended from people who had lived in Hawaii prior to 1778, when the first white settlers arrived. *Rice v Cayetano*, 528 US 495 (2000). (The Court did not address the "validity" of the underlying administrative structure of the office, id at 522.) And the Court has treated governmental preferences in favor of members of recognized Indian tribes as granting a benefit "to Indians not as a discrete racial group, but, rather, as members of quasi-sovereign tribal entities" that are political jurisdictions. *Morton v Mancari*, 417 US 535, 554 (1974).

[83] It is of course possible to prove class-wide disparate treatment, in part by showing a disparate impact on the protected class. But such litigation can be costly, requiring large amounts of data and expert assistance.

of exclusion than simply to enjoin the law on the books. And when the decision makers do not harbor a discriminatory purpose, there will, almost by definition, be some other motivation for their actions, and the question will then arise whether the challenged action can be justified with regard to that legitimate purpose. Disparate-impact cases therefore demand some form of balancing.

These "second-generation" forms of exclusion also implicate a more complex web of causal circumstances. The disparate impact so many facially neutral laws and practices have on minority individuals is tied to intergenerational socioeconomic effects, many of them tied in turn to persistent *de jure* discrimination.[84] But the current Supreme Court has been hostile to the idea that constitutional law has the power, let alone the responsibility, to deal with those effects. Quite to the contrary. Consider the Court's treatment of the Voting Rights Act. Prior to *Shelby County*, the Supreme Court had repeatedly upheld the act's preclearance regime against constitutional challenges.[85] But although the act had been a constitutionally appropriate response to the world of the 1960s, the Court found that "[n]early 50 years later, things have changed dramatically."[86] That change in the world changed the strictures of the Constitution, which required that the act's "'current burdens' must be justified by 'current needs.'"[87] So, too, when it comes to race-conscious affirmative action, the Court has shown itself reluctant to permit its continued use fifty years on from the Second Reconstruction.[88]

Unwinding the intergenerational impact of past discrimination requires tools beyond the largely prohibitory injunctions with which contemporary judges are comfortable and familiar. It requires a re-

---

[84] See generally Ira Katznelson, *When Affirmative Action Was White: An Untold History of Racial Inequality in Twentieth-Century America* (2005). This has certainly been proven true in recent Voting Rights Act litigation challenging first-generation barriers such as voter ID requirements and cutbacks to early voting and same-day registration opportunities. See generally Pamela S. Karlan, *Turnout, Tenuousness, and Getting Results in Section 2 Vote Denial Claims*, 77 Ohio St L J 763 (2016).

[85] See *South Carolina v Katzenbach*, 383 US 301 (1966); *Georgia v United States*, 411 US 526 (1973); *City of Rome v United States*, 446 US 156 (1980); *Lopez v Monterey County*, 525 US 266 (1999).

[86] *Shelby County*, 133 S Ct at 2625.

[87] Id at 2627 (quoting *Northwest Austin Mun. Util. Dist. No 1 v Holder*, 557 US 193, 204 (2009)).

[88] See, e.g., *Grutter v Bollinger*, 539 US 306, 343 (2003) (expressing the Court's view that "25 years from now, the use of racial preferences will no longer be necessary to further the interest approved today").

turn to structural reform litigation or the creation of affirmative entitlements.

By contrast, precisely because the gay community is not discrete and insular generationally,[89] the intergenerational transmission of disadvantage likely plays a minor role with respect to where gay people find themselves today. Gay parents are not more likely than straight parents to have gay children (and gay children are not more likely than straight children to have gay parents).[90] Thus, if discrimination against gay individuals leaves them with fewer resources to devote to their children, the children whose opportunities are limited by that discrimination are themselves far more likely to be straight than to be gay. What intergenerational effect there is on the gay community seems more attributable to straight parents who reject their gay children, and thereby refuse to provide them with the most significant contemporary transfer of wealth from parent to child—namely, educational expenditures[91]—than to external discrimination. There may be cases somewhere down the road where gay individuals raise disparate-impact claims,[92] but at least at present disparate-impact theory seems far less central to the gay rights antidiscrimination project than it has necessarily become to the struggle for racial justice. In short, gay rights claims and racial justice claims are at different points in the "life cycle"[93] of the struggle for legal equality.

C. RIVALROUS VERSUS NONRIVALROUS RIGHTS

Another explanation for the relatively greater success gay rights advocates had achieved in the years before *Masterpiece Cakeshop* lies in

---

[89] See text accompanying notes 60–61.

[90] See William N. Eskridge Jr. and Nan D. Hunter, *Sexuality, Gender, and the Law* ch 3, § 3C (1997).

[91] See John H. Langbein, *The Twentieth-Century Revolution in Family Wealth Transmission*, 86 Mich L Rev 722, 730–36 (1988).

[92] One could frame the *Marriage Equality Cases* as raising a form of disparate-impact claim if one starts from the view that the statutes being challenged did not explicitly discriminate on the basis of sexual orientation (since they simply prevented, or refused to recognize, any marriage between two individuals of the same sex, regardless of their sexual orientations). Whatever else may be true, a ban on same-sex marriage will surely have a disparate impact on gay people, since they are far more likely than their straight counterparts to want to enter into such a marriage. See Suzanne B. Goldberg, *Risky Arguments in Social-Justice Litigation: The Case of Sex Discrimination and Marriage Equality*, 114 Colum L Rev 2087, 2093 (2014) (stating that "[m]ost people understand that the [then-existing marriage] bans primarily affect gay people who want to marry their same-sex partners"). But framing the cases that way seems needlessly artificial.

[93] Siegel, 127 Harv L Rev at 76 (cited in note 28).

the nature of the benefits the two cohorts had been seeking. The federal benefits and marriage licenses gay couples were seeking not only involved governmental exclusion, but they involved nonrivalrous, nonpositional goods. By contrast, many of the entitlements at the heart of the Supreme Court's recent racial-justice jurisprudence have involved scarce opportunities.

At an artificially high level of abstraction, any particular marriage in a jurisdiction with laws against bigamy can be characterized as a rival good—that is, a good "whose consumption by one individual necessarily diminishes the store available for others."[94] Because any one person can be married to only one other person (at least at any one time), a particular marriage excludes all other individuals from marrying one of the spouses. That limit, however, seems wholly unimportant on the societal level. At that level, marriage licenses—indeed, the *institution* of marriage—are nonrivalrous. There is no artificial limit on the number of marriages a jurisdiction can solemnize. Perhaps on an individual level, particular marriages might—at least for the status-conscious, insecure, or envious among us—be viewed as positional goods—that is, ones "whose value depends relatively strongly on how they compare with" the relationships enjoyed "by others."[95] But here too, on the societal level, it does not make sense to treat marriage as a positional good. While no doubt many individuals treat marriage as positional, in the sense that they consider being married important, and look down upon nonmarital relationships for a variety of reasons, there is no reason to think that significant numbers of individuals take the view that marriage is valuable precisely because some people are forbidden from marrying.

To be sure, some opponents of marriage equality argued that extending the right to marry to same-sex couples would deprive opposite-sex couples of something meaningful because it would degrade the institution of marriage as they understood it.[96] But that ar-

---

[94] David Hasen, *Some Consequences of Governmental Provision of Rival Goods*, 34 Va Tax Rev 319, 322 (2014) (defining rival goods).

[95] See Robert H. Frank, *The Demand for Unobservable and Other Nonpositional Goods*, 75 Am Econ Rev 101, 101 (1985) (defining positional goods).

[96] See, e.g., George W. Dent Jr., *The Defense of Traditional Marriage*, 15 J L & Pol 581, 616–23 (1999); William C. Duncan, *Law and Culture: The State Interests in Marriage*, 2 Ave Maria L Rev 153 (2004); Lynne Marie Kohm, *How Will the Proliferation and Recognition of Domestic Partnerships Affect Marriages?*, 4 J L & Fam Stud 105 (2002). In *Constitutional Law as Trademark*, 43 UC Davis L Rev 385 (2009), I analogize this argument to claims of "tarnishment" or "dilution" with respect to intellectual property.

gument got relatively little traction in the courts, perhaps because it was so often accompanied by impermissible expressions of animus toward gay people.[97]

By contrast, the goods at issue in recent Supreme Court decisions involving racial equality are often rivalrous.[98] Consider, for example, the seats in selective university entering classes at issue in *Fisher v University of Texas*[99] or *Schuette v Coalition to Defend Affirmative Action*,[100] or the attractive public-sector jobs at issue in *Ricci v DeStefano*,[101] or the affordable housing at issue in *Texas Department of Housing and Community Affairs v Inclusive Communities Project, Inc.*[102] Moreover, when it comes to selective educational institutions, places in the entering class are not only rival goods; they are positional ones: the scarcity is part of their value.

The voting rights at issue in cases like *Shelby County*, the "new vote dilution" cases working their way up to the Supreme Court,[103] and the

---

[97] For example, the House Report accompanying DOMA praised law restricting marriage to heterosexual couples as "reflect[ing] and honor[ing] a collective moral judgment about human sexuality" that "entails both moral disapproval of homosexuality, and a moral conviction that heterosexuality better comports with traditional (especially Judeo-Christian) morality." HR Rep No 104-664 at 15–16 (1996).

Moreover, the degradation-of-marriage argument was often coupled with the claim that the institution of marriage was designed to ensure that men took responsibility for their children. In *Hernandez v Robles*, 855 NE2d 1 (NY 2006), New York's high court explained that the legislature could have restricted marriage to opposite-sex couples because heterosexual relationships "are all too often casual or temporary" and it would be appropriate "to offer an inducement—in the form of marriage and its attendant benefits—to opposite-sex couples who make a solemn, long-term commitment to each other" in order to protect accidently conceived children. Id at 7. This combination of arguments had the ironic consequences of itself threatening to degrade the institution: "to the extent that the decision to restrict marriage to opposite-sex couples rests on the need to provide an incentive to domesticate otherwise feckless and irresponsible heterosexual men who will not enter into marriage if it is extended to everyone, marriage surely loses some of its luster." Karlan, 43 UC Davis L Rev at 408–9 (cited in note 96).

[98] I leave aside for now the Supreme Court's criminal racial justice docket. After *McCleskey v Kemp*, 481 US 279 (1987), *Whren v United States*, 517 US 806 (1996), and *Utah v Strieff*, 136 S Ct 2056 (2016), the Court seems committed to dealing with racial justice in the criminal sphere only when a litigant is claiming purposeful racial bias. See, e.g., *Pena-Rodriguez v Colorado*, 137 S Ct 855 (2017); *Buck v Davis*, 137 S Ct 759 (2017); *Foster v Chatman*, 136 S Ct 1737 (2016).

[99] 133 S Ct 2411 (2013); see also *Fisher v University of Texas*, 136 S Ct 2198, 2209 (2016) (rejecting Fisher's challenge to the university's use of race in the holistic admissions phase of its process but cautioning that the decision rests on a record that "may limit its value for prospective guidance").

[100] 134 S Ct 1623 (2014) (upholding a Michigan initiative that forbids the consideration of race in university admissions).

[101] 557 US 557 (2009).

[102] 135 S Ct 2507 (2015).

[103] For general discussion of the emergence of a new round of vote denial, see Dale E. Ho, *Voting Rights Litigation After Shelby County: Mechanics and Standards in Section 2 Vote Denial*

racial gerrymandering cases[104] are more complicated. As I have explained elsewhere, the right to vote "has come to embody a nested constellation of concepts: participation (the ability to cast a ballot and have it counted), aggregation (the ability to join with like-minded voters to achieve the election of one's preferred candidates), and governance (the ability to pursue policy preferences within the process of representative decisionmaking)."[105] The initial right to participate *should not* be treated as a scarce good—as Janai Nelson explains, votes themselves "do not involve the allocation of a limited resource; rather, the right to vote can be extended to countless individuals without denying others access to that right."[106] But the ability to elect candidates is inherently a competitive, positional enterprise. Because votes are the currency that produces electoral success, the ability to participate has come to be treated, particularly by the current Republican Party in large parts of the country, as a zero-sum game in which restrictive laws are used to "target African Americans with almost surgical precision,"[107] especially when (as in North Carolina) "African-American race is a better predictor for voting Democratic than party registration."[108]

By their nature, cases that involve rival goods are likely harder to win—and not just because there will be motivated opposing parties litigating hard.[109] These cases can also involve countervailing compelling stories by other claimants to the scarce opportunity. More-

---

Claims, 17 NYU J Legis & Pub Pol'y 675 (2014); Daniel P. Tokaji, *Applying Section 2 to the New Vote Denial*, 50 Harv CR-CL L Rev 439 (2015); Daniel P. Tokaji, *The New Vote Denial: Where Election Reform Meets the Voting Rights Act*, 57 SC L Rev 689 (2006).

[104] See *Cooper v Harris*, 137 S Ct 1455 (2017) (involving a challenge to congressional districts in North Carolina); *Bethune-Hill v Virginia State Bd. of Elections*, 137 S Ct 788 (2017) (involving a challenge to state legislative redistricting in Virginia); *Alabama Legis. Black Caucus v Alabama*, 135 S Ct 1257 (2015) (involving a challenge to state legislative districts in Alabama).

[105] Pamela S. Karlan, *Convictions and Doubts: Retribution, Representation, and the Debate Over Felon Disenfranchisement*, 56 Stan L Rev 1147, 1156 (2004); see generally Pamela S. Karlan, *The Rights to Vote: Some Pessimism About Formalism*, 71 Tex L Rev 1705, 1709–19 (1993) (developing this taxonomy).

[106] Janai S. Nelson, *The Causal Context of Disparate Vote Denial*, 54 BC L Rev 579, 611 (2013).

[107] *North Carolina State Conference of NAACP v McCrory*, 831 F3d 204, 214 (4th Cir 2016).

[108] Id at 225.

[109] Cf. *Horne v Flores*, 557 US 443, 448–49 (2009) (noting that "nominal defendants" in certain kinds of institutional reform litigation "are sometimes happy to be sued and happier still to lose") (quoting Donald L. Horowitz, *Decreeing Organizational Change: Judicial Supervision of Public Institutions*, 1983 Duke L J 1265, 1294–95). In both *United States v Windsor*, 570 US 744 (2013), and *Hollingsworth v Perry*, 570 US 693 (2013), for example, the government conceded the unconstitutionality of the marriage restriction at issue.

over, to the extent that a case implicates other private actors' claims of right, a good that is not inherently rivalrous can nonetheless present the question whether the possessor has a right to exclude.[110] In a sense, that is what happened in *Masterpiece Cakeshop* to the contested wedding cake.

II. Masterpiece Minimalism

In recent Terms, the Supreme Court has adopted a practice of "relisting" cases before it grants review. The Justices meet in conference to decide whether to hear the case a short time after the certiorari-stage filings are complete. While denials of certiorari normally appear on an orders list the following Monday, in recent Terms the Court has taken an additional week in cases where it thinks review might be appropriate. The case is then set for the next conference. "Relists appear to be a mechanism for avoiding improvident grants by allowing the justices and their clerks to double-check for procedural or other obstacles to the resolution of a case on the merits, known as vehicle problems, before granting."[111]

Masterpiece Cakeshop appears to be the all-time leader in relists, with the Court relisting the case on a weekly basis for nearly four months. And it had to have been clear to the Justices that other cases raising the same basic question were rising through the pipeline. So it is surprising that the Court took a vehicle with so many potential obstacles to resolving the question whether the First Amendment requires public accommodations statutes to accommodate religious beliefs.

In the summer of 2012, David Mullins, Charles Craig, and Craig's mother, Deborah Munns, went to the Masterpiece Cakeshop in Lakewood, Colorado. The men were getting married in Massachusetts (Colorado did not then give wedding licenses to same-sex couples)

---

[110] That consideration featured in both *Hurley v Irish-American Gay, Lesbian, and Bisexual Group of Boston*, 515 US 557 (1995), and *Boy Scouts v Dale*, 530 US 640 (2000).

[111] Ralph Mayrell, Michael Kimberly, and John Elwood, *The Statistics of Relists, OT 2016 Edition: Has the Relist Lost Its Mojo? Not Quite*, SCOTUSblog (Sept 27, 2017, 3:37 p.m.), available at https://tinyurl.com/PKJD02. A predecessor case to *Masterpiece Cakeshop*, raising similar issues about the application of antidiscrimination law to refusals to provide services to same-sex weddings, was relisted three times before the Court denied review. See *Elane Photography, LLC v Willock*, No 13-585, https://tinyurl.com/PKJD04 (reflecting the Supreme Court's docket in the case).

and hoped to have a celebration in Colorado when they returned home.[112]

The trio sat down at a small table where photo albums showing the store's wedding cakes were kept.[113] Couples who buy wedding cakes from the shop "may select from one of [its] unique creations that are on display inside the store, or they may request that [the store] design and create something entirely different."[114]

While looking at the pictures, Mullens told Jack Phillips, Masterpiece Cakeshop's owner, that the wedding cake would be for him and Craig.[115] Phillips responded that he would not bake a cake for a same-sex wedding, and the trio left the store without discussing any of the details of the cake they hoped to buy.[116]

Mullens and Craig filed complaints with the Colorado Civil Rights Commission alleging discrimination by Masterpiece and Phillips based on sexual orientation, in violation of the Colorado Anti-Discrimination Act. That act had been amended in 2007 and 2008 to add sexual orientation to the list of protected characteristics.[117] It prohibited covered public accommodations—defined broadly to include any "place of business engaged in any sales to the public and any place offering services . . . to the public"[118]—from refusing a protected individual "the full and equal enjoyment of [its] goods [or] services."[119]

Phillips did not deny that his business was covered by the statute. Nor did he suggest that he could refuse to serve gay people altogether. Indeed, he averred that gay people were "welcome in [his] store to purchase any of my creations, with the exception of a wedding cake for [a] same-sex marriage celebration or reception."[120] He would make

---

[112] *Craig v Masterpiece Cakeshop, Inc.*, 370 P3d 272, 277 (Colo Ct App 2015).

[113] Id at 59.

[114] Id at 161.

[115] Id at 48, 59–60.

[116] Id at 60.

[117] Colorado *could* add gay people to the categories protected by the state's public accommodations statute only because, in *Romer v Evans*, 517 US 620 (1996), the Supreme Court, in Justice Kennedy's first gay rights opinion, had struck down a Colorado constitutional prohibition on providing antidiscrimination protection on the basis of sexual orientation.

[118] Colo Rev Stat § 24-34-601(1).

[119] Colo Rev Stat § 24-34-601(2)(a).

[120] Joint Appendix at 63, *Masterpiece Cakeshop, Ltd. v Colo. Civil Rights Comm'n*, 138 S Ct 1719 (2018) (No 16-111).

"birthday cakes, shower cakes, sell . . . cookies and brownies" to gay people but "just [wouldn't] make cakes for same sex weddings."[121]

That asserted willingness was slightly ambiguous. It was not just "wedding" cakes that the shop refused to supply. Apparently, the shop objected to providing *any* baked good celebrating a gay couple's familial bond: it told a female couple that the shop would not sell them cupcakes once the owner learned that the cupcakes would be served after a "Family Commitment Ceremony" involving the couple and their three children.[122]

Phillips defended his refusal by asserting that "decorating cakes is a form of art and creative expression" and that "to participate in same-sex weddings by using his gifts, time and artistic talent would violate his core beliefs, the instructions of the Bible and be displeasing to God."[123] He argued that "[b]y creating a wedding cake for the couple, I am an *active* participant [in the wedding] and I am associated with the event."[124]

After a hearing, a state administrative law judge ruled against Phillips. The judge rejected both Phillips's claim that applying the Colorado statute to require him to create a cake for a same-sex wedding constituted compelled speech in violation of the First Amendment's Free Speech Clause and his claim that forcing him to bake the case would violate the First Amendment's Free Exercise Clause.

After reviewing the record and discussing Phillips's case at a public meeting, the Colorado Civil Rights Commission adopted the ALJ's initial decision in full.[125] It ordered Phillips to "cease and desist from discriminating against . . . same-sex couples by refusing to sell them wedding cakes or any product [he and the shop] would sell to heterosexual couples."[126] The Colorado Court of Appeals affirmed the commission's order,[127] and the Colorado Supreme Court denied review.[128]

---

[121] Id at 152; see also id at 63.

[122] Id at 113–14. See also *Masterpiece Cakeshop*, 138 S Ct at 1726.

[123] Joint Appendix at 151, *Masterpiece Cakeshop, Ltd. v Colo. Civil Rights Comm'n*, 138 S Ct 1719 (2018) (No 16-111).

[124] Id at 162.

[125] See Pet App at 57a, *Masterpiece Cakeshop, Ltd. v Colo. Civil Rights Comm'n*, 138 S Ct 1719 (2018) (No 16-111).

[126] *Masterpiece Cakeshop*, 138 S Ct at 1726.

[127] *Craig v Masterpiece Cakeshop, Inc.*, 370 P3d 272, 295 (2015).

[128] *Masterpiece Cakeshop, Inc. v Colo. Civil Rights Comm'n*, No 15SC738, 2016 WL 1645027 (Colo, April 25, 2016).

The question presented by Masterpiece Cakeshop's petition for certiorari was "Whether applying Colorado's public accommodations law to compel [Jack] Phillips to create expression that violates his sincerely held religious beliefs about marriage violates the Free Speech or Free Exercise Clauses of the First Amendment."[129] Under existing doctrine, the answer to the free exercise question was straightforward: In *Employment Division v Smith*,[130] the Court had held that the Free Exercise Clause "does not relieve an individual of the obligation to comply with a valid and neutral law of general applicability on the ground that the law proscribes (or prescribes) conduct that his religion prescribes (or proscribes)."[131] The Colorado public accommodations statute was undeniably such a law.[132] Unless the Court was prepared to overrule *Smith*, there was nothing to Phillips's free exercise challenge to the Colorado statute.[133]

As for Phillips's compelled-speech claim, the record was a minefield. First, the question whether baking generally—or baking wedding cakes, specifically—was expressive activity was by no means settled, and before the Court could answer the question presented it would have to answer this subsidiary question. Unlike, for example, the photographer in *Elane Photography, LLC v Willock*,[134] who refused

---

[129] Pet for Cert i, *Masterpiece Cakeshop, Ltd. v Colo. Civil Rights Comm'n*, 138 S Ct 1719 (2018) (No 16-111).

[130] 494 US 872 (1990).

[131] Id at 879. For a discussion of *Smith*'s application to cases involving religious objectors to same-sex marriage, see Stone, *Sex and the Constitution* at 527–28 (cited in note 27).

[132] To avoid trenching on free exercise, the public accommodations statute expressly excluded "a church, synagogue, mosque, or other place that is principally used for religious purposes." Colo Rev Stat § 24-34-601(1).

[133] With respect to *federal* government activity, the Religious Freedom Restoration Act, 42 USC § 2000bb et seq, provides as a statutory matter that "Government shall not substantially burden a person's exercise of religion even if the burden results from a rule of general applicability." Id § 2000bb-1(a). A person so burdened is entitled to an exemption from any statute or rule unless the government "demonstrates that application of the burden to the person (1) is in furtherance of a compelling governmental interest; and (2) is the least restrictive means of furthering that compelling governmental interest." Id § 2000bb-1(b).

Interestingly, although twenty-one states have adopted their own state-law analogs, there is little overlap between that group of states and the twenty-two states that prohibit private discrimination on the basis of sexual orientation: only four of these states provide an exemption. Stone, *Sex and the Constitution* at 528–29 (cited in note 27).

For general discussion of the issue of how RFRAs apply to questions of conscience, see Douglas NeJaime and Reva B. Siegel, *Conscience Wars: Complicity-Based Conscience Claims in Religion and Politics*, 124 Yale L J 2516, 2558–65 (2015); Steve Sanders, *RFRAs and Reasonableness*, 91 Ind L J 243 (2016).

[134] 572 US 1046 (2014) (denying review).

to shoot wedding pictures for gay couples, Phillips could not rely on precedent establishing that baking constituted First Amendment–protected expressive conduct.[135]

And the Court could hardly assume that baking *is* an expressive activity. Maybe nothing says loving like something from the oven, but just as "[c]lean and wholesome bread does not depend upon whether the baker works but ten hours per day or only sixty hours a week,"[136] it is unclear whether the meaning a cake expresses depends on the views of its baker.

Second, Phillips later admitted that selling already-created cakes did not involve protected expressive activity, whatever the content of the cake.[137] But if this is so—and there are strong reasons to agree, else the actual *selling* of any item becomes an expressive act—then it is unclear whether the case actually raised the question presented. The record did not show whether Phillips was being asked to *design* a cake for Mullen and Craig or simply to take an existing design he had already created and produce a replica. He had refused to bake them a cake before any discussion of what they were looking for. If he were simply being asked to replicate an existing design, then the expression inherent in the creation had already occurred, and no new expression was being demanded. Moreover, Phillips's response to the lesbian couple seeking cupcakes suggests that he viewed his expression as consisting in the baking of *any* goods for a wedding involving a gay couple, regardless of the baked goods' appearance. If that were so, then his conception of expression inhered not in wedding cakes but in the creation of any item that could be used for a purpose to which the seller objected. That position would be unpalatable to the Court because it would threaten to exempt from antidiscrimination law virtually any business whose goods could be used for a purpose with which the business disagreed.

At oral argument, the perils of Phillips's position became clear. His counsel tried to draw lines between bakers and chefs, between bakers

---

[135] Compare *Ashcroft v Free Speech Coal.*, 535 US 234, 246 (2002) (referring to "the visual depiction" in a photograph as "an idea" protected for its "serious literary, artistic, political, or scientific value"); *Kaplan v California*, 413 US 115, 119 (1973) (stating that "[t]he Court has applied . . . First Amendment standards . . . to photographs"), with Tr of Oral Arg 14 (Sotomayor, J, asking "when have we ever given [First Amendment] protection to a food?").

[136] *Lochner v New York*, 198 US 45, 57 (1905).

[137] Tr of Oral Arg 5, 10, *Masterpiece Cakeshop, Ltd. v Colo. Civil Rights Comm'n*, 138 S Ct 1719 (2018) (No 16-111).

and makeup artists or tailors, and between bakers and architects.[138] But none of the lines made any real sense. As Justice Kennedy's opinion for the Court was later to explain, "any decision in favor of the baker would have to be sufficiently constrained, lest all purveyors of goods and services who object to gay marriages for moral and religious reasons in effect be allowed to put up signs saying 'no goods or services will be sold if they will be used for gay marriages,' something that would impose a serious stigma on gay persons."[139] Indeed, the problem was actually more acute than that: it is unclear why, once baking is treated as expressive activity, the end use of the baked good is any restriction on the baker's ability to express himself. Why would anniversary cakes be treated differently from wedding cakes? Or could a baker who disapproves of women with children working outside the home refuse to bake any cakes for such women on the grounds that it conveys his approval of their life choices? And what about sellers of other goods who don't want their creations used by people whose way of life they find objectionable? Could an upholster simply refuse to recover chairs for African Americans?

Perhaps recognizing that the Court's decisions upholding the constitutionality of the Civil Rights Act of 1964 had decisively rejected the idea that a business owner could express his views on white supremacy, racial mixing, or the dignity of African Americans by denying them service on equal terms, Phillips and the Solicitor General tried to offer the Court a safety valve with respect to race. The Court had long held that "eradicating racial discrimination" was a "compelling" governmental interest that might justify overriding a private actor's otherwise First Amendment–protected religiously based viewpoint.[140] Thus, they suggested that businesses might not be entitled to accommodation of their objections if the state law required nondiscrimination on account of race.[141] But the Solicitor General seemed unwilling to override expression with respect to any other category of protected individuals.[142]

---

[138] See id at 14, 17–18.

[139] *Masterpiece Cakeshop*, 138 S Ct at 1728–29.

[140] *Bob Jones Univ. v United States*, 461 US 574, 604 (1983).

[141] See Tr of Oral Arg 22–23, 32, *Masterpiece Cakeshop, Ltd. v Colo. Civil Rights Comm'n*, 138 S Ct 1719 (2018) (No 16-111).

[142] See id at 32–33.

A hint of how the Court might extricate itself from the morass came later in the oral argument when Justice Kennedy asked Colorado's lawyer to "disavow" a statement made by one of the commissioners during the open meeting where Phillips's request to stay the remedial order had been addressed. Referring to the discussion at the previous meeting, the commissioner "reiterated" that

> Freedom of religion and religion has been used to justify all kinds of discrimination throughout history, whether it be slavery, whether it be the holocaust, whether it be—I mean, we—we can list hundreds of situations where freedom of religion has been used to justify discrimination. And to me it is one of the most despicable pieces of rhetoric that people can use to—to use their religion to hurt others.[143]

Justice Kennedy asked whether this comment might reflect sufficient "hostility" to religion to require rejection of the commission's decision.[144] The Chief Justice and Justices Gorsuch and Alito quickly jumped onto the point as well.

And that was how the case ultimately was decided. After a fair amount of hand-wringing over how the case presented "difficult questions as to the proper reconciliation" of the state's authority "to protect the rights and dignity of gay persons" and the "right of all persons" under the First Amendment,[145] Justice Kennedy's opinion for the Court announced that the problem with the case was that Phillips had not received "the neutral and respectful consideration of his claims" to which he was entitled.[146] The commission's treatment of his case revealed "some elements of a clear and impermissible hostility toward the sincere religious beliefs that motivated his objection."[147] Justice Kennedy declared that "[t]o describe a man's faith as 'one of the most despicable pieces of rhetoric that people can use' is to disparage his religion in at least two distinct ways: by describing it as despicable, and also by characterizing it as merely rhetorical—something insubstantial and even insincere."[148] And he went on to criticize the other actors in the Colorado system, from the fellow

---

[143] *Masterpiece Cakeshop*, 138 S Ct at 1729.

[144] See Tr of Oral Arg 53, *Masterpiece Cakeshop, Ltd. v Colo. Civil Rights Comm'n*, 138 S Ct 1719 (2018) (No 16-111).

[145] *Masterpiece Cakeshop*, 138 S Ct at 1723.

[146] Id at 1729.

[147] Id.

[148] Id.

commissioners to the Colorado Court of Appeals, for not condemning the commissioner's remark.

Justice Kennedy found further support for the conclusion that "that the Commission's consideration of Phillips' case was neither tolerant nor respectful of Phillips' religious beliefs"[149] in what he claimed was the commission's very different treatment of claims against four other bakers. Those bakers had each refused to bake cakes "with images that conveyed disapproval of same-sex marriage, along with religious text."[150] According to Justice Kennedy, the commission found that the bakers had acted lawfully because "the requested cake[s] included 'wording and images [the baker] deemed derogatory'; 'language and images [the baker] deemed hateful'; or displayed a message the baker 'deemed as discriminatory.'"[151] And the Colorado Court of Appeals, he continued, distinguished these cases from Phillips's by characterizing them as involving refusals to deal "'because of the offensive nature of the requested message,'" rather than because of the customer's religion.[152] Far from reassuring Justice Kennedy that Phillips had been treated fairly, "[t]he Colorado court's attempt to account for the difference in treatment elevates one view of what is offensive over another and itself sends a signal of official disapproval of Phillips' religious beliefs."[153]

But as Justice Kagan pointed out in her concurrence, the cases really were quite different: the other four bakers would have refused to make the cakes that William Jack (the putative buyer) requested for *anyone* regardless of that person's religion.[154] Their position was thus much more similar to Jack Phillips's refusal to sell Halloween-themed baked goods (which he simply would not make at all because of his religious beliefs[155]) than it was to his refusal to sell a cake to Mullen and Craig that he would have sold to any straight couple getting married. And Justice Kennedy had simply misstated the Col-

---

[149] Id at 1731.

[150] Id at 1730.

[151] Id at 1731 (internal citations omitted).

[152] Id (quoting *Craig v Masterpiece Cakeshop, Inc.*, 370 P3d 272, 282 n 8 (Colo Ct App 2015)).

[153] Id.

[154] Id at 1733 (Kagan, J, concurring).

[155] See Joint App at 165, *Masterpiece Cakeshop, Ltd. v Colo. Civil Rights Comm'n*, 138 S Ct 1719 (2018) (No 16-111).

orado Court of Appeals position. It was not saying that *it* viewed the proposed cake messages as offensive; it was explaining that the *bakers* had viewed them as offensive and had denied service because they disapproved of the message and not because of William Jack's religion.

Justice Kennedy's last words on gay rights—one of the defining issues of his time as a Justice—were a plea that courts in the future "recognize that these disputes must be resolved with tolerance, without undue disrespect to sincere religious beliefs, and without subjecting gay persons to indignities when they seek goods and services in an open market."[156] And his last words on the Court altogether came later in June in a short separate concurrence in *Trump v Hawaii*,[157] where his lone citation was to his debut gay rights–related decision, *Romer v Evans*.[158] His final sentence as a Justice insisted that "[a]n anxious world must know that our Government remains committed always to the liberties the Constitution seeks to preserve and protect, so that freedom extends outward, and lasts."[159] But in the end, as with the competing claims for racial equality and freedom to exclude that faced the Warren and Burger Courts, one kind of accommodation will have to give way to the other. And whether the freedom and equality of gay people in America continues to extend outward and endure in the Second Roberts Court remains an open question.

III. Gay Rights in the Second Roberts Court

Two days before Justice Kennedy announced his retirement, the Court turned away an opportunity to answer the questions left open by its decision in *Masterpiece Cakeshop*—this time, in the context of a florist who refused to sell her work "crafted in 'petal, leaf, and loam'" to a couple for their same-sex wedding.[160] And although nothing in the petition in *Arlene's Flowers, Inc. v Washington* suggested a vehicle problem, the Court declined to hear the case on the merits, instead remanding it "for further consideration in light of *Masterpiece*

---

[156] *Masterpiece Cakeshop*, 138 S Ct at 1732.

[157] *Trump v Hawaii*, 138 S Ct 2392, 2423 (2018).

[158] Id at 2423 (Kennedy, J, concurring) (citing *Romer v Evans*, 517 US 620, 632 (1996).

[159] Id at 2424.

[160] *State v Arlene's Flowers, Inc.*, 389 P3d 543, 557 (Wash 2017).

Cakeshop."[161] What light *Masterpiece Cakeshop* could shed on a case not involving a claim of a biased decision maker was left unsaid.

The newly constituted Second Roberts Court will surely have myriad opportunities to address the question of how to reconcile public accommodations statutes and claims for religious accommodation; already, another baker's petition is before the Court.[162] And perhaps at least some of the conservative members of the Court are eager to prune the Court's protections of gay people.[163] But if they do so in the context of state nondiscrimination laws, they will of necessity abandon the claim they have advanced to this point: that the political process, rather than the courts, is the appropriate forum to decide these contested issues. Moreover, what *Masterpiece Cakeshop* showed the Justices, if they hadn't already figured it out, is that drawing constitutional lines reconciling public accommodation laws and religious accommodation claims is a tricky business.

First, even if sympathy for religious belief motivates the Justices, they cannot limit any protection of objectors to those motivated by faith unless the Court revisits *Employment Division v Smith*.[164] And if it were to do so, it would face a raft of problems. To begin, it would have no basis for limiting that exemption to objections involving marriage ceremonies or objections involving sexual orientation. The jurisdictions that prohibit discrimination on the basis of sexual orientation with respect to public accommodations generally extend that prohibition to employment and public services as well. So if a for-profit bakery is entitled to respect for its religious objection to same-sex marriage ceremonies,[165] presumably it is also entitled to fire gay people from jobs as dishwashers or cashiers if the owner objects to

---

[161] *Arlene's Flowers, Inc. v Washington*, 138 S Ct 2671, 2672 (2018) (per curiam).

[162] See Pet for Cert i, *Klein v Oregon Bureau of Labor & Indust.* (No 18-547, filed Oct 19, 2018) (presenting the question "Whether Oregon violated the Free Speech and Free Exercise Clauses of the First Amendment by compelling the Kleins to design and create a custom wedding cake to celebrate a same-sex wedding ritual, in violation of their sincerely held religious beliefs.").

[163] See *Pavan v Smith*, 137 S Ct 2075, 2079 (2017) (Gorsuch, J, joined by Thomas and Alito, JJ, dissenting) (suggesting that *Obergefell* does not require that same-sex couples have the same right as opposite-sex couples to have a biological mother's spouse listed on a child's birth certificate when the child is conceived with donor sperm).

[164] 494 US 872 (1990).

[165] The Court has already held, in the context of statutory claims against the federal government under the Religious Freedom Restoration Act, that for-profit businesses can engage in the exercise of religion. *Burwell v Hobby Lobby Stores, Inc.*, 134 S Ct 2751, 2769 (2014).

working with people he views as sinners. Moreover, cases are now working their way through the system where religious entities are seeking access to public programs and exemptions from the nondiscrimination provisions that apply to all other participants.[166]

Nor could the Court carve out only religious objections involving sexual orientation. Many other characteristics that are protected under state or local nondiscrimination provisions—for example, disability or age or familial status—do not receive heightened scrutiny under federal constitutional law. And Justice Kennedy's gay rights decisions notoriously avoided ever articulating the level of scrutiny to be applied to sexual orientation. So if nondiscrimination provisions can override religious objections only in service of a judicially recognized compelling governmental interest,[167] then businesses would presumably be free to refuse customers or discharge workers who are single parents in light of a religious objection to nonmarital sex or who are disabled if the business owner views the disability as God's judgment of wickedness.[168]

Resolving the issue as a matter of free expression, rather than freedom of religion, has all the same problems and then some because the Court must first articulate a line between expressive and non-expressive work. From a worker's perspective, nearly every job *can* have an expressive dimension. John McPhee ends a famous portrait of a reclusive chef with this description: "His tastes are very fresh and bouncy. He has honor, idealism, a lack of guile. . . . He has character. He has integrity. He applies all these to this manual task. His hands follow what he is."[169] But the Court has never held that an actor's subjective belief is enough to make his actions expressive. In *Rumsfeld v Forum for Acad. & Institutional Rights, Inc. (FAIR)*, for example, the Court unanimously rejected the claim of an association of law schools and faculty members that law schools' enforcement of their nondis-

---

[166] For example, in *Fulton v City of Philadelphia*, 320 F Supp 3d 661 (ED Pa 2018), a federal district court denied a preliminary injunction to two religiously affiliated foster care agencies that were denied contracts because they refused to consider married same-sex couples who applied to become foster parents on the grounds that they had a religious objection to placing children with such couples.

[167] See *Sherbert v Verner*, 374 US 398, 402–3 (1963) (using a compelling-interest test).

[168] See Pauline A. Otieno, *Biblical and Theological Perspectives on Disability: Implications on the Rights of Persons with Disability in Kenya*, 29 Disabilities Stud Q No 4 (2009) (describing biblical views of disability), available at https://tinyurl.com/PDJD102.

[169] John McPhee, *Brigade de Cuisine*, New Yorker, Feb 19, 1979, at 43, 99.

crimination policies with respect to on-campus recruiting was "inherently expressive" conduct.[170] So it is not clear why service businesses' refusals to provide goods to potential customers because of disagreement with the customers' activities is expressive.

To avoid the difficulties in drawing defensible lines, the Justices who wish to create some exemption for religious objectors may be tempted to reprise the *Masterpiece Cakeshop* strategy of finding some nugget in the record that allows them to condemn the fairness of the process by which the nondiscrimination provision was applied, rather than the provision itself. But this may have the ironic consequence that the same Justices who condemned the *Obergefell* majority for tarring the other side as bigots, rather than people of good faith, will now be making precisely those kinds of charges—this time, against state and local officials enforcing nondiscrimination laws.

The Chief Justice ended his dissent in *Obergefell* by declaring that those Americans who favored marriage equality should "by all means celebrate [the] decision," but they should not "celebrate the Constitution. It had nothing to do with it."[171] So it would be a further irony for the Court to impose a set of constitutional constraints on the political process's vindication of those interests.

At least in the near future, then, it seems entirely possible that gains in equality for gay people may come not so much from constitutional claims, but rather from statutory protections. In particular, it will be interesting to see how the professed textualists on the Supreme Court handle an issue looming on the horizon: whether the prohibition in Title VII of the Civil Rights Act of 1964—the same omnibus statute that governed *Newman v Piggie Park*—that prohibits discrimination in employment "because of . . . sex"[172] covers discrimination against gay people. Two *en banc* courts of appeals have recently held that it does, basing their analyses on a combination of straight textualism with an analog to the theory of associational discrimination that informed the Supreme Court's decision in *Loving v Virginia*.[173] Thus, the legal struggle for racial justice may continue to inform the struggle for gay rights even in the second Roberts Court.

---

[170] 547 US 47, 66 (2006).

[171] *Obergefell*, 135 S Ct at 2626 (Roberts, CJ, dissenting).

[172] 42 USC § 2000e-2.

[173] *Zarda v Altitude Express, Inc.*, 883 F3d 100 (2d Cir 2018) (en banc); *Hively v Ivy Tech Community College*, 853 F3d 339 (7th Cir 2017) (en banc).

RANDALL KENNEDY

RECONSIDERING PALMER v THOMPSON

In *Palmer v Thompson*[1] the Supreme Court upheld the constitutionality of a decision by the city of Jackson, Mississippi, to close all public swimming pools. The city maintained that it would be unable to operate racially desegregated pools safely at acceptable expense after a judgment declaring segregated recreational facilities to be unconstitutional.[2] *Palmer* is a judicial injustice. In *Palmer*, as in more notorious delinquencies such as *Plessy v Ferguson*[3] and *Korematsu v United States*,[4]

Randall Kennedy is the Michael R. Klein Professor at Harvard Law School.

Author's note: I thank Katie R. Eyer, Justin Driver, Richard Fallon, Sanford Levinson, Michael Meltsner, Frank Michelman, and Geoffrey Stone for comments on an earlier draft. I am pleased to acknowledge as well the research and editorial assistance of Leilia Bijan, Harvard Law School, JD 2019.

[1] 403 US 217 (1971), aff'g 419 F2d 1222 (5th Cir 1969), aff'g 391 F2d 324 (5th Cir 1967).

[2] Id at 219. *Palmer* has provoked considerable commentary. Particularly illuminating is Katie R. Eyer, *Ideological Drift and the Forgotten History of Intent*, 51 Harv CR-CL L Rev 1 (2016); Ian Haney-López, *Intentional Blindness*, 87 NYU L Rev 1779 (2012); Deborah L. Brake, *When Equality Leaves Everyone Worse Off: The Problem in Leveling Down in Equality Law*, 46 Wm & Mary L Rev 513 (2004); Michael Klarman, *An Interpretative History of Modern Equal Protection*, 90 Mich L Rev 213 (1991); *Closing of Municipal Swimming Pools After a Desegregation Order*, 85 Harv L Rev 86 (1971); Paul Brest, *Palmer v Thompson: An Approach to the Problem of Unconstitutional Legislative Motive*, 1971 Supreme Court Review 95; John Hart Ely, *Legislative and Administrative Motivation in Constitutional Law*, 79 Yale L J 1205 (1970). See also Thomas W. Wright, *Constitutional Law—State Action—Closing Rather Than Desegregating Recreational Facilities*, 13 Wm & Mary L Rev 524 (1971); Robert H. McKnight Jr., *Constitutional Law—Civil Rights—Closing Municipal Swimming Pools in Response to Desegregation Order Does Not Violate Negro Plaintiffs' Thirteenth or Fourteenth Amendment Rights*, 16 Wayne L Rev 1434 (1970); Comment, *Closing Public Pools to Avoid Desegregation: Treading Water*, 58 Georgetown L J 1220 (1970).

[3] 163 US 537 (1896).

[4] 323 US 214 (1944).

---

the Supreme Court and tribunals below showed themselves to be unreliable sentinels when it came to recognizing racist abuses of power. The Court later expressly repudiated *Plessy*[5] and *Korematsu*.[6] It has also jettisoned parts of *Palmer*'s rationale.[7] But the Court has never rejected *Palmer*'s holding, which remains "good law," potentially influencing what counts as valid governmental action.[8]

The *Palmer* Supreme Court affirmed the Fifth Circuit en banc which affirmed a Fifth Circuit panel which affirmed a district court—litigations that stretched across eight long, eventful years from 1963 to 1971. These court rulings reveal much about the racial facts of life in the deep South and the nation during the Second Reconstruction. They discredit courts that have been widely lauded for vindicating the rights of civil rights dissidents, for an effort to uproot segregation in disguise was stymied decisively with assistance from the federal judiciary. The *Palmer* rulings were not only erroneous but profoundly misguided in ways that should prompt negative reassessments of those responsible, including such esteemed figures as Judge Richard Taylor Rives and Justice Hugo L. Black.

Palmer involved the public swimming pool, a facility that aroused particularly ferocious resistance to desegregation. Insistence that there be no desegregation at the pool amounted to a public declaration that, in the eyes of officials, it would be degrading to whites to have to share a bathing and swimming facility with blacks. In addition to that stigmatic harm, discrimination at the pool prompted some youngsters to

---

[5] *Gayle v Browder*, 352 US 903 (1956).

[6] *Trump v Hawaii*, 138 S Ct 2392 (2018).

[7] See text at note 122.

[8] The Department of Justice affirmatively cited *Palmer v Thompson* in its brief to the United States Court of Appeals for the Fourth Circuit in *International Refugee Assistance Project v Trump*, one of the cases stemming from President Donald J. Trump's ban on the entry of travelers from certain countries into the United States. See *International Refugee Assistance Project (IRAP) v Trump*, 857 F3d 554 (4th Cir 2017), vac'd, *Trump v IRAP*, 138 S Ct 353 (2017). The Department of Justice similarly cited *Palmer* in its brief in another of the travel ban cases. See Defendant's Memorandum in Opposition to Plaintiffs' Motion for Temporary Restraining Order, *Hawaii v Trump*, No 17-00050 (D Hawaii 2017). See also *Hawaii v Trump*, 859 F3d 741 (9th Cir 2017), vac'd *Trump v Hawaii*, 138 S Ct 2392. The citation to *Palmer* generated a few sharp rebukes. "[B]y apparently resuscitating *Palmer*," John-Paul Schnapper-Casteras wrote, "the Trump Administration relies upon an odious and obsolete decision." John-Paul Schnapper-Casteras, *The Problem with Palmer* (Take Care Blog, May 7, 2017), archived at https://perma.cc/9N9Z-EYFD. The influence of such negative commentary is unclear, but, in any event, when the travel ban case was eventually heard by the Supreme Court, the Solicitor General's brief on behalf of the United States contained no reference to *Palmer*. See Brief for the Petitioners, *Trump v Hawaii*, No 17-965 (US filed Feb 21, 2018). See also *Trump v Hawaii*, 138 S Ct 2392.

frequent unsupervised locales at which they faced higher risks of danger, leading to tragic injuries or even death.[9]

I. CHALLENGING, DEFENDING, AND DENYING RACIAL DISCRIMINATION IN JACKSON, MISSISSIPPI

Hazel Palmer worked as a maid and became an equal rights dissident out of solidarity with her son who was jailed on account of his activities as a Freedom Rider.[10] Palmer and fellow petitioners claimed that Jackson authorities violated the Equal Protection Clause of the Fourteenth Amendment by closing all of the city's swimming pools in 1963.[11] Prior to the closure, the city operated five pools—four reserved

---

[9] In a sworn affidavit, one of Hazel Palmer's co-plaintiffs, Carolyn Stevens, noted that because of racial discrimination Negro children are forced to swim "in dangerous circumstances." She cited two children who had "recently drowned while swimming in the Pearl River because public bathing facilities and appropriate supervision was not available to them." Affidavit of Carolyn Stevens at 71, Appendix B, Petition for Writ of Certiorari, *Palmer v Thompson*, No 1289 (US filed March 7, 1970). Awareness of deaths by drowning accompanied protests in other locales against racial segregation in pools. See Jeff Wiltse, *Contested Waters: A Social History of Swimming Pools in America* 156 (2007) (discussing three drowning deaths in the Baltimore area in 1953).

Some observers suggest that historical racial discrimination at pools is related to disparities today between whites and blacks in terms of enjoyment of aquatic sports and susceptibility to drowning. See Niraj Chokshi, *Racism at American Pools Isn't New: A Look at a Long History*, NY Times (Aug 1, 2018); Ebony Rosemond, *This Stereotype Is Killing Black Children*, Wash Post (Feb 10, 2017). See also Samuel L. Myers, Ana M. Cuesta, and Yufeng Lai, *Competitive Swimming and Racial Disparities in Drowning*, 44 Rev Black Polit Econ 77 (2017); Julie Gilchrist and Erin Parker, *Racial/Ethnic Disparities in Fatal Unintentional Drowning Among Persons Aged <29 Years—United States, 1999–2010*, Centers for Disease Control and Prevention, Morbidity and Mortality Report (May 16, 2014).

[10] Palmer also contributed significantly to the efforts of the Mississippi Freedom Democratic Party, which sought to give voice to disenfranchised black Mississippians. A remarkable oral interview with Ms. Palmer can be heard at KZSU, *Oral History Interview with Hazel Palmer* (Stanford Libraries 1965), online at https://purl.stanford.edu/ws245qj9293 (Perma archive unavailable). See generally Mississippi Civil Rights Project, *Palmer, Hazel*, archived at https://perma.cc/H7LZ-5STX. See also Charles M. Payne, *I've Got the Light of Freedom: The Organizing Tradition and the Mississippi Freedom Struggle* 317 (California, 1995); John Dittmer, *Local People: The Struggle for Civil Rights in Mississippi* 283 (Illinois, 1995).

Freedom Riders used facilities involved in interstate transportation in such a way as to test compliance with court orders. Black Freedom Riders, for instance, would enter waiting rooms that local laws reserved for whites. Although such barriers were illegal, white supremacists tried to enforce obedience to them anyway. Alpha Zara Palmer, Hazel Palmer's son, was arrested on July 6, 1961, for failing to obey racial restrictions at the Illinois Central Rail Road Terminal in Jackson. See Raymond Arsenault, *Freedom Riders: 1961 and the Struggle for Racial Justice* 562 (Oxford, 2006).

[11] *Palmer*, 403 US at 218–19. The plaintiffs and their amici also claimed that the pool closures violated the Thirteenth Amendment and statutes enforcing its prohibition on slavery and the badges and incidents of slavery. Id at 218–19, 226–27. Although there is substantial merit to that claim, this article limits its analysis to the equal protection issue that emerged in the litigation.

for whites and one reserved for blacks.[12] Racial segregation at the municipal pools was a fragment of a larger structure of racial hierarchy characterized by whites' monopolization of authority and deployment of power to subordinate people of color, especially blacks.[13] In 1961, as part of a multipronged revolt, black plaintiffs challenged racial segregation at Jackson's recreational facilities.[14] They won a declaratory judgment from Judge Sidney Mize, even as he announced that, in his view, no genuine problem existed.

According to Judge Mize, Jackson was a "clean, progressive city . . . noted for its low crime rate and lack of racial friction except for the period in 1961 when the self-styled Freedom Riders made their visits."[15] Offering his explanation for the striking racial separation that constituted a conspicuous feature of the Jackson social landscape, Judge Mize maintained that

> [a]s the city rebuilt from the ashes of the Civil War, its white citizens occupied one area, and its colored citizens chose to live together in another. . . . [M]embers of each race have customarily used the recreational facilities located in close proximity to their homes. The defendants believe that the welfare of both races will best be served if this custom is continued.[16]

Averring that the defendants "do not claim the right to require or enforce separation of the races in any public facility," Judge Mize also deemed it a "fact" that "voluntary separation of the races . . . has op-

---

[12] In 1960, Jackson was home to 150,000 whites and 50,000 blacks. *Clark v Thompson*, 206 F Supp 539, 541 (S D Miss 1962), aff'd 313 F2d 637 (5th Cir 1963), cert denied 376 US 951 (1963). For an excellent article on racial segregation in recreational facilities and efforts to remedy it, see Robert M. McKay, *Segregation and Public Recreation*, 40 Va L Rev 697 (1954).

[13] See Dittmer, *Local People* (cited in note 10); James W. Silver, *Mississippi: The Closed Society* (Mississippi, 1964); Pauli Murray, *States' Laws on Race and Color* (Georgia, 1997).

[14] At points in his opinion, Judge Mize suggested that the plaintiffs were entitled to no relief:

> None of the plaintiffs has been arrested or threatened with arrest under any statute or alleged discriminatory practice attacked in this case. . . . Although each of the plaintiffs has been a resident of Jackson for more than 25 years, there is no evidence that they have been denied the right to use any public recreational facility in that city.

Clark v Thompson, 206 F Supp at 542. Ultimately, however, he declared: "The three plaintiffs are entitled to an adjudication of their personal claims of right to unsegregated use of public recreational facilities." In a prior proceeding, the district court denied the plaintiffs' petition for a three-judge court. See *Clark v Thompson*, 204 F Supp 30 (S D Miss 1962).

[15] Id at 541.

[16] Id.

erated smoothly and apparently to the complete satisfaction of all concerned for many years."[17] Judge Mize recognized that, prior to the lawsuit, there had been some manifestation of dissatisfaction with racial custom in Jackson. He noted the arrest of "two colored girls" detained after refusing a police officer's order to leave a "white" library and the arrest of "a colored boy and girl" in a "white" park.[18] But Judge Mize was unwilling to see the dissidents' actions as bona fide efforts to use public facilities in accordance with federal constitutional standards. Rather he saw them as "deliberate attempt[s] to create racial friction"—"isolated publicity stunts" that did not "represent the will or desire of the . . . Negro citizens of Jackson."[19] Lauding the city officials as "outstanding, high class gentlemen," Judge Mize rejected the plaintiffs' request for injunctive relief, maintaining that the defendants "know now what the law is and what their obligations are."[20]

In May 1962, nine days after Judge Mize's declaratory judgment, the *Jackson Daily News* quoted Mayor Allen C. Thompson as announcing: "We will do all right this year at the swimming pools . . . but if these agitators keep up their pressure, we would have five colored swimming pools because we are not going to have any intermingling."[21] The *Daily News* also reported Mayor Thompson as saying that the city had authority to sell the pools or to close them if they could not be sold. A year later, noting that the city's recreational facilities remained segregated, the *Daily News* reported Mayor Thompson declaring that "neither agitators nor President Kennedy will change the determination of Jackson to retain segregation."[22]

After the Fifth Circuit Court of Appeals affirmed Judge Mize's declaratory judgment, bringing the *Clark* litigation to an end, Jackson

---

[17] Id.

[18] Id.

[19] Id.

[20] Id at 542. According to Judge Mize, "[T]he time now has arrived when the judiciary should not issue injunctions perfunctorily, but should place trust in men of high character that they will obey the mandate of the Court without an injunction hanging over their heads." Id. The statement that the defendants "know now what the law is" seems to be in tension with Judge Mize's declaration elsewhere that the plaintiffs had previously been deprived of no federal constitutional right by the authorities. Although the plaintiffs appealed the district court's denial of class action status, the Fifth Circuit Court of Appeals affirmed. *Clark v Thompson*, 313 F2d 637 (5th Cir 1963). The Supreme Court denied certiorari. *Clark v Thompson*, 376 US 951 (1963).

[21] *Palmer*, 403 US at 250, quoting a report in the *Jackson Daily News*.

[22] Id, quoting the *Jackson Daily News*.

stopped enforcing racial segregation in its auditoriums, zoos, golf courses, and most aspects of its other recreational facilities. Jackson, however, decided to close or divest itself of all municipal swimming pools.[23]

After petitioning to have the pools reopened, albeit on a desegregated basis, Palmer and other black residents filed a new lawsuit. Justifying the city's decision to close its pools, Mayor Thompson declared that desegregated pools could not be operated safely at acceptable expense.[24] United States District Court Judge William Harold Cox credited the city's explanation and dismissed the suit.[25] A panel

---

[23] The city closed all of the pools that it owned. The city surrendered its lease on a pool that a branch of the Young Men's Christian Association (YMCA) proceeded to operate exclusively for white swimmers. There was no finding and there appeared to be no substantial evidence indicating that the city involved itself in the YMCA's discrimination. Another pool once owned by the city was, at the time of oral argument at the Supreme Court, owned and operated by Jackson State College, a historically black institution. *Palmer*, 403 US at 221, 222 n 8, 223.

[24] Mayor Thompson stated:

> Realizing that the personal safety of all of the citizens of the City and the maintenance of law and order would prohibit the operation of swimming pools on an integrated basis, and realizing that the said pools could not be operated economically on an integrated basis, the City made the decision . . . to close all pools owned and operated by the City to members of both races. The City thereby decided not to offer that type of recreational facility to any of its citizens, and it has not done so and does not intend to reopen any of said pools.

Palmer v Thompson, 419 F2d at 1225.

[25] Judge Cox's key factual determinations are as follows:

> The City of Jackson closed all swimming pools owned and operated by it in 1963, following the entry of a declaratory judgement [that all persons were entitled to use public facilities free of racial discrimination, including racial segregation]. No municipal swimming facilities have been opened to any citizen of either race since said time, and the City Council does not intend to reopen or operate any of these swimming facilities on an integrated basis. The personal safety of the citizens of the City and the maintenance of law and order would be endangered by the operation of public swimming pools on an integrated basis. The pools could not be economically operated in that manner.

Palmer v Thompson, 391 F2d 324, 325.

Judge Cox's key legal determinations provided the following:

> The plaintiffs have no constitutional right to require the city of Jackson to maintain or operate specific facilities such as swimming pools, benches in parks, or public restrooms in any particular building. And public facility furnished by the city would have to be available to all citizens regardless of race. As to whether any particular facility will be furnished, the city officials exercise judgment on a matter committed to their wisdom which is not subject to review by any Court in the absence if violation of constitutional rights. . . . No person has a constitutional right to swim in a

of the Fifth Circuit Court of Appeals affirmed unanimously in an opinion written by Judge Richard Taylor Rives.[26] The Fifth Circuit, en banc, affirmed the panel by a seven-to-six vote, with Judge Rives writing for the majority and Judge John Minor Wisdom writing the dissent.[27]

Judge Rives concluded, echoing Judge Cox, that Jackson closed the pools for legitimate reasons of expense and safety. The city, he wrote, "was making the transition in the operation of its recreational facilities from a segregated to an integrated basis" and "had considerable discretion as to how that transition could best be accomplished."[28] The municipality's latitude was even broader, Judge Rives asserted, in that the case involved an unessential public facility.[29] Noting that swimming pools need not be provided at all, Judge Rives stated that the city "meets the test of the equal protection clause when it decides not to offer that type of recreational facility to any of its citizens on the ground that to do so would result in an unsafe and uneconomical operation."[30] He believed that the "[m]otive behind a municipal or legislative action may be examined where the action potentially interferes with . . . constitutionally protected rights."[31] He concluded, however, that upon examination the city's motive was legitimate. The plaintiffs charged that the motive was to avoid desegregated swimming by virtually any means possible, even if that meant closing public swimming pools for everyone. By contrast, Judge Rives and

---

public pool. . . . Where a public facility is closed to members if all races, any issue as to discrimination becomes moot.

Id at 325–26.

[26] The other members of the panel were judges James P. Coleman and John Cooper Godbold.

At around the same time that Judge Rives wrote *Palmer*, Judge Rives also wrote for the majority on a Fifth Circuit panel that faced the same closure issue in a case from Tallahassee, Florida. Judge Wisdom sought to have the case heard en banc alongside *Palmer*. When Tallahassee authorities relented, however, and opened pools on a desegregated basis, the Fifth Circuit dismissed the case as moot. See *Steele v Taft*, 415 F2d 1005 (5th Cir 1969); Joel William Friedman, *Champion of Civil Rights: Judge John Minor Wisdom* 232–33 (Louisiana State, 2009).

[27] *Palmer*, 419 F2d at 1222. Joining Judge Rives in the majority were judges Walter Pettus Gewin, Griffin B. Bell, Claud Feemster Clayton, James P. Coleman, Robert Andrew Ainsworth Jr., David William Dyer, and John Cooper Godbold. After casting his vote, Judge Clayton died.

[28] Id at 1226.

[29] Id.

[30] Id.

[31] Id at 1228.

the Fifth Circuit majority believed that the city's motive was a legitimate one of ensuring "the preservation of order and maintenance of economy."[32]

Judge Rives also emphasized that city authorities closed the pools to everyone, whites and blacks alike. It would be unacceptable, Judge Rives stated, for the city to act in a way that affixed a badge implying racial inequality. He insisted, however, that that is not what had transpired since *all* residents were equally deprived of access to municipal pools.

Judge Wisdom's dissent argued that the city's purpose in closing the pools was to avoid desegregation and that the justifications offered by the city—safety and economy—were merely pretextual. "It is astonishing," Judge Wisdom chided, that the Fifth Circuit accepted "at face value the two excuses the city of Jackson offered."[33] He also repudiated the notion that closing the pools to everyone, blacks and whites alike, obviated the possibility that that act could be a stigmatizing attack against blacks. Just as criminalizing marriage across the race line—a burden on whites and blacks alike—was a reflection and technique of racial subordination, so, too, was preventing desegregated swimming a reflection and technique of racial subordination, especially insofar as the pool closures were imposed in reaction to a court order that affirmed the illegitimacy of segregation.[34] Finally, Judge Wisdom asserted that the city's closure of the pools was retaliatory:

> It has taught Jackson's Negroes a lesson: In Jackson the price of protest is high. Negroes there now know that they risk losing even segregated public facilities if they dare to protest segregation. Negroes will now think twice before protesting segregated . . . facilities. They must first decide whether

---

[32] Id.

[33] Id at 1229 (Wisdom, J, dissenting). According to Judge Wisdom, "the pools were closed not to promote peace but to prevent blacks and whites swimming in the same water." Id at 1230. He dismissed as "frivolous" the claim that the city closed the pools to save money. Id at 1232.

[34] "We should not be misled by the equal application argument. That argument smacks of the repudiated separate but equal doctrine of *Plessy v Ferguson*. We should not be misled by focusing on the city's non-operation of the pools. Closing the pools as an official act to prevent Negroes from enjoying equal status with whites constituted the unlawful state action. It had the same purpose and many of the same effects as maintaining separate pools. . . . It was a reaffirmation of the *Dred Scott* article of faith that Negroes are indeed 'a subordinate or inferior class of beings. . . .'" Id at 1236–37.

they wish to risk living without the facility altogether, and at the same time
engendering further animosity from a white community which has [also]
lost its public facilities. . . .[35]

The Supreme Court affirmed the Fifth Circuit, five to four, with
Justice Black writing for the Court and Justice White writing the main
dissent. Justice Black reasoned that while there was some evidence in
the record that the Jackson pools were closed due to opposition to
racial desegregation, the courts below had concluded that the pools
were closed because city officials believed that, as desegregated facilities, they could not be operated safely and economically and that there
was "substantial evidence in the record" to support that conclusion.[36]
Under the theory pursuant to which he resolved the case, however, the
judicial finding regarding motive became irrelevant. "[N]o case in this
Court," Justice Black declared, "has held that a legislative act may violate equal protection solely because of the motivations of the men
who voted for it."[37] Acknowledging that "there is language in some of
[the Court's] cases . . . which may suggest that the motive or purpose
behind a law is relevant to its constitutionality," he maintained that
"the focus in those cases was on the actual effect of the enactments, not
upon the motivation which led the States to behave as they did."[38]
Here, Justice Black concluded, the "actual effect" of the closure was
unobjectionable under the Equal Protection Clause. The record, he

---

[35] Id at 1236. In his excellent biography of Judge Wisdom, Professor Joel William
Friedman laudably discloses the circumstances surrounding his hero's embarrassing tardiness,
a point aired by Judge Griffin B. Bell in an acerbic concurrence. *Palmer*, 419 F2d at 1228.
Judge Wisdom took nearly two years to file his dissent, an excessive amount of time that tried
the patience of even his closest allies. Friedman, *Champion of Civil Rights* at 235–37 (cited in
note 26). Consequences of delay are difficult to determine and cannot be measured with any
degree of confidence here. It is notable, though, that during the pendency of the *Palmer* litigation much transpired. The composition of the Supreme Court changed dramatically at the
end of the 1960s with the retirements of Chief Justice Earl Warren and Justice Abe Fortas.
The mood of some of the remaining Justices changed, too, exhibited in decreasing solicitude
for civil rights dissidents. One can plausibly speculate that *Palmer* might have turned out
differently had it been decided in 1969 rather than 1971. See Randall Kennedy, *Walker v City
of Birmingham Revisited*, 2017 Supreme Court Review 313, 331 (suggesting that *Walker* would
likely have been resolved differently had it been adjudicated earlier).

[36] *Palmer*, 403 US at 225.

[37] Id at 224. Note Justice Black's observation that "no case in this Court has held that a
legislative act may violate protection solely because of the motivations of the men who voted
for it." So? Is the Supreme Court's case law the totality of the Constitution? Justice Black's
rhetoric, which other Justices have echoed, brims with obnoxious hubris.

[38] Id at 225.

declared, "shows no state action affecting blacks differently from whites."[39]

By contrast, Justice White argued that "shutting down the pools was . . . a most effective expression of official policy that Negroes and whites must not be permitted to mingle together when using the services provided by the city."[40] Stating that he was "quite unpersuaded that . . . it is impermissible to impeach the otherwise valid act of closing municipal swimming pools by resort to evidence of invidious purpose or motive,"[41] Justice White contended that "by closing the pools solely because of the order to desegregate, the city [was] expressing its official view that Negroes are so inferior that they are unfit to share with whites this particular type of public facil-

---

[39] Id. Chief Justice Warren Burger and Justice Harry Blackmun wrote brief concurrences. The Chief Justice stated that, in his view, he was being asked to hold "that the Constitution *requires* that public swimming pools, once opened, may not be closed." Id at 228 (Burger, CJ, concurring) (emphasis added). Eschewing that alleged request, the Chief Justice opined: "We would do a grave disservice . . . were we to require that every decision of local governments to terminate a desirable service be subjected to a microscopic scrutiny for forbidden motives rendering the decision unconstitutional." Id.

The Chief Justice's polemic would be laughable were the stakes not so important. He created a proverbial straw man to knock down. The plaintiffs in no sense requested a holding that the Constitution requires that pools once opened may *never* be closed. They argued instead that it violated the Constitution to close pools with the intent of avoiding desegregation (and in the absence of any compelling reason otherwise to close the pools). Judge Wisdom anticipated (and answered) Chief Justice Burger's concern: "We do not say that a city may never abandon a previously rendered municipal service. If the facts show that the city has acted in good faith for economic or other nonracial reasons, the action would have no overtones of racial degradation, and would therefore not offend the Constitution." *Palmer*, 419 F2d at 1237 n 16.

Similarly spurious is the Chief Justice's invocation of "microscopic scrutiny" for "every decision of local governments to terminate a desirable service." *Palmer* involved not "microscopic scrutiny" but a willingness to act when officials had broadcast clearly the racially invidious aim they sought to attain.

Justice Blackmun stated that he found *Palmer* to be a "hard" case in which "there is much to be said on each side." *Palmer*, 403 US at 228 (Blackmun, J, concurring). Justice Blackmun's papers reveal that he initially drafted an opinion reversing the Fifth Circuit. See Eyer, 51 Harv CR-CL Rev at 32 n 168 (cited in note 2). Ultimately, though, he voted to affirm the Fifth Circuit. He mentioned, among other things, that pools were not essential facilities but were instead merely "nice to have." 403 US at 230 (Blackmun, J, concurring). Judge Rives had also suggested that the character of pools as optional public facilities ought to play a role in determining the legality of closure. That is a bad idea. The Equal Protection Clause should be read as prohibiting invidious racial discrimination regardless of the importance of the facilities or services in dispute. Whether the facilities or services are essential or trivial, it is imperative that government be prohibited from discriminating against people because of their race. Fortunately, courts have reached this conclusion in a number of contexts involving matters that some might see as "merely" symbolic. See, for example, *Hamilton v Alabama*, 376 US 650 (1964) (form of addressing a witness); *Gayle v Browder*, 352 US 903 (1956) (seating on a bus).

[40] *Palmer*, 403 US at 241 (White, J, dissenting).

[41] Id.

ity."[42] According to Justice White, Jackson's "closed pools stand as mute reminders to the community of the official view of Negro inferiority."[43]

II. THE SPECIAL PLACE OF SWIMMING POOLS

One thing that none of the *Palmer* opinions adequately highlight is the special place of the swimming pool in the history of racial conflict in America. More intense opposition to desegregation was focused upon pools than any other site of recreation. Resistance stemmed from various sources. One was whites' fear that they would be contaminated if they swam in the same water as blacks. This apprehension was revealed in an episode in the 1930s that involved Robert Lee Carter, a public high school student in East Orange, New Jersey, who became one of the leading civil rights attorneys in American history. Authorities at Carter's school reserved the swimming pool for white students only Mondays through Thursdays. Black students were only permitted to use the pool on Fridays. "To

---

[42] Id at 266.

[43] Id at 268. Justices William O. Douglas and Thurgood Marshall also authored dissents. After voicing several suggestive propositions, including comments about the pertinence of the Ninth Amendment, Justice Douglas concluded:

> Though a State may discontinue any of its municipal services . . . it may not do so for the purpose of perpetuating or installing apartheid or because it finds life in a multi-racial community difficult or unpleasant. If that is its reason, then abolition of a designated public service becomes a device for perpetuating a segregated way of life. That a State may not do.

Id at 239 (Douglas, J, dissenting).

In his dissent, Justice Marshall lodged three objections. The first was to the Court's equal-application theory. Responding to the argument that the pool closures comported with the Equal Protection Clause because they were racially even-handed, excluding whites as well as blacks, Justice Marshall contended that "when the officials . . . denied a single Negro child the opportunity to go swimming simply because he is a Negro, rights guaranteed to that child by the Fourteenth Amendment were lost. The fact that the color of his skin is used to prevent others from swimming in public pools is irrelevant." Id at 272 (Marshall, J, dissenting). Second, Justice Marshall objected to the suggestion that the management of pools, as unessential public facilities, should somehow be subject to a less demanding constitutional standard than schools as essential public facilities that maintained that since *Brown v Board of Education* recreational facilities and schools had properly received "identical" treatment pursuant to the Fourteenth Amendment. Id. Third, Justice Marshall objected to what he perceived to be the excessive weight that Chief Justice Burger and Justice Blackmun attached to a colloquy with one of the plaintiffs' attorneys. The attorney suggested that Jackson should be forever disabled from discontinuing pool service because of costs stemming from racial difficulties. Id at 230 n *. Chief Justice Burger and Justice Blackmun found this response "disturbing." Justice Marshall noted that no Justice is "bound by any admission of an attorney at oral argument as to his version of the law." Id.

protect the white children from contamination the blacks might have left in the pool," Carter writes, "it was then drained, cleaned and refilled for the use of white students the following Monday."[44] Displaying the resolve that characterized his legal career, Carter solitarily challenged the segregationist routine. "I could not swim at the time," he recalled, "but at every gym class, choked up and near tears with emotion and defiance, I would get in the pool at its shallow end and cling to the side until the period ended."[45]

Racial discrimination at the swimming pool played a formative role in the life of another leading attorney, the formidable William T. Coleman. When Coleman insisted that he be allowed to try out for his public high school swimming team in Philadelphia, authorities disbanded it to avoid the possibility that it might become multiracial.[46]

Resistance to desegregation at pools was also attributable to sex. People disrobe at swimming pools and gaze at others who are similarly bare. At pools, more than any other public setting, the erotic rises close to the surface.[47] White racists nationally viewed the lowering of racial barriers at pools with particular contempt.[48] In northern and midwestern cities in the 1940s and 1950s, racists opposed the presence of blacks at pools with fists, bats, rocks, knives, and guns.[49] In border states, resistance was also fierce. When a judge in 1948 in

---

[44] Robert L. Carter, *A Matter of Law* 14 (New Press, 2005). See also Justin Driver, *The Lawyer's Revolution*, New Republic, March 13, 2006.

[45] Carter, *A Matter of Law* 15 (cited in note 44).

[46] See William T. Coleman, *Counsel for the Situation: Shaping the Law to Realize America's Promise* (Brooking Institution, 2010). Presaging *Palmer*, school officials discriminated by leveling down to create an illusion of equal treatment.

[47] The petitioners' brief to the Supreme Court alludes to "[t]he sexual phobia generated by the possibility of even accidental physical contact between lightly clad black and white bodies in swimming pools . . . is part and parcel of the racial mythology that has done so much to divide us as a people." The authors of the brief cite various sources including W. J. Cash, *The Mind of the South* (Knopf, 1941), and "the novels of William Faulkner." Brief for Petitioners, *Palmer v Thompson*, No 107, *13 (US filed July 21, 1970) at 13.

[48] In 1948, as a leader of the States' Rights Democratic Party (the Dixiecrats), South Carolina Governor Strom Thurmond declared that "there's not enough troops in the army to force the southern people to break down segregation and admit the nigger race into our theaters, into our swimming pools, into our homes, and into our churches." Quoted in Joseph Crespino, *Strom Thurmond's America* 71 (Hill & Wang, 2012). For accounts of racial struggles at pools nationwide, see Wiltse, *Contested Waters* (cited in note 9); Victoria W. Wolcott, *Race, Riots, and Roller Coasters: The Struggle Over Segregated Recreation in America* (Pennsylvania, 2012).

[49] Wiltse, *Contested Waters* at 158 (cited in note 9).

Montgomery, West Virginia, ordered authorities to provide blacks with a pool equal to that offered to whites, officials responded by leveling down: they closed the pool for fourteen years.[50] In 1954 in Maryland, officials refused to desegregate bath houses, bathing facilities, and swimming pools, notwithstanding the Supreme Court's recent holding in *Brown v Board of Education*. Noting that *Brown* did not expressly condemn segregation across the board,[51] a federal district court judge suggested that segregating the races in certain forms of recreation continued to be reasonable. He observed that "[t]he degree of racial feeling or prejudice . . . is probably higher with respect to bathing, swimming, and dancing than with any other interpersonal relations except direct sexual relations."[52] Although reversed on the law, the judge's opinion accurately reflected the vexed racial emotions that attended the prospect of interracial contact at public swimming pools. The volatile history of swimming pool desegregation makes more plausible the belief that the Jackson city authorities could have been honestly prompted by concerns over safety and fiscal responsibility (and not their own segregationist commitments) when they closed the pools. On the other hand, the dense record of obstructionism lends weight to the plaintiffs' contention that while segregationist authorities were willing to cede some venues to desegregation, the sexual aura surrounding swimming and sunbathing prompted them to act differently—more stubbornly and deceitfully—with respect to pools.

III. The Problem of Racially Biased Judicial Recalcitrance

The *Palmer* dissents offer a glimpse of the pervasive racism that enveloped Jackson in the 1960s. Justice White cited several cases substantiating his observation that "[t]he city of Jackson was one of the many places where the consistent line of decisions following from *Brown* had little or no effect."[53] Those cases reveal the actions of state

---

[50] Id at 165.

[51] "It may be that at some time in the near or distant future the Supreme Court will seek to destroy the whole pattern of segregation and adopt the position that the States may no longer provide or require segregated facilities in any field. But it has not done so yet." *Lonesome v Maxwell*, 123 F Supp 193, 205 (D Md 1954).

[52] Id at 202.

[53] See *Palmer*, 403 US at 246 (White, J, dissenting), citing *Thomas v Mississippi*, 380 US 524 (1965); *NAACP v Thompson*, 357 F2d 831 (5th Cir 1966); *Bailey v Patterson*, 369 US 31 (1962); *United States v City of Jackson*, 318 F2d 1 (5th Cir 1963).

and municipal authorities who continued to enforce segregation long after it had been judicially proscribed. *Bailey v Patterson*[54] featured equal rights dissidents who, challenging blatantly illegal racial segregation in transportation facilities, also complained of wholesale violations of their civil liberties by Jackson police. The case also featured Mayor Thompson, who showed himself to be a shrewd defender of the Jim Crow regime. Asked in *Bailey* to explain the racial policy of Jackson with respect to transportation, Mayor Thompson responded:

> It has been the policy of mine as chief law enforcement officer . . . to maintain what has worked over the last hundred years to bring happiness and peace and prosperity to everyone within our city. That has been done by a separation of the races, not segregation. We never refer to it as segregation. . . . Our policy calls for a great deal of give and take. It is agreeable to both the white and the colored.[55]

Notwithstanding the image of reciprocity and consensus portrayed by Mayor Thompson, the cases Justice White cited disclosed a steady flow of unlawful conduct undertaken by authorities who repeatedly proceeded as if it were criminal for people to ignore segregationist custom. These cases reveal numerous instances in which authorities trampled rights, exposing in sobering detail why the anodyne depictions offered by the majority decisions in *Palmer* obscure the perfidy of the pertinent state and city authorities.[56]

The situation in Jackson, however, was even *worse* than portrayed by the *Palmer* dissenters, who left unmentioned the deformed structure

---

[54] 369 US 31 (1962).

[55] *Bailey v Patterson*, 199 F Supp 595, 611 (S D Miss 1961).

[56] Justice White rightly noted that it was "not irrelevant in considering the context in which Jackson's pools were closed, that a statute of the state of Mississippi in effect since 1956 provide[d]:

> That the entire executive branch of the government of the State of Mississippi, and of its subdivisions, and all persons responsible thereto . . . [are hereby] directed and required to prohibit, by any lawful, peaceful and constitutional means, the implementation of or the compliance with the Integration Decisions of the United States Supreme Court [in *Brown v Board of Education* and *Brown v Board of Education II*] and to prohibit by any lawful, peaceful, and constitutional means, the causing of a mixing or integration of the white and Negro races. . . .

Palmer, 403 US at 262 n 16 (White, J, dissenting).

of authority that the plaintiffs confronted,[57] including the judiciary.[58] After the overthrow of Reconstruction in Mississippi and throughout the South, white supremacists succeeded in negating black electoral power through a wide variety of means, including chicanery, fraud, discrimination, intimidation, and violence.[59] The result was Jim Crow tyranny reflected in agencies of governance from which blacks were barred. Although blacks constituted nearly half of the electorate in Mississippi during the first half of the twentieth century, there existed a complete absence of black representation in the state legislature until 1967, when Robert G. Clark became the first African American Mississippi legislator since the 1890s.[60] Although blacks constituted a bit more than a third of the population of Jackson in the early 1960s, there were no black elected officials in Jackson city government until 1985.[61] No blacks were among the officials that decided to close the pools.

Another consequence of Jim Crow tyranny was that anyone seeking to wield public authority in Mississippi was obliged to accommodate white supremacy. This grim reality allowed for some variety inasmuch as white racism occupied a spectrum conditioned by a wide array of factors including ideology, religion, and temperament. The distance between "moderate" segregationists and "extreme" segre-

---

[57] One of the Justices probed this feature of the case at oral argument.

Q: Do they have any colored officials now, in the city? . . .
A: No, Sir.

Transcript, Oral Argument, *Palmer v Thompson*, December 14, 1970 at 40.

[58] Twenty-four judges played a role in resolving *Palmer*. Just one, Justice Thurgood Marshall, was black. He dissented from the Court's ruling. This is not to say that racial identity is determinative of a jurist's thinking. Most of the dissenters in *Palmer* were white. Furthermore, had a black jurist with the proclivities of, say, Justice Clarence Thomas sat in judgment in *Palmer* one can easily imagine him voting with the Court. Cf. *Foster v Chatman*, 136, S Ct 1737 (2016) (Thomas, J, dissenting). Still, the paucity of black jurists empowered to participate in the resolution of the case is related to the sentiments that prompted the pool closure and the judicial response that followed. Put plainly, the dearth of blacks in the judiciary, especially at the time *Palmer* was decided, reflected and reinforced the pervasive racism that afflicted—and still afflicts—the United States.

[59] See Vernon Lane Wharton, *The Negro in Mississippi, 1865–1890* (North Carolina, 1947); J. Morgan Kousser, *The Shaping of Southern Politics: Suffrage Restrictions and the Establishment of the One-Party South, 1880–1910* (Yale, 1974); *South Carolina v Katzenbach*, 383 US 301 (1966).

[60] See Frank R. Parker, *Black Votes Count: Political Empowerment in Mississippi after 1965* 72 (North Carolina, 1990).

[61] Id at 163.

gationists could be considerable. One thing, however, was clear: an individual could not be recognized as an antiracist and nonetheless be elevated to a position of authority.[62]

Judges Sidney Mize and William Harold Cox, the trial judges who adjudicated *Clark v Thompson* and *Palmer v Thompson*, were die-hard segregationists who pose for the legal historian a problem similar to that encountered by the appellate judges that reviewed their rulings: to what extent, if any, are their factual findings trustworthy?[63] Trial

---

[62] Several federal judges in the Deep South distinguished themselves as stalwart antiracists. They did so, however, *after* they attained their judgeships and the attendant security of life tenure. Emblematic is the trajectory of Judge J. Skelly Wright. When President John F. Kennedy proposed to elevate Judge Wright from the District Court to the Fifth Circuit after he had shown himself heroically willing to enforce *Brown v Board of Education* in Louisiana, segregationists vehemently objected. Moving him to an appellate court entailed exile from the South, which is why he finished his admirable career not in his hometown of New Orleans but up north where he sat on the United States Court of Appeals for the District of Columbia Court. See generally Arthur Selwyn Miller, *A Capacity for Outrage: The Judicial Odyssey of J. Skelly Wright* (Praeger, 1984); Jack Bass, *Unlikely Heroes* (Alabama, 1981); Frank T. Read and Lucy S. McGough, *Let Them Be Judged* (Scarecrow, 1978).

[63] Judge Sidney Carr Mize (1888–1965) attended the University of Mississippi School of Law and practiced law in private and public capacities for decades before he was nominated to the United States District Court by President Franklin D. Roosevelt in 1937. When Mize was nominated, it would have been assumed that he supported segregation and the other key bulwarks of the Jim Crow regime. Throughout his judicial career, Judge Mize ratified that assumption. For an assessment of Judge Mize from the perspective of an equal rights dissident, see Gilbert R. Mason, M.D., *Beaches, Blood, and Ballots: A Black Doctor's Civil Rights Struggle* (Mississippi, 2000). For an assessment from the perspective of an advocate for equal rights activists, see Constance Baker Motley, *Equal Justice Under Law: An Autobiography* (Farrar, Straus and Giroux, 1998).

Judge William Harold Cox (1901–88) attended the University of Mississippi Law School and practiced law in a private capacity before being nominated to the United States District Court by President John F. Kennedy in 1961. By then, equal rights activists had succeeded in putting questions regarding racial sentiment on the agenda of concerns when assessing judicial nominees. The Justice Department, headed by Attorney General Robert F. Kennedy, made inquiries and was ultimately satisfied that Judge Cox would conduct himself appropriately. Roy Wilkins, Executive Secretary of the NAACP, voiced a different, darker forecast. He warned that "[f]or 986,000 Negro Mississippians, Judge Cox will be another strand in their barbed wire fence, another cross over their weary shoulders and another rock in the road up which their young people must struggle." Judge Cox showed Wilkins to be prescient. He is reliably reported to have referred to blacks as "niggers" and likened their conduct to that of "chimpanzees." Responding to a question about the punishment he imposed on the racially motivated murders of three equal rights activists, Judge Cox reportedly said: "They killed one nigger, one Jew, and a white man. I gave [the defendants] what I thought they deserved."

See Bass, *Unlikely Heroes* 164–68 (cited in note 62); Carol Caldwell, *Harold Cox: Still Racist After All These Years*, 1 Am Law 1 (July 1979); Gerald M. Stern, *Judge William Harold Cox and the Right to Vote in Clarke County, Mississippi*, in Leon Friedman, ed, *Southern Justice* (Meridian, 1965); note, *Disqualification of Judges for Bias in the Federal Courts*, 79 Harv L Rev 1435, 1450 n 103 (1966), quoting *Time*, Nov 6, 1964 at 44. Judge Cox succeeded Judge Mize as the Chief Judge of the Southern District of Mississippi in 1962 and held that position until 1971. For an early critique of Judge Cox and Judge Mize, and other segregationist federal judges, that bears reading and re-reading, see Comment, *Judicial Performance in the Fifth Circuit*, 73 Yale L J 90 (1963).

judges' findings of fact are typically accorded substantial deference. With Mize and Cox, however, such deference would be misplaced in any case involving a challenge to segregation. Both displayed on numerous occasions animus against antiracist activists and a willingness to use their craft and office to defend the Jim Crow regime, even to the point of engaging in judicial nullification. A striking instance was presented in *Meredith v Fair* involving James Meredith's successful (and heroic) effort to become the first recognized African American to attend the University of Mississippi.[64] When Meredith's application was rejected, the obvious cause was the determination of state officials to prevent any black student from enrolling. Governor Ross Barnett worked closely with other Mississippi officials to block Meredith. Barnett declared publicly and repeatedly that no black would enter Ole Miss or any other "white" school in the state so long as he held office. Overwhelming evidence presented at trial showed that state authorities were committed to barring Meredith on account of his race. Yet Judge Mize found as a "fact" that the University of Mississippi was not a segregated institution, that there was no custom or policy excluding qualified Negroes from the university, and, more specifically, that Meredith was not denied admission because of his race.[65] Reversing the trial court, Judge John Minor Wisdom, writing for the Fifth Circuit, wryly observed that Judge Mize's findings "may startle some people in Mississippi."[66] Because the university's policy of racial exclusion was so evident, Judge Mize's inaccurate account is difficult to chalk up to mere good faith error.[67]

Similarly misguided and misleading was Judge Mize's handling of recreational desegregation. Recall that in *Clark*,[68] Judge Mize de-

---

[64] See Charles W. Eagles, *The Price of Defiance: James Meredith and the Integration of Ole Miss* (North Carolina, 2009). In 1945, Henry S. Murphy, an enlistee in the United States Navy, attended the University of Mississippi for a year. His navy and university records listed him as "white," though he perceived himself to be "colored," like his parents. Murphy did not seek to "pass"; he simply refrained from affirmatively revising the racial perceptions of others. By contrast, Meredith was "black" by all conventional criteria and described himself on his application as "an American-Mississippi Negro Citizen." Id at 20–21.

[65] *Meredith v Fair*, 202 F Supp 224 (S D Miss 1962).

[66] 305 F2d 343, 344 (5th Cir 1962).

[67] As Judge Wisdom observed, "from the moment defendants discovered Meredith was a Negro they engaged in a carefully calculated campaign of delay, harassment, and masterly inactivity." Id. Judge Wisdom described one of Judge Mize's rulings as "clearly erroneous," another as "a clear abuse of judicial discretion," and a third as "manifestly erroneous." Deriding Judge Mize's disregard for truths, Judge Wisdom complained that the case had been tried "in the eerie atmosphere of never-never land." Id at 349, 345.

[68] 206 F Supp 539 (S D Miss 1962).

scribed Jackson as a "clean, progressive" city that had been free of racial friction except for that stirred up by intermeddling civil rights activists; maintained that "voluntary separation of the races . . . [had] operated smoothly and apparently to the complete satisfaction of all for many years"; declined to rule that the plaintiffs had been victims of discrimination; and refused to issue an injunction against the "high class" segregationist defendants.[69] Given his solicitude for Jim Crow oppression, his inability to "find" obvious invidious racial discrimination, and his hostility to equal rights activists "guilty" of simply seeking their due under the federal constitution, it is sensible to approach every aspect of Judge Mize's judicial performance in all race relations cases with alert skepticism.

Judge Cox adjudicated *Palmer* at trial. Like Mize, he was a stalwart defender of white supremacist orthodoxy. Consider his rulings in *NAACP v Thompson*,[70] a case in which activists sought an injunction to restrain Mayor Thompson and other officials from unlawfully harassing them for seeking to exercise their right to access to interstate transportation free of racial impediments. Unsurprisingly, in light of his prejudices, Judge Cox first found an insufficient factual predicate for temporary injunctive relief and then dismissed the complaint altogether. The Fifth Circuit reversed, highlighting Judge Cox's unreliability as a fact finder.[71] Convinced that Mayor Thompson and the other defendants would continue to menace the plaintiffs, the Fifth Circuit issued the injunctive relief that Judge Cox had refused to grant.[72]

---

[69] Id at 541.

[70] *NAACP v Thompson*, 11 Race Rel L Rep 657 (1966).

[71] The Fifth Circuit panel remarked that the record disclosed "a pattern of conduct on the part of the officials of the city of Jackson that leads us to the conclusion that defendants took advantage of every opportunity . . . to break up . . . demonstrations in protest against racial discrimination and that a large number of the arrests had no other motive, and some had no justification whatever, either under municipal, state, or federal law." *NAACP v Thompson*, 357 F2d 831, 838 (5th Cir 1966).

[72] Judge Cox was reversed in race cases with regularity by the Fifth Circuit. See, for example, *United States v Wood*, 295 F2d 772 (5th Cir 1961), and *Congress of Racial Equality v Douglas*, 318 F2d 95 (5th Cir 1963). In *Kennedy v Owen*, 321 F2d 116 (5th Cir 1963), Judge Cox ruled against the federal Department of Justice because, among other things, it addressed certain officials as "circuit clerks" as opposed to "registrars" in a setting in which the distinction was immaterial. The Fifth Circuit reversed Judge Cox and remanded the case to him with instructions to follow. Commenting upon Cox's ruling, Professor Alexander Bickel remarked that it was "farcical . . . straight out of *Jarndyce v. Jarndyce*, or out of Kafka." See Alexander M. Bickel, *Politics and the Warren Court* 74 (Harper & Row, 1965).

Here is the rub: the author of the Fifth Circuit's repudiation of Judge Cox in *Thompson* was none other than Judge Rives, who was also the author of the Fifth Circuit's rulings in *Palmer* that affirmed Judge Cox. A southern-bred, well-connected, widely respected jurist, Rives admitted that he had not always been "pure" with respect to bigotry.[73] Early in his career as an attorney he carried on a brief flirtation with the Ku Klux Klan and later advised registrars on how to thwart blacks seeking to vote. His racial sentiments, however, evolved. Elevated to the Fifth Circuit in 1951 by President Harry S. Truman, Rives became one of "The Four"—the cadre of judges on the Fifth Circuit that most insistently enforced *Brown v Board of Education*.[74] Rives, for example, wrote the opinion in *Browder v Gayle*[75] that invalidated segregation on busses in Alabama, a ruling that brought victory to the Montgomery Bus Boycott that launched the career of Martin Luther King Jr.[76] Rives was a less dogged racial liberal than were his colleagues John Minor Wisdom, Elbert P. Tuttle, or John R. Brown. Nonetheless, allied with them, Rives repeatedly acted to block Cox, Mize, and other segregationist judges from subverting the legal reforms of the Second Reconstruction.[77]

Justice Hugo L. Black—a close jurisprudential ally and personal friend of Judge Rives—was the author of the Supreme Court's opinion in *Palmer*. An Alabamian like Rives, Black had briefly been a member of the Ku Klux Klan. After his elevation to the Supreme Court in 1937, however, he spent the next thirty years repeatedly siding with racial minority litigants seeking judicial validation of their federal constitutional rights. He regrettably joined in the Court's deplorable failure to defend the rights of Japanese Americans forced to submit to curfews and detentions during World War II. Indeed,

---

[73] Bass, *Unlikely Heroes* at 73 (cited in note 62).

[74] The name "The Four" was coined by Judge Benjamin Franklin Cameron, the most outspoken segregationist on the Fifth Circuit. He disapproved of the racial liberalism of his colleagues and accused Chief Judge Elbert P. Tuttle of manipulating assignments so that members of "The Four" would predominate on the three-judge panels hearing key race cases. Id at 231–47 (cited in note 62).

[75] 142 F Supp 707 (M D Ala 1956). The decision was summarily affirmed by the Supreme Court, *Gayle v Browder*, 352 US 903 (1956).

[76] In the aftermath of *Browder*, Judge Rives was ostracized by white Alabamians, including former friends and fellow worshippers at church. Some new enemies even vandalized the grave of Judge Rives's son who had died in an automobile accident. See Bass, *Unlikely Heroes* at 66–83 (cited in note 62).

[77] Read and McGough, *Let Them Be Judged* (cited in note 62).

he wrote *Korematsu v United States*, the Court's key decision in that horrific episode. Black also became the leading critic of the direct-action tactics of black liberation activists, a role that probably made him less sympathetic to the underlying complaints of the dissidents. By the waning days of his judicial career—the period during which he wrote *Palmer*—Black had become a somewhat crabby, thin-skinned, intellectually arthritic jurist who was no longer habitually friendly to progressive reformers seeking to challenge social inequities. Still, for all that, Justice Black was a far cry from—indeed a foe of—segregationists such as Judges Mize and Cox.[78]

The presence of Rives and Black in the *Palmer* majorities complicates the story of the litigation. Racist judicial obstructionism cannot account fully for the outcome. Nor can the remaining responsibility for the outcome be fully attributed to "moderate" jurists of various stripes whose commitment to the enforcement of *Brown* and its progeny was unenthusiastic if not halting. Essential to the majorities at both the court of appeals and the Supreme Court were two of the leading federal judicial racial liberals of the era.[79]

IV. Palmer and the Ghost of Plessy

The Supreme Court took the position that, whatever the motivation behind the pool closure, Jackson authorities did not cause a harm cognizable under the Equal Protection Clause because the city treated everyone the same. But the city did *not* treat everyone the same. It did not racially stigmatize whites but did racially stigmatize blacks. The historical record discloses no protest from whites claiming that the city treated them as a disfavored caste by closing the pools rather than permitting them to share the pools with blacks. Some whites may

---

[78] See generally Roger K. Newman, *Hugo Black: A Biography* (Fordham, 1994); Dennis J. Hutchinson, *Hugo Black Among Friends*, 93 Mich L Rev 1885 (1995).

[79] Solicitor General Erwin Griswold, working under the aegis of Attorney General John N. Mitchell in the administration of President Richard M. Nixon, submitted an amicus curiae brief for the United States urging reversal of the Fifth Circuit. See Brief for the United States as Amicus Curiae, *Palmer v Thompson*, No 107 (US filed Dec 1, 1970). The Solicitor General argued that Jackson's closure of all its swimming facilities to avoid racial desegregation was prohibited by the Fourteenth Amendment. "[T]he clear purpose and effect of the municipality's action, coming on the heels of the [*Clark*] court order, is to prevent commingling of the races . . . thereby depriving the city's citizens of an opportunity to be accepted without regard to race in the use of municipal swimming pools. Thus, the citizens of the city of Jackson are no less segregated now than when dual facilities were maintained." Id at *4.

well have complained about inconvenience to themselves or injustice inflicted upon their black fellow residents. But no appreciable number of whites asserted, as did substantial numbers of blacks, that the closure constituted a racial insult aimed at them. In closing the pools city authorities were seeking to protect whites from the imagined danger and indignity of sharing intimate environs with blacks.

The thinking that triumphed in *Palmer* is disturbingly similar to that which triumphed in *Plessy v Ferguson*.[80] In *Plessy* the Court upheld the constitutionality of a Louisiana law that required racially separate-but-equal accommodations on intrastate railroad cars. The petitioner in that case charged that the law was meant to stigmatize them and did so by removing blacks from the presence of whites (while whites were also simultaneously removed from the presence of blacks). The petitioner in *Plessy* stipulated that the facilities at issue were tangibly "equal" to those reserved for whites. They maintained, though, that Louisiana's requirement of racial separation—its prohibition of racially mixed intrastate train travel—violated the Equal Protection Clause. Louisiana defended its segregation law on the grounds that the law applied to everyone, blacks and whites alike; that the segregated facilities were "equal"; and that the compelled separation was for the convenience of the community as a whole. Upholding the constitutionality of the law, the Court dismissed the petitioner's argument that the law targeted them for insult, thereby denigrating their status as legal equals to the whites. In the Court's view, laws requiring separation in places where whites and blacks were liable to be brought into contact did not necessarily imply the inferiority of either race to the other. "We consider the underlying fallacy of the petitioner's argument," the Court declared, "to consist in the assumption that the enforced separation of the two races stamps the colored race with a badge of inferiority. If this be so, it is not by reason of anything found in the act, but solely because the colored race chooses to put that construction upon it."[81]

The plaintiffs in *Palmer* claimed that the closure of the pools, like the segregation in *Plessy*, was a badge of inferiority purposefully pinned upon colored folk to signal and effectuate their subordinate status. And the Court in *Palmer*, like the Court in *Plessy*, rejected the plain-

---

[80] 163 US 537 (1896).

[81] Id at 551.

tiffs' contention, concluding that they were mistaken, that what they took to be a denigrating stigmata was actually a reasonable policy undertaken in good faith for the benefit of all.

In his famous dissent in *Plessy*, Justice John Marshall Harlan repudiated the claim that racial segregation suggested no implication of illicit racial hierarchy. He dismissed as a "thin disguise" the reference to equality in the mantra of separate but equal. He scoffed at the notion that the segregation law, though imposed on all, created no discrimination against blacks. "Everyone knows," he declared, "that the [segregation statute] had its origins in the purpose not so much to exclude white people from the railroad cars occupied by blacks as to exclude colored people from coaches occupied by . . . white persons. . . . The thing to accomplish was, under the guise of giving equal accommodation for whites and blacks, to compel the latter to keep to themselves."[82]

The same could be said of the swimming pool closure in *Palmer*. The justifications proffered—fear of disorder and expense—were also a "thin disguise." Everyone knew, because Mayor Thompson openly stated, that the purpose of the closure was to avoid desegregation at the pools. The city's aim in truth was not to protect the whole community from violence or financial embarrassment. The authorities never tried operating desegregated pools before giving up on them. The authorities merely verbalized speculation that problems would arise in an effort to salvage as much of the Jim Crow regime as could be saved from the onrushing reforms of the Second Reconstruction. Closing the pools was, as Justice White observed, "a most effective expression of official policy that Negroes and whites must not be permitted to mingle together when using the services provided by the city."[83]

V. Justice Black's Tendentious Handling of Precedent

By the time the Supreme Court faced *Palmer*, lower courts had issued rulings in several cases testing the validity of closures to avoid desegregation. In most, courts declared that while it was unconstitutional to segregate facilities, it was not unconstitutional to

---

[82] Id at 557.

[83] *Palmer*, 403 US at 241 (White, J, dissenting).

close them, regardless of intent. In *City of Montgomery v Gilmore*,[84] in another opinion by Judge Rives, the Fifth Circuit foreshadowed its subsequent holding in *Palmer*. It declared that while segregating parks was a violation of the Equal Protection Clause, closing parks to everyone was not, no matter the animating aim.[85]

One might have reasonably surmised that the Supreme Court was abjuring this line of cases with its decision in *Griffin v County School Board of Prince Edward County*.[86] In *Griffin*, the Supreme Court invalidated actions by a county in Virginia that, in the face of a judicial directive ordering school desegregation, closed its schools (unlike all other counties in the state) and channeled resources to racially exclusive "private" schools. The Court affirmed the district court's injunction prohibiting the county from paying tuition grants and giving tax credits while public schools remained closed. The Court also stated that the district court could, "if necessary to prevent further racial discrimination," require officials to levy taxes to raise funds to reopen the closed schools.

Summing up the reason for the Court's decision, Justice Black observed:

> the record . . . could not be clearer that Prince Edward's public schools were closed and private schools operated in their place with state and county assistance, for one reason, and one reason only: to ensure . . . that white and colored children . . . would not, under any circumstances, go to the same school. Whatever nonracial grounds might support a State's allowing a county to abandon public schools, the object must be a constitutional one, and grounds of race and opposition to desegregation do not qualify as constitutional.[87]

Although there was certainly much in *Griffin* that supported the plaintiffs' position in *Palmer*, Justice Black distinguished the earlier case, saying that it could give "no comfort" to the *Palmer* plaintiffs.[88] To denude *Griffin* of relevance to *Palmer* he narrowed the earlier decision. Justice Black portrayed the constitutional sin that the Court condemned not as any effort concocted for the purpose of evading

---

[84] 277 F2d 364 (5th Cir 1960).

[85] Id. See also *Hampton v City of Jacksonville*, 304 F2d 319 (5th Cir 1962); *Tonkins v City of Greensboro*, 276 F2d 890 (MDNC 1959).

[86] 377 US 218 (1964).

[87] Id at 231.

[88] *Palmer*, 403 US at 222.

court-ordered desegregation but rather as a specific, discrete effort that crucially involved assisting racially exclusive private schools.[89]

This reading of *Griffin* is forced and pinched. It is true that the Court mentions all of the various features of the defendants' scheme in *Griffin*. But does that mean that *Griffin* offered "no comfort" to a plaintiff challenging a similar scheme that varied a little? Neither the one-county feature nor the private-school feature nor the two features combined seem to have been essential to the Court's objection when it decided the case. When it decided *Griffin*, the key objection seems to have been broader. The constitutional sin to which the Court rightly objected was state action intended to evade a desegregation order which was tantamount to state action aimed at evading the Equal Protection Clause of the Constitution.

VI. Palmer and the Problem of Resistance to a Court Order

Jackson maintained that it closed the pools not to avoid desegregation per se but to avoid conditions that would accompany desegregation, namely, threats to public safety and the municipality's finances. The inadequacy of the Court's examination of the city's stated justifications is highlighted by comparing *Palmer* with another case in which authorities cited needs to accommodate popular opposition as rationales for policies objected to as hurtful capitulations.

Watson v Memphis[90] involved a challenge to a plan to desegregate recreational facilities gradually on a facility-by-facility basis. Memphis officials argued that a piecemeal approach was preferable to immediate desegregation and, in any event, permissible as a good faith effort to avoid dangerous turmoil and excessive expense. The district court and Sixth Circuit sided with the city. The Supreme Court reversed in an opinion by Justice Arthur Goldberg. The *Watson* court

---

[89] In *Palmer*, Justice Black stated that in *Griffin*:

> We held that the closing of public schools in just one county while the State helped finance "private schools" was a scheme to perpetuate segregation in education.... Thus the *Griffin* case simply treated the school program for what it was—an operation of Prince Edward County schools under a thinly disguised "private" school system actually planned and carried out by the State and the county to maintain segregated education with public funds.

Id at 222.

[90] 373 US 526 (1963).

noted that, in derogation of the Memphis authorities' fears, there had been no previous indications of appreciable violence when some of the recreational facilities had been desegregated. In *Palmer* the same was true, though the Court made no mention of it. The *Watson* Court noted that "there was no factual evidence to support the bare testimonial speculations that authorities would be unable to cope successfully with any problems" that desegregation might bring.[91] The *Palmer* Court simply accepted "the bare testimonial speculations" posited by officials in Jackson.[92]

Other aspects of *Palmer* reinforced the impression that the excuses offered by officials were merely pretextual. The excuses did not explain the need for a *permanent* closure of the pools. Nor did the excuses explain why the city closed *all* as opposed to merely some of the pools. Nor did the rationales explain why the city did not at least try to offer desegregated pools, giving the public a chance to belie fearful expectations, before permanently closing all of the pools. Similar objections face the city's assertions regarding the feared fiscal consequences of desegregation. As Justice White observed, "[t]he city made no showing that integrated operation [of the pools] would increase the annual loss of at least $11,700—a loss that, prior to 1963, the city purposefully accepted for the benefit of its citizens as long as segregated facilities could be maintained."[93]

Justice White invoked a line of precedent that stands for the proposition that, absent a persuasive argument shouldered by governmental authorities, constitutional rights cannot properly be sacrificed to avoid discord or expense. The seminal case was *Buchanan v Warley*.[94] There the Supreme Court invalidated a law that prohibited real estate transactions in locales predominantly inhabited by residents racially different from prospective buyers. "It is urged," Justice William R. Day wrote, "that this proposed segregation will promote the public peace by preventing race conflicts. Desirable as this is, and important as is the preservation of the public peace, this aim cannot be

---

[91] Id at 536–37.

[92] It bears noting that after the *Watson* Court ordered immediate desegregation of recreational facilities, Memphis officials ordered the closure of all municipal swimming pools. See Laurie B. Green, *Battling the Plantation Mentality: Memphis and the Black Freedom Struggle* 255 (North Carolina, 2007).

[93] 403 US at 258. See also *Closing of Municipal Swimming Pools*, 85 Harv L Rev 86 (cited in note 2).

[94] 245 US 60 (1916).

accomplished by laws or ordinances which deny rights created or protected by the Federal Constitution."[95] A subsequent case involved the
Supreme Court's refusal to suspend desegregation temporarily in a
public high school to avoid strife that was interfering with education—
strife that had occasioned the intervention of the United States military. In its landmark ruling in *Cooper v Aaron*,[96] the Court declared
that "law and order are not . . . to be preserved by depriving the Negro
children of their constitutional rights."

The *Palmer* Court did not disavow *Buchanan* or *Cooper*. But it insisted that the lesson of those cases applied to contexts in which officials were citing disorder or other threats as reasons to override a
constitutional right. The Court maintained that in *Palmer* there was
no such overriding because the plaintiffs had no constitutional right
of access to swimming pools.[97] The plaintiffs did, however, have a constitutional right to be treated as the equals of whites. The plaintiffs
would have had no legitimate equal protection complaint had the city
closed the pools to everyone for reasons that harbored no purpose
to treat African Americans as a separate and inferior caste. But that
was precisely the purpose behind the machinations of the Jackson authorities. They closed the pools to perpetuate racial separateness and
hierarchy by different means.

VII. Leveling Down as a Dubious Equal Protection Remedy

The Court was beguiled by the seeming uniformity of the
closure. "[T]his record," Justice Black admonished, "shows no state
action affecting blacks differently from whites."[98] If everyone suffered
the loss of access to public pools, how could it be said that there was
discrimination against blacks? The answer is that the discrimination
arose from an act, closure of the pools, designed to mark blacks as in-
feriors whom the government should keep apart from whites. Racially invidious governmental motivation inevitably produces stig-

---

[95] Id at 81.

[96] 385 US 1 (1958).

[97] According to Justice Black, "Citizens may not be compelled to forgo their constitutional
rights because officials fear public hostility or desire to save money. . . . But the issue here is
whether black citizens of Jackson *are* being denied their constitutional rights when the city
has closed the public pools to black and white alike." *Palmer*, 403 US at 226.

[98] Id at 225.

matizing effects.[99] What really mattered in *Palmer* was not the swimming pools per se—just as what really mattered in the sit-ins and Freedom Rides was not the hamburgers per se or the seating per se. What really mattered was the social meaning of closing pools *to avoid desegregation*. Contrary to what Chief Justice Burger wrote, the plaintiffs did not assert that it was unconstitutional to close pools once opened.[100] Rather, the plaintiffs insisted that it was unconstitutional to close pools *for the purpose of avoiding desegregation*. The social meaning of closing the pools *for that purpose* was the social meaning of segregation[101]—both were ways of expressing and perpetuating the superiority of whites over blacks.[102] Invidious discrimination is, as Professor Deborah L. Brake notes, "a social practice that evolves over time and has no fixed form."[103] Enforcement of *Brown v Board of Education* and its progeny prevented officials from continuing to inscribe racial hierarchy upon recreation through separate-but-equal in swimming pools. Such enforcement, however, did not entirely quiet segregationists. They responded in Jackson by "leveling down": creating a spurious "equality" by denying everyone access to the pools. The Court deemed this maneuver compatible with the Equal Protection Clause. In the context of *Palmer*, however, "levelling down serve[d] the same function as the prior segregation: it perpetuate[d] social hierarchy and racial separation by preventing whites and blacks from sharing city pools as equals."[104]

The Court awarded Fourteenth Amendment absolution to the Jackson authorities, reasoning that they had treated the races equally by denying everyone access to the public pools. But that absolution was misguided. The Jackson authorities did not accept or permit

---

[99] *Closing of Municipal Swimming Pools* at 90 (cited in note 2).

[100] *Palmer*, 403 US at 228.

[101] Professor Charles L. Black Jr. described "the social meaning of segregation" as "putting . . . the Negro in a position of walled-off inferiority." *The Lawfulness of the Segregation Decisions*, 69 Yale L J 421, 427 (1960).

[102] It is true that the closures were a sign of progress in that *Brown v Board of Education* and its progeny no longer permitted separate but equal public facilities. But segregation itself was a sign of progress in that, in principle, it required provision of services to colored folk if the government offered services to white folk. Segregation, albeit bad, was better than total exclusion. The presence of progress within layers of racial oppression underscores the depth of the problem that racial reformers have faced over the centuries.

[103] Brake, 46 Wm & Mary L Rev at 576 (cited in note 2). Professor Brake's article is, as suggested by the references in the text, wonderfully illuminating.

[104] Id.

racial equality at the pools. Rather, they determined that pools previously allocated racially had now become "unworthy of preservation if [they] must be shared on equal terms with those previously excluded."[105] The authorities did not offer equality through closure; they only imposed yet another form of racial subordination.

Because the closure in *Palmer* burdened whites as well as blacks, some observers intuit that there must have been some bona fide, nonprejudicial reason behind the closure because, after all, the pool closing would cost whites too. A socially dominant group, however, might well initiate or support a policy that hurts it in the short run *if* it believes that, in the long run, the policy will perpetuate its ascendancy. Leveling down "may be a particularly effective way to enforce status hierarchies for the very reason that the higher status group has deprived itself of a material benefit in order to preserve existing status differentials."[106]

VIII. The Problem of Discriminatory Intent

For constitutional theorists the most important facet of *Palmer* is Justice Black's handling of the charge that the Jackson authorities' closure of the pools violated the Equal Protection Clause because, in the absence of any overriding justification, that decision stemmed from a constitutionally prohibited motive, intent, or purpose.[107] "[N]o case in this Court," Justice Black observed, "has held that a legislative act may violate equal protection solely because of the motivations of the men who voted for it."[108] He acknowledged that "there is language in some of our cases . . . which may suggest that the motive or purpose behind a law is relevant to its constitutionality."[109] But he maintained that "the focus in those cases was on the actual effect of the enactments, not upon the motivation which led the States to behave as they did."[110]

---

[105] Id.

[106] Id at 578.

[107] "Motive," "intent," and "purpose" are used here as synonyms. For an analysis differentiating these terms, see Richard H. Fallon Jr., *Constitutionally Forbidden Legislative Intent*, 130 Harv L Rev 523, 535–36 (2016).

[108] *Palmer*, 403 US at 224.

[109] Id at 225.

[110] Id.

Two related problems discredit Justice Black's analysis. One problem is descriptive, the other normative. First, Justice Black's rendition of the Court's relevant case law is again tendentious. There were equal protection cases in which the Court had maintained that it was improper to examine the intent of legislators.[111] In other cases, however, the matter of intent loomed large in the Court's judgment of a challenged act—which is understandable since, as a practical matter, it is difficult to see how, in applying the Equal Protection Clause, judges could sensibly disregard the intent of officials.[112] This is evident in two rulings that Justice Black himself articulated on behalf of the Court. In *Korematsu v United States*, he voiced the Court's justification for the federal government's wholesale removal of all persons of Japanese ancestry from the West Coast during World War II. This program—the largest single instance of racial profiling in American history—made no distinction between citizens and noncitizens of Japanese ancestry and made no attempt to engage in individualized screening. "Pressing public necessity may sometimes justify the existence of such restrictions," he wrote, "racial antagonism never can."[113] A program of detention motivated by an aim to protect the nation during time of war was one thing, he insisted; the outwardly identical program motivated by "racial antagonism" would be wholly

---

[111] See, for example, *Soon Hing v Crowley*, 113 US 703 (1883); *Williams v Mississippi*, 170 US 213 (1898).

[112] In the Supreme Court's first application of the Equal Protection Clause in a race relations case, Justice William Strong wrote in *Strauder v West Virginia*, 100 US 303 (1880), that the Fourteenth Amendment contained a right "most valuable to the colored race—the right to exemption from unfriendly legislation." Id at 308. Examination of purpose would certainly seem to be pertinent to determine whether a given act is "friendly" or "unfriendly." In *Loving v Virginia*, 388 US 1 (1967), the legislation at issue on its face treated blacks and whites symmetrically; it forbade whites from marrying across the color line just like it forbade blacks from marrying across the color line. The Court invalidated the antimiscegenation statute, however, because it was "designed to maintain White Supremacy." Id at 11. In saying that the legislation was "designed" to accomplish a certain end, the Court was necessarily judging the defendant's aim, purpose, motive.

The clearest example of judicial focus on purpose in equal protection jurisprudence arises from cases in which it is alleged that, in the absence of criteria making any reference to race, racial discrimination has nonetheless contaminated the selection of juries. The Supreme Court has long insisted that, as a constitutional matter, no particular racial demography is required on juries. An all-white jury is perfectly valid so long as officials do not seek purposefully to make it all white. See *Neal v Delaware*, 103 US 370 (1880); *Norris v Alabama*, 294 US 587 (1935); *Smith v Texas*, 311 US 128 (1940). See also Ely, 79 Yale L J at 1260 (cited in note 2) ("So long as the Court remains unwilling to order states to take race into account in selecting their jury panels, judicial review must await proof of racial motivation and cannot be triggered by disproportion *per se*.").

[113] *Korematsu*, 323 US at 216.

different. The centrality of discriminatory purpose to the *Griffin* Court's reasoning is also evident despite Justice Black's subsequent obfuscation. Closing a public school on "nonracial grounds" might be permissible, Justice Black intoned in *Griffin*.[114] But wholly impermissible would be closing schools "to ensure . . . that white and colored children would not, under any circumstance, go to the same school."[115]

Second, intent *should* matter in determining the constitutionality of governmental conduct under the Equal Protection Clause. Justice Black tried to separate intent from "the actual effect" of governmental action. Intent, however, colors "the actual effect." It is one thing if the government injures you accidentally or incidentally as officials attempt to pursue some legitimate mission. It is something else entirely if the putatively "same" action is done with the aim of hurting you.[116] As the Court observed in *Gomillion v Lightfoot*,[117] "[a]cts generally lawful may become unlawful when done to accomplish an unlawful end."[118]

Palmer seemed to contend that all facially neutral, evenly administered closures should be acceptable under the Equal Protection Clause no matter what the real purpose behind the closures. Such a contention is misguided. Closing a pool for some nonracial reason will have a different "actual effect" than closing a pool to protect whites from the feared contaminating presence of Negroes. The purpose and effect of the latter closure is to affix a racial brand of subordination. Contrary to what Justice Black suggested, the plaintiffs in *Palmer* did not argue that their rights to equal protection were violated "solely" because of the racist thinking of the authorities in Jackson. The plaintiffs argued that their rights were violated when a consequence of that thinking—the closure of the pools—stigmatized them concretely through a deprivation whose social meaning was different, more burdensome, for blacks than for whites.

Disabled by *Brown* and its progeny from directly segregating the races, Mayor Thompson and his colleagues pursued their segregationist mission by resort to indirect means. Both techniques, how-

---

[114] 377 US at 231.

[115] Id.

[116] See Oliver Wendell Holmes Jr., *The Common Law* 3 (1881) ("[E]ven a dog distinguishes between being stumbled over and being kicked.").

[117] 394 US 339 (1960).

[118] Id at 347.

ever, were invidious discriminations that should have been held to violate the Fourteenth Amendment. The Court did not sufficiently appreciate that invidious racial discrimination can mutate. Chameleon-like, it can change shapes, sounds, and rationales to survive under new conditions. After the invalidation of segregation by *Brown* and its progeny, racist officials could no longer openly resort to compulsory separation and stratification pursuant to the maintenance of pigmentocracy. So they turned to different means of accomplishing the same old mission, including closures that offered a mirage of "equality."

IX. AFTER PALMER

Five years after *Palmer*, the Supreme Court adjudicated a case in which the plaintiffs, black candidates for jobs as police officers in Washington, DC, sued on a variety of statutory and constitutional theories. One was that the city government violated the Equal Protection Clause, even in the absence of discriminatory purpose, by relying upon criteria that adversely affected the pool of black candidates disproportionately and by doing so without showing that those criteria identified skills necessary for satisfactory job performance. In *Washington v Davis*,[119] the Court rejected that theory of *constitutional* liability.[120] In an opinion by Justice White, it ruled that the presence of an intent to discriminate is an essential predicate for an equal protection violation. In Justice White's words, "the invidious quality of [government action] claimed to be racially discriminatory must ultimately be traced to a racially discriminatory purpose."[121] In *Palmer* the Court eschewed inquiry into purpose. But in *Washington* the Court said that, with regard to invoking the Equal Protection Clause, inquiry into purpose was mandatory. Justice White acknowledged that *Palmer* contained "indications to the contrary" of what was being posited in *Washington*.[122] But the actual holding of *Palmer*, he insisted, was consistent with *Washington*: "[Jackson] was not overtly

---

[119] 426 US 229 (1976).

[120] In *Washington* the Court rejected the plaintiffs' disparate-impact theory as a constitutional basis of liability. The Court accepted the plaintiffs' disparate-impact theory as a basis of liability under Title VII of the 1964 Civil Rights Act but concluded that the plaintiff had failed to adduce evidence sufficient to prevail statutorily. A point of continuity, then, between *Palmer* and *Washington* is that in both the plaintiffs lost.

[121] Id at 240.

[122] Id at 242.

or covertly operating segregated pools, and was extending identical treatment to both whites and Negroes."[123] Having exposed the flaws of *Palmer* so witheringly, Justice White now participated uncomplainingly in permitting it to retain an odd vitality.[124]

On June 13, 1975, Jackson finally opened desegregated pools to the public. This happened not as a consequence of legal prescription but rather by dint of other developments.[125] Negrophobia and hostility to blacks' demands for equal rights had declined. Prejudices against blacks remained widespread. But its intensity abated. Many whites continued to fight hard to maintain their racial hegemony. But fewer continued to demand segregation or its surrogates in the old, unvarnished style. Whites in Jackson and elsewhere in the Deep South became embarrassed by naked bigotry and aware that conspicuous racism would alienate powerful potential allies, including prospective investors. Moreover, the enfranchisement of blacks in the aftermath of the Voting Rights Act of 1965 and related events prompted increasing numbers of politicians to pay some attention to the needs and sensibilities of African American voters. When it became clearly more advantageous to open desegregated pools than to keep pools closed, politicians acted accordingly. Reporting on the inauguration of desegregated swimming in Jackson, a journalist observed: "With no fanfare . . . park officials simply swung open the safety gates . . . and let dozens of youngsters escape a broiling sun by plunging into the pools."[126]

X. Why Palmer Remains Significant

The Supreme Court occupies a unique niche in American governance. It is widely viewed as different from, better than, the so-called "political branches." Much of the Court's prestige derives from the popular perception that it is "above politics," that it traffics in more than power and interest, that it is a forum in which the weak and the strong meet as equals before the law, that its special currency is legal wisdom. The Supreme Court is looked to for instruction in how to

---

[123] Id at 243.

[124] It bears noting that Justice Black joined the Court in *Washington v Davis* and expressed no disagreement with Justice White's handling of his *Palmer* opinions.

[125] B. Drummond Ayres Jr., *In the South of the '70's, Jackson Integrates Pools*, NY Times (June 14, 1975).

[126] Id.

understand the guidance offered by common law, statutory law, and constitutional law as applied to knotty conflicts. More than any other figures in government, the Justices are viewed as wise men and women. To many, they are respected teachers. The Supreme Court, Professor John Hart Ely observed, "is preeminently entrusted with the care of the nation's principles."[127]

For some observers, the record of the federal judiciary in the Second Reconstruction is what most buoys their faith in courts.[128] Because of *Brown*, *Loving*, and judicial solicitude for protestors in the early years of the Black Freedom Struggle, the Fifth Circuit and the Supreme Court have been lavishly praised.[129] Those tribunals are entitled to some of the plaudits they have received. Breaking free from tradition is exceedingly difficult even—sometimes especially—for members of governing elites.[130]

There were judges and justices in the '50s, '60s, and '70s of the twentieth century who repudiated racist norms, thereby provoking negative reaction from within and without the legal profession. But hyperbolic objection by critics—and wishful thinking by admirers— have often inflated the image of the federal courts' inclination and capacity as vehicles for racial progressivism.[131] *Palmer* shows that even during the high tide of federal judicial racial enlightenment, neither the Fifth Circuit nor the Supreme Court could realistically be relied

---

[127] Ely, 79 Yale L J at 1260 (cited in note 2).

[128] See, for example, Owen Fiss, *Pillars of Justice: Lawyers and the Liberal Tradition* (Harvard, 2017); Bruce Ackerman, *We the People: The Civil Rights Revolution* (Harvard, 2014).

[129] See, for example, J. Harvie Wilkinson III, *From Brown to Bakke: The Supreme Court and School Integration, 1954–1978* (Oxford, 1979) at 3 (asserting that the Supreme Court "sired" the Civil Rights Movement and became its "unlikely patron."); Fred L. Banks Jr., *The United States Court of Appeals for the Fifth Circuit: A Personal Perspective*, 16 Miss College L R 275, 288 (1996) ("[F]or those of us in the civil rights bar, the Fifth Circuit was, on the whole, a beacon of hope for something approaching justice. More often than not, under the leadership of John Brown, John Minor Wisdom, Richard Rives, and Elbert Parr Tuttle, it answered the call with wisdom, understanding, and determination. Never before had a court played such a vital role in managing social change in such a large region.").

[130] See Randall Kennedy, *J. Skelly Wright and the Racial Desegregation of Louisiana*, 61 Loyola L Rev 57 (2015).

[131] This point has been superbly articulated and substantiated. See, for example, Michael J. Klarman, *Rethinking the Civil Rights and Civil Liberties Revolutions*, 82 Va L Rev 1 (1996); Justin Driver, *The Constitutional Conservatism of the Warren Court*, 100 Calif L Rev 1101 (2012). The sentimental view of the federal judiciary, especially its race relations jurisprudence, is still sufficiently widespread, however, that revisionist realism remains very much needed.

upon in struggles against injustice.[132] Indeed, as *Palmer* shows, these courts could sometimes be downright obtuse.

Care ought to be taken, however, to avoid exaggerating *Palmer's* influence. The ruling's breezy repudiation of judicial focus on discriminatory purpose was itself repudiated five years later in *Washington v Davis*.

It should also be recognized that, albeit regrettable, *Palmer* was not the product of a court engaged in a wholesale abandonment of legal protections for racial minorities. The Term that the Court announced *Palmer*, it also decided *Griggs v Duke Power Company*[133] and *Swann v Charlotte-Mecklenburg Board of Education*[134]—two of the most advanced decisions in the Supreme Court's racial relations jurisprudence. In *Griggs* the Court ratified the disparate-impact theory of liability under Title VII of the Civil Rights Act of 1964. As much a surprise as *Palmer* was a disappointment, *Griggs* embraced an aggressive interpretation of Title VII that was considerably more generous to plaintiffs than a more relaxed reading of the statute might suggest.[135] In *Swann*, despite formidable opposition, the Court upheld the authority of federal judges to order wide-ranging remedies, including busing, to effectuate desegregation in public schools.[136]

Still, *Palmer* casts a disturbing shadow. It teaches that faced with an equal protection challenge, officials can credibly threaten to level down, secure in the knowledge that typically (albeit not always) courts will complacently accept what appears to be uniform deprivation as an allowable form of equal treatment. It teaches that racist recalcitrance pursued artfully can triumph in court. It teaches that, covered by a thin disguise, an act of official bigotry can be repackaged such that the judiciary deems such conduct to be an acceptable act of governance.

---

[132] For other examples of judicial delinquency, see *Swain v Alabama*, 380 US 202 (1965); *Walker v City of Birmingham*, 388 US 307 (1967).

[133] 401 US 424 (1971).

[134] 402 US 1 (1971).

[135] See William N. Eskridge Jr., Philip P. Frickey, and Elizabeth Garrett, *Cases and Materials on Legislation: Statues and the Creation of public Policy* 84 (West, 3d ed 2001) ("Our judgment is that *Griggs* was a more liberal interpretation of Title VII than that which Congress . . . would have wanted in 1971."). See also Michael Evan Gold, *Griggs's Folly: An Essay on the Theory, Problems, and Origin of the Adverse Impact Definition of Employment Discrimination and a Recommendation for Reform*, 7 Indust Rel L J 429 (1985). See also Robert Belton, *The Crusade for Equality in the Workplace: The Griggs v. Duke Power Story* (Kansas, 2014).

[136] See Bernard Schwartz, *Swann's Way: The School Busing Case and the Supreme Court* (Oxford, 1986).

LISA MARSHALL MANHEIM AND
ELIZABETH G. PORTER

THE ELEPHANT IN THE ROOM:
INTENTIONAL VOTER SUPPRESSION

No one tried to sell *Husted v A. Philip Randolph Institute* as a thriller.[1]
The case involved the interpretation of a federal statute—the National Voter Registration Act[2] (NVRA)—that regulates how states
manage the logistics of voter registration.[3] The Court interpreted the
statute to permit a regime in Ohio in which the state presumes that
voters have moved, and accordingly purges them from the rolls, if they
engage in no voting activity for six years, *and* if they fail to return
a postcard to the state confirming their address. What, you might
reasonably ask, is the big deal? The premise of *Husted* would make an
exceedingly dull horror movie.

In fact, *Husted* is significant, and ominous, in a quiet way that
Stephen King could appreciate. On a practical level, *Husted* sanctions
the needless and routine purging from voting rolls of a potentially

Lisa Marshall Manheim is Associate Professor of Law at the University of Washington
School of Law, and Elizabeth G. Porter is Associate Professor of Law and the Charles I.
Stone Professor of Law at the University of Washington School of Law.

AUTHORS' NOTE: We would like to thank Rick Hasen, Justin Levitt, Peter Nicolas, Dan
Tokaji, Kathryn Watts, Rob Yablon, and David Ziff for their insightful suggestions. Special
thanks to Seth Dawson, Christina Jaccard, Emily Parsons, and Adam Sterling for excellent
research assistance.

[1] 138 S Ct 1833 (2018).

[2] Pub L No 103-31, 107 Stat 77 (1993), codified as amended at 52 USC § 20501 et seq.

[3] *Husted*, 138 S Ct at 1841.

very large number of eligible and registered voters. Ohio and other states already have removed hundreds of thousands of voters from voting lists in recent years, typically without persuasive evidence that the removals actually correlate with voter ineligibility.[4] *Husted* opens the door to the adoption of similar or even more stringent purge practices in the future. These reforms tend disproportionately to affect minority and low-income voters.[5] Moreover, their effects are amplified by other voting-related restrictions, with states across the country adopting a wide range of measures making it harder to vote.[6] To a degree that is difficult to measure, this trend undermines the practical ability of eligible voters to cast a ballot and have it counted; it also sends a disturbing message about whether these voters are valued as participants in our democracy.[7]

On a theoretical level, *Husted* is equally concerning. The case represents a culmination of two mutually reinforcing trends: the Supreme Court's deepening ambivalence in matters of voting rights, and a successful propaganda campaign—driven by politically motivated advocates—to persuade legislators and the public that rampant voter

---

[4] See generally Jonathan Brater et al, *Purges: A Growing Threat to the Right to Vote*, Brennan Center for Justice (July 20, 2018), available at https://www.brennancenter.org/sites/default /files/publications/Purges_Growing_Threat_2018.1.pdf (analyzing purge statutes, regulations, and other guidance in forty-nine states).

[5] See, for example, US Commission on Civil Rights, *An Assessment of Minority Voting Rights Access in the US: 2018 Statutory Enforcement Report* **144–57 (Sept 12, 2018), available at https://www.usccr.gov/pubs/2018/Minority_Voting_Access_2018.pdf (documenting disproportionate impact of voter purges in several states, such as Florida's purge of 2012, in which 87 percent of those purged were voters of color).

[6] See, for example, Brief of Amicus Curiae National Association for the Advancement of Colored People and the Ohio State Conference of the NAACP in Support of Respondents, *Husted v A. Philip Randolph Institute*, No 16-980 **6–17 (US filed Sept 22, 2017) (available on Westlaw at 2017 WL 4387145) (describing "History of Voter Suppression in Ohio" and effects on voter engagement); Maggie Astor, *Seven Ways Alabama Has Made It Harder to Vote*, NY Times, available at https://www.nytimes.com/2018/06/23/us/politics/voting-rights-alabama .html (June 23, 2018) (cataloging multiple new vote-restricting measures in Alabama, including the categorization of 340,000 voters as inactive in 2017); Atiba R. Ellis, *Economic Precarity, Race, and Voting Structures*, 104 Ky L J 607, 628 (2016) (discussing effects of "cumulative burdens imposed by the increase in voting regulations").

[7] Anecdotal evidence of these effects abounds. See, for example, Danny Hakim and Michael Wines, *"They Don't Really Want Us to Vote": How Republicans Made It Harder*, NY Times (Nov 3, 2018), available at https://www.nytimes.com/2018/11/03/us/politics/voting-suppression-elections .html#click=https://t.co/Vp9hBuubBZ. Allegations of significant burdens are similarly commonplace. See, for example, Complaint, *Fair Fight Action v Crittenden*, 1:18-cv-05391 (ND Ga filed Nov 27, 2018) (available on Westlaw at 2018 WL 6187610) (complaint filed following 2018 election in Georgia detailing alleged problems). We discuss difficulties with measurement in note 134.

fraud demands suppressive voting restrictions.[8] Together these phenomena have cleared the way for jurisdictions to ratchet up bureaucratic barriers to voting.

It didn't have to be this way. For half a century, the Court has recognized a constitutional right to vote.[9] Yet, a decade ago, in *Crawford v Marion County Election Board*,[10] the Court weakened its enforcement of that right by sustaining the constitutionality of what was, at the time, a relatively novel voter identification law, purportedly aimed at preventing voter fraud.[11] Since then, aided by the acquiescence of a majority of the Supreme Court, the ideology of voter fraud—and the adoption of harshly restrictive measures—has flourished.[12]

The Court's acquiescence would be one thing if these restrictive measures did what they purported to do: prevent the forms of voting fraud, such as in-person voting fraud, that they allegedly target. But as scholars painstakingly have explained, all available evidence indicates that the relevant forms of fraud are empirically so negligible as to be

---

[8] The rise of "voter fraud" theories, advanced by political operatives to justify voting restrictions, has been extensively analyzed. See, for example, Allan J. Lichtman, *The Embattled Vote in America* 180–230 (Harvard, 2018) (describing the prominence of these theories among Republican leaders since the George W. Bush administration); Ari Berman, *Give Us the Ballot: The Modern Struggle for Voting Rights in America* 207–85 (Farrar, Straus and Giroux, 2015) (same); see also id at 264 ("A few unusually candid Republican leaders eventually admitted that fraud wasn't the real issue; race and political power were."); Spencer Overton, *Stealing Democracy: The New Politics of Voter Suppression* 150 & 148–67 (Norton, 2006) (discussing the "conflicting values of voter integrity and voter access" that "increasingly frame today's debates about democracy"). See generally Alexander Keyssar, *The Right to Vote: The Contested History of Democracy in the United States* (Basic Books, 2000); see also id at 263–69 (discussing this history's relevance to the Help America Vote Act of 2002).

[9] See, for example, *Reynolds v Sims*, 377 US 533, 562 (1964) (noting that the right to vote is regarded as "'a fundamental political right, because preservative of all rights'"); see also Section I.B.

[10] 553 US 181 (2008).

[11] See id at 204 (finding the voter identification law "amply justified by the valid interest in protecting the reliability and integrity of the electoral process" (quotation marks omitted)).

[12] For example, as of October 2018, thirty-four states had laws "requesting or requiring voters to show some form of identification at the polls," with the nonpartisan National Conference of State Legislatures characterizing ten of those regimes as "strict." Wendy Underhill, *Voter Identification Requirements/Voter ID Laws*, National Conference of State Legislatures (Oct 31, 2018), available at http://www.ncsl.org/research/elections-and-campaigns/voter-id.aspx; see also *Voter ID: Five Considerations*, 35 *The Canvass: States and Election Reform* 1, 2 (National Conference of State Legislatures, Nov–Dec 2012), available at http://www.ncsl.org/documents/legismgt/elect/Canvass_Nov_Dec_2012_No_35.pdf ("Concern about election fraud is the most commonly cited reason for backing photo ID measures."); Brater et al, *Purges: A Growing Threat to the Right to Vote* at *1 (cited in note 4) (stating that "[a]lmost 4 million more names were purged from the rolls between 2014 and 2016 than between 2006 and 2008").

nonexistent.[13] This reality suggests that another, darker motivation may actually drive many of these efforts. The state procedure at issue in *Husted* provides a possible point of reference. On its face, Ohio's voter-list maintenance regime is a neutral measure that helps to combat fraud and maintain accurate records. Yet measures like Ohio's tend to have the effect, and often the purpose, of suppressing eligible votes.

Alleging that a state has engaged in intentional voter suppression is hardly novel; in recent years, debates over suppressive tactics have become front-page news.[14] Yet in response to this heated public discourse, the Supreme Court has remained aloof; its voting-rights jurisprudence effectively ignores the phenomenon. *Husted* is illustrative. On the one hand, it is the first majority opinion of the Supreme Court even to use the term "voter suppression."[15] On the other, the Court raises the issue only to dismiss it as irrelevant. For their part, the *Husted* plaintiffs thought it best not even to raise the question whether Ohio might have acted with the intention of suppressing their own eligible voters.

We define intentional voter suppression as any action taken with the intent to make it less likely that an eligible voter's ballot will be cast or counted.[16] (We omit the word "intentional" when we mean to refer

---

[13] See, for example, Samuel Issacharoff, *Ballot Bedlam*, 64 Duke L J 1363, 1377–79 (2015) (detailing lack of evidence of in-person voter fraud). In addition, there tends to be a stark disconnect between the rare cases of documented voting fraud (such as those associated with theft of absentee ballots) and the practices that legislatures purport to target through restrictive measures (primarily those associated with in-person voting or voter registration). For further discussion of this disconnect, including how it relates to recent controversies in North Carolina, see notes 105–23 and accompanying text.

[14] See, for example, Michael Wines, *Is Target of New Voting Laws Fraud or Blacks?*, NY Times A1 (July 31, 2016); see also Philip Bump, *Americans See Voter Suppression as a Bigger Problem Than Voter Fraud*, Wash Post (Oct 31, 2018), available at https://www.washingtonpost.com/politics /2018/10/31/americans-see-voter-suppression-bigger-problem-than-voter-fraud/?utm_term =.8adace86f63b.

[15] See *Husted*, 138 S Ct at 1848 (quoting Justice Sotomayor's dissent but finding voter suppression to be not "relevant"). Nor has the Supreme Court ever used the term "vote denial."

[16] The term "voter suppression" tends to overlap with "vote denial," which Daniel Tokaji defines as "practices that prevent people from voting or having their votes counted." Daniel P. Tokaji, *The New Vote Denial: Where Election Reform Meets the Voting Rights Act*, 57 SC L Rev 689, 691 (2006); see also Daniel P. Tokaji, *Applying Section 2 to the New Vote Denial*, 50 Harv CR-CL L Rev 439, 439–40 (2015). We use the term "intentional voter suppression" both to emphasize the individual right-holder (the voter) and also because it tracks the formulation used in *Husted*. In this article, we do not distinguish between the government's "intentions," "purposes," and "motivations," but instead use these terms interchangeably to refer to legislative aims, the underlying values that cause officials to pursue these aims, or both. See Richard H. Fallon Jr., *Constitutionally Forbidden Legislative Intent*, 130 Harv L Rev

to an action that, regardless of intent, is likely to have a suppressive effect.) By "eligible voter," we mean to include every United States citizen residing in a given jurisdiction, subject to a small number of exceptions.[17] So defined, intentional voter suppression has become, for the Supreme Court, the elephant in the room. This metaphor is apt both because the Court has failed to acknowledge the issue and also in light of the embrace of a range of suppressive measures by many in the modern Republican party.[18]

It is not clear how voting-rights proponents should respond. In the past, Congress legislated against the scourge of suppressive election measures.[19] Yet in 2019 the probability of a congressional solution seems negligible. In its absence, citizens' right to vote is left to the vagaries of the states' political processes, and to the courts. As for the latter, recent changes to the Supreme Court's composition make it even less likely that the Court will turn its attention to protecting the right to vote in the near, or even the medium-term, future. Still, now that litigants no longer need to frame their arguments with one eye on Justice Kennedy, there may be more space for the maturation of legal theories to prevent voter suppression, even if those theories do not bear immediate fruit.

To this end, our article proceeds in two parts. In Part I, we place *Husted* in context: as a proxy battle over the fundamental right to vote.

523, 534–36 (2016) (discussing distinctions between these terms). Though this approach sacrifices linguistic precision, it tracks the Supreme Court's use. See id.

[17] These exceptions include eligibility restrictions based on age, residence, felon status, and mental capacity. In a long-standing and well-established line of cases, the Supreme Court approved these exceptions but otherwise insisted that the states provide to each and every one of their citizens access to the ballot booth. See Joseph Fishkin, *Equal Citizenship and the Individual Right to Vote*, 86 Ind L J 1289, 1339–50 (2011) (describing "the story of voting rights in the twentieth century" as one in which courts, legislatures, and the public began to embrace the idea that "each adult citizen was entitled—in virtue of being a citizen—to vote"). For a critique of how states implement felon disenfranchisement, see generally Jessie Allen, *Documentary Disenfranchisement*, 86 Tulane L Rev 389 (2011).

[18] See Issacharoff, 64 Duke L J at 1369 (cited in note 13) ("[T]he single predictor necessary to determine whether a state will impose voter-access restrictions is whether Republicans control the ballot-access process. This is not intended as a normative claim."); see also sources cited in note 8. Still, this political connection is not airtight. Some Republicans have resisted suppressive measures; some Democrats have embraced them. Compare, for example, Berman, *Give Us the Ballot* at 262 (cited in note 8) (discussing Republicans), with Vivian Wang, *Why Deep Blue New York Is "Voter Suppression Land,"* NY Times (Dec 19, 2018), available at https://www.nytimes.com/2018/12/05/us/politics/north-carolina-vote-fraud-absentee.html (discussing Democrats).

[19] See Keyssar, *The Right to Vote* 104–15 (cited in note 8) (describing lead-up to the enactment of the Voting Rights Act). For an insightful history of the VRA, see generally J. Morgan Kousser, *The Strange, Ironic Career of Section 5 of the Voting Rights Act, 1965–2007*, 86 Tex L Rev 667 (2008).

The *Husted* plaintiffs could have framed their claim more broadly—as a direct constitutional challenge to intentionally suppressive measures that Ohio allegedly implemented, at least in part, on a pretense. Yet instead they opted for a narrow and technical argument based on the NVRA. Given the Court's current distaste for the robust enforcement of voting rights, this approach was strategically understandable. But it failed. Rather than providing the *Husted* plaintiffs with the modest relief they sought, the Court's myopic opinion helped to validate the evidentiarily bankrupt narrative of voter fraud. In this sense, *Husted* represents a natural extension of the voting-rights jurisprudence already emergent from the Roberts Court. Against an increasingly aggressive pattern of suppressive voting measures, the Court has shielded its eyes; in response to unfounded allusions to voter fraud, it has opened its arms.

How else might the plaintiffs have framed their claim? In Part II, we sketch an argument that precedent might allow, if only the Court were willing to acknowledge the reality and constitutional implications of intentional voter suppression. More specifically, we turn to the neglected Equal Protection framework developed by the Supreme Court in the voting-rights context, to argue that a state acts unconstitutionally when it engages in intentional voter suppression. Surprisingly, this straightforward principle remains unacknowledged in the doctrine. If accepted, it would require judicial scrutiny of election practices to move beyond talking points, to allow genuine adversarial testing of states' justifications for restrictive measures.

We realize that no intent-based interpretation of the Equal Protection Clause can be a voting-rights panacea. Sometimes, jurisdictions offend the right to vote inadvertently, while acting in good faith, and evidentiary hurdles remain even when a state's offenses are intentional. Moreover, a theory of intentional voter suppression responds to the problems eligible voters may face when casting a ballot; it does not address other problems, such as vote dilution associated with redistricting.[20] Finally, a theory of intentional voter suppression does not directly address the overlapping but distinct problems of race-related suppression.[21] Nevertheless, as we argue below, protection

---

[20] See Daniel P. Tokaji, *Vote Dissociation*, 127 Yale L J F 761, 762 n 9, 763 (2018) (defining "vote denial" and "vote dilution" and introducing the concept of "vote dissociation").

[21] Consider, for example, Samuel R. Bagenstos, *Universalism and Civil Rights (with Notes on Voting Rights After Shelby)*, 123 Yale L J 2838, 2840–41 (2014) (identifying dangers inherent in "universalist responses to civil rights problems").

against intentional voter suppression could prevent further constitutional backsliding and help protect the right to vote.

Subtly, but powerfully, *Husted* confirms the need for the federal courts to take seriously the threat of intentional voter suppression. Unfortunately, the decision also confirms just how difficult it will be, for the foreseeable future, to convince them to do it. In the guise of a bloodless disquisition on statutory interpretation, *Husted* underscores the Supreme Court's willingness to use its limited institutional resources and massive institutional power not to protect voters, but instead to aid and abet a rollback of voting rights.

I. Husted v A. Philip Randolph Institute: Score One for "Voter Fraud"

On its surface, *Husted* is a statutory interpretation case. The plaintiffs in *Husted* did not bring a constitutional claim,[22] and the majority opinion does not rely on, or even exude a whiff of, the fundamental nature of the right to vote.[23] Instead, the opinion trains narrowly on the proper interpretation of a few provisions of the National Voter Registration Act of 1993 (NVRA), commonly known as the "Motor-Voter Act" because of its central mandate that people be able to register to vote at their local department of motor vehicles.[24] In this part, we briefly explain how the majority and dissenting opinions in *Husted* interpret the NVRA. Then we place *Husted* in context. The case is a proxy battle in a larger war—the war for and against the right to vote. And the Court in *Husted* takes a dispiriting position in that war.

A. HUSTED ON ITS OWN MYOPIC TERMS

The question presented in *Husted* was whether Ohio's mechanism for maintaining voter registration lists—which the state adopted in the 1990s and began implementing more aggressively in 2014—vi-

---

[22] See Complaint, *A. Philip Randolph Inst. v Husted*, No 2:16-cv-303, **1–3, 13–15 (SD Ohio filed Apr 6, 2016).

[23] See *Husted*, 138 S Ct at 1848.

[24] Royce Crocker, *The National Voter Registration Act of 1993: History, Implementation, and Effects* 3 (Congressional Research Service, Sept 18, 2013), available at https://fas.org/sgp/crs/misc/R40609.pdf.

olated the National Voter Registration Act.[25] The self-proclaimed purpose of the NVRA was to promote the fundamental right to vote by making it easier for citizens to obtain and maintain voter registration.[26] The Act also requires states to make a reasonable effort to maintain accurate voter rolls, though it prohibits states from doing so by removing registered voters except under particular circumstances.[27]

Widely understood as a civil rights law, the NVRA passed Congress along partisan lines, with only a handful of Republican supporters. Voting-rights advocates, as well as the US Department of Justice, had long used the statute to force states to offer voter registration at a range of public agencies. It therefore seems reasonable that voting-rights advocates, like the plaintiffs in *Husted*, would invoke the NVRA to block state laws that potentially have the result of purging large numbers of eligible, registered voters from polling lists. During the George W. Bush administration, however, conservative theorists began—through litigation and legislation—to recast the NVRA as a stringent anti-voter-fraud law.[28] This reframing reflected a conserva-

---

[25] *Husted*, 138 S Ct at 1841. Although Ohio employed its Supplemental Process every two years since 1994, it began implementing the process annually in 2014, after entering into a settlement following a 2012 lawsuit by two conservative groups, Judicial Watch and True the Vote. See Brief for the Petitioner, *Husted v A. Philip Randolph Institute*, No 16-980, *11 (US filed July 31, 2017) (available on Westlaw at 2017 WL 3412011). For further discussion of this litigation and settlement, see note 190 and accompanying text.

[26] See 52 USC § 20501(a) (finding that "(1) the right of citizens of the United States to vote is a fundamental right," and "(2) it is the duty of the Federal, State, and local governments to promote the exercise of that right"), and § 20501(b)(1) (describing the statute's purposes, including "to establish procedures that will increase the number of eligible citizens who register to vote in elections for Federal office").

[27] See 52 USC § 20507(a)(4) (requiring states to "conduct a general program that makes a reasonable effort to remove the names of ineligible voters from the official lists").

[28] See J. Christian Adams, *A Primer on "Motor Voter": Corrupted Voter Rolls and the Justice Department's Selective Failure to Enforce Federal Mandates*, Heritage Foundation (Sept 25, 2014), available at https://www.heritage.org/election-integrity/report/primer-motor-voter-corrupted -voter-rolls-and-the-justice-departments?_ga = 2.190407339.1043249503.1546456196 -529764859.1546456196#_ftnref8 (explaining how conservative efforts began in 2005 to use Section 8 of the NVRA "to combat corrupted voter rolls and the voter fraud that can flourish because of those corrupted rolls"); Brief of Former Attorneys of the Civil Rights Division of the United States Department of Justice as Amici Curiae in Support of Petitioner, *Husted v A. Philip Randolph Institute*, No 16-980, **4, 13–14 (US filed Aug 7, 2017) (available on Westlaw at 2017 WL 3447772) (attorneys who served in the DOJ Civil Rights Division during the Bush administration describing the agreements they negotiated with local governments requiring the adoption of programs "to keep their voter rolls up to date"); Adam Gitlin and Wendy R. Weiser, *The Justice Department's Voter Fraud Scandal: Lessons*, Brennan Center for Justice (2017), available at https://www.brennancenter.org/sites/default/files/publications/Justice_Department_Voter _Fraud_Scandal_Lessons.pdf (noting that before 2004, the DOJ had asserted only one claim that a state failed to purge its rolls, but "from 2004–2007 it asserted six").

tive movement long in the making,[29] and one that has accelerated under the current administration.[30] According to this view, the NVRA mandates that states implement aggressive measures to remove ineligible voters from the rolls, even if those measures may also have the effect of removing large swaths of eligible voters. Ohio's program is just such a regime.

In this sense, *Husted* represents a struggle for the soul of the NVRA, one fought over the effects the statute has on states' maintenance of voting records. At the outset, the NVRA imposes a requirement: each state must make a "reasonable effort" to remove voters from the registration lists who are ineligible by reason of death or a change of residence.[31] The NVRA specifies that states may meet this obligation by relying on set procedures associated with the US Postal Service's change-of-address data.[32]

But some states, like Ohio, exceed the NVRA's baseline requirement and purge voters more aggressively. These states must ensure that their practices comply with the Act's voter protections. The NVRA requires, for example, that no voter be removed "by reason of [a] failure to vote."[33] This prohibition, which the *Husted* Court refers to as the "Failure-to-Vote Clause," reflected Congress's concerns over states' historical willingness to purge voters for simply not voting, in a manner that "sharply depressed turnout, particularly among blacks

---

[29] See Lichtman, *The Embattled Vote in America* 247–48 (cited in note 8) (recounting a 1980 speech by Paul Weyrich, one of the most influential founders of the modern conservative movement, in which he criticized those who "want everybody to vote" and then explained: "I don't want everyone to vote. Elections are not won by a majority of people. . . . As a matter of fact our leverage in the elections quite candidly goes up as the voting populace goes down."); id (making the connection between these sentiments and more recent measures purportedly meant to combat voter fraud).

[30] See Brief for American History Professors as Amici Curiae in Support of Respondents, *Husted v A. Philip Randolph Institute*, No 16-980, **27–30 (US filed Sept 22, 2017) (available on Westlaw at 2017 WL 4298128) (describing how for "two decades and over three different presidential administrations," the Department of Justice interpreted the NVRA as prohibiting all forms of purging for nonvoting). Indeed, in *Husted* itself, the Department of Justice originally sided with the plaintiffs, arguing that the NVRA prohibited Ohio's purging practice. The DOJ switched sides before the Supreme Court to defend Ohio's practice.

[31] 52 USC § 20507(a)(4)(A)–(B). This program must be "uniform, nondiscriminatory, and in compliance with the Voting Rights Act." Id § 20507(b)(1). The plaintiffs in *Husted* originally alleged that Ohio's Supplemental Process was applied in a nonuniform manner in violation of 52 USC § 20507(b)(1), but the district court rejected that claim and plaintiffs did not renew it on appeal. *A. Philip Randolph Institute v Husted*, 838 F3d 699, 705 n 4 (6th Cir 2016).

[32] 52 USC § 20507(c).

[33] Id § 20507(b)(2).

and immigrants."[34] In 2002, the Help America Vote Act (HAVA) amended this Failure-to-Vote Clause.[35] The resulting statutory language, while awkward, confirms a central mandate: a state can remove registered voters from voting rolls if it has determined they have become ineligible—including as a result of moving out of their voter district—but *not* simply for failing to vote. Moreover, all voters must be notified, and also given an opportunity to reaffirm their eligibility, prior to being removed from voting rolls.[36] In *Husted*, the dispute arose because Ohio's voter-maintenance regime walks a fine line between these various mandates.

Specifically, Ohio is among the states that go beyond the NVRA's baseline of using US Postal Service records to identify voters who may have moved. Under its Supplemental Process, Ohio presumes that a wide swath of voters might have changed residence: anyone who has not participated in an election in the prior two years.[37] This approach captures an enormous number of potential voters; in recent nonpresidential years, Ohio's turnout rate has averaged less than 50 percent.[38] In Ohio's view, this sweeping presumption—based on nothing more than a failure to vote for two years—does not amount to the removal of voters from the rolls for not voting. Instead, it simply equates nonvoting with a possible change of residence. Each year, accordingly, Ohio sends those nonvoters a prepaid, preaddressed return card, as required by the NVRA.[39] Nonvoters who neither return the card, nor vote in four subsequent years, are stricken from Ohio's polling lists.

---

[34] *Husted*, 138 S Ct at 1863 (Sotomayor, J, dissenting) (quotation marks omitted).

[35] Pub L No 107-252, 116 Stat 1666 (2002), codified as amended at 52 USC § 20901 et seq. A motley grab-bag of election reform measures, the HAVA was passed in response to the Florida voting chaos that led to *Bush v Gore*, 531 US 98 (2000). Among other changes, the HAVA amended the "Failure-to-Vote Clause" in a manner that fomented disagreement in *Husted*. See 52 USC § 20507(b)(2).

[36] See 52 USC § 20507(d)(1)(A)–(B). Specifically, the state must receive notification from the voter, or it must wait long enough to verify that the voter has failed to return a postcard *and* subsequently failed to participate in two federal elections. Id.

[37] *Husted*, 138 S Ct at 1840.

[38] See *Voter Turnout in General Elections*, Ohio Secretary of State, available at https://www.sos.state.oh.us/elections/election-results-and-data/historical-election-comparisons/voter-turnout-in-general-elections/#gref.

[39] Even after the Court's decision, the question whether Ohio's postcard complies with the NVRA's requirements remained in dispute. See Order, *A. Randolph Institute v Husted*, No 18-3984 (6th Cir filed Oct 31, 2018) (finding plaintiffs are likely to succeed on the merits of their claim that the postcards sent to Ohio voters do not comply with the NVRA).

The plaintiffs—two voting-rights organizations and one Ohio citizen whose registration was revoked—contended that Ohio's Supplemental Process violated the NVRA. After a divided panel of the Sixth Circuit granted relief to the plaintiffs, and without so much as a circuit split, the Court selected this case out of the massive stack of petitions before it, granted cert, and tidily provided Ohio with the reversal it requested.

Husted yielded a 5–4 majority opinion, two dissents, and a concurrence. Other than Justice Thomas's concurrence, which takes a troubling side road,[40] the opinions can be conceptualized as three concentric circles. The smallest circle represents the majority opinion, written by Justice Alito and joined by the Chief Justice and Justices Kennedy, Thomas, and Gorsuch. With important exceptions, discussed below, the majority opinion focuses so closely on the text of a select few provisions of the NVRA that it practically swims in the ink. It finds that Ohio's Supplemental Process does not violate the NVRA's prohibition on removing registered voters for a failure to vote, given that voters were merely *identified* as possibly ineligible based on their voting inactivity. By construing the Failure-to-Vote Clause so narrowly, the majority presents the NVRA as providing only minimal protections for registered voters facing the possibility of a mistaken purge. Outside of those narrow limitations, according to the Court, "States can use whatever plan they think best."[41]

The principal dissent, by Justice Breyer—joined by Justices Ginsburg, Kagan, and Sotomayor—widens the circle of inquiry. Still predominantly textualist, the dissent patiently argues that the majority's reasoning conflicts with the text and structure of the NVRA because, by relying on a two-year failure to vote as a trigger for the return card, Ohio's regime does target voters for removal from the rolls solely based on their failure to vote.[42] Justice Breyer's dissent also finds Ohio's regime unlawful on an independent ground: because the NVRA requires states to implement a "reasonable" program.[43] Citing a range

---

[40] Justice Thomas joined the majority opinion in full, but concurred to reiterate his view—previously expressed in his dissent in *Arizona v Inter-Tribal Council of Ariz., Inc.*, 570 US 1, 29 (2013) (Thomas, J, dissenting)—that the Constitution allocates authority over voter qualifications exclusively to the states in a manner that renders many federally imposed limits "constitutionally suspect." 138 S Ct at 1849 (Thomas, J, concurring).

[41] Id at 1847.

[42] Id at 1853–55 (Breyer, J, dissenting).

[43] Id at 1857 (Breyer, J, dissenting).

of statistics, Justice Breyer characterizes Ohio's process not as removing a few eligible voters accidentally around the edges, but instead as an aggressive purging mechanism that casts into doubt the registration of hundreds of thousands of likely eligible voters.[44] Such a regime, the dissent argues, simply is not reasonable. After all, "the purpose" of the NVRA "'is not to test the fortitude and determination of the voter, but to discern the will of the majority.'"[45]

The broadest circle is the lone dissent of Justice Sotomayor, who breaks from her colleagues by naming the elephant in the room. As she eloquently puts it, the majority opinion "entirely ignores the history of voter suppression against which the NVRA was enacted and upholds a program that appears to further the very disenfranchisement of minority and low-income voters that Congress set out to eradicate."[46] Citing submissions by amici showing that "the Supplemental Process has disproportionately affected minority, low-income, disabled, and veteran voters,"[47] Justice Sotomayor's dissent characterizes Ohio's voter purging practices as yet another manifestation of the long, often disturbing history of voter suppression in the United States.

B. HUSTED IN CONSTITUTIONAL CONTEXT

On a theoretical level, *Husted* itself breaks no new ground. It is a traditional opinion that applies traditional tools of statutory interpretation. In that sense, it might be easy to dismiss *Husted* as an unremarkable statutory skirmish concerning the minutiae of election administration. In fact, what is remarkable about *Husted* is an absence rather than a presence: the lack of engagement—by litigants and the Court alike—with the fundamental right to vote in a case concerning state procedures that place the registrations of large swaths of eligible voters at risk. Despite this threat to voters' rights, the plaintiffs' claims

---

[44] Id at 1856 (Breyer, J, dissenting) (explaining that more than a million registered voters failed to send back their return cards but that in all likelihood only a small fraction actually had moved).

[45] Id at 1850–51 (Breyer, J, dissenting) (quoting S Rep No 103-6, 103d Cong, 1st Sess 3 (1993)).

[46] Id at 1865 (Sotomayor, J, dissenting); see also id at 1863 (Sotomayor, J, dissenting) ("Congress enacted the NVRA against the backdrop of substantial efforts by States to disenfranchise low-income and minority voters, including programs that purged eligible voters from registration lists because they failed to vote in prior elections.").

[47] Id at 1864.

in *Husted* did not invoke the Constitution; they rested instead on the technical language of the NVRA.

This strategic decision reflects a sober reality: the current Court does not view the Constitution as robustly protecting the right to vote. This was not always the case. In a series of cases decided in the 1960s, including one that Chief Justice Earl Warren later would identify as the most important of his career, the Supreme Court developed a set of constitutionally derived ground rules for state election adminis-tration.[48] This jurisprudence understood the Reconstruction Amend-ments to require, among other things, that states comply with the one-person, one-vote principle;[49] refrain from "fencing out" potential voters because of "the way they may vote";[50] design elections untinged by race-based discrimination;[51] and overcome searching judicial scru-tiny if they ever seek to restrict the franchise.[52]

Throughout these decisions, the Court's logic was sweeping, its rhetoric soaring. In the landmark case of *Harper v Virginia Board of Elections*,[53] for example, the Court construed a state poll tax as an "invidious" voter qualification rather than as a minor administrative restriction,[54] and it insisted, not for the first time, that "'any alleged infringement of the right of citizens to vote must be carefully and meticulously scrutinized.'"[55] According to the Court, the Fourteenth

---

[48] See Earl Warren, *The Memoirs of Chief Justice Earl Warren* 306–8 (Doubleday, 1977) (identifying *Baker v Carr*, 369 US 186 (1962)).

[49] See, for example, *Baker v Carr*, 369 US 186, 208 (1962) (finding justiciable plaintiffs' claims that wide disparities in the number of inhabitants in voting districts violated the Equal Protection Clause); *Reynolds v Sims*, 377 US 533, 568 (1964) (holding that voter apportionment plans that did not apportion seats in the state legislature on a population basis violated the Equal Protection Clause).

[50] *Carrington v Rash*, 380 US 89, 94, 96–97 (1965) (holding that a state may not deny the opportunity to vote to a bona fide resident merely because he is a member of the armed services).

[51] See *Gomillion v Lightfoot*, 364 US 339, 340–41 (1960) (holding that a state's creation of a 28-sided voting district that excluded black voters would violate the Fifteenth Amendment).

[52] See *Harper v Virginia State Board of Elections*, 383 US 663, 667–70 (1966) (holding that a state poll tax did not survive strict Equal Protection scrutiny); *Kramer v Union Free Sch. Dist. No. 15*, 395 US 621, 626–33 (1969) (holding that limits on eligibility to vote in school board election did not survive strict scrutiny).

[53] 383 US 663 (1966).

[54] Id at 668 (quotation marks omitted).

[55] Id at 667 (quoting *Reynolds*, 377 US at 561–62); see also id at 581 (imposing "careful judicial scrutiny" of apportionment statutes and rejecting rational basis review); *Kramer*, 395 US at 626–27 (applying strict scrutiny).

Amendment compelled such rigor.[56] But the Court also alluded to other possible constitutional sources for this mandate, including a deeper, more structural argument: because "'the right to exercise the franchise in a free and unimpaired manner is preservative of other basic civil and political rights.'"[57]

As the Supreme Court was erecting this constitutional scaffolding, Congress constructed a parallel statutory edifice. Enacted in 1965, the Voting Rights Act (VRA) upended election administration for the jurisdictions that its most powerful provisions covered—which, by legislative design, were the jurisdictions most likely to engage in race-based voter suppression.[58] The courts soon became a battleground over the VRA's constitutionality and application, and the Supreme Court embraced Congress's reforms. The Court not only confirmed the Act's constitutionality and expansive reach;[59] it openly celebrated Congress's "inventive" marshaling of "an array of potent weapons" against the scourge of discriminatory election practices, which it referred to emphatically, and repeatedly, as "evil."[60] So understood and applied, the VRA took broad aim at voter suppression. And more than any electoral reform that has come before or since, it proved effective.[61]

---

[56] See *Harper*, 383 US at 670 ("We have long been mindful that where fundamental rights and liberties are asserted under the Equal Protection Clause, classifications which might invade or restrain them must be closely scrutinized and carefully confined.").

[57] Id at 667 (quoting *Reynolds*, 377 US at 561–62); see id at 665 (identifying possible First Amendment implications of voting); see also *Reynolds*, 377 US at 554–55 (addressing the scope of the right to vote and explaining that "[t]he right to vote freely for the candidate of one's choice is of the essence of a democratic society, and any restrictions on that right strike at the heart of representative government"); Richard W. Trotter, *Vote of Confidence: Crawford v. Marion County Election Board, Voter Identification Laws, and the Suppression of a Structural Right*, 16 NYU J Legis & Pub Pol 515, 554–58 (2013) (describing historical bases for a structural right to vote).

[58] See *South Carolina v Katzenbach*, 383 US 301, 310–16 (1966) (describing legislative background of the VRA); id at 315 ("The heart of the Act is a complex scheme of stringent remedies aimed at areas where voting discrimination has been most flagrant."); see also Keyssar, *The Right to Vote* at 111–13 (cited in note 8).

[59] See, for example, *Katzenbach*, 383 US at 327–36 (sustaining constitutionality of various provisions of the VRA); *Katzenbach v Morgan*, 384 US 641, 643–47 (1966) (same); see also *Allen v State Board of Elections*, 393 US 544, 563–71 (1969).

[60] *Katzenbach*, 383 US at 327, 337; see also id at 309, 328, 329, 330, 331, 336, 337 (referring to state-based racial discrimination in elections as "evil").

[61] See, for example, Daniel Hays Lowenstein, Richard L. Hasen, and Daniel P. Tokaji, *Election Law: Cases and Materials* 115 (Carolina Academic Press, 4th ed 2008) ("[T]he Act was spectacularly successful.").

Perversely, however, the VRA's success may have alleviated pressure to rely on the Constitution as a mechanism for vindicating voting rights. Following the *Harper* era, the Court largely focused on the VRA as a vehicle for protecting voters; it did not develop case law addressing the constitutionality of voter suppression.[62] The fact that the Supreme Court never overruled *Lassiter v Department of Social Services*—a case upholding the constitutionality of a literacy test for voting—helps to illustrate the problem.[63] Decades later, this doctrinal stagnation allowed a more conservative Court to retreat from its earlier constitutional commitments.

In 2006, the Court sounded a warning. In *Purcell v Gonzalez*,[64] the Ninth Circuit had enjoined Arizona from enforcing a newly enacted voter-identification requirement, purportedly adopted to prevent fraud. In its response to Arizona's request for expedited relief, the Supreme Court insisted, without citation, that "[v]oter fraud drives honest citizens out of the democratic process and breeds distrust of our government."[65] Invoking, of all cases, *Reynolds v Sims*,[66] the per curiam opinion insisted that "[v]oters who fear their legitimate votes will be outweighed by fraudulent ones will feel disenfranchised."[67]

Purcell's discussion of voter fraud, and its relationship to the right to vote, appeared in dicta. Not so two years later, when the Supreme Court tackled a direct constitutional challenge to a voter identification requirement.[68] By that time, the Supreme Court was well accustomed to selectively employing decades-old Warren Court precedents. And so, in *Crawford v Marion County Election Board*,[69] in disregard—or at least disrespect—for the Court's searching vigilance in *Harper*, the

---

[62] Fishkin, 86 Ind L J at 1322 (cited in note 17) ("In the late 1960s and early 1970s, . . . Congress and the Court transformed the right to vote from a formal, theoretical guarantee into a substantive entitlement of citizenship. By . . . 2008, those precedents were thirty or forty years old. In the intervening years, the Court had surprisingly few opportunities to develop its jurisprudence of vote denial." (citations omitted)).

[63] 360 US 45 (1959). Though the Supreme Court appeared prepared to overrule *Lassiter* in the 1960s, it did not, and the VRA effectively abrogated it. See Bruce Ackerman, *The Living Constitution*, 120 Harv L Rev 1790–91 & n 169 (2007).

[64] 549 US 1 (2006).

[65] Id at 4.

[66] 377 US 533 (1964).

[67] *Purcell*, 549 US at 4.

[68] See *Crawford v Marion County Election Board*, 553 US 181, 185 (2008).

[69] 553 US 181 (2008).

Court sustained Indiana's voting restriction without employing strict scrutiny.[70]

Instead, in a fractured set of opinions, the Court exhibited enormous deference to Indiana's decision to require that voters show photo identification at the polls. It did so even though the plaintiffs in both *Crawford* and *Harper* brought their claims pursuant to the Equal Protection Clause, and even though Indiana's restriction strikingly resembled the poll tax that *Harper* had rejected.[71] The controlling plurality opinion rejected *Harper*'s approach in favor of a malleable framework developed in a separate legal context (one relating to the equal-protection implications of ballot-access restrictions).[72] Concurring in the judgment, in an opinion joined by Justices Thomas and Alito, Justice Scalia followed a similar path.[73] A majority of the Court therefore accepted without skepticism Indiana's claim that concerns over voter fraud justified its voter identification restriction[74]—despite no evidence that in-person voter fraud posed any problem in Indiana,[75] despite no comparable effort by the state to prevent more prevalent forms of voter fraud, and despite evidence that Indiana's legislators may in fact have been motivated, at least in part, by par-

---

[70] Id at 189–202 (Stevens, J) (plurality); see also id at 204–5 (Scalia, J, concurring); Pamela S. Karlan, *Undue Burdens and Potential Opportunities in Voting Rights and Abortion Law*, 93 Ind L J 139, 148 (2018) ("There is simply no way to reconcile the Court's extraordinary deference in *Crawford* and *Purcell* with its earlier skepticism about voting restrictions.").

[71] Both restrictions determined whether an otherwise eligible voter could vote, and both imposed only a minor burden for most of those affected. Compare *Harper*, 383 US at 668 (addressing whether minimal amount of $1.50 poll tax is constitutionally relevant), with *Crawford*, 553 US at 198–99 (Stevens, J) (plurality) (characterizing the burden of obtaining voter identification as minimal but noting that "a somewhat heavier burden may be placed on a limited number of persons").

[72] In so doing, the plurality and concurring Justices in *Crawford* disregarded the strikingly voter-protective language the Court had featured in cases such as *Harper* and *Reynolds*. As Professor Yablon has observed, this approach reflects more generally the Court's downplaying of the severity of regulatory burdens in voting cases. See Robert Yablon, *Voting, Spending, and the Right to Participate*, 111 NW U L Rev 655, 666–67 (2017).

[73] See *Crawford*, 553 US at 204–9 (Scalia, J, concurring in the judgment).

[74] See id at 196 (Stevens, J) (plurality) ("There is no question about the legitimacy or importance of the State's interest in counting only the votes of eligible voters."); see id at 209 (Scalia, J, concurring) ("[T]he State's interests . . . are sufficient to sustain that minimal burden."). In addition to preventing fraud, the state also asserted that the statute was designed to further its efforts at election modernization and safeguarding voter confidence. Id at 192, 197 (Stevens, J) (plurality).

[75] Id at 194 ("The record contains no evidence of any such fraud actually occurring in Indiana at any time in its history.").

tisan concerns.[76] The three concurring Justices would have deferred even further to the state; their approach may foreshadow where the post–Kennedy Court is headed.[77]

In short, the Court concluded that *Harper* had set too strict a standard for Indiana's restriction. In defense of this position, the plurality suggested that the difference between the challenge in *Crawford* and in *Harper* went to the nature of the state's professed interest. In *Harper*, the Court deemed the only identifiable reason for the poll tax to be "invidious."[78] By contrast, Indiana did proffer reasons for its voter ID law—reasons relating to election integrity—that the plaintiffs conceded were legitimate.[79] According to the *Crawford* plurality, then, in the absence of proof that a state's restriction imposes a "severe" burden on voters, a state need only identify a legitimate interest in order to enjoy a sliding, but generally quite deferential, framework for review.[80]

Still, *Crawford* left open a question: what if a plaintiff demonstrates that an *illegitimate* reason—such as intentional voter suppression— served as a significant motivation for the state's restriction? The *Crawford* plurality came close to answering this question. In the end, however, it held back. The plaintiffs framed their arguments primarily in terms of burdens on the voters and how those burdens should be balanced against the state's purported interests; none squarely brought a claim of intentional voter suppression.[81] While the specter of suppression loomed over the *Crawford* proceedings,[82] the Supreme

---

[76] Id at 203–4 (Stevens, J) (plurality) (finding that "[i]t is fair to infer that partisan considerations may have played a significant role in the decision to enact" the law, but upholding the law because it is "supported by valid neutral justifications").

[77] See id at 204–5 (Scalia, J, concurring in the judgment).

[78] *Harper*, 383 US at 668.

[79] See *Crawford*, 553 US at 191 (Stevens, J) (plurality) (noting that petitioners "do not question the legitimacy of the interests the State has identified").

[80] Id at 189–90 (Stevens, J) (plurality) ("[E]venhanded restrictions that protect the integrity and reliability of the electoral process itself are not invidious and satisfy the standard set forth in *Harper*." (quotation marks omitted)).

[81] See Brief for Petitioners, *Crawford v Marion County Election Board*, No 07-21, *29 (US filed Nov 5, 2007) (available on Westlaw at 2007 WL 3276506) (alluding to intent in only vague terms); Brief for Petitioners, *Indiana Democratic Party v Rokita*, No 07-25, **4, 24, 40– 41, 55–56 (US filed Nov 5, 2007) (available on Westlaw at 2007 WL 3276507) (alleging a partisan-based intent to restrict voting but not directly making a claim of intentional voter suppression—for example by insisting that Indiana's purported concern over voter fraud "is only a pretext designed to justify a law that effectively suppresses Democratic turnout").

[82] See, for example, the opening line in the dissenting opinion below: "Let's not beat around the bush: The Indiana voter photo ID law is a not-too-thinly-veiled attempt to discourage

Court ultimately grappled only with the question of how "partisan considerations" might affect the analysis.[83] According to the plurality, *Harper*'s heightened scrutiny might be appropriate if "such considerations had provided the *only* justification."[84] Of course, "partisan considerations," without more, are not necessarily invidious.[85] Given that the plurality's discussion of intent did not explicitly connect the dots—between an intention to advance partisan ends, on the one hand, and an intention to suppress voters, on the other—the *Crawford* Court left open the possibility that a future court could oversee the development of a distinct claim, also grounded in the Equal Protection Clause, directly targeting intentional voter suppression.[86]

For the present, however, *Crawford* has hindered, rather than helped, voting rights. The Court's deferential approach has created a space for states to allege a legitimate rationale—such as budgetary pressures, or concerns over election security—in an effort to conceal more invidious motives.[87] Compounding this problem, *Crawford* imposed a new and stringent evidentiary obligation on the plaintiff. Where *Harper* did not require the plaintiff to prove the negative effect of a voting restriction,[88] *Crawford* insisted that plaintiffs somehow "quantify" the burden on voters, through evidence on the record, in order to ensure meaningful scrutiny.[89] Yet it is extraordinarily difficult to prove the impact of burdens on voters with any degree of precision, particularly when the Court has never clarified how it should be measured.[90]

---

election-day turnout by certain folks believed to skew Democratic." *Crawford v Marion County Election Board*, 472 F3d 949, 954 (7th Cir 2007) (Evans, J, dissenting).

[83] *Crawford*, 553 US at 203 (Stevens, J) (plurality) (emphasis added).

[84] Id (emphasis added).

[85] See generally Justin Levitt, *Intent Is Enough: Invidious Partisanship in Redistricting*, 59 Wm & Mary L Rev 1993 (2018) (distinguishing among kinds of partisan-based intent); see also note 193 (discussing partisanship in the context of intentional voter suppression).

[86] *Crawford* did not, of course, foreclose arguments that the right could also be protected through other provisions of the Constitution.

[87] See, for example, *Katzenbach*, 383 US at 310–16 (describing long history of literacy tests and other voting restrictions that were applied in a discriminatory way to prevent black voters from voting).

[88] *Harper*, 383 US at 668 ("The degree of the discrimination is irrelevant.").

[89] *Crawford*, 553 US at 200 (Stevens, J) (plurality).

[90] See, for example, Justin Levitt, *Long Lines at the Courthouse: Pre-Election Litigation of Election Day Burdens*, 9 Election L J 19, 32 (2010) (identifying some of these gaps in the case law). We discuss difficulties of measurement in note 134.

Perhaps the most troubling feature of *Crawford*, however, was its embrace of an illusion: the myth of voter fraud. Notwithstanding its acknowledgment that the record contained "no evidence" at all of in-person voter fraud occurring in Indiana "at any time in its history,"[91] the *Crawford* plurality recounted a whimsical example of such fraud from nineteenth-century New York, and then made a labored reference to a single voter committing in-person fraud in the more than a century that followed.[92] These two anecdotes were apparently enough to persuade the plurality that "the risk of voter fraud [is] real" and that "it could affect the outcome of a close election."[93] This dubious logic provided a roadmap for jurisdictions to follow to ensure that their voting-related restrictions evade searching review. It gave no corresponding roadmap for voters to challenge these restrictions as intentionally suppressive.

In *Crawford*, the Court severely weakened, if not dismantled, one of the Warren Court's constitutional foundations. This is not a shock: voting rights is hardly the only area in which the Rehnquist and Roberts Courts have undermined preexisting Equal Protection jurisprudence.[94] Moreover, bookending *Crawford* was, and is, a growing collection of opinions, issued by the Rehnquist and now Roberts Courts, knocking down the protections once afforded by the Voting Rights Act.[95] What was once uniquely transformative has become an "inadequate, costly, and often slow method for protecting voting rights,"[96] and even

---

[91] *Crawford*, 553 US at 194 (Stevens, J) (plurality).

[92] See id at 195 & nn 11–12. See also Justin Levitt, *Analysis of Alleged Fraud in Briefs Supporting Crawford Respondents*, Brennan Center for Justice (Dec 31, 2007), available at https://www .brennancenter.org/sites/default/files/legacy/Democracy/Analysis%20of%20Crawford %20Allegations.pdf.

[93] Id at 196 (Stevens, J) (plurality).

[94] See Bertrall L. Ross II, *Democracy and Renewed Distrust: Equal Protection and the Evolving Judicial Concept of Politics*, 101 Cal L Rev 1565, 1570 (2013) ("The jurisprudence of the Rehnquist and Roberts Courts seemed to reflect [a] more cynical conception of politics, as the discrete and insular minorities that were once entitled to protection under the defective pluralism conception of politics became the object of suspicion.").

[95] See, for example, Richard L. Hasen, *Race or Party, Race as Party, or Party All the Time: Three Uneasy Approaches to Conjoined Polarization in Redistricting and Voting Cases*, 59 Wm & Mary L Rev 1837, 1846 (2018) (describing how the Supreme Court started "reining in" broad interpretations of the Voting Rights Act in the 1990s); see also, for example, *Shelby County v Holder*, 570 US 529, 557 (2013); *Bartlett v Strickland*, 556 US 1, 25–26 (2009) (Kennedy, J) (plurality); *Shaw v Reno*, 509 US 630, 649 (1993).

[96] US Commission on Civil Rights, *An Assessment of Minority Voting Rights Access* at *13 (cited in note 5).

what remains of the Act's mandates is under threat.[97] This judicial destruction of voter protections—both constitutional and statutory, on simultaneous tracks—provides ample space for states to initiate suppressive practices. And so they have.

C. HUSTED AGAINST THE BACKDROP OF THE MYTH OF VOTER FRAUD

The 2010 midterm was a landslide, and not just in Congress: Republicans secured control of more state legislative chambers than they had in over half a century.[98] For many of these Republicans, voting restrictions were a legislative priority. From voter ID bills to registration restrictions, from cutbacks in early voting to purging of registration lists, measures making it harder to vote were adopted by approximately two dozen states in less than eight years.[99] In 2011 and 2012 alone, lawmakers across the country introduced nearly 200 restrictive reforms.[100] Often the efforts appeared to be coordinated,[101] and patterns emerged connecting suppressive measures to high concentrations of minority voters.[102] "Voter fraud" became the clarion call of these measures, which appeared to be designed, at least in part, to energize conservative voters and suppress liberal votes.[103] Notwithstanding the occasional gaffe, Republican leaders generally stuck to the script, repeatedly citing the threat of fraud to explain why they were pushing reforms that otherwise seemed to be in tension with accessible and well-functioning elections.[104]

---

[97] See, for example, Nicholas O. Stephanopoulos, *Disparate Impact, Unified Law*, 128 Yale L J at *18 (forthcoming 2019), available at https://papers.ssrn.com/sol3/papers.cfm?abstract_id=3232079 (arguing that Section 2, as it currently is being construed by the federal courts, is in "serious constitutional danger" once the Supreme Court has an opportunity to weigh in).

[98] *Republicans Exceed Expectations in 2010 State Legislative Elections*, National Conference of State Legislatures (Nov 3, 2010), available at http://www.ncsl.org/press-room/republicans-exceed-expectations-in-2010.aspx (noting that following the 2010 elections, "[t]he GOP will now control at least 54 of the 99 state legislative chambers, its highest number since 1952").

[99] *New Voting Restrictions in America*, Brennan Center for Justice (Dec 30, 2018), available at https://www.brennancenter.org/new-voting-restrictions-america.

[100] See Berman, *Give Us the Ballot* at 260 (cited in note 8).

[101] Id at 260–61.

[102] Id at 260.

[103] See, for example, Lorraine C. Minnite, *The Myth of Voter Fraud* 89 (Cornell, 2010) (describing efforts to "tar Democrats with politically motivated fraud allegations in order to suppress the votes of their most vulnerable voters," and characterizing this approach as a "revision of the Southern strategy").

[104] For examples of gaffes, see notes 156–57 and accompanying text; see also Berman, *Give Us the Ballot* at 264 (cited in note 8) (confirming that the usual response is to cite concerns over fraud).

The problem for these leaders—had they been forced to confront it—is that the threat of widespread, relevant voter fraud remains a fantasy. It is true that elections are complicated and that no state has a perfect electoral system. There even is significant evidence that illegal activity may recently have affected America's elections.[105] Yet this evidence of illegality overwhelmingly relates to activities that can be characterized as operating at the "wholesale" level, which the recent wave of restrictive measures tends to completely ignore.[106] Illustrative is the controversy roiling North Carolina after the 2018 congressional elections, which produced credible claims that political organizers conspired to steal absentee ballots, fill them out, and deliver them to the elections board for counting.[107] Requiring identification at the polls could not possibly have stopped this fraud; nor could purging names from the voting rolls. Instead, the sort of fraud that these restrictions purport to target—people voting in multiple jurisdictions, or noncitizens creeping into polling booths—may be thought of as occurring at the "retail" level.[108] And by all reputable accounts this latter sort of fraud is vanishingly rare.[109] This pattern makes sense as a practical matter: Trying to change the outcome of an

---

[105] See, for example, Kathleen Hall Jamieson, *Cyberwar: How Russian Hackers and Trolls Helped Elect a President: What We Don't, Can't, and Do Know* (Oxford, 2018). See also note 107 and accompanying text for a discussion of alleged fraud affecting a 2018 congressional race in North Carolina.

[106] See Issacharoff, 64 Duke L J at 1377 (cited in note 13) (using "wholesale" and "retail" terminology); see also Rudy Mehrbani, *Heritage Fraud Database: An Assessment*, Brennan Center for Justice (2017), available at https://www.brennancenter.org/sites/default/files/publications /HeritageAnalysis_Final.pdf (comparing types of alleged fraud with measures designed to addressed them).

[107] See generally Dylan Scott, *The Bizarre Allegations of Ballot Tampering in One of 2018's Closest House Elections*, Vox (Dec 4, 2018), available at https://www.vox.com/policy-and-politics/2018 /11/30/18119546/north-carolina-9th-district-election-board-bladen-county-leslie-mccrae -dowless (describing allegations). See also Alan Blinder and Michael Wines, *North Carolina Republicans Targeted Voter Fraud: Did They Look at the Wrong Kind?*, NY Times (Dec 5, 2018), available at https://www.nytimes.com/2018/12/05/us/politics/north-carolina-vote-fraud-absentee .html (noting that North Carolina has one of the strictest voter-identification laws in the nation, but quoting a former lawyer for the North Carolina General Assembly as saying that "[t]he history of fraud in North Carolina is mostly in absentee ballots," which are very lightly regulated).

[108] See Issacharoff, 64 Duke L J at 1377 (cited in note 13).

[109] Id. See also, for example, Sharad Goel et al, *One Person, One Vote: Estimating the Prevalence of Double Voting in U.S. Presidential Elections*, Harvard University (Oct 24, 2017), available at https:// scholar.harvard.edu/files/morse/files/1p1v.pdf (performing statistical analysis showing that a maximum of .02% of votes in the 2012 presidential election could have been double votes); Ray Christensen and Thomas J. Schultz, *Identifying Election Fraud Using Orphan and Low-Propensity Voters*, American Politics Research 42, at 313 (Aug 19, 2013) (concluding that "election fraud, if it occurs, is an isolated and rare occurrence").

election through voter impersonation or other retail-level activity "is much like trying to change the salinity of the sea by adding a box of salt."[110] Despite massive efforts dedicated to uncovering this sort of fraud—the sort of fraud that is possibly susceptible to voter ID laws and similar measures—no serious studies demonstrate its existence on a scale that even approaches a threat to state or national elections.[111]

To the contrary, whenever the existence of these types of voter fraud has been tested, it vanishes. Since his election, President Donald J. Trump has consistently bemoaned the impact of voter fraud. Yet his Presidential Advisory Commission on Election Integrity disbanded without having found any significant evidence of fraud.[112] And just a few days after the Court decided *Husted*, a federal district court struck down a Kansas anti-voter-fraud statute that sought to mandate proof of citizenship for voter registration.[113] The district court's 188-page opinion ruling against Kris Kobach (Kansas's secretary of state, and one of the most prominent promoters of the theory of widespread voter fraud) painstakingly detailed the lack of evidence of fraud.[114] The very few cases that Kansas had identified, the court found, were not associated with noncitizens and were "largely explained by administrative confusion, error, or mistake."[115]

While other organizations and politicians continue staunchly to proclaim the existence of widespread, relevant voter fraud,[116] the actual evidence remains negligible. Consider the "Voter Fraud Data-

---

[110] Issacharoff, 64 Duke L J at 1377 (cited in note 13).

[111] See *Debunking the Voter Fraud Myth*, Brennan Center for Justice (Jan 31, 2017), available at https://www.brennancenter.org/sites/default/files/analysis/Briefing_Memo_Debunking_Voter_Fraud_Myth.pdf (collecting research and judicial determinations finding in-person voter fraud is rare to nonexistent).

[112] Michael Tackett and Michael Wines, *Trump Disbands Commission on Voter Fraud*, NY Times (Jan 3, 2018), available at https://www.nytimes.com/2018/01/03/us/politics/trump-voter-fraud-commission.html (noting that "no state has uncovered significant evidence to support the president's claim [that voter fraud explained how Hillary Clinton received more votes than Trump during the 2016 election], and election officials, including many Republicans, have strongly rejected it").

[113] *Fish v Kobach*, 309 F Supp 3d 1048, 1053–54 (D Kan 2018) (finding in favor of plaintiffs on their statutory and constitutional challenges to the Kansas proof-of-citizenship statute).

[114] Id at 1108 (noting the court's finding that "at most, 67 noncitizens registered or attempted to register in Kansas over the last 19 years"); see also id at 1112.

[115] Id at 1102.

[116] See, for example, Catherine Engelbrecht, *A Message from True the Vote's Founder*, True the Vote (2018), available at https://truethevote.org/aboutus (stating that the organization has "spoken out about the misleading messaging of those who insist voter fraud does not exist. It does.").

base" maintained by the Heritage Foundation, a prominent and well-funded conservative nonprofit.[117] Though the foundation claims that the database reveals a broad and pernicious trend of fraud,[118] in fact, the paltry number of alleged instances of alleged voter fraud (fewer than 1,200, as of early 2019), in a database that covers federal and state elections and dates back to 1979, proves the opposite.[119] Perhaps recognizing that these claims wither under scrutiny, theorists who promote fraud as a danger often rely on softer justifications, by claiming that most voter fraud goes undetected—a "tip of the iceberg" theory[120]—or, even further removed, that the *perception* of voter fraud will itself undermine public confidence in the election.[121] These assertions, too, are unsupported.[122] No matter. When states after 2011 began ratcheting up their voting purge practices, concerns over voter fraud—the

---

[117] IRS Form 990, Heritage Foundation (listing revenue at over $92 million for 2015, almost $97 million for 2014, and $112 million for 2013).

[118] Jason Snead, *Instances of Voter Fraud Continue to Mount, Further Compromising Our Elections*, Heritage Foundation (July 3, 2018), available at https://www.heritage.org/election-integrity /commentary/instances-voter-fraud-continue-mount-further-compromising-our (asserting based on database, but without specific support, that "there is substantial evidence that voter fraud not only is real, but affects the outcome of elections throughout the country").

[119] Heritage Foundation, *Election Fraud Database* (Heritage Foundation, Dec 30, 2018), available at https://www.heritage.org/voterfraud (listing, at last check, 1,177 "[p]roven instances of voter fraud"). These numbers are far lower when limited to the forms of fraud possibly affected by restrictions such as voter identification laws. See id; see also *Heritage Fraud Database: An Assessment*, Brennan Center for Justice (Sept 8, 2017), available at https://www.brennancenter .org/sites/default/files/publications/HeritageAnalysis_Final.pdf; Justin Levitt, *A Comprehensive Investigation of Voter Impersonation Finds 31 Credible Incidents Out of One Billion Ballots Cast*, Wash Post (Aug 6, 2014), available at https://www.washingtonpost.com/news/wonk/wp/2014/08/06 /a-comprehensive-investigation-of-voter-impersonation-finds-31-credible-incidents-out-of -one-billion-ballots-cast/?utm_term = .cb49159028a9.

[120] See *Fish*, 309 F Supp 3d at 1102 (noting that "tip of the iceberg" was Kansas's refrain in explaining the lack of direct evidence of noncitizen voter registration); Snead, *Instances of Voter Fraud* (cited in note 118) (asserting without support that "[m]any instances of voter fraud simply go undetected because states do not have adequate procedures to uncover them. Others are never investigated.").

[121] See, for example, Michael Wines, *One Rationale for Voter ID Debunked, GOP Has Another*, NY Times (Mar 23, 2017), available at https://www.nytimes.com/2017/03/23/us/election -fraud-voter-ids.html (stating that rather than arguing that actual voter fraud exists, some Republican legislators "are now saying the perception of fraud, real or otherwise, is an equally serious problem, if not worse"); Engelbrecht, *A Message from True the Vote's Founder* (cited in note 116) (stating without citation that "according to a recent survey 81% of Americans believe that election fraud is a very real problem"); John Fund, *Stealing Elections: How Voter Fraud Threatens Our Democracy* 2 (Encounter Books, 2008) (citing a Rasmussen poll indicating that 17% of Americans "believe that large numbers of ineligible people are allowed to vote").

[122] See Stephen Ansolabehere and Nathaniel Persily, *Vote Fraud in the Eye of the Beholder: The Role of Public Opinion in the Challenge to Voter Identification Requirements*, 121 Harv L Rev 1737, 1750–58 (2008) (presenting empirical research finding fear of voting fraud does not impact voters' participation in the electoral process).

same as those the Court embraced, without evidence, in *Purcell* and *Crawford*—provided a key justification.[123]

This, then, brings us to 2016, and the bleak legal landscape voters faced when determining how to challenge Ohio's Supplemental Process. Not only would a *Crawford*-style constitutional claim have been expensive and difficult to litigate; plaintiffs probably would have lost. A mere reference to voter fraud likely would have swallowed everything. In part, the probable weakness of this claim reflects how difficult it is for plaintiffs to gather evidence of burdens on voters.[124] Yet the problem also runs much deeper. At core, protracted fights over restrictive voting measures frequently are not at all what *Crawford* seems to assume they are—dispassionate, technocratic disagreements over how to best balance burdens and benefits when administering elections. Instead they often track long-running, ideologically charged battles over when, if ever, it is acceptable for a jurisdiction to *try* to make it harder for its own, eligible citizens to vote. In other words, they often track battles over intentional voter suppression. The quandary facing plaintiffs seeking to directly combat intentional voter suppression, however, is that it is not at all clear how such a claim would run. From established case law, *Crawford* provides the closest model. But absent adequate proof of how a voting restriction in fact burdens voters—based on evidence that is hard to produce, under a standard that is hard to understand—*Crawford* is of no use.[125] And in the years since *Crawford* was decided, the Court has given no indication that it is prepared to reconsider its embrace of baseless voter-fraud theories or the corrosively deferential model that such an approach implies.

One understands, then, why the *Husted* plaintiffs opted for a statutory approach. An attack on Ohio's Supplemental Process was unlikely to startle the Court into a course correction, not least of all because it is within the range of reasonable possibilities that Ohio

---

[123] See Brief of Amicus Curiae Judicial Watch in Support of Petitioners, *Husted v A. Philip Randolph Institute*, No 16-980, *2 (US filed Aug 7, 2017) (available on Westlaw at 2017 WL 3447771) (describing Ohio's 2014 changes to its Supplemental Process as protecting the "integrity of elections"). See also, for example, *Many States Are Purging Voters from the Rolls*, Economist (Aug 9 2018), available at https://www.economist.com/united-states/2018/08/09/many-states-are-purging-voters-from-the-rolls (connecting purported prevention of fraud to purge regimes).

[124] We discuss *Crawford*'s requirements of proof in notes 88–90 and accompanying text, and we discuss difficulties associated with measuring burdens in note 134.

[125] See id.

implemented this particular restriction in good faith.[126] It was reasonable for plaintiffs to abandon any effort at advancing the constitutional doctrine in favor of technical claims like those based on the NVRA. Unfortunately, this strategy failed. Instead of providing relief to Ohio voters, *Husted* provides reassurance to purging jurisdictions. In addition, *Husted* once again helps to validate the theory of voter fraud. It frames its whole discussion with a conservative talking point: a Pew study finding that 24 million voter registrations are inaccurate, and 2.75 million people are registered to vote in more than one state.[127] This statistic appeals to promoters of a voter-fraud narrative based on the assumption that these inaccuracies facilitate fraudulent voting. Yet the Court cites no evidence to support this inference. Nor does the opinion cite the next statistic listed by Pew: that "at least 51 million eligible U.S. citizens are unregistered," which is "more than 24 percent of the eligible population."[128]

In short, *Husted*, with its focus on the intricacies of § 20507(d), might seem removed from the incendiary questions of voter fraud, voter suppression, and the fundamental right to vote. In fact, both symbolically and actually, it is a participant in the fray. In this way, *Husted* compounds the bind facing voting-rights proponents, who for decades reasonably have been trying to narrow and adjust their claims to satisfy an increasingly skeptical Court. At this point, it is unclear exactly what democratic gains can be won by statutory small ball. Maybe, therefore, it is time to look to the constitutional future.

II. The Unconstitutionality of Intentional Voter Suppression

The suppressive measures shrouding this decade's elections have generated theories of reform, some aimed at preexisting race-based claims,[129] some at claims focused on the impact of voting mea-

---

[126] We discuss arguments to this effect in note 190.

[127] *Husted*, 138 S Ct at 1838. The citation is to a Pew Center study, *Inaccurate, Costly, and Inefficient: Evidence That America's Voter Registration System Needs an Upgrade* *1, The Pew Center on the States (Feb 2012), available at https://www.pewtrusts.org/~/media/legacy/ uploadedfiles /pcs_assets/2012/pewupgradingvoterregistrationpdf.pdf.

[128] Id.

[129] See, for example, Stephanopoulos, 128 Yale L J at **1–6 (cited in note 97) (addressing Section 2 of the VRA); Dale E. Ho, *Building an Umbrella in a Rainstorm: The New Vote Denial Litigation Since Shelby County*, 127 Yale L J F 799 (2018) (same); Hasen, 59 Wm & Mary L Rev at 1837 (cited in note 95) (same).

sures,[130] and some at proposed claims grounded in partisanship.[131] A few of these theories have been tested in the lower courts, to varying degrees of success.[132] If adopted, many of these proposals would help to counteract intentional suppression through indirect means. But perhaps this is an Occam's Razor moment—a time to consider the most direct route. To this end, we contend that intentional voter suppression by the government presumptively violates the Constitution, full stop. It presumptively violates the Constitution regardless of its interaction with race,[133] regardless of the severity of the burden it imposes on the voter,[134] and regardless of whether it serves partisan ends.[135] The basic contours of this argument may seem too obvious to

---

[130] See, for example, Karlan, 93 Ind L J at 146–48, 151–56 (cited in note 70); Ellis, 104 Ky L J at 610 (cited in note 6); Richard L. Hasen, *Race or Party? How Courts Should Think About Republican Efforts to Make It Harder to Vote in North Carolina and Elsewhere*, 127 Harv L Rev F 58, 62 (2014); see also Fishkin, 86 Ind L J at 1331–32 (cited in note 17).

[131] See, for example, Levitt, 59 Wm & Mary L Rev at 1995 (cited in note 85); Michael S. Kang, *Gerrymandering and the Constitutional Norm Against Government Partisanship*, 116 Mich L Rev 351, 352–59 (2017); Edward B. Foley, *Due Process, Fair Play, and Excessive Partisanship: A New Principle for Judicial Review of Election Laws*, 84 U Chi L Rev 655, 684 n 118 (2017); Edward B. Foley, *Voting Rules and Constitutional Law*, 81 Geo Wash L Rev 1836, 1837 (2013); Lori A. Ringhand, *Voter Viewpoint Discrimination: Reconsidering a First Amendment Challenge to Voter Participation Restrictions*, 13 Election L J 288, 289 (2014).

[132] We discuss, for example, litigants' (thus far unsuccessful) attempts to advance an intent-based theory of "partisan fencing" in notes 135, 137, and 171. Litigants have had more success in the lower courts with some burden-based theories, as well as theories based on Section 2 of the VRA. See notes 113–15 and accompanying text (discussing a burden-based claim) and Stephanopoulos, 128 Yale L J at *6–10 (cited in note 97) (discussing claims based on Section 2). It is not clear how these decisions would hold up if reviewed by the Supreme Court.

[133] This is not to say that voter suppression bears no relationship to race. Both historically and in the present day, the overlap between the two is stark. See generally Hasen, 59 Wm & Mary L Rev at 1837 (cited in note 95) (addressing the intersection of race, party, and voter restrictions); see also Issacharoff, 64 Duke L J at 1363 (cited in note 13) (same). As we discuss below, recognition of a freestanding claim for voter suppression should supplement and help to bolster race-based claims; it would not supplant them.

[134] For a description of some of the obstacles to measuring the impact of burdens on voting, see, for example, Justin Elliott, *What We Don't Know: The Full Effect of Voter Suppression and Voter ID Laws*, Pro Publica (Nov 8, 2016), available at https://projects.propublica.org/electionland /national/what-we-dont-know-the-full-effects-of-voter-suppression/. See also Justin Grimmer et al, *Obstacles to Estimating Voter ID Laws' Effect on Turnout*, J Polit 80.3 (2018) (presenting research identifying flaws in earlier studies which had concluded that voter identification laws suppressed turnout among minority voters). For careful attempts at conducting such a measurement and finding burdens, see Kenneth R. Mayer and Michael G. DeCrescenzo, *Voter ID Study*, Elections Research Center (2018), available at https://elections.wisc.edu/voter-id-study/, and Justin Levitt, *Election Reform: The Pursuit of Unwarranted Election Regulation*, 11 Election L J 97 (2012). See generally Issacharoff, 64 Duke L J at 1377–86 (cited in note 13) (discussing empirical studies).

[135] Often, of course, the intention to suppress votes correlates with an intention to advance partisan interests. See Issacharoff, 64 Duke L J at 1366 (cited in note 13) ("Democrats seem

warrant articulation.[136] Yet neither the Supreme Court nor legal scholars have spoken directly to this issue,[137] and that silence almost certainly hides disagreement as to whether this constitutional prohibition on voter suppression even exists, much less how it should be understood.[138] An articulation is overdue.

A basic case for unconstitutionality rests on three principles: (1) the Constitution contains a generally applicable right to vote; (2) fundamental to any such right is the ability of eligible voters to cast ballots and have them counted; and (3) the Constitution precludes a state from taking actions with the intention of undermining this constitutional right. Taken together, these principles mean that the

---

to do better when voter turnout is higher, and worse when turnout is lower."); see also note 18 and accompanying text. As a result, our proposed claim for intentional voter suppression tends to overlap quite a bit with "partisan fencing" claims and other proposed claims based on partisan-related intent. See notes 137 and 171 and accompanying text. These proposals have much to offer them. Still, in at least in one respect, our claim may be more straightforward than those based in partisanship: it rejects *any* intention to suppress an eligible citizen's vote, regardless of whether officials are targeting a voter "'because of the way [that voter] may vote.'" *One Wisconsin Inst., Inc. v Thomsen*, 198 F Supp 3d 896, 928 (WD Wisc 2016) (quoting *Carrington v Rash*, 380 US 89, 94 (1965), a case central to partisan-fencing theory).

[136] For example, in a Fourth Circuit case addressing the lawfulness of restrictive measures passed in North Carolina, the majority stated dismissively, in a footnote: "Of course, state legislators also cannot impermissibly dilute or deny the votes of opponent political parties." *N. Carolina State Conference of NAACP v McCrory*, 831 F3d 204, 226 (4th Cir 2016). Yet the one case the court cited in support of this proposition does not make this point at all clear. See *Anderson v Celebrezze*, 460 US 780, 793 (1983). See also Hasen, 59 Wm & Mary L Rev at 1877 (cited in note 95) (exploring this same issue); Issacharoff, 64 Duke L J at 1371 (cited in note 13) ("How is it that a mature democracy like the United States still allows basic rules of ballot access to be a battleground for political skirmishing?").

[137] See *Crawford*, 553 US at 203–4 (Stevens, J) (plurality) (discussing the effect of "partisan considerations" without providing a definitive resolution); id (failing to address intentional voter suppression); see generally notes 81–86 and accompanying text. So-called "partisan-fencing" claims help to confirm this lacuna in the law. In a recent Wisconsin case, for example, a district court considering a "partisan-fencing" claim explained that "[a]t the heart of [the case was] plaintiffs' contention that the Wisconsin legislature passed the challenged provisions with the intent to suppress Democratic votes to gain a partisan advantage in future elections." *One Wisconsin Inst., Inc. v Thomsen*, 198 F Supp 3d 896, 927 (WD Wisc 2016). The court appeared sympathetic to these claims; it eventually granted relief to the plaintiffs on other grounds. Yet it seemed uncomfortable with the intent-based approach of a partisan-fencing claim. Referring to the claim as a "novel one," the court bemoaned the failure of either party to direct "the court to precedent—binding or otherwise—that definitively establishes a framework" for adjudication. Id. Eventually, the Court decided that it would treat the partisan-fencing claim as functionally indistinguishable from a *Crawford* claim—and therefore accept the suggestion in *Crawford* that a state's action can survive even if "partly motivated by partisan gain, so long as there were sufficient valid justifications." Id (Stevens, J) (plurality). In reaching this conclusion, however, the district court considered only half of the partisan-fencing claim—the half involving partisanship. It did not explain how *Crawford* could resolve the other half—the allegations of intentional voter suppression. See Section I.B. In short, as to the constitutionality of intentional voter suppression, the law remains unsettled.

[138] See note 137; see also Section I.B.

Constitution prohibits a state from acting with the purpose of making it more difficult for an eligible voter's ballot to be cast or counted—in other words, the Constitution prohibits a state from engaging in intentional voter suppression.[139]

The first of these three principles posits that the Constitution does indeed provide individuals with a broadly applicable right to vote. It maintains that any government administering an election therefore must follow basic, constitutionally imposed ground rules (whatever those rules might be). This first principle is unlikely to elicit sustained opposition. Justices of all ideological stripes have recognized that the Constitution protects an individual's "strong interest in exercising the fundamental political right to vote," as the Court phrased it in 2006 in *Purcell*, which generated no dissents.[140] The Court has identified the Equal Protection Clause as the source of this right, though it has alluded to other possibilities as well.[141] For our purposes, identification of the precise textual hook for this right is less important than the Court's consistent recognition—from *Harper* to *Crawford* and beyond—that the right exists, whatever its scope or strength.[142]

The second of these principles insists that a generally applicable "right to vote" in a democracy must, at a minimum, seek to protect the ability of an eligible voter to cast a ballot and have it counted. Perhaps

---

[139] In reaching this conclusion, we acknowledge the primary role that the Constitution gives states to design and administer elections. See US Const, Art I, § 4, cl 1 (congressional elections); Art II, § 1 & Amend XII (presidential elections); see also *Reynolds v Sims*, 377 US 533, 566 (1963) (indicating that, for nonfederal elections, states are "exercis[ing] power wholly within the domain of state interest" and therefore that these election-related activities, typically, are "insulated from federal judicial review" (quotation marks omitted)). Consider also *Arizona v Inter Tribal Council of Ariz., Inc.*, 570 US 1, 79 (2013) (addressing questions of federalism in the election context). However, any "such insulation [from federal judicial review] is not carried over when state power is used as an instrument for circumventing a federally protected right." *Reynolds*, 377 US at 566 (quotation marks omitted). And, "[u]ndeniably, the Constitution of the United States protects the right of all qualified citizens to vote, in state as well as in federal, elections." Id at 554. See also Section I.B.

[140] *Purcell v Gonzalez*, 549 US 1, 4 (2006) (per curiam) (quotation marks omitted).

[141] See Foley, 84 U Chi L Rev at 657–86 (cited in note 131). Still, the reality is that "[n]one of the foundational voting rights decisions were well-grounded in the text, early history, or structure of the Constitution." Christopher S. Elmendorf, *Undue Burdens on Voter Participation: New Pressures for a Structural Theory of the Right to Vote?*, 35 Hastings Const L Q 643, 649 n 32 (2008). Yet it is well settled that the Constitution protects a generally applicable right to vote. As we will explain, moreover, the three principles undergirding our argument are so basic that they would be applicable even if a future court were to hold that the right to vote derives not from (or not *only* from) the Equal Protection Clause, but from some other source such as the Due Process Clause or the structure of the Constitution.

[142] See Yablon, 111 Nw U L Rev at 679–82 (cited in note 72) (describing the current state of the doctrine, including ambivalence regarding its textual hook).

the Constitution's right to vote protects more—but the argument here is that it does not protect less.[143] This second principle therefore understands the right to vote as both *universal* and *substantive*.[144] It is universal insofar as it applies to every citizen, not simply those the polity wishes to empower. This universalist conception of the right to vote coincides with our use of the term "eligible voter"—employed throughout this article—as referring to every United States citizen residing in a given jurisdiction, subject to only a small number of exceptions.[145] A universalist conception rejects a view that existed prior to the civil rights movement of the 1960s and 1970s, when it "was perfectly within the bounds of ordinary political discourse to argue that some citizens were too ignorant, incompetent, corruptible, racially inferior, or poor to deserve the voting rights of full, first-class citizens."[146]

The second of these principles also advances a conception of the right to vote that is substantive, insofar as its reach does not end with the formal recognition of the right, but extends also to the conditions under which citizens are able to exercise the right. To be clear, this understanding does not require an election regime to accommodate the needs or preferences of every voter seeking to cast a ballot. No constitutional right is absolute; other factors inevitably force compromise and require the right to yield.[147] Yet these factors do not change its nature.

---

[143] In this respect, our view aligns squarely with that of Professor Fishkin, who has argued that—regardless of whether the right to vote also serves structural interests—this right must protect an individual's "right to cast a ballot and have it counted." Fishkin, 86 Ind L J at 1293 (cited in note 17). This proposition does not tend to elicit controversy. With rare exceptions, even those advocating a structural approach to the right to vote accept that it also protects this more basic interest. See id at 1293–94 (confirming that even structuralist views acknowledge, in some form, an individual's right to cast a ballot and have it counted).

[144] See id at 1336–38, 1345–51 (defining "universalism" and "substantive" and using these terms to characterize the evolution of American voting rights law in the twentieth century); see also Keyssar, *The Right to Vote* at 217–30 (cited in note 8) (describing the universalist expansion of the franchise during this same period).

[145] See Fishkin, 86 Ind L J at 1349 (cited in note 17). While there are a number of exceptions to this principle of universality—including those relating to age, residence, felon status, and mental capacity—the brevity of this list underscores just how entrenched this idea has become.

[146] Fishkin, 86 Ind L J at 1342–43 (cited in note 17); see also *Lassiter v Northampton County Board of Elections*, 360 US 45 (1959) (upholding the constitutionality of a literacy test for voting).

[147] See generally Jamal Greene, *The Supreme Court, 2017 Term—Foreword: Rights as Trumps?*, 132 Harv L Rev 30 (2018) (exploring frameworks for adjudicating the limits of constitutional rights).

This second principle—that the Constitution's right to vote protects the ability of an eligible voter to cast a ballot and have it counted—also is unlikely to generate controversy, at least in the courts. Beginning with the landmark Warren Court decisions discussed above, a long and virtually unbroken line of Supreme Court cases has endorsed, at least nominally, this conception of the right.[148] Tellingly, even the parsimonious description of the right to vote advanced by Justice Scalia in *Crawford* (in the concurring opinion joined by Justices Thomas and Alito) proceeded on the understanding that the Constitution's right to vote is both universal and substantive.[149] Again, the Court tends to identify the Equal Protection Clause as the source of this right: one that protects each eligible voter's ability to cast a ballot that will be counted.[150]

This leads, then, to the third principle, which contends that the Constitution prohibits a state from acting with the intention of undermining citizens' right to vote. Any discussion of the constitutional implications of intent is likely to elicit heated disagreement,[151] and deep engagement with this debate exceeds the scope of this article. Suffice it to say, the Supreme Court's precedents generally support the conclusion that once a substantive right is articulated, the Constitution prohibits the government from acting with the intention of undermining that same right, unless the action is adequately tailored to a sufficiently important government interest.[152] Indeed, with re-

---

[148] Compare, for example, *Harper*, 383 US 663, with *Crawford*, 553 US 181; see also Fishkin, 86 Ind L J at 1338–39 (cited in note 17) ("[B]y the 1960s, even those who fiercely opposed black voting rights nearly always found some pretext consistent with universalism on which to justify rules that would exclude blacks from casting ballots." (quotation marks omitted)).

[149] See *Crawford*, 553 US 181, 204–5 (2008) (Scalia, J, concurring).

[150] See, for example, *Purcell v Gonzalez*, 549 US 1, 4 (2006) (citing *Dunn v Blumstein*, 405 US 330, 336 (1972)).

[151] See, for example, Fallon Jr., 130 Harv L Rev at 525–28 (cited in note 16) (surveying some of the issues and debates); Aziz Z. Huq, *What Is Discriminatory Intent?*, 103 Cornell L Rev 1211, 1215 (2018) (aiming to "offer a map of discriminatory intent's competing definitional and evidentiary strands" and provide a critique).

[152] See, for example, *Washington v Davis*, 426 US 229, 239 (1976) (state action taken with the intention of engaging in racial discrimination presumptively violates Equal Protection Clause's prohibition on racial discrimination); *Wallace v Jaffree*, 472 US 38, 59–61 (1985) (state action taken with the intention of promoting religion presumptively violates the First Amendment's probation on promoting religion); *Church of the Lukumi Babalu Aye, Inc. v City of Hialeah*, 508 US 520, 533–35 (1993) (state action taken with the intention of restricting practices because of religious motivation presumptively violates the First Amendment's prohibition on restricting practices because of religious motivation); *Planned Parenthood of Southeastern Pennsylvania v Casey*,

spect to some rights, such as the right under the Equal Protection Clause to be free of race-based discrimination by the state, current doctrine *requires* that a jurisdiction act with impermissible intent before the Court will recognize that the Constitution has been violated.[153]

An intent-based argument becomes even stronger when applied to the right to vote. This is because, unlike most other individual rights conferred by the Constitution, the right to vote necessarily depends on the state's affirmative conduct. Anyone seeking to exercise this fundamental right must rely on the assistance of government officials. There is something particularly constitutionally offensive, in our view, about a government intending to undermine a right whose very existence depends on that government's good graces.

If accepted, these three principles together confirm that the government violates the Constitution if it acts with the intention of suppressing voters. Were the Court to endorse this conclusion, it would break new doctrinal ground.[154] At least two beneficial effects would follow. First, this judicial endorsement would discourage jurisdictions from enacting laws (and politicians from advancing platforms) that explicitly seek to dissuade certain voters from voting. Resistance to a universal conception of voting rights has a fraught and frightening history in the United States.[155] If the courts are not prepared to push back against its resurgence, political discourse may again begin to normalize the idea that jurisdictions should, as a matter of official policy, discourage some groups of people from exercising the franchise. Stated otherwise, it may again become politically acceptable to advocate, openly, for intentional voter suppression.

The 2018 election cycle confirms that such a threat exists. A senator from Mississippi, for example, publicly stated during her re-election campaign that she wanted to make it harder for certain

---

505 US 833, 877 (1992) (plurality opinion) (state action taken with the intention of placing a substantial obstacle in the path of a woman seeking an abortion presumptively violates the Due Process Clause's prohibition of placing a substantial obstacle in the path of a woman seeking an abortion).

[153] See, for example, *Washington v Davis*, 426 US 229, 239 (1976).

[154] See Section I.B.

[155] See, for example, Keyssar, *The Right to Vote* at 102–31 (cited in note 8) (discussing efforts of jurisdictions between the Civil War and World War I to change the "size and contours of the electorate"); id at 206–11 (discussing resistance to racial integration during the 1950s and 1960s as it translated into access to the ballot); see also Fishkin, 86 Ind L J at 1339–51 (cited in note 17) (discussing this history from Reconstruction through the 1970s).

citizens to vote.[156] Meanwhile, a secretary of state from Georgia, while running for governor, expressed concern about the effects on elections if minority voters were successfully able to register.[157] Even after the media widely reported these comments, both politicians won their 2018 elections. Tellingly, nearly a third of those surveyed prior to the midterms—and over half of those identifying as Republican—agreed with the idea that citizens should have to overcome hurdles prior to voting in order to "prove" their interest in doing so.[158] Despite these undercurrents, mainstream political discourse continues to resist brazen attacks on a universal conception of voting.[159] Yet it has acceded to contrary views in the past, and it could do so again in the future.

---

[156] See Michael Brice-Saddler, *GOP Senator: It's a "Great Idea" to Make It Harder for "Liberal Folks" to Vote*, Wash Post (Nov 16, 2018), available at https://www.washingtonpost .com/politics/2018/11/16/cindy-hyde-smith-its-great-idea-make-it-harder-liberal-folks-vote /?utm_term = .9e55d7643a81 (quoting Senator Hyde-Smith as saying, "they remind me that there's a lot of liberal folks in those other schools who maybe we don't want to vote. Maybe we want to make it just a little more difficult. And I think that's a great idea").

[157] See Khushbu Shah, *"Textbook Voter Suppression": Georgia's Bitter Election a Battle Years in the Making*, The Guardian (Nov 10, 2018) (quoting Georgia's secretary of state as saying: "You know the Democrats are working hard, and all these stories about them, you know, registering all these minority voters that are out there and others that are sitting on the sidelines, if they can do that, they can win these elections in November"), available at https://www.theguardian.com/us -news/2018/nov/10/georgia-election-recount-stacey-abrams-brian-kemp.

These comments by Senator Hyde-Smith and the Georgia secretary of state are particularly telling because they do not even bother with the pretense that voting restrictions mean to target voting by ineligible voters. To that end, they track a particularly brazen comment made by Paul Weyrich, a cofounder of the Heritage Foundation who frequently is referred to as a founding father of the modern conservative movement. See note 29. They also track efforts by legislators to question whether all voters' votes should carry the same weight. For accounts suggesting that these efforts have been escalating, see, for example, Jamelle Bouie, *The GOP Sees Rural Voters as More Legitimate Than Urban Voters*, Slate (Dec 7, 2018), available at https://slate.com/news -and-politics/2018/12/wisconsin-power-grab-gop-urban-vs-rural-voters.html; Emily Badger, *Are Rural Voters the "Real" Voters? Wisconsin Republicans Seem to Think So*, NY Times (Dec 6, 2018), available at https://www.nytimes.com/2018/12/06/upshot/wisconsin-republicans-rural -urban-voters.html.

[158] Pew Research Center, *Elections in America: Concerns Over Security, Divisions Over Expanding Access to Voting* (Oct 29, 2018) (indicating that 51% of respondents who are Republican or lean Republican agreed that "[c]itizens should have to prove they want to vote by registering ahead of time").

[159] This resistance is reflected even in the rhetoric of those who, at times, seem to waver. For example, the campaign for Senator Hyde-Smith did not defend her comments seeming to endorse intentional voter suppression but insisted "that the senator was joking and that the video had been altered." Brice-Saddler, *It's a "Great Idea" to Make It Harder for "Liberal Folks" to Vote* (cited in note 156). As for the Georgia secretary of state, he insisted throughout his campaign that he was committed to "secure, accessible, and fair elections for all voters," and further stated that "it has never been easier to register to vote and get engaged in the electoral process in Georgia, and we are incredibly proud to report this new record." Lisa Hagen, *Abrams Campaign Calls on Georgia's Secretary of State to Resign Over Voter Registration Issues*, The Hill (Oct 10,

Acknowledgment by the Court of the unconstitutionality of intentional voter suppression would also prevent jurisdictions from using voter suppression as a defense to other claims. Consider another area of election law: redistricting. Although the law of redistricting is distinct (both conceptually and doctrinally) from the law of intentional voter suppression and other forms of vote denial, it nevertheless helps to illustrate this troubling defensive maneuver. Under the Court's current precedents, a court is much more likely to invalidate a redistricting map if it concludes it is motivated by racial considerations rather than by political considerations.[160] This asymmetry gives map-drawers an incentive to claim that they were motivated by the latter. In North Carolina, for example, legislators' maps repeatedly have been invalidated as racial gerrymanders.[161] In response, political leaders have asserted, with increasing audacity, that their real intent in enacting their revised maps was not to disadvantage racial minorities, but instead to disadvantage Democrats. "I acknowledge freely that this would be a political gerrymander, which is not against the law," one official insisted. "I think electing Republicans is better than electing Democrats. So I drew this map to help foster what I think is better for the country."[162] In the context of vote-denial claims (as opposed to redistricting claims), it is unusual for defenders of restrictive measures to embrace political motivation so openly. But some do appear to be testing the approach out.[163] If the precedent set

---

2018), available at https://thehill.com/homenews/state-watch/411060-abrams-campaign-calls-on-georgias-secretary-of-state-to-resign-over.

[160] Compare, for example, *Cooper v Harris*, 137 S Ct 1455 (2017) (racial motivation), with *Easley v Cromartie*, 532 US 234 (2001) (political motivation). See also note 16 (vote denial).

[161] See *Cooper v Harris*, 137 S Ct 1455, 1455, 1465–66 (2017) (affirming district court's finding of unconstitutional racial gerrymandering in North Carolina's congressional maps, and describing the state's prior history in this regard).

[162] Richard H. Pildes, *Will the Court Ever Address Gerrymandering?*, NY Times (June 18, 2018), available at https://www.nytimes.com/2018/06/18/opinion/will-the-court-ever-address-gerrymandering.html.

[163] In North Carolina, for example, state legislators initially defended the enactment of suppressive measures against charges of intentional race discrimination by implying that their target was not minority voters, but rather prior legislative decisions perceived as making it easier for Democratic voters to vote. See *McCrory*, 831 F3d at 228; see also id at 226. In a separate case, Judge Easterbrook of the Seventh Circuit suggested that Wisconsin could defend its suppressive measures by characterizing them as a tit-for-tat response to prior efforts to expand voting. See Recording of Oral Argument, *One Wisconsin Institute v Thomsen*, No 16-03083 & 16-03091 (7th Cir, Feb 24, 2017), available at http://media.ca7.uscourts.gov/sound/2017/nr.16-3091.16-3091_02_24_2017.mp3; Rick Hasen, *Judge Easterbrook Asks in WI Case: Why Can't Republicans Make "Pro-Republican Changes" to Make It Harder to Vote?*, Election Law Blog (Feb 24, 2017), available at https://electionlawblog.org/?p=91322. See also *Veasey v Abbott*, 830 F3d 216, 303

in the redistricting context is a harbinger of what is to come, absent judicial intervention, in the vote-denial context, then jurisdictions may begin to rely much more heavily on partisan-motivated suppression as a defense. Particularly in jurisdictions where race and party tend to overlap, this defensive maneuver poses significant problems for plaintiffs bringing race-based claims. If a court is willing to accept partisanship as a defense, it becomes even harder for plaintiffs to establish that race-based intentions lie behind a state's actions.[164]

Without more, then, a judicial acknowledgment of the unconstitutionality of intentional voter suppression would have important prophylactic effects. Yet for courts to cut back meaningfully on the patterns of intentional voter suppression that already exist, they also would need to adopt an appropriate framework for claims of intentional voter suppression: one that allows litigants to smoke out impermissible intent, and to receive effective relief. Critical to this effort is a framework that recognizes the structural advantages a jurisdiction has over its voters. In administering elections, jurisdictions must make an enormous number of decisions, large and small, many relating to local conditions. So long as a jurisdiction is making these interlocking decisions in good faith, judicial deference is constitutionally appropriate, and eminently sensible.

Yet deference becomes a menace when a jurisdiction is not acting in good faith. It gives jurisdictions wide latitude to suppress votes in ways that typically escape detection. To cut subtly but sharply into the ability of voters to cast a ballot, for example, a jurisdiction can rely on onerous measures that appear innocuous, or on the cumulative effects of many minor measures. Indeed, jurisdictions used precisely these techniques to engage in "unremitting and ingenious defiance" of the Reconstruction Amendments.[165]

(5th Cir 2016) (Jones, J, dissenting) (defending Texas's voter ID law as "reflect[ing] party politics, not racism"). Other scholars have flagged the problematic nature of this potential defense. See Hasen, 127 Harv L Rev F at 62 (cited in note 130) ("When a legislature passes an election-administration law (outside of the redistricting context) discriminating against a party's voters or otherwise burdening voters, that fact should not be a defense.").

[164] For a discussion of the threats to race-based protections posed by defendants' willingness to cite partisan factors, see generally Hasen, 59 Wm & Mary L Rev at 1837 (cited in note 95); see also id at 1864.

[165] *South Carolina v Katzenbach*, 383 US 301, 309 (1966); see also id at 308–15. Indeed, this dynamic helps to explain the unusual, burden-shifting structure of Section 5 of the VRA. See Lisa Manheim, *Shifting the Burden and Striking a Balance*, Take Care Blog (Nov 16, 2018), available at https://takecareblog.com/blog/shifting-the-burden-and-striking-a-balance. Consider, also, Katie R. Eyer, *Ideological Drift and the Forgotten History of Intent*, 51 Harv CR-CL L Rev 1, 5 (2016)

At the outset, therefore, the framework for voter-suppression claims cannot be so deferential that it allows the mere presence or possibility of legitimate motives to override impermissible intent. Otherwise, a state's empty gesture—an unsupported reference to something like "voter fraud" or "cost reduction"—would neuter these claims before they begin. *Crawford* took a stroll down this path, with its willingness to accept the state's proffered justifications at face value and to overlook questionable motives so long as they were coupled with legitimate ones.[166] Regardless of whether this approach is appropriate in the context of *Crawford* itself,[167] which directly addressed partisanship but did not directly address intentional voter suppression,[168] such deference is not appropriate in response to claims that a state intentionally has made it harder for eligible voters to vote. It is not appropriate even if one reads *Crawford* (incorrectly, we believe) to foreclose any other option in the context of vote-denial claims brought under the Equal Protection Clause.[169]

If a plaintiff proves that a state is acting with a purpose that is unquestionably illegitimate—here, the purpose of suppressing votes—the more appropriate model is the one the Court has adopted for claims of invidious intentional race discrimination.[170] Under this ap-

---

(explaining how, in response to desegregation opinions issued by the Supreme Court, southern school districts could, as a practical matter, engage in "virtually indefinite obstruction" prior to the development of the backstop provided by an intent-based form of judicial review).

[166] See *Crawford*, 553 US at 204 (Stevens, J) (plurality).

[167] For criticisms of this approach, see, for example, Karlan, 93 Ind L J at 148 (cited in note 70) (arguing that *Crawford*'s dismissive treatment of partisan intent "threatened abandonment of meaningful judicial scrutiny").

[168] See notes 81–86 and 169 and accompanying text.

[169] As we discussed above, while intentional voter suppression loomed in the background in *Crawford*, no party brought a claim based directly on that ground. See note 81 and accompanying text. As for the Court's quick and opaque discussion of pretextual intent, it limited this discussion to "partisan" motivations, which, without more, are not necessarily invidious. See notes 83–86 and accompanying text. Of course, in the facts presented in *Crawford* itself, the "partisan" motivations likely *were* invidious, at least in part, given that any partisan advantage to Republican candidates likely depended on the law's suppression of Democratic voters. See *Crawford v Marion County Election Board*, 472 F3d 949, 954 (7th Cir 2007) (Evans, J, dissenting). Nevertheless, the Court did not connect these dots in its own analysis. It therefore did not foreclose the possibility that a future Equal Protection Clause claim—based on the theory that intentional voter suppression played at least a partial role in the government's decision making—would trigger a different level of deference. Even if *Crawford* is read to foreclose this result, courts might consider how different constitutional provisions (such as those emanating from the First Amendment or the Due Process Clause) might protect the right to vote in this way—and whether *Crawford* itself ought to be reconsidered.

[170] See, for example, *Village of Arlington Heights v Metro Housing Development Corp.*, 429 US 252, 271 n 21 (1977) ("Proof that the decision by the Village was motivated in part by a racially

proach, a court will look behind the state's proffered justifications in response to evidence of pretext, and *any* discriminatory legislative intent is sufficient to trigger heightened scrutiny—and will in all likelihood invalidate the law.[171] While this approach may elicit concerns over nuisance litigation, particularly given the political valence of these voting-related claims, the history of claims over intentional race discrimination suggests that such concerns are overblown.[172]

Indeed, if anything, the problem may be the reverse: whether the burden of proof on the plaintiffs would be too onerous, as a practical matter, to surmount. Problems of proof in intent-based cases have plagued plaintiffs for decades,[173] and, if anything, these challenges are growing.[174] Burden shifting may help level the playing field. The heightened tiers of scrutiny that courts use to adjudicate constitutional claims all incorporate a form of burden shifting.[175] Burden shifting also has been essential to statutory frameworks where intent is at issue. Notably, for instance, this was the approach Congress took when it enacted Section 5 of the Voting Rights Act,[176] and at least one

discriminatory purpose would not necessarily have required invalidation of the challenged decision. Such proof would, however, have shifted to the Village the burden of establishing that the same decision would have resulted even had the impermissible purpose not been considered.").

[171] See id. In 2016, a district court rejected a similar argument in response to a so-called partisan-fencing claim. See *One Wisconsin Inst., Inc. v Thomsen*, 198 F Supp 3d 896, 929 (WD Wis 2016) ("*Crawford* . . . foreclose[s] the argument that partisan fencing claims should be handled like claims of intentional race or age discrimination, for which any discriminatory legislative intent is sufficient to invalidate a law."). We believe this treatment of *Crawford* is incorrect, in part because it inappropriately conflates claims based on partisanship with claims based on intentional voter suppression. See notes 135 and 137.

[172] See, for example, Erwin Chemerinsky, *Trump, the Court, and Constitutional Law*, 93 Ind L J 73, 74 (2018) ("Proving discriminatory intent is difficult; rarely will government officials express racist motives.").

[173] See Levitt, 59 Wm & Mary L Rev at 2037–38 (cited in note 85) (describing some of the challenges facing plaintiffs).

[174] See *Trump v Hawaii*, 138 S Ct 2392, 2341–43 (2018) (deferring heavily to the government, even in the face of strong evidence of pretext and unlawful intent); *Abbott v Perez*, 138 S Ct 2305, 2324–25 (2018) (insisting that a state enjoys the presumption of lawful intent, even if it was found to have discriminated in relevant ways in the past). But consider *Masterpiece Cakeshop, Ltd. v Colorado Civil Rights Commission*, 138 S Ct 1719, 1730 (2018) (looking behind facial justification offered for state's decision to conclude that it may have intentionally discriminated on the basis of religion).

[175] See, for example, *Johnson v California*, 543 US 499, 505 (2005) ("Under strict scrutiny, the government has the burden of proving that racial classifications are narrowly tailored measures that further compelling governmental interests." (quotation marks omitted)). For cases in which the governmental action contains no racial classifications on its face, but plaintiffs nevertheless are able to prove race-based intention, see *Village of Arlington Heights*, 429 US at 271 n 21.

[176] See Manheim, *Shifting the Burden* (cited in note 165).

scholar has advocated its use in Section 2 cases.[177] Adopting a burden-shifting framework makes particular sense in the context of voting, given the many practical advantages that a jurisdiction has over plaintiffs, as well as the courts, if the jurisdiction intends to suppress votes.[178]

The approach we have described would help to counteract intentional voter suppression. What it would not do, however, is impose new limitations on what a state may do in administering elections—so long as that state is not taking actions *because of* the burdens its actions may pose to eligible voters. This qualification is critical, as it helps to confirm that an effective claim of intentional voter suppression would not "subject virtually every electoral regulation to strict scrutiny, hamper the ability of States to run efficient and equitable elections, [or] compel federal courts to rewrite state electoral codes."[179] A few illustrations help to explain.

If a state, for example, were to remove voters from its registration lists based in part on the Postal Service's change-of-address data after giving those voters effective notice, this activity, without more, would not give rise to an inference of intentional voter suppression. The NVRA requires states to make a reasonable effort to maintain accurate voter rolls, and it indicates that resort to the Postal Service's data constitutes one way to fulfill this obligation.[180] A state's action in this regard is therefore no more consistent with an intent to suppress than it is with an intent to comply with federal law.[181]

Yet imagine that, in addition, the state were to remove hundreds of thousands of additional voters from the rolls, in a manner that far exceeds federal requirements, even though the state's purported ends could be achieved through far less burdensome means.[182] Imagine that this process is overseen by officials with a demonstrated commit-

---

[177] See generally Stephanopoulos, 128 Yale L J at **1–6, 22–25 (cited in note 97) (advancing this proposal).

[178] See note 165 and accompanying text.

[179] *Clingman v Beaver*, 544 US 581, 593 (2005); see also *Burdick v Takushi*, 504 US 428, 433 (1992); *Pers Admr v Feeney*, 442 US 256, 279 (1979).

[180] See 52 USC §§ 20507(a)(4), 20507(d).

[181] This conclusion naturally leads to another question: is the federal requirement itself tainted by intentional voter suppression? Under our theory, there may at least be an argument that this federal requirement—as set by the NVRA and modified by the HAVA in 2002—should be subject to heightened scrutiny. See notes 28–30 and accompanying text. However, ultimately, compared to the other examples we discuss in this article, there is not as much evidence to support an inference of intentional voter suppression with respect to this federal requirement.

[182] As we discuss in note 188 and accompanying text, the conditions described in this paragraph track how Georgia ran its 2018 elections.

ment to policies that make it harder for people to register and vote—including policies that have triggered successful legal challenges—coupled with little interest in policies that make it easier to vote. Assume that while the state continually cites an interest in "voter fraud" to justify its various removals and restrictions, credible experts insist (without any counterarguments based in evidence) that the actual threats of relevant fraud are so negligible as to be nonexistent. And imagine that the same officials promoting these restrictions stand to benefit, politically, from voter suppression. Finally, for good measure, imagine that the state's highest election official openly expresses concern over the effects on election outcomes if too many people, specifically "all these minority voters that are out there and others that are sitting on the sidelines," are registered and able to vote.[183]

In our view, this cumulative evidence gives rise to an inference of intentional voter suppression. This is an inference, not irrefutable proof. Perhaps the state's true intention was to suppress votes; perhaps it was to fight fraud; perhaps it was a combination of both, or something else altogether. Whatever the case, the state should now bear the burden. More specifically, this evidence should establish a prima facie case: it should be enough for the plaintiffs to prevail and receive relief, if the state is unwilling or unable to rebut it. The state should prevail only if it can survive a heightened form of scrutiny. The exact form of this heightened scrutiny is less important than the basic approach: one that requires the state to justify its practices, based on actual evidence. In this sense, a claim of intentional voter suppression could serve as a complement to a *Crawford*-style claim—with evidence of an intent to suppress, rather than evidence of burdens on the voter, serving as the route to heightened scrutiny. If the Court were to adopt this general framework, one reasonable approach would require the state either to prove it would have taken the same step even if intentional suppression had in no way affected its decision (thereby, in a sense, exiting the heightened scrutiny that the prima facie case had established) or alternatively to identify a sufficiently important governmental interest that is closely served by its purging practices.[184]

---

[183] Khushbu Shah, *"Textbook Voter Suppression": Georgia's Bitter Election a Battle Years in the Making*, The Guardian (Nov 10, 2018). The official who expressed this concern, Brian Kemp, did so while simultaneously serving as Georgia's secretary of state and (successfully) running for governor. Id.

[184] This tracks, loosely, the approach the Court has adopted for claims of intentional race discrimination. See *Village of Arlington Heights*, 429 US at 271 n 21.

Subject to this framework, the state we describe above almost certainly would lose. Unless the state could overcome its burden of proving that it would have taken the same action even if intentional voter suppression played no role at all in its decision making, its invocation of voter fraud would have little chance of success.[185] First, the evidence might reveal the state's invocation of fraud to be pretextual. In a world of heightened scrutiny, a court must reject pretextual state interests.[186] Second, it would be close to impossible for this state to establish that its purge practices represent a tailored way of combating voter fraud. Barring the introduction of evidence that, thus far, not even the fiercest proponents of voter-fraud measures have been able to summon,[187] it would become clear that indiscriminately purging throngs of voters from the rolls is a dramatic overreaction to any threat of fraud that actually exists. Indeed, in light of this analysis, it becomes clear that more than just this state's purge practices would be vulnerable to court challenge. And for good reason. This state is projecting a constellation of suppressive tactics.

The hypothetical above describes how Georgia ran its 2018 elections.[188] A closer case, under our model, emerges from the purge practices sanctioned so breezily in *Husted*. In Ohio, the circumstantial evidence of intentional voter suppression was not nearly as blatant as it was in Georgia. A troubling pattern nevertheless emerged: some

---

[185] The state would almost certainly lose, at least, with respect to the purge practices that go above and beyond what federal law minimally requires. With respect to purge practices required by federal law (see notes 180–81 and accompanying text), the state should be able to escape heightened scrutiny by establishing that it would have taken the same step even if intentional suppression had in no way affected its decision. See note 184 and accompanying text. But consider note 190 (exploring the possibility that a state might be able to use a similar theory, bolstered by a lawsuit, to justify even more aggressive purges); note 181 (exploring the possibility that the federal requirement is itself tainted by intentional voter suppression).

[186] See, for example, *United States v Virginia*, 518 US 515, 535–36 (1996) ("[A] tenable justification must describe actual state purposes, not rationalizations for actions in fact differently grounded.").

[187] See notes 105–23 and accompanying text.

[188] See P. R. Lockhart, *Georgia, 2018's Most Prominent Voting Rights Battleground, Explained*, Vox (Nov 6, 2018), available at https://www.vox.com/policy-and-politics/2018/10/26/18024468 /georgia-voter-suppression-stacey-abrams-brian-kemp-voting-rights; see also Complaint, *Fair Fight Action v Crittenden*, 1:18-cv-05391 (ND Ga filed Nov 27, 2018) (available on Westlaw at 2018 WL 6187610) (complaint filed following 2018 election in Georgia detailing alleged problems and demanding extensive relief); id at ¶ 18 ("The U.S. Commission on Civil Rights, a bipartisan, independent agency, found that among the states previously subject to preclearance by the Voting Rights Act, Georgia was the only state that had implemented voting restrictions in every category the Commission examined: strict requirements for voter identification; documentary proof of U.S. citizenship; purges of voters from voter registration rolls; cuts to early voting; and a raft of closed or relocated polling locations.").

legislators and officials committed to practices that make it harder to vote, even when the policies are found to violate federal law; little corresponding interest in policies that would make voting easier for eligible citizens; references to an interest in combating voter fraud, while all credible evidence indicates a lack of a relevant threat; an apparent overlap of voter suppression with the political fortunes of those in power; and so on.[189] In our view, this probably is enough to make a prima facie case—one that might become still stronger through discovery. The burden would therefore shift to Ohio, which would have the opportunity to prove that an intent to suppress played no determinative role in its decision making. Perhaps, with respect to the Supplemental Process, Ohio could make this showing.[190] In the end, however, if Ohio could not overcome its burden of repudiating impermissible intent, it would face the same predicament as Georgia. It would need to prove, through admissible evidence, that its Supplemental Process was an adequately tailored response to a sufficiently important governmental interest. And in all likelihood, it would suffer a similar loss.

The claim we propose—a claim targeting intentional voter suppression, designed to give litigants a fighting chance—would provide important relief to those affected in states across the country. Some might object on the basis that this approach might tend to favor the electoral prospects of certain candidates: those who tend to benefit from increased turnout of eligible voters.[191] This objection takes on

---

[189] See generally Brief of Amicus Curiae National Association for the Advancement of Colored People and the Ohio State Conference of the NAACP in Support of Respondents, *Husted v A. Philip Randolph Institute*, No 16-980 **6–17 (US filed Sept 22, 2017) (available on Westlaw at 2017 WL 4387145) (describing "History of Voter Suppression in Ohio" and its effects on voter engagement).

[190] Ohio might, for example, argue that the threat of liability motivated its change, pointing to the lawsuit, filed in 2012, seeking to force it to purge more voters from its rolls. See note 25. It might also argue that the history of the Supplemental Process—with its implementation, in one form or another, for decades by both Democrats and Republicans—undercuts an inference of intentional suppression. Still, a court scrutinizing these explanations may find them suspect. Among other considerations, the claims advanced in the 2012 lawsuit were legally weak, Ohio entered into a settlement without filing a single defensive motion, and there appeared to be no bipartisanship associated with Ohio's more aggressive implementation of the Supplemental Process starting in 2014. See id. But consider Brief of Amicus Curiae Judicial Watch in Support of Petitioners, *Husted v A. Philip Randolph Institute*, No 16-980, *2 (US filed Aug 7, 2017) (available on Westlaw at 2017 WL 3447771) (resisting suggestions that the litigation was not genuine and adversarial). On the question of Ohio's intent, it is not clear what, if anything, would be revealed through discovery.

[191] This is similar to the one-way ratchet problem that Professor Hasen has identified in the context of conjoined polarization. See Hasen, 59 Wm & Mary L Rev at 1874 (cited in note 95).

particular potency when it appears that the benefits might run disproportionately to politicians associated with one political party over another (in the current political environment, to Democrats over Republicans).[192] Yet this dynamic—occasionally derided as a "one-way ratchet"—is a natural, and we would argue necessary, consequence of the Constitution's universalist protection of the right to vote.[193]

As with any nascent legal theory, many issues would need refinement to ensure the viability of our proposed claim. Scholars have attempted to advance this discussion with respect to other intent-based claims applicable to voting restrictions, and their work provides a substantial starting point.[194] Yet the goal of this article is not to entertain every complexity and counterargument that may arise from this proposal. Instead, it aims to spark an overdue constitutional conversation about intentional voter suppression.

---

[192] See Issacharoff, 64 Duke L J at 1366 (cited in note 13) (discussing the partisan effects of higher and lower turnouts). But consider note 18 (identifying possible exceptions).

[193] In our view, the asymmetry implied by the "one-way ratchet" derives from the Constitution itself, which protects eligible individuals' right to vote but not states' ability to suppress eligible voters. (This asymmetry exists notwithstanding the primary role that the Constitution gives states to design and administer elections. See note 139.) In this sense, our proposed claim presents no more of a one-way ratchet than any other claim effectuating an individual right. Nevertheless, if adopted, our framework would indeed tend to favor the prospects of candidates and political parties that tend to benefit from increased turnout. Consider, for example, a legislature, controlled by one political party, that acts with the intention of improving its candidates' electoral chances by making it easier for eligible voters to vote. Perhaps this legislature might expand early voting because it concludes that early voters are more likely to vote for its candidates than for those of the opposing party. While this intention is motivated by partisanship, it is not coupled with an intention to suppress votes. Our proposed claim is therefore indifferent to it. Now, however, imagine that members of the opposing party gain control of this same legislature and decide they also want to improve their candidates' chances—by intentionally making it *harder* for eligible voters to vote. On this basis, they vote to eliminate the early-voting reform that the legislature so recently had enacted. In our view, this latter action is unlawful. The newly seated legislature's intention to suppress votes is what renders this measure unconstitutional; the political implications neither condemn it nor save it. This hypothetical helps to illustrate our answer to questions such as those posed by Judge Easterbrook at oral argument, when he asked plaintiffs' counsel the following: "A large part [of] your brief reads as if the argument is: 'When Democrats are in control they are free to expand voting. When Republicans in control they are prohibited from making any pro-Republican changes.' That can't be right. . . . Why are the standards when Republicans are in control any different from when Democrats are in control?" See note 163 for the citations for this quote.

[194] See, for example, Hasen, 127 Harv L Rev F at 58 (cited in note 130); Levitt, 59 Wm & Mary L Rev at 1995 (cited in note 85); Kang, 116 Mich L Rev at 352–59 (cited in note 131); Danielle Lang and J. Gerald Hebert, *A Post-Shelby Strategy: Exposing Discriminatory Intent in Voting Rights Litigation*, 127 Yale L J Forum 779, 785 (2018). See also, for example, Andrew Verstein, *The Jurisprudence of Mixed Motives*, 127 Yale L J 1106, 1108 (2018).

Wherever such a conversation may lead, one of the biggest challenges facing the development of a claim seeking to combat intentional voter suppression is, of course, the current composition of the Supreme Court. As *Husted* confirms, there have been, and likely will continue to be, at least five Justices on the Court with records suggesting, on the one hand, resistance to more assertive forms of judicial review over election administration and, on the other, relative indifference to the threat of voter suppression.[195] As a result, it is implausible to believe that the current Court will develop and define a robust and effective set of doctrines to counteract states' efforts to intentionally suppress votes.

Yet most cases are not adjudicated by the Supreme Court. This is true even in the often high-stakes world of election law, where the rapidity of the election cycle, as well as the occasional willingness of jurisdictions to settle in response to adverse court rulings, ensure that many lower court opinions serve as the final word.[196] Moreover, not all cases proceed on the basis of federal law; protections contained in state constitutional and statutory law may offer analogous, but more viable, avenues for relief.[197] And, of course, today's Supreme Court will not be tomorrow's Supreme Court. In the meantime, unfortunately, the problem of intentional voter suppression does not seem to be going anywhere; the elephant has taken up residence.

III. Conclusion

Many landmark Supreme Court decisions stem from small disputes, such as a baker's refusal to sell a wedding cake.[198] In deciding such cases, the Court elevates mundane facts by projecting them against a vast, constitutional landscape. So, for example, a wedding

---

[195] See Section I.B. There is little reason to believe that either Justice Gorsuch or Justice Kavanaugh will upset this balance in a manner that will lead to increased judicial oversight of voter suppression.

[196] For a prominent example of a lower court granting relief in response to election-administration claims that might have received a less warm reception before the Supreme Court, see *McCrory*, 831 F3d at 233 (concluding that "discriminatory racial intent," at least in part, motivated North Carolina's election reforms); see also *Veasey v Abbott*, 830 F3d 216, 235–42 (5th Cir 2016). See generally Daniel P. Tokaji, *Leave It to the Lower Courts: On Judicial Intervention in Election Administration*, 68 Ohio St L J 1065, 1065 (2007) (arguing "the Supreme Court should exercise exceptional restraint in this area").

[197] See generally Joshua A. Douglas, *The Right to Vote under State Constitutions*, 67 Vand L Rev 89 (2014) (exploring state constitutional provisions explicitly granting the right to vote).

[198] See *Masterpiece Cakeshop, Ltd. v Colorado Civil Rights Commission*, 138 S Ct 1719 (2018).

cake—already symbolic—takes on new layers of constitutional and societal significance. At other times, however, the Court takes the opposite tack. Faced with a case that implicates fundamental constitutional questions, the Court averts its gaze, and instead trains its sight narrowly on subconstitutional minutiae. The result is an opinion that feels straightforward—even, perhaps, a bit dull—but also disconcertingly untethered from the heart of the matter.

In the face of the recent retrenchment of voting rights, plaintiffs have enabled this evasion in the election-law context by framing potentially monumental cases in a narrow way, as occurred in *Husted*. The litigants themselves are not to blame. Their strategies represent a rational response to the refusal of the Rehnquist and Roberts Courts to recognize the wisdom and importance of constitutional traditions emerging out of the horrors that predated the Civil Rights Era. The framing of cases like *Husted* nevertheless makes it difficult to understand just how little the Supreme Court is doing to protect the right to vote. The scope of the problem with the Court's approach, and the true significance of cases like *Husted*, emerges only when, and if, we lift our collective gaze and take in the full panorama.

MELISSA MURRAY

INVERTING ANIMUS: MASTERPIECE CAKESHOP AND THE NEW MINORITIES

I. Introduction

Masterpiece Cakeshop v Colorado Human Rights Commission[1] has been discussed in fairly specific terms—the collision of liberty and equality; or, more particularly, religious freedom versus antidiscrimination norms.[2] This frame is certainly accurate, though hardly exhaustive. There are a number of lenses through which we might understand this case. And, indeed, different lenses may cast the Court's decision in entirely new lights, bringing the decision into conversations that may, at first blush, seem quite distant from the questions presented to the Supreme Court.

With this in mind, in this essay I reframe *Masterpiece Cakeshop* to go beyond the collision of religious liberty and equality to intervene in these other conversations. As I explain, *Masterpiece Cakeshop* gestures toward interesting, though neglected, developments in antidiscrimination law. As claims for religious accommodation have proliferated, those seeking

Melissa Murray is Professor of Law, New York University School of Law.

Author's note: I am indebted to Michelle Adams, Devon Carbado, Doug NeJaime, Russell Robinson, Nelson Tebbe, and Kenji Yoshino for helpful comments and suggestions. All errors are my own.

[1] 138 S Ct 1719 (2018).

[2] See Leslie Kendrick and Micah Schwartzman, Comment, *The Etiquette of Animus*, 132 Harv L Rev 133, 133 (2018); Douglas NeJaime and Reva Siegel, *Religious Exemptions and Antidiscrimination Law in Masterpiece Cakeshop*, 128 Yale L J F 201, 203–4 (2018).

accommodations on religious grounds have sought to frame themselves as dissenters from majoritarian norms. To wit, in seeking an exemption from the ambit of Colorado's public accommodations law, *Masterpiece Cakeshop* petitioner Jack Phillips casts his claims in this light.[3] He seeks an exemption from the law not because he is a bigot who wishes to discriminate against LGBTQ persons, but rather because he is an observant Christian in an increasingly secular culture.[4] In other words, he claims to be a minority in a majoritarian culture. In Phillips's view, by applying the public accommodations law to his conduct, the Colorado Civil Rights Commission impermissibly targeted those whose religious beliefs do not condone same-sex marriage and homosexuality.[5]

Ultimately, the Court did not address the questions presented in the litigation—whether the constitutional commitment to free exercise of religion required an exemption from the ambit of a generally applicable antidiscrimination law and whether Colorado's public accommodations law was aimed at particular religious groups.[6] Instead, the Court concluded that the Colorado Civil Rights Commission had failed to review Phillips's claims with the neutrality to which Phillips was entitled, and in so doing, had exhibited "hostility" to religion, in violation of the First Amendment.[7]

Although the Court decided *Masterpiece Cakeshop* on narrow First Amendment grounds, the decision recalled the Court's equal protection jurisprudence; in particular, the doctrine of unconstitutional animus.[8] In finding that the Commission had reviewed Phillips's claims with hostility, the majority essentially concluded that the state Commission had acted with impermissible animus.

Viewed through the lens of the animus doctrine, *Masterpiece Cakeshop* takes on new contours and, intriguingly, gestures toward inter-

---

[3] See Petition for Writ of Certiorari, *Masterpiece Cakeshop, Ltd v Colo Civil Rights Commission*, No 16-111, *13 (US filed 2018) (available on Westlaw at 2016 WL 3971309) ("Petition for Certiorari").

[4] Id at *25–30.

[5] Id.

[6] Kendrick and Schwartzman, 132 Harv L Rev at 133 (cited in note 2) ("The case presented a legal conflict between LGBT rights and religious liberty. But the Court ducked central questions raised by that conflict."); Adam Liptak, *In Narrow Decision, Supreme Court Sides with Baker Who Turned Away Gay Couple*, NY Times (June 4, 2018), available at https://www.nytimes.com/2018/06/04/us/politics/supreme-court-sides-with-baker-who-turned-away-gay-couple.html.

[7] *Masterpiece Cakeshop*, 138 S Ct at 1728–31.

[8] *Church of Lukumi Babalu Aye v City of Hialeah*, 508 US 520, 540–42 (1993).

esting developments in antidiscrimination law. In *Masterpiece Cakeshop*, the majority deployed the concept of animus to protect Jack Phillips, an individual charged with discriminating against LGBTQ persons. This is perhaps ironic given that, in recent years, the animus doctrine has been used to protect LGBTQ persons from discriminatory state action.[9]

The majority's use of animus to protect Jack Phillips is relevant on a number of fronts. As an initial matter, Phillips, a straight white male Protestant, is among a class of persons who, ordinarily, are not assumed to be among the "discrete and insular minorities"[10] in need of antidiscrimination protections. More importantly, the state Commission deemed to have treated Phillips with impermissible hostility was reviewing charges that Phillips himself had discriminated on the basis of sexual orientation, in violation of Colorado law. In this regard, the majority deployed animus to protect someone alleged to be engaged in discriminatory conduct *against* a class of persons understood to be the subject of antidiscrimination protections.

These aspects of *Masterpiece Cakeshop* are relevant because, in recent years, we have seen the rise of antidiscrimination challenges brought by those who ordinarily might not be considered minorities or members of disadvantaged groups, but who nonetheless claim the protections of antidiscrimination law. In many respects, these recent claims are the direct descendants of the "reverse racism" claims that characterized the initial backlash to affirmative action in the 1970s and 1980s. But, critically, even as these newer antidiscrimination claims share features with the earlier claims, there are striking differences. Like the earlier affirmative action cases, these recent cases involve antidiscrimination claims brought by individuals who are not the imagined subjects of antidiscrimination law's protections. Nevertheless, these newer litigants deploy antidiscrimination law and its principles to vindicate their claims against those who *are* the imagined subjects of antidiscrimination law's protections. The rise of challenges from men's rights groups to all-female co-working spaces, networking events, and other programming is exemplary of this development.[11] Taken together, *Masterpiece Cake-*

---

[9] See, for example, *Romer v Evans*, 517 US 620, 632–36 (1996); *Lawrence v Texas*, 539 US 558, 574–75 (2003); *United States v Windsor*, 570 US 744, 769–70 (2013).

[10] *United States v Carolene Products*, 304 US 144, 152 n 4 (1938).

[11] See Part IV.

shop and these men's rights cases suggest antidiscrimination law's malleability and plasticity—and its limits.

This essay proceeds in four parts. Part I rehearses the facts and disposition of *Masterpiece Cakeshop*. Part II briefly details the animus doctrine and considers the Court's use of animus in *Masterpiece Cakeshop*. As I explain in Part II, in invoking animus to vindicate Jack Phillips's right to neutral review of his claims, the majority departed from, and indeed inverted, the traditional animus analysis in important ways. Part III maintains that *Masterpiece Cakeshop* gestures toward important developments in antidiscrimination law—namely, the use of antidiscrimination doctrine to challenge the actions of those who are ostensibly the intended objects of antidiscrimination law's protections. With this in mind, I focus in Part III on recent cases in which antidiscrimination law has been deployed against all-women's spaces and programming in an effort to vindicate men's rights to be free of gender-based discrimination. Part IV considers the implications of these developments for antidiscrimination law. Part V briefly concludes.

II. Masterpiece Cakeshop v Colorado Civil Rights Commission—the Facts

In July 2012, Charlie Craig and David Mullins visited the Masterpiece Cakeshop in Lakewood, Colorado, to order a cake that would be served at a reception celebrating their marriage.[12] However, when Jack Phillips, the owner of Masterpiece Cakeshop, learned that the requested cake was intended for a party celebrating the couple's same-sex wedding, he refused the couple's business.[13] As Phillips explained to Mullins and Craig, he was a devout Christian, and making a cake intended for the celebration of a same-sex union would contradict his religious convictions, which specified that marriage was a union between a man and a woman.[14] In Phillips's view, there was

---

[12] Brief in Opposition, *Masterpiece Cakeshop, Ltd v Colo Civil Rights Commission*, No 16-111, *1–2 (US filed Nov 6, 2015) (available on Westlaw as 2015 WL 13522772) ("Brief in Opposition"). Because same-sex couples were ineligible for civil marriage in Colorado, the couple planned to travel to Massachusetts to marry. The cake was intended for a reception that they would host for friends and family in Denver upon their return. *Craig v Masterpiece Cakeshop, Inc.*, 370 P3d 272, 276 (Colo App 2015).

[13] Brief in Opposition, *2–3 (cited in note 12).

[14] Id.

nothing untoward about refusing the couple's business on sincerely held religious grounds.[15] After all, in 2012, the state of Colorado did not recognize same-sex marriages, clearly communicating that the marriage itself was unlawful in the eyes of the state.[16]

Regardless of whether their marriage was recognized by the state, Mullins and Craig took umbrage to Phillips's refusal. On September 5, 2012, the couple filed complaints against Masterpiece Cakeshop with the Colorado Civil Rights Division, charging Phillips and Masterpiece Cakeshop with sexual orientation discrimination in violation of the Colorado Anti-Discrimination Act (CADA).[17] CADA prohibits discrimination, including discrimination on the basis of sexual orientation, in places of public accommodation.[18] Phillips countered the charges by arguing that he had not engaged in sexual orientation discrimination, as he was happy to serve gays and lesbians by providing cakes for other (nonmarital) occasions, such as birthdays and baby showers.[19]

Over the course of four years, the dispute proceeded through the Colorado administrative[20] and state court systems, where Mullins and

---

[15] *Masterpiece Cakeshop, Ltd v Colo Civil Rights Commission*, 138 S Ct 1719, 1724 (2018).

[16] Id at 1724.

[17] Joint Appendix, *Masterpiece Cakeshop, Ltd v Colo Civil Rights Commission*, No 16-111, *47–53 (US filed Aug 21, 2017) (available on Westlaw at 2017 WL 4232758) ("Joint Appendix").

[18] CADA provides in relevant part: "It is a discriminatory practice and unlawful for a person, directly or indirectly, to refuse, withhold from, or deny to an individual or a group, because of disability, race, creed, color, sex, sexual orientation, marital status, national origin, or ancestry, the full and equal enjoyment of the goods, services, facilities, privileges, advantages, or accommodations of a place of public accommodation." Colo Rev Stat § 24-34-601(2)(a). The act defines "public accommodation" broadly to include any "place of business engaged in any sales to the public and any place offering services . . . to the public," but excludes "a church, synagogue, mosque, or other place that is principally used for religious purposes." Colo Rev Stat § 24-34-601(1).

[19] Joint Appendix at *152 (cited in note 17).

[20] CADA establishes an administrative system for the resolution of discrimination claims. Complaints of discrimination in violation of CADA are addressed in the first instance by the Colorado Civil Rights Division. The division investigates each claim, and if it finds probable cause that CADA has been violated it will refer the matter to the Colorado Civil Rights Commission. The Commission then decides whether to initiate a formal hearing before a state Administrative Law Judge (ALJ), who will hear evidence and argument before issuing a written decision. See Colo Rev Stat §§ 24-34-306, 24-4-105(14). The ALJ's decision may be appealed to the full Commission, a seven-member appointed body. The Commission holds a public hearing and deliberative session before voting on the case. If the Commission determines that the evidence proves a CADA violation, it may impose remedial measures as provided by statute. See Colo Rev Stat § 24-34-306(9). Available remedies include, inter alia, orders to cease-and-desist a discriminatory policy, to file regular compliance reports with the Commission, and "to take

Craig eventually prevailed.[21] Phillips appealed the decision to the United States Supreme Court,[22] which granted review.[23] At the Court, Phillips repackaged his claims and the attendant arguments. Specifically, he argued that the compliance with CADA, and providing wedding-related goods and services to same-sex couples, constituted compelled speech.[24] In a seven to two decision, a majority of the Court reversed the Commission's decision, ruling on narrow grounds that the Commission did not employ religious neutrality in its evaluation of Phillips's claims, thus violating Jack Phillips's free exercise rights.[25]

The majority's decision did not resolve the central questions of *Masterpiece Cakeshop*—whether baking a cake constituted "speech" for purposes of the First Amendment and, if so, whether the state's efforts to protect the rights and dignity of LGBTQ persons should be prioritized ahead of First Amendment claims of free speech and free exercise of religion. Nevertheless, it raised questions about how reviewing courts should handle religious refusal claims going forward. Writing for the majority, Justice Anthony Kennedy concluded that "[w]hatever the confluence of speech and free exercise principles might be in some cases, the Colorado Civil Rights Commission's consideration of this case was inconsistent with the State's obligation of religious neutrality."[26] According to Kennedy, Colorado was entitled to enforce its "generally applicable" antidiscrimination laws in order to prevent those "who object to gay marriages for moral and religious reasons" to effectively "put up signs saying 'no goods or services will be sold if they will be used for gay marriages,' something that would impose a serious stigma on gay persons."[27] But even as it took steps to enforce its laws, the state was required to provide Phillips with "neutral and respectful consideration"—an obligation that was compromised by the Commission's "clear and impermissible hostility

---

affirmative action, including the posting of notices setting forth the substantive rights of the public." Colo Rev Stat § 24-34-605. The Commission is not permitted to assess money damages or fines. Colo Rev Stat §§ 24-34-306(9), 24-34-605.

[21] *Craig*, 370 P3d at 283.

[22] See Petition for Certiorari (cited in note 3).

[23] See *Masterpiece Cakeshop, Ltd v Colo Civil Rights Commission*, cert granted, 137 S Ct 2290 (2017).

[24] Petition for Certiorari at *i (cited in note 3).

[25] *Masterpiece Cakeshop*, 138 S Ct at 1723–24.

[26] Id at 1723.

[27] Id at 1728–29.

toward the sincere religious beliefs that motivated [Phillips's] objection."[28]

According to Justice Kennedy, the record of the Commission's public hearings was riddled with evidence of the commissioners' "hostility" to Phillips and his religious beliefs. As Kennedy recounted, "[a]t several points during its meeting, commissioners endorsed the view that religious beliefs cannot legitimately be carried into the public sphere or commercial domain, implying that religious beliefs and persons are less than fully welcome in Colorado's business community."[29] While Kennedy conceded that such statements were "susceptible of different interpretations"—including the benign conclusion that "a business cannot refuse to provide services based on sexual orientation, regardless of the proprietor's personal views"—Kennedy sensed something more sinister.[30] At a subsequent public hearing, he explained, another commissioner referenced the previous meeting's discussion, but went further to "disparage Phillips' beliefs."[31] Specifically, the commissioner stated:

> I would also like to reiterate what we said in the hearing or the last meeting. Freedom of religion and religion has been used to justify all kinds of discrimination throughout history, whether it be slavery, whether it be the holocaust, whether it be—I mean, we—we can list hundreds of situations where freedom of religion has been used to justify discrimination. And to me it is one of the most despicable pieces of rhetoric that people can use to—to use their religion to hurt others.[32]

For Kennedy and the majority, this was a bridge too far. The commissioner's statements "disparage[d] [Phillips's] religion in at least two distinct ways: by describing it as despicable, and also by characterizing it as merely rhetorical—something insubstantial and even insincere."[33] Comparing "Phillips' invocation of his sincerely held reli-

---

[28] Id at 1729.

[29] *Masterpiece Cakeshop*, 138 S Ct at 1729. Kennedy pointed to a transcript of one of the Commission's hearings, bristling at one commissioner's suggestion that "Phillips can believe 'what he wants to believe,' but cannot act on his religious beliefs 'if he decides to do business in the state.'" Id. Kennedy noted that the same commissioner soon "restated the same position: '[I]f a businessman wants to do business in the state and he's got an issue with the—the law's impacting his personal belief system, he needs to look at being able to compromise.'" Id.

[30] Id.

[31] Id.

[32] Id.

[33] *Masterpiece Cakeshop*, 138 S Ct at 1729.

gious beliefs to defenses of slavery and the Holocaust" compounded the injury.[34] And while the statement was uttered by only one commissioner, it appeared as though the other commissioners shared their colleague's view of Phillips and his religious beliefs.

As Justice Kennedy observed, the other commissioners did not object to the statement when it was made, nor did they disavow it subsequently.[35] Taken together, the statements made at both hearings were, according to the majority, "inappropriate," "dismissive," and "show[ed] lack of due consideration for Phillips' free exercise rights and the dilemma he faced."[36]

The majority found further evidence of the Commission's hostility toward Phillips and his religious beliefs in the Commission's disposition of three related cases.[37] In all three cases, William Jack attempted to purchase cakes with antigay messages from three Denver, Colorado, bakeries.[38] For example, he requested from Marjorie Silva, the owner of Azucar Bakery, a Bible-shaped cake decorated with an image of two grooms covered by a red X and adorned with the words "God hates sin. Psalm 45:7" and "Homosexuality is a detestable sin. Leviticus 18:22."[39] All three bakeries refused to make cakes with these messages, although Silva offered to sell Jack a Bible-shaped cake and to provide him with an icing bag so that he could decorate the cake as he saw fit.[40] Jack filed claims against the bakeries, alleging that they had denied him service based on his religious beliefs, in violation of Colorado's public accommodations law.[41] In all three cases, the Civil Rights Division concluded that the baker acted lawfully in refusing service because the bakers' objections were rooted in a disdain for the "discriminatory" and "derogatory" messages, rather than in objections to Jack's religious beliefs.[42]

---

[34] Id.

[35] Id at 1729–30 ("The record shows no objection to these comments from other commissioners. And the later state-court ruling reviewing the Commission's decision did not mention those comments, much less express concern with their content. Nor were the comments by the commissioners disavowed in the briefs filed in this Court.").

[36] Id at 1729.

[37] See id at 1728–31.

[38] See id at 1730.

[39] Joint Appendix at *232–33 (cited in note 17).

[40] *Masterpiece Cakeshop*, 138 S Ct at 1748–49 (Ginsburg, J, dissenting); Joint Appendix at *233–34 (cited in note 17).

[41] *Masterpiece Cakeshop*, 138 S Ct at 1748–50 (Ginsburg, J, dissenting).

[42] Id at 1730.

For Kennedy, the "treatment of the conscience-based objections at issue in the[] three cases contrast[ed] with the Commission's treatment of Phillips' objection."[43] Specifically, Kennedy noted a difference in the Commission's approach to Phillips's objections and its approach to the bakers' objections in the *Jack* cases. As Kennedy observed, "[t]he Commission ruled against Phillips in part on the theory that any message the requested wedding cake would carry would be attributed to the customer, not to the baker. Yet the Division did not address this point in any of the other cases with respect to the cakes depicting anti-gay marriage symbolism."[44] Further, in part because each bakery was willing to sell other products, including those depicting Christian themes, the division found no violation of CADA in the *Jack* cases.[45] By contrast, "the Commission dismissed Phillips' willingness to sell 'birthday cakes, shower cakes, [and] cookies and brownies,' to gay and lesbian customers as irrelevant."[46] Taken together, "the Commission's consideration of Phillips' religious objection did not accord with its treatment of these other objections."[47]

In all, Justice Kennedy and the majority concluded that the Commission's statements in the public hearings, coupled with the different treatment of the proprietors in the *Jack* cases, failed to comport with the requirement of government neutrality toward religion. In so doing, the Court reversed the lower court's decision in favor of Craig and Mullins and tabled the broader question of how to resolve future conflicts between LGBT rights and religious liberty.[48]

III. INVERTING ANIMUS

For many, the majority's resolution of *Masterpiece Cakeshop* raises more questions than it answers. But what is most interesting about the opinion is the majority's conclusion that the statements of two commissioners, the Commission's failure to discredit those statements, and its disposition of the *Jack* cases pointed to impermissible "hostility" toward religion.[49] Although the majority rooted its decision

---

[43] Id.

[44] Id.

[45] *Masterpiece Cakeshop*, 138 S Ct at 1730.

[46] Id.

[47] Id.

[48] See id at 1732.

[49] See Part II.

in the general principle that the government may not act on the basis of animosity toward religion,[50] the decision recalled the equal protection doctrine of impermissible animus.

Critically, Kennedy never explicitly invokes the term "animus" in *Masterpiece Cakeshop*. Indeed, the term is only mentioned once in the case—in Justice Gorsuch's concurrence, in which Justice Alito joined. And there it was used only to emphasize that, under Colorado law, "'no such showing of actual' 'animus'—or intent to discriminate against persons in a protected class—was even required in Mr. Phillips's case."[51]

Yet, even if the term "animus" is not explicitly invoked in the opinion, it looms large in the logic of the case—and, indeed, in the cases on which the majority relies. Throughout the majority opinion in *Masterpiece Cakeshop*, Justice Kennedy repeatedly references *Church of Lukumi Babalu Aye v Hialeah*, a First Amendment case in which the Court, with Kennedy writing for the majority, struck down a set of municipal ordinances that, although facially neutral, appeared drawn for the purpose of targeting the Santeria religion and its practice of ritual animal sacrifice.[52] There, in holding that the ordinances were animated by impermissible hostility toward the Santeria religion and its practices, Justice Kennedy, with Justice Stevens concurring, "f[ound] guidance in [the Court's] equal protection cases."[53]

But even leaving aside Kennedy's reliance on *Church of Lukumi Babalu Aye* and its embrace of equal protection principles, the turn to animus is perhaps not surprising given that Kennedy, in his tenure on the Court, has done more than any modern Justice to advance the doctrine of animus in the Court's equal protection jurisprudence.[54] But even if the appeal to animus is not surprising, it is perhaps the greatest irony of *Masterpiece Cakeshop*. Throughout Justice Kennedy's tenure on the Court, his interest in identifying and discrediting impermissible state animus toward "politically unpopular groups" has had the greatest effect in advancing the constitutional rights of

---

[50] *Masterpiece Cakeshop, Ltd v Colo Civil Rights Commission*, 138 S Ct 1719, 1731 (2018) ("[T]he government ... cannot impose regulations that are hostile to the religious beliefs of affected citizens.") (quoting *Church of Lukumi Babalu Aye v City of Hialeah*, 508 US 520, 534 (1993)).

[51] *Masterpiece Cakeshop*, 138 S Ct at 1736–37.

[52] *Church of Lukumi Babalu Aye*, 508 US at 523–34 (1993).

[53] Id at 540.

[54] See Kendrick and Schwartzman, 132 Harv L Rev at 137–38 (cited in note 2); Russell K. Robinson, *Unequal Protection*, 68 Stan L Rev 151, 163–70 (2016).

LGBTQ persons.[55] In this regard, what *is* surprising about the turn to animus in *Masterpiece Cakeshop* is that it is not used to protect the interests of LGBTQ persons, but rather to protect the interests of an evangelical Christian who sought an exemption from the ambit of laws prohibiting sexual orientation discrimination.

The parts that follow detail the Court's animus jurisprudence, much of which has been authored by Justice Kennedy. In tracing the contours of the Court's—and Kennedy's—understanding of animus, parts III.A and III.B consider the origins of the doctrine and its deployment in cases involving LGBTQ rights. With this context in place, Part III.C illuminates the continuity and disjunction between prior iterations of animus and the Court's understanding of animus in *Masterpiece Cakeshop*. As it explains, though the majority opinion's understanding of animus tracks many of the key features of earlier iterations of the animus analysis, it departs from—and inverts—the established vision of animus in important ways.

A. IDENTIFYING ANIMUS: MORENO, CLEBURNE, AND CHURCH OF LUKUMI BABALU AYE

As a formal matter, the concept of animus can be traced to the 1973 opinion *USDA v Moreno*,[56] where the Court struck down an amendment to the Food Stamps Act.[57] The case involved a challenge to a statutory amendment that modified the eligibility requirements for the food stamps program to exclude households composed of "unrelated" persons.[58] The government justified the modification as an effort to minimize benefits fraud, but as the Court noted, the act already had mechanisms for dealing with fraudulent claims.[59] Instead, the government's interest in amending the eligibility criteria stemmed from a more troubling rationale. Though the legislative history on the amendment was scant, "[t]he legislative history that does exist indicates that that amendment was intended to prevent 'hippies' and 'hippie communes' from participating in the food stamp program."[60]

---

[55] See Robinson, 68 Stan L Rev at 171–85 (cited in note 54).

[56] 413 US 528 (1973).

[57] Id at 538.

[58] Id at 529.

[59] Id at 536–37.

[60] Id at 534.

For the *Moreno* majority, antipathy for hippies and hippie communes was insufficient to justify the distinction between households of related persons and those of unrelated persons. As Justice William Brennan concluded, if "the constitutional conception of 'equal protection of the laws' means anything, it must at the very least mean that a bare congressional desire to harm a politically unpopular group cannot constitute a legitimate governmental interest."[61] Put differently, to pass constitutional muster under the Equal Protection Clause, "an enactment must have a public-regarding reason other than to disadvantage a particular group."[62]

Later, in *City of Cleburne v Cleburne Living Center*,[63] the Court reiterated its concerns about animus against disfavored groups.[64] There, the Court considered a city's denial of a special-use zoning permit for the operation of a group home for the developmentally disabled.[65] In finding the denial of the permit unconstitutional, the Court observed that "[t]o withstand equal protection review, legislation that distinguishes between the mentally retarded and others must be rationally related to a legitimate governmental purpose."[66] In this regard, the issue was one of means and ends, with the Court concluding that "[t]he State may not rely on a classification whose relationship to an asserted goal is so attenuated as to render the distinction arbitrary or irrational."[67]

And, critically, the facts of *Cleburne* suggested the irrationality of the city's actions. As the Court noted, the city required a special-use permit for a group home that intended to operate as "[h]ospitals for the insane or feebleminded,"[68] but did not require such permits for other kinds of group homes, like nursing homes, apartment complexes, and fraternity and sorority houses.[69] Though the city tried to justify the distinction by adverting to, among other reasons, "the

---

[61] Id at 534–35.

[62] Dale Carpenter, *Windsor Products: Equal Protection from Animus*, 2013 Supreme Court Review 183, 205.

[63] 473 US 432 (1985).

[64] Id at 449–50.

[65] Id at 435.

[66] Id at 446.

[67] *Cleburne*, 473 US at 446.

[68] Id at 437.

[69] Id at 447.

negative attitudes of the majority of property owners located within 200 feet of the [proposed] facility, as well as ... the fears of elderly residents of the neighborhood," the Court rejected these rationales out of hand:

> [M]ere negative attitudes, or fear, unsubstantiated by factors which are properly cognizable in a zoning proceeding, are not permissible bases for treating a home for the mentally retarded differently from apartment houses, multiple dwellings, and the like.... [T]he City may not avoid the strictures of [the Equal Protection] Clause by deferring to the wishes or objections of some fraction of the body politic.[70]

Although the city of Cleburne had not acted out of a bare desire to harm the cognitively disabled, by responding to the "negative attitudes" of property owners and the "fears of elderly residents of the neighborhood," the city had credited and prioritized these views in its permit deliberations. Regardless of whether they were harbored by the city or by individual members of the community, such "vague and undifferentiated fears" could not justify the different treatment of the cognitively disabled. As Justice Byron White concluded, "[t]he short of it is that requiring the permit in this case appears to us to rest on an irrational prejudice against the mentally retarded."[71]

While *Moreno* and *Cleburne* were equal protection cases, the Court's understanding of animus also surfaced in cases involving religious rights. In *Church of Lukumi Babalu Aye*, Justice Kennedy, writing for himself and Justice Stevens, drew on the logic of the Court's equal protection jurisprudence to invalidate a set of municipal ordinances aimed at prohibiting a Santeria church's use of animal sacrifice in its religious practices.[72] In concluding that the ordinances effectively functioned as a "religious gerrymander,"[73] with the purpose of specifically targeting the practices of this disfavored religious sect, Justice Kennedy, referencing the Court's disparate-impact jurisprudence,[74]

---

[70] Id at 448.

[71] Id at 450.

[72] *Church of Lukumi Babalu Aye*, 508 US at 539–42.

[73] Id at 535.

[74] Specifically, the *Church of Lukumi Babalu Aye* Court cited *Arlington Heights v Metropolitan Housing Development Corporation*, 429 US 252, 266 (1977), and *Personnel Administrator of Massachusetts v Feeney*, 442 US 256, 279 n 24 (1979), for the proposition that both direct and circumstantial evidence could be used to determine whether the challenged ordinances "were enacted 'because of,' not merely 'in spite of,'" their suppression of Santeria religious practice. 508 US at 540.

considered "both direct and circumstantial evidence," including statements made by council members at public hearings disparaging the Santeria religion and pondering what could be done "to prevent the [Santeria] Church from opening?"[75] Taken together, the statements and the ordinances evinced "animosity to Santeria adherents and their religious practices,"[76] and in so doing, violated the requirement of government neutrality toward religion.

In these early cases, the Court emphasized the need to consider broadly the circumstances in which a particular government action arose in order to determine whether impermissible animus was at work. These circumstances might include explicit statements of hostility and animosity, as in *Moreno* and *Church of Lukumi*, as well as circumstantial evidence. In this vein, although the City of Cleburne had never explicitly disparaged the developmentally disabled in the legislative process, the Court concluded that the stark deviations in the permit process required of the Cleburne Living Center, compared to that for other group homes, coupled with the city's solicitude for the "negative attitudes" of community members, suggested that the legislative process had been infected with animus.[77] Put differently, in determining whether impermissible animus was at the root of a government action, the Court considered the broader context and made inferences based on "both direct and circumstantial evidence."[78]

More recently, the Court has relied on context and inference more explicitly in extending the animus doctrine to cases involving the rights claims of gay people.

B. ANIMUS ELABORATED—ROMER AND WINDSOR

In recent years, the animus doctrine has been used to resolve cases involving claims of gay rights.[79] Critically, these opinions have all been authored by Justice Kennedy, and they have all relied on a contextual analysis in determining that impermissible animus was afoot. In *Romer v Evans*,[80] for example, the Court struck down Amendment 2, a

---

[75] Id at 541.

[76] Id at 542.

[77] *Cleburne*, 473 US at 448.

[78] *Church of Lukumi Babalu Aye*, 508 US at 540.

[79] See Robinson, 68 Stan L Rev at 171–74 (cited in note 54).

[80] 517 US 620 (1996).

Colorado voter referendum that amended the state constitution to preclude all legislative, executive, or judicial action intended to shield individuals from discrimination on the basis of "homosexual, lesbian or bisexual orientation, conduct, practices or relationships."[81] Writing for the majority, Justice Kennedy took note of "peculiar" aspects of the challenged amendment.[82] Although the state cited its interests in protecting the liberties of landlords and employers who objected to homosexuality and conserving scarce state resources for fighting other forms of discrimination,[83] the amendment's reach seemed far broader than these narrow justifications.

As an initial matter, the amendment imposed "a broad and undifferentiated disability on a single named group"—lesbian, gay, and bisexual (LGB) persons.[84] As Justice Kennedy noted, "Amendment 2 ... prohibits all legislative, executive or judicial action at any level of state or local government designed to protect [gays and lesbians]."[85] In this vein, the amendment, which "withdr[ew] from homosexuals, but no others, specific legal protection from the injuries caused by discrimination,"[86] treated LGB persons as a "solitary class" and effectively undermined state and local public accommodations laws aimed at protecting against sexual orientation discrimination. In short, the amendment effected a "[s]weeping and comprehensive" change in the legal status of LGB persons[87]—a change that seemed disproportionate to the amendment's purported interests in protecting the liberties of landlords and employers who objected to homosexuality and conserving state resources for fighting other kinds of discrimination.

But it was not solely that Amendment 2 was unprecedented in its breadth. The social and political milieu in which it was enacted gestured toward impermissible discrimination against gay men and lesbians. For example, the record below was replete with evidence that the campaign in favor of Amendment 2 had engaged in derogatory and hostile invective about gays and lesbians. As Professor Martha Nussbaum recounts,

---

[81] Id at 624.

[82] Id at 632.

[83] Id at 635.

[84] Id.

[85] *Romer*, 517 US at 624.

[86] Critically, Amendment 2 was a response to the enactment of sexual orientation antidiscrimination municipal ordinances in progressive Colorado cities like Boulder, Aspen, and Denver. Id at 626–29.

[87] Id at 627.

in promoting the amendment to the voters, an organization called Colorado for Family Values (CFV) organized a campaign aimed at thwarting future acts of "militant gay aggression" and rolling back "special rights" for gays and lesbians.[88] To this end, CFV distributed pamphlets and other campaign material that characterized gays and lesbians as "depraved" and "deviant" and claimed that "gays [ate] feces and dr[ank] raw blood."[89] As one amici noted, "[g]iven the evidence of irrational animus and bigotry in the record below, this Court should conclude ... that a constitutionally illegitimate desire to harm an unpopular group is precisely Amendment 2's objective."[90]

Although these incidents were evident in the record[91]—and would have been known to the Court—the *Romer* majority did not reference them directly in its decision. Instead, the majority concluded that the amendment's impact on the legal status of LGB persons, "raise[d] the inevitable inference that the disadvantage imposed is born of animosity toward the class of persons affected."[92] Indeed, as the Court saw it, "[Amendment 2's] sheer breadth is so discontinuous with the reasons offered for it that the amendment seems inexplicable by anything but animus toward the class it affects."[93]

In *United States v Windsor*,[94] the social and political milieu in which the Defense of Marriage Act (DOMA) was enacted also likely factored into the Court's disposition of the case. There, the Court, with Kennedy again writing for the majority, struck down section 3 of DOMA on the ground that it was enacted for the purpose of disparaging and injuring same-sex couples and their unions, and, as such, was infected with impermissible animus.[95] In making this determination, Kennedy, in terms that reflected the Court's analysis of Amendment 2 in *Romer*, noted that DOMA was an "unusual deviation from the usual tradition

---

[88] Martha C. Nussbaum, *From Disgust to Humanity: Sexual Orientation and Constitutional Law* 101–3 (Oxford, 2010).

[89] Id at 102.

[90] Brief for Amici Curiae Asian American Legal Defense and Education Fund et al, *Romer v Evans*, No 94-1039, *19 (US filed June 19, 1995) (available on Westlaw at 1995 WL 17008434).

[91] See, for example, Brief for Respondents, *Romer v Evans*, No 94-1039, 7–8, 48 & n 33 (US filed June 19, 1995) (available on Westlaw at 1995 WL 417786).

[92] *Romer*, 517 US at 634.

[93] Id at 632.

[94] 570 US 744 (2013).

[95] Id at 769 ("DOMA seeks to injure the very class New York seeks to protect.").

of recognizing and accepting state definitions of marriage."[96] Moreover, the legislative history, which featured statements expressing "both
moral disapproval of homosexuality, and a moral conviction that heterosexuality better comports with a traditional (especially Judeo-
Christian) morality," served as "strong evidence" of DOMA's "avowed
purpose and practical effect of . . . impos[ing] a disadvantage, a separate
status, and . . . a stigma upon all who enter into same-sex marriages made
lawful by the unquestioned authority of the States."[97]

And as in *Romer*, where Amendment 2 was proposed in the wake of
the enactment of municipal public accommodations laws protecting
LGBTQ persons, DOMA was enacted in anticipation of the legalization of same-sex marriages by judicial fiat in Hawaii.[98] Although the
Baehr v Lewin litigation goes unmentioned in the Court's opinion in
Windsor, this context was widely known at the time that DOMA was
enacted, and as challenges to DOMA were litigated.[99] Justice Kennedy
surely would have known these facts, and they, in tandem with the facts
stated in the opinion, likely would have informed his conclusion that
impermissible animus lurked at DOMA's core. Taken together, *Romer*
and *Windsor* build upon the Court's earlier animus cases to suggest that,
even in the absence of a discriminatory "smoking gun," courts may
undertake a contextual analysis in inferring impermissible animus.

C. ANIMUS INVERTED

As the previous parts suggest, the Court's animus doctrine makes
clear that a finding of impermissible animus does not proceed solely
from direct evidence of discriminatory intent, but rather may be inferred from a confluence of factors. In this regard, the Court's failure
to rely on the most direct evidence of discriminatory animus arguably
forged a "thicker," more powerful animus doctrine that focused on the

---

[96] Id at 770.

[97] Id. On this account, Kennedy pointed to DOMA's legislative history, which documented
the view that "it is both appropriate and necessary for Congress to do what it can to defend
the institution of traditional heterosexual marriage. . . ." See id (quoting HR Rep No 104-664,
104th Cong, 2d Sess 12–13 (1996)). The legislative history also revealed that DOMA was
seen as expressing "both moral disapproval of homosexuality, and a moral conviction that
heterosexuality better comports with traditional (especially Judeo-Christian) morality." See
id at 770–71 (HR Rep No 104-664 at 16 (footnote deleted)).

[98] See HR Rep No 104-664 at 4–12.

[99] See Brief of NAACP Legal Defense & Education Fund, Inc. as Amicus Curiae Supporting Respondent Windsor, *United States v Windsor*, No 12-307, *14 (US filed Mar 1, 2013)
(available on Westlaw at 2013 WL 785636).

broader context in which discrimination may occur, rather than on specific incidents of discriminatory harm. With this in mind, the majority's
conclusion in *Masterpiece Cakeshop*—that Jack Phillips and his religious
beliefs were subjected to impermissible animus—is all the more puzzling.

In concluding that the Colorado Civil Rights Commission acted
with religious hostility, depriving Phillips of the neutral treatment to
which he was entitled, Justice Kennedy focused principally on the
statements of two commissioners.[100] This, by itself, was noteworthy. As
Professor Thomas Berg notes, "the [Court's] reliance on contemporaneous statements by the commissioners sits uneasily with the jurisprudence of the majority's conservative members, who tend to focus on
text rather than intent.[101] Nevertheless, according to Kennedy, tran-
scripts of the public hearings at which the Commission reviewed
Phillips's appeal from an administrative law judge's ruling showed that
"commissioners endorsed the view that religious beliefs cannot legitimately be carried into the public sphere or commercial domain."[102] The
implication, Kennedy surmised, was that "religious beliefs and persons
are less than fully welcome in Colorado's business community."[103]

The statements, however, are far less derisive and hostile than the
statements made in support of Amendment 2 or DOMA.[104] At one
point, Commissioner Raju Jairam observed: "I don't think the act
necessarily prevents Mr. Phillips from believing what he wants to
believe. And—but if he decides to do business in the state, he's got to
follow [the law]."[105] In many ways, Jairam's statement simply reflected
the current state of antidiscrimination law, including the Supreme
Court's own jurisprudence, which admits few exemptions to generally
applicable public accommodations laws.[106]

---

[100] *Masterpiece Cakeshop*, 138 S Ct at 1729.

[101] Thomas C. Berg, *Masterpiece Cakeshop: A Romer for Religious Objectors?*, 2018 Cato Sup
Ct Rev 139, 149. Indeed, in *Church of Lukumi*, only Justices Kennedy and Stevens viewed the
contemporaneous statements of Hialeah city council members as reflecting hostility to the
Santeria religion. 508 US at 542 (Kennedy and Stevens, JJ). In so doing, the two Justices drew
a stinging rebuke from Justice Scalia, who wrote a separate concurrence disputing the use of
those statements to infer impermissible animus. Id at 558059 (Scalia, J, concurring).

[102] *Masterpiece Cakeshop*, 138 S Ct at 1729.

[103] Id.

[104] Compare id, with Nussbaum, *From Disgust to Humanity* at 101–3 (cited in note 88)
(discussing the campaign around Amendment 2), and HR Rep No 104-664 at 15–16 (describing the motivation behind the passage of DOMA).

[105] Joint Appendix at *205 (cited in note 17).

[106] See *Masterpiece Cakeshop*, 138 S Ct at 1727 ("[I]t is a general rule that such objections do
not allow business owners and other actors in the economy and in society to deny protected

Indeed, this interpretation is underscored by Jairam's subsequent reference to "the comments made by Justice [Bosson] in [*Elane Photography, LLC v Willock*[107]].[108] *Elane Photography*, like *Masterpiece Cakeshop*, involved wedding vendors (photographers) who refused to photograph a lesbian couple's commitment ceremony because doing so would conflict with their religious views that marriage is a heterosexual union.[109] The New Mexico Supreme Court, in a unanimous decision, upheld the denial of the exemption, concluding that the vendors had discriminated against a same-sex couple when they refused to photograph their commitment ceremony.[110] In a concurring opinion, Justice Bosson affirmed the sincerity of the vendors' religious beliefs, but nonetheless concluded that "[i]n the smaller, more focused world of the marketplace, of commerce, of public accommodation, [objecting wedding vendors] have to channel their conduct, not their beliefs, so as to leave space for other Americans who believe something different. . . . In short, . . . it is the price of citizenship."[111]

It is not surprising that Jairam viewed this statement as "saying that if a businessman wants to do business in the state and he's got an issue with the . . . law's impacting his personal belief system, he needs to look at being able to compromise."[112] Bosson's concurrence essentially restates the general principle that antidiscrimination laws enable pluralism, and as such require compromise. What is surprising, though, is that the majority would equate Jairam's statement with the kinds of hostile views asserted in cases like *Church of Lukumi*, *Windsor*, and *Romer*. Indeed, equating a statement reiterating the underlying principles of antidiscrimination law with "inappropriate and dismissive comments"[113] directed at a particular group distorts and inverts the entire concept of animus.

This distortion is even more evident in Justice Kennedy's discussion of statements made by a second commissioner, Diann Rice. In a

persons equal access to goods and services under a neutral and generally applicable public accommodations law.").

[107] 309 P3d 53 (NM 2013).

[108] Joint Appendix at *207 (cited in note 17) (citing *Elane Photography, LLC v Willock*, 309 P3d 53, 77 (NM 2013) (Bosson concurring)).

[109] *Elane Photography*, 309 P3d at 59–60.

[110] Id at 59.

[111] Id at 80 (Bosson concurring). For further discussion of Justice Bosson's statement, see Kendrick and Schwartzman, 132 Harv L Rev at 139–40 (cited in note 2).

[112] Joint Appendix at *207 (cited in note 17), quoted in *Masterpiece Cakeshop*, 138 S Ct at 1729.

[113] *Masterpiece Cakeshop*, 138 S Ct at 1729.

hearing held a few months after the hearing at which Jairam stated his remarks, Rice noted that "[f]reedom of religion and religion has been used to justify all kinds of discrimination throughout history, whether it be slavery, whether it be the holocaust ... we can list hundreds of situations where freedom of religion has been used to justify discrimination."[114]

For Justice Kennedy, Rice's remarks were an over-the-top expression of hostility and animosity toward Phillips and his religious beliefs—ones that "disparaged" Phillips's belief by "describing it as despicable, and also by characterizing it as merely rhetorical."[115] But, in fact, Rice said nothing about Phillips's beliefs. It was the "use" of religious freedom to justify discrimination that she denounced as despicable. Further, in stating that, historically, religion had been used to justify discrimination, Rice did no more than state an empirical truth. As numerous scholars have documented, in the antebellum South, religion was regularly and widely used to justify and rationalize the enslavement of Africans and African Americans.[116] In the same vein, the view that Jews were responsible for the death of Jesus has fueled anti-Semitism, including anti-Semitism in Nazi Germany.[117]

But it is not just that scholars have acknowledged these facts as empirical truths. The Court itself has done so. In striking down miscegenation bans in *Loving v Virginia*,[118] the Court expressly quoted the Virginia trial court, which defended the ban on the ground that "Almighty God created the races white, black, yellow, malay and red, and he placed them on separate continents. ... The fact that he separated the races shows that he did not intend for the races to mix."[119] Likewise, in *Newman v Piggie Park Enterprises, Inc.*,[120] the Court rejected as "patently frivolous" a restauranteur's claims that serving African Americans, in compliance with the Civil Rights Act of 1964, would con-

---

[114] Id (citing hearing transcript).

[115] Id.

[116] See, for example, Drew Gilpin Faust, *The Ideology of Slavery: Proslavery Thought in the Antebellum South, 1830–1860* 13 (LSU, 1981); Ibram X. Kendi, *Stamped from the Beginning: The Definitive History of Racist Ideas in America* 208–9 (Bold Type, 2016).

[117] See Common Questions About the Holocaust (United States Holocaust Memorial Museum), available at https://www.ushmm.org/educators/teaching-about-the-holocaust/common-questions.

[118] 388 US 1 (1967).

[119] Id at 2–3.

[120] 390 US 400 (1968) (per curiam).

travene his religious beliefs and defy "the will of God."[121] To be sure, in doing so, the Court did not question the sincerity of the believer's views. Instead, it merely found that such beliefs, even if sincerely held, could not be a predicate for avoiding the application of anti-discrimination norms.[122] Meaningfully, the Court in *Masterpiece Cakeshop* cited *Piggie Park* approvingly for the proposition that, "while those religious and philosophical objections are protected, it is a general rule that such objections do not allow business owners and other actors in the economy and in society to deny protected persons equal access to goods and services under a neutral and generally applicable public accommodations law."[123]

The *Masterpiece Cakeshop* Court was not alone in its reliance on *Piggie Park* and its logic. The Commission and its commissioners relied on the Court's pronouncements in both *Loving* and *Piggie Park* and, indeed, reviewed Phillips's claims with those cases firmly in view.[124] If the Court could denounce as "patently frivolous" the claim that sincerely religious beliefs could justify racial discrimination, it is not surprising that a Commission charged with following the law would reiterate the argument in their effort to review a case that raised similar issues about the confluence of religious beliefs and antidiscrimination law. What *is* surprising is that a majority of the *Masterpiece Cakeshop* Court would conclude that articulating these truths about the history of discrimination would by itself constitute discriminatory treatment of religious objectors and their views.

But, for Justice Kennedy, it was not simply the statements of the two commissioners that prompted concern. It was that the other members of the Commission had not subsequently denounced either statement.[125] The commissioners' silence was further amplified by

---

[121] Id at 401–3 & n 5.

[122] Id at 402 n 5; see also *Newman v Piggie Park Enterprises, Inc.*, 256 F Supp 941, 945 (DSC 1966) ("Undoubtedly defendant ... has a constitutional right to espouse the religious beliefs of his own choosing, however, he does not have the absolute right to exercise and practice such beliefs in utter disregard of the clear constitutional rights of other citizens.").

[123] *Masterpiece Cakeshop*, 138 S Ct at 1727.

[124] See Joint Appendix at *198 (cited in note 17) ("[W]hen I thought about this issue, I thought about (inaudible) back not very many decades ago where—to when interracial marriage was—was frowned upon, was not recognized, was actually illegal in some states. And I think that that is the same issue as same sex marriage."); id at *202 ("I mean, I can believe anything I want to believe. But if I'm going to do business here, then I'd better not discriminate.... And to refuse service to somebody is—you know, it is discriminatory in my mind.").

[125] Id at 1729–30.

the Commission's review of the *Jack* cases, where it upheld the rights of bakers to refuse to make cakes with antigay or homophobic messages.[126]

As others, including members of the *Masterpiece Cakeshop* majority, have concluded, the *Jack* cases can be distinguished from Phillips's circumstances on the ground that while Phillips refused service on the ground that he objected to the couple, their marriage, and their sexual orientation, the bakers in the *Jack* cases refused to provide the requested cakes because they objected to the antigay messages, not to the customer or his religious beliefs.[127] On this account, Phillips engaged in discrimination on the basis of sexual orientation, a protected category under CADA, while the bakers had refused service on the ground that they objected to the message (not a protected category). And, meaningfully, at least one baker offered to sell Jack a cake and provide him with the icing and tools that would allow him to inscribe the cake with whatever message he liked.[128]

But it is not simply that the majority's reasoning distorts the concept of animus by reading it broadly to include statements like those uttered by Commissioners Jairam and Rice and the Commission's disposition of a set of distinguishable cases; it is that the majority distorted the analytical framework for determining animus by ignoring the broader social and political context that suggested resistance to, if not hostility toward, same-sex couples and their relationships.[129]

As noted above, in concluding that impermissible animus improperly infected government actions against a particular group, the Court has often considered the broader political and social milieu in which the action arose.[130] Critically, Phillips's refusal to bake a cake for a same-sex wedding was not an isolated event. In recent years, a

---

[126] Id at 1730–31.

[127] Id at 1733 (Kagan, J, concurring) ("The Colorado Anti-Discrimination Act (CADA) makes it unlawful for a place of public accommodation to deny 'the full and equal enjoyment' of goods and services to individuals based on certain characteristics, including sexual orientation and creed. The three bakers in the *Jack* cases did not violate that law. Jack requested them to make a cake (one denigrating gay people and same-sex marriage) that they would not have made for any customer. In refusing that request, the bakers did not single out Jack because of his religion, but instead treated him in the same way they would have treated anyone else—just as CADA requires.").

[128] Id at 1748–49 (Ginsburg, J, dissenting); Joint Appendix at *233–34.

[129] For a similar reaction, see Larry Sager and Nelson Tebbe, *The Reality Principle*, Const Comm (draft on file with author).

[130] See Part III.B.

number of challenges, many of them coordinated by the Alliance Defending Freedom and the Becket Fund, have been filed by religious objectors who seek exemptions or accommodations from the scope of public accommodations laws prohibiting sexual orientation discrimination.[131] Indeed, religious objections to same-sex marriage reached a fever pitch after the Court's June 2015 decision in *Obergefell v Hodges*,[132] where Justice Kennedy, writing for the Court, recognized a right to same-sex marriage. In one widely reported episode, a Kentucky county clerk refused to issue marriage licenses to same-sex couples because doing so would contravene her religious beliefs.[133] Meaningfully, many of these objections to same-sex marriage reflected both moral disapproval of homosexuality, as well as the view that heterosexual marriage better comports with traditional morality than its same-sex counterpart—views that the Court equated with impermissible animus only five years earlier in *United States v Windsor*.[134]

In *Masterpiece Cakeshop*, this context goes unmentioned as Kennedy and the majority focus single-mindedly on Phillips's claims and the treatment he received at the hands of the commissioners. On this account, the relevant context is not the social and political milieu in which LGBTQ people live their lives; it is the social and political milieu that the individual accused of sexual orientation discrimination experiences. Rather than focusing on the context presented in cases like *Windsor* and *Romer*, where the Court inferred hostility toward LGBTQ persons from the political and social climate, the *Masterpiece Cakeshop* majority focuses on the observations and concerns cited by the *Obergefell* dissenters: "Hard questions arise when people of faith exercise religion in ways that may be seen to conflict with the new

---

[131] See Jeremy K. Kessler and David E. Pozen, *The Search for an Egalitarian First Amendment*, 118 Colum L Rev 1953, 1975–76 (2018); Jane C. Timm, *Another Gay Wedding Case Could Go to the Supreme Court. This One's About Flowers*, NBC News (June 4, 2018), available at https://www.nbcnews.com/politics/politics-news/other-gay-wedding-case-could-go-supreme-court-one-s-n879906.

[132] 135 S Ct 2584 (2015). Critically, in that decision, Kennedy anticipated the prospect of religious objections to same-sex marriages: "Many who deem same-sex marriage to be wrong reach that conclusion based on decent and honorable religious or philosophical premises, and neither they nor their beliefs are disparaged here." Id at 2602.

[133] *Kentucky Clerk Jailed Over Gay Marriage Licenses Loses Re-election Bid*, Associated Press (Nov 7, 2018), available at https://www.nbcnews.com/feature/nbc-out/kentucky-clerk-jailed-over-gay-marriage-licenses-loses-re-election-n933451.

[134] 570 US at 771 (noting, in finding animus, that "[t]he House [of Representatives] concluded that DOMA expresses 'both moral disapproval of homosexuality, and a moral conviction that heterosexuality better comports with traditional (especially Judeo-Christian) morality.'").

right to same-sex marriage. . . . Unfortunately, people of faith can take no comfort in the treatment they receive from the [*Obergefell*] majority today."[135]

While the majority's inattentiveness to the broader context in which religious accommodation claims arise distorts the animus analysis, it is the Court's singular focus on Jack Phillips's religious rights that works to invert the animus analysis. As Professor Russell Robinson has observed, in recent years, Justice Kennedy's equal protection jurisprudence has effectively limited the invocation of animus to claims of discrimination brought by LGBTQ people.[136] In this regard, the appeal to animus in cases involving gay rights may serve various ends. As Professor Thomas Berg notes, in both *Romer* and *Windsor*, the Court, with Kennedy writing for the majority, used animus to credit gay rights while studiously avoiding the broader questions of whether sexual orientation discrimination should be subject to heightened scrutiny and whether the right to marry included the right to marry a person of the same sex.[137]

Not only does the appeal to animus avoid the thorny question of whether sexual orientation should be denominated a suspect or quasi-suspect classification, it allows the Court to resolve claims of sexual orientation discrimination without requiring a clear showing of discriminatory intent, as is necessary in cases involving race and gender discrimination that is not reflected in a facial "classification."[138] On this view, the appeal to animus has allowed Kennedy and the Court greater flexibility in resolving cases involving claims of antigay bias. Unfettered by the requirements of the traditional tiers of equal protection scrutiny, with their demands for a clear showing of discriminatory intent, Kennedy can instead rely on context, and indeed, his own intuition that some subtler invidious purpose is afoot, to determine that unconstitutional animus is at work.

While this has provided Kennedy with greater flexibility in resolving cases involving LGBTQ rights, recent cases suggest that it may lead to uneven and inconsistent results. The Court's disposition of *Trump v Hawaii*—the Travel Ban case—is instructive on this point. In *Trump v Hawaii*, Justice Kennedy and four other Justices upheld the Travel Ban

---

[135] *Obergefell*, 135 S Ct at 2625–26 (Roberts, CJ, dissenting).

[136] Robinson, 68 Stan L Rev at 163–70 (cited in note 54).

[137] Berg, 2018 Cato Sup Ct Rev at 139, 148 (cited in note 101).

[138] Robinson, 68 Stan L Rev at 164–65, 171–80 (cited in note 54).

despite overwhelming evidence that the ban reflected anti-Muslim bias.[139] Put simply, despite a broad context from which many inferred impermissible animus toward Muslims, the Court concluded otherwise. Likewise, in *Masterpiece Cakeshop*, the Court also ignored context— but with stunningly different results. By ignoring the broader context of religious accommodations and the growing conflict over LGBTQ rights, Justice Kennedy and the *Masterpiece Cakeshop* majority interpreted the concept of animus broadly so that it might comfortably accommodate Jack Phillips, a business owner accused of discriminating against LGBTQ people.[140]

In this regard, the Court's approach in *Masterpiece Cakeshop* makes clear that the concept of animus may be applied flexibly—and indeed, inverted—to protect a broader range of claimants. With this in mind, what really distinguishes the vision of animus in *Masterpiece Cakeshop* from that which is invoked in Kennedy's earlier animus jurisprudence is the individual who is deemed the object of the state's antipathy. In sharp contrast to earlier animus cases, where the object of the state's antipathy was a historically disfavored group, like gay men and lesbians or a minority religious sect, the object of the state's alleged antipathy in *Masterpiece Cakeshop* is Jack Phillips, an evangelical Christian and a white man who has denied goods and services to two gay men.

On this account, the invocation of animus in *Masterpiece Cakeshop* is notable in at least two respects: the imagined object of the state's antipathy and the degree to which the conception of animus can be expanded to include a wider range of protected classes. Let me take each of these in turn. As an initial matter, it is not often that straight white Protestant men are the imagined subjects of animus. Indeed, in traditional antidiscrimination narratives, such individuals are quite literally "The Man"—an individual with significant social, political, and economic capital and unsurpassed privileges, opportunities, and access.[141] In these narratives, someone like Jack Phillips is more likely

---

[139] 138 S Ct 2392, 2423 (2018) (reversing the Ninth Circuit's preliminary injunction of the travel ban).

[140] In this regard, *Masterpiece Cakeshop* has been understood by some as identifying and crediting "parallels between same-sex couples and religious objectors." Berg, 2018 Cato Sup Ct Rev at 161 (cited in note 101). On this account, same-sex couples and religious objectors share a "fundamental feature of identity ... , the intertwining of that identity with conduct (marrying a partner, acting consistently with God's will), and the painfulness or impossibility of changing that identity or the conduct that necessarily flows from it." Id.

[141] See Eric K. Yamamoto, *Critical Race Praxis: Race Theory and Political Lawyering Practice in Post–Civil Rights America*, 95 Mich L Rev 821, 844–45 (1997).

to be imagined as the oppressor than as the oppressed. And in keeping with this stock narrative, when courts intervene, it is to protect, and prevent harm to, the oppressed—not to protect, or prevent harm to, the oppressor.[142]

With this in mind, cases like *Masterpiece Cakeshop* suggest the inversion of this traditional antidiscrimination narrative. The oppressed victim of discrimination is no longer the "discrete and insular minorities" contemplated in *Carolene Products,*[143] but rather religious objectors who were once trumpeted as a "moral majority," but now cloak themselves as "religious minorities" in need of state protection.[144] In this regard, Christian evangelicals are not simply making a conceptual claim about the amenability of their cause to antidiscrimination law. They are making what amounts to an *empirical* claim that their traditional morals no longer hold sway in majoritarian culture, transforming them into minorities who face discrimination and subordination in public life.

And in Justice Kennedy, such claims seem to have found a receptive ear. Kennedy's use of animus to vindicate Jack Phillips's interests leads to interesting conclusions and inferences. Although Kennedy avoids the question of whether one might infer or intuit animus toward LGBTQ persons from a refusal to furnish a wedding cake for a same-sex marriage, read in tandem with *Obergefell,* the majority opinion suggests that there is a broader climate of hostility and disdain directed toward people of faith—and that the two commissioners' statements are the smoking guns that allow the Court to infer that conservative Christians are a beleaguered minority religious sect subject to invidious discrimination. Put differently, the focus on Phillips, and the inference of a broader climate of disdain toward religion, allows Kennedy to treat conservative Christians the way he treated Santeria adherents in *Church of Lukumi Babalu Aye,* while eliding the broader climate of animus toward LGBT persons.

But while conservative Christians and Santeria adherents are both religious sects, their circumstances could not be more different. Santeria was the very definition of a minority religious sect—a religion so

---

[142] Id.

[143] Id.

[144] See Douglas Laycock, *Religious Liberty for Politically Active Minority Groups: A Response to NeJaime and Siegel,* 125 Yale L J F 369, 370 (2016) ("[T]he sexual revolution has swept away the former religious majority on sexual matters. Religious conservatives make the individual-rights arguments of a minority group because they are a minority group.").

disfavored in its home country of Cuba that it operated underground for centuries.[145] As importantly, in Cuba and in the Hialeah community, Santeria was associated with those of African descent—in essence, a minority religion practiced by racial and ethnic minorities.[146] Not so with conservative Christians, who are predominantly white and free to express their faiths openly, rather than operating underground.[147] The status of conservative Christians in contemporary society also contrasts sharply with that of LGBTQ individuals, who have not only faced historic discrimination, but continue to face discrimination on the basis of sexual orientation in a number of arenas,[148] including in the public marketplace.[149]

In this regard, the vision of animus invoked in *Masterpiece Cakeshop* is a departure from the Court's earlier understanding of animus. Together, these two strains of animus reflect competing theories of antidiscrimination law. The understanding of animus invoked in *Cleburne, Romer, Windsor*, and *Church of Lukumi Babalu Aye* reflects the antisubordination theory of antidiscrimination law. Under this theory, the "guarantees of equal citizenship cannot be realized under conditions of pervasive social stratification."[150] Accordingly, law should be deployed to

---

[145] See *Church of Lukumi Babalu Aye*, 508 US at 524–25. See also Lizette Alvarez, *After Years of Secrecy, Santeria Is Suddenly More Popular. And Public*, NY Times (Jan 27, 1997), available at https://www.nytimes.com/1997/01/27/nyregion/after-years-of-secrecy-santeria-is -suddenly-much-more-popular-and-public.html (discussing the history of underground Santeria worship).

[146] Id. Interestingly, as Professor Larry Cata Backer has shown, the Hialeah city council that promulgated the challenged ordinances identified as Christian and regarded Santeria as an affront to their Christian beliefs. Larry Cata Backer, *The Church of the Lukumi Babalu Aye, Inc. v. City of Hialeah: The Protection of Majority Religions' Privilege at the Nexus of Race, Class, and Ethnicity*, in Leslie C. Griffin, ed, *Law and Religion: Cases in Context* (Aspen, 2010).

[147] Religious Landscape Study (Pew Forum on Religion and Public Life), available at http://www.pewforum.org/religious-landscape-study/racial-and-ethnic-composition/ (noting that an estimated 76% of American Evangelical Protestants identified as white); see also Clyde Haberman, *Religion and Right-Wing Politics: How Evangelicals Reshaped Elections*, NY Times (Oct 28, 2018), available at https://www.nytimes.com/2018/10/28/us/religion-politics -evangelicals.html (describing Evangelical influence in American politics from the Carter Administration to the present).

[148] See, e.g., Brief of Amici Curiae Ilan H. Meyer et al, *Masterpiece Cakeshop v Colorado Civil Rights Comm.*, No 16-111, at 10–12; Pizer et al, *Evidence of Persistent and Pervasive Workplace Discrimination Against LGBT People*, 45 Loyola LA L Rev 715, 721–28 (2012); A. Tilcsik, *Pride and Prejudice: Employment Discrimination Against Openly Gay Men in the United States*, 117 Am J Soc 586, 586–626 (2011).

[149] See Brief of Amici Curiae Ilan H. Meyer et al, *Masterpiece Cakeshop v Colorado Civil Rights Comm.*, No 16-111, at 12–20 (discussing discrimination against LGB persons in the marketplace, as well as the impact of such discrimination and stigma).

[150] Jack M. Balkin and Reva B. Siegel, *American Civil Rights Tradition: Anticlassification or Antisubordination?*, 58 U Miami L Rev 9, 9 (2003).

"reform institutions and practices that enforce the secondary social status of historically oppressed groups."[151] On this logic, the Court's identification of animus in *Romer* and *Windsor* began the process of disrupting and dismantling other legal impediments to full citizenship for LGBTQ persons—and, indeed, *Romer* begat *Lawrence v Texas*[152] and the decriminalization of same-sex sodomy and *Windsor* begat *Obergefell* and the legalization of same-sex marriage. Likewise, the invocation of animus in *Church of Lukumi* began the process of identifying the state-sanctioned hostility that prevented Santeria adherents from enjoying the fruits of full citizenship.

While the majority's inversion of animus in *Masterpiece Cakeshop* is out of step with the logic of these earlier animus cases, it is utterly consistent with developments in other areas of antidiscrimination law, namely, the trajectory of race and gender discrimination. As Professor Russell Robinson has noted, in the context of the constitutional equal protection, the traditional mechanisms vindicating minority rights have, in recent years, been deployed in service of a "color-blind" vision of antidiscrimination law.[153] This vision of antidiscrimination law, Robinson contends, views *any* classification on the basis of a protected trait with skepticism and, as such, is frequently hostile to classifications that serve benign or remedial interests.[154] The Court's use of strict scrutiny in race discrimination cases bears this out. As Robinson explains, "when strict scrutiny appears in the Court's race jurisprudence today, it is almost invariably on behalf of white litigants such as Abigail Fisher [the respondent in *Fisher v University of Texas*[155]], who wield it to dismantle affirmative action policies. For the last thirty years ... strict scrutiny has been the principal tool of civil rights retrenchment, protecting whites rather than blacks and Latinos."[156] Critically, the Court's disparate-impact jurisprudence has complemented this vision of color-blindness. As Professor Ian Haney-López observes, the Court no longer focuses on the background and context in which discrimination is claimed, but rather demands that minori-

---

[151] Id at 9.

[152] 539 US 558 (2003).

[153] Robinson, 68 Stan L Rev at 172–74 (cited in note 54).

[154] Id.

[155] 570 US 297 (2013).

[156] Robinson, 68 Stan L Rev at 172–73 (cited in note 54).

ties provide clear evidence of discriminatory intent in order to prevail on a claim of disparate impact.[157]

This jurisprudential context provides a useful lens through which to understand the implications and consequences of inversion of the animus doctrine in *Masterpiece Cakeshop*. As an initial matter, though cases like *Moreno* and *Romer* framed animus narrowly to encompass an irrational and impermissible "bare desire to harm,"[158] *Masterpiece Cakeshop* expands our understanding significantly to include statements of empirical truths that, at worst, might be characterized as uncivil or skeptical. As importantly, in recent years, the Court's invocation of animus relied upon contextual analysis and inferential reasoning to identify and redress discrimination against LGBTQ people. As scholars have noted, the invocation of animus to vindicate the rights of LGBTQ persons is a stark contrast to traditional equal protection and disparate-impact analysis, the doctrinal areas most likely to be invoked for the resolution of claims of racial and gender discrimination, where reliance on context and inference is disfavored.[159] In *Masterpiece Cakeshop*, however, animus's amenability to claims of LGBTQ discrimination is utterly absent as the Court ignores the background and context of resistance to *Obergefell* and same-sex marriage, and the discrimination that LGBTQ persons face more generally, in favor of a narrative that suggests that Christian evangelicals seeking accommodations from the application of antidiscrimination law are the persons most in need of the Court's protections.

The disposition of *Masterpiece Cakeshop* makes clear the malleability of animus—and the antidiscrimination narrative more generally. Less attentive to the broader social context in which discrimination may occur, animus, as deployed in *Masterpiece Cakeshop*, is no longer a shield used to protect LGBTQ persons. Instead, it functions to protect those who, in the pursuit of their sincerely held religious beliefs, seek to avoid the state's mandate against sexual orientation discrimination. In the same vein, the demand for clear evidence of discriminatory intent, coupled with the rigid application of strict scrutiny to programs that employ racial classifications for benign purposes, ensures that traditional equal protection frameworks offer uneven protection against race and gender discrimination. Indeed, as Professor Robinson observes, the

---

[157] See Ian Haney-López, *Intentional Blindness*, 87 NYU L Rev 1779, 1784–88 (2012).

[158] *Moreno*, 413 US at 534–35; *Romer*, 517 US at 634–35.

[159] See Robinson, 68 Stan L Rev at 171–85 (cited in note 54).

traditional equal protection frameworks have functioned as "tool[s] of civil rights retrenchment, protecting whites rather than blacks and Latinos."[160]

In this regard, it is not just that the animus doctrine may function elastically to vindicate a broader range of claims; it is that the anti-discrimination narrative writ large is elastic and capable of expanding to accommodate new visions of what it means to be a minority in need of judicial protection. To illustrate this claim, in the following part, I shift from *Masterpiece Cakeshop* and the context of constitutional law to consider an emerging area of antidiscrimination challenges—state-level statutory claims of gender-based discrimination brought by men against women-only spaces and programming.

IV. THE SECOND SEX?

The inversion of the animus doctrine in *Masterpiece Cakeshop* raises questions about the future of animus doctrine. As discussed above, the majority's use of animus in *Masterpiece Cakeshop* neglects the contextual inquiry that the Court has undertaken in previous cases where it relied on animus to vindicate the claims of disfavored groups. Because the Court does not reflect on the background context in which the challenged action arises, and accepts the view of Christian conservatives as religious minorities, the concept of animus may be deployed broadly to include groups who would not necessarily be considered disfavored, and, indeed, to include those who are alleged to have engaged in discrimination against a disfavored group.

In this regard, the Court's use of animus in *Masterpiece Cakeshop* recalls developments in other areas of antidiscrimination law. To be clear, in these other antidiscrimination contexts, animus doctrine is largely irrelevant, as protections for vulnerable groups proceed from state-level statutes that prohibit discrimination on the basis of certain characteristics. Nevertheless, as this Part maintains, these developments recall *Masterpiece Cakeshop* in that they demonstrate the use of antidiscrimination law and its principles by those who ordinarily would not be considered members of disadvantaged groups against those who are ostensibly the contemplated subjects of antidiscrimination law's protections.

To be clear, this development is not wholly unprecedented. Indeed, the seeds of this trend were sown earlier in opposition to affirmative

---

[160] Id at 172–73.

action, where nonminorities argued that benign preferences for racial minorities amounted to "reverse racism."[161] And, famously, some of the most successful claims of gender discrimination were brought by men who argued that sex-role stereotyping negatively impacted men *and* women.[162]

Even in these circumstances, however, the claims of discrimination were more familiar. For example, in the affirmative action context, the claims of discrimination were directed at state actors, whose use of benign racial preferences, it was argued, constituted discrimination against nonminorities.[163] Likewise, in the gender discrimination context, the claims raised by male litigants were directed at state actors and were intended to dismantle durable gender stereotypes that affected men and women alike.[164]

While this latest iteration of antidiscrimination claims has some of the same features as its predecessors, there are striking differences. Like the earlier affirmative action cases, these recent cases involve antidiscrimination claims brought by individuals who are not the traditional subjects of antidiscrimination law's protections. Nevertheless, these litigants deploy antidiscrimination law and its principles to vindicate their claims against those who *are* the traditional subjects of antidiscrimination law's protections.

Some of the complaints lodged simply challenge the existence of any program or benefit that is restricted to women. For example, in 1985, a male plaintiff sued a car wash and nightclub in Orange County, California, on the ground that "Ladies' Day" and "Ladies' Night" women-only discounts constituted sex-based discrimination,

---

[161] See Robert S. Chang, *Reverse Racism: Affirmative Action, the Family, and the Dream That Is America*, 23 Hastings Const L Q 1115, 1117 (1996); Ronald Walters, *Affirmative Action and the Politics of Concept Appropriation*, 38 Howard L J 587, 604 (1995); Naomi Schoenbaum, *The Case for Symmetry in Antidiscrimination Law*, 2017 Wis L Rev 69, 94–95 & n 111 (2017).

[162] See, for example, *Craig v Boren*, 429 US 190 (1976) (male plaintiff brought suit challenging sale of alcohol to males below the age of twenty-one, but only to females below the age of eighteen); *Weinberger v Wiesenfeld*, 420 US 636 (1975) (male plaintiff sued on behalf of himself and other widowers claiming that Social Security Act unconstitutionally discriminated against men because it denied widowers benefits that widows received upon their spouse's death); *Califano v Goldfarb*, 430 US 199 (1977) (male plaintiff was denied survivor benefits pursuant to statute that mandated surviving widowers must prove they had received over half their financial support from their wives, while widows were provided benefits regardless of their financial dependence).

[163] See, e.g., *Fisher v University of Texas at Austin*, 136 S Ct 2198 (2016) (*Fisher II*); *Fisher v University of Texas at Austin*, 570 US 297 (2013) (*Fisher I*).

[164] See *Craig*, 429 US at 208–9; *Wiesenfeld*, 420 US at 642–43.

in violation of California's Unruh Act, which prohibits discrimination based on a wide range of characteristics, including sex.[165] The California Supreme Court found for the plaintiffs, holding that the Unruh Act ought to be given a "liberal construction."[166] As the court held, "arbitrary sex discrimination by businesses is per se injurious," and "men and women alike suffer from the stereotypes perpetuated by sex-based differential treatment."[167] Indeed, the court noted that as long as businesses were allowed to create policies in this way that impermissibly distinguished between the sexes, these stereotypes would flourish—even if defendants had not consciously enacted the policy as a discriminatory measure.[168] As the court found, this was not a situation where public policy warranted differential treatment for men and women—for example, in the case of public restrooms[169]— but rather an arbitrarily discriminatory pricing policy based on impermissible stereotype.[170]

The California high court's logic in *Koire*, and its liberal interpretation of the Unruh Act, has fueled a range of high-profile suits against benefits and discounts aimed exclusively at women. For example, in 2009, the Oakland A's settled for $510,000 a gender discrimination claim brought by men's rights activists under the Unruh Act.[171] The team's alleged violation was sponsoring a Mother's Day giveaway where the first 7,500 women received a commemorative cap.[172] No-

---

[165] *Koire v Metro Car Wash*, 707 P2d 195, 195–96 (Cal 1985).

[166] Id at 196, 204.

[167] Id at 200–01.

[168] Id at 201.

[169] To wit, the acceptability of sex segregation in public restrooms has provided strong support for limiting restroom access for transgender and gender-nonconforming persons. See, for example, *Johnston v Univ of Pittsburgh*, 97 F Supp 3d 657, 672–73 (WD Penn 2015) (upholding a university's "policy of requiring students to use sex-segregated bathroom and locker room facilities based on students' natal or birth sex, rather than their gender identity"); Jessica A. Clarke, *They, Them, and Theirs*, 132 Harv L Rev 894, 981–83 (2019) (discussing the challenges that individuals with nonbinary gender identities face when public facilities such as restrooms are sex-segregated). For broader discussion of "urinary segregation," see Mary Anne Case, *Why Not Abolish Laws of Urinary Segregation?*, in Harvey Molotch and Laura Noren, eds, *Toilet: Public Restrooms and the Politics of Sharing* (NYU, 2010).

[170] *Koire*, 707 P2d at 203–4.

[171] Joe Kukura, *Man Wins $500K from A's for Mother's Day Snub*, NBC Bay Area (June 17, 2009), available at https://www.nbcbayarea.com/news/local/As-Fan-Denied-Moms-Day-Hat-Wins-In-Court-.html; Chris Metinko, *San Diego Lawyer and A's Settle Class-Action Sex Discrimination Lawsuit*, East Bay Times (June 17, 2009), available at https://www.eastbaytimes.com/2009/06/17/san-diego-lawyer-and-as-settleclass-action-sex-discrimination-lawsuit/.

[172] Id.

tably, the plaintiff in the suit filed a series of challenges against other major league baseball teams objecting to similar Mother's Day promotions.[173]

But, more frequently, these challenges are not simply aimed at "Ladies' Night" and other marketing events that provide discounts or special benefits exclusively to women. Instead, suits under the Unruh Act and other state and municipal laws prohibiting gender discrimination challenge programs that target women to the exclusion of men for the specific purpose of redressing the impact of historic discrimination against women, as well as dismantling structural impediments to women's ability to achieve equality in employment and other crucial aspects of society.

Consider, for example, the Department of Education's 2018 investigation of Yale University for allegedly violating Title IX,[174] which prohibits sex-based discrimination in education programs or activities that receive Federal financial assistance.[175] The alleged violation? Yale sponsors programs and scholarships for women.[176] Among the offending programs are the Women Faculty Forum, an organization aimed at supporting women faculty, who have been historically underrepresented in the ranks of the professorate (and at Yale, specifically);[177] Yale Women Innovators; Smart Women Securities; Women Empowering Women Leadership Conference; and the Yale Women's Campaign School, a nonpartisan and issue-neutral organization that aims to "increase the number and influence of women in elected and appointed office in the United States and around the globe."[178] The investigation was prompted by a complaint lodged by a men's rights advocate.[179]

More recently, the rise of women-only co-working spaces, networking events, and professional development networks has prompted cries of impermissible gender discrimination from men's rights groups. For example, in 2018, it was reported that the New York City Com-

---

[173] Id.

[174] Hailey Fuchs and Jingyi Cui, *Federal Office of Civil Rights Investigates Yale*, Yale Daily News (May 15, 2018), available at https://yaledailynews.com/blog/2018/05/15/federal-office-of-civil-rights-investigates-yale/.

[175] Title IX of the Education Amendments of 1972, 20 USC § 1681 et seq.

[176] Fuchs and Cui, *Federal Office of Civil Rights Investigates Yale* (cited in note 174).

[177] Id; see Mission (Women Faculty Forum), available at https://dev.wff.yale.edu/structure.

[178] Fuchs and Cui, *Federal Office of Civil Rights Investigates Yale* (cited in note 174); see Women's Campaign School at Yale University, available at https://www.wcsyale.org/.

[179] See Fuchs and Cui, *Federal Office of Civil Rights Investigates Yale* (cited in note 174).

mission on Human Rights was investigating the Wing, a prominent women-only co-working site with offices in major metropolitan areas.[180] According to reports, the co-working site, which does not admit men as members and does not allow men to attend its networking events, violated the New York City Human Rights Law.[181] Represented by a prominent law firm, Boies Schiller Flexner, the Wing has entered into "discussions" with the NYCCHR in the hope of avoiding an investigation.[182] But similar women-only co-working spaces have not been as fortunate.

In 2013, Women on Course, a women-only group aimed at expanding the number of women playing golf for recreational and professional networking purposes, faced similar challenges.[183] Golf, which has long been a staple of professional networking, has largely been viewed as the province of men.[184] By introducing women to the sport in an all-female setting, and facilitating friendship- and network-building among women, Women on Course aimed to make the sport both a recreational and professional development outlet for more women.[185] Unfortunately, the same vocal men's rights activist group that sued the major league baseball teams over their Mother's Day promotions, called the National Coalition for Men (NCFM), sued Women on Course on the ground that in limiting their events to women, the

---

[180] Katherine Rosman, *Is Women-Only Club the Wing Discriminating in a Bad Way?* (Mar 28, 2018), available at https://www.nytimes.com/2018/03/28/style/the-wing-investigation.html.

[181] Id; J. K. Trotter, *The New York Human Rights Commission Is Investigating The Wing*, Jezebel (Mar 26, 2018), available at https://jezebel.com/the-new-york-human-rights-com mission-is-investigating-t-1823334726. Audrey Gelman, a founder of the Wing, told the *New York Times* that the Wing does employ men. Id. The Wing's website notes that "The Wing is an equal opportunity employer and prohibits discrimination and harassment of any kind." Careers (The Wing), available at https://www.the-wing.com/careers/).

[182] Rosman, *Is Women-Only Club the Wing Discriminating in a Bad Way?* (cited in note 180).

[183] Hannah Levintova, *These Men's Rights Activists Are Suing Women's Groups for Meeting Without Men*, Mother Jones (Jan 15, 2016), available at https://www.motherjones.com/politics /2016/01/men-rights-unruh-act-women-discrimination/.

[184] The popular imagination surrounding golf has historically been so gendered that women whose husbands spend too much time on the course have been caricatured as "golf widows." See Golf Widow (Merriam-Webster Dictionary), available at https://www.merriam-webster.com /dictionary/golf%20widow. Augusta National Golf Club, which has hosted the Masters tournament for over 80 years, did not admit a woman member until 2012. Bill Pennington, *Augusta National Takes an Unexpected Turn Toward Women's Golf*, NY Times (Apr 4, 2018), available at https://www.nytimes.com/2018/04/04/sports/golf/augusta-national-womens-tournament .html.

[185] Jordyn Holman, *Men Cry Discrimination in Legal Attack on Women's Organizations*, Bloomberg (May 11, 2018), available at https://www.bloomberg.com/news/articles/2018-05-11/men-cry -discrimination-in-legal-attack-on-women-s-organizations.

group violated California's Unruh Act.[186] Donna Hoffman, the founder of Women on Course, quickly settled the suit.[187] Women on Course was shortly thereafter acquired by Bill Casper Golf, which eventually shuttered the organization.

In a similar vein, in 2017, members of the NCFM brought suit against Ladies Get Paid, a for-profit organization that provides salary negotiation training and professional advancement tools to women in an effort to promote gender wage equity.[188] In the lawsuit, two men claimed gender discrimination under the Unruh Act when they were barred from attending Ladies Get Paid events that were limited to women.[189] In their filings, the claimants characterized their exclusion from the event as "repugnant and unlawful as businesses being involved in a 'Caucasian Night' or a 'Heterosexual Night.'"[190] Ultimately, Claire Wasserman, the founder of Ladies Get Paid, settled the suit—crowd-sourcing and borrowing from a parent to do so.[191] As part of the settlement, she changed the group's policy to admit men.[192] And while Ladies Get Paid continues to operate, the group has no plans to host future events in California,[193] where NCFM is based[194] and where the Unruh Act defines gender discrimination to include women-only spaces.[195] As Wasserman explains, men's rights claims have "a chilling effect overall on the efforts of marginalized groups looking for safe spaces."[196]

---

[186] Levintova, *These Men's Rights Activists are Suing Women's Groups for Meeting Without Men* (cited in note 183).

[187] Id.

[188] Judith Ohikuare, *"Ladies Get Sued": How a Civil Rights Law Could End Women-Only Events*, Refinery 29 (May 25, 2018), available at https://www.refinery29.com/2018/05/199558 /ladies-get-paid-unruhcivil-rights-act-lawsuit.

[189] Id.

[190] Complaint for Injunctive Relief and Damages, *Allison v Red Door Epicurean, LLC*, No 2017-00036282, 1–3 (Cal Sup filed Sept 28, 2017).

[191] Ohikuare, *"Ladies Get Sued": How a Civil Rights Law Could End Women-Only Events* (cited in note 188).

[192] Id.

[193] Id.

[194] See National Coalition for Men (NCFM), available at https://ncfm.org/.

[195] Some women's organizations targeted by the NCFM have discussed a legislative push to amend the Unruh Act in such a way as to permit women-only spaces and programming. See Mari Payton, Dorian Hargrove, and Tom Jones, *Gender Discrimination? Men Are Suing Women for Not Letting Them into Women-Only Events*, NBC 7 San Diego (Apr 26 2018), available at https://www .nbcsandiego.com/news/local/Gender-Discrimination-Men-Are-Suing-Women-For-Not -Letting-Them-Into-Women-Only-Events-480880911.html.

[196] Ohikuare, *"Ladies Get Sued": How a Civil Rights Law Could End Women-Only Events* (cited in note 188).

Other groups agree. In a corollary to Ladies Get Paid, members of NCFM sued ChicCEO, an organization focused on providing women with the skills and network necessary to start their own businesses.[197] The organization settled the matter, but later downsized, citing the financial and personal costs associated with the lawsuit.[198] Likewise, in response to a letter threatening a lawsuit, Geek Girl, a California-based group that sponsors events for women in tech fields, modified their marketing approach to downplay their role as a hub for women in tech fields to ensure that they would not run afoul of state and local gender discrimination statutes.[199] And in 2018, in response to a lawsuit brought by NCFM activist Rich Allison challenging the city of San Diego's Girls' Empowerment Camp, a two-day camp meant to expose young women to careers in fire service and public safety agencies,[200] the city canceled the camp.[201]

It is worth noting that most of the organizations that have sued in these cases operate in fields and industries—business and entrepreneurship, tech, fire safety, and public safety—where women comprise a minority of those employed.[202] Despite the fact that many of the fields in which these women-only networking groups are operating are male-dominated, NCFM and its representatives insist that such lawsuits are necessary because "[m]en are often ignored, discriminated against, and denied entry to these business conferences, networking events . . . solely because of their sex."[203]

---

[197] Levintova, *These Men's Rights Activists are Suing Women's Groups for Meeting Without Men* (cited in note 183).

[198] Id.

[199] Id.

[200] Karen Kucher, *Girls Empowerment Camp Canceled After Attorney Claims It Violates Anti-Discrimination Laws*, San Diego Union-Tribune (Feb 27, 2018), available at http://www.sandiegouniontribune.com/news/public-safety/sd-me-camp-cancelled-20180226-story.html.

[201] The city ultimately reopened the camp, this time explicitly opening the event to all genders. Press Release, Mayor Kevin L. Faulconer, *Mayor Faulconer Reinstates Fire-Rescue Department's Girls Empowerment Camp* (Mar 6, 2018), available at https://www.sandiego.gov/mayor/news/releases/mayor-faulconer-reinstates-fire-rescuedepartment's-girls-empowerment-camp; Karen Kucher, *A Week After It Was Canceled, Girls' Empowerment Camp Reinstated, Expanded*, San Diego Union-Tribune (Mar 6, 2018), available at http://www.sandiegouniontribune.com/news/publicsafety/sd-me-camp-reinstated-20180306-story.html.

[202] See Employment and Earnings by Occupation (United States Department of Labor, 2016), available at https://www.dol.gov/wb/occupations_interactive_txt.htm (finding that women make up only a small percentage of business executives, computer scientists, engineers, firefighters, and police officers).

[203] See Sara Ashley O'Brien, *Women-in-Tech Events Are Anti-Male, Say Men's Rights Activists*, CNN (Aug 12, 2015), available at https://money.cnn.com/2015/08/11/technology/mens-rights-activist-chic-ceo/.

* * *

In some ways, these men's rights lawsuits may simply reflect the peculiarities of the antidiscrimination statutes under which they arise. As a number of commentators have noted, California's Unruh Act, the statute under which almost all of the men's rights challenges discussed were brought, is purposefully broad and has been interpreted expansively in order to deter discrimination.[204]

With this in mind, the men's rights cases may also reflect the particular failings of antidiscrimination law. By this I mean that the men's rights cases are of a piece with the majority opinion in *Masterpiece Cakeshop*. In *Masterpiece Cakeshop*, a majority of the Court deployed the animus doctrine to protect and defend Jack Phillips, a Christian conservative who allegedly engaged in discrimination against a same-sex couple. By the Court's logic, the state arbitral tribunal had acted with impermissible animus in reviewing Phillips's claim for a religious exemption from the ambit of Colorado's public accommodations law. In deploying the animus doctrine in Phillips's favor, the Court appeared to credit the view advanced by conservative commentators that, in an increasingly secular society, Christians have come to occupy minority status, and that discrimination against religious believers is more problematic and pernicious than discrimination against LGBT persons. Put differently, *Masterpiece Cakeshop* reflects the inversion and distortion of the animus doctrine to protect as a minority a person allegedly engaged in discrimination against sexual minorities.

In the men's rights cases, male plaintiffs deploy the force of state antidiscrimination laws against women-only groups and events on the ground that gender-exclusive programming violates the terms of antidiscrimination laws. While these claims have been successful as a matter of law, we might understand them to evince a similar inversion and distortion of the spirit of antidiscrimination law. That is, in these cases, men's rights advocates deploy antidiscrimination law to frustrate efforts to dismantle the systemic and institutional impediments that prevent minority groups from achieving the full benefits of citizenship. In this regard, just as the decision in *Masterpiece Cakeshop* suggested a more

---

[204] Levintova, *These Men's Rights Activists are Suing Women's Groups for Meeting Without Men* (cited in note 183). The Unruh Act provides that "[a]ll persons within the jurisdiction of this state are free and equal, and no matter what their sex, race, color, religion, ancestry, national origin, disability, medical condition, marital status, or sexual orientation are entitled to the full and equal accommodations, advantages, facilities, privileges, or services in all business establishments of any kind whatsoever." Unruh Civil Rights Act, Cal Civ Code § 51(b).

limited view of the animus doctrine—one where context is overlooked and a white, straight Christian may be understood as the object of the state's antipathy—the men's rights cases suggest a more limited view of antidiscrimination law—one that is focused almost exclusively on formal equality, rather than on a more contextual understanding of the conditions necessary for equal citizenship.

These competing visions of antidiscrimination law are reflected in two theoretical frames: the anticlassification theory and the antisubordination theory.[205] The anticlassification view of antidiscrimination law maintains that the harm of discrimination is in "classify[ing] people either overtly or surreptitiously on the basis of a forbidden category: for example, their race."[206] In this regard, anticlassificationists trumpet the appeal of so-called "color-blindness," or, more generally, "trait-blindness"—a general skepticism of classifications made on the basis of a protected trait, even if done for benign purposes.[207] By contrast, the antisubordination theory contends that the harm of discrimination is in "practices that enforce the secondary social status of historically oppressed groups."[208] Under this logic, classifications that expand opportunities for members of traditionally subordinated groups would be accepted and even encouraged. Indeed, the expansive text and interpretation of California's Unruh Act was animated by antisubordinationist impulses—to deter the sort of discrimination that would prevent underrepresented groups from participating fully in public life.[209]

The men's rights lawsuits more clearly evince the triumph of anticlassification values over antisubordination values in their utter disdain for the goals and priorities of the groups and programs challenged under state antidiscrimination law statutes. In the men's rights suits, it matters not that women are underrepresented in certain fields, or that the prospect of their advancement in particular arenas may be frustrated by systemic and institutional dynamics that historically have privileged and prioritized men. In short, the context in which the

---

[205] For a discussion of anticlassification and antisubordination principles and their interaction with American civil rights jurisprudence, consider Balkin and Siegel, 58 U Miami L Rev 9 (cited in note 150); Reva B. Siegel, *Equality Talk: Antisubordination and Anticlassification Values in Constitutional Struggles Over Brown*, 117 Harv L Rev 1470 (2004).

[206] Balkin and Siegel, 58 U Miami L Rev at 10 (cited in note 150).

[207] See Jessica L. Roberts, *Protecting Privacy to Prevent Discrimination*, 56 Wm & Mary L Rev 2123–24 (2014).

[208] Balkin and Siegel, 58 U Miami L Rev at 9 (cited in note 150).

[209] See Sande L. Buhai, *One Hundred Years of Equality: Saving California's Statutory Ban on Arbitrary Discrimination by Businesses*, 36 USF L Rev 109, 113–15 (2001).

classification arises, and the purposes for which it is deployed, are utterly irrelevant. The only relevant consideration is that the challenged program classifies on the basis of sex.

Masterpiece Cakeshop, by contrast, appears to embrace more of an antisubordinationist logic. To the extent the majority opinion credits Phillips's framing of himself and his situation as a religious minority in a majoritarian secular culture, then the opinion might be understood to reflect an antisubordination ethos.[210] That is, the identification of animus is intended to prevent the state's subordination of Phillips, as well as those like him who do not adhere to the tenets of majoritarian culture.

Although *Masterpiece Cakeshop*'s use of animus to protect and defend Jack Phillips suggests, at first blush, an antisubordinationist bent, its inattentiveness to questions of context also reflects an anticlassificationist ethos—indeed, a "color-blindness" for religion. In determining that the commissioners' statements and actions evince impermissible animus toward religious objectors, the majority's opinion cares not for whether, as an empirical matter, there is a broader context of hostility toward Christian evangelicals that might justify increased skepticism of the Commission's statements and actions. Rather, the majority took statements that were factually correct and read into them a veneer of hostility and derision that was not readily apparent to most observers. Indeed, the only attempt to contextualize the issue of hostility to religion was in the majority's consideration of the *Jack* cases, which presented circumstances where business owners objected to the customer's antigay message, not to the customer or his religious beliefs. Put differently, unlike the earlier cases where the Court looked to the broader social context in which minority groups operated in order to infer animus, the majority in *Masterpiece Cakeshop* instead focused narrowly on the commissioners' (true) statements and their disposition of three related, though distinct, cases to conclude that Jack Phillips has experienced the kind of discrimination that the Constitution deems actionable.

Viewed through this lens, both the men's rights cases and *Masterpiece Cakeshop* reveal both the rigidity of the anticlassification vision of antidiscrimination law and the plasticity and malleability of animus

---

[210] Some have argued that *Masterpiece Cakeshop* suggests antisubordinationist impulses as well. See Sager and Tebbe, Const Comm (draft on file with author) (cited in note 129). And to the extent that Jack Phillips understands himself to be a minority in a majoritarian secular society, the Court's crediting of his claims may reflect an antisubordinationist ethos as well.

doctrine more generally. The anticlassification vision, which has been ascendant in constitutional law and in some statutory approaches to antidiscrimination law,[211] is rigid in its narrow focus on treating groups alike, irrespective of the differing social circumstances in which the groups operate. Unlike the antisubordination frame, which considers whether conditions of *equity* exist, the anticlassification frame insists upon *equality*, and in so doing, refuses to acknowledge the structural circumstances—indeed, the context—that might make equality elusive for certain groups.

And in their rigid and reflexive disavowal of context, both the men's rights cases and *Masterpiece Cakeshop* evince the plasticity and malleability of the antidiscrimination project more generally. Both cases make clear that while we may think of minority status as a relatively fixed concept, in fact the question of who counts as a minority is constantly shifting and open to contest. In the same vein, even as we insist that antidiscrimination laws should be limited to "real" discrimination, there is no consensus as to what constitutes "real" discrimination. For the men's rights groups that have prevailed against women-only events and programming, discrimination is simply the exclusion from these events. It is not the historic subordination and marginalization that makes such programming urgent and necessary. Likewise, the discrimination to be corrected—at least for now—in *Masterpiece Cakeshop* is not the marginalization of LGBTQ persons in the marketplace, but rather the slights, whether real or imagined, that those who object to same-sex marriage and homosexuality experience when they seek an exemption from the ambit of antidiscrimination law.

V. Conclusion

Taken together, *Masterpiece Cakeshop* and the men's rights gender discrimination cases suggest an effort to suppress the antisubordination vision of antidiscrimination law, in favor of a more individualized, less contextual, anticlassification frame. Put differently, these cases reflect, perhaps to different degrees, the weaponization of antidiscrimination law against those who were once the objects of its protections.

---

[211] See id at 72 n 15, 79–80 (discussing statutory law); Balkin and Siegel, 58 U Miami L Rev at 10 (discussing constitutional law) (cited in note 150).

This weaponization speaks to a broader trend that goes beyond antidiscrimination law. In recent years, various strands of constitutional law and statutory doctrine that were once aimed at protecting the rights of minorities and those who espoused unpopular views and ideas have been "weaponized" for the purpose of shutting down these groups, their views, and their claims. Legal scholars have made much of the weaponization of the First Amendment, once the champion of religious minorities and those trumpeting unpopular viewpoints, to protect corporations and business interests.[212] Indeed, in the most recent Court term, the First Amendment was deployed to further weaken public unions[213] and to limit the force of consumer protection laws aimed at transparency in the provision of reproductive healthcare.[214] The trajectory of arbitration and alternative dispute-resolution mechanisms also bears this out. Originally intended to widen avenues for access to justice, mandatory arbitration clauses have more recently become a potent means for limiting individuals' ability to seek adjudication of legal claims.[215]

With this in mind, *Masterpiece Cakeshop* is not simply a punt on the broader question of whether commitments to religious liberty should dwarf equality principles, as some have suggested. Although the decision was narrow and cabined, it gestured toward developing trends in antidiscrimination law—trends that are consistent with a broader trajectory in which powerful constituencies have been able to mobilize law to vindicate their interests, while marginalizing the interests of individuals and groups once deemed in need of the law's protection.

---

[212] See, for example, Kessler and Pozen, 118 Colum L Rev at 1975–77 (cited in note 131); Samuel R. Bagenstos, *The Unrelenting Libertarian Challenge to Public Accommodations Law*, 66 Stan L Rev 1205 (2014); Frederick Mark Gedicks and Rebecca G. Van Tassell, *Of Burdens and Baselines: Hobby Lobby's Puzzling Footnote 37*, in Micah Schwartzman, Chad Flanders, and Zoë Robinson, eds, *The Rise of Corporate Religious Liberty* 323 (Oxford, 2016); Leslie Kendrick, *First Amendment Expansionism*, 56 Wm & Mary L Rev 1199 (2015); Elizabeth Sepper, *Free Exercise Lochnerism*, 115 Colum L Rev 1453 (2015); Amanda Shanor, *The New Lochner*, 2016 Wis L Rev 133; Nelson Tebbe, *Religion and Marriage Equality Statutes*, 9 Harv L & Pol Rev 25 (2015); Jedediah Purdy, *Neoliberal Constitutionalism: Lochnerism for a New Economy*, 77 L & Contemp Probs 195 (2014); Adam Liptak, *How Conservatives Weaponized the First Amendment*, NY Times (June 30, 2018), available at https://www.nytimes.com/2018/06/30/us/politics/first-amendment -conservatives-supreme-court.html.

[213] See *Janus v AFSCME*, 138 S Ct 2448, 2486 (2018).

[214] See *National Institute of Family & Life Advocates v Becerra*, 138 S Ct 2361, 2378 (2018).

[215] See *Epic Systems Corp. v Lewis*, 138 S Ct 1612, 1637, 1643–44 (2018) (Ginsburg, J, dissenting).

VIKRAM DAVID AMAR

"CLARIFYING" MURPHY'S LAW: DID SOMETHING GO WRONG IN RECONCILING COMMANDEERING AND CONDITIONAL PREEMPTION DOCTRINES?

Murphy v National Collegiate Athletic Association[1] is perplexing. The Court, 7–2, emphatically held that key provisions of the federal Professional and Amateur Sports Protection Act[2] (PASPA) did not operate as permissible federal preemption but instead unconstitutionally commandeered state legislative processes in violation of federalism principles, and by a 6–3 margin ruled that no other part of the Act was severable. But interested parties sought more than a definitive result— they wanted a ruling that carefully explained how commandeering and preemption doctrines fit together,[3] and in this respect consumers of

---

Vikram David Amar is Dean and Iwan Foundation Professor of Law, University of Illinois College of Law.

AUTHOR'S NOTE: The author thanks Alan Brownstein, Evan Caminker, Carlton Larson, Arden Rowell, and David Strauss for their insightful comments on earlier versions.

[1] 138 S Ct 1461 (2018).

[2] Pub L No 102-559, 106 Stat 4227 (1992), codified at 28 USC § 3701 et seq, held unconstitutional by *Murphy v National Collegiate Athletic Association*, 138 S Ct 1461 (2018).

[3] See Transcript of Oral Argument, *Murphy v National Collegiate Athletic Association*, Nos 16-476, 16-477 (Dec 4, 2017) at 66 (federal government urging Court not to "[]blur the clear line between preemption and commandeering") ("*Murphy* Oral Argument").

the Court's work product may feel disappointed. At times *Murphy* defined unconstitutional commandeering in incredibly broad terms— to include federal laws "that direct[ ] ... the States ... to refrain from enacting a regulation of the conduct of activities occurring within their borders."[4] And yet every congressional enactment that properly accomplishes federal preemption either explicitly or implicitly "direct[s] the States [ ] to ... refrain from ... regulation" of some kind.[5] While it is far too late in the day to believe Congress can simply command states to adopt or maintain, as state law, policies desired by the federal government, it would be revolutionary to suggest Congress cannot cabin states' sovereign actions when states affirmatively regulate private actors—through new state-law restrictions or partial repeal of old ones—in a domain located within Congress's enumerated powers. So some of *Murphy*'s sweeping language cannot be taken at face value.

Not all of *Murphy*'s proclamations are problematic on account of breadth, but that doesn't make the result any easier to decipher. Even when they are considerably narrower, the Court's assertions sometimes conflict with each other, and at key points the analysis leans in helpful directions but stops short of adequate explanation.

Some analysts may be tempted to see *Murphy* as an idiosyncratic decision with no significant impact on future cases. But reading opinions as meaningless is always risky, and also disrespectful to the Court. How might *Murphy* alter federalism disputes going forward? Some will want to read it as implicitly overruling seminal cases recognizing Congress's fundamental power to preempt conditionally. Or interjecting new judicial scrutiny of congressional intent when Congress undertakes to partner with the states in "cooperative federalism," the term often used to describe conditional federal funding as well as conditional preemption. Or maybe *Murphy* introduces a new substantive limit on certain types of cooperative federalism by preventing Congress from imposing overly tough choices on states. These readings, while possible, attribute a lot of unarticulated ambition to

---

[4] *Murphy*, 138 S Ct at 1479. See also id at 1478 (PASPA is unconstitutional because it "unequivocally dictates what a state legislature . . . may not do," which distinguishes it from statutes in earlier cases in which Congress had not "commanded state legislatures to . . . refrain from enacting state law.").

[5] Id at 1479. In the same vein, *Murphy*'s suggestion that the "basic principle [is] that Congress cannot issue direct orders to state legislatures," see id at 1478, is undeniably overbroad unless the Court means to overturn scores of federal statutes preempting states from regulating in certain ways or in certain areas. See Part III.B.

the Court, and an ambition that, importantly, doesn't fit well into preexisting federalism doctrine and that would create problems down the road.

I argue that the best reading of *Murphy* is one under which Congress's conditional preemption powers remain intact but can be exercised only when Congress lays out its conditions with clarity—just as Congress must do in the companion strand of cooperative federalism doctrine, conditional funding. This account explains *Murphy*'s outcome and builds on the facts and a great deal of language drawn from the entire majority opinion, relating both to the "merits" and to severability.[6] Under my interpretation, *Murphy*'s result is defensible (because Congress did not clearly lay out the conditions with which states had to comply to prevent preemptive federal law from coming into effect) and forges important new federalism doctrine. But it is new doctrine that complements rather than upends longstanding federalism traditions. Because my reading does not disregard, insult, or even minimize what the Court did or said, yet neither does it ascribe to the Court a wish to dramatically, problematically, and silently revamp the balance of state and federal power, I think it represents the most responsible path forward until the Court revisits matters.

I. THE BACKGROUND

PASPA, titled by Congress as "An Act [t]o prohibit sports gambling under State law," makes it "unlawful" in 28 USC § 3702(1) for a state or any of its subdivisions "to sponsor, operate, advertise, promote, license, or authorize by law or compact . . . a lottery, sweepstakes, or other betting, gambling, or wagering scheme based . . . on" competitive sporting events.[7] A separate, related provision but one not challenged as independently unconstitutional, § 3702(2), also makes it "unlawful" for "a [private] person" to undertake sports-gambling schemes—provided the person is doing so "pursuant to the law or compact of a governmental entity."[8] PASPA does not itself crimi-

---

[6] See Part III.C.

[7] 28 USC § 3702(1).

[8] 28 USC § 3702(2).

nalize any sports-gambling schemes[9] under federal law, but does allow the Attorney General, as well as professional and amateur sports organizations, to bring civil actions to enjoin violations of sections 3702(1) and 3702(2).[10] Moreover, separate provisions of Title 18 of the U.S. Code make it a federal crime to engage in a variety of interstate gambling activities (not specifically limited to sports gambling) that are unlawful under state law where they occur.

When PASPA was enacted in 1992, nearly every state prohibited sports gambling—albeit with different civil and criminal enforcement regimes. Four states (Delaware, Montana, Nevada, and Oregon) allowed some types of sports gambling, and these activities were grandfathered so as to be unaffected by PASPA.[11] Another provision, in effect, allowed New Jersey in particular to legalize sports gambling post-PASPA, but only in Atlantic City casinos and only if the state chose to do so within a year of PASPA's enactment.[12]

New Jersey failed to invoke that option. Instead, two decades later, in 2011, New Jersey voters amended that state's constitution to permit the legislature to "authorize" sports betting more broadly, at casinos and racetracks throughout the state.[13]

Following this state constitutional amendment, the New Jersey legislature enacted the Sports Wagering Law of 2012,[14] which permitted state-licensed entities to facilitate "wagering at casinos and racetracks on the results of certain professional or collegiate sports or athletic events."[15] Various sports organizations promptly sued the Governor of New Jersey, alleging New Jersey's constitutional amendment and implementing statute had violated PASPA. The de-

---

[9] From now on, I, like the Justices, generally refer to "sports-gambling schemes," a statutory term that presumably connotes some level of size and organization of the sports-gambling enterprise, simply as "sports gambling."

[10] 28 USC § 3703 ("A civil action to enjoin a violation of section 3702 may be commenced ... by the Attorney General of the United States, or by a professional sports organization or amateur sports organization whose competitive game is alleged to be the basis of such violation.").

[11] 28 USC § 3704(a)(1)–(2); *Murphy*, 138 S Ct at 1471.

[12] 28 USC § 3704(a)(3); *Murphy*, 138 S Ct at 1471.

[13] See NJ Const, Art IV, § 7, cl 2(D)–(E).

[14] 2011 NJ Sess Law Serv 231, codified at NJ Rev Stat § 5:12A-1–6 (2013), invalidated by *National Collegiate Athletic Association v Governor of NJ*, 730 F3d 208 (3d Cir 2013).

[15] Id.

fendants countered that, among other things,[16] PASPA's provision making state authorization or licensing of sports gambling unlawful violated the anticommandeering principle—which is rooted in the Tenth Amendment and constitutional structure—that was recognized by the Court in *New York v United States*[17] and again in *Printz v United States*.[18] The district court rejected this defense, and the U.S. Court of Appeals for the Third Circuit, with one of the three judges dissenting in a case now known as *Christie I*, affirmed.[19] *Christie I* viewed PASPA as an exercise of Congress's power under the Commerce Clause to preempt inconsistent state law, and observed that, unlike the statute invalidated in *New York*, PASPA "does not require or coerce [ ] states to lift a finger—they are not required to pass laws, to take title to anything, ... or to in any way enforce federal law."[20] The court rejected defendants' suggestion that PASPA effectively obligated states to maintain laws banning sports gambling, reasoning that the mere absence or repeal of state-law prohibitions does not, by itself, constitute "authoriz[ing]" or "licens[ing]" within the meaning of § 3702(1).[21]

New Jersey unsuccessfully sought review in the Supreme Court. In opposing certiorari, the United States stated that although New Jersey's actions had violated PASPA, the Act does not require a state to "leave in place the state-law prohibitions against sports gambling

---

[16] Among the most interesting of the other grounds for challenging PASPA that never made their way to the Court was the idea that Congress impermissibly favored the states in which sports gambling was grandfathered. Although the Court has frowned on laws that single out a small number of states for adverse treatment, see *Shelby County v Holder*, 570 US 529 (2013), perhaps in part because victimized states cannot protect themselves in Congress, the Justices have (sensibly) viewed things differently when the states being singled out are being helped, not hurt, in which case a national majority in Congress can easily undo the favorable treatment if it wants. See, for example, *United States v Ptasynski*, 462 US 74 (1983).

[17] 505 US 144 (1992).

[18] 521 US 898 (1997).

[19] *National Collegiate Athletic Association v Governor of NJ*, 730 F3d 208 (3d Cir 2013) ("*Christie I*").

[20] Id at 231 (emphasis omitted).

[21] Id at 232. The court also concluded that, even if § 3702(1)'s directive to states to refrain from authorizing or licensing sports gambling were struck down, § 3702(2)'s federal regulation of private individuals engaging in sports-gambling activity when it is undertaken pursuant to state law would survive, such that "even if the provision that offends New Jersey . . . were excised from PASPA, [the federal statute] would still plainly render [New Jersey's] Sports Wagering Law inoperative by prohibiting private parties from engaging in gambling schemes." Id at 236.

that it had chosen to adopt prior to PASPA's enactment. To the contrary, New Jersey is free to repeal those prohibitions in whole or in part."[22]

Shortly thereafter, New Jersey tried again. The 2014 New Jersey Act in controversy in *Murphy* declares itself to be a repealer[23] and not an attempt to authorize, license, sponsor, operate, advertise, or promote sports gambling. As the Supreme Court would observe:

> Specifically, it repeals the provisions of state law prohibiting sports gambling insofar as they concern[] the "placement and acceptance of wagers" on sporting events by persons 21 years of age or older at a horseracing track or a casino or gambling house in Atlantic City. The new law also specified that the repeal was effective only as to wagers on sporting events not involving a New Jersey college team or a collegiate event taking place in the State.[24]

The repealer 2014 Act was challenged in federal court by the NCAA and others as again violating PASPA's prohibition on a state "authoriz[ing]" and "licens[ing]" sports gambling. New Jersey once more defended by arguing that, inasmuch as PASPA seeks to negate the 2014 New Jersey law, PASPA constitutes impermissible federal "commandeering" of state legislatures. After the lower courts (including the Third Circuit sitting en banc in a case styled as *Christie II*)[25] rejected this commandeering argument, New Jersey officials sought and obtained Supreme Court review. The Court reversed, with Justice Alito writing for the Court, Justice Breyer concurring in part and dissenting in part, and Justice Ginsburg, joined by Justice Sotomayor and in part by Justice Breyer, dissenting.

II. The Supreme Court Opinions

Before reaching the merits of the commandeering claim, the Court said it first had to "examine [PASPA's] meaning," because "[t]he parties advance dueling interpretations [of the statute], and this dispute has an important bearing on the constitutional issue that we must decide."[26] Differing statutory constructions were central to re-

---

[22] Brief for the United States in Opposition, *Christie v National Collegiate Athletic Association*, No 13-967, *11 (US filed May 14, 2014).

[23] 2014 NJ Sess Law Serv 62, codified at NJ Rev Stat § 5:12A-7–9 (2014), repealed and replaced by 2018 NJ Sess Law Serv 33.

[24] *Murphy*, 138 S Ct at 1472 (citation omitted).

[25] *National Collegiate Athletic Association v Governor of NJ*, 832 F3d 389 (3d Cir 2016) ("*Christie II*").

[26] *Murphy*, 138 S Ct at 1473.

solving *Murphy*, but significant work is required to understand the "important bearing" the statutory interpretation dispute may have had on the constitutional question.

In a nutshell, New Jersey said PASPA banned the state from repealing any or all state-law sports-gambling prohibitions. New Jersey's argument was that because "[o]ne of the accepted meanings of the term 'authorize' ... is 'permit,'" it follows that "any state law that has the effect of permitting sports gambling, including a law totally or partially repealing a prior prohibition, amounts to an authorization."[27]

Importantly, as the Court observed, all parties agreed "that [§ 3702(1)] is unconstitutional if it means what [New Jersey] claim[s]."[28] Respondents rejected New Jersey's assertion that PASPA bans all modifications of state-law sports-gambling restrictions, but the Court expressed uncertainty about the contours of respondents' reading: "[J]ust how far [respondents] think a modification could go is not clear. They write that a State 'can ... repeal or enhance [laws prohibiting sports gambling] without running afoul of PASPA' but that it cannot 'partially repeal' a general prohibition for only one or two preferred providers, or only as to sports-gambling schemes conducted by the state."[29]

The federal government, like the respondents, argued that PASPA prohibits only certain "selective" repeals that leave the general prohibition in place but that confer on some particular entities permission to engage in conduct that is otherwise illegal.[30] But again, according to the Court, the federal government's interpretation "[likewise] does not set out any clear rule for distinguishing between partial repeals that constitute [ ] 'authorization' of sports gambling and those that are permissible," beyond a suggestion that it would be permissible under PASPA for a state to limit sports gambling to persons over twenty-one but to otherwise deregulate it.[31]

After laying all this out, Justice Alito's majority opinion then concludes, flatly: "In [the Court's] view, petitioners' interpretation is correct: When a State *completely or partially* repeals old laws banning

---

[27] Id.

[28] Id.

[29] Id (final alteration in original).

[30] *Murphy*, 138 S Ct at 1474.

[31] Id.

sports gambling, it 'authorize[s]' that activity" within the meaning of PASPA.[32] That could have ended much of the matter, given the acknowledgment by all the parties that if PASPA bans complete repeals (as the Court said it thinks PASPA does), PASPA is unconstitutional. But then, in a pivotal passage, the Court opined that even if Congress in enacting § 3702(1) did *not* seek to prohibit complete repeals but instead sought only to prohibit *some kinds of partial* repeals by states, as the respondents and federal government urged, there would still exist a fatal commandeering problem:

> The respondents and United States argue [invoking the canon of constitutional avoidance] that even if there is some doubt about the correctness of their interpretation of the anti-authorization provision, that interpretation should be adopted in order to avoid any anticommandeering problem that would arise if the provision were construed to require States to maintain their laws prohibiting sports gambling.... The plausibility of the alternative interpretations is debatable, *but even if the law could be interpreted as respondents and the United States suggest, it would still violate the anticommandeering principle*, as we now explain.[33]

As Ricky and Lucy Ricardo taught generations of TV viewers, it is in the explaining that things get interesting.

Justice Alito's commandeering analysis began by observing that while Congress's laws are supreme and preemptive when Congress acts pursuant to its enumerated powers,[34] the anticommandeering doctrine reflects "the decision [in the Constitution] to withhold from Congress the power to issue orders directly to the States."[35] This structural principle was invoked by the Court first in *New York*, where the Justices ruled that Congress could not require a state to enact "regulat[ions] according to the instructions of Congress" on pain of having to "take title to [and accept potential liability from] low-level radioactive waste" generated in the state.[36] The *Murphy* majority reiterated *New York*'s admonition that "even a particularly strong federal interest would [not] enable Congress to command a state government to enact *state* regulation."[37]

---

[32] Id (emphasis added and final alteration in original).

[33] Id at 1475 (emphasis added).

[34] *Murphy*, 138 S Ct at 1476.

[35] Id at 1475.

[36] Id at 1476 (quotation marks omitted), citing *New York*, 505 US at 153.

[37] Id at 1476 (emphasis in original and quotation marks omitted).

After describing the Court's extension of *New York*'s anticommandeering principle to state executive officials five years later in *Printz*, Justice Alito's *Murphy* opinion summarized, "[w]ithout attempting a complete survey,"[38] three of the functional justifications underlying *New York* and *Printz*: (1) a dual protection against tyranny;[39] (2) a facilitation of political accountability;[40] and (3) a barrier to federal cost-shifting to states.[41] Purporting to apply these principles, the Court emphatically proclaimed:

> [T]he PASPA provision at issue here—prohibiting state authorization of sports gambling—violates the anticommandeering rule. That provision unequivocally dictates what a state legislature may and may not do. . . . [S]tate legislatures are put under the direct control of Congress. It is as if federal officers were installed in state legislative chambers and were armed with the authority to stop legislators from voting on any offending proposals. A more direct affront to state sovereignty is not easy to imagine.[42]

Addressing potential counterarguments, the Court first took up the notion that while Congress cannot compel a state to enact legislation, "prohibiting a State from enacting new laws is another matter."[43] The Court found "[t]his distinction [to be] empty," observing that "[i]t was a matter of happenstance that the laws challenged in *New York* and *Printz* commanded 'affirmative' action,"[44] because there is no difference between Congress ordering states to affirmatively criminalize sports gambling and ordering them to preserve their existing prohibitions.[45] The Court next distinguished various cases relied on by PASPA's defenders, saying these cases rightly did not find commandeering because "[n]one concerned laws

---

[38] *Murphy*, 138 S Ct at 1477.

[39] Id.

[40] Id.

[41] Id.

[42] *Murphy*, 138 S Ct at 1478.

[43] Id.

[44] Id.

[45] Id. It is hard to imagine that respondents and the United States really did suggest that Congress could always prevent states from enacting new laws, given, as the Court had already pointed out, all parties conceded that if PASPA banned complete repeals and required states to maintain their prohibitions completely in force, there would be a commandeering problem. Instead, a fairer reading of the respondents'/federal government's position (which, for brevity, I sometimes refer to henceforth simply as the federal government's position) is that Congress enjoyed power to prohibit states from enacting the particular *kind* of law New Jersey enacted.

that directed the States either to enact or refrain from enacting a regulation of the conduct of activities occurring within their borders."[46] As I observed earlier, this breathtakingly broad articulation of commandeering—to include laws that direct states to refrain from regulation—creates a challenge in understanding *Murphy*, because all federal laws that successfully accomplish federal preemption in effect and often on their face "direct[ ] . . . States [ ] to . . . refrain from . . . regulation" in some manner.[47]

But the Court explained that PASPA does not validly preempt New Jersey's 2014 Act because PASPA's anti-authorization provision "does not confer any federal rights on private actors interested in conducting sports gambling operations . . . [n]or does it impose any federal restrictions on private actors."[48] The Court contrasted PASPA in this regard with the federal law upheld in *Morales v Trans World Airlines, Inc.*,[49] which blocked states from regulating air carrier rates and in so doing "confer[red] on . . . carriers[ ] a federal right to engage in certain conduct subject only to certain (federal) constraints."[50] Permissible preemption, according to the Court, exists only where Congress regulates private activity by creating federal rights for, or imposing federal duties on, private actors. The same analysis, the Court said, requires that PASPA's ban on state "licensing" of gambling also be characterized as impermissible commandeering: "Just as Congress lacks the power to order a state legislature not to enact a law authorizing sports gambling, it may not order a state legislature to refrain from enacting a law licensing sports gambling."[51]

And "[e]ven if the prohibition of state licensing were not itself unconstitutional, [the Court did] not think it could be severed from the invalid provision forbidding state authorization."[52] Indeed, the Court didn't think *any* other part of PASPA could be severed. Regarding severability, the Court seemed first to decide that § 3702(2)—the part

---

[46] *Murphy*, 138 S Ct at 1479.

[47] Id.

[48] Id at 1481.

[49] 504 US 374 (1992).

[50] *Murphy*, 138 S Ct at 1480.

[51] Id at 1482. The Court never even hinted at what it thinks licensing, as distinguished from authorizing, means under PASPA, and so I shall not spend time on that question either, except to say that some of the most famous preemption cases in the US Reports, like *Gibbons v Ogden*, 22 US (9 Wheat) 1 (1824), involve federal laws displacing state licensing schemes.

[52] *Murphy*, 138 S Ct at 1482 n 29.

of PASPA that makes it illegal under federal law for private entities to undertake sports-gambling activities under the auspices of state law—was not severable because this private-party prohibition was supposed to operate "in tandem" with the prohibition on state authorization and licensing:

> If a State attempted to authorize particular private entities to engage in sports gambling, the State could be sued under § 3702(1), and the private entity could be sued at the same time under § 3702(2). . . . But if . . . Congress lacks the authority to prohibit a state from legalizing sports gambling, the prohibition of private conduct under § 3702(2) ceases to implement any coherent federal policy.[53]

The Court went further, saying that § 3702(2), "if . . . severed from § 3702(1), [would] implement[ ] a perverse policy that undermines whatever policy is favored by the people of a State"[54] by making unlawful under federal law that which a state's people would like to permit. "We do not think that Congress ever contemplated that such a weird result would come to pass."[55]

The part of § 3702(1) that prohibits states themselves from "operating," "sponsoring," or "promoting" sports gambling was similarly unseverable:[56] because state-maintained gambling had been thought to be "more benign" than other forms of gambling, "[p]rohibiting the States from engaging in commercial [gambling] activities that are [now] permitted for private parties would [ ] have been unusual, and it is unclear what might justify such disparate treatment."[57] Neither, thought the Court, could the part of § 3702(1) prohibiting state "advertising" of sports gambling be severed: "If th[is] provision[ ] were allowed to stand, federal law would forbid the advertising of an activity that is legal under both federal and state law, and that is something that Congress has rarely done. . . . [W]e do not think that Congress would want the advertising provisions to stand if the remainder of PASPA must fall."[58]

Justice Breyer joined the majority on the anticommandeering analysis, but not on severability. He thought it perfectly sensible that

---

[53] Id at 1483.

[54] Id.

[55] Id at 1484.

[56] *Murphy*, 138 S Ct at 1483.

[57] Id at 1482–83.

[58] Id at 1484.

Congress would prohibit private activity that nonetheless is authorized or licensed under state law, because Congress's overarching goal was to "keep sports gambling from spreading."[59] Although Congress "may have [reasonably] preferred that state authorities enforce state law [rules] forbidding sports gambling" without federal law and the federal government having to get involved, § 3702(2) could easily be seen as "a backup."[60] Justice Ginsburg, joined by Justice Sotomayor and in part by Justice Breyer, said many of the same things Justice Breyer did on severability, criticizing the majority for "deploy[ing] a wrecking ball" to PASPA.[61]

Justice Thomas concurred entirely in the majority opinion, but also wrote separately to express his misgivings about "our modern severability precedents."[62] Justice Thomas observed that the question severability doctrine requires courts to ask—"'[w]ould Congress still have passed' the valid sections 'had it known' about the constitutional invalidity of the other portions of the statute?"—"appear[s] to be in tension with traditional limits on judicial authority"[63] both because it tasks courts not with determining what a statute means but with making a "nebulous inquiry into hypothetical congressional intent,"[64] and because it "often requires courts to weigh in on statutory provisions that no [current] party has standing to challenge, bringing courts dangerously close to issuing advisory opinions."[65] Notwithstanding these concerns, Justice Thomas joined the majority's application of existing severability doctrine because, among other reasons, "no party in this case has asked us to reconsider these precedents."[66]

---

[59] *Murphy*, 138 S Ct at 1488 (Breyer, J, concurring in part and dissenting in part).

[60] Id.

[61] Id at 1489 (Ginsburg, J, dissenting). Although Justices Ginsburg and Sotomayor dissented entirely, signaling disagreement with the Court on the merits of the commandeering analysis, oddly enough they did not explain how they understood commandeering differently than the majority. The closest they came was to characterize the challenged parts of § 3702(1) as "*alleged* 'commandeering,'" see id at 1490 (Ginsburg, J, dissenting) (emphasis added), which prompted the majority to respond that "the dissent apparently disagrees with our holding that the provisions forbidding state authorization and licensing violate the anticommandeering principle, but it provides no explanation for its position." Id at 1482 n 30.

[62] *Murphy*, 138 S Ct at 1485 (Thomas, J, concurring).

[63] Id (Thomas, J, concurring).

[64] Id at 1486 (Thomas, J, concurring).

[65] Id at 1487 (Thomas, J, concurring).

[66] *Murphy*, 138 S Ct (Thomas, J, concurring).

III. Of Commandeering and Preemption

A. A ban on complete repeal of state-law sports-gambling prohibitions would constitute commandeering

This much is clear, and was agreed upon by all the parties: A state must be free to completely repeal its prohibitions of sports gambling, or any other activity, if it chooses. That is, in the unusual case where states wish to desist from exercising sovereign power altogether over something or someone, congressional directives to states to refrain from passing laws ending regulation, entitlement programs, or taxation[67] would constitute commandeering. In this regard, although the Court overstated things by calling the action/inaction distinction "empty,"[68] the Court was right to find the action/inaction line inadequate, in that the distinction fails to account for a situation in which Congress commandeers not by requiring new legislative action, but by preventing a state from exiting a regulatory sphere. The key question is not whether the state is being forced in formal terms to enact anything new today, but whether the state is being forced to exercise its sovereign power, in either a new or continuing fashion.

B. A ban on specified partial repeals of state-law prohibition of sports gambling would not constitute commandeering

But to suggest, from this starting point, that Congress necessarily commandeered when it tried (according to the federal government's reading of PASPA) to prevent states from disallowing some kinds of sports gambling while allowing others is dubious. This is so because a partial repeal can just as easily be viewed not in terms of a repeal, but in terms of a continued (albeit partial) regulation of private activity.[69]

---

[67] The anticommandeering rule should apply to all three settings. Compare Matthew D. Adler and Seth F. Kreimer, *The New Etiquette of Federalism: New York, Printz, and Yeskey*, 1998 Supreme Court Review 71, 92–93 (*"New Etiquette"*) (discussing the application of the anticommandeering principle to entitlement program mandates).

[68] As Adler and Kreimer demonstrate, the distinction does have some utility in the ordinary situation. See Adler and Kreimer, *New Etiquette* at 92–95 (cited in note 67). But even they, who themselves propose a strong version of this action/inaction distinction, acknowledge that "[u]ndoubtedly, [ ] refinements to the basic distinction between action and inaction will emerge if the Court explicitly adopts that distinction and persists in the anticommandeering jurisprudence." Id at 95 n 80.

[69] The respondents and United States might have benefited by explicitly and repeatedly characterizing the 2014 Act not as a partial repeal, but as a continuing, albeit narrower, exercise of regulatory authority by New Jersey.

And, of course, Congress can prevent states from regulating private individuals when such state regulation is inconsistent with federal objectives, at least where (as here) Congress enjoys the power to regulate the particular field of activity itself. We call that preemption. And for these purposes it shouldn't matter that a state has chosen to deregulate to some extent, provided that it is still in fact regulating; Congress preempts less-than-comprehensive state regulation all the time. For example, in *Morales v Trans World Airlines, Inc.*,[70] cited favorably by *Murphy*, the Court upheld Congress's decision to preempt states from regulating airlines rates, even though Congress did not preempt states from regulating some other aspects of airline operations. And no one would doubt that Congress, instead of prohibiting states from regulating airline rates entirely, could have taken the lesser step of preventing states from imposing certain *kinds* of rate regulations. What matters, in determining whether a state law can be preempted, is not the state regulatory baseline; it is whether the state has chosen to exercise (new or continued) state regulatory power (either comprehensively or selectively) in a field over which Congress has been given the authority to make, and has in fact made, regulatory decisions that conflict with the state's choices.

To see the fundamental difference between PASPA—as the federal government sought to interpret it—and the laws struck down in *New York* and *Printz*, consider what the state desired to do in each of the three cases, and ask whether that state objective is something Congress has the power to override. In *New York*, the state apparently wanted to refrain, at least in the short term, from regulating radioactive waste within its borders. The Court rightly held that New York could make that decision. In *Printz*, the state's local law enforcement officials seemingly didn't want to perform any Brady Act handgun-purchase background checks. The Court similarly held states had that choice. In *Murphy*, New Jersey wanted to prohibit some types of sports gambling but not others. We thus need ask: does Congress have the power to prevent New Jersey from accomplishing that disparate treatment? Although Congress may not be able to require New Jersey to extend its prohibition of sports gambling to the persons or activities New Jersey seeks to leave alone,[71] certainly

---

[70] 504 US 374 (1992).

[71] Compare *Linda R. S. v Richard D.*, 410 US 614 (1973).

Congress can tell New Jersey it cannot enforce its prohibitions of the gambling it does seek to regulate, because such disparate treatment is displaced by federal law. In other words, Congress can lawfully put New Jersey to a choice between regulating in a way that is consistent with Congress's desires that there not be certain kinds of regulatory winners and losers, or not regulating at all.

If this is true, was there something unlawful about the *way* Congress put New Jersey to the choice?[72] This brings us to the heart of the controversy about the *Murphy* outcome: why, under the federal government's reading of PASPA, was the statute deemed to be commandeering rather than permissible preemption? According to the federal government, PASPA is best read (or at least best read in light of constitutional avoidance principles) to mean: (1) states can continue to prohibit sports gambling, and if they do they won't be preempted by federal law—indeed, federal criminal law will continue to reinforce some of the prohibitions by making some actions that are illegal under state law criminal under federal law; (2) states can repeal their prohibitions on sports gambling entirely if they like; (3) they may not enforce a selective repeal of their prohibitions in a way that favors certain entities, such as casinos and racetracks; and (4) if they do selectively repeal and discriminate in favor of some entities, state law will be preempted by federal law, and federal law will kick in to prohibit sports gambling by those favored entities.

Is there a problem with this structure? Each of the listed components is rational and permissible standing alone, and also in connection with the others.[73] For starters, under current doctrine Congress enjoys power to regulate interstate—or intrastate—sports gambling; such gambling is an economic activity with profound effects on the national economy.[74] Thus Congress can regulate sports gambling

---

[72] Compare *Murphy*, 138 S Ct at 1488 (Breyer, J, concurring in part and dissenting in part) ("[T]he only problem with the challenged part of § 3702(1) lies in its means, not its end.").

[73] With or without the kind of helpful statutory summary outlined in the preceding paragraph, when a court reviews Congress's actions in regulating, or conditionally regulating, economic activity under the Commerce Clause, the court applies rational basis review, under which it should seek to understand how the statute might be rational and coherent even in the absence of explicit explanation.

[74] See, for example, *United States v Lopez*, 514 US 549 (1995); *Gonzales v Raich*, 545 US 1 (2005). But see Justice Thomas's dissent in *Raich*, 545 US at 57–75 (Thomas, J, dissenting), and concurrence in *Murphy*, 138 S Ct at 1485–87 (Thomas, J, concurring), which harken back to pre–New Deal understandings of federal Commerce Clause authority.

comprehensively, allow states to regulate it, or direct that the field stay unregulated, either partially or altogether. Nor is Congress's decision to piggyback on (and essentially incorporate by reference) certain state prohibitions of various gambling activities in some criminal provisions of Title 18 problematic; federal statutes in many settings permissibly reinforce state prohibitions by providing that if state law makes something illegal, then federal law will too.[75] Similarly unremarkable is Congress's prohibition of state discrimination that favors certain market participants; since Congress could have ousted states altogether, Congress can allow states to regulate but place limits on the kind of selective regulation allowed.[76]

All of that brings us to the last key feature, the provision by which federal regulatory authority—heretofore unexercised—applies to impose civil prohibitions on sports-gambling activities that someone might seek to undertake pursuant to a state law that impermissibly confers favorable treatment. This last aspect—by which federal law applies when state law seeks not to—may be less common in federal statutes, but it is also grounded firmly in preemption caselaw, and indeed is fundamentally similar to the statutory devices challenged and upheld in *Virginia Surface Mining and Reclamation Association v Hodel*[77] and *Federal Energy Regulatory Commission v Mississippi*[78] (*FERC*), two cases in which the Court explicitly rejected commandeering challenges,[79] and that were expressly reaffirmed in *New York*, and then in *Murphy* itself.[80] In *Hodel* and *FERC*, Congress adopted some policy parameters and gave states a right of first refusal to regulate

---

[75] See, for example, *United States v Sharpnack*, 355 US 286 (1958); 18 USC § 13; 18 USC § 43; 27 USC § 122. See also Vikram David Amar, *Indirect Effects of Direct Election: A Structural Examination of the Seventeenth Amendment*, 49 Vand L Rev 1347, 1366–72 (1996) (discussing incorporation of state law into federal law).

[76] See Brief for the United States as Amicus Curiae Supporting Respondents, *Murphy v National Collegiate Athletic Association*, Nos 16-476 and 16-477, *25 n 7 (US filed Oct 23, 2017) (citing statutes that do not oust states from regulating an activity but that prevent states from discriminating in various respects in their regulation).

[77] 452 US 264 (1981).

[78] 456 US 742 (1982).

[79] *Hodel*, 452 US at 288 ("[T]here can be no suggestion that the Act commandeers the legislative processes of the States."); *FERC*, 456 US at 769 ("In short, Titles I and II do not involve the compelled exercise of Mississippi's sovereign powers.").

[80] *New York*, 505 US at 167 ("[W]here Congress has the authority to regulate private activity under the Commerce Clause, we have recognized Congress' power to offer States the choice of regulating that activity according to federal standards or having state law preempted by federal regulation.") (citing *Hodel*, 452 US at 288; *FERC*, 456 US at 764–65); *Murphy*, 138 S Ct at 1479 ("In *Hodel* ... the federal law, which involved what has been called

according to them. Because the states were not required to do anything, and if they chose not to regulate pursuant to federal desires the
federal government would undertake the regulatory burden itself,
the Court characterized Congress's invitations to states as "cooperative federalism," and rejected any claim of impermissible commandeering.

We might describe the notion that federal law applies only when
states choose not to accept Congress's invitation to regulate pursuant
to federal objectives as "inverse incorporation" of state law. In such
situations, it is the absence, rather than the presence, of state regulation that triggers the applicability of federal law. While this feature
might strike some observers as unconventional, *inverse incorporation
is the heart of conditional preemption*. States are given an option, but
if they decline to take regulatory charge pursuant to federal standards, then federal law and enforcement is a backstop. In basic terms,
conditional preemption (which perhaps more accurately should be
called conditional nonpreemption) is very similar to its sibling, conditional federal spending. In both settings, states are offered a deal
in which they are given something (latitude to operate without federal preemption and dollars, respectively) in exchange for regulating
in ways that are consistent with federal policy objectives. Together,
these two doctrines make up a large part of the "cooperative federalism" the Supreme Court embraced in *Hodel*, *FERC*, and many other
decisions.

Like the statutes at issue in *Hodel* and *FERC*, PASPA (under the
federal government's reading) articulates Congress's basic policy
preferences—namely, that sports-gambling operations be prohibited
under state law and that in no event shall they be permitted on a
selective basis. PASPA reflects a federal view that if states embody
these federal preferences in state law, states are well situated, utilizing
their enforcement resources and exercising permissible enforcement
discretion tailored to their local conditions, to discharge federal
objectives. But if states turn down the federal deal and decide not to
undertake this role, but instead attempt to favor certain actors in
contravention of congressional policy, then federal law—and federal
enforcement—will step in and ensure entities favored under state law
do not benefit from their favored status. States can act consistently

---

'cooperative federalism,' by no means commandeered the state legislative process. . . . [I]n
FERC . . . the federal law in question issued no command to a state legislature.").

with federal objectives, the reward for which is that the federal government will stay its hand; if states decide otherwise, their law is displaced by federal regulation.[81]

When things are framed this way, we can see that the *Murphy* Court did not convincingly articulate a reason for viewing § 3702(1) as commandeering rather than preemption. Justice Alito's opinion rejects preemption as a defense of the provision because, he says, the statute "certainly does not confer any federal rights on private actors interested in conducting sports gambling operations ... [n]or does it impose any federal restrictions on private actors."[82] But under the federal government's reading of PASPA, the statute creates conditional federal rights for and conditional federal duties on private actors: § 3702(1) of PASPA confers a federal right to be free from disparate treatment ("authorization") by states with respect to sports gambling, and § 3702(2) of PASPA imposes a federal duty not to take advantage of favorable disparate treatment in which states might attempt to engage.[83]

C. ALTHOUGH CONGRESS COULD HAVE PERMISSIBLY ACCOMPLISHED
   PASPA'S GOALS, THE OFFER CONGRESS MADE TO THE STATES IN
   PASPA WAS INSUFFICIENTLY CLEAR

In light of the foregoing discussion, how can *Murphy*'s outcome be explained, much less defended? As noted earlier, conditional preemption power is analytically quite similar to the conditional funding power also enjoyed by Congress. In both settings, Congress offers a deal that avoids the commandeering problem because states are free to accept or reject. But one of the key teachings of conditional

---

[81] A question arises under PASPA: Why would Congress seek both to block states from discriminating and also to undo any such discrimination using federal enforcement? As the NCAA's brief and Justice Breyer's separate writing suggest, such an approach might have been adopted out of an abundance of caution and a desire to make sure that beneficiaries of state discrimination understood they would not be allowed to benefit by it. See Brief for Respondents, *Murphy v National Collegiate Athletic Association*, Nos 16-476 and 16-477, *56 (US filed Oct 16, 2017); *Murphy*, 138 S Ct at 1488 (Breyer, J, concurring in part and dissenting in part).

[82] *Murphy*, 138 S Ct at 1481.

[83] The *Murphy* Court acknowledges that § 3702(2) in PASPA itself contains federal duties but suggests that since this is not the challenged provision of PASPA it doesn't matter whether this section can be understood as permissible preemption. Id. But, of course, it shouldn't matter how Congress breaks up the sections in an Act, and the relevant constitutional question is whether the statute operating as a whole should properly be understood as preempting, rather than commandeering, state regulatory power.

funding doctrine is that, in order for a deal not to be coercive, the terms of the bargain offered to the states must be laid out "unambiguously, [so that] States [are able] to exercise their choice knowingly, cognizant of the consequences of their participation."[84] Could and should this concept carry over from conditional spending to its close relative in the cooperative federalism family—conditional preemption? And is this the key respect in which PASPA was constitutionally problematic (even if Congress was trying to accomplish what the federal government said it was)? I believe so.

But how, exactly, was the deal offered by PASPA problematically unclear? Under the respondents' and federal government's reading, PASPA tells states that they can repeal their sports-gambling prohibitions in whole and sometimes in part, *but does not tell them what kinds of partial repeals are disallowed.* The Court was clearly frustrated by the imprecision in this regard, and returned to this aspect of the statute more often than any other. Oral argument time was devoted to it,[85] and the opinion itself mentions either the inscrutability of the partial repeal option, or the way in which New Jersey relied on federal (mis)representations concerning that option, more than a half dozen separate times throughout. For example, as to vagueness, the Court itself added the following emphasis when quoting from the lower court: "[The Third Circuit felt it] need not ... articulate a line whereby a partial repeal of a sports wagering ban amounts to an authorization under PASPA, *if indeed such a line could be drawn.*"[86] In characterizing the briefs, the Court said that under respondents' reading of the statute it is "not clear" "how far [a state] could go" in modifying preexisting state law.[87] The Court similarly remarked that "[the United States] does not set out any clear rule for distinguishing between partial repeals that constitute the 'authorization' of sports gambling and those that are permissible. [All it says is] that a State could 'eliminat[e] prohibitions on sports gambling involving wagers by adults or wagers below a certain dollar threshold.'"[88] To

---

[84] See *South Dakota v Dole*, 483 US 203, 207 (1987).

[85] See *Murphy* Oral Argument at 58–59 (cited in note 3) (Justice Gorsuch asking: "But where is the line? The Third Circuit said *de minimis* private gambling isn't covered. On page 30 of your brief, you indicate maybe the state could have a certain dollar threshold, and that wouldn't be authorizing. ... [W]here does the government draw the line?").

[86] *Murphy*, 138 S Ct at 1472–73 (emphasis and ellipses in original).

[87] Id at 1473.

[88] Id at 1474 (final alteration in original).

the same effect: "Respondents and the United States tell us that the PASPA ban on state authorization allows complete repeals, but beyond that they identify no clear line[s]."[89] And at the end of its statutory meaning discussion, the Court characterized the level of unclarity present under the respondents'/federal government's interpretation as a "nebulous regime."[90]

As to the (unfair) position in which this put states, the Court leaned on the representation the federal government made in *Christie I*, saying that the United States "told this Court that PASPA does not require New Jersey 'to leave in place the state-law prohibitions against sports gambling that it had chosen to adopt prior to PASPA's enactment. To the contrary, New Jersey is free to repeal those prohibitions in whole or in part.' "[91] At the oral argument in *Murphy*, Justice Ginsburg even asked the federal government whether this representation in the first brief in opposition to certiorari was inaccurate.[92] Further reinforcing the idea that New Jersey was unfairly treated, *Murphy* described New Jersey's 2014 Act as having "*[p]ick[ed] up on the suggestion* [by the federal government] that a partial repeal would be allowed."[93]

The Court's concern here was understandable. Neither the respondents nor the federal government offered a clear line differentiating permissible from impermissible partial repeals, much less a line that could be teased from the word "authorize" in PASPA. There was no thorough explanation—by reference to PASPA's text, structure, or even legislative history—of why age or dollars-at-risk classifications are permitted, but classifications concerning different types of institutions are not. This imprecision made it hard if not impossible for New Jersey to know what the federal deal permitted and disallowed. The state was left to guess in adopting its laws, and if it guessed wrong, it would have wasted its time and energy.[94]

---

[89] Id at 1475. The Court even seemed to belittle the NCAA's statutory reading by saying it offered a "*primary*" meaning of the word "authorize." Id at 1473 (emphasis in original).

[90] *Murphy*, 138 S Ct at 1475.

[91] Id at 1472.

[92] See *Murphy* Oral Argument at 63 (cited in note 3).

[93] *Murphy*, 138 S Ct at 1472 (emphasis added).

[94] See *Pennhurst State School and Hospital v Halderman*, 451 US 1, 25 (1981) ("The crucial inquiry, however, is not whether a State would [ever] knowingly undertake [a particular] obligation, but whether Congress spoke so clearly that we can fairly say that the State could make an informed choice.").

Conditional preemption, like conditional spending, is about pre-serving choice on the part of states when the federal government seeks to partner with them. In both settings, Congress is offering a carrot (in the case of conditional funding, it is dollars, and in the case of conditional preemption, it is Congress's willingness to stay out and let states exercise some substantive and enforcement discre-tion) if states assist in implementing federal objectives. Thus, clarity of terms is just as important to facilitate choice in conditional preemp-tion as in conditional funding. Requiring, in conditional preemption, that Congress lay out its conditions unambiguously would therefore fit neatly into federalism doctrine more generally. And such a re-quirement explains and justifies the result in *Murphy* without over-reading the ruling. On top of that, it dovetails nicely with another of the stated justifications of anticommandeering doctrine, facilitating accountability: it would be problematic for state citizens to blame their state for a deal that, because of vagueness in federal drafting, turned out to be costly in unforeseeable ways.

To be sure, absence of clarity is a problem that creates costs for states whenever federal law may end up displacing state law. In so-called "conflict" preemption and "field" preemption that involves no conditional bargains, for instance, Congress makes decisions against a backdrop of existing and evolving state law, and when the meaning of the new federal statute is unclear, states may not know which of their current or future laws will be displaced. But as problematic as imprecision in those settings may be, it is at least arguably more un-fair to states to be vague when, as in cooperative federalism, the fed-eral government is purporting, directly or indirectly, to offer states a choice—a deal—to partner with Washington, DC, by undertaking responsibility that the federal government will otherwise need to as-sume. That, after all, is why we have a distinctive clarity requirement in the conditional spending arena already. Offering states terms of involvement and then imposing different terms than they might rea-sonably have expected is wrong for the same reasons that the law more generally resolves ambiguities in contractual settings against the drafter.[95]

Perhaps requiring Congress to express its intent to preempt in un-mistakable terms, and also to define the scope of preemption clearly, would make sense for preemption settings more generally. But it would

---

[95] See Restatement (Second) of Contracts § 206 (1981).

be a rational first step for the Court to take to harmonize conditional spending and conditional preemption by requiring particular clarity in both settings, where the applicability of federal law will depend on legislative choices states are being encouraged—indeed invited—to make.

Thus, it is one thing for Congress to say to a state, "we are regulating in a particular way, and you can't conflict with our regulation" (conflict preemption), or "we may regulate by particular means, so you must steer clear from the whole area" (express field preemption), when the ways, means, and areas in question are fuzzy. Or, even, for Congress to say, "if you don't regulate along certain particular lines, we will regulate the matter ourselves" even though the substance of any subsequent Congressional regulation is not necessarily foreseeable. Imprecision in any of these settings is troubling enough. But it is yet another thing for Congress to say to a state, "if you choose not to regulate along particular lines, we will regulate the matter ourselves" when the lines along which states are being asked to affirmatively regulate are themselves nigh impossible to discern. As the Court has said in the conditional spending context, "[t]he canon [requiring clarity] applies with greatest force where . . . a State's [own] potential obligations under [an] Act are largely indeterminate."[96]

So if PASPA has offered states a cooperative federalism deal in which states could not meaningfully exercise choice because what is allowed and what is forbidden are unclear, what should the remedy be? In both *Pennhurst State School and Hospital v Halderman*[97] and *Sebelius*,[98] the two most prominent Spending Clause cases of this kind, the Court refused to enforce unclear terms of the purported federal-state deal. In *Murphy*, then, even if the federal government's reading of the statute is the one that best reflects what Congress sought to accomplish, since Congress did not clearly set out that reading in clear enough terms when the deal was offered, states are not bound.[99]

---

[96] *Pennhurst*, 451 US at 24.

[97] 451 US 1 (1981).

[98] *National Federation of Independent Business v Sebelius*, 567 US 519 (2012).

[99] There is a question—one that I flag but needn't resolve here—about whether, going forward, litigation and executive branch pronouncements can cure vagueness in the cooperative federalism context, such that states can be put on sufficient notice of their obligations and the federal law consequences of their failure to abide by them even if the original congressional enactment was lacking in the constitutionally required clarity. In other (e.g.,

Accordingly, if the meaning of "authorize" in § 3702(1) and the meaning of "pursuant to state law" under § 3702(2) (which is keyed to the meaning of "authorize") are unclear, then those provisions are simply unenforceable. Importantly, unclarity pervades both sections—if states don't know what they are prohibited from doing under § 3702(1), they don't know what will trigger unwanted federal involvement under § 3702(2). And if these two provisions fall, then the Court's determination that the rest of PASPA must fall as well is plausible in a way that is not true under the majority's reasoning, which finds a substantive constitutional flaw in § 3702(1) but no constitutional problem with § 3702(2).[100]

D. WHY ALTERNATIVE EXPLANATIONS ARE INFERIOR

1. *Could the Court be abandoning Hodel and FERC and conditional preemption?* It is of course possible that the Court was not troubled by PASPA's lack of clarity so much as by the very idea of conditional preemption that constitutes part of cooperative federalism. To explore this possibility, we need to delve into these seminal *Hodel* and *FERC* cases on conditional preemption a bit more deeply.

---

due process or First Amendment) vagueness contexts, judicial interpretations—especially by state courts, which are not encumbered by Article III limits on advisory opinions and the like—of a statute can put individuals on notice as to the meaning of a law and thus avoid the problem of vagueness in future disputes. But query whether in the federalism context, where other plain statement rules such as that announced in *Gregory v Ashcroft*, 501 US 452 (1992) are designed to make sure Congress has carefully considered state interests, Congress itself has to be the one to fix any vague conditions problem. The Court hasn't had occasion to discuss this in any depth in the conditional spending arena; my instinct is that whatever possibility there is for congressional unclarity to be cured later (and prospectively) by the executive branch in litigation or elsewhere (assuming the executive branch's efforts don't conflict with the meaning of the statute), the approach in conditional preemption should track that in conditional spending. And in *Murphy* itself, even if the Court wanted in dicta to help ease the vagueness of PASPA in the future, it would not have been able to do so because even by the end of the litigation no one could clearly answer the question: Precisely what kinds of selective decisions by states constitute "authorization"?

[100] Putting aside PASPA's specifics and looking more abstractly at *Murphy*'s methodology on severability, we see that the Court asked whether the invalidation of provision A (the "authorization" provision of § 3702(1)) dooms the continued application of provision B (the regulation of private gambling in § 3702(2)), and then asked, if B is doomed, what does that mean for provision C (the ban on state operation of gambling schemes)? Such an approach seems sound in general terms. The only observation I might make here has to do with sequence. If in a given case the Court invalidates A, and then upholds rather than invalidates B because B is independent of A, and then invalidates C because C is dependent upon A, the Court should double back to ask whether B is dependent upon C even if it is not directly dependent on A.

Hodel involved the Surface Mining Act,[101] "a comprehensive statute designed to 'establish a nationwide program to protect society and the environment from the adverse effects of surface coal mining operations.'"[102] The statute provided for a "two-stage program" of regulation. In the interim stage, the Secretary of the Interior was to immediately promulgate and enforce some of the Act's environmental protection performance standards; in the permanent phase, each state was required to have a regulatory program that ensured "compliance with the full panoply of federal enforcement standards, with enforcement responsibility lying with either the State or Federal Government."[103] A state that wished to maintain permanent regulatory authority over surface coal mining operations occurring inside the state was required to submit for the Secretary's approval a proposed program demonstrating the state's willingness and capacity to enforce federal environmental standards.[104] If a state proved unable or unwilling to submit or implement a satisfactory permanent program, the Secretary was required under the Act to develop federal regulations—which of course would have preemptive effect— for the state.[105]

In rejecting a commandeering challenge, the Court emphasized that under the Act the

> States are not compelled to enforce [federal environmental] standards, to expend any state funds, or to participate in the federal regulatory program in any manner whatsoever. If a State does not wish to submit a proposed permanent program that complies with the Act . . . the full regulatory burden will be borne by the Federal Government. Thus, there can be no suggestion that the Act commandeers the legislative processes of the States by directly compelling them to enact and enforce a federal regulatory program.[106]

The next year the Court took up *FERC v Mississippi*, involving the Public Utility Regulatory Policies Act of 1978[107] (PURPA)—a statute designed to help combat the nationwide energy crisis. Titles I

---

[101] 30 USC § 1201 et seq.

[102] *Hodel*, 452 US at 268.

[103] Id at 269.

[104] Id at 271 (quotation marks omitted).

[105] Id at 272.

[106] *Hodel*, 452 US at 288.

[107] 16 USC § 2601 et seq.

and III of PURPA directed state utility regulatory commissions and nonregulated utilities to "consider" adopting and implementing specific "rate design" and regulatory standards, and required state commissions to follow certain notice and comment procedures when acting on proposed federal standards, and to provide an explanation if they chose not to adopt the federal standards.[108]

In rejecting the notion that PURPA impermissibly commandeered, the Court observed that "Titles I and III of PURPA require only *consideration* of federal standards. And if a State has no utilities commission, or simply stops regulating in the field, it need not even entertain the federal proposals."[109] The Court then reminded that "the commerce power permits Congress to pre-empt the States entirely in the regulation of private utilities," and that the case poses essentially the same issue already addressed in *Hodel*, where "the Federal Government could have pre-empted all surface mining regulations [but] instead . . . allowed the States to enter the field if they promulgated regulations consistent with federal standards," and where the Court held that "the Surface Mining Act should [not] become constitutionally suspect simply because Congress chose to allow the States a regulatory role."[110]

Echoing *Hodel*, the *FERC* Court said that because "Congress could have pre-empted the field . . . PURPA should not be invalid simply because, out of deference to state authority, Congress adopted a less intrusive scheme and allowed the States to continue regulating in the area on the condition that they consider the suggested federal standards."[111]

The reasoning of *Hodel* and *FERC* was affirmed by the Court in *New York*, the granddaddy of commandeering cases. The *New York* Court characterized *Hodel* as a case "where Congress ha[d] the authority to regulate private activity under the Commerce Clause [and

---

[108] See *FERC*, 456 US at 746–48.

[109] Id at 764 (emphasis in original).

[110] Id.

[111] Id at 765–66 (emphasis omitted). The Court said: "In a sense, then, this case is only one step beyond *Hodel v. Virginia Surface Mining & Recl. Assn.*, . . ." Id at 764. But what it should have said is that PURPA is one step *shy* of the statute in *Hodel*. In the Surface Mining Act, Congress told states to "adopt or be preempted"; in PURPA, Congress told states to "consider adopting or be preempted." Neither is commandeering because states are always free to say no and suffer the preemption, but it is hard to see how having to consider something in order to avoid preemption is more onerous than having to adopt a measure in order to avoid preemption.

thus could permissibly] offer States the choice of regulating that activity according to federal standards or having state law pre-empted by federal regulation."[112] Quoting from *Hodel*, the *New York* Court called such choices Congress gives states to regulate according to federal parameters or face preemption "program[s] of cooperative federalism,"[113] and observed that such arrangements are "replicated in numerous federal statutory schemes,"[114] including the Clean Water Act,[115] the Resource Conservation and Recovery Act of 1976[116] (RCRA), the Alaska National Interest Lands Conservation Act,[117] and the Occupational Safety and Health Act of 1970[118] (OSHA). Under such cooperative programs, "residents of the State retain the ultimate decision as to whether or not the State will" participate in adopting and implementing federal policy objectives.[119]

The *New York* Court more than affirmed *Hodel*; it *applied Hodel* in upholding the part of the Low-Level Radioactive Waste Policy Amendments Act of 1985 by which Congress threatened, via its Commerce Clause power, to deny noncooperating states access to regional compacts and disposal sites. Said the Court:

> Where federal regulation of private activity is within the scope of the Commerce Clause, we have recognized the ability of Congress to offer States the choice of regulating that activity according to federal standards or having state law pre-empted by federal regulation. *Hodel* . . . Th[at] is the choice presented to . . . States [by this aspect of the radioactive waste law]. [Under such circumstances] [t]he affected states are not compelled by Congress to regulate.[120]

As for *FERC*, the *New York* Court indicated that the same reasoning dictated the same result:

---

[112] *New York*, 505 US at 167.

[113] Id.

[114] Id.

[115] 33 USC § 1251 et seq.

[116] 42 USC § 6901 et seq.

[117] 16 USC § 3101 et seq.

[118] 29 USC § 651 et seq. See also Energy Policy Act of 2005 § 216 codified at 16 USC § 824; Roderick M. Hills Jr., *The Political Economy of Cooperative Federalism: Why State Autonomy Makes Sense and "Dual Sovereignty" Doesn't*, 96 Mich L Rev 813, 866–71 (1997) (*"Political Economy"*).

[119] *New York*, 505 US at 168.

[120] Id at 173–74.

As in *Hodel*, the *[FERC]* Court upheld the statute at issue because it did not view the statute as . . . a command. The Court emphasized: "Titles I and III of [the Public Utility Regulatory Policies Act of 1978 (PURPA)] require *only consideration* of federal standards. And if a State has no utilities commission, or simply stops regulating in the field, it need not even entertain the federal proposals."[121]

None of this understanding of *Hodel* or *FERC* was challenged by Justice Alito in *Murphy*; indeed, his opinion expressly reaffirmed the permissibility of cooperative federalism schemes like that represented by *Hodel*: "[T]he federal law [in *Hodel*], which involved what has been called 'cooperative federalism,' by no means commandeered the state legislative process" because Congress "offered States the choice of 'either implement[ing]' the federal program 'or else yield[ing] to a federally administered regulatory program. . . . If a State did not 'wish'" to cooperate, the federal authorities would take over and the state government would not be burdened.[122] *Murphy*'s opinion was similarly embracing of *FERC*, observing that in that case "the federal law in question issued no command to a state legislature."[123]

There are certainly jurists and scholars who seek to expand commandeering doctrine in ill-defined but ambitious ways (which would in turn shrink federal preemption power) in order to give greater effect to state policy choices in areas such as drug criminalization[124] and immigration enforcement.[125] And there is some language in *Murphy* that seems at odds with the very premises of *Hodel* and the inverse incorporation idea more generally.[126] So one cannot reject out of hand the possibility that the *Murphy* Court is dissatisfied with the preexisting contours of commandeering doctrine and would decide *Hodel* differently if it arose today.

But overturning *Hodel* would mean rejecting the conditional preemption part of cooperative federalism in a variety of statutory settings, including those mentioned by *New York*, which would be quite

---

[121] Id at 161–62 (emphasis and final alteration in original).

[122] *Murphy*, 138 S Ct at 1479 (second, third, and final alteration in original).

[123] Id.

[124] See, for example, *Conant v Walters*, 309 F3d 629, 645–46 (9th Cir 2002) (Kozinski, J, concurring).

[125] See generally Vikram David Amar, *A Guided Tour Through the United States v. California Lawsuit Challenging Some of California's "Sanctuary" Policies* (Justia: Verdict, June 1, 2018), available online at https://verdict.justia.com/2018/06/01/a-guided-tour-through-the-united-states-v-california-lawsuit-challenging-some-of-californias-sanctuary-policies.

[126] See Part III.D.2.a.

momentous in the real world. More importantly, eliminating this kind of cooperative federalism would not necessarily serve a states' rights agenda. True, the federal government would be unable to threaten preemption to induce states to take on federal policies and preserve federal enforcement resources. But this route could also push the federal government into preempting state law right out of the gate and imposing one-size-fits-all solutions that ignore local needs. Indeed, in *FERC*, the Court made exactly that point in responding to the dissent's suggestion that Congress's use of the cooperative federalism device ought not to be allowed in PURPA.[127]

2. Is the Court implicitly adding doctrinal requirements for the invocation of conditional preemption that can distinguish Murphy from Hodel/FERC-type cases? If *Hodel/FERC* remain good law, we must ask whether, apart from my focus on the absence of clarity in PASPA, the laws upheld in those cases might differ from PASPA in other relevant respects.[128] To be sure, some scholars do believe that cooperative federalism doctrines need to be augmented by additional judicial requirements if the Court wants to prevent *New York* and *Printz* from becoming empty gestures. For example, Professors Adler and Kreimer have written that "the constitutional permissibility of conditional spending and conditional preemption threaten[] to make the anticommandeering rule of *Printz* and *New York* a practical nullity."[129] Professor Hills has similarly observed: "If there are no [additional] limits on Congress's power to use conditional preemption, then *New York* is a meaningless formality. . . ."[130] But I am not convinced that new requirements, at least new substantive limitations, on conditional preemption are necessarily required.

The two most frequent normative explanations for the anticommandeering rule the Court has offered are antityranny and accountability. The accountability rationale doesn't explain why comman-

---

[127] *FERC*, 456 US at 765 n 29 ("Justice O'Connor's partial dissent's response to this is peculiar. . . . PURPA, of course, *permits* the States to play a continued role in the utilities field, and gives full force to the States' ultimate policy choices. Certainly, it is a curious type of federalism that encourages Congress to pre-empt a field entirely, when its preference is to let the States retain the primary regulatory role.") (emphasis in original).

[128] One reason why answering this question is tricky is that the *Murphy* Court never even tried to explain why PASPA isn't like the laws in those cases. That is, the Court distinguished the Mining Act and the Power Act from the commandeering take-title provision of the Radioactive Waste Act, but it never doubled back to distinguish PASPA from the Mining Act and the Power Act.

[129] Adler and Kreimer, *New Etiquette* at 106 (cited in note 67).

[130] Hills, *Political Economy* (cited in note 118).

deering is bad but conditional preemption and conditional funding are not. All three blur accountability, and perhaps overt commands by the federal government are *easier* to see than are threats to withhold money or aggressively preempt state law. But antityranny can help distinguish commandeering from cooperative federalism. For states to remain effective watchdogs they need (1) credibility in the eyes of the people, (2) time to express themselves,[131] and, relatedly, (3) room to show they can be better than the federal government at fashioning public policy. As long as states have a technical choice to decline offers of cooperation, even at a significant cost, they retain more credibility than they would if the electorate saw them as commandable by the federal government; watchdogs cannot be seen to be lapdogs. Moreover, commandeering in theory can eat up literally all of a legislature's (or executive branch's) time, whereas states can choose—again, even if there are costs—to decline cooperative federalism so as to leave time and resources to express their opposition to the federal government and to pass and enforce laws demonstrating the value they add to the federalist system. While—as Evan Caminker has rightly observed[132]—it is politically unlikely that commandeering would reach the point of consuming all state legislative and executive resources, consider the slippery-slope reasoning of *McCulloch v Maryland*,[133] in some sense the flip-side of commandeering doctrine. Similarly moved by an historical and structural analysis of the Constitution, the *McCulloch* Court held that because the power to tax involves the power to destroy, states could not tax the federal government at all, even if one small tax wouldn't substantially impair federal operations. The power to command also involves the power to destroy in a way that the power to preempt does not quite, and if the federal government can command a little, it can command a lot. Thus, it should not be permitted to command at all.[134]

No doubt preemption—and threats of preemption—can shrink the public policy playing field in which states can deploy their time

---

[131] This need for states to be able to speak out should not be confused with the "expressive" interpretation of commandeering doctrine, which refers to the message the Court (rather than states) is making in this area. See Adler and Kreimer, *New Etiquette* at 133–34 (cited in note 67).

[132] Evan H. Caminker, *Printz, State Sovereignty, and the Limits of Formalism*, 1997 Supreme Court Review 199, 210–11.

[133] 17 US (4 Wheat) 316 (1819).

[134] Compare Lynn A. Baker, *Conditional Spending After Lopez*, 95 Colum L Rev 1911, 1934 (1995) ("an offer is ... different from a mandate").

and resources to show their stuff. But since the modern Court has made clear[135] that there are limits to Congress's substantive enumerated powers, Congress cannot—even in theory—preempt states from undertaking all regulation. Thus, states can, if they want to, stand up to Congress by speaking their minds, and by enacting laws that demonstrate an alternative approach to good government.[136]

To say that additional substantive limits on the invocation of conditional preemption are not necessary is not to say they might not be worth considering. I have my doubts, but it is enough for present purposes to know that commandeering doctrine can exist as a coherent and meaningful body of law even without them. Such a conclusion informs my consideration of possible doctrinal enhancements, to which I now turn.

a) A requirement of good intent. One possible substantive constraint on conditional preemption that some might try to argue explains *Murphy*'s result involves congressional motive. That PASPA's objectives could be rational does not mean that Congress's *intent* in the sports-gambling arena is necessarily legitimate, insofar as Congress might be seen to be unfairly trying to foist[137] onto states the costs of prohibiting sports gambling. I raise this possibility largely because of the pejorative way the *Murphy* Court characterized § 3702(2)—the part of PASPA that makes it unlawful under federal law for private parties to engage in sports gambling, but only if the gambling is undertaken "pursuant to state law." The Court characterized Congress's goal of having "private conduct violate[] federal law only if it is permitted by state law"[138] as "strange,"[139] "weird,"[140] "[in]coherent,"[141] and "perverse."[142] *Murphy*'s critical discussion of this notion occurred in the severability section and not in the Court's dis-

---

[135] See, for example, *United States v Lopez*, 514 US 549 (1995); *United States v Morrison*, 529 US 598 (2000).

[136] The sanctuary jurisdiction movement discussed in Part IV may be a good illustration of that.

[137] See *Curb Your Enthusiasm: Foisted!*, season nine, episode 1 (episode aired Oct 1, 2017).

[138] *Murphy*, 138 S Ct at 1483.

[139] Id.

[140] Id at 1484.

[141] Id at 1483.

[142] *Murphy*, 138 S Ct at 1483. See also *Murphy* Oral Argument at 38 (cited in note 3) (during oral argument, Chief Justice Roberts stated that this was "a very odd way to phrase something").

cussion of why PASPA constitutes commandeering, but the feature
of § 3702(2) the Court seemed to find troubling would exist regardless of whether § 3702(1) were upheld or struck down; even if the
Court found that PASPA's ban on state authorization did *not* amount
to commandeering, under PASPA's § 3702(2) "private conduct violates federal law only if it is permitted by state law." If that is a strange,
weird, incoherent, or perverse aspect of PASPA, the problem exists no matter how narrowly or broadly one defines "authorize" in
§ 3702(1).

But if Congress's instinct to use inverse incorporation (as I have
defined it) in PASPA is illegitimate, so too would it be illegitimate
in *Hodel* (and *FERC* too). In *Hodel*, private conduct would violate
federal law (a permanent federal program) only if it were permitted
by state law (which has turned down the federal offer to adopt an
acceptable permanent state program).[143] From one vantage point, the
federal government might be seen to be "using" states. But from
another, states are given a right of first refusal. The federal government could have gone straight ahead and displaced state law, but it
wanted to see if the states would choose to be involved—and be
empowered—so that local conditions and needs might get more
nuanced attention. That's why the Court found *Hodel*'s and *FERC*'s
schemes to be permissible, in those cases themselves, and then again
in *New York* and in *Murphy*. And in *FERC* the Court was candid in
acknowledging that Congress's actions in this realm are "designed to
induce state action."[144] So the federal desire to obtain a benefit can't
make a deal inherently illicit, since both parties are trying to get
something from the other.

Yet there is an aspect of PASPA that might be thought to distinguish it from the statute in *Hodel*, at least. In *Hodel*, private parties
were going to be regulated pursuant to a set of predetermined federal
environmental policies whether the states or the federal authorities

---

[143] Many other statutes operate the same way. For example, in the Clean Water Act, the EPA
provides states with substantial guidance in the drafting of water-quality standards. See generally
33 USC § 1251 et seq (setting forth model water-quality standards). Moreover, 33 USC § 1313
requires, inter alia, that state authorities periodically review water-quality standards and secure
the EPA's approval of any revisions in the standards. If the EPA recommends changes to the
standards and a state fails to comply with that recommendation, the Act authorizes the EPA to
promulgate water-quality standards for the state. 33 USC § 1313(c). See also *Arkansas v
Oklahoma*, 503 US 91 (1992).

[144] *FERC*, 456 US at 766.

would be the ones implementing those policies. While enforcement priorities and discretion would differ, the essential policy being implemented wouldn't change.

What is unusual about PASPA (even as the federal government sought to understand it) is that if states repeal their sports-gambling regulations entirely (as is their right), there arises a regulatory vacuum. This is because, under PASPA, a complete repeal by a state does not constitute impermissible discrimination or authorization, and accordingly no private activity is made unlawful under federal law.[145] How is it legitimate for Congress to enact legislation that indicates a preference or at least a tolerance for complete state prohibition of sports gambling, and that steps in to fill a regulatory void if states impermissibly discriminate against and in favor of some persons with regard to sports gambling, but that leaves the field completely unregulated if states pull out altogether?[146] Can the oddity of such a scheme indicate that Congress is simply "playing chicken" with the states to strong-arm them into maintaining their absolute (or near absolute) prohibitions? And wouldn't Congress be acting disingenuously to suggest that it prefers an absence of regulation to selective state prohibition?

---

[145] A complete regulatory vacuum could arise if a state forthrightly repealed all its sports-gambling prohibitions or if a state undertook a selective repeal that violates PASPA and—in response to an injunction prohibiting discriminatory enforcement—decided not to enforce any of its remaining prohibitions. While the presence of a regulatory vacuum ought not by itself doom PASPA, it is possible that there is less of a regulatory vacuum under PASPA than New Jersey and the Court seemed to assume. The NCAA at argument suggested—but refrained from actually arguing—that "pursuant to" may be broader than "authorized by" state law, such that a complete repeal by a state could trigger a full-blown federal prohibition of sports gambling in that state. See *Murphy* Oral Argument at 43 (cited in note 3). New Jersey and the federal government, by contrast, were clear in their views that "pursuant to" state law referred back to § 3702(1)'s prohibition on state authorization, licensing, etc., but would not cover state decisions to deregulate entirely. See id at 15–16 (New Jersey stating that "[s]ubsection 2 is another side of the same coin because subsection 2 says pursuant to law. The law that's referred to in subsection 1 we say is something that the states can do and . . . Congress, if Congress chose to prevent it, [ ] would be unconstitutional."); id at 62–64 (United States conceding that complete state repeal would lead to sports-gambling schemes being unregulated under both state and federal law, at least for the time being). The NCAA's musing that "pursuant to" might include "unregulated by" seems like a tough sell. A much more natural reading would seem to link the "pursuant to" language to the specific language of § 3702(1). Moreover, the NCAA's suggestion may raise more problems for PASPA than it solves: because it is certainly not clear that "pursuant to" is broader than the state actions referred to in § 3702(1), the essential flaw in PASPA—its failure to put states on notice of what they can and cannot do that will then trigger the application of preemptive federal law—would remain, and indeed might be exacerbated.

[146] At argument Justices seemed puzzled by this feature of a vacuum. See *Murphy* Oral Argument at 60, 62–63, 65–66 (cited in note 3).

It is conceivable that this seeming oddity—and not the more generic idea that federal law applies where state law does not—is what
troubled the Court and what inclined it to be dubious of PASPA .[147]
But unlike a concern over statutory clarity, concern about Congress's
intent in this arena would be factually misplaced and doctrinally
detrimental, such that without more explanation from the Court, I
am disinclined to believe that is what was driving the Court's bottom
line. For starters, what would "disingenuous" even mean in this setting? As noted above, both parties in a deal are always trying to get
concessions from the other side. Perhaps (but only perhaps) Congress was "bluffing" when it enacted PASPA, in that it would not
prefer an unregulated world to a world in which states discriminate in
favor of certain gambling operators. But perhaps also states were
playing chicken when they gave information to Congress prior to
PASPA about the kind of deal they might accept—they may not have
been interested in discriminating in favor of certain gambling operators and would have refrained from such discrimination whether
or not the federal government stayed out of the field.

Second, the Court doesn't seem to police bluffing or insist on sincerity in the conditional spending context. For example, in the seminal

---

[147] A related possibility is that the Court was troubled by the fact that if a state repealed all
regulation of sports gambling, private actors in the state would be unregulated but the state
would, under PASPA, be treated worse because it could not operate a gambling scheme itself.
But while the Court, in its severability analysis, found "unclear what might justify such
disparate treatment," *Murphy*, 138 S Ct at 1483, the Court never said that such differential
treatment would be unconstitutional. New Jersey, of course, did not seek to repeal all of its
sports-gambling prohibitions, so it could not itself claim to be victimized in this respect.
Moreover, even if treating states worse than private parties under federal law in some
circumstances violates federalism norms in the Constitution, and even if that bothered the
Court, there is no language in the opinion suggesting how such a scheme would amount
to "commandeering of state legislative processes"—the central vice the Court found in
PASPA—when the state's real complaint would be that it is blocked from engaging in non-
legislative activities (i.e., operating a gambling scheme).

Perhaps the possibility of disparate treatment against states is one reason why the Court felt it
could not embrace the federal government's interpretation of PASPA, but the Court never
suggested so. Indeed, to the extent that the Court elaborated on any constitutional difficulty in
prohibiting states from themselves participating in gambling schemes, the Court did so, again,
in terms of absence of clarity: "The line between authorization, licensing and operation, on the
one hand, and sponsorship and promotion, on the other, is too uncertain. It is unlikely that
Congress would have wanted to prohibit such an ill-defined category of state conduct." Murphy,
138 S Ct at 1483. Finally, if the Court's true concern was with PASPA's potential disparate
treatment against states, the majority would have had to more fully engage the NCAA's suggestion that a complete repeal by a state would have made all private sports gambling illegal
under federal law, see note 145, a reading that would diminish if not eliminate any disparate
treatment against states.

funding case of *South Dakota v Dole*,[148] it may well have been that Congress would prefer to fund highway construction rather than not, even if states—for whatever reason[149]—were reluctant to raise their drinking ages to twenty-one. (In the same vein, states might have been willing to raise their drinking ages to twenty-five to get the highway funding, but Congress sold out too cheaply.) Again, in any deal setting, each side is shrewdly trying to get whatever it can.

Indeed, if we were worried about sincerity in cooperative federalism, spending would likely be an area where we should impose a sincerity requirement, because in that realm we acknowledge that Congress often uses money to accomplish things it isn't otherwise permitted to do. As the Court observed in *FERC*, Congress in conditional spending can be trying to get states to do its bidding "in areas that otherwise would be beyond Congress' regulatory authority."[150] If that motive isn't illicit, it's hard to see what should be.

On top of all that, in *Murphy* itself, there is no particular reason to think Congress was being insincere. Remember, as *Hodel* itself notes, that Congress can displace state regulation even when there is no affirmative federal regulatory scheme to replace it (a kind of so-called "field preemption"). Sometimes Congress wants an area of commercial activity to remain unregulated. That is likely not true with respect to sports gambling, but perhaps if states choose to pull out altogether, Congress needs some time to craft a substitute national regulatory scheme.[151] If Congress can say "regulate according to these policies otherwise we will," it can also say "regulate according to these policies or we will figure out our next steps." For example, in *New York v United States*, the Court cited instances like the Clean Water Act, under which if states refuse to do what the federal government asked, federal regulatory entities are then empowered to impose rules of their own, but the specific content of the rules is not known at the time states choose whether to partner.[152] And in *FERC*, the Court noted even more overtly that the situation states confronted was one in which Congress had "failed to provide an alter-

---

[148] 483 US 203 (1987).

[149] For example, a state constitution might have a prohibition on age discrimination.

[150] *FERC*, 456 US at 766.

[151] See *Murphy* Oral Argument at 64 (cited in note 3) (United States suggesting that "if states start lifting their prohibitions as a whole, ... Congress may well want to revisit that.").

[152] See Clean Water Act, 33 USC § 1251 et seq.

native regulatory mechanism to police the area in the event of state default."[153]

Consider also the important reality that in the sports-gambling realm—as in every other regulatory arena—Congress has more than one objective. To be sure, keeping sports gambling from getting out of hand is one important objective, and coming up with the right national approach might take time and study. But another important congressional objective is to make sure the wrong actors aren't controlling sports-gambling operations. Congress may, for historical reasons among others, distrust states to do the picking and choosing. Challengers of PASPA say the federal government has not adopted a policy other than trying to force states to do its bidding,[154] but under the United States's reading, PASPA does embody a coherent policy—the prohibition of certain kinds of favoritism by states.[155] This second objective may be sufficiently strong that Congress prefers a (temporarily) unregulated world to one that remains regulated but in which states are selecting winners and losers. To put things more formally, Congress's first choice might be state prohibition without selective exceptions, coupled with state enforcement. Its second choice might be state withdrawal from the field with the possibility of future comprehensive federal regulation. And its least preferred policy choice might be to permit states to pick and choose. If this accurately explains Congress's rank order of preferences, having federal law kick in only in the third scenario, when and to the extent that a state impermissibly discriminates, makes sense. Perhaps it would have been wiser for Congress to have provided more federal regulation of private activity that would spring into effect if a state withdrew altogether, but the scheme I describe above—which corresponds to the federal government's reading of PASPA—is certainly not irrational and does not necessarily reflect an improper motive.[156]

---

[153] *FERC*, 456 US at 766.

[154] See *Murphy* Oral Argument at 21 (cited in note 3). See also id at 54 (United States characterizing New Jersey's position to be that there is "no federal policy").

[155] See id at 55 (United States observing that "States are to take their hands off of that particular part of interstate commerce").

[156] This is not to deny that Congress might have wanted to discourage states from pulling out altogether by creating a temporary vacuum if they were to do so. But in all cooperative federalism settings, Congress is trying to encourage states to help it accomplish federal objectives—it's a deal, not a giveaway. Another possible bad motive concerns an impermissible federal intent to stifle state expression—the federal government can block what states do, but not what message states try to send. The Court alluded to this issue in discussing the

b) A requirement of nonadhesion. Perhaps the *Murphy* Court felt the problem was not that what Congress was trying to do was bad, but that, as a substantive matter, the options facing the states do not constitute a true choice, in a way that differentiates this case from *Hodel* or *FERC*.[157] The notion would be that forcing states that want to permit more sports gambling to repeal their laws altogether, rather than being able to selectively deregulate, puts states in an untenable position, since completely unregulated sports gambling poses many dangers.

There is no modern Supreme Court case squarely holding that a deal offered by Congress to states is invalid simply because it is too adhesive. Some folks seem to read the Medicaid portion of *National Federation of Independent Business v Sebelius*[158] to mean that if a particular deal Congress offers in fact places too much pressure on state fiscs, then states needn't live up to the agreement.[159] And the Court's mention of how the Medicaid expansion placed a "gun" to the states' heads may contribute to that impression.[160] But a careful reading of *Sebelius* indicates that a sufficient reason Obamacare was deemed coercive was that Congress was imposing new terms onto a pre-existing deal. (Seeking to enforce terms not agreed upon is analytically coercive regardless of the amount of money at stake.) That is, any federal coercion present was a function of a lack of meaningful notice to, and thus consent by, the states, not necessarily a function of

---

"promot[ion]" and "advertis[ing]" provisions of PASPA. But the Court did not find any part of PASPA (much less the whole statute) unconstitutional on the ground that it impermissibly sought to stifle state speech, and certainly never linked any censorial concern with the determination that the words "authorize" and "license" amounted to impermissible commandeering.

[157] See *Murphy* Oral Argument at 62 (cited in note 3) (Chief Justice Roberts telling United States "that's not a real choice").

[158] 567 US 519 (2012).

[159] Compare James F. Blumstein, *Enforcing Limits on the Affordable Care Act's Mandated Medicaid Expansion: The Coercion Principle and the Clear Notice Rule*, 2012 Cato S Ct Rev 67, 78 ("The Court in *NFIB*, for the first time, held that legal, judicially enforceable [substantive] limits on such federal power exist and applied those limits to invalidate the ACA's expanded Medicaid [statute]."); see also Samuel R. Bagenstos, *The Anti-Leveraging Principle and the Spending Clause after NFIB*, 101 Georgetown L J 861, 870 (2013) (arguing that economic duress is part of what accounts for the *Sebelius* result) ("*Anti-Leveraging Principle*"); *Sebelius*, 567 US at 625–26 (Ginsburg, J, concurring in part and dissenting in part) (asserting that one of the "premises" on which Chief Justice Roberts's opinion "rests" is that "the threatened loss of funding is so large").

[160] *Sebelius*, 567 US at 581.

any substantive unfairness that enforcing the terms of an agreed-upon deal would visit upon the states.

In holding that Congress could not discontinue Medicaid funding to states that were unwilling to cover additional classes of persons, the Court had to confront the federal government's argument that states agreed when they joined Medicaid that Congress would have latitude to make changes to the funding scheme.[161] Such an argument, if successful, would have defeated the states' challenge. Tellingly, Chief Justice Roberts[162] at that point did *not* say that agreement by states in 1965 could not cure a problem of undue economic pressure in 2011. Instead, he said states were never given notice in 1965 of the kinds of changes involved in Obamacare. This suggests that had there been clear notice that the coverage requirements might expand greatly within the program, states would have to live with the deal they struck. He characterized Medicaid as one continuing program in which the states had essentially been told they would receive money on an ongoing basis, subject to minor coverage and funding modifications, until the program was formally repealed. He thus identified the problem with Obamacare's expansion of Medicaid as the federal government's having "surpris[ed] participating States with post-acceptance or 'retroactive' conditions. . . . A State could hardly anticipate that Congress's reservation [in the original Medicaid Act] of the right to 'alter' or 'amend' the Medicaid program included the power to transform it so dramatically."[163]

Some analysts[164] (and dissenting Justice Ginsburg[165]) are inclined to think that while absence of notice was an ingredient in Chief Justice Roberts's analysis, it was not sufficient, and that the magnitude of state reliance was also an essential factor in the outcome of the case. But absence of notice alone can fully justify Chief Justice Roberts's bottom line in *Sebelius*, just as it explains the outcome in

---

[161] Id at 582–84 ("[T]he Government claims that the Medicaid expansion is properly viewed merely as a modification of the existing program because the States agreed that Congress could change the terms of Medicaid when they signed on in the first place.").

[162] His opinion is the key one. See Bagenstos, *Anti-Leveraging Principle* at 867 (cited in note 159).

[163] *Sebelius*, 567 US at 584. See also 42 USC § 1304 (reserving, in the original Medicaid Act, Congress's right to "alter, amend or repeal any provision").

[164] See, for example, Bagenstos, *Anti-Leveraging Principle* at 890–91 (cited in note 159).

[165] See *Sebelius*, 567 US at 625–42 (Ginsburg, J, concurring in part and dissenting in part) (identifying lack of notice as a "premise" of Chief Justice Roberts's opinion but suggesting reliance by the states was also necessary to the majority's analysis).

other cases, like *Pennhurst State School and Hospital v Halderman*,[166] where the economic stakes were not very large but the absence of notice nonetheless freed states of having to comply with federally imposed conditions. Whether in *Sebelius* the Chief's belief "that states could not [or should not] have anticipated such a fundamental change is [factually] unpersuasive," and whether his understanding of the Medicaid deal is accurate "as a positive matter … [or] as a normative matter,"[167] that was how Chief Justice Roberts understood the bargain. And any mistake of fact on his part, while unfortunate, does not upend federalism doctrine in the way a broader reading of *Sebelius* (or *Murphy*, for that matter) would.

My notice-based reading of *Sebelius* is buttressed significantly by the fact that Chief Justice Roberts apparently conceded Justice Ginsburg's claim that Congress could have lawfully repealed Medicaid and replaced it with Obamacare. Chief Justice Roberts replied to that assertion not by saying that repeal today would be unconstitutional, but only that it would be politically difficult.[168] Yet repeal/replace would impose the same substantive duress on states—the same "gun" to their heads—as did Obamacare. The only legal difference between the two is that Congress in the original Medicaid act reserved for itself the right to "repeal … any provision." While the kind of "alter[ations]" and "amend[ments]" Congress and the states had in mind in 1965 may be open to debate, "repeal" is more textually straightforward.

None of this is to say that the large "amount-in-controversy" (the size of the "gun," so to speak) was not germane to Chief Justice Roberts's analysis. But, in context, his mention of the financial pressure and reliance under which states were operating could (and I think should) be understood simply as a relevant observation to help establish that Obamacare wasn't the kind of relatively minor "amendment" or "alteration" of the ongoing program as to which states had been put on notice in 1965 that Congress was empowered to make.

In the future the Court might squarely hold that a discontinuation of federal funding violates the conditional funding doctrine even though clear notice was given to states at the relevant time period— simply because the economic harm to states would be too large. But

---

[166] 451 US 1 (1981),

[167] Bagenstos, *Anti-Leveraging Principle* at 890–91 (cited in note 159).

[168] *Sebelius*, 567 US at 583 n 14.

Sebelius (in keeping with prior cases like *Pennhurst*) can be understood simply in terms of inadequate notice.

The fact that the Court up until now has not invalidated a deal offered by Congress on substantive unfairness grounds does not foreclose the possibility that the *Murphy* Court was in fact motivated by a concern that in PASPA states were being presented with a Hobson's choice. But the Court did not talk in those terms. And the substantive unfairness of PASPA's deal would be a poor basis on which to defend *Murphy*. Remember that states, if they comply with PASPA's nondiscrimination limitations, retain important discretionary enforcement discretion,[169] and also the power to make some substantive decisions (because under the federal government's reading of PASPA some decisions about age and other bases for discrimination remain in state hands). Moreover, by abiding by PASPA, a state keeps the federal government out of the business of regulating sports gambling in the state. So the deal is not entirely one-sided.[170]

On top of all this, Congress, like many states, may not prefer a completely unregulated sports-gambling market in the long term. Nor may the federal government want to bear the full cost of enforcement.[171] So states have leverage too—they can repeal their prohibitions altogether, and feel reasonably comfortable that some new regulatory arrangement that might take better account of their desires may be adopted.

More fundamentally, in keeping with preemption doctrine generally, *Hodel* itself makes clear that states can be forced by the specter of preemption to make policy choices they'd rather avoid: in rejecting the notion that cooperative federalism violates the Tenth Amendment when applied to traditional police power arenas like land use, the Court reminded that "although such Congressional enactments obviously curtail or prohibit the States' prerogatives to make legis-

---

[169] See *Murphy* Oral Argument at 22–25 (cited in note 3) (Justice Ginsburg asked New Jersey: "[M]ay I just ask you to qualify . . . 'must enforce'? Because the Third Circuit . . . said each state is free to decide how much of a law enforcement priority it wants to make of sports gambling." Justice Sotomayor also asked: "Does the injunction tell the governor that he has to enforce this law? . . . I don't see it anywhere telling the governor he has to enforce these prohibitions.").

[170] See id at 49–51 (NCAA commenting on the federalism virtues of flexibility: "If you want to regulate this in 46 different ways, have at it," and "rather than have a one-size-fits-all federal felony where everybody's going to get the same exact sentence, hav[e] a system where . . . one state makes it a misdemeanor, another makes it a felony").

[171] See note 156 and accompanying text.

lative choices respecting subjects the States may consider important, the Supremacy Clause permits no other result."[172] In *New York v United States*, for example, had Congress told states it would preempt them altogether from the field of nuclear waste regulation if they did not deal—consistently with federal objectives—with the waste generated within their boundaries, many states would have felt pressured and constrained. But such is the nature of federal supremacy over certain subject matters.

This was made all the more explicit in *FERC*, where the Court rejected Justice O'Connor's dissenting notion that the choice was substantively too difficult for states. As the majority wrote emphatically:

> We recognize ... that the choice put to the States—that of either abandoning regulation of the field altogether or considering the federal standards—may be a difficult one. And that is particularly true when Congress, as is the case here, has failed to provide an alternative regulatory mechanism to police the area in the event of state default. Yet ... it cannot be constitutionally determinative that the federal regulation is likely to move the States to act in a given way, or even to "coerc[e] the States" into assuming a regulatory role ... [While] it may be unlikely that the States will or easily can abandon regulation of public utilities to avoid PURPA's requirements. ... [T]his does not change the constitutional analysis.[173]

It would be hard to conclude the deal offered in PASPA was sharper than those in *Hodel* and *FERC*—land-use preemption and a threat of a utility regulation vacuum are certainly not child's play.

None of this means that all deals offered in the name of cooperative federalism are necessarily fair game. For example, suppose Congress said: "If you selectively (de)regulate sports gambling, you are preempted from regulating employment discrimination." Many would be troubled by the lack of a logical relationship between the cooperation the federal government is seeking, and the sanction for noncooperation. In the conditional spending arena, the Court has insisted upon a nexus between the condition Congress attaches to the use of the federal funds and the purpose for which the funds are being expended in the first place.[174] Without such a nexus, as the Court observed in *New York*, Congress could too easily use spending to

---

[172] *Hodel*, 452 US at 290.

[173] *FERC*, 456 US at 766–67 (first alteration in original, citations omitted).

[174] See *Dole*, 483 US at 207.

accomplish objectives not within Article I's enumerated powers.[175] This could be a concern in conditional preemption as well: Imagine that Congress threatened to preempt employment regulation unless states made it a crime to possess a gun near a school. And even where, as in my example of employment regulation and gaming regulation, Congress enjoys the unilateral power to preempt both the area in which it seeks state involvement and the area in which it threatens to preempt, a nexus requirement may be worth considering. Scholars have pointed out analytic challenges in constructing and implementing a germaneness requirement,[176] but these may be surmountable.[177] The Court has yet to insist on a nexus in conditional preemption, but in any event such a nexus requirement would be satisfied by PASPA.

E. A CLARITY-BASED READING OF MURPHY WOULD NOT UNFAIRLY BURDEN CONGRESS NOR REQUIRE ABANDONMENT OF EARLIER COURT DECISIONS

Requiring Congress to articulate the terms of a deal clearly is not the same thing as imposing a "Simon says" rule requiring particular words to be used, something the *Murphy* Court seemed uninterested in doing. A cursory reading of *Murphy* might lead one to think that what was problematic to the Court about PASPA is § 3702(1)'s making it "unlawful" for a state to authorize sports gambling. If this "unlawful" language were construed to mean that a state legislature's act of passing such a measure was itself a violation of federal law—a violation that could be enjoined or punished—rather than to mean (as it does) only that such a state legislative enactment is not legally valid or enforceable, federalism values would indeed be violated. And perhaps Congress should—out of respect for the communicative function of state legislatures—generally draft its preemption laws in terms of validity and enforceability, rather than in terms of the (un)lawfulness of state policy, even if we all know that "unlawful" means not that a statute cannot be passed but only that it cannot be en-

---

[175] Imagine, for example, a law conditioning all state social-services funding on states' making it a crime to possess a gun near a school.

[176] See Adler and Kreimer, *New Etiquette* at 105 (cited in note 67).

[177] The Court seeks to deal with these challenges in, for example, the Takings cases of *Nollan v Cal. Coastal Commission*, 483 US 825 (1987), and *Dolan v City of Tigard*, 512 US 374 (1994).

forced.[178] But the *Murphy* Court does not appear to believe that the particular phrasing of any law violates federalism—it said as much in citing approvingly to *Morales v TWA*.[179] In *Morales*, the Court upheld a statute beginning with the words "[N]o State . . . shall enact . . . any law . . . "—words that direct/constrain legislative activity even more overtly than Congress's use of "unlawful" does in PASPA.[180] And yet, in discussing *Morales*, the *Murphy* Court observed that effects—not particular formulations—determine permissible preemption.[181]

A clarity requirement also doesn't mean that Congress must act with hyper-specificity, or that states can be subjected to no uncertainty about how their decisions will interact with federal regulatory power. In *Hodel*, for example, there was a federal approval requirement, and so states might be disappointed to put in effort only to be rejected. But they were put on notice that such rejection was possible, and more importantly the statute laid out the procedures, timelines, and criteria for federal approval or rejection.[182] In *FERC*, the federal standards were clear, and so too were the requirements of how and when they should be considered.[183] And the same is true for the other statutes cited in *New York* as examples of permissible conditional preemption. In PASPA itself, if Congress had in mind the particular kinds of selective regulatory decisions it wanted states to avoid mak-

---

[178] Compare *Tenney v Brandhove*, 341 US 367 (1951) (discussing limits on enjoining legislatures).

[179] *Murphy*, 138 S Ct at 1480, citing *Morales v TWA*, 504 US 374 (1992).

[180] Id. Indeed, the words in PASPA found to constitute commandeering—that neither a "State" nor its "subdivision[s]" may "authorize" or "license"—do not speak to legislative action in particular, but are more naturally read to constrain only what a state does by way of enforcement, not what it says by way of enactment. Nowhere does the *Murphy* opinion suggest PASPA's words target state legislatures per se.

[181] Id. In the same vein, one might be tempted to think the popular title of PASPA ("An Act to Prohibit Gambling Under State Law") "fak[ed] out" the Court and led it to find commandeering where none existed, cf. *Clinton v City of New York*, 524 US 417, 468 (1998) (Scalia, J, dissenting), yet the *Murphy* Court didn't seem to make anything of the title.

[182] See *Hodel*, 452 US at 271–72 ("The proposed program must demonstrate that the state legislature has enacted laws implementing the environmental protection standards established by the Act and accompanying regulations, and that the State has administrative and technical ability to enforce these standards. The Secretary must approve or disapprove each such program in accordance with time schedules and procedures established by §§ 503(b)(c).") (citations omitted).

[183] *FERC*, 456 US at 746–47 ("Section 111(d) of the Act . . . requires each state regulatory authority and nonregulated utility to consider the use of six different approaches to structuring rates. . . . The Act directed each state authority and nonregulated utility to consider these factors not later than two years after PURPA's enactment, that is, by November 8, 1980, and provided that the authority or utility by November 9, 1981, was to have made a decision whether to adopt the standards.").

ing, it could and should have laid them out without use of the inscrutable "authorize" language.

The case in the past two decades that most arguably involved insufficiently clear conditional preemption is *EPA v EME Homer City Generation*.[184] The Clean Air Act[185] (CAA) says that states must submit to the EPA State Implementation Plans (SIPs) that meet certain requirements within three years after National Ambient Air Quality Standards (NAAQS) are issued, and the EPA then must decide whether a state's SIP is adequate. If no adequate SIP is submitted, the EPA is directed to come up with a Federal Implementation Plan (FIP). Proper SIPs are supposed to comply with the so-called Good Neighbor policy, which requires states to have a plan to avoid downwind pollution. States argued that in order to submit acceptable SIPs, they needed guidance from EPA about how much downwind pollution sources in their respective states were allowed to generate. The lower court agreed, saying that "[e]xpecting any one State to develop a 'comprehensive solution' to the 'collective problem' of interstate air pollution without first receiving EPA's guidance was ... 'set[ting] the States up to fail.'"[186] The Supreme Court disagreed, saying that no matter how sensible it might be to give states federal guidance before states had to submit their SIPs, the duties and timelines for states were clear in the Act, and a reviewing court's "task is to apply the text [of the statute], not to improve upon it."[187] Quoting from a dissenting judge below, the Court observed that "the Act does not require EPA to furnish upwind States with information of any kind about their good neighbor obligations before a FIP issues. Instead, a SIP's failure to satisfy the Good Neighbor Provision, without more, triggers EPA's obligation to issue a federal plan within two years."[188]

Justice Scalia (joined by Justice Thomas) dissented, accusing the "majority [of] reliev[ing] EPA of any obligation to announce novel interpretations of the Good Neighbor Provision before the States must submit plans that are required to comply with those interpre-

---

[184] 572 US 489 (2014).

[185] 42 USC § 7401.

[186] *Homer*, 572 US at 508 (final alteration in original), quoting *EME Homer City Generation v EPA*, 696 F3d 7, 36–37 (DC Cir 2012).

[187] Id at 508–9 (alteration in original).

[188] Id at 509 (citation omitted), citing *EME Homer City Generation v EPA*, 696 F3d at 47 (Rogers, J, dissenting).

tations."[189] He explained: "[It is unfair to require private] parties to divine the agency's interpretations in advance or else be held liable when the agency announces its interpretations for the first time. . . . That principle applies *a fortiori* to a regulatory regime that rests on principles of cooperative federalism."[190]

To the extent that *Murphy* implicitly overrules any prior ruling, it would not be *Hodel* or *FERC* or any of the cases that recognize broad preemption powers, but *Homer*, a case mentioned neither by the Court nor by the petitioners' or respondents' briefs. But if one might want to try to reconcile *Murphy* and *Homer*, there are three possible arguments to make—each of which has some force but none of which is fully persuasive. First, the *Homer* case was exclusively argued in statutory interpretation terms. No one raised a constitutional objection, and while Justice Scalia used the word "commandeer" in his critique of the majority's reasoning,[191] he did not argue that the CAA violated the Constitution. By contrast, in *Murphy*, the entire conversation is on whether PASPA amounts to an unconstitutional commandeering, and the statutory interpretation question arises in the context of that constitutional inquiry. Second, in the CAA states are put on notice that the EPA can reject their SIPs— states must factor that possibility into whether they think it is worth their time to go through the SIP process. By contrast, PASPA does not contemplate any federal approval of state actions; the fact that the PASPA deal is posed to states in static rather than dynamic terms might affect instincts about what states should be able to reasonably count on. Third, with regard to any SIP in question, the federal government didn't give any particular (and arguably misleading) guidance on which the state might have based its actions and wasted its time. In *Murphy*, the federal government's representation in the *Christie I* litigation that "partial repeals" were permissible served to underscore the vagueness of the term "authorize," and seemed to be of equitable relevance to the Court.[192]

One potentially pedantic question remains. As I have noted earlier, the aspect of *Murphy* that cries out perhaps most loudly for explanation is Justice Alito's view that PASPA constitutes commandeer-

---

[189] Id at 525 (Scalia, J, dissenting).

[190] *Homer*, 572 US at 539 (Scalia, J, dissenting).

[191] Id at 538.

[192] See Part III.C.

ing in spite of the federal government's statutory reading.[193] The United States, it will be recalled, invoked *Ashwander*[194] avoidance principles to construe PASPA so as to steer clear of the commandeering problem that arises if PASPA prohibits complete repeals. To reach and justify its outcome, the *Murphy* majority had to have a reason for deciding that *Ashwander* doesn't save PASPA. Does the account of *Murphy* I offer here—focusing on Congress's failure to adequately lay out the terms of conditional preemption—explain why the federal government's invocation of *Ashwander* was unavailing? Technically, yes, in the sense that perhaps the United States's reading was the best one to adopt to steer clear of a commandeering issue, but not one that the Court was permitted to embrace because this reading would create its own distinct federalism problems due to lack of clarity.[195] And once the federal government's reading is off the table, we are back to New Jersey's interpretation of the statute—one that prohibits even complete repeal—that raises the insurmountable commandeering problems.

My interpretation of *Murphy* may not square entirely with the Court's statement that "*even if the law could be interpreted as respondents and the United States suggest, it would still violate the anticommandeering principle.*"[196] But note that "could be" is not the same as "is." Perhaps the Court was intimating that the federal government's interpretation "could be" embraced but for another problem (like vagueness), so it can't be. Certainly it would have been better had the Court said: "Even if the respondents and the United States are right about what PASPA, best read, means, we cannot embrace that reading because it was not clearly articulated by Congress." In any event, my approach explains *Murphy*'s result and most if not all of its language. And I'm not sure anyone can make sense of every sentence the *Murphy* Court uttered, an ironic reality for an opinion that is itself best read to be about Congress's unclarity.

---

[193] See text following note 72.

[194] *Ashwander v Tenn. Valley Authority*, 297 US 288 (1936).

[195] In the Spending Clause arena, for example, we do not allow the federal government to cure constitutionally vague conditions imposed by Congress—as in *Pennhurst* or *Sebelius*—by advancing a more well-defined interpretation of the conditions coupled with an invocation of *Ashwander*.

[196] *Murphy*, 138 S Ct at 1475 (emphasis added).

IV. Implications for Commandeering Doctrine Generally

Many Court watchers were interested in *Murphy* because of other arenas in which states are challenging federal laws on anticommandeering grounds, especially in the so-called "sanctuary" jurisdiction setting, but also others.[197] The sanctuary jurisdiction clashes with the federal government typically involve state executive officials rather than state legislatures, so *Printz*—rather than *New York v United States*—is the key precedent. But *Printz* itself is so firmly premised on *New York* that any development concerning the meaning and vitality of *New York* is important. And in *Murphy* seven Justices, including two who might have been expected to join the dissenters in *New York* itself,[198] reaffirmed *New York*'s teachings.

And in so doing, the Court once again made clear, in the middle of its justifications for the prohibition on commandeering, that "the anticommandeering rule promotes political accountability,"[199] preventing states from being improperly blamed for unpopular policies that in reality are dictated by federal actors. As I mention above, like many other scholars, I have generally been unconvinced by the accountability rationale, primarily because it fails to adequately explain why conditional funding and conditional preemption are permitted.[200]

For me, that antityranny explanation has always carried more weight, but if accountability remains the (or even a) touchstone, this has implications for the current debate and litigation over so-called "sanctuary" jurisdictions. One of the specific issues in the multiple lawsuits between the federal government and states/cities involves 8 USC § 1373, which says in pertinent part that a "... State, or local

---

[197] See, for example, Mark Brnovich, *Betting on Federalism: Murphy v. NCAA and the Future of Sports Gambling*, 2018 Cato S Ct Rev 247, 262–67; Kimberly Strawbridge Robinson, *Christie Case Could Topple Sanctuary Cities, Marijuana Laws* (Bloomberg BNA, Nov 29, 2017), online at https://www.bna.com/christie-case-topple-n73014472637/); *Brackeen v Zinke*, 2018 WL 4927908 (ND Tex).

[198] Some analysts might speculate that Justices Breyer and Kagan joined *Murphy* in order to be able to more easily argue for protection of sanctuary jurisdictions.

[199] *Murphy*, 138 S Ct at 1477.

[200] All three blur accountability lines, and I've seen no convincing empirical work suggesting that voters are more confused by commandeering than by federal monies or threatened federal preemption. Indeed, it would seem easier for state officials to explain—"they forced us to do it"—in commandeering settings than to explain why the money was too much to turn down, especially since voters think governments (including state governments) can and should tighten their belts anyway.

government entity or official may not prohibit, or in any way restrict, any government entity or official from [maintaining,] sending to, or receiving from, [federal immigration authorities] information regarding the citizenship or immigration status, lawful or unlawful, of any individual."[201] In short, the statute prevents a state or local government from having a policy or practice that forbids maintaining or giving to the federal government information on the immigration status of individuals.

The cities and states that decline to accede to the requirements of § 1373 would seem to be on solid footing when they invoke accountability concerns.[202] Although some kinds of information demands might not implicate accountability concerns,[203] the ones at issue today[204] do. Sanctuary jurisdictions often explain their decisions to become sanctuaries by arguing that all residents are safer and healthier if undocumented residents feel free to report crimes to police and to avail themselves of other public resources (e.g., health clinics and schools) without fear that local authorities are actively working in concert with the federal deportation efforts. If local officials are not able to publicly and credibly proclaim and publicize that they will not provide information (or other support) to federal authorities, undocumented persons may clam up or fail to seek health and education services (whether or not the undocumented persons know the details of any support the locals provide). The electorate may blame the resulting possible local increases in unsolved crime and public health problems on local officials rather than the federal officials making the demands. Or, at least, this corruption of accountability is as plausible as it was in *New York* and *Printz*.[205]

---

[201] 8 USC § 1373(a).

[202] They are also on solid antityranny ground since states are trying to make a political point with sanctuary policies.

[203] See, for example, *Printz*, 521 US at 936 (O'Connor, J, concurring) (citing to a federal statute "requiring state and local law enforcement agencies to report cases of missing children to the Department of Justice" and observing that "the Court appropriately refrains from deciding whether other purely ministerial reporting requirements imposed by Congress on state and local authorities pursuant to its Commerce Clause powers are similarly invalid.").

[204] See 8 USC § 1373. In some litigation, the United States has also asserted demands that states detain noncitizens to enable federal authorities to question or arrest these individuals; detainer demands are even more likely to be held to be commandeering under *Printz* than information demands.

[205] This fact will make it harder, though not necessarily impossible, for the Court to create a rigorous "information-demand exception" to *Printz* that might apply to 8 USC § 1373. There remains the question of a possible "immigration exception" to *Printz*; compare *Trump*

And, of course, more generally, *Murphy*'s forceful affirmation of anticommandeering principles generally suggests the Court will not be open to gimmicky ways of distinguishing *New York* or *Printz*. In this regard, it bears mention also that *Murphy* represents the first case in which the Court has applied the anticommandeering principle to strike down a federal law that was not associated with progressive policies in the way environmental protection and gun control are, a fact that might portend the durability of the doctrine.

Beyond the sanctuary arena, it is not clear to me what clear effect *Murphy* should have on lower courts adjudicating claims of commandeering. With regard to the state decriminalization of marijuana or instances in which the meaning and effect of federal tax law depend on state tax decisions, it is not remotely clear to me that the federal government is commanding states to do anything,[206] although there is, as noted throughout this article, some loose language in *Murphy* that may be seized upon to assert broad claims.[207]

---

v Hawaii, 138 S Ct 2392 (2018). But remember that one feature of *New York*, and presumably *Printz* too, is that the anticommandeering rule is absolute and not subject to balancing: As the Court reminded in *Murphy*: "'[N]o Member of the Court ha[d] ever suggested' that even 'a particularly strong federal interest' 'would enable Congress to command a state government to enact *state* [legislation].'" *Murphy*, 138 S Ct at 1476 (emphasis and second alteration in original). An immigration exception would seem inconsistent with this categorical prohibition. Another issue regarding commandeering and sanctuary jurisdictions involves intrastate control, see Vikram David Amar, *Federalism Friction in the First Year of the Trump Presidency*, 45 Hastings Const L Q 401, 409–11 (2018). This issue of intrastate control was not, of course, the focal point of the dispute in *Murphy*. But Justice Alito's opinion did recognize—in the course of rejecting one the federal government's arguments—that commandeering by the federal government can take the form of interfering with a state's decision about how much autonomy to give its local actors. *Murphy*, 138 S Ct at 1483.

[206] In the marijuana setting, for example, the federal government is criminalizing drug use (and could preempt all or part of the marijuana regulation field), but as far as I know it is not telling states that they can't or must regulate or tax marijuana in any particular ways. Nor is the federal government saying the Controlled Substance Act's meaning changes depending on choices states make as to their laws. Compare the Obama administration's Memorandum for all United States Attorneys, *Guidance Regarding Marijuana Enforcement* (Aug 29, 2013) (incorporating state law for enforcement purposes). As for state taxes, see Neil H. Buchanan, *The Double-Taxation Bogeyman Rides Again* (Dorf on Law, Oct 20, 2017), online at http://www.dorfonlaw.org/2017/10/the-double-taxation-bogeyman-rides-again.html. Federal tax treatment may sometimes turn on state-law choices, but I am not aware of any problematic unclarity in that realm. It bears noting that the *Murphy* Court cited *South Carolina v Baker*, 485 US 505 (1998), approvingly, saying that the federal statute there made federal tax treatment turn on state law, but seeing no inherent problem with this.

[207] See *Brackeen v Zinke*, 2018 WL 4927908 (ND Tex).

LAURA K. DONOHUE

FUNCTIONAL EQUIVALENCE AND RESIDUAL RIGHTS POST-CARPENTER: FRAMING A TEST CONSISTENT WITH PRECEDENT AND ORIGINAL MEANING

I. INTRODUCTION

The evolution of Fourth Amendment doctrine over the past century bears a striking resemblance to Hamlet's descent into insanity. Step by step, faced by increasingly sophisticated technologies, the Court has crafted rules, exceptions, and exceptions to the exceptions, until we find ourselves in an incoherent world that bears little relationship to the original rights it encompasses.

The Founders introduced the Fourth Amendment to secure liberty.[1] The clause reinforced the right of the people, as sovereign, to determine the conditions under which the government could intrude

Laura K. Donohue is Professor of Law, Georgetown Law.

AUTHOR'S NOTE: Special thanks to Jeremy McCabe at the Georgetown Law Library for his assistance in cite checking, formatting the footnotes, and obtaining materials used in this article. Nadia Asancheyev, George Farahat, Katrina Kleck, and Allen Tran further assisted with formatting and cite checking. I am indebted to Randy Barnett, Jennifer Daskal, John Facciola, Jennifer Granick, Bob Litt, Allegra McLeod, Michael Mosman, Abbe Smith, Lawrence Solum, Geoffrey Stone, and David Vladeck for their thoughtful critique.

[1] 1 Annals of Congress 443, 446, 449 (June 8, 1789).

in their lives.[2] The interests at stake went well beyond the physical world. As Justice Brandeis famously observed in his dissent in *Olmstead v United States*, the Framers "sought to protect Americans in their beliefs, their thoughts, their emotions and their sensations."[3] Any intrusion had to be justified. For that, a general warrant would be insufficient. Even a particularized one had to meet the requirements in the second part of the clause: probable cause demonstrated to an independent magistrate, supported by oath or affirmation, and "particularly describing the places to be searched, and the persons or things to be seized."[4] Outside of these conditions, or a known felon in flight, the Fourth Amendment created an absolute bar.[5] It was not, as the Court suggested in 1948 and repeated seventy years later in *Carpenter v United States*, an effort "to place obstacles in the way of a too permeating police surveillance."[6] It was government surveillance of the privacies of life itself that was forbidden, outside of constitutional strictures.[7]

For decades, the Court adopted a property-based approach, tying the doctrine to common-law trespass, which prioritized the question of whether a physical intrusion had occurred "on a constitutionally protected area."[8] When confronted with its first wiretapping case, the Court's failure was not in recognizing that telephone wires lay outside the home, which they clearly do, but in failing to recognize that through wiretapping, the government gained access to the intimate details of the speakers' lives—details ensconced in their persons, houses, papers, and effects.

---

[2] *Camara v Municipal Court of City and County of San Francisco*, 387 US 523, 528 (1967); *Boyd v United States*, 116 US 616, 630 (1886). See also Raymond Shih Ray Ku, *The Founders' Privacy: The Fourth Amendment and the Power of Technological Surveillance*, 86 Minn L Rev 1325, 1326 (2002).

[3] *Olmstead v United States*, 277 US 438, 476 (1928) (Brandeis, J, dissenting).

[4] US Const, Amend IV.

[5] Laura K. Donohue, *The Original Fourth Amendment*, 83 U Chi L Rev 1181 (2016). See also *Carpenter v United States*, 138 S Ct 2206, 2243 (2018) (Thomas, J, dissenting).

[6] *United States v Di Re*, 332 US 581, 595 (1948); *Carpenter*, 138 S Ct at 2214 (majority); *Camara*, 3887 US at 528, quoted in *Carpenter*, 138 S Ct at 2213.

[7] See *Segura v United States*, 468 US 796, 810 (1984) ("But the home is sacred in Fourth Amendment terms not primarily because of the occupants' possessory interests in the premises, but because of their privacy interests in the activities that take place within.").

[8] See *United States v Jones*, 565 US 400, 405, 406 n 3 (2012); *Carpenter*, 138 S Ct at 2213. See also *Kyllo v United States*, 533 US 27, 34–35 (2001); *Carpenter*, 138 S Ct at 2236 (Thomas, J, dissenting).

In 1967, *Katz v United States* did nothing to address this deficiency.[9] Instead, it took the doctrine further from its original purpose, placing it in a make-believe land of relativistic determinations.[10] If there is a silver lining to be taken from the Court's recent decision in *Carpenter*, it is that multiple Justices acknowledged the problems created by *Katz* and its progeny.[11] Justice Thomas launched a devastating attack on the earlier decision, stating, "The *Katz* test has no basis in the text or history of the Fourth Amendment."[12] His complaints are well-founded.

Not only is the test from Justice Harlan's concurrence in *Katz* inconsistent with the original meaning of the Fourth Amendment, but as a matter of constitutional pluralism, it has proven deeply problematic. If, as the Court stated in 2006, "the ultimate touchstone of the Fourth Amendment is 'reasonableness,'"[13] then it falls to judges to make the call of what is "more" or "less" reasonable. This puts them squarely in the realm of policy-making, risking public confidence in the workings of the Court.[14] In the decades that followed *Katz*, the Court repeatedly ignored societal standards, substituting its own judgment for that of elected representatives and narrowing protections afforded to the people.[15] The

---

[9] *Katz v United States*, 389 US 347 (1967).

[10] See Randy E. Barnett and Evan D. Bernick, *The Letter and the Spirit: A Unified Theory of Originalism*, 107 Georgetown L J 1 (2018) (arguing that originalist constitutional construction should be informed by the original function or purpose of the relevant provision).

[11] See *Carpenter*, 138 S Ct at 2236 (Thomas, J, dissenting); id at 2261–65 (Gorsuch, J, dissenting). See also *Minnesota v Carter*, 525 US 83, 97 (1998) (Scalia, J, concurring).

[12] *Carpenter*, 138 S Ct at 2236 (Thomas, J, dissenting). See also id at 2238–45 (discussing many ways in which *Katz* departed from the original meaning of the Fourth Amendment).

[13] *Brigham City v Stuart*, 547 US 398, 403 (2006).

[14] See *Carpenter*, 138 S Ct. at 2236 (Thomas, J, dissenting) (arguing that *Katz* "invites courts to make judgments about policy, not law."); id at 2264 (the right to bring a claim does not "depend on whether a judge happens to agree that your subjective expectation to privacy is a 'reasonable' one."); id at 2265 (Gorsuch, J, dissenting) ("When judges abandon legal judgment for political will . . . [we] risk undermining public confidence in the courts themselves."); id ("Deciding what privacy interests *should* be recognized often calls for a pure policy choice . . . which calls for the exercise of raw political will belonging to legislatures, not the legal judgment proper to courts.").

[15] In *California v Ciraola*, the Court held there is no "reasonable expectation of privacy" in an enclosed yard, as even fences "might not shield [marijuana plants] from the eyes of a citizen or a policeman perched on the top of a truck or a two-level bus," despite state laws making it illegal to ride on top of a truck, trespass on others' property, or climb fences without the owner's consent. See *California v Ciraolo*, 476 US 207, 209, 214 (1986); 1981 Cal Stat 3149, 3155, codified at Cal Veh Code § 21712 (adding Subsection (b), stating that "No person shall ride on any vehicle or upon any portion thereof not designed or intended for the use of passengers,"); 1982 Cal Stat 4709, codified at Cal Veh Code § 23116 (passed Sept 22,

result is a doctrine that is much maligned for logical fallacies, in-consistency, and unmanageability.[16]

Along the way, the judiciary carved out broad exceptions, foremost amongst which is the third-party doctrine. In *Katz*, Justice White presaged its evolution, arguing that knowingly exposing information to others implies an assumption of risk that the other party may later disgorge it.[17] For him, the Fourth Amendment had nothing to say about unreliable associates. Drawing an analogy to informant doctrine,

---

1982, making it illegal for a minor to be in the back of a flatbed truck); 1961 Cal Stat 2919, codified at Cal Penal Code § 602.5 (unauthorized entry of property); 1981 Cal Stat 980, 988, codified at Cal Penal Code § 602 (trespass upon fenced, cultivated land). This last provision is reflected in numerous local ordinances. See, for example, Orange County, California, County Code § 3-8-24. In *United States v Dunn*, the Court determined that it was "reasonable" for a Drug Enforcement Agency agent to cross a perimeter fence, an interior fence, and a barbed wire fence, to peer inside a barn that was located on private property a half mile from any road, before crossing another barbed wire fence and a wooden fence to look inside a second structure. See *United States v Dunn*, 480 US 294, 297 (1987). The Court ignored state and federal judicial decisions that considered barns to be within the curtilage. See, for example, *Luman v State*, 629 P2d 1275, 1276 (Okla Crim App 1981); *United States v Berrong*, 712 F2d 1370, 1374 (11th Cir 1983); *Rosencranz v United States*, 356 F2d 310, 313 (1st Cir 1966); *Walker v United States*, 225 F3d 447; *United States v Swann*, 377 F Supp 1305, 1306 (Md 1974); *United States v King*, 305 F Supp 630, 634 (ND Miss 1969), and dozens of further cases cited in *Dunn*, 480 US at 308–9 (Brennan, J, dissenting). It also ignored state law making it illegal to trespass on private property if given notice. See Tex Penal Code Ann § 30.05 (1980). In *California v Greenwood*, the Court decided that it was not "reasonable" to consider garbage within the Fourth Amendment on the grounds that bags left out on the curb are "readily ac-cessible to animals, children, scavengers, snoops, and other members of the public," despite local ordinances making it illegal for anyone to go through peoples' garbage. See *California v Greenwood*, 486 US 35 (1988); California, Laguna Beach, Municipal Code § 7.16.060(b).

[16] *Carpenter*, 138 S Ct at 2244 (Thomas, J, dissenting). Scholars are scathing in their crit-icism. See, for example, Daniel J. Solove, *Nothing to Hide: The False Tradeoff Between Privacy and Security* (Yale, 2011); Amitai Etzioni, *A Cyber Age Privacy Doctrine: More Coherent, Less Subjective, and Operational*, 80 Brooklyn L Rev 1263 (2015); Steven M. Bellovin et al, *When Enough Is Enough: Location Tracking, Mosaic Theory, and Machine Learning*, 8 NYU J L & Liberty 556 (2014); David Gray and Danielle Citron, *The Right to Quantitative Privacy*, 98 Minn L Rev 62, 70 (2013); Paul Ohm, *The Fourth Amendment in a World Without Privacy*, 81 Miss L J 1309 (2012); Andrew William Bagley, *Don't Be Evil: The Fourth Amendment in the Age of Google, National Security, and Digital Papers and Effects*, 21 Albany L J Sci & Tech 153 (2011); Priscilla J. Smith et al, *When Machines Are Watching: How Warrantless Use of GPS Surveillance Technology Violates the Fourth Amendment Right Against Unreasonable Searches*, 121 Yale L J Online 177, 177 (2011); John J. Brogan, *Facing the Music: The Dubious Constitu-tionality of Facial Recognition*, 25 Hastings Comm & Ent L J 65, 73 (2002); Ku, 86 Minn L Rev at 1327 (cited in note 2); Christopher Slobogin, *Peeping Techno-Toms and the Fourth Amendment: Seeing Through Kyllo's Rules Governing Technological Surveillance*, 86 Minn L Rev 1393 (2002); Daniel J. Solove, *Digital Dossiers and the Dissipation of Fourth Amendment Privacy*, 75 S Cal L Rev 1083 (2002).

[17] *Katz*, 389 US at 363 n ** (1967) (White, J, concurring) ("When one man speaks to another he takes all the risks ordinarily inherent in so doing, including the risk that the man to whom he speaks will make public what he has heard. The Fourth Amendment does not protect against unreliable . . . associates.").

the Court subsequently decided that anything you tell anyone else—
even if necessary for the day-to-day running of a household or living in
the modern world—does not fall within the protections of the Fourth
Amendment. *Miller v United States* and *Smith v Maryland* dealt, respectively, with banking and telephone records.[18] But the rule quickly
expanded to encapsulate almost any record entrusted to others.

Intellectually diverse scholars have roundly denounced third-party
doctrine.[19] Professor Wayne LaFave declared *Miller* "dead wrong,"
"a mockery of the Fourth Amendment."[20] Professor Daniel Solove
considered it "one of the most serious threats to privacy in the digital
age."[21] Professor Randy Barnett has called for "[b]oth the third-party
doctrine of *Smith* and the 'reasonable expectation of privacy' approach of *Katz* . . . to be adapted to modern circumstances."[22] As
Justice Gorsuch observed in *Carpenter*, the exception eviscerated
Fourth Amendment doctrine, leaving it unprepared for the modern
age: "Even our most private documents—those that, in other eras, we
would have locked safely in a desk drawer or destroyed—now reside
on third party servers."[23] It is ludicrous to think that these documents
are not private.

Now we have, with *Carpenter*, an exception to the exception, saying
that location data are, well, special and that other things might be
special too, but we can't say right now just what falls into that camp.[24]
This article observes that while the Court had little choice but to
grant certiorari and to find location data protected under the Fourth

---

[18] *Smith v Maryland*, 442 US 735, 745 (1979); *United States v Miller*, 425 US 435, 443 (1976).

[19] See Orin S. Kerr, *The Case for the Third-Party Doctrine*, 107 Mich L Rev 561, 563 n 5 (2009) (observing that "[a] list of every article or book that has criticized the doctrine would make . . . the world's longest law review footnote").

[20] Wayne R. LaFave, 1 *Search and Seizure: A Treatise on the Fourth Amendment* § 2.7(c) at 747 (Thomson West, 4th ed 2004), cited and quoted in Kerr, 107 Mich L Rev at 564 (cited in note 19).

[21] Daniel J. Solove, *Fourth Amendment Codification and Professor Kerr's Misguided Call for Judicial Deference*, 74 Fordham L Rev 747, 753 (2005), cited and quoted in Kerr, 107 Mich L Rev at 564 n 10 (cited in note 19). See also *Carpenter*, 138 S Ct at 2264 (Gorsuch, J, dissenting).

[22] Randy E. Barnett, *Why the NSA Data Seizures Are Unconstitutional*, 38 Harv J L & Pub Pol 3, 16 (2015).

[23] *Carpenter*, 138 S Ct at 2262 (Gorsuch, J, dissenting) (writing that *Miller* and *Smith* proved "[a] doubtful application of *Katz* that lets the government search almost whatever it wants whenever it wants.").

[24] See id at 2217, 2223 (majority).

Amendment, the reasoning it adopted exacerbated doctrinal weaknesses and created profound challenges for judiciary going forward.

The *Carpenter* Court held that warrantless access to seven or more days of cell site location information (CSLI) constitutes a violation of the reasonable expectation of privacy that individuals have in the whole of their physical movements.[25] But the grounds on which the Court drew a line—the "deeply revealing nature of [CSLI], its depth, breadth, and comprehensive reach, and the inescapable and automatic nature of its collection"[26]—are not unique to location data. They characterize all sorts of digital records—including those at issue in *Miller* and *Smith*, belying the majority's claim that the decision leaves third-party doctrine intact. Instead of avoiding *Katz*'s pitfalls, the Court emphasized voluntary assumption of risk, doubling down on the subjective nature of judicial interpretation. Even as it declared the warrantless search of CSLI unreasonable, it introduced myriad questions that will push the lower courts into uncharted territory. Without clear direction, the decision is likely to lead to further chaos, fragmentation in the circuits, and reversals in the courts of appeals—far from the predictability and certainty essential to rule of law.

To mitigate the risk and take account of the significant challenges ahead, this article proposes that, going forward, courts eschew voluntary assumption of risk. An outgrowth of open space and informant doctrines, the approach imported analogical fallacies into the Court's jurisprudence and turned a blind eye to the implications of new technologies. The perfunctory application of voluntariness to third-party records further eviscerated the constitutional protections extended to private and commercial papers at the founding. The lack of clarity in *Carpenter* between what can be understood as "device-use compulsion" and "record-creation compulsion," and the insertion of the judiciary into that determination, forces judges into a policy-making role. The Court's emphasis on novel technologies will further confound efforts to adjudicate Fourth Amendment claims in a consistent manner.

To address problems created by *Carpenter*, this article advocates a property-based approach in which the Court extends the rule of functional equivalence, which characterizes home and border searches,

---

[25] Id at 2219–20, 2223.
[26] Id at 2223.

to digital papers. The multifactor test employed in *Carpenter*—the volume of information, its revealing nature, its retroactivity, its near perfect recall, the length of time it was collected, and its precision—underscores the extent to which information reveals the "privacies of life." While such factors may explain why data are considered within the construct of "papers," they are neither necessary nor sufficient. Just as the Court has been clear that technology conveying information about the interior of a home triggers Fourth Amendment protections regardless of whether it exposes intimate details, so, too, should the search of digital papers be sufficient to find them constitutionally protected—regardless of the level of intimacy revealed.

In ascertaining who owns digital documents and records, the Court can employ a *but for* analysis, asking whether the material would exist but for the right-holder's actions. In the context of CSLI, the right-holder buys the phone, charges it, turns it on, and decides when and where to carry it. It is up to the right-holder to decide with whom the resulting location information is shared. Indeed, an individual could not even contract to provide the information to others absent the original right. Simultaneously, the owner has a separate claim on the third party to perform a particular service (in exchange for money), which only exists within the contractual relationship.

To determine whether, by providing access to information, the right-holders divest themselves of their ownership interest in the data, as Justice Gorsuch recognized in *Carpenter*, the law of bailment and positive law have the potential to play a crucial role.[27] English common law has long recognized that possession is insufficient to extinguish a property owner's residual rights.[28] A bailor and bailee both hold rights in the same property.[29] CSLI closely mirrors a

---

[27] *Carpenter*, 138 S Ct at 2268 (Gorsuch, J, dissenting).

[28] See Frederick Pollock and Frederic William Maitland, 2 *History of English Law Before the Time of Edward I* 169 (Cambridge, 2d ed 1898).

[29] See, for example, Oliver Wendell Holmes Jr., *The Bailee at Common Law*, in *The Common Law* 164 (Little, Brown, 1881); Joseph H. Beale Jr., *The Carrier's Liability*, 11 Harv L Rev 158 (1887); Thomas Atkins Street, 2 *The Early Law of Bailment*, in 2 *Foundations of Legal Liability* 251 (Edward Thompson, 1906); Percy Bordwell, *Property in Chattels II: Property in the Bailor*, 29 Harv L Rev 501 (1916); Percy Bordwell, *Property in Chattels III: Property in the Bailee*, 29 Harv L Rev 731 (1916); Eric G. M. Fletcher, *The Carrier's Liability* (Stevens & Sons, 1932); W. S. Holdsworth, 3 *A History of English Law* 336 (Methuen, 3d ed 1923); Theodore F. T. Plucknett, *A Concise History of the Common Law* 451–52 (Little, Brown, 5th ed 1956). See also G. W. Paton, *Bailment in the Common Law* 48 (Stevens & Sons, 1952); C. H. S. Fifoot, *History and Sources of the Common Law: Tort and Contract* 157–66 (Stevens & Sons, 1949); Samuel Stoljar, *The Early History of Bailment*, 1 Am J Legal Hist 5 (1957).

bailment in locatio rei, in which a considerable amount of control is provided to the possessor, without altering the right-holder's power—in this case, over his or her location information. Positive law, in turn, may prove probative in regard to the existence of a property right: where federal or state law has *acknowledged a property right* and placed a correlative *duty of noninterference* on others, government intrusions may constitute a search or seizure within the meaning of the Fourth Amendment. The approach advocated has the advantage of clarity, adaptation to the modern world, and the restoration of core Fourth Amendment rights protected at the founding.

II. Carpenter: A Case That Had to Happen

In 2018, the Court had little choice but to confront the issues raised in *Carpenter*. Use of CSLI had become widespread. Enormously powerful, it allowed law enforcement the ability to find suspects, to place them near crimes, to verify (or undermine) alibis, to discover what people had done (and with whom), and to discover behavioral patterns. Simultaneously, it did not fit well within either statutory law or Fourth Amendment doctrine—a situation exacerbated by the Court's decisions in *Riley v California* and *United States v Jones*.[30] Faced with a jurisprudence that denied constitutional protections, defied common sense, and sent contradictory messages, lower courts struggled with how to apply *Katz*. Central to the debate was whether telephone users voluntarily divulged location information to others—a question rooted in informant doctrine and bedeviled by the contemporary dependence on mobile devices.

A. STATUTORY FRAMING

As CSLI came of age, it was not immediately apparent whether statutory provisions authorized law enforcement to collect it. The government began by arguing that it fell within the criminal pen register and trap and trace provisions (PRTT).[31] But virtually every court to confront the question rejected this approach, not least because the Communications Assistance for Law Enforcement Act

---

[30] *Riley v California*, 134 S Ct 2473 (2014), taken in conjunction with *United States v Wurie*, 728 F3d 1 (2013), cert granted 134 S Ct 999 (2014); *United States v Jones*, 565 US 400 (2012).

[31] 18 USC §§ 3121–27.

(CALEA) expressly forbade the use of pen register statutes to collect location data.[32]

In 1994, Congress had passed CALEA to require service providers to be able to provide law enforcement with information for which it had legal authorization.[33] The hearings aired significant worry about the government's potential use of service providers' records to track individuals. During his testimony, Federal Bureau of Investigation (FBI) Director Louis Freeh acknowledged this concern, declared that the government had no intention of collecting location data, and offered to make it clear in the statutory language that the caller's location would be excluded.[34] Congress adopted Freeh's clarification almost verbatim.[35] But the statute, which stated that information may not be collected "solely pursuant" to PRTT provisions, appeared to leave open the possibility of a separate authorization. The govern-

---

[32] Communications Assistance for Law Enforcement Act (CALEA), Pub L No 103-414 § 103(a)(2)(b), 108 Stat 4279, 4280–81 (1994). See, for example, *In re Applications of the United States for Orders Pursuant to Title 18, United States Code, Section 2703(d)*, 509 F Supp 2d 64 (D Mass 2007); *In re Application of United States for an Order Authorizing Disclosure of Location Based Services*, 2007 WL 2086663 (SD Tex); *In re Application of the United States for an Order Authorizing the Disclosure of Prospective Cell Site Information*, 412 F Supp 2d 947 (ED Wis 2006); *In re Application of the United States for an Order Authorizing Installation and Use of a Pen Register*, 415 F Supp 2d 211 (WDNY 2006); *In re Application of United States for an Order for Prospective Cell Site Location Information on a Certain Cellular Telephone*, 2006 WL 468300 (SDNY); *In re United States*, 2006 WL 1876847 (ND Ind); *In re United States*, 441 F Supp 2d 816 (SD Tex 2006); *In re Authorizing the Use of a Pen Register*, 384 F Supp 2d 562 (EDNY 2005); *In re Application for Pen Register and Trap/Trace Device with Cell Site Location Authority*, 396 F Supp 2d 747 (SD Tex 2005); *In re Application of the United States for an Order*, 396 F Supp 2d 294 (EDNY 2005).

[33] Within four years, service providers had to be able to provide law enforcement agencies with "access call-identifying information that is reasonably available to the carrier—(A) before, during, or immediately after the transmission of a wire or electronic communication (or at such later time as may be acceptable to the government); and (B) in a manner that allows it to be associated with the communication to which it pertains, except that, with regard to information acquired solely pursuant to the authority for pen registers and trap and trace devices (as defined in [18 USC § 3127])." 47 USC § 1002(a)(2). See 47 USC § 1001 note.

[34] See *Digital Telephony and Law Enforcement Access to Advanced Telecommunications Technologies and Services: Joint Hearings on H.R. 4922 and S. 2375 before the Subcommittee on Technology and the Law of the Senate Judiciary Committee and the Subcommittee on Civil and Constitutional Rights of the House Judiciary Committee*, 103d Cong, 2d Sess 29–34 (1994) (Statement of FBI Director Freeh).

[35] 47 USC § 1002(a)(2). See also *Communications Assistance for Law Enforcement Act*, HR Rep No 103-827, Part I, 103d Cong, 2d Sess 17 (1994), reprinted in 1994 USCCAN 3489, 3497 (The bill "[e]xpressly provides that the authority for pen registers and trap and trace devices cannot be used to obtain tracking and location information, other than that which can be determined from the phone number.").

ment quickly turned to an alternative anchor: the Stored Communications Act (SCA).[36]

The key question under the SCA was whether the collection of CSLI turned a phone into a "tracking device" or whether what was being sought was merely a "record."[37] If the phone was understood as a tracking device, the statute exempted the data from disclosure under 18 USC § 2703.[38] Courts thus paid careful attention to how accurately the technology conveyed location.[39]

For real-time or prospective information, courts considered the phone to be acting as a tracking device and thus outside the SCA, with the result that probable cause and a warrant would be required to obtain the data.[40] In contrast, numerous courts considered *historic*

---

[36] Stored Communications Act (SCA), 18 USC § 2701 et seq. See, for example, *In re Application of the United States for an Order for Disclosure of Telecommunications Records and Authorizing the Use of a Pen Register and Trap and Trace*, 405 F Supp 2d 435, 436 (EDNY 2005). Some courts rejected the argument that the government could apply under different statutory provisions, saying that CALEA sought to foreclose other options. See *In re Application of the United States for an Order Authorizing the Release of Prospective Cell Site Information*, 407 F Supp 2d 134 (DDC 2006).

[37] See, for example, *People v Hall*, 823 NYS 2d 334 (NY 2006); *In re Application of United States for an Order for Prospective Cell Site Location Information on a Certain Cellular Telephone*, 460 F Supp 2d 448 (SDNY 2006); *In re Application for an Order Authorizing the Extension and Use of a Pen Register Device*, 2007 WL 397129 (ED Cal); *In re Application of United States for an Order Relating to Target Phone 2*, 733 F Supp 2d 939, 942–43 (ND Ill 2009).

[38] The statute defined "electronic communication" as "any transfer of signs, signals, writing, images, sounds, data, or intelligence of any nature transmitted in whole or in part by a wire, radio, electromagnetic, photoelectric or photooptical system that affects interstate or foreign commerce, but does *not* include . . . (C) any communication from a tracking device (as defined in section 3117 of this title)." 18 USC § 2510(12) (emphasis added). That section defined "tracking device" as "an electronic or mechanical device which permits the tracking of the movement of a person or object." 18 USC § 3117. If a mobile phone is a tracking device, then the electronic signals from it do not count as "electronic communications" for SCA purposes—so 18 USC § 2703(d) is inapplicable.

[39] See, for example, *In re Application of the United States for an Order*, 396 F Supp 2d at 310; *In re Application of the United States for an Order for Disclosure of Telecommunications Records and Authorizing the Use of a Pen Register and Trap and Trace*, 405 F Supp 2d at 438; *In re Application of the Unites States for an Order*, 411 F Supp 2d 678, 679–80 (WD La 2006); *In re Application of the United States for Orders Authorizing the Installation and Use of Pen Registers and Caller Identification Devices on Telephone Numbers*, 416 F Supp 2d 390, 396 (D Md 2006); *In re United States for an Order*, 433 F Supp 2d 804, 806 (SD Tex 2006); *United States v Bermudez*, 2006 WL 3197181 (SD Ind).

[40] See, for example, *In re Application of the United States for an Order Authorizing Disclosure of Location Information of a Specified Wireless Telephone*, 849 F Supp 2d 526, 575 (D Md 2011); *In re Application of United States for an Order*, 2009 WL 1530195, *3–4 (EDNY); *In re United States*, 416 F Supp 2d at 397; *Bermudez*, 2006 WL 3197181, *7 (noting that 18 USC § 2703 does not allow real-time tracking); *In re United States*, 441 F Supp 2d at 828; *In re Application of the United States for an Order Authorizing Disclosure of Prospective Cell Site Information*, 2006 WL 2871743, *6 (ED Wis) (18 USC § 2703 is only retrospective); *United States v*

CSLI to be a "record" under 18 USC § 2703.[41] Here, the government only had to meet the requirements in § 2703(d). The government argued that because the information was derived from wire (not electronic) communications, the tracking device exception did not apply.[42] As for tower dumps (i.e., a record of every phone using a particular tower), courts generally considered them to qualify as a search under the Fourth Amendment.[43] The collection of information on innocent citizens and the volume of information mattered: in some requests, providers turned over up to 150,000 telephone numbers in a given area at a particular time.[44]

B. DOCTRINAL PLACEMENT

Like the statutory realm, the Court's jurisprudence did not provide an easy fit for CSLI, which fell somewhere between public versus private space and third-party doctrine (both of which consistently ignored the impact of technology on Fourth Amendment rights) and more recent decisions that had begun to acknowledge the privacy interests at stake.[45] The shadow of *Katz*, and the subjective nature of the reasonableness test, loomed large.

1. *First analogical fallacy: the application of assumption of risk and fairness (from public space doctrine) to location tracking.* The Supreme Court has long held that observation outdoors does not constitute

---

Espudo, 954 F Supp 2d 1029, 1036–37 (SD Cal 2013) (prospective CSLI does not create a "record" under 2703, which is only for data already captured). But see *United States v Powell*, 943 F Supp 2d 759, 777 (ED Mich 2013) (deciding a mobile phone is not a tracking device because it is not owned by the government and 18 USC § 3117 is geared toward installation). Courts have, for prospective CSLI, tended to resolve the question under *Knotts* and the public/private distinction, and not within the third-party context. See, for example, *United States v Forest*, 355 F3d 942, 950–52 (6th Cir 2004). One court has found that even if an individual has a reasonable expectation of privacy in real-time location data, the government does not violate it by arresting her, without a warrant, while she is traveling with the target of the surveillance. See *United States v Peters*, 333 F Supp 3d 366, 376–78 (D Vt 2018).

[41] See, for example, *In re United States for an Order Authorizing the Use of Two Pen Register and Trap and Trace Devices*, 632 F Supp 2d 202, 207 (EDNY 2008); *In re Application of the United States for an Order Authorizing the Disclosure of Cell Site Location Information*, 2009 WL 8231744 (ED Ky).

[42] *In re Application of United States for an Order Directing a Provider of Electronic Communication Service to Disclose Records to Government*, 620 F3d 304, 310 (3d Cir 2010).

[43] See, for example, *In re United States ex rel Order Pursuant to 18 U.S.C. Section 2703(d)*, 930 F Supp 2d 698, 702 (SD Tex 2012); *In re Application of United States for an Order Pursuant to 18 USC § 2703(d)*, 964 F Supp 2d 674, 678 (SDNY 2013).

[44] *In re Application of United States*, 964 F Supp 2d at 678.

[45] See also *Carpenter*, 138 S Ct at 2215–16, 2218–19 (discussing *Knotts* and *Jones*).

a search.[46] Following *Katz*, it came to include anything that could be seen from the air or on the ground—from greenhouses missing roof tiles to cars traveling along thoroughfares.[47] These cases often downplayed the privacy implications of new technologies, even lauding their use for ensuring more accurate information.[48]

The Court's argument as to why individuals had no reasonable expectation of privacy in public ultimately turned on a two-part argument grounded in assumed risk and fairness. First, what an individual knowingly exposed to others was different from what he or she sought to keep private. By deciding to go outside and get into a car, individuals knowingly ran the risk that others would be able to observe them. Second, a basic principle of fairness applied: it would be strange to tell a police officer that she must close her eyes or cover her ears to block what anyone else could see or hear.[49] Traveling in public therefore fell outside the protections of the Fourth Amendment.

CSLI, at first glance, appeared to come within the public/private distinction: if there was no privacy interest in a global positioning

---

[46] See, for example, *Hester v United States*, 265 US 57 (1924) (observation of open fields does not constitute a search); *Air Pollution Variance Board v Western Alfalfa Corp.*, 416 US 861 (1974) (conducting opacity test on smoke coming out of a stack up to a quarter of a mile away does not constitute a search); *Oliver v United States*, 466 US 170, 178 (1984) ("[A]n individual may not legitimately demand privacy for activities conducted out of doors in fields, except in the area immediately surrounding the home."); *United States v Dunn*, 480 US 294, 304 (1987) ("Under *Oliver* and *Hester*, there is no constitutional difference between police observations conducted while in a public place and while standing in the open fields."); *California v Greenwood*, 486 US 35, 40 (1988) (citations omitted) (examination of garbage left at the curb does not constitute a search on the grounds that it is "readily accessible to animals, children, scavengers, snoops, and other members of the public").

[47] See *California v Ciraolo*, 476 US 207, 211 (1986) (noting that even high fences "might not shield [marijuana plants] from the eyes of a citizen or a policeman perched on the top of a truck or a two-level bus."); *Dow Chemical Co. v United States*, 476 US 227, 236, 239 (1986) (drawing a distinction between private and public space and holding that while the company had a "reasonable, legitimate, and objective expectation of privacy within the interior of its covered buildings," it did not have one in regard to areas visible outside the structure); *Florida v Riley*, 488 US 445 (1989) (holding that areas visible from the air were not protected under the Fourth Amendment); *Cardwell v Lewis*, 417 US 583, 590 (1974) (plurality) ("A car has little capacity for escaping public scrutiny. It travels public thoroughfares where its occupants and its contents are in plain view."); *United States v Karo*, 468 US 705 (1984); *United States v Knotts*, 460 US 276 (1983). Compare *United States v Michael*, 622 F2d 744 (5th Cir 1980) (holding that warrantless installation of a beeper outside of exigent circumstances required prior judicial authorization), rehearing granted, 628 F2d 931 (5th Cir 1980), rev'd, 645 F2d 252 (5th Cir 1981) (holding that installation of a beeper requires only reasonable suspicion).

[48] See, for example, *Knotts*, 460 US at 282 ("Nothing in the Fourth Amendment prohibited the police from augmenting the sensory faculties bestowed upon them at birth with such enhancement as science and technology afforded them in this case.").

[49] See also *Katz*, 389 US at 361 (Harlan, J, concurring) (considering actions in public to lay outside Fourth Amendment protections).

system (GPS) chip on a car, why would it be any different in regard to a GPS chip in a telephone? Either way, the information revealed the location of an individual in public space. GPS, moreover, is accurate within centimeters. Why should CSLI, which is *less* accurate, come within the protections of the Fourth Amendment?

The picture, though, was more complicated. For one, cars generally do not follow individuals inside the curtilage of the home. Phones do. For another, the ubiquity of mobile devices resulted in the generation of terabytes of information about millions of people for lengthy periods of time. This raised deeper privacy implications than someone watching a car drive by. It was unclear, though, whether and how this distinction impacted the doctrine. If there were no interests implicated at the front end, what created the back-end right? The only doctrinally relevant question was whether it was a search at the outset.[50] In addition, unlike GPS systems or RFID chips, for mobile devices, law enforcement did not have to *do* or *attach* anything to the individual or vehicle in order to obtain extensive amounts of information.[51] It was not entirely clear how this cut. Finally, both parts of the Court's logic for the public/private distinction—that upon entering the public sphere an individual assumed the risk that other citizens could observe them, and that there was something fundamentally unfair about disadvantaging law enforcement in comparison to others—rang somewhat hollow when *no* person actually could observe an individual twenty-four hours a day, seven days a week, for months, or even years without end.

2. *Second analogical fallacy: the application of assumption of risk and voluntariness (from informant doctrine) to third-party records.* The second jurisprudential home, third-party doctrine, proved equally problematic. It derived from cases dealing with informers that predated *Katz* and continued in its wake.[52] Like open space doctrine, the informant cases saw technology not as deepening any expectation of privacy, but merely as enhancing human capabilities and offering a

---

[50] See *United States v Graham*, 846 F Supp 2d 384 (D Md 2012).

[51] *In re Application of the United States for an Order for Disclosure of Telecommunications Records and Authorizing the Use of a Pen Register and Trap and Trace*, 405 F Supp 2d 435, 449 (SDNY 2005).

[52] For informant cases prior to *Katz*, see *On Lee v United States*, 343 US 747 (1952); *Lopez v United States*, 373 US 427 (1963); *Hoffa v United States*, 385 US 293 (1966); *Lewis v United States*, 385 US 206 (1966). For cases following *Katz*, see *United States v White*, 401 US 745 (1971); *United States v Caceres*, 440 US 741 (1979).

more efficient way to get (more) accurate information.[53] They also followed a parallel assumption-of-risk argument: voluntarily confiding information in others meant that an individual essentially consented to the possibility that the other person would divulge the information to others.[54]

Katz did nothing to alter the calculation. In 1971, the Court maintained its stance in *United States v White*, in which a prosecutor introduced a recorded conversation between an informer and a suspect at trial.[55] Justice White, writing for the Court, explained, "[O]ne contemplating illegal activities must realize and risk that his companions may be reporting to the police. . . . [I]f he has no doubts, or allays them, or risks what doubt he has, the risk is his."[56]

In *Miller*, Justice Powell, writing for the Court, cited back to the informant cases to exempt third-party business records from the protections of the Fourth Amendment:

> This Court has held repeatedly that the Fourth Amendment does not prohibit the obtaining of information revealed to a third party and conveyed by him to Government authorities, even if the information is revealed on the assumption that it will be used only for a limited purpose and the confidence placed in the third party will not be betrayed.[57]

For the Court, just as criminals assumed the risk in telling others of their plans that someone would pass on that information, so, too, did the decision to provide financial information to a bank deprive it of Fourth Amendment protections. The key was that the data were

---

[53] See, for example, *Lopez v United States*, 373 US 427, 438–39 (1963) (the Constitution does not recognize a right to probe "flaws in the agent's memory, or to challenge the agent's credibility without being beset by corroborating evidence that is not susceptible of impeachment."); *White*, 401 US at 751–52 (plurality) ("If the law gives no protection to the wrongdoer whose trusted accomplice is or becomes a police agent, neither should it protect him when that same agent has recorded or transmitted the conversations"); id at 753 (arguing that the Court should not "be too ready to erect constitutional barriers to relevant and probative evidence which is also accurate and reliable.").

[54] See *On Lee v United States*, 343 US at 751–53 (by confiding information to an undercover agent on whom a microphone had been placed, On Lee consented to the possibility that law enforcement would overhear the conversation); *Lopez*, 373 US at 438–39 (use of a recording device did nothing to alter the assumption of risk); *Hoffa*, 385 US at 303 ("The risk of being overheard by an eavesdropper or betrayed by an informer . . . is the kind of risk we necessarily assume whenever we speak.").

[55] *White*, 401 US at 746–47 (plurality).

[56] Id at 752.

[57] *United States v Miller*, 425 US 435, 443 (1976). In *Carpenter*, Gorsuch asks what theory underlies the assumption of risk argument in third-party doctrine tying it back, potentially, to tort law. See *Carpenter*, 138 S Ct at 2263 (Gorsuch, J, dissenting).

voluntarily divulged, indicating that the individual consented to the possibility that they would be provided to others.[58] By applying this logic to third-party business records, the Court employed an analogical fallacy with profound implications.

Most critically, by equating spoken words with "papers and effects," the Court buried an essential Fourth Amendment protection. At the founding, "papers" had a privileged place in the Constitution, reflecting the contemporary view that such documents were protected from government inspection.[59] In the 1765 case of *Entick v Carrington*, Lord Camden famously reflected, "Papers are the owner's goods and chattels: they are his dearest property; and are so far from enduring a seizure, that they will hardly bear an inspection."[60] The Father of Candor seized on the case and loosed a vitriolic attack on the Crown: "What then, can be more excruciating torture, than to have the lowest of mankind . . . enter suddenly into [Entick's] house, and forcibly carry away his scrutores, with all his papers of every kind, under a pretence of law."[61] Entry mattered. But of equal importance was doing so *to access Entick's papers*. Reeling from the trials associated with the Crown's effort to apprehend Entick and "the authors, printers, and publishers" of *North Britain No. 45*, Parliament passed a resolution condemning the Crown's actions and expressing strong protections for private and commercial documents.[62] Edmund Burke wrote, "The lawful secrets *of business and friendship* were rendered inviolable, by the [Parliamentary] resolution for condemning the seizure of papers."[63]

---

[58] *Miller*, 425 US at 442 ("All of the documents obtained . . . contain only information voluntarily conveyed to the banks.").

[59] Donald A. Dripps, *"Dearest Property": Digital Evidence and the History of Private "Papers" as Special Objects of Search and Seizure*, 103 J Crim L & Criminol 49 (2013); Thomas K. Clancy, *What Does the Fourth Amendment Protect: Property, Privacy, or Security?*, 33 Wake Forest L Rev 307 (1998).

[60] *Entick v Carrington*, 19 Howell St Tr 1030 (KB 1765).

[61] Father of Candor, *A Letter Concerning Libels, Warrants, the Seisure of Papers, and Sureties for the Peace of Behavior* (7th ed 1770) (first published in 1764 as *An enquiry into the doctrine lately propagated concerning libels, warrents, and the seizure of papers*, with likely authorship John Almon).

[62] *The General Warrant on Which John Wilkes Was Arrested, 30 April 1763*, in D. B. Horn, ed, *English Historical Documents 1714–1815* 61, 61–62 (Methuen, 1967). See also Donohue, 83 U Chi L Rev at 1196–1207 (cited in note 5).

[63] 1 Edmund Burke, *A Short Account of a Late Short Administration* (1766), in *The Works of the Right Honorable Edmund Burke* 265, 265 (1865), quoted in Dripps, 103 J Crim L & Criminol at 72 (cited in note 59) (emphasis added).

Americans were equally appalled at the Crown's reach.[64] Papers—whether social, personal, or commercial—were sacrosanct.[65] Accordingly, the new state constitutions, as well as the federal constitution, protected "papers."[66] For nearly a century, there was no effort made by Congress to obtain personal or business-related documents. It was not until 1863 that the first statute appeared, authorizing warrants to obtain "any invoices, books, or papers" related to undutied goods.[67] It was an enormous departure from the status quo—and from *Entick*, which was still good law.[68] Whether or not it was "reasonable" to obtain commercial papers was of no consequence. The government *could not obtain them at all*. Accordingly, the *Boyd* Court flatly rejected the statute, noting that it was the first time in the history of England or the United States that a legislature had tried to search and seize, or to compel the production, of "a man's private papers . . . for the purpose of using them in evidence against him in a criminal case."[69] Forcing the production of papers "would be subversive of all the comforts of society."[70]

The *Boyd* Court got it right: alteration did have profound consequences. Starting with *Miller*, the ability of the people to engage in commercial relationships within the protections of the Fourth Amendment sharply eroded. The *Miller* Court failed to acknowledge that what was potentially at stake was all of a person's business records—effectively eviscerating a critical constitutional right.

The analogical reasoning underlying third-party doctrine also failed to appreciate that there was a world of difference between confiding illegal behavior in (supposed) coconspirators, and engaging in an entirely legal, contractual relationship to conduct business. The information entrusted to a bank was provided for a specific, legal purpose. The customers' financial records were not publicly available. Indeed, banks were under *a legal obligation* not to allow the information

---

[64] Donohue, 83 U Chi L Rev at 1257–60 (cited in note 5).

[65] H. Brian Holland, *A Cognitive Theory of the Third-Party Doctrine and Digital Papers*, 91 Temple L Rev 55, 60 (2018).

[66] See Pa Const of 1776, Decl of Rights Art X (superseded 1790); NH Const of 1783, Bill of Rights Art XIX; Vt Const of 1777, Decl of Rights Art XI (superseded 1793); Ma Const of 1780, Part the First: Declaration of Rights Art XIV; US Const, Amend IV.

[67] See Act of Mar 3, 1863, ch 76, 12 Stat 737, 740.

[68] See generally Dripps, 103 J Crim L & Criminol at 72 (cited in note 59).

[69] *Boyd v United States*, 116 US 616, 622 (1886).

[70] Id at 628.

to be made public. Although Congress responded to *Miller* with the Right to Financial Privacy Act, the Court held its course.[71]

Another weakness in the analogy centered on consent. In *Miller*, as aforementioned, the Court assumed that, like the criminal confiding in potential accomplices, the person with a bank account knew that the bank might turn the information over to others.[72] This argument performs a sleight of hand: consenting to give the bank access to financial data for a specific use is not the same as consenting to the company releasing it to the public at large—much less to the government.[73] To the contrary, it is a limited disclosure for a specific, contractual purpose.

Finally, the analogical reasoning failed in regard to its emphasis on voluntariness. It assumed that, just like confiding in coconspirators, submitting financial information to the bank was voluntary.[74] The Court did *not* consider whether *banking* itself was voluntary in the modern world. Nor did it give any credence to the fact that the Bank Secrecy Act *required* the bank to obtain consumer information and maintain certain records.[75] For the Court, "The depositor [took] the risk, in revealing his affairs to another, that the information [would] be conveyed by that person to the Government."[76]

To summarize, analogizing between informant doctrine and third-party records buried a critical constitutional protection for commercial "papers"; equated legal, contractual relationships with the secret whisperings of criminals (thereby denying the former protection); assumed that consenting to provide information to a third party for a limited, legal purpose amounted to acquiescing to government

---

[71] Right to Financial Privacy Act of 1978, Pub L No 95-630, 92 Stat 3641.

[72] See also *Carpenter*, 138 S Ct at 2263 (Gorsuch, J, dissenting) ("Consenting to give a third party access to private papers that remain my property is not the same thing as consenting to a *search of those papers by the government*.") (emphasis in original); id (citing and quoting Kerr, 107 Mich L Rev at 588 ("So long as a person knows that they are disclosing information to a third party, their choice to do so is voluntary and the consent valid") (cited in note 19).

[73] See also *Smith v Maryland*, 442 US 735, 749 (1979) (Marshall, J, dissenting) ("Privacy is not a discrete commodity, possessed absolutely or not at all. Those who disclose certain facts to a bank or phone company for a limited business purpose need not assume that this information will be released to other persons for other purposes").

[74] *Miller*, 425 US at 442 ("[a]ll of the documents obtained, including financial statements and deposit slips, contain only information *voluntarily* conveyed to the banks and exposed to their employees in the ordinary course of business.") (emphasis added).

[75] Id at 442–43.

[76] Id at 443 (citing *White*, *Hoffa*, and *Lopez*).

search of the material; and presumed that conducting business as part of the ordinary affairs of modern life was voluntary.

As they confronted CSLI, the lower courts wrestled with the voluntariness component, seeing it as the linchpin for ascertaining whether third-party doctrine applied. They questioned the extent to which individuals freely elected either to carry phones or to provide their location to the service provider.[77] With precious little guidance from *Katz* or its progeny, the decisions ended up all over the map.

Some judges considered the provision of CSLI to be voluntary.[78] Others came out on the other side.[79] One of the most notable cases arose in 2008 in the Third Circuit, where *all* of the magistrate judges in the Western District of Pennsylvania, in a highly unusual move, cosigned an opinion rejecting a § 2703(d) order for historical cell site data.[80] The decision turned on whether customers voluntarily provided location information. The court recognized the ubiquitous use of cell phones and observed that users do not share their location "in any meaningful way."[81] "[W]hen a cell phone user receives a call," moreover, "he hasn't voluntarily exposed anything at all."[82] The court considered the phone to be a tracking device, for which a warrant was

---

[77] See, for example, *In re Application of the United States for an Order for Disclosure of Telecommunications Records and Authorizing the Use of a Pen Register and Trap and Trace*, 405 F Supp 2d at 449; *In re Application of the United States for an Order Authorizing the Disclosure of Cell Site Location Information*, 2009 WL 8231744 (ED Ky).

[78] See, for example, *United States v Gordon*, 2012 WL 8499876 (DDC) (upholding); *United States v Ruby*, 2013 WL 544888 (SD Cal) (upholding six weeks of CSLI on grounds they are business records/not protected under *Smith* and *Miller*); *United States v Rigmaiden*, 2013 WL 1932800 (D Ariz) (*Smith* and *Miller* control); *United States v Denard*, 24 F3d 599 (5th Cir 2013).

[79] See, for example, *In re Application of United States for an Order Directing a Provider of Electronic Communication Service to Disclose Records to Government*, 620 F3d 304 (3rd Cir 2010); *In re United States for Historical Cell Site Data*, 747 F Supp 2d 827 (SD Tex 2010).

[80] *In re United States for an Order Directing a Provider of Electronic Communication Service to Disclose Records to the Government*, 534 F Supp 2d 585 (WD Pa 2008). The appellate court commented, "This is unique in the author's experience of more than three decades on this court and demonstrates the impressive level of support Magistrate Judge Lenihan's opinion has among her colleagues." *In re Application for an Order*, 620 F3d at 308.

[81] *In re Application for an Order*, 620 F3d at 317. See also *In re United States*, 534 F Supp 2d at 589 ("Our individual cell phones now come with us everywhere: not only on the streets, but in (a) business, financial, medical and other offices; (b) restaurants, theaters and other venues of leisure activity; (c) churches, synagogues and other places of religious affiliation; and (d) our homes and those of our family members, friends, and personal and professional associates.").

[82] *In re Application for an Order*, 620 F3d at 317–18.

required.[83] Rule 41, amended by the Supreme Court in 2006, provided for the installation and use of a tracking device, for a renewable period not to exceed forty-five days.[84] Failure to meet these requirements resulted in exclusion of the evidence.[85]

The government appealed the magistrates' decision to the District Court, which, recognizing the complex issues in the case, affirmed the decision in a short, two-page order, kicking it up to the Court of Appeals for de novo review. The Third Circuit concurred, saying that the magistrate had the discretion to require a warrant.[86] The government could not force a disclosure with less if a court considered the records to be more sensitive.

3. *Addressing the technology gap: Jones, Riley, and disarray.* The subjective nature of the test from *Katz*, in concert with technological advances and inherent doctrinal hostility to acknowledging any resultant constitutional implications, created a world in which "the right of the people to be secure" against government inspection steadily narrowed. The dissonance between the supposed reasonableness test and reality demanded attention. But as the Supreme Court began acknowledging the deeper privacy interests in mobile telephone–related technologies, the application of *Katz* to location tracking was thrown into further doubt.

One of the most important cases, *United States v Jones*, originated in the 2010 case of *United States v Maynard*. The FBI placed a GPS device on a suspected drug dealer's car while it was on private property and then tracked the position of the car every ten seconds for twenty-eight days, without a warrant. The D.C. Circuit held that the tracking amounted to a search, which was per se unreasonable and thus, absent a warrant, violated the Fourth Amendment.[87] Writing for the panel, Judge Douglas Ginsburg zeroed in on one of the analogical fallacies in open space doctrine: he concluded that Jones had not knowingly exposed his behavior to the public "because the likelihood anyone

---

[83] *In re United States*, 534 F Supp 2d at 613–14.

[84] Id at 592.

[85] Id.

[86] *In re Application for an Order*, 620 F3d at 317.

[87] *United States v Maynard*, 615 F3d 544, 555–56 (DC Cir 2010), rehearing en banc denied, *United States v Jones*, 625 F3d 766 (DC Cir 2010) (mem), cert denied, *Maynard v United States*, 131 S Ct 671 (2010) (mem).

will observe all those movements is effectively nil."[88] While, perhaps, physically possible, a reasonable person would not expect a government agent to tail them twenty-four hours a day for a month.

The Supreme Court granted cert in *Maynard* (renamed *Jones*) and ultimately decided the case based on trespass.[89] Two concurrences, though, created a "shadow majority" that cast doubt on location tracking and the future of third-party doctrine.

In her concurring opinion, Justice Sotomayor wrote, "GPS monitoring generates a precise, comprehensive record of a person's public movements that reflects a wealth of detail about her familial, political, professional, religious, and sexual associations."[90] Sotomayor indicated that she might go so far as to reconsider third-party doctrine altogether, noting that it was "ill-suited to the digital age, in which people reveal a great deal of information about themselves to third parties in the course of carrying out mundane tasks."[91]

Justice Alito, in a concurring opinion joined by Justices Ginsburg, Breyer, and Kagan, similarly raised arguments that challenged location tracking and third-party doctrine. "[W]hat is really important," he suggested, is "the *use* of a GPS for the purpose of long-term tracking."[92] The majority's approach led "to incongruous results."[93] Under the open space doctrine, no Fourth Amendment interest would be implicated if law enforcement had followed the car, even longer, from the air and the ground. So why would the installation of a GPS chip yield a different result?[94] What would the constitutional analysis have been if law enforcement had simply tracked a GPS system already installed in the car?[95] Alito expressed concern at myriad "new devices that permit the monitoring of a person's movements," acknowledging that "cell phones and other wireless devices now permit wireless carriers to track and record the location of users," which implicated more than 322 million wireless devices.[96] The point at which

---

[88] *Maynard*, 615 F3d at 558, 563.

[89] *United States v Jones*, 565 US 400 (2012).

[90] Id at 417 (Sotomayor, J, concurring).

[91] Id.

[92] *Jones*, 565 US at 424 (Alito, J, concurring).

[93] Id at 425.

[94] Id.

[95] Id at 426.

[96] *Jones*, 565 US at 428.

the tracking became a search "was surely crossed before the 4-week mark."[97]

Two years after *Jones*, the Supreme Court again wrestled with how to apply *Katz* in a way that took account of the intrusiveness of mobile technologies. *Riley v California* focused on another exception carved out by the Court post-*Katz*: search incident to arrest.[98] In *Riley*, a law enforcement officer stopped the petitioner for a traffic violation, leading to an arrest on weapons charges.[99] During the arrest, the officer, discovering a mobile phone in Riley's pants pocket, scrolled through it and found photographs, videos, and language suggesting involvement in gang activity.[100] Based in part on the data uncovered, the government prosecuted him for a prior shooting with a sentence enhancement for membership in the Bloods.[101]

The Supreme Court objected, carving out (yet another) exception to an exception: officers may search an individual incident to arrest without a warrant, but if they want to inspect a telephone they must first obtain a warrant.[102] The immense storage capacity of cell phones had "several interrelated consequences for privacy": they collect more information in one place than present in isolated records; the volume at stake in even one category of information may be enormous; data held on the device can stretch back for years; and the records provide a detailed and comprehensive view into an individual's private life.[103]

Together, *Jones* and *Riley* indicated judicial disquiet at how the exceptions carved out post-*Katz* had failed to take account of the

---

[97] Id at 431.

[98] *Riley v California*, 134 S Ct 2473 (2014), taken in conjunction with *United States v Wurie*, 728 F3d 1 (2013), cert granted 134 S Ct 999 (2014). See also *Chimel v California*, 395 US 752, 762–63 (1969) (requiring a search incident to arrest be restricted to the area of the arrestee's immediate control as justified by the need for officer safety and preservation of evidence); *United States v Robinson*, 414 US 218, 235 (1973) (holding, "[t]he authority to search the person incident to a lawful custodial arrest, while based upon the need to disarm and to discover evidence, does not depend on what a court may later decide was the probability in a particular arrest situation that weapons or evidence would in fact be found upon the person of the suspect."); *United States v Chadwick*, 433 US 1, 15 (1977) (limiting the search incident to arrest exception to "personal property ... immediately associated with the person of the arrestee.").

[99] *Riley*, 134 S Ct at 2480.

[100] Id.

[101] Id at 2481.

[102] Id at 2485.

[103] *Riley*, 134 S Ct at 2489–91.

impact of new technologies on Fourth Amendment rights. But they did not squarely address the underlying doctrinal concerns.

4. *Growing judicial tension.* In the aftermath of *Jones*, the Fifth, Sixth, Tenth, and Eleventh Circuits held that historic CSLI amounted to information voluntarily conveyed to a third party and thus controlled by *Miller* and *Smith* and not abrogated by *Jones*.[104] Simultaneously, the judiciary expressed significant frustration and concern. In 2017, the Tenth Circuit raised alarm at the implications, writing, "[W]e, too, fear the Orwellian-style surveillance state that could emerge from unfettered government collection of personal data."[105] But "until the Supreme Court instructs us otherwise, we are bound to follow its

---

[104] See *United States v Richardson*, 732 Fed Appx 822, 828 (11th Cir 2018) (per curiam) (holding warrantless acquisition of cell-tower data as outside the Fourth Amendment); *United States v Banks*, 884 F3d 998, 1011–13 (10th Cir 2018) (finding a state court order for historical and real-time tracking consistent with statutory requirements and exigent circumstances); *United States v Thompson*, 866 F3d 1149, 1156–59 (10th Cir 2017), cert granted, 138 S Ct 2706 (stating covered by *Smith/Miller*); *United States v Carpenter*, 819 F3d 880, 887–88 (6th Cir 2016) (adding the content/noncontent distinction, saying that *Smith* is mainly about noncontent and concluding, "The business records here fall on the unprotected side of this line. Those records say nothing about the content of any calls."); *United States v Davis*, 785 F3d 498, 511 (11th Cir 2015) (en banc) (there is "no reason to conclude that cell phone users lack facts about the functions of cell towers or about telephone providers' recording cell tower usage."); *United States v Graham*, 824 F3d 421, 424–26 (4th Cir 2016) (en banc) (overturning panel on third-party grounds); *In re Application of the United States for Historical Cell Site Data*, 724 F3d 600, 614, 610, 613–14 (5th Cir 2013) (even though user "does not directly inform his service provider of the location of the nearest cell phone tower," it is the company that holds the information, demonstrating that the customer "knowingly exposes his activities" to the third party. Additionally, use of a mobile phone is "entirely voluntary."); *United States v Skinner*, 690 F3d 772, 777 (6th Cir 2012) (defendant has no "reasonable expectation of privacy in the data given off by his voluntarily procured pay-as-you-go cell phone."). Compare *United States v Riley*, 858 F3d 1012, 1018 (6th Cir 2017) (Court of Appeals held that police officers did not conduct search under Fourth Amendment when it tracked real-time GPS coordinates of firearm defendant's cell phone for seven hours on date of his arrest), and *United States v Forest*, 355 F3d 942, 950–52 (6th Cir 2004) (rejecting *Miller/Smith* but applying *Knotts* to find no reasonable expectation of privacy in CSLI and holding that coconspirator lacked standing to bring a constitutional claim simply because he also was being tracked when they were together). Numerous district court cases followed suit. See, for example, *United States v Jones*, 2018 WL 3212073 (ED Ky); *United States v Serrano*, 2017 WL 3055244 (SDNY); *United States v Rosario*, 2017 WL 2117534 (ND Ill); *United States v Adkinson*, 2017 WL 1318420, *5 (SD Ind); *United States v Lambis*, 197 F Supp 3d 606, 615 (SDNY 2016); *United States v Wheeler*, 169 F Supp 3d 896, 910 (ED Wis 2016); *United States v Lang*, 78 F Supp 3d 830, 836 (ND Ill 2015); *United States v Rogers*, 71 F Supp 3d 745 (ND Ill 2014); *United States v Moreno-Nevarez*, 2013 WL 5631017, *2 (SD Cal); *United States v Money*, 2013 WL 412626 (ED Ky); *United States v Caraballo*, 963 F Supp 2d 341 (D Vt 2013); *United States v Degaule*, 797 F Supp 2d 1332 (ND Ga 2011); *United States v Benford*, 2010 WL 1266507, *2–3 (ND Ind); *United States v Navas*, 640 F Supp 2d 256 (SDNY 2009), rev'd in part on other grounds, *United States v Navas*, 597 F3d 492 (2d Cir 2010); *In re Applications of United States for Orders Pursuant to Title 18, US Code, Section 2703(d)*, 509 F Supp 2d 81 (D Mass 2007).

[105] *United States v Thompson*, 866 F3d 1149, 1159 (10th Cir 2017) (also writing, "Thompson raises valid concerns about the third-party doctrine in the digital age."). See also *Carpenter*, 819 F3d 893–94 (Stranch concurring in the judgment but rejecting the reasoning) (writing "the sheer quantity of sensitive information procured without a warrant in this case raises

third-party doctrine precedents."[106] The Fourth Circuit reflected, "The Supreme Court may in the future limit, or even eliminate, the third-party doctrine. . . . But without a change in controlling law," their hands were tied.[107]

Scathing criticism of third-party doctrine followed. In the Fourth Circuit, Judge Wynn stated there was "no reason to think that a cell phone user is aware of his CSLI or that he is conveying it," and noted that such information was recorded even when users receive calls, taking no action of their own.[108] In the Eleventh Circuit Judge Martin wrote that the "application of the third-party doctrine threatens to allow the government access to a staggering amount of information that surely must be protected under the Fourth Amendment."[109] Several state supreme courts flatly contradicted the Supreme Court, holding that there *is* a reasonable expectation of privacy in real time or historic CSLI under state constitutional provisions nearly identical to the Fourth Amendment.[110]

In the Sixth Circuit, *United States v Carpenter* reflected the growing confusion and concern among the lower courts. A man arrested for a series of robberies confessed to the crime and identified fifteen

---

Fourth Amendment concerns of the type the Supreme Court acknowledged in *United States v Jones*," and observing that "the addition of cellular (not to mention internet) communication has left courts struggling to determine if (and how) existing [Fourth Amendment] tests apply or whether new tests should be framed," but finding, nevertheless, that the good faith exception to the exclusionary rule applied).

[106] *Thompson*, 866 F3d at 1154.

[107] *United States v Graham*, 824 F3d at 425–26.

[108] Id at 445 (Wynn, J, concurring).

[109] *United States v (Quartavious) Davis*, 785 F3d 498, 535 (11th Cir 2015) (en banc) (Martin dissenting).

[110] See *Commonwealth v Holley*, 87 NE3d 77 (Mass 2017); *Jones v United States*, 168 A3d 703 (DC 2017); *State v Copes*, 165 A3d 418 (Md 2017); *Commonwealth v Fulgiam*, 73 NE3d 798 (Mass 2017); *State v Lunsford*, 141 A3d 270 (NJ 2016); *State v Simmons*, 143 A3d 819 (Me 2016); *Tracey v State*, 152 So 3d 504 (Fla 2014); *Commonwealth v Augustine*, 4 NE3d 846 (Mass 2014); *State v Earls*, 70 A3d 630 (NJ 2013). But see *Zanders v State*, 73 NE3d 178 (Ind 2017), vac'd, 138 S Ct 2206 (2018); *Hankston v State*, 517 SW3d 112 (Tex Crim App 2018); *Love v State*, 543 SW3d 835 (Tex Crim App 2018); *State v Jenkins*, 884 NW2d 429 (Neb 2016); *Marchman v State*, 787 SE2d 734 (Ga 2016); *Taylor v State*, 371 P3d 1036 (Nev 2016); *State v Simmons*, 143 A3d 819 (Me 2016); *Ford v State*, 477 SW3d 321 (Tex Crim App 2015); *Ross v State*, 769 SE2d 43 (Ga 2015); *State v Griffin*, 834 NW2d 688 (Minn 2013). Compare *State v Subdiaz-Osorio*, 849 NW2d 748, 768 (Wis 2014) (declining to address "whether society is prepared to recognize as reasonable an expectation of privacy in cell phone location data," and determining instead that the tracking at issue in the case fell within the exigent circumstances exception); *Commonwealth v Estabrook*, 38 NE3d 231 (Mass 2015) (determining that six hours of CSLI falls short of constitutional search requirements).

accomplices, providing some of their mobile numbers to the FBI.[111] Prosecutors used the SCA to apply for court orders to produce geolocational data for several suspects, including Timothy Carpenter.[112] The government obtained three orders for sixteen different phones, including "[a]ll subscriber information, toll records and call detail records including listed and unlisted numbers dialed or otherwise transmitted to and from [the] target telephones" as well as "cell site information for the target telephones at call origination and at call termination for incoming and outgoing calls."[113]

The request amounted to 127 days of Carpenter's records,[114] which was at the low end of the spectrum in terms of the length of surveillance and the amount of CSLI information obtained. In *United States v Rogers*, for example, a case in the Northern District of Illinois, the government secured three orders for historic CSLI, with a total of 430 days of continuous surveillance of two phones.[115] In *United States v Jones*, which arose in the Eastern District of Kentucky, the numbers were even starker: two warrants issued in relation to thirteen different numbers sought historical CSLI for 739 days.[116]

In the face of the significant inroads into privacy, a doctrinal morass, and open judicial frustration, the Supreme Court had little choice but to grant certiorari. But even as it reached the right answer, it did so in a way that failed either to inter third-party doctrine or to begin to rationalize Fourth Amendment law.

III. The Problem with Carpenter

Carpenter can best be understood as a 5+1 decision, in which the Court recognized that the whole of one's movements over a seven-

---

[111] *Carpenter*, 138 S Ct at 2218.

[112] Id.

[113] *Carpenter*, 819 F3d at 884.

[114] Id at 886.

[115] *United States v Rogers*, 71 F Supp 3d 745 (ND Ill) (first order under § 2703(d) for Rogers's historic records covering June 1, 2012 to March 29, 2013 (302 days); second order for CSLI from Curtis's phone covering June 1, 2012 to April 10, 2013 (333 days); third order for both phones covering March 29, 2013 to August 13, 2013 (128 more days), bringing the total for both phones to 430 days in a row).

[116] *United States v Jones*, 2018 WL 3212073, *8 (ED Ky). The Nov 16, 2015 warrant authorized search and seizure in relation to thirteen different telephone numbers, including, inter alia, historical collection of CSLI and cell tower identification records for call transmissions, all available text/SMS records (including contents), GPS location records, and roaming records covering September 21, 2013 to September 30, 2015 (DTC wireless's records), while the March 28, 2016 warrant authorized similar search and seizure as obtained from AT&T, which included CSLI, but not the content of communications. Id at *1.

day period are protected by the Fourth Amendment. In an opinion authored by Chief Justice Roberts, the five-Justice majority applied *Katz* to establish that individuals have a reasonable expectation of privacy in location information held by service providers, carving out an exception to third-party doctrine.[117] Justice Gorsuch, in his dissent, also would have protected the information under the Fourth Amendment, but he was deeply unsatisfied with the Court's rationale.

Gorsuch got it right. The decision failed to address the doctrinal morass and created significant uncertainty for lower courts going forward. The factors that distinguish location data apply equally well to numerous types of digital records—including those at issue in *Miller* and *Smith*, raising questions about whether *Carpenter* has overturned third-party doctrine in all but name. The factors employed by the Court rely on subjective determinations, pushing the judiciary even more firmly into a policy-making realm. In its dogged adherence to voluntariness, itself the result of an analogical fallacy, the Court vacillated between device-use compulsion and record-creation compulsion, further obfuscating the doctrine. It provided no guidance whatsoever as to what qualifies as a (reasonable) search of records that now fall within the exception to the exception.

A. CSLI: AN EXCEPTION TO AN EXCEPTION

For the majority in *Carpenter*, the nature of location data loomed large. "[D]etailed, encyclopedic, and effortlessly compiled,"[118] the Court wrote, the fact that CSLI was "held by a third-party" was insufficient to deny Fourth Amendment protection.[119] In short, "accessing seven days of CSLI constitutes a Fourth Amendment search."[120]

Jones played a central role in the Court's reasoning in two ways. First, Roberts adopted the shadow majority in the prior case as though it had been the grounds on which it had been decided, writing, "A majority of this Court has already recognized that individuals have

---

[117] *Carpenter*, 138 S Ct 2206, 2217 (2018) ("[A]n individual maintains a legitimate expectation of privacy in the record of his physical movements as captured through CSLI.").

[118] Id at 2209.

[119] Id at 2211.

[120] Id at 2217 n 3. In *Commonwealth v Estabrook*, 38 NE3d 231, 237 (Mass 2015), a state court held that where the state has complied with statutory requirements for required disclosure of customer communications or records, it may obtain up to six hours of person's CSLI without search warrant.

a reasonable expectation of privacy in the whole of their physical movements."[121] As Justice Kennedy pointed out in his dissent, in so doing, the Court treated the concurrences as though they were the holding.[122]

Second, *Carpenter* picked up on language in *Jones*, recognizing the degree to which location data shed light on individuals' private lives and the role that resource constraints have historically played (indirectly) on what society was prepared to recognize as reasonable.[123] Just because records were held by a third party did not negate the character of the information: "time-stamped data provides an intimate window into a person's life, revealing not only his particular movements, but through them his 'familial, political, professional, religious, and sexual associations.'"[124] They could be accessed at the touch of a button "at practically no expense," making CSLI an "even greater privacy concern[] than the GPS monitoring of a vehicle."[125] The issue was not just one of public activity:

> A cell phone faithfully follows its owner beyond public thoroughfares and into private residences, doctor's offices, political headquarters, and other potentially revealing locales. [] Accordingly, when the Government tracks the location of a cell phone it achieves near perfect surveillance, as if it had attached an ankle monitor to the phone's user.[126]

These qualities, Roberts concluded, paired with factors if not unique to CSLI then certainly characteristic of it, were sufficient to overcome third-party doctrine.

B. WHENCE, THIRD-PARTY DOCTRINE?

To fit its decision within the existing doctrine, the Court reinterpreted *Miller* and *Smith* as applying a balancing test within which CSLI

---

[121] *Carpenter*, 138 S Ct at 2209–10, citing *United States v Jones*, 565 US 400, 430, 415 (2012) (Alito, J, concurring and Sotomayor, J, concurring).

[122] *Carpenter*, 138 S Ct at 2231 (Kennedy, J, dissenting), citing *Jones*, 565 US at 404.

[123] *Carpenter*, 138 S Ct at 2217 (majority) (prior to digitization, it was costly to pursue suspects for any extended period of time; resultantly, "society's expectation has been that law enforcement agents and others would not—and indeed, in the main, simply could not—secretly monitor and catalogue every single movement of an individual's car for a very long period.").

[124] Id, citing *Jones*, 565 US at 415 (Sotomayor, J, concurring).

[125] Id.

[126] Id at 2218.

could be distinguished. For the majority, these cases were not just about whether an individual had shared information, but also about the nature of the documents as weighed against any legitimate expectation of privacy in the information conveyed.

For the former, the nature of the documents, the Court concluded that the material at issue in CSLI was different in kind than data considered in the prior cases. *Miller* centered on "negotiable instruments to be used in commercial transactions," while the telephone records in *Smith* provided little by way of "identifying information."[127] In contrast, CSLI fell into its own, distinct category, identified by a number of factors: (*a*) the number of people implicated,[128] (*b*) the volume of information,[129] (*c*) the revealing nature of the information,[130] (*d*) the lack of resource constraints in obtaining it,[131] (*e*) the retroactive nature of the data,[132] (*f*) the near perfect recall,[133]

---

[127] Id at 2219.

[128] Id at 2215 ("The Government's [reliance on third-party doctrine] fails to contend with the seismic shifts in digital technology that made possible the tracking of not only Carpenter's location but also everyone else's, not for a short period but for years and years."); id at 2218 ("[B]ecause location information is continually logged for all of the 400 million devices in the United States—not just those belonging to persons who might happen to come under investigation—this newfound tracking capacity runs against everyone.").

[129] Id at 2211–12 (observing the increasing amount of data collected, its use for business purposes ranging from testing the network to applying roaming charges, the increasingly dense cell site coverage, and the increasing number of ways in which the phone was used (e.g., texting and routine data connections) that required location information).

[130] Id at 2216 (CSLI "is detailed, encyclopedic, and effortlessly compiled."); id at 2218 (CSLI "gives police access to a category of information otherwise unknowable."); id at 2220 (CSLI "implicates privacy concerns far beyond those considered in *Smith* and *Miller*.").

[131] Id at 2217 ("[P]rior to the digital age, law enforcement might have pursued a suspect for a brief stretch, but doing so 'for any extended period of time was difficult and costly and therefore rarely undertaken.'"); id at 2217–18 ("[Now] cell phone tracking is remarkably easy, cheap, and efficient compared to traditional investigative tools. With just the click of a button, the Government can access each carrier's deep repository of historical location information at practically no expense."). See also *Jones*, 565 US at 417–18 (Sotomayor, J, concurring); id at 429 (Alito, J, concurring).

[132] *Carpenter*, 138 S Ct at 2218 (majority) ("[T]he Government can now travel back in time to retrace a person's whereabouts, subject only to the retention policies of the wireless carriers, which currently maintain records for up to five years.").

[133] Id at 2219 ("Unlike the nosy neighbor who keeps an eye on comings and goings, they are ever alert, and their memory is nearly infallible. There is a world of difference between the limited types of personal information addressed in *Smith* and *Miller* and the exhaustive chronicle of location information casually collected by wireless carriers today. The Government thus is not asking for a straightforward application of the third-party doctrine, but instead a significant extension of it to a distinct category of information.").

(g) the potential length of time for which information can be obtained,[134] and (h) the increasing precision.[135]

For the latter, the expectation of privacy, the Court concluded that the user did not voluntarily convey the information in the same way that a user provided the numbers dialed to the phone company or financial records to a bank. The Court reasoned that mobile phones have become a pervasive part of daily life and an integral part of living in the modern world. Throughout the day, phones automatically log onto cell towers, which means that users do not have to *do* anything to have their location recorded.[136] In fact, users do not have an option *not* to create a record.[137] Because conveying the information is not left to the user's discretion, there has been no assumption of risk.[138]

The Court's reinterpretation of *Miller* and *Smith* was met with incredulity by Justices Kennedy, Alito, and Gorsuch in their dissents. For Kennedy, relinquishing the information "to a third party was the entire basis for concluding that the defendants in those cases lacked a reasonable expectation of privacy."[139] The earlier cases were best read as limiting the damage done by *Katz*, placing "necessary limits on the ability of individuals to assert fourth Amendment interests in property to which they lack a 'requisite connection.'"[140] For Kennedy and

---

[134] Id at 2218 (noting that no probable cause is required at the outset for what turns out to be the potential to trail someone every moment of every day for five years).

[135] Id at 2218–19 ("[T]he rule the Court adopts 'must take account of more sophisticated systems that are already in use or in development.' While the records in this case reflect the state of technology at the start of the decade, the accuracy of CSLI is rapidly approaching GPS-level precision.").

[136] *Carpenter*, 138 S Ct at 2220 ("Virtually any activity on the phone generates CSLI, including incoming calls, texts, or e-mails and countless other data connections that a phone automatically makes when checking for news, weather, or social media updates. Apart from disconnecting the phone from the network, there is no way to avoid leaving behind a trail of location data.").

[137] Id ("Apart from disconnecting the phone from the network, there is no way to avoid leaving behind a trail of location data.").

[138] Id ("[I]n no meaningful sense does the user voluntarily 'assume[] the risk' of turning over a comprehensive dossier of his physical movements."), quoting *Smith v Maryland*, 442 US 735, 745 (1979).

[139] Id at 2232 (Kennedy, J, dissenting). See also id at 2228 (reading *Miller* and *Smith* as considering the "absence of property law analogues" not as part of a balancing test, but as "dispositive of privacy expectations.").

[140] *Carpenter*, 138 S Ct at 2227, quoted and cited id at 2260 (Alito, J, dissenting). See also id at 2259 (Alito, J, dissenting) (writing with *Katz*, "the sharp boundary between personal and third-party rights was tested.").

Alito, *Miller* and *Smith* did not so much create a new doctrine as rectify the uncertainty created by *Katz*.[141]

Like Kennedy and Alito, Justice Gorsuch read the foundational third-party cases as categorically establishing that individuals have no reasonable expectation of privacy in records held by third parties, "even if the information is revealed on the assumption that it will be used only for a limited purpose and the confidence placed in the third-party will not be betrayed."[142] *Miller* and *Smith* did not "distinguish between *kinds* of information disclosed to third parties [or] require courts to decide whether to 'extend' those decisions to particular classes of information, depending on their sensitivity."[143] They were simply poorly decided—an example of an irrational doctrine. Gorsuch observed, "People often do reasonably expect that information they entrust to third parties, especially information subject to confidentiality agreements, will be kept private."[144]

Justice Kennedy further charged that the Court misapplied even its own misinterpretation of *Miller* and *Smith*: cell site records were not *more* invasive of privacy than financial and telephone records, they were *less* so.[145]

> What persons purchase and to whom they talk might disclose how much money they make; the political and religious organizations to which they donate; whether they have visited a psychiatrist, plastic surgeon, abortion clinic, or AIDS treatment center; whether they go to gay bars or straight ones; and who are their closest friends and family members. The troves of intimate information the Government can and does obtain using financial records and telephone records dwarfs what can be gathered from cell-site records.[146]

Kennedy was correct that the type of information at stake in financial records can be incredibly invasive. This does not mean, though, that the majority was wrong. It does suggest that in a digital age, CSLI is not so unique. The test applied by the Court could apply equally well to a range of records—including those at issue in the foundational third-party cases. How one views the invasiveness of the information

---

[141] See id at 2228 (Kennedy, J, dissenting); id at 2260 (Alito, J, dissenting).

[142] *United States v Miller*, 425 US 435, 443 (1976), cited and quoted in *Carpenter*, 138 S Ct at 2262 (Gorsuch, J, dissenting).

[143] *Carpenter*, 138 S Ct at 2262 (Gorsuch, J, dissenting).

[144] Id.

[145] Id at 2232 (Kennedy, J, dissenting).

[146] Id.

has a lot to do with perspective, underscoring the subjectivity inherent in the Court's approach and illustrating why it will be so difficult to implement going forward.

1. *Broadly applicable.* The *Carpenter* majority claimed that CSLI is different from other kinds of information held by third parties. In its effort to avoid overturning third-party doctrine, however, the majority failed to acknowledge the applicability of its approach to many types of consumer data. The multifactor test applies just as easily to telephony metadata collection which, ostensibly, is the *same type of information* at issue in *Smith*, raising questions about whether *Carpenter* actually overturned third-party doctrine.

Let's start with the number of people implicated, one of the defining factors of CSLI. The same is true of telephony metadata. There are 265.9 million mobile phone users in the United States.[147] These devices generate detailed information about who is in contact with each user, implicating hundreds of millions of people.

Like location data, the volume of communications at issue is enormous and rapidly increasing. In addition to expanding mobile phone use, approximately 224.3 million mobile phone users have Smartphones that run sophisticated applications, which provide further ways for users to communicate with each other.[148] The top app, Facebook, is on 78 percent of all Smartphones.[149] The company has a tremendous reach: in October 2018, the Pew Research Center reported that approximately two-thirds of all adults in the United States use Facebook.[150] Users can send and receive messages to anyone on the network using Facebook Messenger, the mobile phone's browser, the Facebook SMS Service, or third-party apps.[151] The company collects

---

[147] MaXab, *How Many Cell Phone Subscribers in the US 2018* (Media Tech Reviews, Mar 20, 2018), online at http://www.mediatechreviews.com/how-many-cell-phone-subscribers-the -us. This number is expected to increase. *Share of Americans Using a Personal Cell Phone Users in 2018, by Age* (Statista), online at https://www.statista.com/statistics/231612/number-of-cell -phone-users-usa.

[148] *Smartphone* (Techopedia), online at https://www.techopedia.com/definition/2977/smart phone.

[149] MaXab, *How Many Cell Phone Subscribers* (cited in note 147).

[150] John Gramlich, *8 Facts About Americans and Facebook* (Pew Research Center, Oct 24, 2018), online at http://www.pewresearch.org/fact-tank/2018/10/24/facts-about-americans -and-facebook (reporting that 68 percent of American adults use Facebook, with 74 percent visiting the site daily).

[151] *Six Ways to Send Facebook Messages Without Messenger* (Dr. Fone), online at https:// drfone.wondershare.com/facebook/send-facebook-messages-without-messenger.html.

logs of all communications—including data on individuals who do not even have a Facebook account, gleaned from their inclusion in users' contact lists.[152] Facebook is only one company in a rapidly growing social media market in which some 3 billion people worldwide (approximately one-third of the population on earth) are expected to take part by 2021.[153]

The information that can be extracted from the associated telephony metadata can be far more invasive than location data. Even one-off communications can reveal hobbies, interests, relationships, and beliefs. Patterns impart degrees of intimacy. Using network analytics, relationships can be mapped into nodes and networks and analyzed.[154] Communities previously hidden from view can be detected.[155] Power structures and levels of influence can be identified.[156] Social networks, of course, are not static. Future interactions, col-

---

[152] Gabriel J. X. Dance, Michael LaFoergia, and Nicholas Confessore, *As Facebook Raised a Privacy Wall, It Carved an Opening for Tech Giants* (NY Times, Dec 18, 2018), online at https://www.nytimes.com/2018/12/18/technology/facebook-privacy.html?action=click&module=Top%20Stories&pgtype=Homepage; Kurt Wagner, *This Is How Facebook Collects Data on You Even if You Don't Have an Account* (Recode, Apr 20, 2018), online at https://www.recode.net/2018/4/20/17254312/facebook-shadow-profiles-data-collection-non-users-mark-zuckerberg.

[153] *Mobile Social Media—Statistics & Facts* (Statista), online at https://www.statista.com/topics/2478/mobile-social-networks.

[154] See Greg Statell, *How the NSA Uses Social Network Analysis to Map Terrorist Networks* (Digital Tonto, June 12, 2013), online at https://www.digitaltonto.com/2013/how-the-nsa-uses-social-network-analysis-to-map-terrorist-networks; Amir Gandomi and Murtaza Haider, *Beyond the Hype: Big Data Concepts, Methods, and Analytics,* 35 Intl J Info Management 137 (2015); Julia Heidemann, Mathias Klier, and Florian Probst, *Online Social Networks: A Survey of a Global Phenomenon, Computer Networks,* 56 Computer Networks 3866 (2012).

[155] Charu C. Aggarwal, *An Introduction to Social Network Data Analytics* (Springer, 2011). See also *Community Detection Algorithms* (Neo4j), online at https://neo4j.com/docs/graph-algorithms/current/algorithms/community.

[156] Degree centrality counts how many neighbors a node within a network has. *Degree Centrality* (Network Science), online at https://www.sci.unich.it/~francesc/teaching/network/degree.html. Betweenness centrality reveals how information flows through a network—that is, nodes that provide a bridge between different parts of the network. *The Betweenness Centrality Algorithm* (Neo4j), online at https://neo4j.com/docs/graph-algorithms/current/algorithms/betweenness-centrality. Closeness centrality indicates the most efficient spread of information through a network, that is, how close they are to the relevant nodes. *The Closeness Centrality Algorithm* (Neo4j), online at https://neo4j.com/docs/graph-algorithms/current/algorithms/closeness-centrality. Eigenvector centrality looks at the importance of a node in terms of the importance of nodes with which it is linked. It is a way of ranking importance in a network. *Eigenvector Centrality* (Network Science), online at https://www.sci.unich.it/~francesc/teaching/network/eigenvector.html. See also Lei Tang and Huan Liu, *Community Detection and Mining in Social Media,* in Jiawei Han et al, eds, *Synthesis Lectures on Data Mining and Knowledge Discovery* 1–137 (Morgan and Claypool, 2010).

laboration, and influence can be estimated, based on latent data.[157] Using regression equations and machine learning, observers can predict what people are likely to do, *even when the subjects themselves are not aware of their patterns.*[158] The more information that is collected, the more accurate such predictions become.[159]

Massive amounts of data are being produced by social media companies such as Facebook, Twitter, and WhatsApp. That information already has been used to predict influenza, stock market trends, and customer attitudes, as well as spiritual beliefs and political views.[160] Over the past five years, there has been an explosion in scholarly articles and book chapters focused on exploiting social network analytics in the criminal context as well.[161] The technique can be effective in identifying critical nodes, which law enforcement can then target to disrupt criminal enterprises.[162]

---

[157] See David Liben-Nowell and Jon Kleinberg, *The Link Prediction Problem for Social Networks*, in Donald Kraft, ed, *Proceedings of the Twelfth International Conference on Information and Knowledge Management* 556 (ACM, 2003).

[158] See Jianqing Fan, Fang Han, and Han Liu, *Challenges of Big Data Analysis*, 1 Natl Sci Rev 293, 293 (2014).

[159] Id at 297–98.

[160] Id at 296–97 .

[161] See, for example, Giulia Berlosconi, *Social Network Analysis and Crime Prevention*, in Benoit Le Clerc and Ernesto U. Savano, eds, *Crime Prevention in the 21st Century* 129 (Springer, 2017); Morgan Burcher, *Social Network Analysis as a Tool for Criminal Intelligence*, 21 Trends in Organized Crime 278 (2018); David A. Bright, Catherine Greenhill, and Natalya Levenkova, *Dismantling Criminal Networks: Can Node Attributes Play a Role?*, in Carlo Morselli, ed, *Crime and Networks* 148 (Routledge, 2013); Francesco Calderoni, *Identifying Mafia Bosses from Meeting Attendance*, in Anthony J. Masys, ed, *Networks and Network Analysis for Defence and Security* 27 (Springer, 2014); Francesco Calderoni, *Predicting Organized Crime Leaders*, in Gisela Bichler and Aili E. Malm, eds, *Disrupting Criminal Networks: Network Analysis in Crime Prevention* 89 (First Forum, 2015); David Décary-Hétu, *Information Exchange Paths in IRC Hacking Chat Rooms*, in Carlo Morselli, ed, *Crime and Networks* 218 (Routledge, 2014); Paul A. C. Duijn and Peter P. H. M. Klerks, *Social Network Analysis Applied to Criminal Networks: Recent Developments in Dutch Law Enforcement*, in Anthony J. Masys, ed, *Networks and Network Analysis for Defence and Security* 121 (Springer, 2014); Jenny C. Piquette, Chris M. Smith, and Andrew V. Papachristos, *Social Network Analysis of Urban Street Gangs*, in Gerben Bruinsma and David Weisburd, eds, *Encyclopedia of Criminology and Criminal Justice* 4981 (Springer, 2014); David A. Bright et al, *Networks Within Networks: Using Multiple Link Types to Examine Network Structure and Identify Key Actors in a Drug Trafficking Operation*, 16 Global Crime 219 (2015).

[162] Burcher, 21 Trends in Organized Crime at 278 (cited in note 161). Instead of focusing on low-level criminals, for instance, law enforcement could use metadata to identify the key members of Mara Salvatrucha (MS-13), a violent criminal gang formed in the 1980s in Los Angeles. They could then call those individuals in for questioning, subject them to more detailed scrutiny, put out false information about them to undermine their position within the organization, or prosecute them in an effort to imprison them and thus interrupt the network.

Like location data, the resource constraints in obtaining telephony metadata and subjecting it to targeted queries or sophisticated algorithms are rapidly diminishing. In the past, it might not have been possible to record most, or even all, of an individual's relationships and communications. Now, not only is it possible, but big data and massive computing power have put technology in hyperdrive. What might have taken days, or even months, of analysis, can now be done at the push of a button.

All of this information, moreover, like location data, is retroactive in that it relates to communications in the past. And while CSLI provides near-perfect recall, telephony metadata reproduce *exactly* what happened, recording at precisely what time, on which date, an individual was in contact with which number or entity. And it is available for weeks, months, or even years at a time. The only limit is that of the cell phone provider or the app itself.

By all the factors laid out by the Court in *Carpenter*, pen register and trap and trace data prove equally, if not even more, invasive than location information. If the intent of the Court is to be believed (i.e., to restore some sort of equilibrium between society and law enforcement), then such records *must* be included in the exception to the exception. A similar argument could be made about banking records, which were at issue in *Miller*.[163]

In *Carpenter*, the Court tried to draw a distinction between location information and telephony metadata based on voluntariness.[164] This

---

[163] Banking records implicate nearly every American. The volume of information held by banks is enormous and can be extremely revealing in terms of individuals' private lives. As technology has progressed, fewer and fewer resource constraints exist for obtaining, and analyzing, significant amounts of data. Banking records are just as precise as telephony metadata, and they can be obtained for activity that occurred decades before. As with mobile telephones, it is not an option in the current age not to have a bank account; nor is it voluntary, in any sense of the word, not to confide certain information to banks—particularly information that is required by statute. Banking records look remarkably like location data, in terms of the factors laid out by the Court in *Carpenter*. See also *Carpenter*, 138 S Ct at 2233 (Kennedy, J, dissenting) ("Financial records are of vast scope. Banks and credit card companies keep a comprehensive account of almost every transaction an individual makes on a daily basis. ... And the decision whether to transact with banks and credit card companies is no more or less voluntary than the decision whether to use a cell phone."); id at 2224 (arguing that the Court has drawn an "unprincipled and unworkable line between cell-site records on the one hand and financial and telephonic records on the other.").

[164] *Carpenter*, 138 S Ct at 2220 (majority). See also *Carpenter*, 138 S Ct at 2227–30 (Kennedy, J, dissenting) (noting that by voluntarily conveying information to the respective companies, the defendants in *Miller* and *Smith* "'assumed the risk that the information would be divulged to police,'" and arguing that Carpenter similarly lacked any reasonable expectation of privacy in CSLI).

assertion, however, does not survive scrutiny. For the distinction to hold, one of two things would have to be true: either having a phone must be optional, or providing the numbers to the company must be at the user's discretion. Neither is accurate. As for the former, 99.28 percent of adults aged eighteen to twenty-nine have a mobile phone.[165] As the Court recognized in *Riley*, the devices have become an indispensable part of living in society. In regard to the latter, users cannot mask the numbers that they call. Companies must have this information to connect them to the other party, and vice versa. Providing it to the company is not voluntary in any sense of the word.[166]

In sum, the factors considered by the Court as (ostensibly) unique to CSLI apply equally well to telephony metadata—and banking data[167]—making the claim that the Court left *Miller* and *Smith* untouched ring somewhat hollow.[168] Applying the *Carpenter* test, it is difficult to see any distinction between many types of third-party documents.[169] With this in mind, Justice Alito's critique, that the Court's "revolutionary" holding fractured the "pillars of Fourth Amendment law," seems about right.[170]

2. *Unknowable.* Not only do many different kinds of digital records meet the test laid out in *Carpenter*—including the records at issue in the foundational third-party cases—but it is impossible to say with any certainty how the courts will apply the logic adopted. The Court's approach requires a case-by-case analysis in which unanswerable questions are presented. Because it is based on a bad analogy and highly indeterminate concepts, such as voluntariness and reasonableness, it will prove difficult to implement in any sort of consistent manner.[171]

---

[165] *Share of Americans Using a Personal Cell Phone Users in 2018, by Age* (Statista) (cited in note 147).

[166] A third possibility might be that telephone users voluntarily call *certain numbers.* This argument, though, is at odds with the Court's acknowledgment in *Riley* that a phone is concomitant to living in society. It makes no sense to then turn around and say that it is *not* actually necessary to use it to be part of that society.

[167] See note 163.

[168] As Justice Gorsuch laments, *Carpenter* only made matters worse, placing "*Smith* and *Miller* on life support and supplement[ing] them with a new and multilayered inquiry that seems to be only *Katz*-squared." *Carpenter*, 138 S Ct at 2272 (Gorsuch, J, dissenting).

[169] The same could be said of educational assessments, employment records, and the like. So, too, does it apply to other forms of metadata, such as IP addresses, websites visited, or text and email contacts.

[170] *Carpenter*, 138 S Ct at 2247 (Alito, J, dissenting).

[171] See also id at 2261 (recognizing that the reasoning of the majority will require the Court to take every case and subject each type of information to qualifications, further entangling Fourth Amendment jurisprudence).

a) Which records? Like many of the lower courts that confronted CSLI, the *Carpenter* court emphasized voluntary assumption of risk. In doing so, it perpetuated the false analogy between informant doctrine and third-party business records. As explained above, this conflation subordinates the constitutional right to security in "papers"; ignores the difference between admitting illegal activity to a coconspirator and engaging in a legal, contractual relationship; assumes consent for a limited purpose means consent to government surveillance; and sidesteps the extent to which commercial relations are an essential part of ordinary life. It is an awful analogy.

The Court discussed two kinds of potentially compelled (or voluntary) actions: use of a mobile phone, and the generation of location records *while* using the phone.[172] It did not provide guidelines for how to think about these two categories going forward; nor did it address their relative importance or how to gauge greater or lesser degrees of compulsion.

Consider, first, what could be termed device-use compulsion. Noting that carrying a phone is not an option in the contemporary context, the Court neglected to enquire (*a*) whether other mobile devices are "voluntarily" used, or (*b*) whether records connected to the technologies contained on (specifically) mobile telephones fall within the exception.

For (*a*), a colorable case could be made that *many* other kinds of nontelephonic mobile devices are critical in the contemporary environment. The computer on which I am writing this article is essential to my work. It would be almost impossible to undertake modern legal scholarship without one. The same could be said of the use of computers in many different fields. As a matter of private use, computers are used for everything from shopping, entertainment, and scheduling dates with friends, to cooking, buying bus, train, and plane tickets, and planning vacations. They have become a pervasive part of ordinary life. In 2016, the American Community Survey determined that 89 percent of American households have a computer, making it, in the Census Bureau's estimation, "a common feature of everyday

---

[172] Although I do not here go into detail, it is worth noting that the way in which the Court referred to compulsion versus voluntary action departs significantly from philosophical treatment of these areas. In *Carpenter*, what the Court appears to mean by these concepts relates to technical requirements of participation in modern society.

life."[173] Under *Carpenter*, does this mean that Fourth Amendment protection extends to records associated with computers?

For that matter, are *all* electronic devices, which store digital information, (in)voluntary in a modern era? If not, how do we distinguish between those that are and those that are not? The Court provides no basis on which to calculate which devices are coerced by the circumstances of life. What level of necessity is required? How pervasive must they be? How will voluntariness be determined? By the number of people using the technology? By the percentage of the population? *Carpenter* clarifies none of this.

Perhaps, turning to (*b*), voluntariness has to do not with the phone itself, but with the specific function the phone performs. If so, then it is not clear if the Court's reasoning is limited to the traditional place of the phone in contacting others in society—for personal or business purposes—or whether it has something to do with the *types of technologies* typically contained on the telephone. For the former, the primary use is found in the function of the device *as a phone*. So, in order to exist in modern life (i.e., to be part of society), perhaps the underlying theory is that we must carry one in order to be in contact with others. Or perhaps it is just use of the phone when it operates *as a tracking device* that qualifies for protection. But if that is the case, then all photographs that include geolocational metadata, and applications like Yelp, Flixter, or Foursquare, which rely on location information, also are protected. What if the voluntariness is not limited to location data? If use of the mobile telephone is not voluntary (under *Riley* and *Carpenter*), for reasons related to taking part in society, then wouldn't this encompass other functions the phone performs, such as social media?

And who is to make the voluntariness determination? From *Carpenter*, it appears that the Court has this responsibility. But judges' experiences will shape the answer. For some, social media may be a complete mystery, not at all part of their daily interactions. For others, Facebook may be an indispensable part of their social life. For those of a younger generation, who see Facebook as something that their grandparents do, their world may revolve around Snapchat, Instagram, and YouTube. For them, participation is not voluntary. It

---

[173] Camille Ryan, *Computer and Internet Use in the United States: 2016* (US Census Bureau, Aug 8, 2018), online at https://www.census.gov/content/dam/Census/library/publications/2018/acs/ACS-39.pdf.

is required for participating in, and being part of, society.[174] Justices may see it quite differently. The result will further entrench the judiciary in policy determinations.

Perhaps what the Court meant in *Carpenter* was that voluntariness relates not to the device, but to the production of records themselves, a sort of record-creation compulsion: that is, users do not have a meaningful choice whether to convey their location to a service provider.[175] But this is a distinctly odd way to think about what one does when one uses a mobile device. The argument is that by having the device, you are locked into transmitting your location to the internet service provider (ISP) to get service. But by using the device in certain ways—ways equally central to the role of the device in modern society—you also are locked into transmitting all sorts of different kinds of data.

Consider, for instance, Internet Protocol (IP) addresses, which are dynamically assigned to a device when you go online. When you are at home, it is assigned by your ISP. But that number can change as quickly as a power outage, when the server is turned off. As soon as you leave home and use a different network to go online, a new (temporary) IP address is assigned.[176] You can try to mask your IP address by using a Virtual Private Network (VPN) Service, the Onion Router (Tor) (a network that allows users to disguise their identity by using multiple servers and encryption), a proxy server, or free/public WiFi.[177] But most users are not this sophisticated and are left with the default IP address, which reveals their location.

So, under *Carpenter*, does this mean that IP addresses are included? If so, then how about Uniform Resource Locators (URLs)? By using a browser to visit web pages, you may (unwittingly) record the URLs in your browser cache, the operating system cache, the router cache, *and* the ISP cache.[178] Are you providing that information voluntarily or not? If the carrying of the phone is not voluntary, and the access

---

[174] See discussion in note 172.

[175] *Carpenter*, 138 S Ct at 2220 (majority).

[176] See, for example, *My IP Address Is:* (WhatIsMyIPAddress.com), online at https://whatis myipaddress.com.

[177] *How to Hide Your IP Address* (WhatIsMyIPAddress.com), online at https://whatismy ipaddress.com/hide-ip.

[178] Maneesha Wijesinghe, *What Happens When You Type a URL in the Browser and Press Enter?* (Medium, Apr 25, 2017), online at https://medium.com/@maneesha.wijesinghe1/what-happens -when-you-type-an-url-in-the-browser-and-press-enter-bb0aa2449c1a.

it provides to the online world similarly compelled, then it seems as though it ought to be considered within the domain of the Fourth Amendment. As in the case of CSLI, it is simply a by-product of actions you take in the real world—in this case, the decision to go online.

With so many different questions left unanswered by *Carpenter* about how to think about device-use compulsion and record-production compulsion, it will be up to the courts to answer them and to gauge voluntariness—entrenching courts ever more firmly in the policy-making realm and leading to unpredictable results.

b) When is a search reasonable? In *Carpenter*, the Court held that seven days of CSLI required a warrant. For Justice Kennedy, this (apparently arbitrary) distinction was "illogical" and would "frustrate principled application of the Fourth Amendment."[179] Worse, the Court had collapsed its determination that obtaining CSLI constituted a search and the analysis of whether or not it was "reasonable."[180] For Kennedy, the proper approach would have been to remand the case to address the "important and difficult issues" that marked the second query.[181] Underlying his critique was the Court's failure to address the role of technology not just in determining whether a search had occurred, but whether it was one that society was prepared to recognize as reasonable. That lack of precision regarding the role of technology raised myriad questions that will further frustrate efforts to implement the decision in a reliable manner.

The majority in *Carpenter* went some length to note that "seismic shifts in digital" technologies had created CSLI—a form of information hitherto unknown.[182] When confronted by "new concerns wrought by digital technology," the Court had to be careful not to reflexively extend precedent.[183] The majority was critical of the gov-

---

[179] *Carpenter*, 138 S Ct at 2224 (Kennedy, J, dissenting) ("[T]he Government crosses a constitutional line when it obtains a court's approval to issue a subpoena for more than six days of cell-site records in order to determine whether a person was within several hundred city blocks of a crime scene.").

[180] Id at 2235 ("Having concluded . . . that the Government searched Carpenter when it obtained cell-site records from his cell phone service providers, the proper resolution of this case should have been to remand for the Court of Appeals to determine in the first instance whether the search was reasonable.").

[181] Id.

[182] Id at 2219 (majority).

[183] *Carpenter*, 138 S Ct at 2222.

ernment, and Kennedy, for failing to grasp the implications of the "new technology."[184] There was a "world of difference between the limited types of personal information addressed in *Smith* and *Miller* and the exhaustive chronicle of location information" now available.[185] The Court also had to be mindful "of more sophisticated [technologies] that were already in use or in development."[186]

The majority's language suggested that the *novelty* of the technology mattered—that is, the extent to which the technology in question departed from previous circumstances.[187] It was not clear whether the chief complaint was the impact of new technologies or the creation of new types of records.[188] Neither, as a limitation going forward, is persuasive.

While the factors laid out in *Carpenter* underscored the impact of one "new" technology that had resulted in near-universal 24/7 location tracking, in other situations, perhaps the prior limitation is merely one of storage capacity, or battery life—or whether information is shared, an algorithm created, or an old technology applied to a new context. Perhaps it has nothing to do with the novelty of the technology in question.

If it *is* only "new" technologies, how do we draw the line? This is a hard question. The *Carpenter* court stated, for example, that its decision did not reach traditional cameras.[189] But a camera with still image capabilities and limited memory is a different animal than one with video capabilities and virtually unlimited memory. Still more are these different from cameras with infrared vision, remote rotation, and powerful zoom functions, or that capture not just video, but audio as well. Yet more distant are cameras paired with biometric identification systems, or linked to extensive online databases providing de-

---

[184] Id at 2219.

[185] Id.

[186] Id at 2218. See also id at 2223 ("As Justice Brandeis explained in his famous dissent, the Court is obligated . . . to ensure that the 'progress of science' does not erode Fourth Amendment protections.") (citations omitted).

[187] See, for example, *Carpenter*, 138 S Ct at 2217 (comparing tailing a suspect "[p]rior to the digital age" to the contemporary use of technology).

[188] On the one hand, the Court focused on the technology itself, as well as the state of the technology. Id at 2219–20. On the other hand, it observed "a world of difference between the limited types of personal information addressed in *Smith* and *Miller* and the exhaustive chronicle of location information casually collected by wireless carries today," referring to CSLI as "an entirely different species of business record." Id at 2219, 2222.

[189] Id at 2220.

tailed, personally identifiable information. Even further are such cameras mounted on a drone and not tied to one place. Nevertheless, the government considers all of these to be one technology, at times not even deigning to issue a new privacy impact assessment when the nature of the recordings, capacity, or capabilities change.[190]

Or perhaps the Court, applying a rule of functional equivalence, would only include technologies that allow for the constructive search of what was traditionally found to be unreasonable when subject to a physical search. The Court has used this approach in related areas. The protections of the home, for instance, extend to anywhere that functions in the same manner, regardless of whether it amounts to an actual "house."[191]

Functional equivalence has been particularly important for giving courts latitude to take account of new technologies. Air travel did not exist at the founding, but as individuals began using airports, the Court extended the border exception to the "functional equivalent" of the border: interior airports employed as ports of entry.[192] Where technology has made it possible to conduct a search that otherwise would require entry and thereby exposes the home to inspection, the Court again has applied a rule of functional equivalence.[193] Accord-

---

[190] The Department of Justice's (DOJ) Federal Bureau of Investigation operates the Next Generation Identification–Interstate Photo System (NGI-IPS) and an internal unit called Facial Analysis, Comparison and Evaluation (FACE) Services. Although DOJ developed a Privacy Impact Assessment in 2008 for NGI-IPS, it did not update it as the system integrated new technologies, nor did it publish a PIA on FACE Services. US Government Accountability Office, *Face Recognition Technology: FBI Should Better Ensure Privacy and Accuracy* (May 16, 2016), online at https://www.gao.gov/products/GAO-16-267. See also Laura K. Donohue, *Technological Leap, Statutory Gap, and Constitutional Abyss: Remote Biometric Identification Comes of Age*, 97 Minn L Rev 407 (2012) (noting the absence of PIAs despite the addition of new technologies).

[191] See, for example, *United States v Dunn*, 480 US 294, 301 n 4 (1987) (defining curtilage as an area "harbor[ing] those intimate activities associated with domestic life and the privacies of the home."); *United States v McDonald*, 335 US 451 (1948) (regarding a locked common area of a rooming house to be within the Fourth Amendment).

[192] *Torres v Puerto Rico*, 442 US 465 (1979) (holding that the search of an individual arriving in the Commonwealth of Puerto Rico from the United States did not satisfy Fourth Amendment requirements because there was no functional equivalent to an international border of the United States); *Almeida-Sanchez v United States*, 413 US 266, 273 (1973) ("[A] search of the passengers and cargo of an airplane arriving at a St. Louis airport after a nonstop flight from Mexico City would clearly be the functional equivalent of a border search.").

[193] See also Barnett and Bernick, 107 Georgetown L J at 3 (cited in note 10) (arguing for a commitment to "the functions, purposes, goals, [and] aims" of constitutional clauses in ascertaining the meaning of the Constitution); Paul Ohm, *The Many Revolutions of Carpenter*, Harv J L & Tech at 34 (forthcoming 2019), online at https://osf.io/preprints/lawarxiv/bsedj /download (articulating a rule of technological equivalence as: "The Court in the past has

ingly, in *United States v Knotts*, the Court considered a beeper tracked along a public road to fall outside Fourth Amendment protections; but then, in *United States v Karo*, the Court held that the moment at which a beeper crossed the threshold, a search had occurred.[194] Whether or not law enforcement actually entered the domicile, they could infer that the can of ether being tracked was inside.[195] Similarly, in *Kyllo*, the Court determined that the use of a thermal imaging device to read the heat signatures of exterior walls constituted a search within the meaning of the Fourth Amendment.[196] Justice Scalia, writing for the Court, rejected the government's argument that it was constitutional because the thermal device did not uncover "intimate details." Using it violated a categorical protection: "In the home, our cases show, all details are intimate details, because the entire area is held safe from prying government eyes."[197] Lower courts have adopted the same approach for other technologies that reveal what happens inside the home.[198]

In *Carpenter*, the Court favorably cited back to *Kyllo*, acknowledging "[a]s technology has enhanced the Government's capacity to encroach upon areas normally guarded from inquisitive eyes," the Court has tried to ensure the protections guaranteed at the founding.[199] In dicta, the Court went on to accept that the examination of digitized letters would constitute a search. It considered email "a sensible ex-

---

held that information in a particular, traditional privacy context is protected by the Fourth Amendment. A technology produces information that is a modern-day equivalent to the information produced in the traditional context of step one. The information in the modern context is also protected by the Fourth Amendment.").

[194] *United States v Karo*, 468 US 705, 715 (1984) ("[H]ad a DEA agent thought it useful to enter the Taos residence to verify that the ether was actually in the house and had he done so surreptitiously and without a warrant, there is little doubt that he would have engaged in an unreasonable search within the meaning of the Fourth Amendment.... [T]he result is the same where, without a warrant, the Government surreptitiously employs an electronic device to obtain information that it could not have obtained by observation from outside the curtilage of the house."); *Knotts*, 460 US at 281 ("A person traveling in an automobile on public thoroughfares has no reasonable expectation of privacy in his movements from one place to another.").

[195] *Karo*, 468 US at 714–15. See also *Kyllo v United States*, 533 US 27, 36 (2001) (Scalia, J, for the majority) (stating that in *Karo* "the police 'inferred' from the activation of a beeper that a certain can of ether was in the home.").

[196] *Kyllo*, 533 US at 29.

[197] Id at 37–38. See also *Florida v Jardines*, 569 US 1 (2013).

[198] See *Naperville Smart Meter Awareness v Naperville*, 900 F3d 521 (7th Cir 2018).

[199] *Carpenter*, 138 S Ct at 2214.

ception," an example of "the modern-day equivalents of an individual's own 'papers' or 'effects.'"[200]

The challenge in understanding *Carpenter* in light of the rule of functional equivalence is that *Miller* and *Smith* eviscerated the protections afforded to "papers." Yet it appears that *Carpenter* eliminated third-party doctrine in all but name. So, going forward, if we apply the rule of functional equivalence, how do we understand "papers," or for that matter, "effects," in a digital age? Do text messages count? Or instant messages? Or chats in multiplayer online games?

Perhaps the technologies that allow for constructive search of traditional categories provide a minimum. If so, how far out does the new rule go? Again, in dicta, the Court noted that whatever rule the Court adopts must take account of increasingly sophisticated technologies.[201] But how sophisticated do they need to be? Which (new) technologies constitute a search, but do not fall afoul of the reasonableness determination? How is the decision to be reached? In collapsing its analysis, the Court failed to provide a reliable way for the lower courts to draw a line, even as it cemented them into a policy-making realm.[202]

IV. Residual Property Rights

While *Carpenter* unquestionably represents a departure from familiar doctrinal landmarks, it leaves us at somewhat of a loss. How should we chart a future course concerning personal, digital information held by companies in a post-*Katz*, post-*Miller* and *Smith*, post-*Carpenter* era?

Consistent with the previous discussion, the voluntary assumption of risk is a nonstarter. Continued use of it will confound efforts to provide consistency across the circuits. In addition to the analogical fallacies at work in the decision, *Carpenter* fails to provide guidance on device-use compulsion and record-creation compulsion, both of

---

[200] Id at 2222, citing and quoting id at 2230 (Kennedy, J, dissenting), citing *United States v Warshak*, 631 F3d 266, 283–88 (6th Cir 2010).

[201] *Carpenter*, 138 S Ct at 2218–19 (majority).

[202] Gorsuch raised myriad further questions that bedevil the holding. See *Carpenter*, 138 S Ct at 2266–67 (Gorsuch, J, dissenting) (concluding, "In the end, our lower court colleagues are left with two amorphous balancing tests, a series of weighty and incommensurable principles to consider in them, and a few illustrative examples that seem little more than the product of judicial intuition.").

which, in any event, rely on complex policy determinations. This approach further draws courts into value judgments, running the risk that the public will lose confidence in the judiciary.

No better does the "novel technology" approach fare. As argued above, it is beset by hard questions, including how to understand what counts as a "new" technology. As digitization becomes widespread, this approach will become less and less relevant. New forms of information that previously did not even exist will become available, which implicates interests ostensibly protected by the Fourth Amendment.

Given these potentially insuperable difficulties, the judiciary ought seriously to consider returning to constitutional first principles: a property-rights-based approach. As the Supreme Court observed, "One virtue of the Fourth Amendment's property-rights baseline is that it keeps easy cases easy."[203] Just as the Court in *Karo* and *Kyllo* adopted a rule of functional equivalence in regard to the home, it can embrace a similar approach to papers. A central question then becomes which digital documents come within constitutional protections. A property-rights approach helps to answer that question. This is the path favored by Gorsuch in *Carpenter*.[204] He drew on bailment and positive law, asking what kind of legal interest would be sufficient to generate ownership rights and what sources of law would help to determine the answer.[205] In the balance of this article, I identify important reasons why the Court should consider adopting a property-rights approach.

A. GENERATION, OWNERSHIP, AND POSSESSION

As the dissents in *Carpenter* observed, the Fourth Amendment has at its core a right in one's own property that stems from the inclusion

---

[203] *Florida v Jardines*, 569 US 1, 12 (2013).

[204] Gorsuch envisioned three possible futures: the Court could doggedly hold to precedent, it could reevaluate the world post-*Katz*, or it could chart a new course. *Carpenter*, 138 S Ct at 2262 (Gorsuch, J, dissenting). The first amounted to "A doubtful application of *Katz* that lets the government search almost whatever it wants whenever it wants." Id at 2264. The second was problematic, as the issue was *Katz* in the first place. Id. The third offered the most promising way forward. See id at 2267–72.

[205] Id at 2268. See also William Baude and James Stern, *The Positive Law Model of the Fourth Amendment*, 129 Harv L Rev 1821 (2016) (arguing that a Fourth Amendment search only occurs where a private party could not lawfully perform the action undertaken by the government); Richard Re, *The Positive Law Floor*, 129 Harv L Rev F 313 (2016) (arguing in juxtaposition to Baude and Stern that positive law creates a floor, not a ceiling, on Fourth Amendment protections).

of *"their* persons, houses, papers, and effects."[206] The text does not refer to a right exercised in relation to the property of others.[207] It thus requires the Court to ask *whose* property was searched.

This approach is consistent with *Katz*, which, as the Supreme Court has recognized, did not extinguish the role of property rights in the Fourth Amendment.[208] Even the "legitimation" of *Katz*'s "expectations" test(s) "must have a source outside the Fourth Amendment, either by reference to concepts of real or personal property or to understandings that are recognized and permitted by society."[209] From this, we can conclude that even under existing precedent, *ownership rights still matter*.

Can individuals have an ownership interest in *digital* documents or records? The answer here is plainly yes. Federal statutes routinely treat "data," "digital data," "digital content," and "digital assets" as property.[210] The same is true at a state level: since 2013, forty-six states have enacted laws governing access to digital assets ranging from email, social media accounts, and microblogging to electronically stored information.[211] State statutes also create a private right of action to redress the unauthorized collection, retention, disclosure,

---

[206] US Const, Amend IV; *Carpenter*, 138 S Ct at 2260 (Alito, J, dissenting) (The Fourth Amendment protects *"their* persons, houses, papers, and effects"—not those of others) (emphasis in original); id at 2235 (Thomas, J, dissenting) ("The Fourth Amendment guarantees individuals the right to be secure from unreasonable searches of *'their* persons, houses, papers, and effects.'") (emphasis in original); id at 2227 (Kennedy, J, dissenting) ("the Fourth Amendment's protections must remain tethered to the text of that Amendment, which, again, protects only a person's own 'persons, houses, papers, and effects.'").

[207] *Carpenter*, 138 S Ct at 2227 (Kennedy, J, dissenting).

[208] *Rakas v Illinois*, 439 US 128, 143–44 n 12 (1978) ("Expectations of privacy protected by the Fourth Amendment . . . need not be based on a common-law interest in real or personal property, or on the invasion of such an interest. These ideas were rejected [in]. . . *Katz*. [] But by focusing on legitimate expectations of privacy in Fourth Amendment jurisprudence, the Court has not altogether abandoned use of property concepts in determining the presence or absence of the privacy interests protected by that Amendment."). See also *Carpenter*, 138 S Ct at 2227 (Kennedy, J, dissenting) (writing, "'property concepts' are . . . fundamental 'in determining the presence or absence of the privacy interests protected by'" the Fourth Amendment and that even in *Katz*, the property-based concept remained).

[209] *Rakas*, 439 US at 144 n 12.

[210] See, for example, *Other Digital Content* (Copyright.gov), online at https://www.copyright.gov/registration/other-digital-content; Health Insurance Portability and Accountability Act of 1996 (HIPPA), Pub L No 104-191, 110 Stat 1936.

[211] *Access to Digital Assets of Decedents* (National Conference of State Legislatures, Dec 3, 2018), online at http://www.ncsl.org/research/telecommunications-and-information-technology/access-to-digital-assets-of-decedents.aspx.

and destruction of biometric data.[212] As a matter of Supreme Court jurisprudence, the rule of functional equivalence applies: at a minimum, the types of matters that historically would have been protected, if digitized, fall within the Fourth Amendment. Scholars, too, appear to be nearly universal in their agreement.[213] To the extent, then, that third-party doctrine eviscerated a foundational right to security of one's digital personal or commercial papers, it undermined rights secured at the founding.

Papers encompass the intimacies of life that arise, at least in part, from an individual's actions and decisions: writing a letter, keeping a diary, dictating a memo, engaging in business transactions, and going about one's daily business. The fact that they are held on parchment or online matters naught. Such documents would not exist *but for* the actions of the owner. The (traditional) position of the letter-writer, diary-keeper, or individual engaged in commercial activity matters. Digital records mirror what happens in the world—what people think, say, do, and believe. They arise from the right-holder's actions.

The question, "who owns this information?" relates not just to the concept of ownership itself, but also to the relationship between the holder of the right and others. This leads to a critical insight: *If it is up to an individual to determine with whom information generated by them is shared, then that person holds the original right.* An individual could not contract to provide the information without power over the data.[214] Under such circumstances, the right at issue can be understood, at least in part, according to the actions of the right-holder.

---

[212] See, for example, the Biometric Information Privacy Act, 740 ILCS 14/1 et seq, which was recently upheld in *Rosenbach v Six Flags Entertainment Corp.*, 2019 WL 323902 (Ill).

[213] See Pamela Samuelson, *Privacy as Intellectual Property?*, 52 Stan L Rev 1125, 1130 (arguing that people think about personal data as property); Megan Blass, *The New Data Marketplace: Protecting Personal Data, Electronic Communications, and Individual Privacy in the Age of Mass Surveillance through a Return to a Property-Based Approach to the Fourth Amendment*, 42 Hastings Const L Q 577, 592 (2015) ("Personal data and electronic communications … are an extension of the individual and the home. … [They] are closely tied to the privacies of life or intimate activities that are traditionally associated with the home . . . and deserve continued protection under the Fourth Amendment."); Wendy K. Mariner, *Reconsidering Constitutional Protection for Health Information Privacy*, 18 U Pa J Const L 975, 978 (2016) (arguing that the dependence on sharing personal health information electronically should be reflected in Fourth Amendment doctrine); Edina Harbinja, *Legal Nature of Emails: A Comparative Perspective*, 14 Duke L & Tech Rev 227 (2016) (arguing that email accounts "can be analogized to the paper on which letters are written.").

[214] See Wesley Newcomb Hohfeld, *Fundamental Legal Conceptions as Applied in Judicial Reasoning* 10 (Yale, 1923) (Walter Wheeler Cook, ed) (articulating the juridical incidents (i.e., privileges, claims, powers, and immunities) embedded in the concept of a right).

Consider freedom of movement. It is the right-holder's exercise of this freedom that generates location data, which would not exist *but for* the individual's actions: purchasing a mobile device, charging it, turning it on, carrying it, and going to particular places at particular times. If the individual did not have an original right to the information, he or she could not contract to share it with an ISP. It would not be hers to provide. However, it clearly *is* hers to provide.

Simultaneously, the right-holder has a claim on the company with whom she contracts to provide communications in a timely, efficient, and consistent manner. That is the whole point of having a mobile device: to be able to use the telephone whenever and wherever one chooses. This claim-right *does not exist independent of the individual's contractual relationship with the company.* The salient question is whether, *by providing it* to the service provider, the right-holder somehow *loses* her ownership interest in the information.[215] Here, the law of bailment and positive law may play an important role.

1. *Bailment and contractual obligations.* "[T]he fact that a third-party has access to or possession of your papers and effects," Justice Gorsuch wrote in *Carpenter*, "does not necessarily eliminate your interest in them."[216] Gorsuch's insight is important. History and precedent strongly support distinguishing between ownership and possession in regard to property rights. English law has long favored the former—a preference embedded in the concept of bailment.[217]

By the end of the Middle Ages, common law recognized a bailor's property interest in goods held by others.[218] In such instances, an

---

[215] In cases where an individual writes a letter (or email) and sends it to another person, then the recipient would have the right to reveal the information. The government can only gain access to the document via consent (of either the sender or the recipient) or a particularized warrant. The carrier, however, as the discussion that follows explains, is in a different position: namely, bailment upon consideration.

[216] *Carpenter*, 138 S Ct at 2268 (Gorsuch, J, dissenting). It creates a bailment—that is, "delivery of personal property by one person (the bailor), to another (the bailee), who holds the property for a certain purpose." Id, quoting and citing *Black's Law Dictionary* 169 (West, 10th ed 2014). See also Richard A. Lord, 19 *Williston on Contracts* § 53:1 (West, 4th ed Nov 2018 update) ("A bailment may be defined as the rightful possession of goods by one who is not the owner."); James Schouler, *A Treatise on the Law of Bailments Including Pledge, Innkeepers and Carriers* 2 n 2 (Little, Brown, 1905) (defining bailment as "A delivery of some chattel by one party to another, to be held according to the special purpose of the delivery, and to be returned or delivered over when that special purpose is accomplished."). If the bailee, who has a legal duty to keep the property safe, fails to do so or violates the bailor's instructions, he is liable for conversion. Id at 2269. He cites state cases: *Goad v Harris*, 207 Ala 357, 92 So 546 (1922); *Knight v Seney*, 124 NE 813, 815–16 (Ill 1919); *Baxter v Woodward*, 158 NW 137, 139 (Mich 1916).

[217] Pollock and Maitland, 2 *History of English Law* at *152 (cited in note 28).

[218] Id at *177.

owner "deliver[ed] possession of his chattel to another,"[219] altering custody without transferring ownership.[220] The bailee (temporarily) held the property for some purpose (e.g., use, enjoyment, or safe-keeping).[221]

Where the law shifted over time was in regard to liability, recovery, and types of bailment. Thus Ranulf de Glanvill, Chief Justiciar under Henry II, wrote in the twelfth century in the first recognized treatise on English law that the commodatary (the bailee in a *commodatus*, see discussion below) was held to strict liability.[222] In the thirteenth century, Bracton's *De Legibus et Consuetudinibus Angliae* took a less aggressive stance, holding the depositary liable only in the case of *dolus*—that is, deceit or bad faith.[223] Due diligence, in some cases, would be sufficient. In 1601, however, Edward Coke, the first lord chief justice of England, essentially returned to Glanvill's approach when he examined a writ of *detinue* against a bailee from whom the goods in question had been stolen by force.[224] Coke, finding no distinction between the duty to keep chattel and to keep chattel safely, held the bailee to a standard of strict liability for the items in his possession.[225]

For the next century, Coke's approach in *Southcote's case* held. But in 1703, Lord Chief Justice of England John Holt, drawing in part from Roman law, repudiated Coke's standard and laid down a series of principles that formed the basis for the modern law of bailment.[226] In 1781, the English jurist William Jones built upon Holt's principles,

---

[219] Id at *168. Bailment vests when content of chattels are made visible to bailee. *Bowdon v Pelleter*, 17 YB 8 Edw II (41 Seldon Society) 136 (1315).

[220] Pollock and Maitland, 2 *History of English Law* at *168 (cited in note 28).

[221] See id at *169; Schouler, *A Treatise on the Law of Bailments* § 1 at 1 (cited in note 216).

[222] Ranulf de Glanvill, *Tractatus de legibus et Consuetudinibus Regni Anglie* book 10, ch 13 (*Treatise on the Laws and Customs of the Kingdom of England*) (1554).

[223] Henrici de Bracton, 2 *De Legibus et Consuetudinibus Angliae (On the Laws and Customs of England)* fol 99 b at 111 (Hein, 1990) (Travers Twiss, ed).

[224] *Southcote's Case*, 76 Eng Rep 1061 (KB 1601).

[225] Id at 1062.

[226] *Coggs v Bernard*, 92 Eng Rep 107, 110 (1703) ("[T]o shew that the tenor of the law was always otherwise, I shall give a history of the authorities in the books in this matter, and by them shew, that there never was any such resolution given before *Southcote's case*."). See also William F. Elliott, *A Treatise on the Law of Bailments and Carriers* 3 (Bobbs-Merrill, 1914); Thomas Beven, 2 *Negligence in Law* 746–48 (Stevens and Haynes, 3d ed 1908) (critiquing Oliver Wendell Holmes's sui generis understanding of English common law). But see Holmes, *The Common Law* at 179–85 (cited in note 29) (generally supporting Coke).

finding in the temporary nature of bailment a certain (albeit limited) duty to the bailor.[227] Like Holt, Jones considered different forms of bailment based on the relationship between bailor and bailee.[228] Supreme Court Justice Joseph Story augmented Jones, cementing the foundation for the contemporary era.[229]

Throughout this time, bailment was thought of as a type of contractual relationship, even where no formal contract had been signed.[230] Simultaneously, it was not merely a right ex contractu; the common law conveyed it.[231] The bailee had possession, while the bailor retained residual ownership rights.[232]

A number of implications followed. A bailor could sue in detinue to recover chattel wrongfully detained.[233] Although the bailee was merely a custodian, he maintained remedies against anyone who tried to disturb his possession.[234] The bailee thus had something more than

---

[227] William Jones, *Essay on the Law of Bailments* 5 (Nichols, 1781).

[228] See id.

[229] Joseph Story, *Commentaries on the Law of Bailments* v–vii (Hilliard and Brown, 1832).

[230] Id at 2 ("[A] bailment is a delivery of a thing in trust or some special object or purpose, and upon a contract, expressed or implied, to conform to the object or purpose of the trust."); Henry John Stephen, 2 *New Commentaries on the Laws of England (Partly Founded on Blackstone)* at 129 (John S. Voorhies, 1st Am ed 1843) ("Bailment . . . is delivery of goods for some particular purpose, or on mere deposit, upon a contract express or implied, that, after the purpose has been performed, they shall be re-delivered to the bailor, or otherwise dealt with according to his directions."); Edwin Charles Goddard, *Outlines of the Law of Bailments and Carriers* § 1 at 1 (Callaghan, 1904) ("A *bailment* is a contract relation resulting from the delivery of personal chattels by the owner, called the bailor, to a second person, called the bailee, for a specific purpose, upon the accomplishment of which the chattels are to be dealt with according to the owner's direction."); Elliot, *A Treatise on the Law* at 1 (cited in note 226) ("A bailment may be defined as a contract by which the possession of personal property is temporarily transferred from the owner to another for the accomplishment of some special purpose.").

[231] See William K. Laidlaw, *Principles of Bailment*, 16 Cornell L Q 286, 287 (1931) ("Although it is frequently said that bailment is founded upon contract, the actual decisions show that it is not so founded."). See also Alice Erh-Soon Tay, *The Essence of a Bailment: Contract, Agreement or Possession?*, 5 Sydney L Rev 239, 239 (1966).

[232] English law had long recognized these dual rights. See Bracton, 2 *On the Laws and Customs of England* fol 103 b at 144–45 (Bracton wrote, "An action [*vi bonorum raptorum*], on account of movables carried off by force or robbed, is allowed to the owner of a thing or to him from whose custody they have been carried off and who has entered into contract of payment in relation to their owner, so that he has an interest to bring the action.") (cited in note 223), cited and quoted in Bordwell, 29 Harv L Rev at 510 (cited in note 29). Pollock and Maitland, 2 *The History of English Law* at *172 (cited in note 28) ("[T]he action of detinue is a vindication based upon a proprietary right.").

[233] Id at *173. See also Samuel Stoljar, *The Early History of Bailment*, 1 Am J Legal Hist 5 (1957).

[234] Pollock and Maitland, 2 *The History of English Law* at *170 (cited in note 28).

mere possession: he had an interest in the property, and a responsibility for its safety.[235] The bailee *and* the bailor could go after a third party to protect their interests.[236] Bailment further distinguished ownership not just from possession, but from the *right to possess*.[237] As the English jurist Frederick Pollock and Justice Robert Samuel Wright of the Queen's Bench Division explained in the late nineteenth century,

> Right to possession (sometimes called constructive "possession,") . . . is one of the constituent elements of the complete right of property; though it may be in a different person from the general owner, and though a person's right of property may continue during a temporary suspension of his right to possession, as in the case of a bailment for a term. Being a part of the right or property it is said not to be lost, even by a general abandonment of the thing.[238]

Applied to CSLI, if we assume, arguendo, that digital records ought to be treated in the same manner as goods or chattel, under a theory of bailment, the fact that a company holds customer data does not necessarily mean that the individual has alienated his property interest in the record.[239] Nor does an independent right of action by the company against others who attempt to obtain the information necessarily erase the underlying ownership interest. Even should Verizon, for example, *agree* to let other companies use CSLI to market

---

[235] Id at *169. See also Bracton, 2 *On the Laws and Customs of England* fol 151 (cited in note 223), quoted and cited in both Pollock and Maitland, 2 *The History of English Law* at *169 (cited in note 28), and Holmes, *The Common Law* at 168 (cited in note 29); Federick Pollock and Robert Samuel Wright, *An Essay on Possession in the Common Law, Part 3* at 145 (Clarendon, 1888).

[236] As the English Year Books related, "In these actions two rights may be concerned—the right of possession, as is the case where a thing is robbed or stolen from the possession of one who had no right of property in it (for instance, where the thing has been lent, bailed, or let); and the right of property, as is the case where a thing is stolen or robbed from the possession of one to whom the property in it belongs." William Joseph Wittaker, ed, 7 *Seldon Society Publications: The Mirror of Justices* 57 (Bernard Quaritch, 1895).

[237] Pollock and Wright, *An Essay on Possession in the Common Law* at 145 (cited in note 235); Pollock and Maitland, 2 *The History of English Law* at *151 (cited in note 28).

[238] Pollock and Wright, *An Essay on Possession in the Common Law* at 145 (cited in note 235).

[239] This is how the Federal Trade Commission treats data held by service providers. In their case against Facebook, even though the company possessed the information, when customers chose to leave the platform, they retained the right to delete their data. See Complaint, *In the Matter of Facebook, Inc.*, Docket No C-, File No 092 3184, online at https://www.ftc.gov/sites/default/files/documents/cases/2011/11/111129facebookcmpt.pdf; Agreement Containing Consent Order, *In the Matter of Facebook, Inc.*, File No 092 3184, online at https://www.ftc.gov/sites/default/files/documents/cases/2011/11/111129facebookagree.pdf.

goods to the customer, as a categorical matter, the law of bailment might still recognize the customer's underlying property rights. As long as the rights of ownership have not been sold in a market overt, the owner retains residual rights. As Pollock and Maitland explained, "the owner cannot be deprived of his ownership by any transaction between other persons, even though he has parted with possession, and for a time with the right to possess."[240]

To ascertain whether the individual who carries a mobile device retains an ownership interest in the record of his or her movements, the relationship between the original rights-owner (i.e., the person with the original right to contract with others to provide access to the information) and the entity possessing the property requires further scrutiny.

2. *Digital records as a "bailment upon consideration."* Modern law recognizes different kinds of relationships between bailor and bailee. Although historically they carried differing levels of liability (for the bailee), they did not alter the ownership interest. The court asked what duty was owed *by the one who possesses the goods.* Among the kinds of bailment recognized by eighteenth- and nineteenth-century treatise writers, the ones most relevant to CSLI are included in bailment upon consideration—specifically, contracts related to hiring.[241] They sub-

---

[240] Pollock and Maitland, 2 *The History of English Law* at *153 (cited in note 28).

[241] By the eighteenth century, at least five kinds of bailment had come to be recognized in common law. Jones, *Essay on the Law of Bailments* at 35 (cited in note 227); James Kent, 2 *Commentaries on American Law* 558 (O. Halsted, 2d ed 1832). In *Coggs v Bernard*, though, Holt distinguished "six sorts of bailments," which included depositum, commodatum; locatio et conductio; vadium (pawn or pledge); delivery of goods or chattels to be transported for a reward; and delivery of goods or chattels gratis. *Coggs v Bernard*, 92 Eng Rep 107, 109 (1703). *Depositam* dealt with situations in which a deposit was made without reward for recovery. Kent, 2 *Commentaries on American Law* at 560 (cited in note 241). In *Coggs v Bernard*, Lord Holt established that only ordinary care and diligence is expected. *Coggs*, 92 Eng Rep at 110. *Mandatum* amounted to a gratuitous commission, wherein "the mandatary undertakes to do some act about the thing bailed." Kent, 2 *Commentaries on American Law* at 558 (cited in note 241). If the bailee were to transport movable goods, he was only responsible for gross negligence or a breach of good faith. "But if he undertakes to perform some work relating to it, he is then bound to use a degree of diligence and attention suitable to the undertaking and adequate to the performance of it." Id at 569–70. *Commodatum* was a loan for use without payment, wherein the item was to be restored *in specie* (e.g., a horse, carriage, or book). The bailee had a higher duty of care to return the same goods. Id at 446–49. *Vadium* was a pawn or pledge, such as when something "is bailed to a creditor as a security for a debt." Id at 437. The bailee was required "to take ordinary care, and is answerable for ordinary neglect, and no more." Id at 449. *Locatio*, which entails "hiring for a reward," is of three types: *locatio rei* (where the bailee, in return for money, has temporary use of the item); *locatio operis faciendi*, in which work and labor is done, or care and attention bestowed by the bailee on the materials bailed, in return for compensation; and *locatio operis mercium vehendarum* (in which goods are bailed

divide into bailments involving: (*a*) use of a thing (*locatio rei*), (*b*) work on a thing (*locatio operis faciendi*), (*c*) the keeping of a thing (*locatio custodiae*), and (*d*) the transportation of an item (*locatio operis mercium vehendarum*).[242] How does CSLI look in this context? The strongest argument places location data in the first category, while two others provide further insight.

Just as telecommunication service providers only have access to customers' location while they are paying for the service, the bailee in *locatio rei* "gains a qualified property in the thing hired, and the [owner] an absolute property in the price."[243] Professor James Kent observed, "This is a contract in daily use in the common business of life."[244]

As the Court in *Riley* and *Carpenter* was at pains to point out, mobile phones have become a part of daily life. The owner of the phone generates the data and signs a contract to provide it to others. Customers pay for the service, giving companies *temporary* access to their location, in return for which the customer is able to make use of the mobile devices. Companies, in turn, are responsible for ensuring that others do *not* gain access to the information. Failure to safeguard the data creates a liability, not unlike the one established in *locatio rei*.

At no point does the company gain power over the individual's freedom of movement, generation of data, or authority to contract. Once the agreement ends, the company no longer has access to the (former) customer's location. Nor could the company dictate with whom future movements could be shared. In no sense has the ISP gained the authority to alter the customer's privileges or claims. No

---

to public carrier or private person or transport, in return for either a stipulated or implied reward). Kent, 2 *Commentaries on American Law* at 558, 585–86 (cited in note 241). Modern treatises classify bailments slightly differently. See Lord, 19 *Williston on Contracts* § 53:3 (cited in note 216). The most recent American treatise on bailment, published in 1914, placed all bailments in two categories: gratuitous bailments (i.e., for the benefit of one party) and bailments upon consideration. Elliott, *A Treatise on the Law* at 4–5 (cited in note 226). Of the former, those for the benefit of the bailor divide into deposits and mandates. Those for the benefit of the bailee alone are considered *commodates*. Elliott, *A Treatise on the Law* at 4 (cited in note 226). Bailments upon consideration for mutual benefit divide into two categories: *vadium* (pledges) and contracts of hiring.

[242] Elliott, *A Treatise on the Law* at 4–5 (cited in note 226). *Locatio custodiae* applies less directly to CSLI, as it signifies the keeping of a specific item that is then returned to the customer intact.

[243] Kent, 2 *Commentaries on American Law* at 586 (cited in note 241).

[244] Id.

more so could the ISP itself collect future location data, without express permission. The fact that a consumer has granted access for a limited purpose (providing services) does nothing to divest the individual of her underlying privilege. To the contrary, the company's ability to obtain and use such records rests entirely on the original claim-right exercised by the customer as against the company. It is a bailment for consideration structured in a manner consistent with *locatio rei*.

CSLI also shares characteristics with a second kind of bailment: *locatio operis faciendi*, in which work is done, or care and attention bestowed, by the bailee on the materials bailed, in return for compensation. At least part of the service provided by telecommunications companies relates to the use that is made of the records. Verizon temporarily obtains the information, which it uses to provide better services to its customers. Part of the advantage to the customer is that in the future, calls will be provided more efficiently, with fewer gaps in coverage. While not as complete an account as *locatio rei*, this approach takes account of potentially broader controls over how the information is used by the ISP.

Under a third kind of bailment for consideration, *locatio operis mercium vehendarum*, goods are bailed to a public carrier, a private person, or a transportation service, in return for either a stipulated or implied reward. To the extent that modern telecommunications companies carry communications, there is room for further consideration. Postmasters, for example, historically fell within this category, within which they had a higher duty of care—precisely because of their relationship to the intimate details of individuals' lives. This was the logic adopted by the Court in *Ex parte Jackson*, where it held that private papers were still protected "wherever they may be."[245] It mattered naught that the government itself held the documents (qua the postal service). When sealed from public inspection, letters fell within constitutional protections.[246]

The divergent theories of liability that depend upon the position of the bailor, as well as degrees of negligence, came to be replaced in the

---

[245] Id, quoting *Ex Parte Jackson*, 96 US 727, 733 (1877).

[246] Applying this approach to the contemporary era, Gorsuch wrote, "Just because you entrust your data—in some cases, your modern-day papers and effects—to a third party may not mean you lose any Fourth Amendment interest in its contents." *Carpenter*, 138 S Ct at 2269.

American context by a uniform negligence standard.[247] Keeping in mind concerns about data breaches, the duty placed on ISPs again is remarkably consistent with the traditional responsibilities of a bailment upon consideration. The categories shed light on the different types of relationships contemplated by the law, in which residual ownership rights have historically been maintained by the courts.

3. *Points of convergence and divergence.* In *Carpenter*, Justices Kennedy and Alito largely agreed with Gorsuch in regard to digital documents qua property and the potential role of bailment in a digital age. For Kennedy, "modern-day equivalents of an individual's own 'papers or 'effects' . . . are held by a third-party" as a "bailment."[248] He considered such matters covered by the Fourth Amendment, even where they might run afoul of third-party doctrine.[249] The point of disagreement was whether CSLI involved *that* sort of bailment.[250] For Kennedy, it did not: "The businesses were not bailees or custodians of the records, with a duty to hold the records for the defendants' use."[251] Justice Alito similarly noted that bailment may apply to certain types of records entrusted to others, but not to CSLI.[252]

Their arguments are difficult to sustain in light of the structure of bailment and how CSLI works. Their logic centered on the level of control exhibited by the companies. Alito noted that Carpenter,

> had no right to prevent the company from creating or keeping the information in its records. [He] had no right to demand that the providers destroy the records, no right to prevent the providers from destroying the records, and, indeed, no right to modify the records in any way whatsoever (or to prevent the providers from modifying the records). Carpenter, in short, has no meaningful control over [CSLI].[253]

But the law of bailment recognizes that the possessor not only exercises control over material so bailed, but also has a series of *rights*

---

[247] Richard H. Helmholz, *Bailment Theories and the Liability of Bailees: The Elusive Uniform Standard of Reasonable Care*, 41 Kan L Rev 97, 97 (1992). See also Sheldon D. Elliott, *Degrees of Negligence*, 6 S Cal L Rev 91 (1933).

[248] *Carpenter*, 138 S Ct at 2230 (Kennedy, J, dissenting).

[249] Id (writing, "*Miller* and *Smith* may not apply when the Government obtains the modern-day equivalents of an individual's own 'papers' or 'effects,' even when those papers or effects are held by a third-party.").

[250] Id.

[251] Id at 2228 (Kennedy, J, dissenting).

[252] *Carpenter*, 138 S Ct at 2259 n 6 (Alito, J, dissenting).

[253] Id at 2257 (Alito, J, dissenting). See also id at 2228–29 (Kennedy, J, dissenting).

related to that control. Indeed, to even be considered a bailee, *Williston on Contracts* notes, "one must have both *physical control* of goods and *intent to exercise that control*."[254] The bailment itself "depends on the degree of control and possession, and there must be such a full transfer, actual or constructive, of the property to the bailee as to exclude the possession of the owner and all other persons and give the bailee the sole custody and control of the goods."[255] In such circumstances, though, it is "only possession of property" that is transferred.[256] "[T]he bailor remains the true owner."[257]

It is not necessary to fully satisfy the ancient, or even modern, law of bailment to recognize that it provides a solid, well-grounded way of thinking about property in a digital era. Some forms of customer data are only brought into being by a third party and do not rely on others' actions for their existence. Others are unique *to the customer*, to which the company has access. CSLI is of the second sort, in that it wholly depends upon the customer's decision to purchase a phone, the customer's use of his property, the customer's movements, and the customer's decision to contract with a company to provide services to the customer. Even after providing location data, the customer is free to share it with others through various apps. And once the contract ends, the service provider no longer has the right to obtain the information. Instead, the consumer decides where it will reside. CSLI is in a different category from that of traditional police surveillance. It is one intimately grounded in property rights.

B. THE ROLE AND LIMITS OF POSITIVE LAW

In *Carpenter*, Justice Gorsuch emphasized that positive law (federal and state) may play a role in helping to establish Fourth Amendment interests.[258] This, too, offers a promising approach for understanding property rights in an advanced technological age.

Where federal statutory law or regulatory measures have *privileged certain actors' control over information* and *denied access to the information to others*, government intrusions may constitute a search or seizure

---

[254] Lord, 19 *Williston on Contracts* § 53:2 (cited in note 216) (emphasis added).

[255] Id.

[256] Id.

[257] Id.

[258] *Carpenter*, 138 S Ct at 2270 (Gorsuch, J, dissenting).

within the meaning of the Fourth Amendment.[259] This approach is similar to a formulation offered by Professor William Baud and Professor James Stern, who argue that the salient question for Fourth Amendment purposes is "whether it was unlawful for an ordinary private actor to do what the government's agents did."[260] But it distinguishes between the *privilege* held by the right-holder and the *duty of noninterference* placed on others. In doing so, it recognizes that it is important first to acknowledge *who* holds the right of consent and, second, whether the law establishes an *expectation of security against interference* (based on the obligation on others *not* to access the information absent the right-holder's consent).

This distinction is constitutionally meaningful. Where an individual has a privileged position, such that they may grant (or withhold) access to the property in question, the law recognizes ownership: in other words, these are "their" papers or effects. Similarly, where private actors have been *denied* access absent the right-holder's consent, then the privilege owner's *security* in relation to "*their*" *papers* has been established. Should a private actor access the information without the privilege-holder's consent, it would be a violation of the duty owed by the other party to the privilege-holder.

From this, it is logically consistent to conclude that should the *government* try to access the same information, that security also would be violated. Absent a special carve-out for an obligation owed by the privilege-holder to the government, to the extent that the privilege-holder has the right to security of their papers, it may be said to set an expectation of security against all comers.

In fact, there may be an even *higher* burden that the government must meet to gain access to information in which the privilege owner has been granted security.[261] The government, after all, has massive resources and a monopoly on coercion backed by violence. It can imprison people, take their money, forfeit their property, and even

---

[259] Professors Baude and Stern offer a straightforward distinction between search and seizure, which strikes me as correct: the former "requires an action generally likely to obtain information," while the latter "requires an assertion of physical control." Baude and Stern, 129 Harv L Rev at 1833 (cited in note 205). As they observe, there must be a distinction—otherwise the addition of "seizure" would be surplusage. Id at 1832–33.

[260] Id at 1826.

[261] See also Re, 129 Harv L Rev F at 314 (cited in note 205) (writing, "[G]overnment action is different—and often more deserving of regulation—than similar conduct by private parties.").

take their lives. Private actors (as a matter of law) cannot. The Fourth Amendment itself places restrictions on the government in an effort to restrict the exercise of power and, in so doing, to protect liberty. Positive law thus may help to demarcate constitutional limits.

How does this look in the context of CSLI? Federal laws routinely create rights in intangible things, thereby restricting private actors.[262] The 1996 Telecommunications Act, for example, places a duty on carriers "to protect the confidentiality of proprietary information of, and relating to . . . customers."[263] The statute goes on to lay out the confidentiality of customer proprietary network data, limiting its use, disclosure, or access to the direct provision of services.[264] As Gorsuch noted in *Carpenter*, service providers cannot use, disclose, or give others access to customer proprietary network information without the consent of the customer, except as needed for ordinary business purposes.[265] They must provide it, when the customer requests, to anyone designated by the customer.[266] Where a company fails to protect customer data, the statute provides for a private cause of action.[267] Surveying these measures, he concluded, "Plainly, customers have substantial legal interests in this information, including at least some right to include, exclude, and control its use. Those interests might even rise to the level of a property right."[268]

While federal statutory measures may provide the strongest evidence in support of property rights (in regard to placing a duty of noninterference on others—including, arguendo, the government), state laws also may be probative. Where states have taken certain steps to establish property rights, acknowledging a privilege held by the rights-holder, the courts should at least consider such measures in their analysis. This approach may help to identify constitutional limits on doctrines ill-suited to the digital age.

---

[262] Health care providers, for instance, are required to protect all "individually identifiable health information" relating to an individual's past, present, or future physical or mental health or condition, in any media in which it is held. Health Insurance Portability and Accountability Act of 1996, Pub L No 104-191, §§ 262, 110 Stat 1936, 2021, 2023, 2029–30.

[263] 47 USC § 222(a).

[264] 47 USC § 222(c)(1).

[265] *Carpenter*, 138 S Ct 2272 (Gorsuch, J, dissenting), citing 47 USC § 222(c)(1).

[266] *Carpenter*, 138 S Ct 2272, citing 47 USC § 222(c)(2).

[267] *Carpenter*, 138 S Ct 2272, citing 47 USC § 207.

[268] *Carpenter*, 138 S Ct 2272.

Consider open space doctrine. Many states have responded to the privacy invasions occasioned by Unmanned Aerial Systems (UAS) by extending trespass laws to include the airspace above the land.[269] California forbids "constructive trespass" onto private property, which does *not* require physical entry into the airspace above private property for a right of action.[270] It is illegal "to capture any type of visual image, sound recording, or other physical impression of the plaintiff engaging in a private, personal, or familial activity."[271] Not only is the person who conducts the constructive trespass liable for punitive damages, but also anyone who "directs, solicits, actually induces, or actually causes another person, regardless of whether there is an employer-employee relationship" to commit the offense.[272]

These and myriad similar state provisions suggest an outer limit to open space doctrine, extending property rights to the constructive trespass of the airspace above private land and placing a duty of non-interference on others—thus protecting the property owners' enjoyment of their land. While not conclusive, such measures surely are at least probative in understanding the associated property rights when the same restrictions are violated by the government.

This may be particularly true when state provisions expressly forbid state and local *governments* from interfering with property rights. More than eighteen states, for instance, require that law enforcement obtain a warrant before using UAS as part of their investigatory powers.[273] Where data are collected outside of a warrant, most states include a suppression remedy.[274] Some go so far as to allow for a civil cause of action against officials, with significant penalties for the dissemination

---

[269] See, for example, Cal Civ Code § 1708.8(a); La Rev Stat Ann § 14:63; Nev Rev Stat § 493.103(1); Or Rev Stat § 837.380(1); Tenn Code Ann § 39-14-405(d). See also Laura K. Donohue, *A Tale of Two Sovereigns: Federal and State Use and Regulation of Unmanned Aircraft Systems*, in Kimon P. Valavanis and George J. Vachtsevanos, eds, *Handbook of Unmanned Aerial Vehicles* (Springer, 2d ed forthcoming 2020), online at https://papers.ssrn.com/sol3/papers.cfm?abstract_id=2943018.

[270] Cal Civ Code § 1708.8(b). See also NC Gen Stat § 15A-300.1(b).

[271] Cal Civ Code § 1708.8(a).

[272] Cal Civ Code § 1708.8(e).

[273] See, for example, Alaska Stat Ann § 18.65.901(1); Fla Stat § 934.50(3)(b); Idaho Code § 21-213(2)(a); 725 ILCS 167/15(2); Ind Code § 35-33-5-9(a); 25 Me Rev Stat Ann § 4501(4)(B); Mont Code Ann § 46-5-109(1); Nev Rev Stat § 493.112(2); Or Rev Stat §§ 837.310, 837.320; Va Code § 19.2-60.1(B).

[274] See, for example, Nev Rev Stat § 493.112(4); Tenn Code Ann § 39-13-609(e)(2).

of material obtained via warrantless surveillance. In North Carolina, the target of the surveillance is entitled to $5,000 for *every* photograph or video illegally disseminated by any government agency or employee.[275] States also forbid and/or tightly regulate UAS use of biometric identification technologies, infrared imaging, video analytics, and enhanced visual aids.[276]

More specifically, in regard to CSLI, some states preclude law enforcement from accessing information generated by electronic devices without proper legal process. The 2015 California Electronic Communications Privacy Act (CalECPA) creates a property right in digital assets, that is, digitally stored content and online accounts, such as photographs, text messages, postings, spreadsheets, word documents, email, and myriad other digital formats and their associated metadata.[277] Lawmakers introduced the statute to curb ballooning law enforcement requests for commercial third-party records.[278]

Looking to state law to establish property rights (and thereby gauge constitutional entitlements) is consistent with the Court's jurisprudence. The Fifth and Fourteenth Amendments refer to "property," but the Constitution says nothing about *whether* ownership rights exist, much less their scope.[279] Courts make this determination by looking to state and local law.[280] Regulatory takings determinations turn on two sources: the state's property law, and the reasonable expectations of owners as "shaped by the State's law of property—i.e., whether and to what degree the State's law has accorded legal rec-

---

[275] NC Gen Stat § 15A-300.1(e).

[276] See, for example, 20 Vt Stat Ann § 4622(d)(2); 25 Me Rev Stat Ann § 4501(5)(D).

[277] California Electronic Communications Privacy Act, 2015 Cal Stat 5110, codified at Cal Penal Code § 1546 et seq.

[278] See *SB 178 Fact Sheet (Leno and Anderson)* (ACLU of Northern California, Sept 2, 2015), online at https://www.aclunc.org/sites/default/files/SB%20178%20CalECPA%20Fact %20Sheet_1.pdf (noting, inter alia, a 70 percent increase for location data from AT&T within the past year and a 52 percent increase in requests to Twitter).

[279] See US Const, Amend V ("No person shall . . . be deprived of . . . property, without due process of law; nor shall private property be taken for public use, without just compensation."); US Const, Amend XIV ("[N]or shall any State deprive any person of . . . property, without due process of law."). See also *Phillips v Washington Legal Foundation*, 524 US 156, 164 (1998) (holding that the Fifth Amendment protects but does not create property interests), quoting *Board of Regents of State Colleges v Roth*, 408 US 564, 577 (1972).

[280] *United States v Powelson*, 319 US 266, 279 (1943) (Justice Douglas writing for the Court, noting that although "the meaning of 'property' as used in . . . the Fifth Amendment is a federal question, it will normally obtain its content by reference to local law." See also *United States v Causby*, 328 US 256, 266 (1946), quoting and citing *Powelson*).

ognition and protection" to the property owner's interests.[281] Even states may not avoid confiscatory regulations takings claims by disavowing property interests historically recognized under their laws.[282] The query is not limited to economic value. As an annotation from the *American Law Reports* explains, it incorporates "a group of rights that a so-called owner exercises in his or her domination of [the item], such as the right to possess, use, and dispose of it."[283]

The Court's Fifth and Fourteenth Amendment jurisprudence underscores the importance of the protections extended to property.[284] What is included may expand over time: liberty and property "relate to the whole domain of social and economic fact, and the statesmen who founded this Nation knew too well that only a stagnant society remains unchanged."[285] Liberty means not just "freedom from bodily restraint but also the right of the individual to contract, to engage in any of the common occupations of life, to acquire useful knowledge, to marry, establish a home . . . to worship God according to the dictates of his own conscience, and generally to enjoy those privileges long recognized . . . as essential to the orderly pursuit of happiness by free men."[286]

As a matter of Fourth Amendment doctrine, positive law may create a floor, but not a ceiling, for constitutional rights.[287] Once the law has established a privilege in the right-holder and placed a duty of noninterference on others, it is for the government to demonstrate that it has the right to violate security of property. But a heavier burden may be on them, in light of their particular position of power over the people.

---

[281] *Lucas v South Carolina Coastal Council*, 505 US 1003, 1016 n 7 (1992). See also id at 1027.

[282] *Phillips*, 524 US at 167, citing id at 1029.

[283] Ann K. Wooster, Annotation, *What Constitutes Taking of Property Requiring Compensation Under Takings—Supreme Court Cases*; 10 ALR Fed 2d 231, 257 (2006).

[284] See *Board of Regents of State Colleges*, 408 US at 571 ("'Liberty' and 'property' are broad and majestic terms. They are among the '(g)reat (constitutional) concepts . . . purposely left to gather meaning from experience'"), quoting *National Mutual Insurance Co. v Tidewater Transfer Co.*, 337 US 582, 646 (Frankfurter, J, dissenting).

[285] *Board of Regents of State Colleges*, 408 US at 571.

[286] *Meyer v Nebraska*, 262 US 390, 399 (1923).

[287] I agree here with Professor Re, who proposes that the Court learn from how legislatures treat private parties without being limited by them: "[W]hen the law has made a deliberate choice to protect against certain intrusions on privacy and security by private parties, then police should have to adduce some kind of justification for undertaking a similar intrusion." See Re, 129 Harv L Rev F at 313 (cited in note 205). Accordingly, I disagree with Professors Baude and Stern who see the positive law inquiry as a ceiling, not a floor. See Baude and Stern, 129 Harv L Rev at 1888 (cited in note 205).

Elected representatives, of course, do not hold the final determination of constitutional protections. That falls to the judiciary. As Justice Scalia declared in *Jones*, "we must 'assur[e] preservation of that degree of privacy against government that existed when the Fourth Amendment was adopted.'"[288] In *Carpenter*, Gorsuch agreed, noting that *Ex parte Jackson* reflected this principle. He explained that in *Jackson*,

> this Court said that "[n]o law of Congress" could authorize letter carriers "to invade the secrecy of letters." So the post office couldn't impose a regulation dictating that those mailing letters surrender all legal interests in them once they're deposited in a mailbox. If that is right, *Jackson* suggests the existence of a constitutional floor below which Fourth Amendment rights may not descend.[289]

Congress is constitutionally prohibited from granting warrantless access to houses or papers, absent cause.[290]

In addition to helping to secure rights guaranteed at the founding, adapting them to modern times, and providing a standard consistent with judicial precedent, appealing to positive law to gauge property rights for Fourth Amendment purposes has at least three policy advantages. First, it offers clarity. Where relevant laws have been adopted, the Court can look to them as part of their calculus. Second, it helps to insulate the courts from policy-making, freeing them to focus on matters of law. The Court's prior refusal to take account of statutory law in determining what society considers more or less reasonable resulted in contradictory and counterintuitive results that continue to undermine judicial credibility. Just as it was illegal in California in the 1980s to cross fences or to trawl through a neighbor's trash, it is now illegal to obtain digital assets, or to record what happens on private land, even when the recording takes place outside the property line and in public view. Third, the positive law approach acknowledges the role played by the legislature in responding to new and emerging technologies. This was one of the dissents' primary concerns in *Carpen-*

---

[288] *United States v Jones*, 565 US 400, 406 (2012), quoting *Kyllo v United States*, 533 US 27, 34 (2001), cited in *Carpenter*, 138 S Ct at 2271 (Gorsuch, J, dissenting). See also *Pennsylvania Coal Co. v Mahon*, 260 US 393, 413 (1922) ("The greatest weight is given to the judgment of the legislature but it always is open to interested parties to contend that the legislature has gone beyond its constitutional powers.").

[289] *Carpenter*, 138 S Ct at 2270, quoting *Ex parte Jackson*, 96 US 727, 733 (1877).

[290] See *Carpenter*, 138 S Ct at 2271.

ter.[291] For Kennedy, "The last thing the Court should do is incorporate an arbitrary and outside limit—in this case six days' worth of cell-site records—and use it as the foundation for a new constitutional framework."[292] Asking whether positive law establishes a privilege, however, and whether there is a duty of noninterference—and using this as probative as to whether a property right (as held against the government) exists—is a very different kind of exercise, and one entirely compatible with the dissents' view that it is relevant to, but not dispositive of, the property interests at stake.[293]

V. The Way Forward

In 1910 Sir Winston Churchill inveighed: "Let us . . . go forward together. Advance with courage, and the cause of the people shall prevail."[294] Such is the moment at which we stand, that the Court simply must find a way to ensure, at a minimum, the rights that were guaranteed by the Constitution at the founding. How, then, should we think about digitization and the Fourth Amendment going forward?[295]

Voluntariness and assumption of risk do not have a central role to play. The application of open space doctrine to location tracking rested on a faulty analogy. Unlike cars, mobile devices follow you into the home. The approach ignored the impact of new technologies on rights—in contrast to the Court's recognition in *Jones*, *Riley*, and *Carpenter* of the deeper privacy interests at stake. Other citizens, moreover, cannot track you twenty-four hours a day, seven days a week,

---

[291] See, for example, id at 2261 (Alito, J, dissenting); id at 2233 (Kennedy, J, dissenting).

[292] *Carpenter*, 138 S Ct at 2233 (Kennedy, J, dissenting).

[293] See, for example, id at 2242–43 (Thomas, J, dissenting); id at 2227–28 (Kennedy, J, dissenting).

[294] Sir Winston Churchill, *The Lords and the Budget*, in Robert Rhodes James, ed, *Churchill Speaks: Winston S. Churchill in Peace and War Collected Speeches, 1897–1963*, at 185, 189 (Chelsea House, 1980) (speech given at the Manchester Free Trade Hall on Mar 19, 1910).

[295] Since *Carpenter*, courts have exempted prior, warrantless collection based on good faith, exigent circumstances, and reliance on binding precedent. See *United States v Joyner*, 899 F3d 1199, 1204–05 (11th Cir 2018); *United States v Chavez*, 894 F3d 593, 608 (4th Cir 2018); *United States v Curtis*, 901 F3d 846, 848 (7th Cir 2018); *United States v Zodhiates*, 901 F3d 137, 143 (2d Cir 2018); *United States v Chambers*, 2018 WL 4523607, *1–2 (2d Cir), rem'd from *Chambers v United States*, 138 S Ct 2705 (2018) (mem). But see *United States v Thompson*, 866 F3d 1149 (10th Cir 2017), vac'd and rehearing granted by *Thompson v United States*, 138 S Ct 2706 (mem) (2018); *United States v Stimler*, 864 F3d 253 (3d Cir 2017), vac'd and rehearing granted by *United States v Goldstein*, 902 F3d 411 (3d Cir) (mem).

for years. If they did, it would be downright creepy. And however much an individual uses technology does not mean that others can see it: from network security and encryption to the use of passwords and consent clauses, users protect their data in myriad ways.

The assumption of risk and voluntariness argument drawn from informant doctrine also falls short. This approach, which formed the core of third-party doctrine, decimated constitutional protections extended to papers. It ignored the difference between engaging in illegal activity and forming legal, contractual relationships. It (erroneously) equated consenting to give a company access to one's personal information with consenting to give the government access. And it assumed that not using a bank or having a telephone were viable options in the modern world. As the Court noted in *Riley* and emphasized again in *Carpenter*, mobile devices are not voluntary. Ordinary citizens cannot go through their day without encountering Amazon, much less phones or computers.[296] Any effort by the Courts to parse which devices or apps are more or less voluntary will put the judiciary ever more firmly in the policy-making realm, risking future public confidence.

A more promising approach going forward is for the Court to adopt a property-based approach, which, happily, is compatible with both precedent and the original meaning of the text. Digital documents and records constitute "papers" within the meaning of the Fourth Amendment, such that their warrantless acquisition and analysis is per se unreasonable.[297] This approach applies the rule of functional

---

[296] See Kashmir Hill, *I Tried to Block Amazon from My Life: It Was Impossible* (Gizmodo, Jan 22, 2019), online at https://gizmodo.com/i-tried-to-block-amazon-from-my-life-it-was-impossible-1830565336.

[297] In *Carpenter*, Justices Kennedy and Alito considered compulsory process to support *Miller*, *Smith*, and third-party doctrine. For Kennedy, the reason that the government could use a subpoena to compel individuals to release information within their control was because it differed "from a warrant in its force and intrusive power." *Carpenter*, 138 S Ct at 2228 (Kennedy, J, dissenting). He explained: "While a warrant allows the Government to enter and seize and make the examination itself, a subpoena simply requires the person to whom it is directed to make the disclosure." Kennedy's argument was not strictly accurate. In requesting 128 days of records, the government sought *all* location data on the target, not just one discrete piece of information. Once served with a § 2703(d) order, the companies were forced to comply. Additionally, in the 1946 case of *Oklahoma Press Publishing Co. v Walling*, the Supreme Court established that the Fourth Amendment applies to the compelled production of documents. See *Oklahoma Press Publishing Co. v Walling*, 327 US 186 (1946). Orders must "be sufficiently limited in scope, relevant in purpose, and specific in directive so that compliance will not be unreasonably burdensome." *Donovan v Lone Steer, Inc.*, 464 US 408, 415 (1984), quoting *See v City of Seattle*, 387 US 541, 544 (1967). See also *Carpenter*, 138 S Ct at 2228 (Kennedy, J, dissenting); id at 2255

equivalence, already adopted in regard to "houses," to another, enumerated category.[298] It recognizes that while digitization has altered the world in which we live, it has not impacted guaranteed rights. In *Carpenter*, the Court balked at leaving individuals "at the mercy of advancing technology."[299] As Gorsuch observed, it is not just "the specific rights known at the founding" that come within Fourth Amendment protections, but also "their modern analogues."[300]

To the extent that the factors employed by the Court to evaluate CSLI (e.g., its volume, revealing nature, retroactivity, near perfect recall, temporal extent, and precision) are relevant, it is not in making some sort of relativistic determination, but in illustrating the extent to which digital records reveal the same intimacies of life traditionally protected under the Fourth Amendment. This approach is consistent with *Riley* and *Jones*, where the Court recognized the revelatory nature of the information at stake. While probative in terms of whether digital documents or records are included in "papers," however, the degree of invasiveness is neither necessary nor sufficient. The Court does not rest constructive search on the quality of information: in *Kyllo*, it did not matter whether measuring heat levels revealed the type of "intimacies of life" traditionally protected. It was the government's access to *anything* in the home—including information that allowed it to draw inferences—that constituted a violation. The Court took the same position in *Karo*.

Instead, in determining who owns digital records, the Court should consider adopting a *but for* approach: where the underlying data arise from the actions of an individual, and that person has the original legal right to determine whether and with whom it is shared, they hold an ownership interest in it. This provides a clear line. For situations involving third parties, the law of bailment upon consideration offers a way to distinguish between ownership and possession and to evaluate whether the owner has divested himself of the right of ownership.

(Alito, J, dissenting). CSLI reveals much more than the information being sought, and the Court has never held that a subpoena can elicit records in which the suspect has a reasonable expectation of privacy. Id at 2221 (majority). See also id at 2271 (Gorsuch, J, dissenting) (establishing as his fifth proposition that a constitutional floor may prevent efforts to circumvent Fourth Amendment requirements through subpoenas).

[298] See *United States v Karo*, 468 US 705, 715 (1984), and *Kyllo v United States*, 533 US 27, 34 (2001).

[299] *Carpenter*, 138 S Ct at 2214.

[300] Id at 2271 (Gorsuch, J, dissenting).

To the extent that positive law recognizes and protects the right of ownership, it speaks to a constitutional minimum. Here, courts should look to the establishment of a privilege in the right-holder and the corresponding duty held by private citizens—and, by extension, the government—to noninterference absent consent or appropriate (constitutional) process. This approach draws attention to the requirements of ownership (in "their" papers) and security, restoring rights secured at the founding. It adapts the Fourth Amendment to the modern age. And it is consistent with *Katz*, which recognized property interests and suggested that societal expectations matter—in this case, as acknowledged by legislators. Beyond this, it offers clarity and insulates judges from making policy determinations, allowing them to focus on matters of law, even as it takes account of judicial concerns that the legislature play a role in mediating new technologies. In sum, as the Court develops its jurisprudence post-*Carpenter*, it should consider acknowledging the gravitational force of the original Fourth Amendment in protecting essential rights in a digital age.

EVAN CAMINKER

LOCATION TRACKING AND DIGITAL DATA: CAN CARPENTER BUILD A STABLE PRIVACY DOCTRINE?

In *Carpenter v United States*,[1] the Supreme Court struggled to modernize twentieth-century search and seizure precedents for the "Cyber Age."[2] Twice previously this decade the Court had tweaked Fourth Amendment doctrine to keep pace with advancing technology, requiring a search warrant before the government can either peruse the contents of a cell phone seized incident to arrest[3] or use a GPS tracker to follow a car's long-term movements.[4] This time, the

Evan Caminker is the Branch Rickey Collegiate Professor of Law and former Dean, University of Michigan Law School.

AUTHOR'S NOTE: I briefed and argued *Carpenter* on behalf of the United States before the Sixth Circuit Court of Appeals while I was on academic leave and serving as a Special Assistant United States Attorney in the Eastern District of Michigan. Once the Supreme Court granted certiorari, I played no further role in strategizing about, briefing, or arguing the case. This article does not discuss, reflect, or reveal any inside information about the litigation. All of the ideas expressed here are entirely my own, and they do not necessarily reflect any views or even speculation of the United States. I thank Vik Amar, Eve Brensike Primus, Don Herzog, Jerry Israel, David Moran, Deeva Shah, and Geof Stone for valuable input on earlier drafts, and Sam Mancina and the University of Michigan Law Library for excellent research assistance.

[1] 138 S Ct 2206 (2018).

[2] Id at 2224 (Kennedy, J, dissenting).

[3] *Riley v California*, 134 S Ct 2473 (2014).

[4] *United States v Jones*, 565 US 400 (2012) (twenty-eight-day tracking).

Court asked what the Fourth Amendment requires when law enforcement seeks cell phone records revealing the user's approximate location when his cell phone connects to local cell towers. The Court's answer "is a familiar one—get a warrant."[5]

Familiar, yes; but easy, no: the Court split 5–4 with four separate dissenting opinions spanning 115 pages. The case reflects a fundamental clash between long-standing doctrinal approaches and new surveillance and digital information technologies. The government today has unprecedentedly sophisticated ways of seeing, hearing, and tracking people, ways that were unimaginable to the Fourth Amendment's Framers. The question is whether and how the Court should adjust constitutional doctrines to maintain some historical or reasonable equilibrium between privacy and law enforcement, or whether legislatures should be the guardians of privacy in the face of technological innovation.

The Court addressed this question in *Carpenter* at a time when its existing doctrinal approaches are both stressed and uncertain. The Court's primary framework protects individuals from unwarranted invasions of their "reasonable expectation of privacy," a doctrine first announced fifty-plus years ago in *Katz v United States*,[6] and then refined a decade later in *United States v Miller*[7] and *Smith v Maryland*[8] through the third-party doctrine that withheld protection for information voluntarily disclosed to others. Both of these doctrines have come under withering attack from different quarters: *Katz* for protecting privacy too freely, *Miller-Smith* for withdrawing that protection too rigidly, and both for being textually and conceptually ungrounded. Perhaps in response to these criticisms, some Justices recently revived an older framework, most famously articulated in *Olmstead v United States*,[9] holding that the Fourth Amendment protects people only against physical intrusions on or in "material things—the

---

[5] *Carpenter*, 138 S Ct at 2221.

[6] 389 US 347, 360–61 (1967) (Harlan, J, concurring) (requiring warrant to eavesdrop electronically on phone conversations).

[7] 425 US 435 (1976) (holding customer lacks Fourth Amendment interest in bank's records showing his financial transactions).

[8] 442 US 735 (1979) (holding phone customer lacks Fourth Amendment interest in phone company's records showing whom he called).

[9] 277 US 438 (1928) (rejecting challenge to government wiretapping of phone conversations).

person, the house, his papers, or his effects."[10] This test too has raised questions of scope and principled application.[11]

Lurking in the background, moreover, are competing motivations for Fourth Amendment doctrine: to protect atomistic privacy and security interests of individual citizens, and to regulate government conduct that might threaten such values.[12] The atomistic approach suffuses through the doctrine today, for example, by limiting Fourth Amendment standing to people whose rights were arguably violated by, rather than who were just incriminated by, a questionable search.[13] But the regulatory approach has its own foothold, most notably in the exclusionary remedy designed generally to deter illegal searching rather than to vindicate individual rights[14]—and some claim anew that a regulatory approach is required to address privacy threats of the modern age.[15]

What makes the *Carpenter* decision a potential game changer is that neither the *Katz* nor *Olmstead* doctrines, whether viewed through an atomistic or regulatory lens, previously seemed hospitable to many novel Fourth Amendment claims arising in the digital age. Today, given widespread use of the internet, the cloud, corporate digital-data storage, internet-connected personal devices, and related technologies, a huge amount of personal and sensitive information is stored somewhere in the digital records of an institutional third party, be it a phone company, internet service provider, bank, credit-card company, social media giant, phone applications manager, online retailer, wearable technology company, or medical provider.[16] And govern-

---

[10] Id at 464.

[11] See Orin S. Kerr, *The Curious History of Fourth Amendment Searches*, 2012 Supreme Court Review 67, 90–93 (exploring ambiguities).

[12] See, for example, Anthony G. Amsterdam, *Perspectives on the Fourth Amendment*, 58 Minn L Rev 349, 367 (1974) ("Does [the Amendment] safeguard *my* person and *your* house and *her* papers and *his* effects against unreasonable searches and seizures; or is it essentially a regulatory canon requiring government to order its law enforcement procedures in a fashion that keeps us collectively secure in our persons, houses, papers, and effects, against unreasonable searches and seizures?").

[13] *Rakas v Illinois*, 439 US 128, 133–38 (1978).

[14] Both the deterrence focus of the exclusionary rule, and its burgeoning exception for good-faith violations, reflect this approach. See *Davis v United States*, 564 US 229, 236–39 (2011).

[15] See, for example, Daniel J. Solove, *Fourth Amendment Pragmatism*, 51 BC L Rev 1511 (2010); Donald A. Dripps, *Perspectives on the Fourth Amendment Forty Years Later: Toward the Realization of an Inclusive Regulatory Model*, 100 Minn L Rev 1885 (2016).

[16] "Use of the Internet is vital for a wide range of routine activities in today's world— finding and applying for work, obtaining government services, engaging in commerce,

ment officials regularly subpoena documents containing this information, without warrants or probable cause, in early-stage crime investigations. Prior to this decision, *Katz*'s reasonable expectations–based approach, as limited by the third-party doctrine, did not protect the privacy interests of the targets of such investigations because the targets had voluntarily shared their information with the third party, thus relinquishing any erstwhile claim to privacy. And the older/revised *Olmstead* property invasion–based approach did not protect the targets' privacy interests because the records being secured weren't "their . . . papers [or] effects" but belonged to the third party.

In his majority opinion in *Carpenter*, Chief Justice Roberts redirected the *Katz* route to require the government to obtain search warrants before securing location-revealing cell phone records, by broadening the scope of privacy interests and narrowing the exception carved out by the third-party doctrine. The issues are complicated and the opinions long. My goal here is to analyze carefully the Court's approach, to explain and critically evaluate its reasoning, to highlight remaining important questions, and to project future directions.

Like Justice Gorsuch in dissent, "I do not begin to claim all the answers today."[17] But my main conclusions are these: To find a Fourth Amendment search, the Court substantially refashioned (though it claimed otherwise) *Katz*'s progeny to replace relatively definitive-though-controversial rules with multivariate standards, primarily by emphasizing the comparative sensitivity of location information; this shift makes doctrine more flexible and hospitable to digital privacy claims but also less coherent and clear. And at key points the Court's reasoning appears to reflect a regulatory as well as atomistic attitude toward privacy protection, motivated to forestall an Orwellian future of rampant surveillance of everyone's movements and activities. The Court purported to move cautiously, crafting a self-described "narrow" opinion addressing cell phone location records and little else, persistently labeling cell phone tracking "novel" and "unique" and creating a "qualitatively different category" of

---

communicating with friends and family, and gathering information on just about anything, to take but a few examples." *United States v LaCoste*, 821 F3d 1187, 1191 (9th Cir 2016).

[17] *Carpenter*, 138 S Ct at 2268 (Gorsuch, J, dissenting).

sensitive records.[18] But the opinion's reasoning opens the door for lower courts and future Court decisions to protect privacy well beyond this category.

As for the required justification, "get a warrant" is the familiar route for full-scale searches. But it is also a novel approach to requests for private document production, and the Court's ruling raises interesting and either underappreciated or unanticipated questions about broader categories of subpoenas as well. The more broadly the warrant requirement applies, the more it will frustrate "many legitimate and valuable investigative practices upon which law enforcement has rightfully come to rely."[19] So even if the Court's *Katz*-expanding reasoning invites further privacy protection over time, I predict that at some point the warrant's constraint on law enforcement efforts will likely curb that momentum. *Carpenter* takes a strong first step toward digital privacy protection, but the length of the stride remains unclear.

Part I sets the stage by briefly sketching the litigation, existing doctrinal approaches, and the five separate opinions in the case. Part II examines the Court's conclusion that acquiring customers' cell phone records from their service provider constitutes a Fourth Amendment "search" because it violates their reasonable expectation of privacy. Part III examines the Court's conclusion that such searches require a probable cause–backed warrant rather than the lesser showing typically required for document subpoenas, and it considers the majority opinion's potential effect on first-party subpoenas as well. In my view, the Court's path to both conclusions is bumpy at best, though perhaps understandably so as the Court heads in a new direction across fast-changing technological terrain.[20]

If nothing else, *Carpenter* means that a majority of the Justices are searching to find ways to better protect privacy in the modern age. And by retooling long-standing precedent to be more adaptive to privacy concerns, the decision invites much more open and free-spirited dia-

---

[18] Id at 2216–17 (majority).

[19] Id at 2247 (Alito, J, dissenting).

[20] Amsterdam, 58 Minn L Rev at 352 (cited in note 12) (the Court sometimes decides cases based on a new approach "even though it is not prepared to announce the new principle in terms of comparable generality with the old, still less to say how much the old must be displaced and whether or how the old and new can be accommodated.").

logue among lower courts, as they confront what Justice Alito aptly anticipates will be a continuing "blizzard of litigation."[21] We'll find out soon enough whether the decision works a shift in constitutional doctrine that is as "seismic" as the shift in the technology it's chasing.[22]

I. Carpenter's Backdrop and Decision

A. CELL-PHONE TRACKING A CELL PHONE THIEF

You really couldn't make up better facts: Timothy Carpenter used his cell phone to help his confederates steal cell phones, and then the government used his cell phone records to help to put him in a prison cell.[23]

In April 2011, police arrested four men suspected of joining a larger, rotating crew committing a months-long string of armed robberies during which they stole brand new cell phones from Radio Shack and T-Mobile stores in Michigan and Ohio. One arrestee confessed and squealed on half-brothers "Little Tim" Carpenter and "Big Tim" Sanders, plus others, providing the FBI with many of the group's cell phone numbers.

Federal officials applied under the Stored Communications Act[24] (SCA) for a court order to obtain Carpenter's and his accomplices' cell phone records for the months covering the crime spree. Specifically, the officials wanted call detail records indicating the phone numbers the men called at what times, and also records indicating which cell phone towers the phones used when the men made or received those calls—otherwise known as cell-site location information, or CSLI.

Cell phones transmit radio signals to cell sites (antennas) mounted on cell towers. Each tower typically has three or six cell sites spread around it in a circle, creating separate sectors that carve the space surrounding the tower into pie-slice-shaped service areas. More sectors create narrower pie slices, and closer towers create shorter slices. When the phone sends or receives a call, text message, or other

---

[21] *Carpenter*, 138 S Ct at 2247 (Alito, J, dissenting).

[22] Id at 2219 (majority).

[23] See generally id at 2211–13; *Carpenter v United States*, 819 F3d 880, 884–85 (6th Cir 2016).

[24] 18 USC §§ 2701–12 (2012).

data, the phone signals the local cell site with the strongest signal.[25] That's usually the nearest tower, so the phone typically connects to the cell site located at the tip of the service area in which the phone resides.[26] Wireless carriers can detect and record which phones connect to which of their cell sites at what times. For various business reasons, such as detecting coverage problems and billing for roaming charges, they maintain records containing their customers' CSLI for up to several years.

The SCA authorizes judges to compel production of cell phone records when government provides "specific and articulable facts showing that there are reasonable grounds to believe" the records sought "are relevant and material to an ongoing criminal investigation"[27]—a significantly weaker showing than the probable cause typically required for a search warrant, though more than required for a grand jury subpoena. Agents requested 152 days of CSLI records from Carpenter's primary carrier MetroPCS (which produced 127), and seven days of records from roaming-in-Ohio carrier Sprint (which produced two, all it had). The records indicated that Carpenter placed cell phone calls from within a half-mile to two miles from several of the robberies just before or while they occurred, corroborating reports that Carpenter was typically the "lookout" who used his phone to signal the actual robbers when to enter the targeted stores.

Combining this location information with other evidence, the United States charged Carpenter with six counts of robbery, Sanders with two counts, and both with related gun offenses. Both defendants moved to suppress Sprint's CSLI data,[28] arguing that its procurement without a probable cause–backed search warrant violated the Fourth Amendment. The district court denied the motion, and at trial the government introduced a few of the CSLI records to locate the

---

[25] Unless turned off or in "airplane mode," the phone continually sends out registration pings to nearby cell sites, measuring in advance the relative strength of available connections so it is ready to go. Aaron Blank, *The Limitations and Admissibility of Using Historical Cellular Site Data to Track the Location of a Cellular Phone*, Richmond J L & Tech 1, 5 (2011).

[26] Weather, topography, and obstructions such as buildings and trees can sometimes cause cell phones to connect to a tower that isn't the nearest one. Id at 6–7.

[27] 18 USC § 2703(d).

[28] Following the Court's lead, *Carpenter*, 138 S Ct at 2219 (referencing "Sprint Corporation and its competitors"), I'll use Sprint to refer to the carriers (including MetroPCS) involved in this case and also generic wireless carriers.

The defendants did not seek to suppress the call detail records linked to the cell-site data.

defendants near some of the robberies when they occurred. A jury found both men guilty, and the court sentenced Carpenter to over 116 years' imprisonment (note: if you rob a store, don't let a buddy use a gun).

The Court of Appeals for the Sixth Circuit affirmed, holding that compelling Sprint to produce CSLI records does not constitute a Fourth Amendment search.[29] This ruling was predictably consistent with other Court of Appeals rulings, because then-binding Supreme Court precedent was fairly clear.[30] But there were equally clear signs of a storm brewing within the Court over the direction of doctrine and its suitability for the digital age. And when the Court granted review despite the lack of a circuit split, one could easily forecast a tempest ahead.[31]

B. COMPETING FOURTH AMENDMENT FRAMEWORKS

The Fourth Amendment declares "[t]he right of the people to be secure in their persons, houses, papers, and effects against unreasonable searches and seizures shall not be violated. . . ."[32] The Court over time, and internally today, has split between two quite different doctrinal frameworks and motivating visions.

---

[29] *Carpenter*, 819 F3d at 886–90.

[30] *In re Application of United States for an Order Directing a Provider of Electronic Comm'n Service to Disclose Records to Gov't*, 620 F3d 304 (3d Cir 2010); *In re Application of United States for Historical Cell Site Data*, 724 F3d 600 (5th Cir 2013); *United States v Davis*, 785 F3d 498 (11th Cir 2015) (en banc); *United States v Graham*, 824 F3d 421 (4th Cir 2016) (en banc); *United States v Thompson*, 866 F3d 1149 (10th Cir 2017).

[31] Sanders did not petition for certiorari alongside Carpenter, despite his own fourteen-year sentence. Of course, even a Supreme Court victory would not likely help the half-brothers' plight. Upon remand, Carpenter will (and Sanders would have) likely confront the argument that his CSLI records were still admissible at trial based on the good-faith exception to the exclusionary rule, as the government reasonably followed the SCA's procedures. See *Illinois v Krull*, 480 US 340, 349 (1987) (good-faith exception applies when officials act "in objectively reasonable reliance on a statute" unless it is "clearly unconstitutional"); *United States v Warshak*, 631 F3d 266, 288–89 (6th Cir 2010) (applying good-faith exception to e-mail content records secured under the SCA despite ruling that procuring e-mail content requires a warrant); *United States v Pembrook*, 876 F3d 812, 823 (6th Cir 2017) (applying exception to CSLI records based on alternative argument that no binding judicial precedent then required a warrant). Carpenter will also likely face strong arguments, as Sanders would have too, that the CSLI evidence was cumulative so any error was harmless. See Brief for the United States, *United States v Carpenter*, Nos 15-1572 & 14-1805, *40–47 (6th Cir, filed May 6, 2015) archived at https://perma.cc/78RV-KT83 (*Carpenter* 6th Cir Brief) (advancing good-faith exception and harmless error arguments).

[32] US Const, Amend IV.

1. *The Katz framework: privacy and public exposure.* In *Katz*, FBI agents eavesdropped on the defendant's phone call by placing an electronic listening device on the outside of a public telephone booth. Because the "Fourth Amendment protects people, not places,"[33] the Court announced, it didn't matter that the government had left untouched Katz's person, houses, papers, or effects. As Justice Harlan famously restated the rule in his concurring opinion, a person enjoys a Fourth Amendment protected interest if she has "exhibited an actual (subjective) expectation of privacy and . . . the expectation [is] one that society is prepared to recognize as 'reasonable.'"[34] By shutting the phone-booth door behind him, Katz reasonably expected his conversation would remain private except for the person he was calling.[35] The Court has embraced and applied Justice Harlan's two-part "reasonable expectation of privacy" test ever since.[36]

But from the very beginning, the Court made clear that public disclosure defeats potential Fourth Amendment protection. As *Katz* put it, the Fourth Amendment does not protect "objects, activities, or statements that [a person] exposes to the 'plain view' of outsiders."[37] This principle manifests itself in several ways, two of which are central here:

Exposure of public movements: Revealing yourself to the general public extinguishes any erstwhile privacy interest in your location or visible activities. In *United States v Knotts*,[38] police used a "beeper" planted in a container of chloroform, after visual surveillance failed, to help track a vehicle used by suspected drug manufacturers. The Court held that the tracking did not constitute a search, reasoning that Knotts could not reasonably expect privacy "in his movements from one place to another" because "he voluntarily conveyed to anyone who wanted to look" his route, stops along the way, and final destination.[39] The Court has since invoked this reasoning to deny

---

[33] 389 US at 351.

[34] Id at 361 (Harlan, J, concurring).

[35] Id.

[36] See, for example, *Terry v Ohio*, 392 US 1, 9 (1968); *Smith*, 442 US at 740.

[37] *Katz*, 389 US at 361 (Harlan, J, concurring); see id at 351 (majority) ("What a person knowingly exposes to the public, even in his own home or office, is not a subject of Fourth Amendment protection.").

[38] 460 US 276 (1983).

[39] *Knotts*, 460 US at 281–82.

privacy protection for movement and activities in a variety of contexts where "anyone who wants to look" can see what's going on.[40]

And yet *Knotts* cryptically hinted at a possible limit to what "anyone" can see, as different rules might apply to "dragnet type" twenty-four-hour surveillance practices.[41] Three decades later in *United States v Jones*,[42] five Justices turned the hint into a full-blown alarm. Suspecting Jones of drug trafficking, agents surreptitiously attached a GPS tracking device to his car and remotely monitored the car's movements for twenty-eight days.[43] Justice Scalia wrote the majority opinion, holding that physically affixing the device to the car constituted a Fourth Amendment search under *Olmstead*'s invasion-of-property approach.[44] But Justice Sotomayor (for herself, after joining the majority) and Justice Alito (for himself and Justices Ginsburg, Breyer, and Kagan, rejecting the majority) penned *Katz*-driven concurring opinions, recognizing that modern technologies enable police to track a car without physically intruding upon it.[45] After focusing on ways that GPS location information can reveal sensitive information, they posited that "longer term GPS monitoring in investigations of most offenses impinges on expectations of privacy."[46]

This shadow majority of five Justices embraced what many call a "mosaic" theory: even though discrete movements or locations lack Fourth Amendment protection after being "disclosed to the public at large,"[47] a substantial aggregation of those movements can rise to the level of a protected interest. While privacy advocates cheered this nonprecedential endorsement,[48] critics viewed the mosaic approach

---

[40] See, for example, *California v Ciraolo*, 476 US 207, 213–15 (1986) (no search where police in private plane flew over defendant's yard and spotted marijuana, because defendant voluntarily exposed backyard to visual observation from publicly navigable airspace); *Florida v Riley*, 488 US 445, 449 (1989) (same for helicopter flyover).

[41] *Knotts*, 460 US at 283–84.

[42] 565 US 400 (2012).

[43] Agents exceeded their search warrant authority by attaching the device too late and in the wrong jurisdiction. 565 US at 402–3.

[44] Id at 404. See text accompanying notes 61–63.

[45] Id at 414–15 (Sotomayor, J, concurring).

[46] Id at 430 (Alito, J, concurring in the judgment); id at 415 (Sotomayor, J, concurring).

[47] *Carpenter*, 138 S Ct at 2215.

[48] See, for example, Christopher Slobogin, *Making the Most of United States v. Jones in a Surveillance Society: A Statutory Implementation of Mosaic Theory*, 8 Duke J Const'l L & Pub Pol (Special Issue) 1 (2012); Paul Rosenzweig, *In Defense of the Mosaic Theory* (LawFare, Nov 29, 2017), archived at https://perma.cc/RYX5-DUVS.

as "upend[ing] decades of settled doctrine"[49] and raising significant conceptual and pragmatic questions.[50] Thus the *Jones* concurrences created substantial uncertainty about *Knotts*'s heretofore bright-line public exposure doctrine.

Exposure of third-party records: The Fourth Amendment likewise does not protect information that is willingly disclosed to a third party and then obtained by the government from that party. In *United States v Miller*, federal agents who suspected Miller of running an illegal whiskey distillery subpoenaed his banks to produce his financial records, including some checks, deposit slips, and other account documentation. The Court rejected Miller's Fourth Amendment challenge to the subpoenas, holding that he lacked any reasonable expectation of privacy in the banks' records and therefore he was not "searched" under *Katz*.[51] He had "voluntarily conveyed" the sought-after information to the banks and "exposed [it] to their employees in the ordinary course of business."[52] Miller thus took the risk that the banks would share that information with the government.

Three years later in *Smith v Maryland* the police, suspecting Smith of making badgering phone calls to a woman he had robbed, asked a telephone company to install at its central office a pen register corresponding to Smith's home landline.[53] The pen register recorded only the outgoing phone numbers he dialed, not the content of any communications.[54] The Court rejected Smith's Fourth Amendment challenge to the warrantless request because Smith voluntarily revealed the called numbers to the phone company through his dialing. Smith lacked a subjective expectation of privacy, knowing he had to convey the numbers to complete his calls, and knowing the company could make and keep records of his calls.[55] And, in any event, any subjective expectation of privacy would not be objectively reasonable, as "a person has no legitimate expectation of privacy in information he

---

[49] Matthew B. Kugler and Lior Jacob Strahilevitz, *Actual Expectations of Privacy, Fourth Amendment Doctrine, and the Mosaic Theory*, 2015 Supreme Court Review 205, 209.

[50] See, for example, Orin S. Kerr, *The Mosaic Theory of the Fourth Amendment*, 111 Mich L Rev 311 (2012) (explaining and largely criticizing the mosaic approach).

[51] *Miller*, 425 US at 437–40.

[52] Id at 442.

[53] *Smith*, 442 US at 737.

[54] Id at 741.

[55] Id at 742–43.

voluntarily turns over to third parties."[56] So again, the pen register's use was not a search under *Katz*.

The seminal *Miller-Smith* decisions established the third-party doctrine that cabins *Katz*. As *Miller* summarized:

> the Fourth Amendment does not prohibit the obtaining of information revealed to a third party and conveyed by him to Government authorities, even if the information is revealed on the assumption that it will be used only for a limited purpose and the confidence placed in the third party will not be betrayed.[57]

Scholars haven't been kind to this doctrine, to say the least, claiming that the doctrine's all-or-nothing treatment of disclosure clashes with any reasonable conception of reasonable expectations.[58] For some critics, *Miller* and *Smith* were wrong when decided; for others, their legacy became increasingly untenable as third parties' digital creation and retention of personal records burgeoned over time. As currently applied to a world in which countless companies digitally store vast amounts of personal information about virtually everyone—including but not limited to records of communications, purchases, finances, computer searches, car operations, media viewing, home and wearable technology use, travel, and medical histories[59]—the doctrine forestalls Fourth Amendment protection and gives government access basically for the asking. After Justice Sotomayor's concurrence in *Jones* echoed this chorus of criticism by proclaiming "it may be necessary to reconsider" the third-party doctrine because the "approach is ill suited to the digital age,"[60] the *Miller-Smith* edifice suddenly wobbled.

2. *The Olmstead framework: property-focused tetrad intrusions.* Along with questions about *Katz*'s "public exposure" principles came questions about *Katz* itself. Because the reasonable expectations of privacy test isn't constrained by the textual tetrad of persons, houses, papers, or effects, Justices inclined toward textual or originalist interpretation predictably looked elsewhere for guidance.

---

[56] Id at 743–44.

[57] *Miller*, 425 US at 443.

[58] See note 170.

[59] See, for example, Stephen E. Henderson, *Our Records Panopticon and the American Bar Association Standards for Criminal Justice*, 66 Okla L Rev 699, 704–7 (2014); id at 704 ("If we step back and think of our everyday experiences, it is easy to see that very significant information about each of us is recorded by third parties that used to be recorded by no one.").

[60] 565 US at 417 (Sotomayor, J, concurring).

In *Jones*, Justice Scalia resurrected *Olmstead*'s property-based approach. In *Olmstead*, the Court rejected a Fourth Amendment challenge to government wiretapping of home and office phone lines used by bootlegging suspects. The Court held that the "amendment itself shows that the search is to be of material things—the person, the house, his papers, or his effects"[61] rather than intangible things such as sounds or sights. In addition, the Court continued, a search occurs only upon "an actual physical invasion" of such material things.[62] Because the agents tapped Olmstead's phone lines "without any trespass upon [his] property,"[63] they conducted no Fourth Amendment search. In *Jones*, Justice Scalia (with four other Justices) applied this test in holding that when agents attached a GPS tracking device to Jones's car, they "physically occup[ied] private property for the purpose of obtaining information" and therefore searched the car.[64]

Justice Scalia posited that this tetrad-invasion approach, in which the Fourth Amendment primarily protects property rather than privacy interests, could coexist with *Katz*.[65] But there is no question that he and other like-minded Justices (presumably including his successor Justice Gorsuch) hoped never to rely on *Katz* going forward, adding additional uncertainty to the mix.[66] Thus, the fissures within *Katz* and its progeny and the resurgence of the property-based approach raised questions about whether and how *Carpenter* might build new doctrine for the digital age.

C. OVERVIEW OF CARPENTER'S OPINIONS

1. *The Court (Chief Justice Roberts, joined by Justices Ginsburg, Breyer, Sotomayor, and Kagan).* Chief Justice Roberts's opinion for the Court applied the *Katz* framework, concluding that when the government acquired Carpenter's cell-site records, it "searched" him

---

[61] *Olmstead*, 277 US at 464.

[62] Id at 466.

[63] Id at 457.

[64] 565 US at 404.

[65] Id at 409.

[66] As recounted earlier, in *Jones* four Justices embraced the property-based framework, four the reasonable-expectations framework, and one both. In *Florida v Jardines*, 569 US 1 (2013), five Justices held that police searched Jardines's home when they lingered at his front door with a drug-sniffing dog because they thereby physically invaded the house's curtilage without license to do so, three of these Justices held that the lingering was also a search because it invaded Jardines's *Katz*-based reasonable expectation of privacy, and the other four Justices held none of the above.

by invading his reasonable expectation of privacy in information about his whereabouts. The Court invoked some "basic guideposts" for *Katz*'s application: the Fourth Amendment seeks to secure the "'privacies of life' against 'arbitrary power'" and "'to place obstacles in the way of a too permeating police surveillance.'"[67] When confronting "innovations in surveillance tools," Roberts explained, the Court seeks to "'assure[ ] preservation of that degree of privacy against Government that existed when the Fourth Amendment was adopted.'"[68]

Following these guideposts, the Court decided that Carpenter had a protected privacy interest in CSLI data revealing his movements over a week or more, but left open the question for shorter durations.[69] Roberts explained that location information is sufficiently continuous and precise that the records essentially tracked Carpenter back in time to provide an "all-encompassing record of [his] whereabouts"[70]—sufficient to potentially reveal "not only his particular movements, but through them his 'familial, political, professional, religious, and sexual associations.'"[71] Such long-term tracking, Roberts noted, goes beyond what people normally expect to expose publicly as they move around. Embracing the mosaic theory, the Court cabined *Knotts* and recognized Carpenter's reasonable expectation of privacy "in the whole of his physical movements."[72]

The Court then held, for the first time, that the *Miller-Smith* third-party doctrine did not encompass a particular category of stored records. First, given the widespread use of and need for cell phones today, Roberts maintained that CSLI is not voluntarily shared in the same way as bank records and phone calls. Second, he argued, location records are more sensitive than bank and call records. "There is a world of difference," he explained, "between the limited types of personal information addressed in *Smith* and *Miller* and the exhaustive chronicle of location information casually collected by wireless carriers today."[73] Thus, "[i]n light of the deeply revealing nature of

---

[67] *Carpenter*, 138 S Ct at 2214, quoting *Boyd v United States*, 116 US 616, 630 (1886), and *United States v Di Re*, 332 US 581, 595 (1948), respectively.

[68] *Carpenter*, 138 S Ct at 2214, quoting *Kyllo v United States*, 533 US 27, 34 (2001).

[69] *Carpenter*, 138 S Ct at 2217 n 3.

[70] Id at 2217.

[71] Id, quoting *Jones*, 565 US at 415 (Sotomayor, J, concurring).

[72] *Carpenter*, 138 S Ct at 2219.

[73] Id.

CSLI, its depth, breadth, and comprehensive reach, and the inescapable and automatic nature of its collection, the fact that such information is gathered by a third party does not make it any less deserving of Fourth Amendment protection."[74] As a result, Carpenter's location information "was the product of a search."[75]

Absent exigent circumstances, the Court further held, such a search requires a warrant backed by probable cause.[76] The Court dismissed the suggestion that because the SCA requires Sprint or other carriers to produce the CSLI records itself, the lesser Fourth Amendment standard of relevance and nonburdensomeness typically required for subpoenas *duces tecum* (and satisfied by SCA orders) should apply. The Court concluded this lesser standard is not appropriate where the target retains a *Katz*-based privacy interest in the records being sought, a "rare case" justifying the stricter warrant requirement.[77]

2. Justice Kennedy's dissent (joined by Justices Thomas and Alito). Justice Kennedy wrote the primary (and his very last) dissent. The main thrust of his argument was that the Court applied *Katz* too expansively and the "public exposure" precedents too narrowly. Justice Kennedy defended the *Miller-Smith* third-party doctrine, arguing first that it faithfully reflects the notion that people cannot claim a privacy interest in papers or effects that are not theirs, and second that the doctrine accords with the government's traditional authority to use (warrantless) subpoenas to obtain documents.[78] Carpenter, Justice Kennedy argued, loses under this doctrine because he does not own, possess, or control Sprint's CSLI records in any meaningful sense.[79]

The Court finds otherwise, Justice Kennedy continued, only by misreading its "public exposure" precedents. While he questioned the Court's use of the *Jones* concurrences to supersede *Knotts*'s privacy waiver for public movements,[80] he trained his fire on the Court's "transform[ing] *Miller* and *Smith* into an unprincipled and unwork-

---

[74] Id at 2223.

[75] Id at 2217.

[76] *Carpenter*, 138 S Ct at 2221. The SCA's statutory standard fell "well short" of the required showing. Id.

[77] Id at 2221–22.

[78] Id at 2227–29 (Kennedy, J, dissenting).

[79] Id at 2229–30 (Kennedy, J, dissenting).

[80] *Carpenter*, 138 S Ct at 2231 (Kennedy, J, dissenting).

able doctrine."[81] In his view, *Miller-Smith* established a bright-line rule extinguishing privacy interests in shared information, rather than a balancing test taking sensitivity into account.[82] And even so, he maintained, the Court erred in its arbitrary judgments that location information is more sensitive than financial and phone call records, that location records are cheaper and easier to acquire, and that cell phone use is less "voluntary" than using banks or credit cards.[83]

Because technological change has "complex effects on crime and law enforcement" and can influence both property norms and expectations of privacy, Justice Kennedy would defer to Congress' judgment in enacting the SCA, which he believed "weighed the privacy interests at stake and imposed a judicial check to prevent executive overreach."[84] Kennedy closed by worrying that the Court's decision would negatively affect law enforcement, noting that access to CSLI is "an important investigative tool for solving serious crimes" and is often "indispensable" in the early stages of an investigation before the government can develop probable cause supporting a warrant.[85]

3. *Justice Thomas's dissent.* Justice Thomas also maintained that the key issue is not "whether" a search occurred (yes), but "whose" property was searched.[86] Although Sprint was "searched," Thomas insisted that Carpenter was not "searched" because neither property, tort, contract, nor federal statutory law supports Carpenter's claim that Sprint's records are *his* papers or effects.[87]

But Justice Thomas wrote separately primarily to lambast *Katz*, which "has no basis in the text or history of the Fourth Amendment" and "invites courts to make judgments about policy, not law."[88] First, he argued, the reasonable expectation of privacy test has no plausible foundation in Fourth Amendment text because it distorts the original meaning of "search," wrongly focuses on privacy rather than property, reads the tetrad list out of the text, excises the word "their"

---

[81] Id at 2230 (Kennedy, J, dissenting).

[82] Id at 2232 (Kennedy, J, dissenting).

[83] Id at 2232–33 (Kennedy, J, dissenting).

[84] *Carpenter*, 138 S Ct at 2233 (Kennedy, J, dissenting).

[85] Id at 2233–34 (Kennedy, J, dissenting).

[86] Id at 2235 (Thomas, J, dissenting).

[87] Id at 2242–43 (Thomas, J, dissenting).

[88] *Carpenter*, 138 S Ct at 2236 (Thomas, J, dissenting).

modifying the tetrad, and wrongly applies "unreasonable" to define searches rather than to justify them.[89] Second, he argued, the *Katz* test has proven unworkable in practice, which he illustrated by stringing together a long list of scholarly epithets, including my favorite, "a mass of contradictions and obscurities."[90] It is not clear, he observed, whether privacy expectations are to be measured empirically or normatively, and (even worse) neither measure is any good.[91] The nicest thing Justice Thomas called *Katz* is a "failed experiment," one that the Court, he maintained, is duty-bound to reconsider.[92] If that happens, it's not hard to guess what Justice Thomas will do.

4. *Justice Alito's dissent (joined by Justice Thomas).* Justice Alito piled on by also attacking the Court's decision to let Carpenter object to the search of a third party's property, arguing that neither the constitutional text nor a proper reading of *Miller-Smith* permits this, and insisting that neither federal statute nor any other law gives Carpenter "any meaningful property-based connection to the cell-site records owned by his provider."[93]

Justice Alito's primary target, however, was the Court's decision to require a warrant for the "search" it defined. To Alito, the Court ignored the basic distinction between a traditional search in which government agents rummage through protected spaces or things, and a constructive search in which government agents simply request the target to produce specified documents. Alito traced the history of subpoenas from British practice through the founding,[94] concluding that "the Fourth Amendment, as originally understood, did not apply to the compulsory production of documents at all."[95] He acknowledged that the Court's doctrine does not reflect this view; instead, document subpoenas must satisfy the Fourth Amendment's "reasonableness" requirement[96]—but they do so when they satisfy the much-relaxed standard of being limited in scope, relevant in purpose,

---

[89] Id at 2238, 2239–40, 2241, 2241–42, 2243–44 (Thomas, J, dissenting).

[90] Id at 2244 (Thomas, J, dissenting).

[91] Id at 2245–46 (Thomas, J, dissenting).

[92] *Carpenter*, 138 S Ct at 2246 (Thomas, J, dissenting).

[93] Id at 2257–60, 2260 (Alito, J, dissenting).

[94] Id at 2247–52 (Alito, J, dissenting).

[95] Id at 2250 (Alito, J, dissenting).

[96] *Carpenter*, 138 S Ct at 2252–57 (Alito, J, dissenting).

and not unreasonably burdensome.[97] SCA orders easily pass this test.[98]

After lamenting the Court's failure to defer to legislative judgments regarding privacy and technology, Justice Alito concluded that "[t]he desire to make a statement about privacy in the digital age does not justify the consequences [of thwarting important law enforcement investigations] that today's decision is likely to produce."[99]

5. *Justice Gorsuch's dissent—or concurrence dressed as a dissent.* Justice Gorsuch also jumped on the *Katz*-bashing bandwagon. He maintained that both the Fourth Amendment's "plain terms" and history show that the "framers chose not to protect privacy in some ethereal way" but only in "particular places and things," meaning the textual tetrad.[100] He also characterized the *Katz* test as both undetermined and indeterminate: after five decades of doctrinal dominance "we still don't even know" whether the test poses an empirical or a normative question,[101] and insufficiently guided judges have reached decisions that are "often unpredictable—and sometimes unbelievable,"[102] inevitably resting on their "own curious judgment."[103] Moreover, he declared, the *Miller-Smith* gloss is "not only wrong, but horribly wrong,"[104] whether the question about post-sharing expectations is empirical or normative, which itself is unclear.[105] And beyond that, he insisted, the Court's effort to tweak and apply *Katz* and *Miller-Smith* to the facts in *Carpenter* made matters worse, now dictating two "amorphous balancing tests"—"*Katz*-squared"[106]—weighing incom-

[97] Id at 2256 (Alito, J, dissenting).

[98] Id at 2255 (Alito, J, dissenting).

[99] Id at 2261 (Alito, J, dissenting).

[100] *Carpenter*, 138 S Ct at 2264 (Gorsuch, J, dissenting).

[101] Id at 2265 (Gorsuch, J, dissenting).

[102] Id at 2266 (Gorsuch, J, dissenting), poking fun in particular at *Florida v Riley*'s approval of police snooping around residential backyards via hovering helicopter, 488 US 455 (1989), and *California v Greenwood*'s approval of police rummaging through curbed trash ahead of the raccoons, 486 US 35 (1988).

[103] *Carpenter*, 138 S Ct at 2266 (Gorsuch, J, dissenting).

[104] Id at 2262 (Gorsuch, J, dissenting), quoting Orin S. Kerr, *The Case for the Third-Party Doctrine*, 107 Mich L Rev 561, 564 (2009).

[105] *Carpenter*, 138 S Ct at 2262–63 (Gorsuch, J, dissenting), quoting William Baude and James Y. Stern, *The Positive Law Model of the Fourth Amendment*, 129 Harv L Rev 1821, 1872 (2016).

[106] *Carpenter*, 138 S Ct at 2272 (Gorsuch, J, dissenting).

mensurable variables.[107] But at least Justice Gorsuch graciously allowed that the *Carpenter* majority's doctrinal mishmash was not the Court's fault because, he opined, "this is where *Katz* inevitably leads."[108]

Justice Gorsuch then spent the bulk of his opinion sketching out a potential argument on Carpenter's behalf that purported to protect his privacy interests while remaining true to the traditional property-based framework.[109] The approach combines (1) old-school bailment principles that demonstrate an individual does not necessarily abdicate Fourth Amendment protections for property merely by voluntarily sharing it, (2) a more recent recognition that positive law can create property rights in intangible things such as digital records, and (3) a specific claim that a federal statute prohibiting wireless carriers from publicly sharing their customers' location information[110] might be such a law.[111] The combination, Justice Gorsuch suggested, might give customers a form of bailed ownership interest such that the CSLI records become (at least in part) *their* papers or effects for Fourth Amendment purposes.[112] And perhaps, he continued, this model might generalize to other types of third-party digital records as well. In the end, though, Justice Gorsuch dissented rather than concurred after concluding that Carpenter failed to present any property or positive law-based claim in the courts below.[113]

---

[107] Id at 2267 (Gorsuch, J, dissenting).

[108] Id (Gorsuch, J, dissenting).

[109] I plan to address more fully the promises and pitfalls of Justice Gorsuch's proposed approach in a separate essay. See Evan Caminker, *Rebuilding Carpenter on Property Law Foundations: Justice Gorsuch's Proposed Approach to Protecting Privacy in the Digital Age* (unpublished manuscript, 2018) (on file with author). Given interpretative trends and shifting membership, this approach may reflect an ascendant position on the Court. In my view, while Justice Gorsuch suggests creative ways to update the *Olmstead* approach to better address privacy threats of the digital age, significant questions remain.

[110] Telecommunications Act of 1996, 47 USC § 222.

[111] *Carpenter*, 138 S Ct at 2267–71 (Gorsuch, J, dissenting).

[112] Id at 2272 (Gorsuch, J, dissenting). It is worth nothing that Justice Gorsuch would part company here with his fellow dissenters, all of whom reject this conclusion. See id at 2229–30 (Kennedy, J, dissenting); id at 2242–43 (Thomas, J, dissenting); id at 2257–59 (Alito, J, dissenting).

[113] Carpenter's new counsel (the ACLU) briefed this statutory claim to the Supreme Court. Brief for Petitioner, *Carpenter v United States*, No 16-402, *33–35 (US, filed Aug 7, 2017) (available on Westlaw at 2017 WL 3575179) ("*Carpenter* Petr's Brief"). But Carpenter never mentioned any statutory claim or broader property rights claim before either the district court or court of appeals. Indeed, his district court brief supporting his motion to suppress (joining his co-defendant) never once uses the word "property," and his Sixth Circuit brief uses the term only three times and only when describing the charged robberies. Defendant Timothy Sanders's Motion in Limine to Suppress Cell Phone Data, *United States v Sanders*,

II. Building a New Search Doctrine for Cell Phone Location Records

Carpenter's majority (and Justice Gorsuch) clearly recognized that current doctrinal protections do not "fit neatly" with modern forms of digital data or data analytics.[114] Under the *Katz*-based approach, Chief Justice Roberts explained, "requests for cell-site records lie at the intersection of two lines of cases"[115]—an odd locution when the public and third-party exposure lines don't intersect but rather both lead directly away from Fourth Amendment protection. But Roberts redirected both doctrinal paths, creating more flexible routes of reasoning that better respond to digital data's oft-sensitive nature and the circumstances of its sharing. And while Roberts described the Court's doctrinal revisions as narrow, their rationales appear to leave room for extension to a much broader set of digital records and privacy concerns.

A. LOCATION INFORMATION AND THE THREAT TO PRIVACY: RECORD, REALITY, AND RULING FOR THE FUTURE

Carpenter's privacy claim is straightforward: Sprint's CSLI records reveal his phone's general location at many moments over a long period of time, enabling someone studying those records to infer some activities and associations he might rather keep confidential. CSLI's capacity to threaten his personal privacy depends on how precisely it determines location, how frequently Sprint records phone-tower connections, and for how long Sprint stores the data. Chief Justice Roberts's opinion of the Court depicted CSLI as rivaling GPS tracking in these respects, providing a "detailed chronicle" of a person's physical presence "every moment of every day for five years."[116]

This alarming claim of "near perfect surveillance"[117] is futuristic, projecting well beyond the record data from 2011 and even beyond

---

Case No 12-cr-20218 (ED Mich, filed Nov 21, 2013) (joined by Carpenter); Appellant's Brief, *United States v Carpenter*, No 15-1572, *3, 41 (6th Cir, filed Mar 2, 2015). So if the doctrine of argument forfeiture means anything (a fair question), it surely applies here.

[114] *Carpenter*, 138 S Ct at 2214.

[115] Id.

[116] Id at 2220; id at 2218 (comparing phone to ankle monitor).

[117] Id at 2218.

present-day reality. To be sure, CSLI data are certainly trending toward greater precision and frequency. But Chief Justice Roberts's willingness to pretend the future is already here (and likely exaggerate it) suggests two things: first, a desire to get ahead of the technology curve rather than rule from behind, reflecting a regulatory rather than atomistic attitude toward Fourth Amendment protection in this context; and, second, an effort to describe the privacy intrusion as particularly acute, so as to limit the precedential scope of the ruling.

1. *Precision of recorded locations.* Given the spacing of cell towers where Carpenter made and received phone calls, the CSLI data merely "locate[d] the defendants' cellphones within a 120- (or sometimes 60-) degree radial wedge extending between one-half mile and two miles in length."[118] Those service areas are "between around a dozen and several hundred city blocks" and "up to 40 times more imprecise" in rural areas.[119] And nothing indicates where in a particular service area the phone was located at any point in time.[120] The location information in the record is therefore "as much as 12,500 times less accurate than the GPS data in *Jones*."[121]

And yet the Court felt unconstrained by the record, declaring that it "'must take account of more sophisticated systems that are already in use or in development.'"[122] Even so, the Court seemed quite aggressive in describing those systems as "rapidly approaching GPS-level preci-

---

[118] *Carpenter v United States*, 819 F3d 880, 889 (6th Cir 2016).

[119] *Carpenter*, 138 S Ct at 2225 (Kennedy, J, dissenting); see also Stephen E. Henderson, *Carpenter v. United States and the Fourth Amendment: The Best Way Forward*, 26 Wm & Mary Bill of Rts J 495, 501 (2017) (calculating service area to range from 0.1 square miles to 4.2 square miles).

[120] See Joint Appendix, *United States v Carpenter*, No 16-402, *86–88 (US filed Aug 7, 2017) (available on Westlaw at 2017 WL 3614549) ("*Carpenter* Appendix") (testimony of Agent Hess): "Q: [Y]ou are not able to say that the phone was at a particular place, right? A: Correct. Q: What you would really say at best is that it is somewhere within that area that could be a half-mile to a mile in distance from the tower and then [as wide as the far crossing line] connecting those two, right? A: Right. . . . [The phone] would be within the footprint of that tower on that sector."

[121] *Carpenter*, 819 F3d at 889. The Court protested that the government could "deduce" when Carpenter "was at the site of the robberies," information "accurate enough to highlight" during closing argument. *Carpenter*, 138 S Ct at 2218. Yes—except the prosecutor's reference to "at the site" meant nothing more than somewhere in the "exact" or "right sector" for a nearby cell tower. *Carpenter* Appendix at *56 (cited in note 120) (government's closing argument).

[122] *Carpenter*, 138 S Ct at 2218, quoting *Kyllo*, 533 US at 36.

sion."[123] Since Carpenter's crime spree, carriers have installed more cell sites so that "the geographic area covered by each cell sector has shrunk, particularly in urban areas."[124] But how much will service areas likely continue to shrink? Even six times the present would leave most service areas measuring two to fifty blocks.[125] And what about other technological developments that might slow or reverse this trend by *reducing* reliance on local cell-site connections?[126]

The Court pointed to "new technology measuring the time and angle of signals hitting their towers" giving carriers "the capability to pinpoint a phone's location within 50 meters."[127] But the cited briefs contain scant evidence that these newer capabilities will ever be regularly used (except when law enforcement requests real-time tracking), or the resulting data will be regularly recorded and stored.[128] The most supportive data show that Verizon keeps more-precise-than-mere-service-area data for just eight days,[129] and one can only speculate if and

---

[123] *Carpenter*, 138 S Ct at 2219.

[124] Id.

[125] Carpenter's own data source (updated) reports a 52 percent increase in cell sites over the past decade (to 323,448) by the end of 2017, and projects another 800,000 or so small cells (typically deployed on streetlights or utility poles, with much smaller service areas) by 2026. CTIA, *The State of Wireless 2018* *20 (2018), archived at https://perma.cc/7QGZ-6EKA. As implied, small cells create much smaller service areas, such as "one floor of a building, the waiting room of an office, or a single home," *Graham v United States*, 824 F3d 421, 448 (4th Cir 2016) (en banc) (Wynn dissenting).

[126] Brief for the United States, *United States v Carpenter*, No 16-402, *27 (US filed Sept 25, 2017) (available on Westlaw at 2017 WL 4311113) ("*Carpenter* US Brief") (discussing device-to-device calling and wi-fi calling, neither of which creates CSLI). See, for example, Tom Simonite, *Future Smartphones Won't Need Cell Towers to Connect* (MIT Tech Rev, Sept 29, 2014), archived at https://perma.cc/HH7T-HZY8 (discussing device-to-device direct connections for shorter-distance data connections).

[127] *Carpenter*, 138 S Ct at 2219, citing Brief for Amici Curiae Electronic Frontier Foundation et al, *United States v Carpenter*, No 16-402, *12 (US filed Aug 14, 2017) (available on Westlaw at 2017 WL 4512266) ("*Carpenter* EFF Amici Brief"). This claim of precision depends on the distance between cell towers. For example, see Phil Locke, *Cell Tower Triangulation—How It Works* (Wrongful Conviction Blog, June 1, 2012), archived at https://perma.cc/R8FK-FYUT (concluding from triangulation modeling "it is possible to determine a phone location to within an area of 'about' ¾ square mile[s]").

[128] For example, the amicus brief the Court cited for this capability in turn cites congressional testimony that describes the process but says only that any use or recording of such data depends on individual carriers' policies, which are not described. *Carpenter* EFF Amici Brief at *11 & n 24 (cited in note 127).

[129] Craig Silliman, *Technology and Shifting Privacy Expectations (Perspective)* (Bloomberg Law, Oct 7, 2016), archived at https://perma.cc/N8N4-XJV5; see also Tom Jackman, *Experts Say Law Enforcement's Use of Cellphone Records Can Be Inaccurate* (Wash Post, June 27, 2014), archived at https://perma.cc/8PU6-2F9B (observing "phone companies do not save GPS or triangulation for an individual phone").

when carriers will find business reasons to record and store more precise location records for long periods of time.[130]

2. *Frequency of recorded connections.* The records in this case showed Carpenter's phone connections only when he made or received phone calls.[131] Admittedly, Carpenter apparently breathed through his phone, making or receiving enough calls to average 101 recorded connections per day[132]—well above average.[133]

Chief Justice Roberts characterized Carpenter's monitoring as far more continuous, claiming that his carriers recorded his cell-tower and sector usage "[e]ach time the phone connects to a cell site."[134] This parrots Carpenter's and his amici's non-record-based (and hence not adversarially tested) assertions that "in recent years phone companies have also collected location information from the transmission of text messages and routine data connections."[135] "Collected," perhaps; but the sources cited in Carpenter's and supportive amici briefs do not connect the dots all the way to long-term *storage* that would

---

[130] See Henderson, 26 Wm & Mary Bill of Rts J at 498 n 19 (cited in note 119) ("But such a precise location [using triangulation and signal strength] will typically not be calculated, let alone recorded in records later received by law enforcement, at least not based upon current business practices.").

An online search for recent federal or state decisions indicating that the government had requested and received historical CSLI data reflecting such triangulation technology reveals none. A few courts discuss such technology only to clarify that the produced records did not include any pinpoint location data. See, for example, *Zanders v State*, 73 NE3d 178, 182 (Ind 2017) (discussing triangulation and other technologies but noting that no "high-resolution location data" were involved in case); *Commonwealth v Augustine*, 4 NE3d 846, 855 (Mass 2014) (same). Agents sometimes request triangulation to assist with prospective or "real-time" CSLI tracking. See, for example, *United States v Alarcon*, 2016 WL 2844164, *1 (D Minn).

[131] That's all the government asked for. See *Carpenter*, 138 S Ct at 2212; *Carpenter* US Brief at *7 (cited in note 126) ("The records . . . did not contain any cell-site information for text messages or for times when petitioner's phone was turned on but was not being used to connect a call."). And indeed that's all Sprint and MetroPCS recorded. Id.

[132] *Carpenter*, 138 S Ct at 2212.

[133] A year earlier the average was ten connections per day (five calls). See Amanda Lenhart, *Cell Phones and American Adults* (Pew Research Center, Sept 2, 2010), archived at https://perma.cc/DSM6-XXMH.

[134] *Carpenter*, 138 S Ct at 2211; id at 2212 (repeated almost verbatim). The Court attributed this claim to FBI Agent Hess's trial testimony, id at 2212, and yet Hess was crystal clear that by "connection" he meant only actively making or receiving phone calls. *Carpenter* Appendix at *61 (cited in note 120) (testimony of Agent Hess) ("Q: So if the phone is just in my pocket, and I'm not calling and no one is calling me, you couldn't really do this? A: Right. It's not populated in the call detail records. Q: Even though it might be communicating in there, — A: That's correct.").

[135] *Carpenter*, 138 S Ct at 2212.

produce records covering "every moment of every day for five years."[136]

This projection of continuous long-term CSLI monitoring is, at a minimum, overconfident. It will probably soon be true for some people at some times in some places; but it is generally still quite a way off.

3. *What can CSLI reveal?* Location data threaten privacy to the extent an observer can (1) compare tower service areas with local maps and (2) determine what places the target visited and how long she stayed there and then (3) infer what she might have been doing there and why.[137] The Court warned that, "[a]s with GPS information, the time-stamped data provides an intimate window into a person's life, revealing not only his particular movements, but through them his 'familial, political, professional, religious, and sexual associations.'"[138] But this GPS comparison exaggerates the capacity for (2) and (3) above. On this record, the typical service area for Carpenter's CSLI "contains about 1000 buildings."[139] Cut that in half—indeed, cut it in hundreds—it's still hard to infer these details with any confidence. So current or even near-future projected CSLI records cannot easily determine the kinds of personal associations about which the Court expressed worry, at least not without significant nonlocation data obtained elsewhere.[140]

That said, there is no question that current CSLI can be used to infer with reasonable confidence *some* sensitive facts. For example, even imprecise data can reveal whether the target visits the same general locations repeatedly, or not. And imprecise data can indicate where a cell phone is *not* (not near one's workplace during the day,

---

[136] Id at 2218.

[137] The Court rhetorically embellishes the capacity to infer by repeatedly describing CSLI location monitoring as "surveillance." See, for example, *Carpenter*, 138 S Ct at 2217–18. That term implies "being watched," as if CSLI can determine not just *where* you are located (however precisely), but also *what* you are doing and *with whom*, as opposed to leaving this to inference. Of course, that is not what the data show.

[138] Id at 2217, quoting *Jones*, 565 US at 415 (Sotomayor, J, concurring).

[139] *Carpenter* US Brief at *25 (cited in note 126).

[140] For example, while the ACLU claimed before the Sixth Circuit that Carpenter's cell phone records placed him at church at a particular time, that claim was based partly on information Carpenter himself provided rather than only on the records themselves. See *Carpenter* 6th Cir Brief at 33 n 4. Without such additional information, CSLI data "does not paint the 'intimate portrait of personal, social, religious, medical, and other activities and interactions'" that Carpenter claims. *United States v Davis*, 785 F3d 498, 515 (11th Cir 2015) (en banc) (citation omitted).

not near one's home all night). Moreover, the Court may appropriately worry about current trends. Surely the Court correctly concluded that CSLI "has afforded law enforcement a powerful new tool" that "*risks* Government encroachment of the sort the Framers . . . drafted the Fourth Amendment to prevent."[141]

4. *Record, reality, and ruling for the future.* Given clear trends and risks, why did Chief Justice Roberts apparently feel a need to embellish CSLI's actual level of intrusion, both in terms of precision and continuity? Perhaps for two reasons.

First, the aggressive depiction of CSLI tracking suggests a regulatory approach to privacy doctrine, reflecting a desire to cabin worrisome surveillance even before the technology reaches highly invasive levels. Given the typical time lag between the development/deployment of new privacy-threatening technology and judicial (especially Supreme Court) review, law enforcement activities might well impinge upon should-be-protected privacy interests for quite some time before courts confined to actual record-based threats catch up.[142] The desire to forestall a "'too permeating police surveillance'"[143] heralds an increasingly regulatory approach to modern surveillance threats, leading the Court to anticipate protections required for atomistic privacy values.

To be sure, the Court does not always rule forward in this manner.[144] Hesitation in the face of technology lag may reflect hope that

---

[141] *Carpenter*, 138 S Ct at 2223 (emphasis added). The far greater risk here involves a myriad and growing number of cell phone applications whose operators collect phone users' location information, sometimes to deliver tailored services (such as local weather news or driving directions) but oftentimes just to collect the information so they can sell it en masse to companies for commercial purposes (such as to provide businesses and advertisers with clues about consumer behavior). Again it's not clear that the app operators store the information in user-identifiable form; rather, the data are typically anonymized before bulk resale. But in some cases a dedicated analyst, once armed with a lot of other facts about particular people's movements and location patterns, can reverse-engineer educated guesses as to which individuals actually made which tracked movements. These apps frequently track location through GPS coordinates, far more precise than CSLI. See, for example, Jennifer Valentino-DeVries et al, *Your Apps Know Where You Were Last Night, and They're Not Keeping It Secret* (NYT, Dec 10, 2018), archived at https://perma.cc/98FB-KTXZ (discussing practices and providing examples). Of course, while not necessarily easy to do, users can adjust their cell phone settings to disable the location services that enable such tracking, either wholesale or piecemeal and either indefinitely or for particular periods of time. Id.

[142] See, for example, Neil Richards, *The Third-Party Doctrine and the Future of the Cloud*, 94 Wash U L Rev 1441, 1448, 1464–65 (2017) (describing and applying the "Fourth Amendment lag problem" to digital data and related technology).

[143] *Carpenter*, 138 S Ct at 2214 (citation omitted).

[144] See, for example, *Maryland v King*, 569 US 435, 464 (2013) (joined by Roberts, CJ) (refusing to consider future improvements in DNA testing that might further compromise

legislative bodies, arguably better suited to project and regulate for the future, will step up.[145] But given the conjectured technology growth curve and no congressional action in sight, the Court may reasonably have thought the time to intervene was now.

Of course, Chief Justice Roberts could have candidly recognized that both the monitoring to which Carpenter was actually subjected and the most common location monitoring available today remain quite imprecise and episodic compared to GPS-level tracking, and yet still expressed concern for doctrinal time lag as a reason to rule forward by modifying doctrine prophylactically. Lack of candor comes with a cost; the Court's exaggerated claims will likely be accepted at face value by lower courts, and the underlying technological reality will continue to escape judicial scrutiny.[146]

But here lies the second possible motive for embellishment. The more precise and continuous the Court depicts CSLI tracking, the easier it is to claim both that it violates reasonable expectations of privacy, and that it is distinguishable from more conventional surveillance techniques and other types of third-party records. Let's now see how strong those claims are.

B. A MOSAIC PRIVACY INTEREST IN THE "WHOLE OF ONE'S
PUBLIC MOVEMENTS"

Given this futuristic description of CSLI data, the Court easily found that historical location monitoring implicates a *Katz*-based privacy interest. The more difficult question is whether that interest dissipates because the phone user shares his location information, either with the public around him or with Sprint.

---

privacy, despite acknowledging that "science can always progress further, and those progressions may have Fourth Amendment consequences"); *Silverman v United States*, 365 US 505, 508–9 (1961) (refusing to consider "recent and projected developments in the science of electronics" despite foreseeable "Fourth Amendment implications of these and other frightening paraphernalia").

[145] See, for example, Jeffrey S. Sutton, *Courts, Rights, and New Technology: Judging in an Ever-Changing World*, 8 NYU J L & Lib 261, 274–75 (2014) (although "courts have no license to abdicate their duty to enforce constitutional guarantees based on the complexities of new technology," there are virtues associated with deferring to (and presumably encouraging) legislative intervention).

[146] See, for example, *United States v Curtis*, 901 F3d 846, 847 (7th Cir 2018) (accepting without question that CSLI "is capable of 'pinpoint[ing] a phone's location within 50 meters'" and carriers "can collect CSLI as frequently as several times a minute"), quoting and then citing *Carpenter*, 138 S Ct at 2219, 2211–12.

The "public exposure" doctrine holds that people lack a reasonable expectation of privacy in movements or activities that they publicly expose to "anyone who wants to look."[147] The majority in *Carpenter*, however, embraced a form of the mosaic approach championed by the shadow majority of concurring Justices in *Jones*, and announced that heretofore "individuals have a reasonable expectation of privacy in the *whole of their physical movements*."[148] In other words, while *each* public movement may be exposed and hence unprotected by *Katz*, the *aggregate* of such movements may qualify for Fourth Amendment protection. Given that "[t]he sum of an infinite number of zero-value parts is also zero,"[149] how did the Court add this up?

First, Chief Justice Roberts redefined the question. Rather than follow *Katz* and *Knotts* by asking whether public sojourners reasonably expect they are exposing their *discrete* movements to *any* one, meaning to different people at different places and times,[150] the Court in *Carpenter* asked whether the sojourners reasonably expect they are exposing their *entire set* of movements to any *one*, meaning to a single person who sees it all. The question shifted from what bits and pieces of information the sojourners knowingly reveal to random people, to what they might expect a single-but-dedicated viewer to learn from what they reveal.

And the Court answered "not so much." Personal surveillance by law enforcement or private tails using only conventional tools and techniques is both difficult and costly. As a result, people reasonably expect that "law enforcement agents and others would not—and indeed, in the main, simply could not—secretly monitor and catalogue every single movement of an [individual] for a very long period."[151] So, while people do not reasonably expect privacy in any *discrete* movement (or perhaps a short series of movements), people do reasonably expect that no one is systematically viewing the "whole" of

---

[147] See text accompanying notes 38–40.

[148] *Carpenter*, 138 S Ct at 2217 (emphasis added).

[149] *United States v Jones*, 625 F3d 766, 769 (DC Cir 2010) (Sentelle dissenting from denial of rehearing en banc).

[150] See *Katz*, 389 US at 351 (exposure to "public"); id at 361 (Harlan, J, concurring) (exposure to "outsiders"); *Knotts*, 468 US at 281 (exposure to "anyone who wanted to look").

[151] *Carpenter*, 138 S Ct at 2217, quoting *Jones*, 565 US at 430 (Alito, J, concurring in the judgment).

their physical movements over any extended period of time.[152] Even for the police, this is wildly inefficient except in extraordinary circumstances.

Second, Roberts emphasized the potential sensitivity of location information. Knowing *all* of someone's movements, a dedicated viewer might be able to construct a "mosaic" of discrete data points from which to infer things about the sojourner that society reasonably believes she should be able to keep to herself—such as her "'familial, political, professional, religious, and sexual associations.'"[153]

Third, Roberts highlighted how easily government can leverage Sprint's CSLI-based monitoring powers. Compared to both "nosy neighbors" and government agents using traditional surveillance techniques, Sprint is a potentially super-powerful tracker due to features of CSLI technology. After all, "[c]ell phone tracking" by the government "is remarkably easy, cheap, and efficient"[154] because Sprint has already done the work. Moreover, the ability to search stored records "gives police access to a category of information otherwise unknowable."[155] Normally, agents can surveil targets only from the moment of suspicion and going forward; stored CSLI data let agents "travel back in time to retrace a person's whereabouts."[156] Although police can always interview eyewitnesses about a suspect's prior movements, such efforts are limited by "the frailties of recollection,"[157] whereas Sprint's memory is "nearly infallible."[158] Another consideration, unmentioned by the Court, is that agents seeking to reconstruct someone's prior movements may have a hard time figuring out who might be plausible human eyewitnesses to interview, but the agents can easily consult the universe of plausibly "witnessing" service providers. In sum, government access to Sprint's records will almost assuredly reveal a more comprehensive and accurate story of the target's movements than whatever can likely be pieced together

---

[152] *Carpenter*, 138 S Ct at 2217.

[153] Id, quoting *Jones*, 565 US at 415 (Sotomayor, J, concurring).

[154] *Carpenter*, 138 S Ct at 2217–18; see also id at 2218 (asserting government can access CSLI "at practically no expense").

[155] Id.

[156] Id.

[157] Id.

[158] *Carpenter*, 138 S Ct at 2219.

through more traditional investigative efforts—precisely why the government wants such access.

The Court's first-ever embrace of a mosaic-defined search has been roundly praised by privacy advocates clamoring for change, and it is truly a significant doctrinal shift. And perhaps not surprisingly, as an initial step in a novel direction, the majority opinion is under-theorized, or at least underexplained. Most fundamentally, the Court did not address or resolve the long-standing conceptual ambiguity underlying *Katz* that so frustrated the dissents. Does the mosaic test assess *empirical* expectations—suggesting that when I walk down the street, I don't *predict* that a single person will see my entire route even though I do predict that lots of different people may collectively see every single step along the way? Or does the test reflect a *normative* standard—suggesting that I *shouldn't assume the risk* that any one person will see the entire route (thereby potentially learning something about my familial/political/professional/religious/sexual affiliations or proclivities), even though I assume the risk that each step is discretely revealed? Nor did the Court clarify an ambiguity raised by *Jones*'s separate opinions by specifying the baseline against which it measures how much monitoring information—whether assessed empirically or normatively—is too much. Is the mosaic-triggered privacy interest invaded when I am monitored for a longer period than I (would or should) expect to be seen by law enforcement officers trying to surveil me; or for a longer period than I (would or should) expect to be seen by a single "nosy neighbor"?[159] Perhaps we will learn more as the doctrine unfolds; but the Court may leave well enough alone,

---

[159] Rather than pick one baseline, the Court referred to both: society expects that "law enforcement agents *and* others would not" and could not monitor the target's entire journey. Id at 2217 (emphasis added). But whether viewed empirically or normatively, these baselines might be quite different. Orin Kerr, for example, traces the law enforcement baseline to Justice Alito in *Jones*, traces the private "others" baseline to the court of appeals in that case, traces yet a third baseline (when the government can learn intimate details "more or less at will") to Justice Sotomayor in *Jones*, notes that the approaches are materially different, and further pinpoints ambiguities within each formulation. Kerr, 111 Mich L Rev at 330–31 (cited in note 50). By acting as if the *Jones* shadow majority had already established the "whole of one's public movements" principle, the *Carpenter* Court avoided the need to explain its views further.

The approach previously espoused by Justice Alito in *Jones*, employing a what-would-law-enforcement-do-through-traditional-surveillance baseline, might hinge (empirical or normative) expectations to the crime being investigated. He ponders whether the more serious the offense, the longer and more intense surveillance would/should be expected. *Jones*, 565 US at 431 (Alito, J, concurring in the judgment). This would add another conceptual trick. The Fourth Amendment protects innocent people too, but how can one of them possibly speculate

sidestepping these underlying questions as it has done with *Katz* for decades.[160]

The mosaic approach, by its very nature, invites line-drawing to distinguish location monitoring that reveals the "whole of one's public movements" from monitoring that merely reveals discrete "publicly exposed" movements unprotected under *Knotts*. The rationale for mosaic-based protection does not justify covering shorter-term CSLI requests. The fewer location data points available, the harder it is to discern patterns or sequences and therefore to infer particular activities, and the more likely it is the target could reasonably expect (empirically and normatively) to be personally viewed throughout that period.[161]

As with other doctrinal questions that hinge on aggregated events or the passage of time (for example, how long may a nonwarrant arrestee be detained prior to a judicial probable cause determination[162]), the Court must establish some cut-off point for when *Knotts*-approved monitoring ends and search-triggering monitoring begins. In *Carpenter*, the Court proclaimed that "accessing seven days of CSLI constitutes a Fourth Amendment search," leaving for another

about how long she would/should expect to be surveilled if she needs to know the severity of an offense she did not commit?

Throughout this discussion the Court also implicitly evinced little care for *Katz*'s "subjective expectation of privacy" component. The Court concluded that Carpenter did not truly expose his long-term location information in the relevant sense; but the Court seemed entirely uninterested in whether Carpenter manifested any intent to keep to himself the underlying kinds of information the Court worried his movements will reveal. For all we know, Carpenter was quite open about his family relations, political views, professional associations, religious views and practices, and sexual interests—perhaps all revealed through his Facebook postings and personal attire (such as wearing a cross or yarmulke, rainbow pin, and gang colors). See generally Orin S. Kerr, *Katz Has Only One Step: The Irrelevance of Subjective Expectations*, 82 U Chi L Rev 113 (2015) (observing demise of subjective test).

[160] That said, the obvious difficulties applying the empirical baseline to any specific instance of long-term monitoring, see *United States v Cuevas-Perez*, 640 F3d 272, 282–83 (7th Cir 2011) (Flaum concurring) (concluding "probabilistic" mosaic approach is "unworkable"), coupled with the Court's not doing so here, strongly suggests the *Carpenter* majority is thinking in normative terms.

[161] As Justice Alito concluded in *Jones*, "relatively short-term monitoring of a person's movements on public streets accords with expectations of privacy that our society has recognized as reasonable." 565 US at 430 (Alito, J, concurring in the judgment). Even Justice Sotomayor, who in *Jones* flagged her concern about "short-term" as well as "longer term" GPS monitoring, id at 415–17 (Sotomayor, J, concurring), still recognized that only "aggregated" records of movements could generate privacy-threatening inferences. Id at 416; see also id at 415 (expressing concern over "comprehensive record of a person's public movements"); id at 416 (expressing concern over "substantial quantum of intimate information").

[162] See *Riverside v McLaughlin*, 500 US 44 (1991) (imposing presumptive forty-eight-hour limit to detention before postarrest probable cause hearing).

day whether government may obtain historical CSLI for a shorter period "free from Fourth Amendment scrutiny, and if so, how long that period might be."[163] One could imagine the Court ultimately embracing a broad prophylactic rule that *any* CLSI request constitutes a search, in part to avoid the appearance of drawing arbitrary lines.[164] I anticipate, however, that the Court will maintain some cut-off point—likely a week, but at least a day or two—both to reflect the underlying mosaic-based justification and, as described below, to balance privacy with law enforcement interests.[165]

Of course, any such cut-off point raises further line-drawing issues as well—some raised by many duration-defined doctrines,[166] but others tailored to the novelty of applying a mosaic approach to law enforcement. Traditionally, courts have looked at a discrete interaction between police and a person or tetrad object and asked

---

[163] *Carpenter*, 138 S Ct at 2217 n 3. The Court apparently focused on a week because the shorter of the two records requests was for a week's worth of data. See id. The Court did not address Justice Gorsuch's poke that Sprint provided only two days of records (because Carpenter's trip to Ohio that triggered roaming was brief) and his query why the search should be measured by the information requested rather than the information actually acquired. See id at 2266–67 (Gorsuch, J, dissenting).

[164] The Court could have also reached this point through a different route, ruling that any CSLI is too much based on a concern about tracking targets in private homes. In *United States v Karo*, 468 US 705 (1984), the Court cabined *Knotts* and held that location monitoring becomes a search when it fixes the target in a private residence such that the government learns "a critical fact about the interior of the premises that the Government . . . could not have otherwise obtained without a warrant." Id at 715. If the Court doubled down on its claim of GPS-like precision, CSLI could suggest that the target entered a home. Because officials would have no way of predicting that in advance, the records might contain some Fourth Amendment–protected as well as some publicly exposed data points. See *Tracey v Florida*, 152 So3d 504, 524 (2014). To be sure, the Court in *Karo* held the public data pings admissible while suppressing the private pings. But on those different facts it was easy to separate the two; here it might be very difficult. Moreover, a broader prophylactic rule would better protect targets who never become criminal defendants.

[165] See text accompanying note 266. Requiring a warrant for short-term CSLI monitoring might hinder criminal investigations much more severely than requiring a warrant only for long-term monitoring.

The non-search status for short-term historical monitoring should also apply to short-term tracking deployed to locate a target in real time. Such tracking might aid law enforcement in arresting her, or rescuing a kidnapping victim, or even providing an alibi for a recent crime. But a short sequence of location fixes (whether through cell tower usage or GPS pings) hardly seems sufficient to lay bare her "privacies of life" by revealing the "whole" of her public movements.

[166] For example, consider remedies. Agents do not search me when they obtain six consecutive days of Sprint's CSLI records for my phone, but they search you when they obtain seven consecutive days. Is your exclusionary rule remedy suppressing records for all seven days, or only the seventh (or perhaps only the first, or only one day of your choice, or of the government's choice)? Is your civil remedy damages for one day or one week of illegal searching? Put differently, have you suffered a single indivisible illegal search, or a legal search for six days and an illegal one for the seventh?

whether that interaction constitutes a Fourth Amendment search. Here, we're left wondering whether that's still true (such that only a single long-term records request from a single third party can create a search-triggering mosaic), or whether a search can be produced by the aggregation of different enforcement activities across time, motives, sovereigns, technologies, etc. For example, suppose Agent Amy requests five days of Sprint's records for your phone. When, if at all, may Agent Barb later ask Sprint for the next three days? Never? Only after a certain amount of time has elapsed? Only when investigating a different crime? Only if Agent Barb represents a different law enforcement agency, or even a different sovereign? And what if two different third-party carriers are involved: suppose given your movements and roaming your phone connects to Sprint towers for four consecutive days and then MetroPCS towers for the next four. Agent Carol requests these four-day series of records from both Sprint and MetroPCS. Both carriers have been searched;[167] have you?[168]

An atomistic view of mosaic theory supports aggregating all of these various information requests for the purpose of defining a search—from your perspective, you don't care whether your nosy neighbor or the police have pieced together the privacy-threatening mosaic from one long stare or many momentary glances. But that means that whether Agent Esther searches you may depend on the completely independent and even then-unknown interactions between many other agents and many other third parties. That's conceptually unsettling, to say the least, let alone a pragmatic quagmire both for officers trying to comply with the Fourth Amendment and for courts trying to sort things through after the fact. I suspect here again that a regulatory perspective will win the day, with the

---

[167] Though subject only to the much relaxed standard for document subpoenas. See text accompanying notes 281–82.

[168] To press the point even further, consider aggregating requests for different kinds of third-party records. For a week-long period, Agent Darcy requests records revealing some of your credit card purchases, some swipes of your building entrance passkey, some passages on toll roads, and some internet protocol addresses, and then she views some surveillance tapes from near your house and office—all of which directly or incidentally reveal timed location information, and which collectively add up to 101 data points per day to match Carpenter's prolific phone use. Now all of those third parties have been searched; again, have you?

For other pragmatic challenges posed by mosaic-required line drawing, see Kerr, 111 Mich L Rev at 328–43, 346–48, 330–31 (cited in note 50); Lucas Issacharoff and Kyle Wirshba, *Restoring Reason to the Third Party Doctrine*, 100 Minn L Rev 987, 1003 (2016) (concluding that mosaic theory "works better as a metaphor than as a constitutional doctrine" due to "impracticality as an administrable standard").

Court favoring easier-to-implement bright-line rules over harder-to-measure-and-enforce aggregation rules, even though the latter more directly track atomistic and mosaic-defined privacy concerns.

C. MODIFYING THE MILLER-SMITH THIRD-PARTY DOCTRINE TO PROTECT CSLI RECORDS

So Carpenter's legitimate claim to privacy in the whole of his public movements overcame *Katz*'s caveat about publicly exposed activities. But he still faced the third-party doctrine's independent caveat that " 'a person has no legitimate expectation of privacy in information he voluntarily turns over to third parties' " even just " 'for a limited purpose,' "[169] and therefore acquiring such information is not a Fourth Amendment search.

As noted earlier, the *Miller-Smith* mantra that voluntary sharing automatically defeases privacy has been criticized by scholars on a wide variety of grounds,[170] some echoed by Justice Gorsuch's dissent.[171] As an empirical statement of the expectations people generally hold, the doctrine is "quite dubious";[172] surely at least sometimes we expect people or even companies to keep our shared private information to themselves.[173] And as a normative statement of when people are entitled to expect postsharing privacy, "the notion that the answer might be 'never' seems a pretty unattractive societal prescription."[174] Scholars have proposed many different rules to determine

---

[169] *Carpenter*, 138 S Ct at 2216, quoting *Smith*, 442 US at 743–44, and then *Miller*, 425 US at 443.

[170] For a small subset of voluminous critical commentary, see Kerr, 107 Mich L Rev at 563 n 5 (cited in note 104) (collecting sources criticizing the doctrine); Jane Bambauer, *Other People's Papers*, 94 Tex L Rev 205, 208 & n 18 and 214–15 nn 50–51 (2015) (criticizing doctrine and collecting sources).

[171] *Carpenter*, 138 S Ct at 2262–63 (Gorsuch, J, dissenting).

[172] Id at 2263 (Gorsuch, J, dissenting), quoting Baude and Stern, 129 Harv L Rev at 1872 (cited in note 105); see also Kugler and Strahilevitz, 2015 Supreme Court Review at 255 (cited in note 49) (explaining survey data indicate third-party doctrine holds disproportionate appeal to older Americans and has an "apparent lack of resonance with younger Americans").

[173] Context matters: if I tell a friend funny stories about my addiction to college football, I'd generally expect her (absent special admonition) to share them with whomever she sees fit; but if I tell her painful stories about emotional anxieties, I'd generally expect her to keep quiet or perhaps share only with her spouse. And the down-the-line recipient matters: if I confess suicidal thoughts, I'd expect my friend to keep quiet if I insist or perhaps reveal them to my wife or an appropriate caretaker, but not reveal them to my students or my young children.

[174] *Carpenter*, 138 S Ct at 2263 (Gorsuch, J, dissenting); see id at 2262–64 (canvassing and critiquing application of various assumption-of-risk norms). When the Court acknowledged

when sharing does not extinguish privacy interests.[175] Whatever the best approach,[176] it is difficult to rally around a simplistic, binary answer—other than for the sake of being simplistic and binary.[177] While voluntarily sharing "objects, activities, or statements" with others may *sometimes* extinguish privacy interests under *Katz* because "no intention to keep them to himself has been exhibited,"[178] the properly nuanced question is when and why.

In *Carpenter*, Chief Justice Roberts did not accept Justice Sotomayor's suggestion in *Jones* that the Court "reconsider" the entire third-party doctrine as being "ill-suited to the digital age."[179] But Roberts confidently announced that the Court "decline[d] to *extend Smith* and *Miller* to cover these novel circumstances" and that the information's possession by a third party "does not by itself overcome" the user's Fourth Amendment claim.[180] Roberts offered two reasons not to apply the third-party doctrine to CSLI: the information revealed was both highly sensitive and not truly shared volun-

---

in *Katz* that a person cannot claim Fourth Amendment protection for things she "knowingly exposes to the public," 389 US at 351, the Court may well have considered only remarks/activities shared with natural persons, including both any intended recipients of the remarks or viewers of the activities, and also any inadvertent hearers or viewers in a private home or public space such as a park or restaurant. When nine years later *Miller* extrapolated this assumption of risk to encompass information exposed to business entities, changed membership may have made the Court less attuned to privacy interests (though Justices Stewart and White were in the majority for both decisions).

[175] For example, sharing with a company via automated processes where the information is not typically monitored by people, sharing with a person or company who is an "information fiduciary" owing an obligation of silence, sharing information that is particularly sensitive, sharing information for clearly limited purposes, and more. See, for example, Susan Brenner and Leo Clarke, *Fourth Amendment Protection for Shared Privacy Rights in Stored Transactional Data*, 14 J L & Pol 211, 215–16 (2006) (sharing should not trigger third-party doctrine if customer has broadly defined "trust-based" relationship and a confidentiality agreement with the third party and if the data are maintained at least in part for and are accessible by the customer).

[176] I'm inclined to frame the question this way: if you share information A with person B under circumstances C, do you have a right to complain if B shares your information with person D under circumstances E? That is more a normative than empirical inquiry, though empirics about observed social norms play a role. Borrowing an example from my colleague Don Herzog, I suspect it is pretty unusual for a stranger to poke around in the garbage I place on the curb for pickup, and I would think it quite weird if one did so; but I also think I couldn't persuasively *complain* that she violated my right of privacy.

[177] And as Justice Gorsuch notes, privacy "always wins" is just as clear as "always loses." *Carpenter*, 138 S Ct at 2264 (Gorsuch, J, dissenting).

[178] *Katz*, 389 US at 361 (Harlan, J, concurring).

[179] *Jones*, 565 US at 417 (Sotomayor, J, concurring); id at 418 (suggesting doctrine should "cease[ ] to treat secrecy as a prerequisite for privacy").

[180] *Carpenter*, 138 S Ct at 2217 (emphasis added).

tarily. Because the latter is more traditional terrain, I will address that argument first.

1. *Protecting involuntarily shared information.* The Court offered two seemingly simple reasons why Carpenter cannot reasonably be said to have "voluntarily" shared his location information with Sprint. But neither the reasons nor their analytical roles are as simple as they first appear.

Here are the Court's two arguments in their entirety as to why "[c]ell phone location information is not truly 'shared' as one normally understands the term."[181] First, what I will call the macro-involuntary argument: "cell phones and the services they provide are 'such a pervasive and insistent part of daily life' that carrying one is indispensable to participation in modern society."[182] And, second, what I will call the micro-involuntary argument:

> [A] cell phone logs a cell-site record by dint of its operation, without any affirmative act on the part of the user beyond powering up. Virtually any activity on the phone generates CSLI, including incoming calls, texts, or e-mails and countless other data connections that a phone automatically makes when checking for news, weather, or social media updates. Apart from disconnecting the phone from the network, there is no way to avoid leaving behind a trail of location data.[183]

Thus, Roberts reasoned, "in no meaningful sense does the user voluntarily 'assume[ ] the risk' of turning over a comprehensive dossier of his physical movements."[184]

The macro-involuntary argument says everyone needs a cell phone today. Because you need to use your phone, doing so ought not be viewed as a volitional act that "voluntarily" shares the information required to make the phone work.

This is a normative rather than factual claim. The Court cannot mean that using a cell phone is *literally* indispensable to modern life; until quite recently we managed to survive without one. That said, smartphones surely make negotiating daily activities significantly easier, more efficient, more fun, and even safer for all the obvious reasons—constant communicability, easier information retrieval,

---

[181] Id at 2220.

[182] Id, quoting *Riley v California*, 134 S Ct 2473, 2484 (2014).

[183] *Carpenter*, 138 S Ct at 2220.

[184] Id at 2220, quoting *Smith*, 442 US at 745.

faster driving directions, instant Starbucks gratification, and the like. The Court makes a normative judgment that a cell phone's important and convenient functions are so compelling today that we act *as if* we have no real choice, despite the downside of enabling location monitoring. Frankly, I act that way too: I carry my phone everywhere I go, as long as my teenage daughters are around to remind me how to use it. As a matter of social reality, the Court's judgment strikes me as reasonable.[185]

That said, I think the dissents in *Miller* and *Smith* were equally reasonable in claiming that people must use banks and landlines.[186] The Court in *Carpenter* offered no reason to distinguish among these arguable imperatives of daily life, nor thoughts on the comparative societal necessity of using credit cards, computers, cars, or cardiologists. So whether the macro-involuntary argument implicates any of these core features of modern living is not yet clear.

Perhaps the Court's micro-involuntary argument distinguishes CSLI from the rest: cell phones constantly communicate your location "without any affirmative act on the part of the user beyond powering up."[187] The point, I gather, is that you can't effectively self-regulate to control when or whether you share your location, without turning your phone off. If the Court's view is that its macro- and micro-level arguments *together* distinguish *Miller-Smith* (and other third-party digital data), that's probably right. You volitionally provide documents to (or today establish internet connections with) your bank, you dial phones, you swipe or hand over credit cards, you confide in your cardiologist, etc. Maybe some background computer func-

---

[185] Though the conclusion that we all need our cell phones also strikes me as for-this-train-only; somehow I doubt the Court will now conclude that all service-provider agreements are contracts of adhesion.

[186] See *Miller*, 425 US at 451 (Brennan, J, dissenting) ("[I]t is impossible to participate in the economic life of contemporary society without maintaining a bank account.") (citation omitted); *Smith*, 442 US at 750 (Marshall, J, dissenting) (claiming that using landline phones "for many has become a personal or professional necessity" and "individuals have no realistic alternative"); see also *Carpenter*, 138 S Ct at 2233 (Kennedy, J, dissenting) ("[T]he decision whether to transact with banks and credit card companies is no more or less voluntary than the decision whether to use a cell phone.").

Of course, there were alternative ways to keep some specific transactions private in the 1970s; you could pay for your mistress's abortion using cash or a traveler's check, and schedule that abortion from the corner payphone. Similarly, for discrete and highly sensitive trips today, you can temporarily place your phone in airplane mode.

[187] *Carpenter*, 138 S Ct at 2220. Again, this assumes, outside the record, that carriers routinely record such data exchanges other than incoming and outgoing phone calls (which clearly require affirmative acts).

tions and car black-box communications are equally automated, but perhaps even they fail the micro-involuntary test because, unlike phone connections, you intentionally turn on your laptops and start your cars before you use them.

But it is not clear that the Court intends to exclude from the third-party doctrine only technologies that are *both* socially necessary and automated. The two exceptions don't fit well together. If you have no (socially realistic) choice but to use a cell phone that lets your carrier track your location, why should the Court additionally insist for Fourth Amendment protection that the device transmits information automatically? It seems odd to conclude that you still voluntarily share your location for third-party doctrine purposes even when you intentionally place a call knowing that doing so triggers a record, when your making such phone calls "is indispensable" to modern living.

Alternatively, perhaps the Court views its macro- and micro-involuntary arguments as separately sufficient (rather than jointly necessary) to exempt technology from the *Miller-Smith* rule. Understood this way, you would waive your reasonable expectation of privacy only if you *both* enjoyed and exercised a real choice to use a cell phone in the first place, *and* did something volitional each time that your phone generates CSLI. This alternative reading is far more privacy-protective, further narrowing the sharing exception to *Katz*. But as noted above, it raises questions about the continuing vitality of *Miller* and *Smith* themselves given the realistic need to use banks and phones.[188]

---

[188] Consider this four-square comparison, which for the sake of illustration assumes that credit cards are "indispensable" for modern living but Fitbit health monitors and voice-activated TVs are not.

	micro-level = automatic data sharing	micro-level = volitional data sharing
macro-level → use is necessary	(1) CSLI	(2) using credit cards
macro-level → use is discretionary	(3) Fitbit health monitors	(4) voice-activated TVs

If the macro- and micro-involuntary arguments are necessary conditions to avoid the third-party doctrine, then only (1) CSLI remains protected under *Katz*. If the macro- and micro-involuntary arguments are separately sufficient, then (1) CSLI, (2) credit cards, and (3) Fitbits all remain *Katz*-protected. Given the potential sizes of categories (2) and (3), that is a huge difference.

The Court didn't say what it means[189]—and, indeed, it's possible the Court had neither alternative in mind. Perhaps the Court intended only to make two arguments against voluntary sharing that carry the day for this particular technology, remaining open to different antisharing arguments for other technologies. Although we know that Carpenter didn't voluntarily share his location data with Sprint, we "do not know," as Justice Gorsuch surely grew tired of lamenting,[190] just how doctrine has changed to make this so. As is often the case when the Court marks out a new path, we await further direction.

2. *Protecting especially sensitive information.* The Court could have stopped right here: *Miller-Smith* does not apply because there was no voluntary sharing, period. Instead, the Court injected data sensitivity into the third-party equation. Actually, Chief Justice Roberts claimed that the doctrine already considers sensitivity:

> The third-party doctrine partly stems from the notion that an individual has a reduced expectation of privacy in information knowingly shared with another. But the fact of "diminished privacy interests does not mean that the Fourth Amendment falls out of the picture entirely." *Riley [v California*[191]]. *Smith* and *Miller*, after all, did not rely solely on the act of sharing. Instead, they considered "the nature of the particular documents sought" to determine whether "there is a legitimate 'expectation of privacy' concerning their contents." *Miller*, 425 U.S., at 442.[192]

But this claim is forced, quoting non-third-party cases out of context.[193] Rather, the Court has repeatedly explained that sharing in-

---

[189] The locution "In the first place, . . . Second, . . . As a result . . ." does not help. Id at 2220.

[190] Id at 2266, 2267, 2272 (Gorsuch, J, dissenting).

[191] 134 S Ct 2473, 2488 (2014).

[192] *Carpenter*, 138 S Ct at 2219 (majority). Some scholars agree that case law already reflects, if only implicitly, some emphasis on information sensitivity. See, for example, Michael Gentithes, *The End of Miller's Time: How Sensitivity Can Categorize Third Party Data After Carpenter*, 53 Ga L Rev *14–16 (forthcoming 2019), archived at https://perma.cc /6SYG-Q4TQ (referencing cases protecting communicative content, medical records, and hotel rooms). Current law aside, some scholars believe sensitivity should be considered going forward. See, for example, id at 24–25 (proposing new test should evaluate information on "sensitivity continuum" reflecting mosaic approach); Kugler and Strahilevitz, 2015 Supreme Court Review at 212 (cited in note 49) (advocating a *Katz* prong 1 focusing on general expectations of privacy, and a *Katz* prong 2 focusing on the sensitivity of the collected information, both measured in part by survey research).

[193] The quotation from *Riley* about "diminished" interests refers to arrestees rather than third-party records. And the Court's subsequent claim that *Jones* "already show[ed] special solicitude for location information in the third-party context" is equally misplaced, as *Jones* is likewise not a third-party records case. *Carpenter*, 138 S Ct at 2219.

formation completely extinguishes rather than merely diminishes privacy interests, as the dissenters pointed out[194] (and as Roberts, apparently inadvertently, recited elsewhere in his opinion[195]).

True, *Miller* looked at the "nature of the particular documents sought," but context shows it did so to determine whether the documents were shared with the bank, not whether they were especially sensitive.[196] In *Carpenter*, Roberts noted *Miller*'s caution that the "checks were 'not confidential communications but negotiable instruments to be used in commercial transactions.'"[197] But *Miller*'s point was that all of the information shared with the bank was *conveyed to the bank itself*, rather than kept "confidential" from the bank but conveyed to the bank so the bank could pass it along to another recipient (which apparently doesn't count as third-party sharing with the bank).[198]

The Court's claim that *Smith* considered sensitivity also overreads that decision. *Smith* did note the limited capabilities of a pen register,

---

[194] See id at 2226, 2232 (Kennedy, J, dissenting) (interpreting *Miller-Smith* as categorical rule); id at 2262, 2272 (Gorsuch, J, dissenting) (same).

[195] "We have previously held that 'a person has no legitimate expectation of privacy in information he voluntarily turns over to third parties.'" Id at 2216 (majority). That's not a novel characterization for the Chief Justice. See, for example, *Georgia v Randolph*, 547 US 103, 128 (2006) (Roberts, CJ, dissenting) ("If an individual shares information, papers, or places with another, he assumes the risk that the other person will in turn share access to that information or those papers or places with the government"—note no mention of sensitivity at all) (emphasis omitted).

[196] Here is the full quotation:

> [I]in *Katz* the Court also stressed that "[w]hat a person knowingly exposes to the public . . . is not a subject of Fourth Amendment protection." We must examine the nature of the particular documents sought to be protected in order to determine whether there is a legitimate "expectation of privacy" concerning their contents.

Miller, 425 US at 442 (citation omitted).

[197] *Carpenter*, 138 S Ct at 2216, quoting *Miller*, 425 US at 442.

[198] See *Miller*, 425 US at 442 ("All of the documents obtained, including financial statements and deposit slips, contain only information voluntarily conveyed to the banks and exposed to their employees in the ordinary course of business.").

Recall that *Miller* was applying *Katz*, where the caller was *not* held to convey the content of his call to his phone company; rather, the company (like the postmaster for letters) was merely an intermediary tasked with passing the confidential communicative content to Katz's bookie. *Miller* just references, though distinguishes, the general rule that communicative content shared with intermediaries whose function is to pass the content to someone else (phone calls, letters, now e-mails) is not *shared with the intermediaries* in the way that triggers third-party waiver. See, for example, Wayne R. LaFave et al, 2 *Criminal Procedure* § 4.4(c) at 525 (West, 4th ed 2015).

and telephone call logs reveal little in the way of "identifying information."[199] But again the Court's language suggests that its point was to distinguish *Katz* and to show that the information revealed in call logs is information conveyed to the phone company, unlike communicative content for which the company is merely a transmitting intermediary. And the Court then concluded that Smith's privacy interest in the noncontent information was extinguished, not because it was nonsensitive, but because by making calls he "voluntarily conveyed numerical information to the telephone company and 'exposed' that information to its equipment in the ordinary course of business."[200]

Of course, in *Smith* the Court did not state that the third-party doctrine would apply to the caller's substantive message had the phone company created and stored a copy of that message after forwarding it to the caller's intended recipient. And while lower courts' subsequent decisions protecting various forms of communicative content typically invoke the just-described technical distinction between conveying to an intended recipient versus an intermediary,[201] those decisions might well reflect a sense that the Court would bend its brightly articulated line as necessary in order to maintain *Katz*-based protection for highly sensitive information such as personal communications. So perhaps lower courts' sensitivity to sensitivity quietly shaped the outer contours of *Miller-Smith* through the years. But even if so, Chief Justice Roberts in *Carpenter* unabashedly and explicitly injected a sensitivity analysis for the first time into what used to be described as an inquiry focused solely on voluntary exposure. Both the doctrine (at least substantially) and its articulation (quite clearly) have changed. As Justice Gorsuch put the point, we now have "*Katz*-squared."[202]

3. *Miller-Smith revised: but how?* How should courts square *Katz* in the future? The Court in *Carpenter* said there are two separate rationales underlying the third-party doctrine—lack of special sensitivity and voluntary exposure—and that CSLI triggers nei-

---

[199] *Carpenter*, 138 S Ct at 2219 (citation omitted).

[200] *Smith*, 442 US at 744.

[201] See, for example, *United States v Warshak*, 631 F3d 266, 288 (6th Cir 2010) (concluding e-mail content is protected because internet service provider transmitting content is "an *intermediary*, not the intended recipient of the emails").

[202] *Carpenter*, 138 S Ct at 2272 (Gorsuch, J, dissenting).

ther.[203] As with its involuntary arguments, however, the Court does not explain how the two rationales relate as part of the overall doctrine.

The Court might mean that the third-party doctrine applies when *either* of the two rationales is present. In other words, if highly sensitive information was voluntarily conveyed (think Fitbit health data), *or* if nonsensitive information was involuntarily shared (perhaps computer internet protocol addresses?), then the privacy interest dissipates. This reading fits with the Court's decision to address both variables, rather than to end its analysis after finding no voluntary sharing.

Or, the Court might mean that privacy dissipates only if *both* rationales apply, and the information is both voluntarily shared *and* nonsensitive. That seems perfectly logical too, though it seems less likely because it would mean that the third-party doctrine can *never* apply to sensitive information, no matter how clearly it was voluntarily shared (think of Carpenter posting his own location history on Facebook, or celebrities publishing tell-all memoirs).

And then there is a third possibility, raised and criticized by the dissents: an open-ended multifactor test. Justice Gorsuch, for example, lamented a "*second Katz*-like balancing inquiry, asking whether the fact of disclosure . . . outweighs privacy interests in the 'category of information' so disclosed."[204] Justice Kennedy also viewed the Court as announcing a balancing test that encompassed both privacy interests and CSLI tracking properties by "considering intimacy, comprehensiveness, expense, retrospectivity, and voluntariness."[205] Of course, the Court often articulates doctrine through multifactor tests, but Justice Kennedy feared that this one would particularly put "the law on a new and unstable foundation"[206] as lower courts would be left to figure out for themselves how the doctrinal variables relate when they address other surveillance technologies and types of digital data.

---

[203] Id at 2219–20 (majority).

[204] Id at 2267 (Gorsuch, J, dissenting) (emphasis in original).

[205] Id at 2234 (Kennedy, J, dissenting); see id at 2231 (the Court "establish[es] a balancing test" weighing "the privacy interests at stake" against "the fact that the information has been disclosed").

[206] *Carpenter*, 138 S Ct at 2234 (Kennedy, J, dissenting).

As Professor Anthony Amsterdam sagely admonished just before *Miller-Smith* emerged, scholarly critics should tread softly when the Supreme Court first steps onto an intuitively defensible but under-theorized new doctrinal path. Sometimes the Court recognizes that "the application of clear and consistent [existing] theories would produce unacceptable results" and a new direction is appropriate, even though the Court is not prepared to announce the new doctrine with the same level of specificity as the old doctrine, or to explain the extent to which the new doctrine displaces or can be accommodated with the old.[207] I am sympathetic to the Court's enterprise, even while recognizing the many unsatisfying aspects of its explanations. Unlike scholars, however, lower courts may not "take a sabbatical, or otherwise procrastinate till muddy waters clear";[208] they must now decide how to pave this new path while awaiting further blueprints.

D. LOCATION MONITORING EXCEPTIONALISM—OR DISMANTLING THE THIRD-PARTY DOCTRINE?

Privacy advocates hail *Carpenter* as heralding a broad Fourth Amendment reformation for the digital age. By recognizing new privacy interests and softening the third-party doctrine, they predict, hopefully, that the new approach will eventually constrain other intrusive technologies and protect other types of personal records.[209]

The decision itself, however, admits no such thing. Indeed, the Court's opinion suggests the opposite—that perhaps its privacy-protecting analysis covers CSLI and little else. Given "the deeply revealing nature of CSLI, its depth, breadth, and comprehensive reach, and the inescapable and automatic nature of its collection,"[210] Chief Justice Roberts repeatedly claimed that long-term historical location information is "unique," "qualitatively different," a "world of difference" from *Miller* and *Smith*, and an "entirely different species"

---

[207] Amsterdam, 58 Minn L Rev at 351, 352 (cited in note 12).

[208] Id at 352.

[209] See, for example, Sharon Bradford Franklin, *Carpenter and the End of Bulk Surveillance of Americans* (LawFare, July 25, 2018), archived at https://perma.cc/X6F6-75MP; Louise Matsakis, *The Supreme Court Just Greatly Strengthened Digital Privacy* (Wired, June 22, 2008), archived at https://perma.cc/UV9S-PK5X; Paul Ohm, *The Broad Reach of Carpenter v. United States* (Just Security, June 27, 2018), archived at https://perma.cc/8LJQ-BN6B.

[210] *Carpenter*, 138 S Ct at 2223.

of business record.[211] A search warrant will be required, he maintained, only in a "rare case."[212] As Roberts summarized the Court's
holding:

> Our decision today is a narrow one. We do not express a view on matters
> not before us: real-time CSLI or "tower dumps" (a download of infor-
> mation on all the devices that connected to a particular cell site during a
> particular interval). We do not disturb the application of *Smith* and *Miller*
> or call into question conventional surveillance techniques and tools, such as
> security cameras. Nor do we address other business records that might
> incidentally reveal location information. Further, our opinion does not
> consider other collection techniques involving foreign affairs or national
> security. As Justice Frankfurter noted when considering new innovations
> in airplanes and radios, the Court must tread carefully in such cases, to
> ensure that we do not "embarrass the future."[213]

In truth, though, the Court's underlying reasoning may not be so
easy to cabin to CSLI; and it is not at all clear that the Justices in the
majority would want to do so. Let's consider how stable and deeply
rooted the Court's proposed or suggested distinctions might be.

1. *Other forms of direct location monitoring.* The Court's reasoning sends this clear message: government's use in domestic criminal
investigations of tracking technologies that reveal a target's relatively
precise historical locations over an extended period of time now
triggers a Fourth Amendment search. This includes CSLI data, GPS
tracking, and future equivalents, whether the technology tracks the
target personally[214] or through her phones,[215] cars,[216] or anything else

---

[211] Id at 2217, 2216, 2219, 2222.

[212] Id at 2222.

[213] Id at 2220 (citation omitted). This caution rests in substantial tension with the Court's
aggressiveness in describing CSLI as approaching GPS-level tracking. See Part II.A.

[214] For example, law enforcement agencies increasingly use various technologies to track
individuals directly, including aerial surveillance drones and body cameras linked with facial
recognition software. Rachel Levinson-Waldman, *Hiding in Plain Sight: A Fourth Amendment
Framework for Analyzing Government Surveillance in Public*, 66 Emory L J 527, 539–44 (2017)
(video cameras and drones); id at 547 (body cameras).

[215] I use my cell phone for driving directions, finding coffee shops and gas stations, and
sometimes (shh, don't tell them) tracking my teen daughters; all of these functions share my
or another phone's GPS coordinates with a third party.

[216] For example, fixed-place license plate readers or intersection cameras can identify and
record car traffic. Levinson-Waldman, 66 Emory L J at 544–47 (cited in note 214) (noting
ICE use of license plate readers). And smart boxes and dashboard infotainment services installed in cars can transmit information about car location and operation to manufacturers
and other third parties. Michael J. D. Vermeer, Dulani Woods, and Brian A. Jackson,
Identifying Law Enforcement Needs for Access to Digital Evidence in Remote Data Centers *22

that frequently accompanies her as she moves;[217] and this conclusion surely governs government-initiated monitoring as well as accessing third-party location records. (As explained earlier, I suspect the Court will maintain at least some durational trigger, excluding short-term monitoring from Fourth Amendment coverage.)[218]

The Court's insistence that it does *not* "call into question conventional surveillance techniques and tools, such as security cameras," raises interesting questions.[219] I assume "conventional" techniques include old-fashioned eyes-on personalized surveillance of the sort Justice Alito compared to GPS tracking in his *Jones* concurrence, potentially involving "a large team of agents, multiple vehicles, and perhaps aerial assistance."[220] At first glance, it would seem that such conventional, personalized surveillance should be subject to the same durational limits as more high-tech location monitoring. After all, around-the-clock personal surveillance reveals at least the same "privacies of life" and is "reasonably unexpected" to the same degree.[221] So

---

(Rand, 2018), archived at https://perma.cc/7ANK-TB3Z (noting that "Carfax, Hertz, and other vehicle-related companies collect vehicle histories, including oil changes, vehicle locations, and potentially even snapshots from an in-car camera that could have evidentiary utility").

[217] For example, Fitbits and other body-worn biometric assessment devices generally track movement and location, among other things. Andrew Guthrie Ferguson, *The "Smart" Fourth Amendment*, 102 Cornell L Rev 547, 558–59 (2017).

[218] See text accompanying note 165. Because the Court assumed (contra the record) that CSLI reveals the user's location pretty much continuously, the Court had no need to consider whether it might have felt differently about a week's worth of records if each day produced significantly fewer data points. If a different tracking technology fixed the target's location just once per hour or once per day, perhaps the Court would recognize that only a longer period of location monitoring would pose a sufficient mosaic-based privacy risk to constitute a Fourth Amendment search.

[219] As noted above, I assume that even "conventional tools" such as security cameras no longer qualify as "conventional surveillance techniques" once their videos or photos are aggregated into a long-term database that is searchable through facial recognition technology so as to constitute a form of historical location tracking. The distinction is less clear for long-term surveillance through an around-the-clock video camera feed targeting suspects' homes. Compare, for example, *United States v Houston*, 813 F3d 282, 287–88 (6th Cir 2016) (holding that 24/7 video monitoring of suspect's home for ten-week period was not a Fourth Amendment search), with *State v Jones*, 903 NW2d 101, 113 (SD 2017) (holding that similar video monitoring for eight-week period was a search); see also *United States v Kubasiak*, 2018 WL 4846761, *6–7 (ED Wis) (holding that *Carpenter's* reasoning does not apply to four-month and 24/7 video camera surveillance of defendant's backyard).

[220] *Jones*, 565 US at 429 (Alito, J, concurring in the judgment).

[221] See Slobogin, 8 Duke J Const'l L & Pub Pol at 27 (cited in note 48) (recognizing that naked-eye "[o]vert surveillance by the police can be just as intrusive as covert tracking or monitoring"). These conclusions apply as well to private surveillance, for example where a private detective is hired to confirm a spouse is cheating or unfit to parent.

if a week-long CSLI request (or shorter, if the Court later shrinks the duration trigger for a search) violates Carpenter's reasonable expectation of privacy, why not also a same-length old-school stakeout and tail, or a same-length use of low-tech tools such as fixed-position security and traffic cameras?

But the Court's refusal to question conventional or low-tech surveillance is no surprise. Calling old-school tailing a search would significantly hamper what heretofore has been universally considered good investigative policing. And there is no sign that the Court intended that, as evidenced by its repeated references to CSLI tracking being "unique." What explains this?

Perhaps this again reflects a regulatory rather than atomistic bent, given how much the Court emphasized CSLI's detailed, comprehensive, infallible, cheap, and retrospective nature. It is hard to see why these features make high-tech surveillance categorically more privacy-revealing from the *target's* atomistic perspective. First, good old-school surveillance might be just as detailed and comprehensive—and potentially more so, because it can reveal not just the target's location but also how she appears, what she's doing, and with whom. Second, while CSLI is nearly infallible, good traditional surveillance might produce records that are not far off, especially if cameras are used and observations are meticulously documented. And, in any event, the Court has previously rejected the normatively dubious proposition that targets can expect privacy due to witnesses' faulty recall.[222] Third, the fact that CSLI tracking is relatively cheap doesn't add to a target's privacy intrusion for a comparably long surveillance. Finally, the fact that CSLI records can effectively turn back time is similarly atomistically irrelevant, as there is no reason to think that the target's activities for some week in the past are categorically more revealing than for some week in the present. Overall, it's hard to see why the target's atomistic privacy expectation in the whole of her public movements for any particular span of time turns on whether the government uses high-tech or low-tech location-monitoring measures.

That said, these features plus more may lead government to *track more people* using CSLI than it would track using only traditional

---

[222] See, for example, *Lopez v United States*, 373 US 427, 439 (1963) (admitting in evidence undercover agent's electronic recording of conversation because defendant has no "constitutional right to rely on possible flaws in the agent's memory" and assumes risk that witness's testimony will be "accurately reproduced in court"); *Smith*, 442 US at 744–45 (explaining that shift from human operator to automated switchboard does not affect privacy analysis).

measures, such that a CSLI tracking regime might be more privacy-intrusive *in the aggregate*, even if not so for individual targets. Though not as hassle-free as some suggest,[223] seeking CLSI from Sprint avoids typical hurdles to setting up a successful stakeout and tail. First and foremost, it is far less costly for the government. Traditional surveillance efforts typically require money, manpower, and equipment; generally, the longer the effort, the higher the cost. Resource constraints limit how much around-the-clock surveillance law enforcement can handle, forcing officials to prioritize and to intensively track only relatively important targets. Comparatively costless access to CSLI records will likely lead government to monitor the movements of many more suspects for less significant crimes. Second, CSLI tracking avoids any risk of community pushback for establishing longer-term eyes-on surveillance operations that might inconvenience or otherwise irritate neighboring residents or workers.[224] Third, CSLI data can *locate* as well as follow a target if her cell phone number is known, whereas traditional surveillance works only if agents already know where the target can be found so they can start the tail. For these reasons, agents might employ high-tech tracking even though they would not otherwise choose to bear the costs of low-tech alternatives—especially where, by hypothesis, they do not yet have probable cause to support their intuitions.[225] Finally, CSLI is more user-friendly in a different way: being able to discover a target's past rather than only her present/future locations enables agents to focus on the time frame that best fits their investigatory goals and to access information that is "otherwise unknowable."[226] Therefore, the Court could reasonably worry that the capacity for high-tech track-

---

[223] Compare *Carpenter*, 138 S Ct at 2218 ("with just the click of a button"), with Vermeer, Woods, and Jackson, *Identifying Law Enforcement Needs* (cited in note 216) (canvassing difficulties law enforcement faces in securing digital data from third-party service providers). It also costs something for officials to decipher the data, with experts mapping towers onto real locations.

[224] See *Jones*, 565 US at 416 (Sotomayor, J, concurring) (explaining that, because GPS monitoring is cheap and "proceeds surreptitiously, it evades the ordinary checks that constrain abusive police practices: 'limited police resources and community hostility'") (citation omitted).

[225] Using surveillance cameras might also cost little at the margin, if the costs of installing and maintaining the cameras are borne by others as with private store security cameras; or if the government uses cameras that it previously mounted on utility poles or over traffic lights, etc.

[226] As noted earlier, see text accompanying notes 157–58, it will likely be comparatively difficult and costly to reconstruct the target's past movements through nosy neighbors' eyewitness testimony.

ing will encourage officials to do it more often and hence acquire far more sensitive location information about people in the aggregate, even if the extent of any given intrusion is the same.

This explanation fits the Court's expressed desire "to place obstacles in the way of a too permeating police surveillance."[227] While the Court focused primarily on CSLI's capacity for individual-target intrusion, at key points the opinion also suggested concern for the overall flow of information to the government. For example, as Chief Justice Roberts noted, "[t]he Government's position fails to contend with the seismic shifts in digital technology that made possible the tracking of not only Carpenter's location but also everyone else's, not for a short period but for years and years."[228] One can almost hear a background whisper of "Big Brother" throughout the analysis, as well as in Justice Sotomayor's earlier warning in *Jones* about government gathering intimate information "more or less at will."[229]

Concerns over frequency do not typically play a role in determining whether an investigatory method constitutes an atomistically intrusive search. But, in the end, I suspect such concerns are driving much of the distinction here between high- and low-tech surveillance methods for those Justices who worry that the former "may 'alter the relationship between citizen and government in a way that is inimical to democratic society.' "[230] If so, this doctrinal line will likely remain stable over time.[231]

2. *Other types of sensitive third-party records.* The Court also purported in *Carpenter* neither to "disturb the application of *Smith* and *Miller*" nor to "address other business records that might incidentally reveal location information," let alone to address records that reveal nonlocation information.[232] The *Smith-Miller* category

---

[227] *Carpenter*, 138 S Ct at 2214 (citation omitted)

[228] Id at 2219.

[229] *Jones*, 565 US at 416 (Sotomayor, J, concurring); id (questioning the "appropriateness of entrusting to the Executive, in the absence of any oversight from a coordinate branch, a tool so amenable to misuse").

[230] Id (citation omitted).

[231] And this might provide a reason to treat "tower dumps," a "download of information on all the devices that connected to a particular cell site during a particular interval," differently from short-term historical or real-time tracking of a single target. *Carpenter*, 138 S Ct at 2220. While the intrusion per individual is the same, the aggregate information grab by the government is vastly greater for tower dumps.

[232] Id. As Carpenter did not move to suppress the information contained in his carriers' records showing the phone numbers he dialed, he presented no direct challenge to *Smith*.

obviously includes sensitive financial and call-record information; the second category includes such things as credit card swipes, ATM withdrawals, and computer wi-fi connections through IP addresses; and the third category includes such things as accountant, utility, medical, and internet-of-things records.[233] The dissenters rightly pressed back by asking why location information is more sensitive and deserving of Fourth Amendment protection than, say, credit card or phone records.[234] After all, many private facts can be inferred from these other types of records as well.

In response, Chief Justice Roberts did not address the comparison between location and phone call, financial, or other information in the abstract. Instead, he purported to distinguish *Miller* and *Smith* by emphasizing the quantity as well as the quality of the CSLI at stake. Rather than information about "a person's movement at a particular time," this case is "about a detailed chronicle of a person's physical presence compiled every day, every moment, over several years" and thus "implicates privacy concerns far beyond those considered in *Smith* and *Miller*."[235]

But that compares a truckload of apples to a handful of oranges. The proper question, one would think, is whether a week of location monitoring works a qualitatively greater privacy intrusion than a week of phone call records or credit card purchases.[236] As to that comparison, the dissenters either were agnostic[237] or thought quite the opposite.[238] Reasonable people clearly can reasonably disagree.[239]

---

[233] While many of these examples reveal information linked to fixed locations (e.g., in-person bank transactions, landline phones, home-based utility or appliance usage, in-person doctor visits), the location sensitivity is typically dwarfed by other privacy concerns.

[234] Id at 2224, 2229, 2232–33 (Kennedy, J, dissenting); id at 2267 (Gorsuch, J, dissenting).

[235] Id at 2220 (majority).

[236] I'm accepting here the Court's focus on number of days as the proper metric, but perhaps one ought to compare X number of location data points with X number of phone calls or X number of purchases, whether they take the same or different time periods to generate.

[237] "Why is someone's location when using a phone so much more sensitive than who he was talking to (*Smith*) or what financial transactions he engaged in (*Miller*)? I do not know. . . ." *Carpenter*, 138 S Ct at 2262 (Gorsuch, J, dissenting).

[238] Because who you call and what you buy can reveal so much about what you do and with whom, "[t]he troves of intimate information the Government can and does obtain using financial records and telephone records dwarfs what can be gathered from cell-site records." Id at 2232 (Kennedy, J, dissenting).

[239] Surveys show people are sensitive about location information as well as many other kinds of surveillance and third-party records, with some ranking their various sensitivities quite differently than do others. See, for example, Christopher Slobogin, *Privacy at Risk: The*

And if Justice Kennedy is correct that the Court intends CSLI's operative properties of "comprehensiveness, expense, [and] retrospectivity" to weigh in the balance, those too are a wash. Whether the government seeks CSLI records or call, banking, or credit card records, it is just requesting similarly stored information from a different record-holder. For each category of information, officials can collect all stored records fairly effortlessly, going far back in time.[240]

In the end, while location information is surely *different* from other kinds of information, whether it is categorically *more sensitive* reflects a multifaceted subjective judgment.[241] And there is still the question of *how* sensitive information must be to trigger Fourth Amendment protection. Is protection limited to mosaic-creating information, meaning the records reveal something (how much is unclear) about someone's familial, political, professional, religious, and sexual associations? Or should protection be triggered for highly sensitive information that offers little mosaic-creating potential, such as records of third-party DNA testing revealing someone's ancestry composition and a genetic proclivity for adult-onset vision loss?[242]

A close friend and brilliant lawyer undoubtedly spoke for many when he summarized the Court's reasoning as follows: historical location monitoring "feels kind of invasive to me, so it must be subject to the 4th Amendment." Put differently, short of defining a search by social survey data (which would raise conceptual and methodological quandaries),[243] the Court's *Katz*-based approach in *Carpenter*, in the

---

New Government Surveillance and the Fourth Amendment 183–85 (Chicago, 2007) (survey results ranking sensitivity over twenty types of transactional records); Kugler and Strahilevitz, 2015 Supreme Court Review at 239 (cited in note 49) ("Contemporary polling on sensitivity produces a hierarchy that many readers will find intuitive . . . [but] some readers may prefer to construct the hierarchy differently than the median citizen does").

[240] The comparison between CSLI and call records is particularly salient, since Sprint keeps these types of information in the exact same records and therefore one is no more comprehensive, cheap, and historical (or infallible, for that matter) than the other.

[241] See Kugler and Strahilevitz, 2015 Supreme Court Review at 237 (cited in note 49) ("Determining what information counts as sensitive requires numerous subjective judgments. Sensitivity depends a great deal on context, on the identity of the recipient of the information, on the preferences of the data privacy subject, the risks posed by present or future disclosure, and the priors of the person evaluating the information.").

[242] Consider *Carpenter*, 138 S Ct at 2262 (Gorsuch, J, dissenting) (musing that, despite the apparent applicability of *Miller-Smith*, the notion that agents can "secure your DNA from 23andMe without a warrant or probable cause . . . strikes most lawyers and judges today—me included—as pretty unlikely").

[243] See, for example, Christopher Slobogin and Joseph E. Schumacher, *Reasonable Expectations of Privacy and Autonomy in Fourth Amendment Cases: An Empirical Look at "Understandings Recognized*

words of Justice Gorsuch, inevitably entails some intuitive judgment based on "I do not know [what] and the Court does not say."[244]

Is the Court serious about hewing to its articulated line and ensuring that exceptions to the *Miller-Smith* doctrine will be "rare"? Only time will tell. But there is no question the line will be tested early and often. In addition to privacy advocates, every criminal defendant whose investigation includes *any* third-party record request, or *any* more than *de minimis* surveillance, will surely press the claim. And lower courts now can listen. While they were previously bound mechanically to apply both the *Knotts* and *Miller-Smith* exposure rules, the amorphous nature of the Court's new doctrinal tests now gives judges license, if not permission, to deviate, to innovate, and even to anticipate technological change.

Perhaps that is precisely what the majority intended. The Court could have buttressed its cautionary prose by resting its conclusion on far narrower grounds, deploying reasoning less likely to invite open-ended interpretation than its mosaic approach coupled with sensitivity considerations.[245] But by embracing a broader if more uncertain approach, the majority can benefit from unleashed lower-court efforts to help map *Carpenter*'s new doctrinal paths. While the doctrine remains unsettled, law enforcement officers will likely err on the side of securing search warrants. And where they cannot or do not get warrants, the officers' reasonable mistakes (viewed in hindsight, if

---

and Permitted by Society," 42 Duke L J 727 (1993) (empirically testing how people rate different searches' intrusiveness); Jeremy A. Blumenthal, Meera Adya, and Jacqueline Mogle, *The Multiple Dimensions of Privacy: Testing Lay "Expectations of Privacy,"* 11 U Pa J Const L 331 (2009) (updating and modifying survey methodology and analysis).

[244] *Carpenter*, 138 S Ct at 2262 (Gorsuch, J, dissenting).

[245] The Court could have distinguished *Knotts* by embracing a private space–protective prophylactic rule based on *United States v Karo*, 468 US 705 (1984), see note 164; or distinguished *Miller-Smith* just by its micro-involuntary argument (automated connectivity rather than volitionally triggered sharing) and stopped there, see text accompanying note 192.

Or here is a third narrow path: the Court could have held that Carpenter did not actually share (voluntarily or otherwise) the information extracted from Sprint's records because he didn't know the specific towers/sectors his phone signaled when in use. To be sure, sometimes we are deemed (under current doctrine) to share information that we don't *actively* know in the sense of being consciously aware of it in the moment; for example, when we swipe a credit card at a gas station and we functionally transmit the store's address to American Express even though we don't really know that address, or we hit "call back" or "Mom's office" on our smartphones and functionally transmit the corresponding call numbers even though we don't currently remember them. See *In re United States for Historical Cell Site Data*, 724 F3d 600, 613 (5th Cir 2013). But in those and similar contexts, we know we can easily find out the content of the data we are transmitting. Here, by contrast, Carpenter *could not* realistically have known or learned the specific towers/sectors his phone signaled when in use because of the way cell service works. See note 26 and accompanying text.

and when *Carpenter*'s coverage expands) will be excused under the good-faith exception to the exclusionary rule. From the Court's perspective, what's not to like?[246]

III. GET A WARRANT

After all that, had the Court concluded that the warrantless search of Sprint's CSLI records was not "unreasonable" under the Fourth Amendment, perhaps its uncertain narrowing of *Katz*'s carve-outs for public or third-party exposure would be much ado about nothing. The Court could have found the search justified because the government satisfied the mid-level "reasonable suspicion" standard, or the lower-level standard for compulsory document production, or even the SCA's own requirement of "specific and articulable facts showing reasonable grounds to believe" that the records were "relevant and material to an ongoing criminal investigation."[247] But the Court confidently announced that "the Government's obligation" to justify this search "is a familiar one—get a warrant."[248] Although this conclusion might be familiar, in this context it is far from axiomatic.

Indeed, the Court might profitably have refrained from addressing this issue at all, instead remanding for further lower-court consideration. Although a Fourth Amendment search typically triggers a warrant requirement, it does not always do so; and critics of the third-party doctrine have taken different positions on the issue.[249] Lower courts through the years have paid much less attention to the justification than to the search question.[250] And, in particular, few courts

---

[246] And of course, while courts debate and refine the new mosaic approach and narrowed third-party doctrine, other actors may explore their own interventions. Congress, state legislatures, and state courts may create positive law protections for privacy interests in third-party records that would overlay any Fourth Amendment protection (or, under the alternative property-based approach Justice Gorsuch tentatively advanced, that would themselves create new property interests deserving Fourth Amendment protection, see text accompanying notes 109–12). And perhaps service providers seeking to assuage old customers and woo new ones will consider storing far fewer name-identified records for far fewer days, limiting the information a search would reveal.

[247] See discussion in Parts III.B and III.C.

[248] *Carpenter*, 138 S Ct at 2221. The Court acknowledged that case-specific exceptions may support warrantless searches in conventionally recognized exigent circumstances, such as "pursu[ing] a fleeing suspect, protect[ing] individuals who are threatened with imminent harm, or prevent[ing] the imminent destruction of evidence." Id at 2222–23.

[249] See note 276 and accompanying text.

[250] For most courts (including the Sixth Circuit here) the second question became moot after finding there was no Fourth Amendment search to justify.

have meaningfully considered the dissents' primary argument (discussed below) that the traditional standard governing subpoenas *duces decum* should apply.[251] Despite professing caution when deciding the search question, the Court appeared decidedly uninterested in what lower courts, or even Congress, might have to say about Fourth Amendment reasonableness after they consider the Court's new view of the privacy interests at stake.[252]

Although the warrant requirement typically follows a newly defined search, the connection here is worth a closer look for two reasons. First, for Justices who care (and surely some do), the trade-off between privacy protection and law enforcement interests may undergird the desire to keep "[o]ur decision today . . . a narrow one." Requiring probable cause for long-term CSLI tracking will, unsurprisingly, hinder and sometimes thwart investigations into various crimes. Applying the same requirement to single-data-point or very short-term tracking (historical or prospective) will expand and amplify the burden while protecting, by definition, thinner mosaic-based privacy interests. And applying the same requirement to a much broader swath of third-party records will magnify those costs considerably, as law enforcement is far more dependent on early-investigation access to certain other records for certain types of crimes. Obviously, the privacy/enforcement trade-off has no formal place within the Court's search analysis. But as a matter of simple prediction, I suspect the Court will be reluctant to extend *Carpenter*'s new search definition to encompass short-term location tracking or financial, phone, and other forms of communications metadata if the warrant requirement would inevitably apply.

Second, Chief Justice Roberts's response to the dissents' pressure to apply the much more relaxed reasonableness standard traditionally governing subpoena-compelled production of documents may have implications well beyond this case. While articulating a new sensi-

---

[251] None of the five Court of Appeals decisions did so. See note 30.

[252] Lower courts might have looked to experience from the nine states that by statute or constitutional provision currently require warrants to obtain CSLI. See *Carpenter* Petr's Brief at *22 & n 11 (cited in note 113).

And prompted by the Court's holding that a search occurred, perhaps Congress would have amended the Stored Communications Act to require a showing greater than investigatory relevance but still short of probable cause, a decision potentially deserving deference down the road. See *United States v Di Re*, 332 US 581, 585 (1948) (noting Court has "be[en] reluctant to decide that a search thus authorized by Congress was unreasonable"); *Jones*, 565 US at 429–30 (Alito, J, concurring in the judgment) (suggesting preference for legislative resolution).

tivity constraint on third-party subpoenas to protect Carpenter's CSLI, the Court (perhaps inadvertently) raised questions as to whether and how that same constraint may apply to a broad array of first-party subpoenas as well.

A. THE WARRANT REQUIREMENT AND EARLY-STAGE CRIMINAL INVESTIGATIONS

Police use CSLI tracking because it works; and not just to solve store thefts.[253] "Historical cell tower location records are routinely used to investigate the full gamut of state and federal crimes, including child abductions, bombings, kidnappings, murders, robberies, sex offenses, and terrorism-related offenses."[254] For example, historical CSLI was recently used to identify the person alleged to have mailed pipe bombs to various Democratic officials and supporters and CNN.[255]

Surely, at times police have used SCA court orders to secure historical CSLI even where they had sufficient probable cause to secure a warrant.[256] But CSLI is generally requested during the early stages of criminal investigations, when police lack probable cause with respect to any given suspect.[257] Many lower courts have described the government's use of location data in solving serious crimes where the stories make clear the data were very helpful long before officials could establish probable cause.[258] Early access to location information is particularly useful to determine who among several potential

---

[253] Those who have characterized Carpenter's spree of cell phone robberies as relatively mundane might be forgetting or at least underappreciating the gang's frequent use of a gun.

[254] *United States v Davis*, 785 F3d 498, 518 (11th Cir 2015) (en banc) (citing cases).

[255] After federal agents identified a possible suspect, they used his historical CSLI records to confirm he had signaled a cell tower in the vicinity of the post office used to mail some of the packages (and then they apparently used real-time cell-tower tracking to locate and arrest him). Kara Scannell, Evan Perez, and Shimon Prokupecz, *How the Alleged Bomber Was Caught* (CNN, Oct 27, 2018), archived at https://perma.cc/6Y56-GHWL.

[256] Some commentators assert that was true for *Carpenter*. See Lior Strahilevitz and Matthew Tokson, *Quick Reactions to Today's Carpenter Oral Argument—Post 2* (Concurring Opinions, Nov 29, 2017), archived at https://perma.cc/A85G-M7K3 ("There probably was probable cause in *Smith v. Maryland*, and in *Carpenter*, for that matter."). I'm dubious as to the latter, especially given the breadth of the records request.

[257] *Davis*, 785 F3d at 518; see also id ("In such cases, [SCA] § 2703(d) orders—like other forms of compulsory process not subject to the search warrant procedure—help to build probable cause against the guilty, deflect suspicion from the innocent, aid in the search for truth, and judiciously allocate scarce investigative resources.").

[258] See, for example, *United States v Pembrook*, 876 F3d 812, 816–19 (6th Cir 2017) (using CSLI initially to identify common phones near two jewelry heists that were over 150 miles

suspects deserves further scrutiny,[259] to exclude potential suspects where a wrong accusation might stymie the investigation or cause other harms,[260] and to identify members and significant places (e.g., for meetings, hideouts, and stashes) for criminal groups such as gangs, mobs, and other conspiracies.[261]

Some privacy advocates assert that a warrant requirement will have little impact on criminal investigations, claiming that officials can almost always establish probable cause if they just work a little harder.[262] That strikes me as quite optimistic, as more sober privacy experts concede.[263] More likely, sometimes additional sleuthing will produce probable cause to support a warrant for CSLI records; and sometimes it will not, leaving the records unobtainable.[264]

---

apart and finding a recently activated prepaid "burner" phone with no associated name; call detail records then identified the perpetrators).

[259] See, for example, *United States v Reynolds*, 626 Fed Appx 610, 612 (6th Cir 2015) (identifying one among several plausible suspects because only he was in the vicinity of the house where and when a computer downloaded child pornography).

[260] For example, quietly ruling out a father or boyfriend as a child kidnapping suspect because CSLI shows he was not near the abduction scene, where a false accusation or even just further investigation might both preclude his good-faith assistance and create a long-term family rift. See *Davis*, 785 F3d at 518 (noting that CSLI can reveal that "an individual suspect was . . . far away in another city or state").

[261] See Jim Baker, recorded in *The Lawfare Podcast: Jim Baker and Orin Kerr on the Carpenter Ruling* (Lawfare, June 30, 2018), archived at https://perma.cc/8P4G-RH2U.

[262] Aziz Huq, *The Latest Supreme Court Decision Is Being Hailed as a Big Victory for Digital Privacy. It's Not* (Vox, June 23, 2018), archived at https://perma.cc/R895-XL9N (explaining that CSLI data are "routinely relevant to conspiracy charges" and asserting that in such cases "it will often be very easy for the police to meet the (exceedingly weak) probable cause standard"); see also *Davis*, 785 F3d at 543 (Martin dissenting) ("But if my view of the Fourth Amendment were to prevail, all the officers in this case had to do was get a warrant for this search. That is no great burden.").

[263] As Jane Bambauer advises, "[m]ost [privacy] scholars know that recognizing access to third-party records as a full-fledged search requiring a warrant and probable cause is an unworkable solution. Police need some way to build up suspicion about a suspect, and keeping every last third-party record off limits until the case progresses to probable cause would unacceptably frustrate investigations." Bambauer, 94 Tex L Rev at 215 (cited in note 170); id at 216–17 ("If courts open the definition of 'search' to cover more things, they must have the latitude to work exclusively within the Reasonableness Clause of the Fourth Amendment and to avoid the Warrant Clause.").

[264] Two potential unintended consequences are worth noting. First, where agents do the extra work and manage to develop probable cause to support a CSLI records request, might the agents then consider broadening the scope of their intended search? Armed with probable cause, why not also seek even more precise GPS data created by location or driving-directions apps? Or also seek the content of text messages or e-mails sent or received within a few days of the crime? Once agents have probable cause to believe location records would reveal evidence of criminality, they likely also have probable cause to believe GPS data and text and e-mail content would do so as well.

Second, many conventional sleuthing efforts are prone to error and stereotyping, and they tend to disproportionately focus on poor and minorities communities—tendencies

Expanding Carpenter's search definition to include single-data-point or very short-term CSLI monitoring would not only protect records less susceptible to privacy-threatening mosaic creation,[265] but also make it harder for police to use CSLI precisely when it offers the most unique investigative benefits, such as checking to see whether a phone was near a single relevant place at a single relevant time.[266] In other words, the privacy/law enforcement trade-off is quite sensitive to monitoring duration.

That said, it is worth noting that although both long- and short-term CSLI records requests are useful for investigating many *different* types of crime, they are not crucial for investigating any *particular* type of crime. So the inevitable costs to law enforcement will likely be distributed across many different kinds of criminal investigations. And, of course, access to location records for use in criminal investigations is relatively new.

By contrast, the impediment to effective and efficient investigations would likely both be more widespread and have a greater impact on particular crimes if the Supreme Court or lower courts broaden *Carpenter*'s "narrow" ruling to hold that securing other types of third-party records likewise requires a warrant. Many other types of third-party records (especially financial, credit card purchases, internet protocol addresses, and phone/text noncontent metadata) are routinely relied upon in early-stage investigations.[267] And certain types of crimes would largely defy successful prosecution without early access to such third-party records. Obvious examples include white-collar financial crimes, identity theft, "[m]alicious hacking, possession of child pornography, laundering money through gambling websites, and insider trading," which among other crimes "leave very few clues in the physical world."[268] And proactive efforts to identify and thwart

---

that digital records generally avoid. See Bambauer, 94 Tex L Rev at 244–48 (cited in note 170); see also Andrew Guthrie Ferguson, *Big Data and Predictive Reasonable Suspicion*, 163 U Penn L Rev 327, 391 (2015) ("The accuracy that big data provides not only increases the likelihood that police target the right suspects, but also, in turn, prevents the resulting physical, face-to-face interactions [of conventional policing] that generate tension.").

[265] See note 161 and accompanying text.

[266] See notes 259–60 and accompanying text.

[267] See *Carpenter*, 138 S Ct at 2229 (Kennedy, J, dissenting) (referencing crimes ranging from drug trafficking to health-care fraud to tax evasion).

[268] Bambauer, 94 Tex L Rev at 249 (cited in note 170); id ("Some crimes offer little hope of detection without the aid of third-party data."); Christopher Slobogin, *Transaction Surveillance by the Government*, 75 Miss L J 139, 185–86 (2005) (explaining that "requiring a uniform

potential acts of terrorism require lots of background location and movement data from which computer algorithms can predict conventional behavior in order to discern unconventional and perhaps threatening aberrations.[269]

The ultimate impediments to law enforcement efforts posed by requiring a warrant to access CSLI and other third-party records cannot easily be quantified, though surely they are real. The Court has previously voiced concern over these impediments when protecting grand juries' long-standing authority to compel access to documentary evidence in order to determine whether there is probable cause to believe a crime was committed; requiring a warrant up front "would stop much if not all investigation in the public interest at the threshold of inquiry."[270] Justice Alito echoed this concern in *Carpenter*, warning that requiring search warrants for document production requests "will seriously damage, if not destroy, their utility."[271]

Perhaps that alarm is a bit dramatic. But whatever impact *Carpenter*'s warrant requirement will have on criminal investigations where early-stage CSLI data could be useful, the impact of further extending *Carpenter*'s search analysis to protect short-term CSLI and especially other third-party records—assuming the warrant requirement comes along for the ride—will be broader and sharper. That recognition at least invites a closer look at the warrant requirement's plausible alternatives, if only for future consideration.

B. WHY NOT IMPOSE A MID-LEVEL REASONABLENESS STANDARD?

The Fourth Amendment prohibits unreasonable searches, not warrantless ones. The United States argued that the SCA's "reasonable grounds to believe . . . relevant" standard, perhaps somewhat

---

standard of probable cause for all [third-party] records searches . . . provides far too much protection for some types of information" because certain kinds of investigations "would probably never get off the ground"); Wayne R. LaFave, 2 *Search and Seizure: A Treatise on the Fourth Amendment* § 4.13 at 1081 (West, 5th ed 2012) (noting IRS subpoena power "is critical to determining tax liability properly").

[269] See Baker, *Jim Baker and Orin Kerr on the Carpenter Ruling* (cited in note 261).

[270] *Oklahoma Press Pub. Co. v Walling*, 327 US 186, 213 (1946); see also, for example, *United States v R. Enterprises, Inc.*, 498 US 292, 297 (1991) ("[T]he government cannot be required to justify the issuance of a grand jury subpoena by presenting evidence sufficient to establish probable cause because the very purpose of requesting the information is to ascertain whether probable cause exists.").

[271] *Carpenter*, 138 S Ct at 2256 (Alito, J, dissenting); see id at 2257 (Alito, J, dissenting) ("Today a skeptical majority decides to put that understanding to the test.").

less stringent than the more commonplace "reasonable suspicion" standard, is a more appropriate measure of constitutional reasonableness for CSLI searches than is probable cause.[272] The Court has previously signaled that a subprobable-cause standard suffices in exceptional circumstances involving "special law enforcement needs, diminished expectations of privacy, minimal intrusions, or the like."[273] The United States claimed that cell phone users' privacy interests are at least somewhat diminished, the document request to a third party visits only "minimal intrusions" upon the target, and law enforcement's heavy reliance on early-stage access to records before it can establish probable cause presents a special need. And over the past few decades, the Supreme Court has been increasingly receptive to nonwarrant reasonableness determinations.[274]

But the *Carpenter* Court wasted no words—literally zero—rejecting this argument. Presumably the Court, having described CSLI tracking as uniquely invasive and involuntary, simply rejected the premise of "diminished" expectations and "minimal" intrusions.[275]

---

[272] *Carpenter* US Brief at *50–55 (cited in note 126).

[273] *Maryland v King*, 569 US 435, 447 (2013), citing *Illinois v McArthur*, 531 US 326, 330 (2001); see *Riley v California*, 134 S Ct 2473, 2484 (2014) ("Absent more precise guidance from the founding era, we generally determine whether to exempt a given type of search from the warrant requirement 'by assessing, on the one hand, the degree to which it intrudes upon an individual's privacy and, on the other, the degree to which it is needed for the promotion of legitimate governmental interests.'"), citing *Wyoming v Houghton*, 526 US 295, 300 (1999); *United States v Martinez-Fuerte*, 428 US 543, 561 (1976) ("[T]he Fourth Amendment imposes no irreducible requirement of such suspicion.") (citation omitted).

[274] See, for example, Tinsley E. Yarbrough, *The Rehnquist Court and the Constitution* 222–27 (Oxford, 2000) (canvassing Rehnquist Court decisions upholding warrantless searches in various contexts).

[275] Perhaps the Court found the warrant requirement additionally attractive for ensuring that the decision to invade privacy is made by a judge. But if the Court required only reasonable suspicion or some other intermediate standard to CSLI requests, agents would still need to seek a court order to comply with the SCA.

For other third-party records requests, the traditional subpoena process might frequently lead to judicial preclearance. Many statutes (including the SCA) either require or permit under many circumstances third parties served with a subpoena seeking customer information to notify the customer. See Ellen S. Podgor et al, *White Collar Crime* § 17.5 at 576 (West, 2d ed 2018). When a customer receives notice, she can move in court to quash the subpoena—formerly on grounds of overbreadth, harassment, and the like; but after *Carpenter* presumably to protect her own reasonable expectation of privacy. Id § 16.9 (D) at 514–15; id § 16.12(G) at 563.

And where the first-party target does not receive such notice, the third-party record-holder can move to quash the subpoena itself, perhaps increasingly motivated by marketplace pressures to protect consumer confidentiality. Conventional Fourth Amendment standing rules appear to preclude the company from raising the target's claim as well as its own. *Rakas v Illinois*, 439 US 128, 133–34 (1978). Perhaps in this atypical context, how-

That was predictable here. But if the search holding ultimately extends to other types of third-party records, then the same question will arise there. After emphatically requiring a warrant here, the Court may feel compelled to apply the same rule for all other third-party record searches, even though there might be a more persuasive argument for diminished expectations (due to some measure of voluntariness) and minimal intrusions (due to lesser sensitivity) in other contexts. And many privacy scholars critical of *Miller-Smith*'s reach have advocated reasonable suspicion or some other intermediary or graduated standard rather than across-the-board probable cause as properly balancing the competing privacy and law enforcement interests.[276] The Court could have been more cautious, reserving some flexibility for itself and lower courts facing challenges to other record requests, by conceding room for nuance. But the Court's self-described caution in keeping its search holding narrow found no visible expression here.

Of course, there is another plausible explanation. As described above, a broadly applied warrant requirement for third-party record requests likely would significantly hamper many criminal investigations, especially for particular crimes such as child pornography, tax fraud, financial crimes, internet hacking, and the like. Perhaps the Supreme Court wants the apparent remedial consequences to discourage lower courts (and its future self) from expanding its Fourth Amendment search finding beyond what it portrays as continuous, precise, and long-term location monitoring. Put differently, if it might be difficult to find principled ways to cabin the Court's

---

ever, Sprint should have third-party standing to champion the rights of a customer who receives no advance notice of the search, and indeed will never learn about it unless she is ultimately prosecuted based on its fruits. But see *Microsoft Corp. v United States Dep't of Justice*, 233 F Supp 3d 887, 912 (WD Wash 2017) (denying service provider third-party standing to represent non-noticed customers' Fourth Amendment interests).

[276] See, for example, Slobogin, 75 Miss L J at 169 (cited in note 268) (matching different types of records with either a probable cause, reasonable suspicion, or relevance requirement); Stephen E. Henderson, *Beyond the (Current) Fourth Amendment: Protecting Third-Party Information, Third Parties, and the Rest of Us Too*, 34 Pepperdine L Rev 975, 1025 (2007) (after canvassing nine relevant factors, advocating "flexible reasonableness criterion that considers the totality of the circumstances"). See also Bambauer, 94 Tex L Rev at 242 (cited in note 170) (expressing discomfort that an across-the-board warrant requirement for third-party records would mean "a policeman might be able to holler at a person, forcibly spin him around, press him to the hood of a car, and publicly feel up his entire body more easily than he could get access to his Amazon records"; and advocating "[m]ore modest reforms" than an across-the-board warrant requirement to avoid "adding a new set of paradoxes.").

reasoning to "rare" cases like this, perhaps these real-world implications stemming from a warrant requirement will encourage courts
to try harder.[277] This hypothesized disincentive might not be pretty,
but it could be potent.

C. WHY NOT IMPOSE THE LOW-LEVEL REASONABLENESS STANDARD FOR DOCUMENT SUBPOENAS?

The United States also argued, and this time three dissenting
Justices (most vociferously Justice Alito) agreed, that to be constitutionally reasonable a CSLI records request need satisfy only the
much-less-than-probable-cause standard applicable to a conventional subpoena *duces tecum*.[278] For both CSLI and other compulsory
records requests, officials demand that the request recipient produce
the specified documents, rather than themselves enter the recipient's
space and rummage around until they find and take the documents.

Justice Alito, after spending many pages arguing that "the Fourth
Amendment, as originally understood, did not apply to the compulsory production of documents at all,"[279] conceded that in the late
nineteenth century the Court began to view compulsory process as a
type of "figurative" or "constructive" Fourth Amendment search.[280]
But the Court has long applied a different and lower standard of
reasonableness to constructive rather than full-blown rummage
searches: while the latter generally require a probable cause–backed

---

[277] See Akhil Reed Amar, *Fourth Amendment First Principles*, 107 Harv L Rev 757, 769
(1994) ("Because it creates an unreasonable mandate for all searches, the warrant requirement
leads judges to artificially constrain the scope of the Amendment itself by narrowly defining
'search' and 'seizure.'").

[278] *Carpenter* US Brief at *44–50 (cited at note 126); *Carpenter*, 138 S Ct at 2228–29
(Kennedy, J, dissenting); id at 2247–57 (Alito, J, dissenting).

[279] *Carpenter*, 138 S Ct at 2250 (Alito, J, dissenting). According to Alito, a request to
produce is neither a textual "search" nor "seizure." Id at 2251 (Alito, J, dissenting). And the
Founders opposed the Crown's practice of general warrants because "[p]rivate area after
private area becomes exposed to the officers' eyes as they rummage through the owner's
property in their hunt for the object or objects of the search." Id (Alito, J, dissenting). A
request to produce raises no such privacy concerns, beyond revealing the secured object's
contents. And no historical evidence supports the Fourth Amendment's application to
compulsory process. Id at 2252 (Alito, J, dissenting). Justice Gorsuch appears more equivocal
on this latter point, noting there may be no good historical evidence either way in the form of
common law decisions. Id at 2271 (Gorsuch, J, dissenting).

[280] *Carpenter*, 138 S Ct at 2254 (Alito, J, dissenting); see generally id at 2252–54 (tracing
history).

search warrant, the former require only that a subpoena or similar court order demanding documents "'be sufficiently limited in scope, relevant in purpose, and specific in directive so that compliance will not be unreasonably burdensome.'"[281] This lower standard, which I will refer to as the "burdensome" test, reflects a "'basic compromise' between the 'public interest' in every man's evidence and the private interest 'of men to be free from officious meddling.'"[282]

This compromise is essential, Justice Alito maintained, to law enforcement's ability to investigate crime. As noted previously, various forms of compulsory process (including grand jury, legislative, administrative subpoenas and similar law enforcement document demands) are used regularly "to determine '*whether* there is probable cause to believe a crime has been committed,'" which by definition means that they are not supported by probable cause.[283] After citing numerous cases in which the Court across many decades has applied the lower burdensome standard to document subpoenas issued to third parties for their business records,[284] Justice Alito concluded that the same standard should govern here—especially because he thought it quite odd for Carpenter to enjoy greater Fourth Amendment protection than Sprint does in Sprint's own records.[285]

Not so odd at all, rejoined the Court. Almost all of Justice Alito's cited examples either "contemplated requests for evidence implicat-

---

[281] Id at 2255 (Alito, J, dissenting), quoting *Donovan v Lone Steer, Inc.*, 464 US 408, 415 (1984); see also *Oklahoma Press*, 327 US at 209 (holding that subpoena satisfies Fourth Amendment reasonableness if "the investigation is authorized by Congress, is for a purpose Congress can order, and the documents sought are relevant to the inquiry," and the "specification of the documents to be produced [is] adequate, but not excessive, for the purposes of the relevant inquiry"). The lower standard also reflects the fact that the subpoena recipient has an "opportunity to present objections" to a judicial officer before producing the records, which further minimizes the intrusion. Id at 195.

[282] *Carpenter*, 138 S Ct at 2254 (Alito, J, dissenting), quoting *Oklahoma Press*, 327 US at 213. Mild differences in the constitutional standards applied to different subpoena sources, see Podgor, *White Collar Crime* § 17.4(A) at 570 (cited in note 275), are not important for present purposes, and none of the opinions in *Carpenter* distinguished among them. See, for example, *Carpenter*, 138 S Ct at 2234 (Kennedy, J, dissenting) (referencing decision's impact on "the subpoena practices of federal and state grand juries, legislatures, and other investigative bodies" as well as the "court-approved compulsory process in this case").

[283] *Carpenter*, 138 S Ct at 2256 (Alito, J, dissenting).

[284] Id at 2254 (Alito, J, dissenting).

[285] Id at 2256 (Alito, J, dissenting) (citation omitted). Justice Alito's assertion that the Stored Communications Act order for Sprint's records regarding Carpenter satisfied that standard is hard to contest, given the Act's required showing of relevance is more stringent, and Sprint could produce the records without much effort. Id at 2255 (Alito, J, dissenting).

ing diminished privacy interests" because the sought-after information had been publicly exposed, or requests for "a corporation's own books" containing information such as "corporate tax or payroll ledgers."[286] The lone exception is *Miller*, where the Court had already determined that Miller lacked a cognizable privacy interest in the bank records.[287] This observation's relevance, presumably, is that the Court had sometimes justified applying the lower burdensome standard to traditional corporate records on the ground that legislatures have a special interest in regulating the corporations whose formation they authorized, and such regulations could realistically be enforced only through self-revelation of internal corporate operations—basically, creating a form of reduced expectations of privacy in core corporate activities.[288]

Once again Chief Justice Roberts was a bit aggressive in characterizing precedent. Even assuming that corporations have diminished privacy interests in their own tax, payroll, and similar business records, at least two of the cited decisions addressed types of records that seem far afield and are awash with sensitivity concerns.[289] Moreover,

---

[286] Id at 2221–22 (majority).

[287] *Carpenter*, 138 S Ct at 2221–22.

[288] See, for example, *Oklahoma Press*, 327 US at 204–5 (explaining that private corporations are historically subject to "broad visitorial power" and "Congress may exercise wide investigative power over them, analogous to the visitorial power of the incorporating state"); *United States v Morton Salt*, 338 US 632, 652 (1950) ("corporations can claim no equality with individuals in the enjoyment of privacy"); LaFave, 2 *Search and Seizure* § 4.13(e) at 1085 (cited in note 268).

[289] Wayne R. LaFave et al, 3 *Criminal Procedure* § 8.7(a) at 34 n 38.550 (West, 4th ed, 2018–19 Pocket Part) ("LaFave 2018–19 Pocket Part § 8.7(a)") ("However, not all of the cases cited involved corporate records, not all involved business records, and not all involved business regulations."). The Court described *United States v Powell*, 379 US 48 (1964), as regarding "corporate tax records," *Carpenter*, 138 S Ct at 2221 n 5, without acknowledging that the demanded tax documents may include records pertaining to "a variety of non-business activities (e.g., charitable contributions and medical expenses)." LaFave 2018–19 Pocket Part § 8.7(a) at 23 (cited earlier in this note). And the Court describes *McPhaul v United States*, 364 US 372 (1960), as regarding "books and records of an organization," *Carpenter*, 138 S Ct at 2221 n 5, without letting on that the House Un-American Activities Committee was seeking "all records, correspondence and memoranda" pertaining to the Civil Rights Congress's structure, affiliation with other organizations, and all monies received or expended by it to determine whether the Civil Rights Congress was "being used for subversive purposes" and "affiliated with known Communist organizations." *McPhaul*, 364 US at 381.

Importantly, even *Miller* does not clearly state that the customer, had he retained a reasonable expectation of privacy in his banks' records, would have been entitled to insist on a warrant. The court of appeals had held that Miller possessed a sufficient Fourth Amendment interest to challenge the subpoenas that produced those records, but the subpoenas were defective (because they were issued by the wrong entity and for a date when the grand jury was not in session), and

Roberts ignored an entire body of lower-court cases applying the burdensome standard to subpoenas seeking sensitive information equally far afield from traditional corporate records.[290] So claiming that "this Court has never held that the Government may subpoena third parties for records in which the suspect has a reasonable expectation of privacy"[291] means less than at first appears.[292]

The Court's stronger response is that the burdensome standard is simply too weak to adequately protect the privacy interests at stake. The "critical issue . . . [is] that CSLI is an entirely different species of business record—something that implicates basic Fourth Amendment concerns about arbitrary government power much more di-

---

therefore Miller was not afforded "sufficient 'legal process.'" *United States v Miller*, 500 F2d 751, 758 (5th Cir 1974) (citation omitted). The Supreme Court reversed after finding Miller lacked Fourth Amendment standing to challenge the subpoenas. But the Court did not clearly indicate that if Miller retained a privacy interest affording him standing he could insist on a search warrant rather than just properly issued subpoenas. See *Miller*, 425 US at 445 (holding that Miller's motion to suppress was correctly denied "since he possessed no Fourth Amendment interest that could be vindicated by a challenge to the subpoenas"); id at 451 (Brennan, J, dissenting) (decrying government access to bank records "'without any judicial control as to relevancy or other traditional requirements of legal process'") (citation omitted); compare id at 456 (Marshall, J, dissenting) (asserting that statute mandating that banks maintain customers' records triggers "warrant and probable cause" requirement, and customers have standing to complain). The Court also ignored another line of cases discussing other potential constitutional limits on the subpoena power, in which the targets did not even raise Fourth Amendment concerns notwithstanding the obviously sensitive nature of the requested documents. The *Carpenter* Court's claim that it had never previously upheld a third-party subpoena for records in which first parties retained a privacy interest is at least "inconsistent" with these other cases. LaFave 2018–19 Pocket Part § 8.7(a) at 23–25 (cited earlier in this note). See, for example, *Branzburg v Hayes*, 408 US 665 (1972) (rejecting First Amendment challenge to subpoenas issued to newspaper reporters for interview notes); see also *Fisher v United States*, 425 US 391, 401 n 7 (1976) (rejecting Fifth Amendment challenge to business records; flagging "[s]pecial problems of privacy which might be presented by subpoena of a personal diary," but only because of an overbreadth concern for rummaging rather than a privacy concern for the requested information), citing *United States v Bennett*, 409 F2d 888, 897 (2d Cir 1969).

[290] Podgor, *White Collar Crime* § 16.10(D) at 534–35 (cited in note 275) ("A long line of lower court rulings have upheld grand jury subpoenas demanding from individuals personal records and correspondence, including emails stored on a computer."); LaFave 2018–19 Pocket Part § 8.7(a) at 25 (cited in note 289) (noting that Court's rule would also "require rejection of a body of federal lower court precedent also not discussed in the *Carpenter* opinions"); id at 35–36 nn 38.780–38.820 (citing and discussing cases).

[291] *Carpenter*, 138 S Ct at 2221.

[292] See also id at 2228–29 (Kennedy, J, dissenting) ("[I]t is well established that subpoenas may be used to obtain a wide variety of records held by businesses, even when the records contain private information.").

rectly than corporate tax or payroll ledgers."[293] Moreover, Justice Alito's position would prove too much, Roberts continued, because then the warrant requirement would *never* protect any type of self-producible record no matter the privacy interest retained in it. Rather, "private letters, digital contents of a cell phone—any personal information reduced to document form, in fact—may be collected by subpoena" so long as the request isn't too burdensome.[294] Surely that's not right; and the Court noted that even Justice Kennedy "declines to adopt the radical implications of this theory, leaving open the question whether the warrant requirement applies when the Government obtains the modern-day equivalents of an individual's own 'papers' or 'effects,' even when those papers or effects are held by a third party."[295] Such an exception would sensibly "prevent the subpoena doctrine from overcoming any reasonable expectation of privacy."[296]

Thus, the Court reached its purportedly humble conclusion: just as these individual papers and effects receive full Fourth Amendment protection, "[w]e simply think that such protection should extend as well to a detailed log of a person's movements over several years."[297] Government can continue using subpoenas in the "overwhelming majority" of investigations, but a warrant is required "in the rare case" where the suspect retains a legitimate privacy interest in third-party records.

But here again, the Court may have bitten off more than it wants to chew. While the Court affirmed that a warrant would heretofore be required for the modern-day equivalents of an individual's own papers or effects in third-party hands, it is unclear why the Court's logic doesn't equally apply to (1) such papers even when in the hands of the first rather than third party, and (2) other types of sensitive documents as well. If so, the warrant-over-subpoena rule announced here might have much broader application than the Court admitted.

---

[293] Id at 2222 (majority).

[294] Id.

[295] *Carpenter*, 138 S Ct at 2222.

[296] Id.

[297] Id.

D. DID THE COURT (INADVERTENTLY) MODIFY SUBPOENA DOCTRINE
   MORE GENERALLY?

A thought experiment: what if the government subpoenaed Carpenter directly, ordering him to turn over documents he personally possessed that revealed his historical movements? Perhaps his cell phone maintained such records within itself or in the cloud.[298] Perhaps his job required him to keep detailed location records.[299] Perhaps he exercised his federal statutory right under the Telecommunications Act of 1996 and requested Sprint to send him a copy of their records.[300] Most intriguingly, perhaps the government earlier ordered him by subpoena to obtain a copy of Sprint's records precisely so that the government could then demand that he turn them over.[301]

One might fight the hypothetical, as government officials would usually prefer to get potentially incriminating records from third rather than first parties. If asked directly, the target might destroy or alter the evidence, alert co-conspirators, etc. And he might also refuse to comply, claiming that the act of producing the records would itself violate his privilege against self-incrimination.[302] But these worries won't always arise. Here, Carpenter would not likely despoil the CSLI records knowing that Sprint has an accurate copy, and perhaps the government does not mind him knowing he's been fingered. And Carpenter may have no valid Fifth Amendment objection, either because his possession of the documents is a foregone conclusion,[303] or he has been granted immunity, or the records might incriminate someone else but not him.

---

[298] Chief Justice Roberts himself suggested this possibility in *Riley*, noting that "[h]istoric location information is a standard feature on many smart phones . . . ." 134 S Ct at 2490. See also Huq, *Decision Is Being Hailed* (cited in note 262) ("Locational data is held not only by [the] telephone company. It is also contained on a person's phone, even if she chooses to disable locational tracking.").

[299] For example, perhaps he's a cross-country truck driver who takes constant notes of time and location to prove that he's neither shirking nor exceeding maximum permissible driving hours.

[300] 47 USC § 222.

[301] See LaFave 2018–19 Pocket Part § 8.7(a) at 20–21, 30 nn 38.280–38.290 (cited in note 289) (noting this possibility).

[302] *United States v Hubbell*, 530 US 27, 36 (2000) ("[T]he act of producing documents in response to a subpoena may have a compelled testimonial aspect.").

[303] Id at 44.

The point is that the government could seek the same CSLI directly from Carpenter, and it would make no sense for the Court, based on its own reasoning, to grant him less privacy protection for the copy he possesses than for Sprint's original. So the heightened protection for CSLI necessarily applies to first-party as well as third-party subpoenas.[304] And indeed this conclusion flows naturally from the Court's endorsement of Justice Kennedy's caveat: if the warrant requirement shields a target's papers or effects "*even when*" they are held by a third party,[305] surely it also shields them when they remain with the target herself. This in itself is a significant statement: heretofore first parties served document subpoenas were generally thought protected by the same low-level burdensome standard as their third-party counterparts.[306] *Carpenter*—perhaps inadvertently—suggests otherwise.

This, then, raises the question: how broadly applicable is this warrant requirement that supersedes first-party subpoenas? Following the Court's language, it is at least expansive enough to include the "modern-day equivalents" of papers and effects, and presumably the original forms as well. This clearly addresses Justice Kennedy's reference to letters and e-mails.[307] But the Court also wanted to cover Justice Alito's broader reference to "private letters, digital contents of a cell phone—*any personal information reduced to document form*, in fact."[308] This sounds pretty broad.

Perhaps the adjectives "individual's own" and "personal" suggest the Court would stop short of saying that *anything* that's technically a tetrad paper or effect now deserves warrant-level rather than subpoena-level protection. Perhaps "personal" papers such as diaries and letters are in, whereas "impersonal" papers such as drug ledgers

---

[304] Otherwise, the Court's holding has no bite. The government could always force targets to get a copy of their "own" records from any and all third parties as a prelude to producing them to the government in response to a subpoena *duces tecum*—and the foregone conclusion doctrine would take the Fifth Amendment privilege out of the picture.

[305] *Carpenter*, 138 S Ct at 2222 (emphasis added).

[306] See, for example, Kerr, *Initial Reactions to Carpenter v. United States* (USC Law Legal Studies Paper No 18-14, July 6, 2018), archived at https://perma.cc/2SZV-TSKJ ("A [first-party] recipient does have Fourth Amendment rights at stake, but he can challenge the subpoena only on the ground that it is overbroad or compliance is overly burdensome.").

[307] *Carpenter*, 138 S Ct at 2230 (Kennedy, J, dissenting).

[308] Id at 2222 (majority) (emphasis added). For his part, Justice Gorsuch would appear to protect from warrantless subpoenas all records that are "sufficiently similar to letters in the mail." Id at 2271 (Gorsuch, J, dissenting).

and porn magazines are out. But it isn't clear where this line comes from, nor where one would draw it (intimate photos? appointment books? the Kamasutra?). The Fourth Amendment text offers no help: all papers and effects appear on the same footing, and indeed the whole point of the *Katz* test is to identify and place other privacy interests on the *same* footing as papers and effects, not on some higher plane. So the Court again seems to invite a sensitivity test, whereby future courts must decide if various documents or effects are sufficiently "personal" to qualify for warrant rather than subpoena-level protection.[309] A broad definition could significantly ratchet up the showing required to serve a large swath of first-party document subpoenas.

Maybe the Fifth Amendment's privilege against self-incrimination renders this largely an academic discussion, as the act of production doctrine typically presents a separate and high barrier for government to hurdle. But, as already noted, there may well be circumstances that naturally (or government can manufacture to) counter the Fifth Amendment claim, and then the level of Fourth Amendment protection becomes significant. This is another question for judges to work through, with little guidance from the Court. And even the Court's assurance that CSLI presents the "rare case" applies only to "records held by a third party"; it offers no guidance on how rare it should be for first-party document requests to require a warrant.

And now let us return to corporations and organizations, which have no Fifth Amendment rights.[310] Many entities generate and house all sorts of documents containing sensitive information that seem far

---

[309] Justice Thomas observes that the original meaning of "papers" might exclude *business* records that don't reveal "'personal or speech-related confidences.'" Id at 2241 n 8 (Thomas, J, dissenting), quoting Eric Schnapper, *Unreasonable Searches and Seizures of Papers*, 71 Va L Rev 869, 923–24 (1985). This statement leaves unclear whether that original meaning might also exclude a similar category of *nonbusiness* records possessed by individuals. Either way, Justice Thomas's observation implies that any such insufficiently personal or speech-related documents receive no Fourth Amendment protection at all, not that they are protected but only as second-class citizens.

Of course there is nothing inherently odd about hinging the required justification on the nature or extent of privacy invasions. That happens with rummage searches, where it takes more to search someone's body cavities than pockets. But those privacy invasions are measured by the nature of the *search* (body or pockets), not the nature of the *information* that will be revealed (drugs or passwords). Police do not, for example, need greater suspicion to search a house known to be stuffed with personal effects than a house known to be almost empty.

[310] Wayne R. LaFave et al, 3 *Criminal Procedure* § 8.12(b) at 349 (West, 4th ed 2015) (describing entity exception to self-incrimination privilege).

afield from the kinds of "corporate tax and payroll ledgers" used to rationalize the weaker protection for general business records. What about subpoenas requesting state election precincts to produce voting records during a voter fraud investigation; or subpoenas requesting dioceses to produce priests' personnel records during a sexual abuse investigation?[311] With perhaps some debate and handwringing, heretofore documents of these kinds have been considered subject to warrantless subpoena.[312] But these are not standard business documents of the sort traditionally deemed to have diminished privacy interests, and indeed they might contain very sensitive and "personal" information about the organization, people within it, and even people outside of it.

So, in the end, the Court's understandable desire not to let subpoena doctrine circumvent a CSLI warrant requirement seems to land us here: the Fourth Amendment's warrant requirement extends to compulsory process served on third parties or first parties ordering them to produce either all traditional papers and effects, or at least the "personal" subset thereof, as well as their modern-day equiva-

---

[311] See *Society of Jesus of New England v Commonwealth*, 808 NE2d 272 (Mass 2004) (rejecting motion to quash such a subpoena on free exercise of religion grounds; Fourth Amendment challenge not even raised).

[312] See, for example, Christopher Slobogin, *Subpoenas and Privacy*, 54 DePaul L Rev 805, 844 (2005) (noting that Fourth Amendment provides "minimal protection against document subpoenas, whether addressed to third parties or to the target of an investigation, and whether aimed at organizational or personal records").

Courts moved to protect personal privacy interests implicated by subpoenas issued to corporations or their officers generally do so, if at all, by ensuring the information is requested in good faith or tightening the required showing of relevance—not by requiring a showing of anything approaching probable cause. See, for example, *In re McVane v FDIC*, 44 F3d 1127, 1131 (2d Cir 1995) (requiring "more exacting scrutiny" of relevance where government seeks personal financial records of family members of corporate director suspects); *In re Administrative Subpoena (Doe)*, 253 F3d 256, 270–71 (6th Cir 2001) (enforcing subpoena requesting personal financial documents of children of doctor suspected of health-care fraud where request was "sufficiently narrowly-tailored to pass the reasonable relevance standard"). This approach applies even where companies claim that compliance will chill exercise of their or others' First Amendment rights. See, for example, LaFave, 3 Criminal Procedure § 8.8(d) at 229–43 (cited in note 310) (canvassing cases); id § 8.8(d) at 231 ("With few exceptions [generally involving fishing expeditions], such challenges have not succeeded in obtaining the quashing of the grand jury directive"); *In re Grand Jury Subpoena (Glassdoor, Inc.)*, 875 F3d 1179, 1188 (9th Cir 2017) (applying a "good-faith" test and rejecting application of heightened "substantial connection" relevancy test to subpoena requesting identity and credit card/billing information for anonymous on-line reviewers).

It is worth nothing that "[i]n white collar cases, subpoenas commonly require production of such potentially private items as 'reminder pads, notepads, diaries, calendars, day books, telephone directories, [and] telephone call logs.'" Podgor, *White Collar Crime* § 16.11(A) at 539 n 146 (citation omitted) (cited in note 275).

lents. Perhaps this extension is troubling, as it might unsettle long-standing understandings and practices;[313] and perhaps instead it is welcome, as necessary to conform those practices to fully protect Fourth Amendment interests.[314] But it seems clear that the Court was not well positioned in *Carpenter* to think this important issue through. And at the very least, the ambiguity invites widespread but good-faith resistance by those served with any and all subpoenas, until the questions are sorted out.

Finally, what do we make of this observation by Justice Alito: if the Fourth Amendment (and warrant requirement) "applies to the compelled production of documents, then it must also apply to the compelled production of testimony—an outcome that we have repeatedly rejected and which, if accepted, would send much of the field of criminal procedure into a tailspin"?[315] That extension certainly makes superficial sense. Suppose the government subpoenas Carpenter's co-defendant and half-brother Sanders to testify as to Carpenter's whereabouts over a week-long period.[316] Assuming they spent lots of time together, Sanders's testimony might threaten Carpenter's reasonable privacy interests just as much as any sensitive document might. In addition to revealing a great deal about Carpenter's location and movements (along with what he did where and with whom), Sanders might also have surreptitiously read Carpenter's diary and snooped throughout his house, learning additional sensitive information that Carpenter did not voluntarily share. Why should the government need a probable cause–backed warrant to se-

---

[313] Marty Lederman, *Carpenter's Curiosities (and Its Potential to Unsettle Longstanding Fourth Amendment Doctrines)* (Balkanization, June 26, 2018), archived at https://perma.cc/2NTR -NXUB (*Carpenter's* potential for "fundamental transformation of national subpoena practices (and other compulsory process practices) remains to be seen").

[314] See, for example, Slobogin, 54 DePaul L Rev at 845 (cited in note 312) (advocating that Fourth Amendment *should* be "interpreted to demand that all 'papers' that contain personal information—whether held by the subject or by a third-party institution—be afforded protection similar to that extended to the individual's house, person, and effects").

[315] *Carpenter*, 138 S Ct at 2251 n 1 (Alito, J, dissenting), referencing *United States v Dionisio*, 410 US 1, 9 (1973) ("It is clear that a subpoena to appear before a grand jury is not a 'seizure' in the Fourth Amendment sense, even though that summons may be inconvenient or burdensome.").

[316] Sanders could not refuse merely because testifying "might prove embarrassing or result in an unwelcome disclosure of his personal affairs." *United States v Calandra*, 414 US 338, 353 (1974). And the Fifth Amendment would offer Sanders no shield if the questions were carefully designed not to elicit answers that could incriminate him, or if the government immunized his testimony in advance.

cure Carpenter's CSLI records from Sprint, but not need to meet even "the minimal requirement of 'reasonableness' "[317] to secure Sanders's testimony?

Advocates for overturning or cabining *Miller-Smith* primarily justify treating documents and live testimony differently by invoking a norm of counterparty autonomy. For Sanders, as a human being with his own interests and motivations, autonomy over information is central to "personhood." This autonomy principle, they claim, entitles Sanders to do what he wants with what he knows, and the principle assertedly trumps Carpenter's expectation of privacy. By contrast, the argument runs, Sprint as an institution lacks the "personhood" underpinning an autonomy claim, so Sprint has no valued reason to squeal that can trump Carpenter's privacy interests.[318]

This proffered distinction raises more questions than I can address here, such as what autonomy entails, who gets to claim it, and why it ostensibly supersedes privacy values across the board. For now, I will just highlight two concerns. First, why would we say that Sanders's autonomy interest in sharing his thoughts with the government (so strong as to override Carpenter's privacy concerns) is greater than his autonomy interest in sharing documents that he possesses? And, even more fundamentally, why would autonomy play a role here at all,

---

[317] *Dionisio*, 410 US at 15.

[318] See, for example, Slobogin, 75 Miss L J at 185–86 (cited in note 268):

> The reason we should treat interviews differently from records requests is not because privacy is somehow irrelevant in the former situation, but because the target's interest in privacy is countered by an even stronger interest—the third party's autonomy. Human information sources . . . should have a right to decide what to do with the information they possess; in such cases, the subject's privacy interest is outweighed by the source's autonomy interest. When the third party is an impersonal record-holder, on the other hand, concerns about denigrating "personhood" through limitations on when information may be revealed are non-existent.

See also ABA Standards for Criminal Justice: Law Enforcement Access to Third Party Records 39 (3d ed 2013), archived at https://perma.cc/8CUC-3JUZ (asserting that "an individual [possessing information about a target] has an autonomy and free speech interest in choosing to share information that will often trump any privacy interest" of that target; but "the balance in cases involving institutional record-holders is different"). Compare Henderson, 34 Pepperdine L Rev at 1012 (cited in note 276) (questioning distinction between third-party records and recollections and arguing that third-party doctrine should be modified to restrict government access to both—which concededly "makes the adoption of a rational third-party doctrine more far-reaching than one might have imagined").

One might also suggest that, in general, live testimony is more fallible than documentary evidence. But that is contingent on the nature of the evidence; maybe so for CSLI, and maybe not for other kinds of documents. And, in any event, it is not the Fourth Amendment's job to regulate evidentiary quality. See note 222 and accompanying text.

when by hypothesis Sanders does not *want* to either testify or produce documents, and he is being forced to do so by threat of contempt? It seems paradoxical to distinguish between Sanders and Sprint based on Sanders's autonomy when he is not legally permitted to exercise it.

And this distinction seems especially vulnerable in this case, because Sprint looks an awful lot like an (admittedly alert and ever-present) eyewitness being called to testify as to what it knows about Carpenter's whereabouts. As the Court recounts the transaction and especially the involuntary nature of the information flow, and given that Carpenter himself does not (and cannot) know the information that Sprint is actually recording,[319] one can fairly describe the transaction as follows: Carpenter wants his cell phone to connect to Sprint's towers so the phone will function as contracted. Every now and then, sometimes consciously (phone calls) and sometimes not (background app refreshing), Carpenter essentially waves his hand and says "hey Sprint, here I am, figure out your nearest cell tower so you can direct some radio signals my way." And Sprint says "Okay, and I'll write myself a note recording which tower we use, so I can keep track for business purposes." And now the government wants Sprint to share that information, either by producing the written notes or by having someone testify as to what they say. At some point, the distinction between Sprint qua third-party record-holder and Sprint qua neighbor-with-good-notes seems thin indeed.

Of course Justice Alito correctly implied that there is no way the Court would ever lead law enforcement into a "tailspin" by requiring warrants for subpoenas *ad testificandum*, and I am not suggesting that *Carpenter* will inevitably slip down that slope. But absent a persuasive answer to the question, the argument highlights the ever-growing pile of seemingly fuzzy distinctions required to keep this decision's ripple effects "rare."

IV. Conclusion

Justice Breyer was doubly correct in conceding at oral argument that "this is an open box. We know not where we go."[320] We don't know how modern surveillance methods and digital technology

---

[319] See note 26 and accompanying text.

[320] Transcript of Oral Argument, *Carpenter v United States*, No 16-402, 35 (Nov 29, 2017), archived at https://perma.cc/EYN8-3XYE.

will progress; and we don't know where Fourth Amendment doctrine will take us after *Carpenter*. It is certainly possible that this decision will eventually be viewed "as being as important as *Olmstead* and *Katz* in the overall arc of technological privacy";[321] the Court's initial embrace of the mosaic theory alone might qualify for such recognition. But the scope of overall doctrinal and practical change will turn on many factors and future decisions.

A majority of the Court is clearly motivated to tackle the challenges that new technologies present to "ensure that the 'progress of science' does not erode Fourth Amendment protections."[322] And while the Court's holding is self-professedly narrow, much of its reasoning is neither narrow nor clear. Many criminal defendants and privacy advocates are already lining up to press further expansions of *Katz* as a bulwark against digital and other technological threats to privacy.

But lurking in the background of this decision—and the forefront of law enforcement minds around the country—is a concern that reasonable and early government access to at least short-term CSLI and certain types of third-party (and perhaps first-party) records is crucial for investigating, prosecuting, and perhaps even forestalling crime. Privacy is a paramount societal value; security is too. And if the Court consistently applies a warrant requirement wherever third-party records implicate first-party Fourth Amendment interests, then any accommodation for law enforcement needs will necessarily come through the continuing life, in some form or another, of the *Miller-Smith* framework. For this reason, in my view, excited reports that "the third-party doctrine is almost dead"[323] are greatly exaggerated. The Court has surely unsettled the old balance to combat new digital threats. It will take time for the Court to construct a new one.

---

[321] Ohm, *The Broad Reach of Carpenter* (cited in note 209).

[322] *Carpenter*, 138 S Ct at 2223, quoting *Olmstead*, 277 US at 473–74.

[323] Ohm, *The Broad Reach of Carpenter* (cited in note 209).